All in One®

Recommended by Teachers
Trusted by Toppers

GEOGRAPHY
Class 11

AF814219

EVERYTHING YOU NEED TO SCORE

- Simplified Theory
- NCERT, Diksha & Other Imp. Ques.
- CBQs; MCQs, A-R, Source Based
- Sample Question Papers

CBSE Exams 2026

Authors
Kumari Priya
Shruti Sharma

arihant
SUCCESS AND NOTHING LESS

arihant
SUCCESS AND NOTHING LESS

ARIHANT PRAKASHAN
(School Division Series)

卐 ADMINISTRATIVE & PRODUCTION OFFICES

Regd. Office
'Ramchhaya' 4577/15, Agarwal Road, Darya Ganj, New Delhi -110002
Tele: 011- 47630600, 43518550; Fax: 011- 23280316

卐 *Head Office*
Kalindi, TP Nagar, Meerut (UP) - 250002, Tel: 0121-7156203, 7156204

卐 SALES & SUPPORT OFFICES
Agra, Ahmedabad, Bengaluru, Bareilly, Chennai, Delhi, Guwahati, Hyderabad, Jaipur, Jhansi, Kolkata, Lucknow, Nagpur & Pune.

PO No : TXT-XX-XXXXXXX-X-XX

Published By Arihant Publications (India) Ltd.

For further information about the books published by Arihant, log on to www.arihantbooks.com or e-mail at info@arihantbooks.com
Follow us on

卐 PRICE ₹ 495.00

PRODUCTION TEAM

Publishing Managers
Mahendra Singh Rawat & Keshav Mohan

Cover Designer
Salman Shaikh

Inner Designer
Ankit Tyagi

Project Head
Shivam Gupta

Page Layouting
Jashoda

Proof Reader
Priya

Index *cum* Study Planner

PART A FUNDAMENTALS OF PHYSICAL GEOGRAPHY

Studied | Revised | Exam ready

UNIT 6

PART B INDIA : PHYSICAL ENVIRONMENT

UNIT 7

UNIT 8

One Book- Endless Features

to Help you Succeed

Complete Theory in Each Chapter

Each chapter has Complete, Easy to Understand and Simplified theory covering latest syllabus and rationalised NCERT Textbook. Theory is developed in such a way that it is suitable for all types of learners.

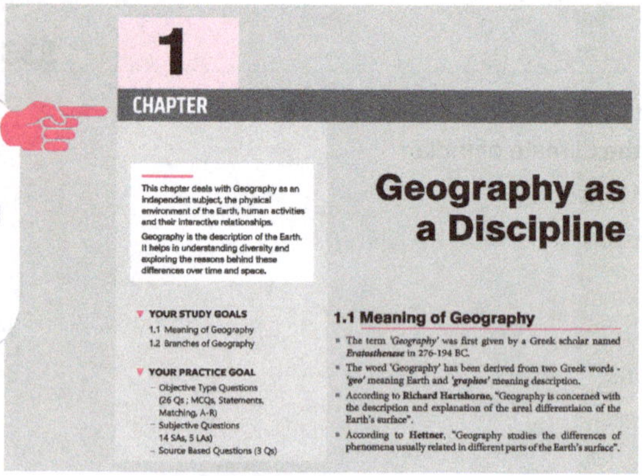

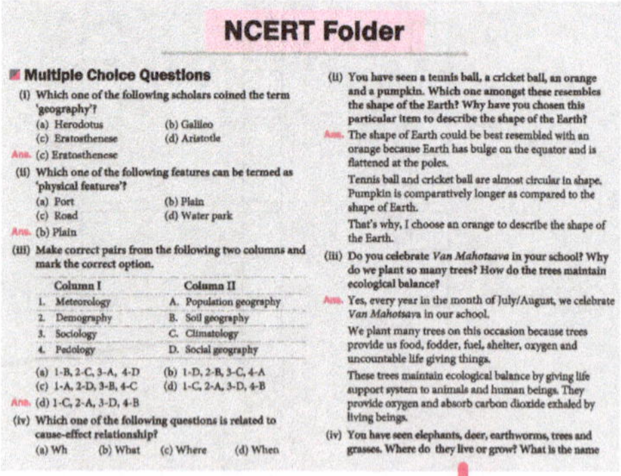

NCERT Folder

Complete explanations of all the questions of NCERT Exercises.

Quick Test 1

1. Who coined the term geography?
2. How did human societies develop their cultural features?
3. What does the relationship between the physical environment and human societies indicate?
4. Which question makes geography a discipline of science?
5. Name any two fields of geography.

Quick Test

A set of 4-6 Questions given in between the text, helps students to remain connected with the text while studying. They can instantly assess themselves for their understanding.

Mind Map

A quick revision visual tool for the complete chapter.

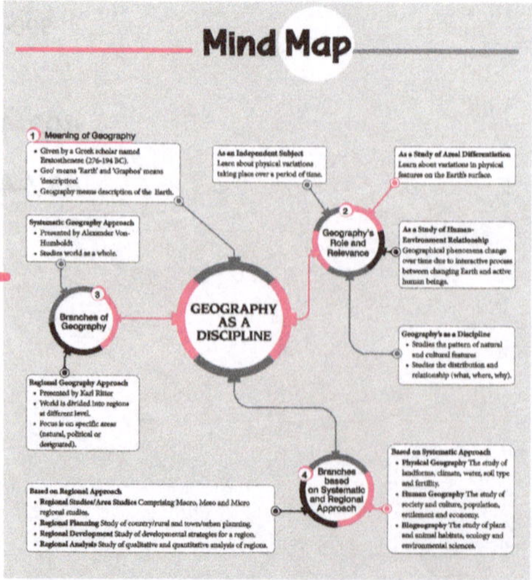

One Book- Endless Features
to Help you Succeed

Exam Pattern Questions

Chapter Practice have all types of questions; Objective Type Questions, SA & LA Type Questions.

Exam Pattern Questions

Objective Type Questions

Multiple Choice Questions (MCQs)

1. The term 'Geography' was coined by Eratosthenese in
(a) 300- 250 BC (b) 250- 222 BC
(c) 276- 194 BC (d) 200-270 BC
2. Which one of the following question is related to identification of pattern of natural and cultural features found on the Earth's surface?
(a) Where (b) What (c) Why (d) When
3. .... attempts spatial synthesis.
(a) History (b) Anthropology
(c) Geography (d) Economics
4. Who draws, produces and studies maps?
(a) Researcher
(b) Cartographer
(c) Demographer
(d) Analyst

SELF ASSESSMENT TEST

Objective Type Questions

1. Who considered geography as study of differences of phenomena?
(a) Erastosthenes (b) Galileo (c) Hettner (d) Richard Hartshorne
2. Geographical phenomena are ....
(a) Static (b) Dynamic (c) Passive (d) None of these
3. Which of the following is not a method to study geography?
(a) Cartography (b) Geographical thought
(c) Quantitative revolution (d) Field survey method
4. Quantitative approach in geography includes fields like
(i) Sustainable development (ii) GIS and GPS
(iii) Human Ecology (iv) Field survey methods
Choose the correct option.
(a) Only (i) (b) Both (ii) and (iv) (c) Both (i) and (iii) (d) Only (iv)

Self Assessment Test

Complete Test of chapter in Exam format.

Sample Question Papers

To make students practice of examination in real sense, there are 3 Sample Question Papers at the end. All these Sample Questions Papers are exactly prepared on the latest syllabus & pattern of examination.

SAMPLE QUESTION PAPER 1

A Highly Simulated Sample Question Paper for CBSE Class XI

(SOLVED)

GEOGRAPHY

General Instructions

- This question paper contains 30 questions. All questions are compulsory.
- This question paper is divided into five sections - Sections A, B, C, D and E.
- Section A - Questions no. 1 to 17 are Multiple Choice (MCQ) Type Questions carrying 1 mark each.
- Section B - Questions no. 18 and 19 are Source Based Questions carrying 3 marks each.
- Section C - Questions no. 20 to 23 are Short Answer (SA) Type Questions carrying 3 marks each. Answer to these questions shall be written in 80 to 100 words.
- Section D - Questions no. 24 to 28 are Long Answer (LA) Type Questions carrying 5 marks each. Answer to these questions shall be written in 120 to 150 words.
- Section E - Questions no. 29 and 30 are Map Based Questions. Carrying 5 marks each.

Time : 3 hours | Max. Marks : 70

SECTION A

1. A branch of physical geography called as climatology deals with which of the following. (1)
(a) Geology (b) Hydrology (c) Meteorology (d) Pedology
2. The term given to the study of map making .... (1)
(a) Researcher (b) Analyst (c) Cartography (d) Demography

Latest Course Structure

Fundamentals of Physical Geography

Chapter No	Chapter Name	Marks Allocated
	Unit - I Geography as a Discipline	
1	Geography As a Discipline	3
	Unit - II The Earth	
2	The Origin and Evolution of the Earth	9
3	Interior of the Earth	
4	Distribution of oceans and continents	
	Unit - III Landforms	
5	Geomorphic Processes	6
6	Landform and their Evolution	
	Unit - IV Climate	
7	Composition and Structure of Atmosphere	8
8	Solar Radiation, Heat balance and Temperature	
9	Atmospheric Circulations and Weather Systems	
10	Water in the Atmosphere	
11	World Climate and Climate Change (To be tested through internal assessments in the form of project and presentation)	
	Unit - V Water (Oceans)	
12	Water (Oceans)	4
13	Movements of Ocean Water	
	Unit - VI Life on the Earth	
14	Biodiversity and Conservation (To be tested through internal assessments in the form of project and presentation)	-
	Map Work	5
	Total	**35**

India : Physical Environment

Chapter No	Chapter Name	Marks Allocated
	Unit - I Introduction	
1	India-Location	5
	Unit - II Physiography	
2	Structure and Physiography	13
3	Drainage System	
	Unit - III Climate Vegetation and Soil	
4	Climate	12
5	Natural Vegetation	
	Unit - IV Natural Hazards and Disasters: Causes Consequences and Management	
6	Natural Hazards and Disasters (To be tested through internal assessment in the form of Projects and presentation)	–
	Map	5
	Total	**35**

COURSE CONTENT

Book- Fundamentals of Physical Geography

Unit 1: Geography as a Discipline

Chapter 1 Geography as a Discipline

- Introduction to Geography as a discipline
- Geography as an integrating discipline: Spatial and Temporal synthesis
- Approaches to study Geography: Systematic and Regional
- Branches of Geography: Physical Geography, Human Geography and Bio Geography
- Physical Geography and its importance.

Unit 2: The Earth

Chapter 2 The Origin and Evolution of The Earth

- Origin and evolution of the earth
- Early theories: Origin of the Earth
- Modern Theories: Origin of the universe
- Formation of Stars and Planets
- Evolution of the Earth: Lithosphere, Atmosphere and Hydrosphere
- Origin of Life

Chapter 3 Interior of the Earth

- Sources of Information about the Interior of the Earth (Direct and Indirect)
- Earthquakes: Earthquake Waves, Shadow zones, Types, Scales to measure earthquake intensity, effects, frequency of earthquake occurrences
- Structure of the Earth
- Volcanoes and Volcanic landforms

Chapter 4 Distribution of Oceans and Continents

- Continental Drift Theory, and Evidence in support of Continental Drift and Force for Drift
- Post Drift Studies
- Ocean Floor Configuration
- Distribution of Earthquakes and Volcanoes
- Concept of Seafloor Spreading
- Plate Tectonics: Types of Plate boundaries, Rate and forces for the Plate Movement
- Movement of the Indian Plate

Unit 3: Landforms

Chapter 5 Geomorphic processes

- Geomorphic processes: Exogenic and Endogenic
- Endogenic Process: Diastrophism, Volcanism
- Exogenic Processes Weathering, landslides.
- Soil: Processes and factors of Soil Formation

Chapter 6 Landforms and their Evolution

- Running water: Erosional and Depositional Landforms
- Wind: Erosional and Depositional Landforms

Unit 4: Climate

Chapter 7 Composition and Structure of Atmosphere

- Atmosphere- composition and structure; elements of weather and climate

Chapter 8 Solar Radiation, Heat Balance and Temperature

- Solar radiation: Variability of Insolation.
- Processes of Heating and Cooling of Atmosphere
- Terrestrial Radiation
- Heat budget of the earth
- Temperature- Factors controlling temperature; Horizontal distribution of temperature; Inversion of temperature

Chapter 9 Atmospheric Circulation and Weather Systems

- Atmospheric Pressure: Horizontal and Vertical Variation of Pressure
- Forces affecting velocity and direction of Wind
- General Circulation of the atmosphere: Pressure belts; Winds: Planetary, Seasonal and Local; Air masses and Fronts; Tropical and Extratropical cyclones; Thunderstorms and Tornadoes

Chapter 10 Water in the Atmosphere

- Humidity-Absolute and Relative humidity
- Evaporation and condensation-
- Different Forms of Condensation: dew, frost, fog, mist and cloud;
- Precipitation
- Types of Rainfall and world distribution of rainfall

Chapter 11 World Climate and Climate Change

(To be tested through internal assessments in the form of project and presentation)

Unit 5: Water (Oceans)

Chapter 12 Water (Oceans)

- Hydrological Cycle
- Major and Minor Relief Features of the Ocean Floor
- Temperature and Salinity of Ocean Waters: Factors, Horizontal and Vertical distribution of temperature and Salinity

Chapter 13 Movements of Ocean Water

- Movements of ocean water- Waves, Tides and Currents.

Unit 6: Life on the Earth

Chapter 14 Biodiversity and Conservation
(To be tested through internal assessments in the form of project and presentation)

Book- India- Physical Environment

Unit 1: Introduction

Chapter 1 **India** — Location, Size, Latitudinal and Longitudinal extent, Indian Standard time, India and its neighbours

Unit 2: Physiography

Chapter 2 **Structure and Physiography**

- Physiographic Divisions: (1) The Northern and North-eastern Mountains (2) The Northern Plain (3) The Peninsular Plateau (4) The Indian Desert (5) The Coastal Plains (6) The Islands.

Chapter 3 **Drainage System**

- Drainage patterns
- Concepts of River basin, Catchment Area, Watershed
- Drainage and River systems of India: the Himalayan and the Peninsular
- Extent of Usability of River Water- linking of rivers, problems in using river water and water pollution

Unit 3: Climate, Vegetation and Soil

Chapter 4 **Climate**

- Weather and climate
- Unity and diversity in the Monsoon Climate
- Factors determining the climate of India
- The Nature and characteristics on Indian Monsoon
- The Rhythm of Seasons
- Distribution of Rainfall
- Monsoon and the Economic Life in India
- Global Warming

Chapter 5 **Natural Vegetation**

- Natural vegetation - Introduction
- Forest types and distribution
- Conservation of forests
- Wildlife; conservation; biosphere reserves

Unit 4: Hazards and Disasters: Causes, Consequences and Management

Chapter 6 **Natural Hazards and Disasters**
(To be tested through internal assessment in the form of Projects and presentation)

Book- Geography Practical Part I

Chapter 1 **Introduction to Maps**

- Essentials of map making
- History of map making
- Maps -types
- Uses of maps

Chapter 2 **Map Scale**

- Scales-methods and construction
- Conversion of scale

Chapter 3 **Latitude, Longitude and Time**

- Drawing of Parallels of latitude and Meridians of longitude
- Longitude and time
- International date line

Chapter 4 Map Projections

- Map projection- typology, construction and properties of projection: Conical with one standard parallel and Mercator's projection. (only two projections)

Chapter 5 Topographical Maps

- Study of topographic maps (1 : 50,000 or 1 : 25,000 Survey of India maps); Conventional Symbols, contour cross section and identification of landforms-slopes, hills, valleys, waterfall, cliffs; distribution of settlements

Chapter 6 Introduction to Remote Sensing

- Satellite imageries, stages in remote sensing data-acquisition, platform and sensors and data products, (photographic and digital)

Map Items for locating and labelling on outline political World Map Fundamentals of Physical Geography

Chapter No Chapter Name	Map Work	
4 Distribution of oceans and continents	• Political Map of all Continents of the world. • Major Oceans of the world: Indian Ocean, Pacific Ocean, Atlantic Ocean, Arctic Ocean, Southern Ocean • Major lithospheric plates and Minor lithospheric plates, Ring of fire (Pacific Ocean), Mid-Atlantic Ridge.	
9 Atmospheric Circulations and Weather Systems	Major Hot Deserts of the world: • Mojave Desert- Nevada, US • Sahara- Africa • Thar desert- India	• Patagonian Desert- Argentina • Gobi Desert- Mongolia, Asia • Great Victoria desert- Australia
12 Water (Oceans)	• Major Seas • Baltic sea • Mediterranean Sea • Red sea • Bay of Fundy (Canada)-Famous for the highest tides in the world	• Black sea • Caspian Sea • North Sea
13 Movements of Ocean Water	OCEAN CURRENTS-Cold currents • Humboldt c. • California c. • Falkland c. • Canaries c. • West Australian c. • Oyashio c. • Labrador c.	Warm currents • Alaska c. • Brazilian c. • Aughlas c. • Kuroshio c. • Gulf stream c.
14	Ecological Hotspots • Eastern Himalaya, India	
Biodiversity and Conservation	• Western ghats, India • Eastern Madagascar, Africa • Atlantic forest, Brazil	• Indonesia, Asia • Upper Guinean forests, Africa • Tropical Andes

Map items for locating and labelling on outline political map of India
India : Physical Environment

Chapter No Chapter Name	Map Work
1 India- Location	• Latitudinal extent of India • Longitudinal extent of India • Standard Meridian of India • Important latitude passing through India (Tropic of Cancer) • Southern Most Point of main land of India (Kanya Kumari)
2 Atmospheric Circulations and Weather Systems	• **Mountains:** Karakoram Range, Garo- Khasi- Jaintia hills, Aravalli Range, Vindhyan Range, Satpura Range, Western ghats & Eastern ghats • **Peaks:** K2, Kanchenjunga, Nandadevi, Nanga Parvat, Namcha Barwa and Anaimud • **Passes:** Shipkila, Nathula, Palghat, Bhor ghat and Thal ghat • **Plateaus:** Malwa, Chhotnagpur, Meghalaya and Deccan Plateau. • **Coastal Plains:** Saurashtra, Konkan, North and South Kanara, Malabar, Coromandel and Northern Circars • Islands: Andaman & Nicobar Islands and Lakshadweep Islands
3 Drainage System	• **Rivers:** Brahmaputra, Indus, Satluj, Ganga, Yamuna, Chambal, Damodar Mahanadi, Krishna, Kaveri, Godavari, Narmada, Tapti and Luni • **Lakes:** (Identification)Wular, Sambhar, Chilika, Kolleru, Pulicat & Vembanad • **Straits, Bays , Gulfs:** Palk Strait, Rann of Kachch, Gulf of Kachch, Gulf of Mannar & Gulf of Khambat
4 Claimate	• Area with highest temperature in India • Area with lowest temperature in India • Area with highest rainfall in India • Area with lowest rainfall in India
5 Natural Vegetation	(Identification on an outline map of India) Tropical evergreen, Tropical deciduous, Tropical] thorn, Montane and Littoral/Swamp forests. Wildlife reserves: (locating and labeling) • **National Parks**: Corbett, Kaziranga, Ranthambore. Shivpuri, Simlipal • **Bird Sanctuaries**: Keoladev Ghana and Ranganathitto • **Wildlife Sanctuaries**: Periyar, Rajaji, Mudumalai, Dachigam

1

CHAPTER

Geography as a Discipline

This chapter deals with Geography as an independent subject, the physical environment of the Earth, human activities and their interactive relationships.

Geography is the description of the Earth. It helps in understanding diversity and exploring the reasons behind these differences over time and space.

YOUR STUDY GOALS

1.1 Meaning of Geography
1.2 Branches of Geography

YOUR PRACTICE GOAL

- Objective Type Questions (26 Qs ; MCQs, Statements, Matching, A-R)
- Subjective Questions 14 SAs, 5 LAs)
- Source Based Questions (3 Qs)

1.1 Meaning of Geography

- The term *'Geography'* was first given by a Greek scholar named ***Eratosthenese*** in 276-194 BC.
- The word 'Geography' has been derived from two Greek words - ***'geo'*** meaning Earth and ***'graphos'*** meaning description.
- According to **Richard Hartshorne**, "Geography is concerned with the description and explanation of the areal differentiaion of the Earth's surface".
- According to **Hettner**, "Geography studies the differences of phenomena usually related in different parts of the Earth's surface".

Geography as an Independent Subject

- In geography, we learn about the physical variations that are taking place over a period of time.
- In geography, we learn about the relationship between geographical condition and socio-cultural development.

Geography as a Study of Areal Differentiation[1]

- The **Earth's surface** is not uniform, it has variations in its physical features. There are mountains, hills, valleys, plains, plateaus, oceans, lakes, deserts, etc.

1 Areal Differentiation It is the process of distinguishing one geographical area from another based on its unique physical and cultural characteristics.

- Geography is used to study prevailing variations in different forms on the Earth's surface and their relationship with humans.
- There is a close relation between physical environment and social/cultural features as the impact of climate, availability of resources and topography can be seen over social and cultural features.
- The physical environment has provided the base on which human society evolved.
- There are villages, cities, ports, roads, railways, markets and many other elements created by humans, across the entire period of cultural development.
- Human society perform their creative skills with the tools and techniques they invented and evolved in the process of their cultural development. For example variation in cropping pattern of region is related to the soil, climate, demands of market, capacity of farmer to invest and technological inputs.
- To understand geography, we not only focus on the variation but also on the **association** with other factors which cause these variations.

Geography as a Study of Human-Environment Relationship

- The geographical phenomena (human and physical) are not fixed and keep on changing.
- They change over time as a result of interactive process between *changing Earth* and *active human beings*. Thus, geography studies the interaction between the *nature* and *human* as a whole.
- Human is the integral part of nature. Nature has imprints of humans which can be seen on food, clothing, shelter and occupation.
- Primitive societies are good example to observe the close relationship between nature and human. They survived on **'Natural means'** of subsistence i.e. edible plants and animals.
- With modernisation and technological advancement, humans started producing food using natural resources like land, soil and water.
- Primitive societies were dependent only on physical environment for their sustenance whereas modern societies have modified their natural environment by technology.
- With the help of technology, humans moved from **the stage of necessity** to **the stage of freedom**.
- With this interactive relationship between human and nature, we find-**Humanised *nature*** and ***Naturalised human* beings**.

Geography as a Discipline

- Geography as a discipline is concerned with three sets of questions which are
  - Identification of the patterns of natural and cultural features found over the Earth i.e. **WHAT?**
  - Distribution of human cultural and natural features over the surface of the Earth i.e. **WHERE?**
  - Explanation or casual relationship between features and processes and phenomena i.e. **WHY?**
- The first two questions (**WHERE? AND WHAT?**) discuss about the distributional and locational details of the natural and cultural features. It provides information of what is the feature and where it is located.
- The third question, (**WHY?**) is what makes geography a discipline of science.
- Geography as a discipline is related to space and studies pattern of distribution, location and concentration of phenomena over space.

- Geography as a discipline enables us to grasp reality in totality by integrating the physical, temporal(time), human and spatial (location) dimensions of the Earth.

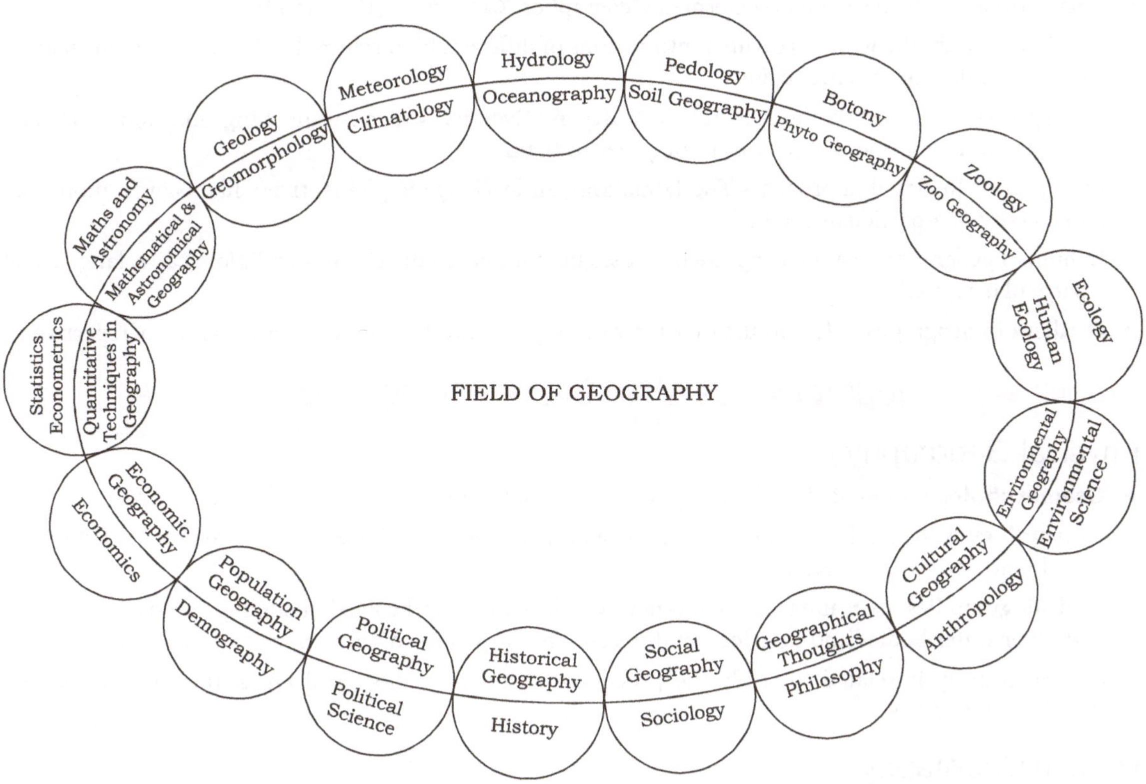

▲ *Geography and its Relation with Other Disciplines*

Quick Test 1

1. Who coined the term geography?
2. How did human societies develop their cultural features?
3. What does the relationship between the physical environment and human societies indicate?
4. Which question makes geography a discipline of science?
5. Name any two fields of geography.

1.2 Branches of Geography

Geography as an interdisciplinary subject has two approaches. These are

Systematic Approach

- It was introduced by ***Alexander Von Humboldt*** (1769-1859), a German Geographer.
- This approach involves the study of specific geographical phenomena or theme across the world, without necessarily focusing on any particular location.
- This approach focuses on understanding the general patterns and process that are applicable globally. For example, different types of forests like equatorial rainforests, sandalwood forests and monsoon forests will be studied, described and mapped globally.

Regional Approach

- This approach was developed by German Geographer ***Karl Ritter*** (1779-1859).
- In this approach, the world is divided into regions of different hierarchical levels. These regions may be natural, political or specific regions.
- This approach is based on the principle of **Unity in Diversity**, which means things may look different, we try to find common patterns and categories in them.
- Examples of Regional approach - The Himalayas, Indo-Gangetic plains, rivers like Ganga, monsoon, biodiversity of a particular region.
- In human geography, regional approach focuses on population distribution, religion, caste, language of a particular region'.
- **Dualism** in geography refers to the division of discipline into two broad approaches or perspective.

Branches of Geography Based on Systematic Approach

Physical Geography

- **Geomorphology** is devoted to the study of landforms, their evolution and related processes.
- **Climatology** is the study of structure of atmosphere, meteorology[2], elements of weather and climates, and climatic types and regions.
- **Hydrology** studies the realm (reach) of water over the surface of the Earth including oceans, lakes, rivers and other water bodies and its effect on different life forms including humans and their activities.
- **Soil geography** is related to study the processes of soil formation, soil types, their fertility status, distribution and uses.

Human Geography

- **Social and cultural geography** focuses on studying how society interacts with and is influenced by space as well as the cultural aspects that society contributed to its surroundings.
- **Population and settlement geography** (rural and urban) studies population growth, distribution, density, sex ratio, migration, etc. Settlement geography studies the characteristics of rural and urban settlements.
- **Economic geography** studies economic activities including agriculture, industry, tourism, trade and transport, infrastructure and services.
- **Historical geography** studies the historic processes that has shaped the Earth and the human society. Every region has gone through some past experiences before attaining present day status.
- **Political geography** studies political events and boundaries, space relations between neighbouring political units, political behaviour of population and election scenario.

Biogeography

- The interaction between physical geography and human geography has led to the development of Biogeography.
- It includes plant geography, zoo geography, pedology[3], ecology and environment.
- **Plant geography** studies spatial pattern of natural vegetation in their habitats.
- **Zoo geography** studies spatial patterns and geographic characteristics of animals and their habitat.

2 Meteorology The branch of science concerned with the process and phenomena of atmosphere, especially as a means of forecasting the weather.

3 Pedology It is the study of soils in their natural environment.

- **Ecology/ecosystem** is the scientific study of habitats and characteristics of species.
- **Environmental geography** studies the concerns related to the environmental problems like land degradation, pollution and concerns for conservation.

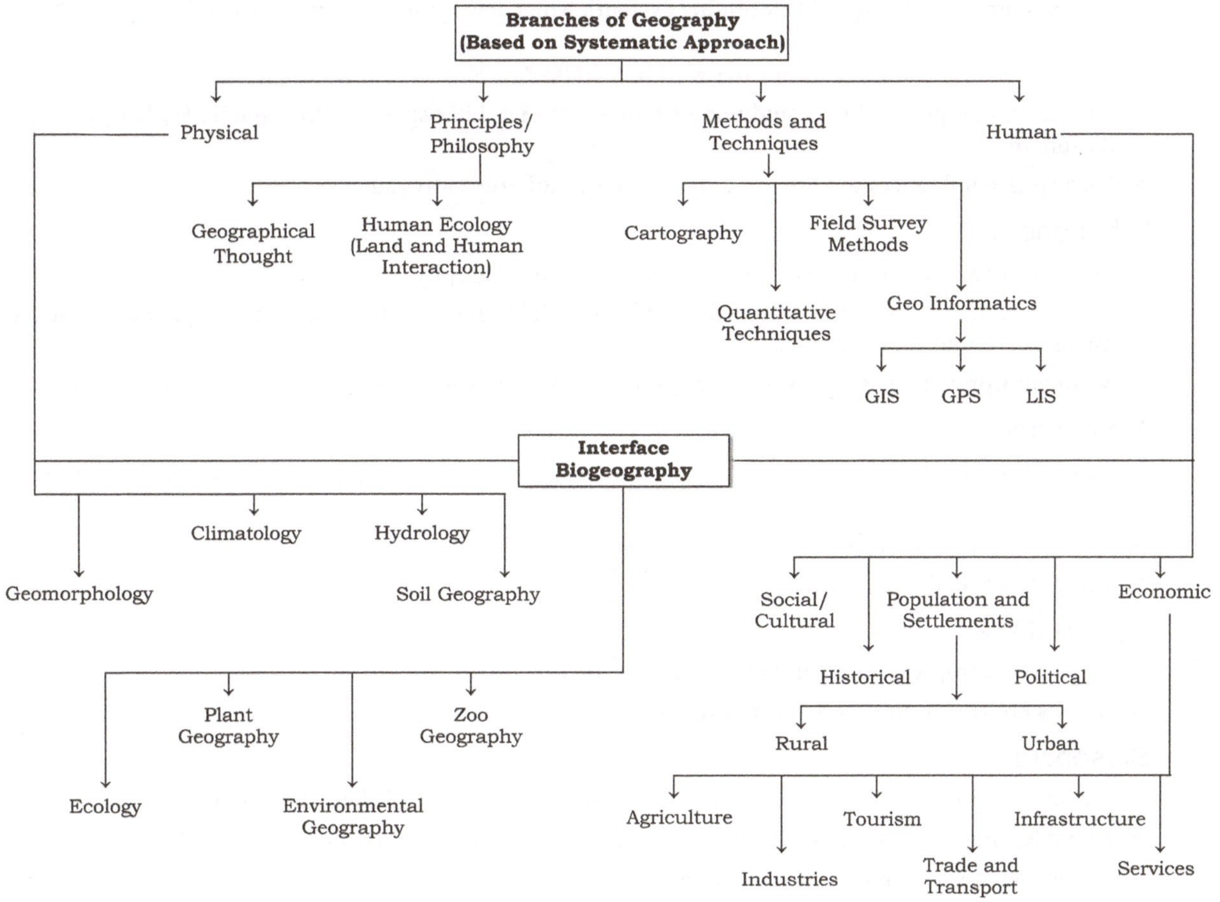

▲ *Branches of Geography Based on Systematic Approach*

Branches of Geography Based on Regional Approach

(i) **Regional studies/area studies** comprises *Macro*, *Meso* and *Micro* regional studies.

(ii) **Regional planning** comprises country/rural and town/urban planning.

(iii) **Regional development** comprises smart city projects, sustainable development, economic development.

(iv) **Regional analysis** comprises policy formulation, environment management.

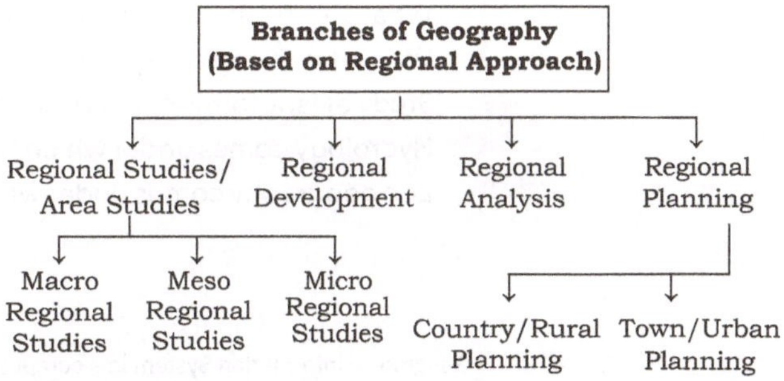

▲ *Branches of Geography Based on Regional Approach*

There are two aspects which are common to every discipline, which are

(i) **Philosophy**

(a) Geographical thought.

(b) Land and human interaction/human ecology.

(ii) **Methods and Techniques**

(a) Cartography including computer cartography.

(b) Quantitative techniques/statistical techniques.

(c) Field survey methods.

(d) Geo-informatics comprising techniques such as remote sensing, GIS[4] (Geographic Information System), GPS[5] (Global Positioning System), which has application in the field of navigation[6]

Physical Geography and its Importance

- Physical geography includes study of all four sphere i.e. Lithosphere, Atmosphere, Hydrosphere and Biosphere.
- Each sphere influences the life of human beings in different ways such as

Lithosphere

- Comprises various landforms, drainage, relief and physiography.
- Various human activities are carried out like - agricultural activities are done on plains, forest and minerals are found in plateaus.
- Mountains provides pastures, tourist spot and are the source of rivers providing water to the lowlands.

Atmosphere

- Comprises structure and composition of atmosphere, temperature, winds, precipitation, pressure, climate, etc.
- Climate influences our house type, clothing and food we eat.
- Temperature and precipitation control the density of forest and type of grassland.

Hydrosphere

- Includes oceans, seas, lakes and associated features.
- Oceans are rich in minerals and resources.

Biosphere

- Includes the life forms of human beings and macro-organisms and their sustaining mechanism.
- Examples may include - food chain, ecological parameter and ecological balance.
- **Pedogenesis** is the process of soil formation.
- Soil formation depends upon the parent rock, climate, biological activities and time.
- **Time** is an important factor in Pedogenesis, that helps in the development of soil profile and soil maturity.

Quick Test 2

1. What are the two approaches in the geography?
2. Who introduced the systematic approach of geography?
3. Study of landforms comes under which sphere?
4. Hydrology comes under which branch of geography?
5. Zoo geography comes under which branch of geography?

---

4 GIS Geographic Information System is a computer system for capturing, storing and displaying data related to positions on the Earth's surface.

5 GPS Global Positioning System is a satellite-based navigation system that helps to determine the precise location anywhere on the Earth.

6 Navigation It is the method of determining position, distance and direction while travelling from one place to another.

Mind Map

GEOGRAPHY AS A DISCIPLINE

1 Meaning of Geography

- Given by a Greek scholar named Eratosthenese (276-194 BC).
- Geo' means 'Earth' and 'Graphos' means 'description'.
- Geography means description of the Earth.

2 Geography's Role and Relevance

As an Independent Subject
Learn about physical variations taking place over a period of time.

As a Study of Areal Differentiation
Learn about variations in physical features on the Earth's surface.

As a Study of Human-Environment Relationship
Geographical phenomena change over time due to interactive process between changing Earth and active human beings.

Geography's as a Discipline
- Studies the pattern of natural and cultural features
- Studies the distribution and relationship (what, where, why).

3 Branches of Geography

Systematic Geography Approach
- Presented by Alexander Von-Humboldt
- Studies world as a whole.

Regional Geography Approach
- Presented by Karl Ritter
- World is divided into regions at different level.
- Focus is on specific areas (natural, political or designated).

4 Branches based on Systematic and Regional Approach

Based on Systematic Approach
- **Physical Geography** The study of landforms, climate, water, soil type and fertility.
- **Human Geography** The study of society and culture, population, settlement and economy.
- **Biogeography** The study of plant and animal habitats, ecology and environmental sciences.

Based on Regional Approach
- **Regional Studies/Area Studies** Comprising Macro, Meso and Micro regional studies.
- **Regional Planning** Study of country/rural and town/urban planning.
- **Regional Development** Study of developmental strategies for a region.
- **Regional Analysis** Study of qualitative and quantitative analysis of regions.

NCERT Folder

Multiple Choice Questions

(i) **Which one of the following scholars coined the term 'geography'?**

(a) Herodotus (b) Galileo
(c) Eratosthenese (d) Aristotle

Ans. (c) Eratosthenese

(ii) **Which one of the following features can be termed as 'physical features'?**

(a) Port (b) Plain
(c) Road (d) Water park

Ans. (b) Plain

(iii) **Make correct pairs from the following two columns and mark the correct option.**

Column I	Column II
1. Meteorology	A. Population geography
2. Demography	B. Soil geography
3. Sociology	C. Climatology
4. Pedology	D. Social geography

(a) 1-B, 2-C, 3-A, 4-D (b) 1-D, 2-B, 3-C, 4-A
(c) 1-A, 2-D, 3-B, 4-C (d) 1-C, 2-A, 3-D, 4-B

Ans. (d) 1-C, 2-A, 3-D, 4-B

(iv) **Which one of the following questions is related to cause-effect relationship?**

(a) Why (b) What (c) Where (d) When

Ans. (a) Why

(v) **Which one of the following disciplines attempts temporal synthesis?**

(a) Sociology (b) Anthropology
(c) Geography (d) History

Ans. (d) History

Answer the following questions in about 30 words

(i) **What important cultural features do you observe while going to school? Are they similar or dissimilar? Should they be included in the study of geography or not? If yes, why?**

Ans. When we go to school, we observe cultural features like temple, pond, shops, theatres, housing complex, etc.

All these features are dissimilar. They should be included in the study of geography because these features are human made features and play an important role in understanding human geography.

(ii) **You have seen a tennis ball, a cricket ball, an orange and a pumpkin. Which one amongst these resembles the shape of the Earth? Why have you chosen this particular item to describe the shape of the Earth?**

Ans. The shape of Earth could be best resembled with an orange because Earth has bulge on the equator and is flattened at the poles.

Tennis ball and cricket ball are almost circular in shape. Pumpkin is comparatively longer as compared to the shape of Earth.

That's why, I choose an orange to describe the shape of the Earth.

(iii) **Do you celebrate *Van Mahotsava* in your school? Why do we plant so many trees? How do the trees maintain ecological balance?**

Ans. Yes, every year in the month of July/August, we celebrate *Van Mahotsava* in our school.

We plant many trees on this occasion because trees provide us food, fodder, fuel, shelter, oxygen and uncountable life giving things.

These trees maintain ecological balance by giving life support system to animals and human beings. They provide oxygen and absorb carbon dioxide exhaled by living beings.

(iv) **You have seen elephants, deer, earthworms, trees and grasses. Where do they live or grow? What is the name given to this sphere? Can you describe some of the important features of this sphere?**

Ans. Elephants, deer, earthworms, trees and grasses live or grow in forests which is a part of biosphere.

Some important features of this biosphere are

- It is full of animal and plant species.
- It is the combination of lithosphere, hydrosphere and atmosphere where life is possible.
- Plants and animals are the biotic elements while soil, water, air, etc are abiotic elements of biosphere.

(v) **How much time do you take to reach your school from your house? Had the school been located across the road from your house, how much time would you have taken to reach school? What is the effect of the distance between your residence and the school or the time taken in commuting? Can you convert time into space and vice-versa?**

Ans. To reach my school, it takes around 30 minutes.

If my school is located across the road from my house then I could reach it within five minutes.

If the distance is longer between my residence and school then it will affect my studies as I have to travel for longer time to reach to school.

Time can be converted into space and vice-versa, as it depends on the length of journey e.g. the distance is 5 km and it takes 20 minutes to reach. It can also be said that school is 20 minutes away (if one travels from bicycle).

Answer the following questions in about 150 words

(i) **You observe every day in your surroundings that there is variation in natural as well as cultural phenomena. All the trees are not of the same variety. All the birds and animals you see are different. All these different elements are found on the Earth. Can you now argue that geography is the study of 'areal differentiation'?**

Ans. By observing different types of variations in natural and cultural phenomena, it is right to say that geography is the study of 'areal differentiation'. There is variation on the surface of the Earth both in physical and cultural environments. Variations could be observed in flora and fauna, landforms, climate and in lifestyle of human beings.

Geography studies both variations and their associations with other factors that causes these variations. But it will be absolutely wrong to say that geography is the study of only 'areal differentiation'. Geography as a discipline is related to space and takes note of spatial characteristics and attributes.

It studies the patterns of distribution, location and concentration of phenomena over space and interprets them by providing explanations and these patterns.

Geography also takes note of the interaction between ever changing Earth and untiring and ever active human beings. It helps in understanding the reality in totality in its spatial perspective. Geography, thus, not only takes note of the differences in the phenomena from place to place but integrates them holistically which may be different at other places.

(ii) **You have already studied geography, history, civics and economics as parts of social studies. Attempt an integration of these disciplines highlighting their interface.**

Ans. Geography is a discipline of synthesis. Each social study subject has interface with one another. All the social sciences like geography, history, civics, economics study different aspects of social reality.

Integration of these disciplines is discussed below

Geography and History

The geographical factors have modified the cause of history in different aspects of world. History of geographical thoughts as a mother branch of geography is inducted universally in its curriculum.

Geography and Political Science

Political science is the study of territories, people and sovereignty. On the other hand, political geography studies the state in the form of spatial unit alongwith people and their political behaviours.

Geography and Economics

Economics studies basic attributes of the economy like production, distribution, exchange, etc. Each of these have close link to economic geography.

Exam Pattern Questions

Objective Type Questions

Multiple Choice Questions (MCQs)

1. The term 'Geography' was coined by Eratosthenese in

(a) 300- 250 BC (b) 250- 222 BC
(c) 276- 194 BC (d) 200-270 BC

2. Which one of the following question is related to identification of pattern of natural and cultural features found on the Earth's surface?

(a) Where (b) What (c) Why (d) When

3. .... attempts spatial synthesis.

(a) History (b) Anthropology
(c) Geography (d) Economics

4. Who draws, produces and studies maps?

(a) Researcher
(b) Cartographer
(c) Demographer
(d) Analyst

5. **Study of population growth, distribution and density comes under which branch of human geography?**
(a) Economic Geography
(b) Political Geography
(c) Population and Settlement Geography
(d) Soil Geography

6. **The interface between Physical Geography and Human Geography has led to the development of which branch?**
(a) Zoology (b) Biogeography
(c) Climatology (d) Hydrology

7. **Which of the following scholars considered geography as study of areal differentiation?**
(a) Hettner (b) Richard Hartshorne
(c) Aristotle (d) Galileo

8. **Which of the following is included in lithosphere?**
(a) Ocean (b) Winds
(c) Food chain (d) Landforms

9. **Which of the following pair controls the density of forest and quality of grasslands?**
(a) Rock and precipitation
(b) Temperature and pressure
(c) Temperature and precipitation
(d) Climate and relief

10. **Pedogenesis refers to** **CBSE Diksha**
(a) the process of soil formation as regulated by the effects of place, environment and history.
(b) the study of Earth's landform, terrain and the process that guide these changes.
(c) the study of interactions and impacts between humans and natural world.
(d) the study of physical composition of the rocks.

11. **Read the following statement carefully and answer the question that follows.**

"Human is an integral part of nature and nature has imprints of human"

Which among the following explanation is not correct?
(a) Human and nature interacts accordingly.
(b) No connection is there between humans and nature.
(c) Humans and nature coexist.
(d) Imprints of nature can be seen on humans.

12. **How many pairs are incorrectly matched?**

	Branch		Application
(i)	Hydrology	–	Oceans
(ii)	Geomorphology	–	Landforms
(iii)	Climatology	–	Ecology
(iv)	Biogeography	–	Climatic Regions

(a) Only (i) (b) Only (ii)
(c) All of these (d) None of these

13. **Which of the following pairs is incorrect?**
(a) Philosophy – Geographical Thought
(b) Political Science – Political Geography
(c) Botany – Phyto Geography
(d) Anthropology – Economic Geography

14. **Consider the following statements.**
I. In regional approach, a phenomenon is studied world over as a whole and then the topologies are identified.
II. In systematic approach, world is divided into regions and phenomena in a region are studied in a holistic manner.

Which of the above statement/statements is/are correct?
(a) Only I (b) Only II
(c) Both I and II (d) None of these

15. **Which of the following statements given below is/are correct?**
I. Biogeography is branch of geography based on regional approach.
II. Biogeography has developed due to interface between physical and human geography.

Codes
(a) Only I (b) Only II
(c) Both I and II (d) None of these

16. **Consider the following statements.**
I. Human beings moved from the 'stages of necessity to stages of freedom'.
II. Human beings created new possibilities in collaboration with the nature.

Which of the above statements is/are correct?
(a) Both I and II (b) Only II
(c) Only I (d) None of these

17. **Consider the following statements.**
I. The nature of geographical phenomena is fixed.
II. The nature of geographical phenomena is dynamic.

Which of the above statements is/are correct?
(a) Only I (b) Both I and II
(c) Only II (d) None of these

18. **Consider the following statements and choose the incorrect one.**

Statement I Plant geography studies problems like land degradation, pollution, habitat loss.

Statement II Plant geography studies spatial pattern of natural vegetation in their habitat.

Options
(a) Only statement I is incorrect
(b) Both statements I and II are incorrect
(c) Statement II is incorrect
(d) None of the above

Match the Following

19.

List I		List II
A. Alexander von Humboldt	1.	Regional Approach
B. Karl Ritter	2.	Coined-term Geography
C. Erastosthenese	3.	Systematic Approach

Codes

	A	B	C		A	B	C
(a)	1	2	3	(b)	3	1	2
(c)	2	3	1	(d)	2	1	3

20.

List I (Branch of Geography)		List II (Associated fields)
A. Geomorphology	1.	Tourism
B. Soil Geography	2.	Mountains
C. Economic Geography	3.	Pedogenesis
D. Social/Cultural Geography	4.	Cultural Diversity

Codes

	A	B	C	D		A	B	C	D
(a)	2	3	1	4	(b)	3	2	1	4
(c)	2	1	3	4	(d)	2	1	4	3

21.

List I (Feature)		List II (Spheres)
A. Drainage	1.	Atmosphere
B. Temperature	2.	Hydrosphere
C. Oceans	3.	Biosphere
D. Food chain	4.	Lithosphere

Codes

	A	B	C	D
(a)	4	3	2	1
(b)	2	3	4	1
(c)	2	4	1	3
(d)	4	1	2	3

22.

List I (Approaches)		List II (Application)
A. Regional Planning	1.	GIS and GPS
B. Philosophy	2.	Urban Planning
C. Regional Development	3.	Geographical Thought
D. Methods and Techniques	4.	Smart City Projects

Codes

	A	B	C	D		A	B	C	D
(a)	3	2	4	1	(b)	4	1	2	3
(c)	2	3	4	1	(d)	1	2	3	4

Assertion-Reason

Directions (Q. Nos. 23-26) In the questions given below are two statements labelled as Assertion (A) and other is labelled as Reason (R). In the context of two statements which one of the following is correct?

Codes

(a) Both A and R are true, but R is not the correct explanation of A

(b) Both A and R are true and R is the correct explanation of A

(c) Both A and R are incorrect

(d) A is correct, but R is incorrect

23. **Assertion** (A) Time is an important factor in pedogenesis.

Reason (R) Time provides maturity to soils and helps in development of soil profile.

24. **Assertion** (A) Climate influences life of human beings.

Reason (R) Temperature and precipitation affect density of forests and quality of grassland.

25. **Assertion** (A) "Geography is an integrated discipline that studies relation between Human and nature".

Reason (R) "Geography examines both physical features of the Earth and human activities, making it interdisciplinary in nature".

26. **Assertion** (A) Regional approach in geography helps in understanding the unique characteristics of different areas of the Earth's surface.

Reason (R) Regional approach focuses only on the physical aspects of regions, ignoring cultural and economic factors.

Answers

1. (c) 276- 194 BC
2. (b) What
3. (c) Geography
4. (b) Cartographer
5. (c) Population and Settlement Geography
6. (b) Biogeography
7. (b) Richard Hartshorne
8. (d) Landforms

9. (c) Temperature and precipitation
10. (a) the process of soil formation as regulated by the effects of place, environment and history.
11. (b) No connection is there between humans and nature.
12. (b) Only (ii)
13. (d) Anthropology – Economic Geography
14. (d) None of these
15. (b) Only II
16. (a) Both I and II
17. (c) Only II
18. (a) Only statement I is incorrect
19. (b)
20. (a)
21. (d)
22. (c)
23. (b) Both A and R are true and R is the correct explanation of A
24. (a) Both A and R are true, but R is not the correct explanation of A
25. (b) Both A and R are true and R is the correct explanation of A
26. (d) A is correct, but R is incorrect

Subjective Questions

Short Answer Type Questions

1. 'Geography should be studied as an independent subject'. Explain why? **Competency Based Que**

Ans. We should study geography as an independent subject to understand about the physical environment of the Earth, human activities and their interactive relationship. As an independent subject, it is easier to study its various dimensions and its impact on human life. It reveals the relationship between the geographical pattern and socio-cultural development.

We study geography to understand about the changes that occur in our life and how our lives are affected by our surroundings. We depend upon the resources to sustain ourselves in the surrounding areas. There are variations in the natural resources, technological development, adaptation and modification of physical environment, social organisation and cultural development.

Hence, to understand these variations and linkage between these, it is necessary to study the geography as an independent subject.

2. 'Geography is considered as the study of the Earth's surface'. Justify the statement. **Competency Based Que**

Ans. Geography is considered as the study of the Earth's surface as the word 'geography' has been derived from two root words from Greek language; *geo* (Earth) and *graphos* (Description). Put together, they mean description of the Earth.

As we know that the Earth's surface is not uniform. It has variations in its physical features. There are mountains, hills, valleys, plains, plateaus, oceans, lakes, deserts and wilderness. There are variations in its social and cultural features too. There are villages, cities, roads, railways, ports, markets and many other elements created by human beings across the entire period of their cultural development.

Geography as an independent subject discuss about the physical environment of the Earth, human activities and their interactive relationships. All these are the aspects of earth's surface. Thus, we can say that geography is considered as the study of the Earth's surface.

3. How many categories of questions the geography is concerned with? Explain.

Ans. Geography as a discipline is concerned with three sets of questions which are

(i) Identification of the patterns of natural and cultural features as found over the surface of the Earth, i.e. What?

(ii) Distribution of human/cultural and natural features over the surface of the Earth i.e. Where?

(iii) Explanation or casual relationships between features and processes and phenomena i.e. Why?

4. "Geography is a discipline of synthesis." Justify the statement. **Competency Based Que**

Ans. Geography is considered a discipline of synthesis because it integrates and combines knowledge from various natural and social sciences to understand the complex relationships between people, places and the environment. Unlike other fields, which may focus on specific aspects of reality, geography seeks to understand the world as a whole.

Geography attempts spatial synthesis, meaning it studies how physical features (like landforms, climate and ecosystems) and human activities (such as cities, cultures and economies) are interconnected in a given space. Geography's holistic approach recognises that the world functions as a system of interdependencies. For example, geography acknowledges how transportation networks, advancements in communication technologies and media influence the social, economic and environmental landscapes.

5. How is understanding of reality the only objective of all sciences?

Ans. Understanding the reality is the only objective of all sciences. Geography attempts to comprehend this reality in its totality. It does not attempt to study different phenomena in isolation but it attempts to study by integrating them with one another.

In same way, all the sciences whether natural or social have basic objective of understanding the reality. Sciences like geology, pedology, zoology and a number of sister disciplines of social science like economy, political science and history study different aspects of Earth's surface.

6. What are the elements which have been created by human being during the period of development?

Ans. There are many elements created by humans during the period of development. These elements include villages, cities, roads, railways, ports and markets.

- **Villages** Settlements where people live and engage in agricultural and other activities.
- **Cities** Larger, more complex settlements with advanced infrastructure and diverse economic activities.
- **Roads** Pathways constructed to connect different places, facilitating transportation and communication.
- **Railways** Systems of trains and tracks that connect cities and regions, improving mobility and trade.
- **Ports** Harbors or dock areas used for the docking of ships and facilitating trade and transportation by sea.
- **Markets** Places where goods and services are exchanged, supporting economic activity and trade.

These elements reflect human efforts to modify and shape the physical environment for better living conditions, economic activities and cultural development.

7. How do human and environment influence each other? Explain.

Ans. Human is an integral part of his environment/ nature. In the same way nature has the imprints of human since ancient times.

Nature has influenced different aspects of human life. The imprints of nature can be noticed on food, clothing, shelter and occupation of humans.

But with adaptation and modification human started to live with his environment. He invented different technologies to modify and change his environment. For example, different farming techniques and equipments are used to grow crops from the soil provided by nature. With the help of advanced technologies, human extract and utilise different natural resources provided by nature.

But when the environment gets disturbed beyond its limit, it can cause disasters. Thus, human and environment influence each other.

8. 'We now find humanised nature and naturalised human beings'. What are the changes do you observe from primitive to present society? Competency Based Que

Ans. It is true that human gets naturalised by nature and nature gets humanised by human beings.

The following changes explain this statement

- Since ancient times human was greatly dependent on his environment/nature to fulfil his basic needs, like food, clothing, shelter and occupation. That was the period of naturalised human beings.
- With the passage of time, human beings have come to terms with nature through adaptation and modification.
- The present society has passed the stage of primitive societies, which were directly dependent on their immediate physical environment for sustenance.
- Present societies have modified their natural environment by inventing and using technology and thus, have expanded the horizon of their operation by appropriating and utilising the resources provided by nature.
- As technology gradually developed, humans were able to break free from the limitations of their physical environment. This is the period of humanised nature.
- But still nature has its greater impact on human activities. Thus, we now find humanised nature and naturalised human beings.

9. "Imprints of nature can be noticed on food, clothing and shelter." Justify the statement briefly. Competency Based Que

Ans. The imprints of nature on food, clothing and shelter reflect how the environment influences human life. Food habits are shaped by local climate and available resources, such as rice in tropical regions and wheat in temperate areas. Clothing styles are adapted to the weather, like wool in cold climates and cotton in hot regions. Similarly, shelter designs reflect the environment, with materials and architecture suited to local conditions, like stilt houses in flood-prone areas and earth-shattered homes in arid regions demonstrating the profound impact of nature on human necessities.

10. How is geography considered as an integrated discipline? **CBSE Diksha**

Ans. Geography is an integrated discipline because it bridges natural and social sciences, studying the Earth's physical features (like landforms, climate) and their interactions with human activities (such as settlements, economies). It combines tools and methods from both fields to understand complex spatial relationships and processes that shape the environment and human societies. As a discipline of synthesis, geography attempts spatial synthesis by recognising the world as a system of interdependencies.

11. How physical and human geography differs? Explain.

Ans. Physical geography studies natural features of the Earth, such as climate, landforms, vegetation and water bodies. It examines the physical processes that shape the environment and the resulting landscapes. Human geography, on the other hand, focuses on human activities and their impacts on the environment, including culture, economy, urbanisation and political organisation. Together, they offer a holistic view of the world, highlighting the complete interactions between human societies and the natural environment.

12. How does atmosphere influences life on the Earth?

Ans. The atmosphere plays a vital role in influencing life on earth. It regulates the planet's climate by controlling, pressure, winds, precipitation and climate. The atmosphere drives weather patterns and the hydrological cycle, which in turn impact agriculture, water resources and ecosystems. Additionally, atmospheric gases like oxygen and carbon dioxide are essential for respiration and photosynthesis which supports life forms from plants to humans. The atmosphere's protective layer also shields life from harmful solar radiation.

13. Define regional approach and explain its various parts.

Ans. Regional approach was developed by German geographer Karl Ritter (1779-1859). In regional approach, the world is divided into regions at different hierarchical levels and then all the geographical phenomena in a particular region are studied.

These regions may be natural, political or designated region. The phenomena in a region are studied in a holistic manner searching for unity in diversity.

Various parts of regional approach are as follows

- **Regional Studies/Area Studies** Comprising *Macro*, *Meso* and *Micro* regional studies.
- **Regional Planning** Comprising country/rural and town/ urban planning.
- **Regional Development** Comprising smart city projects, sustainable and economic development.
- **Regional Analysis** Comprising policy formulation and environment management.

14. How is physical geography different from biogeography? Explain.

Ans. Physical geography is different from biogeography in the following ways

Basis	Physical Geography	Biogeography
Meaning	It has developed as a subject concerned with the study of evolution and management of natural resources.	It has emerged as a result of the interface between physical and human geography.
Branches	It has four branches i.e. geomorphology, climatology, hydrology and soil geography.	It has four branches i.e. plant geography, zoo geography, ecology and environmental geography.
Subject matter	It studies abiotic elements of the Earth.	It studies biotic elements of the Earth.

Long Answer Type Questions

1 Both physical and human factors are dynamic not static. Elucidate. **Competency Based Que**

Ans. The geographical phenomena, both physical and human, are not static but highly dynamic. They change over time as a result of the interactive processes between ever changing Earth and ever active human beings.

Relationship between Physical Environment and Human

- Relation between human and nature is changing continuously. Primitive human societies were directly dependent on their immediate environment. Human beings have come to terms with nature through adaptation and modification.
- The present societies have passed the stage of primitive societies and have modified their natural environment by inventing and using technology.
- On the other hand, due to fast pace of resource utilisation and changing climate, physical environment is also changing.
- Interaction between the physical environment and human beings has put their imprints everywhere and created new possibilities in collaboration with nature.
- Hence, the association and inter-relationships between phenomena which is resulting from the interaction between human beings and their physical environment witness the dynamism.

2 'Geography is a discipline of different approaches'. Analyse the statement. **Competency Based Que**

Ans. Geography is a discipline of different approaches as the major approaches to study geography have been systematic and regional approach.

- **Systematic Approach** It is often applied when researchers seek to understand the global distribution and patterns of a particular geographical feature. This approach was popularised by Alexander Von Humboldt, a German Geographer in the late 18th and early 19th centuries (1769-1859).

In this approach, the focus is on understanding a single type of geographical phenomenon, such as climate, vegetation, or population, on a global scale. Researchers identify typologies or spatial patterns across the entire globe, providing a broad framework for understanding how different phenomena interact.

- **Regional Approach** It was developed by Karl Ritter. Rather than looking at a single geographical phenomenon on a global scale, this approach divides the world into distinct regions-each of which is analysed in detail to understand the spatial relationships of different phenomena within that region. Regions can be classified in various ways-natural (such as climatic regions or biomes), political (such as countries or states), or even designated regions (such as cultural or economic regions).

  Once a region is defined, all geographical phenomena within that area are studied holistically, meaning that researchers analyse how different elements-climate, vegetation, population, economic activities and cultural practices-interact with each other within the specific context of that region. The goal of the regional approach is to understand the unity of diverse phenomena in a given area. This approach emphasises the uniqueness of a region while recognising that it is shaped by multiple factors working together.

3 How is physical geography important for human life?

Ans. Physical geography includes the study of lithosphere, atmosphere, hydrosphere and biosphere. Each element is very important for human beings and influence the life of human beings in various ways

- **Lithosphere** comprises various landforms, drainage, relief and physiography. These things provide the bases for the development of all types of human activities, i.e. plains are utilised for agricultural activities, plateaus provide forest and minerals. Mountains provide pastures, tourist spots and sources of rivers providing water to lowlands.
- **Atmosphere** includes its structure and composition, temperature, pressure, winds, precipitation, climate, etc. Climate influences our house types, clothing and food habits. It has a wider impact on vegetation, cropping pattern, livestock farming and some stone industries, etc. Temperature and precipitation also ensure the density of forests and quality of grasslands.
- **Hydrosphere** includes oceans, seas, lakes and associated features with water realm. We study oceans which are the storehouse of resources. Besides fish and other sea-food, oceans are rich in mineral resources.
- **Biosphere** covers the life forms of human beings and macro-organisms and their sustaining mechanism, i.e. food chain, ecological parameters and ecological balance. Soils are formed through the process of pedogenesis and depend upon the parent rocks, climate, biological activities and time. Time provides maturity to soils and helps in the development of soil profile. Soils are renewable resources, which influence a number of economic activities such as agriculture. They also provide basis for the biosphere accomodating plants, animals and micro-organisms.

4. "Human geography is crucial for analysing how people interact with the environment". Support the statement with suitable example. Competency Based Que

Ans. Human geography is crucial for analysing how people interact with the environment. It examines how geographic features influence human activities, such as agriculture, urbanisation and industrialisation, while also exploring the impact of human decisions on natural landscapes. By studying patterns of settlement, migration and resource utilisation, human geography offers insights into economic development, cultural practices and social organisation. It also addresses challenges like climate change, urban sprawl and resource depletion, encouraging sustainable development. Human geography helps policymakers create strategies to balance human needs with environmental conservation.

Additionally, it helps in understanding cultural differences and promoting global cooperation by studying how societies adapt to various geographic contexts. Ultimately, human geography bridges natural and social sciences, providing a comprehensive view of how human life is shaped by and shapes the Earth.

5. Explain how human geography contributes to solving global issues such as climate change, urbanisation and resource management.

Ans. Human geography plays a key role in addressing global challenges like climate change, urbanisation and resource management by analysing human-environment interactions. It helps in understanding the spatial distribution of populations, resource use and economic activities, all of which are crucial for sustainable development. By studying patterns of urban growth, human geography provides insights into managing urban sprawl, transportation, and housing, which are essential for planning future cities. It also focuses on the impact of human activities on natural resources, guiding the creation of policies for sustainable resource management.

In terms of climate change, human geography assesses how different regions contribute to greenhouse gas emissions and how populations are vulnerable to climate impacts like sea-level rise and extreme weather. These insights inform strategies for mitigation and adaptation, making human geography essential in the global effort to address these critical issues.

Source Based Questions

1. Read the passage carefully and answer the questions that follow.

Geography is a discipline of synthesis. It attempts spatial synthesis and history attempts temporal synthesis. Its approach is holistic in nature. It recognises the fact that the world is a system of interdependencies. The present world is being perceived as a global village. The distances have been reduced by better means of transportation increasing accessibility. The audio-visual media and information technology have enriched the data base. Technology has provided better chances of monitoring natural phenomena as well as the economic and social parameters.

Every discipline, concerned with scientific knowledge is linked with geography as many of their elements vary over space. Geography helps in understanding the reality in totality in its spatial perspective. Geography, thus, not only takes note of the differences in the phenomena from place to place but integrates them holistically which may be different at other places. A geographer is required to have a broad understanding of all the related fields, to be able to logically integrate them. This integration can be understood with some examples. Geography influences historical events. Spatial distance itself has been a very potent factor to alter the course of history of the world. Spatial depth provided defence to many countries, particularly in the last century. In traditional warfare, countries with large size in area, gain time at the cost of space.

(i) Which of the following technology has made the world a global village?

(a) Internet (b) Air Transport
(c) Satellite Communication (d) All of these

Ans. (d) All of these

(ii) Which of the following is the most important feature of geography?

(a) It is derived from three disciplines
(b) It is dynamic in nature
(c) It has no interface with natural sciences
(d) Geography does not help in understanding reality

Ans. (b) It is dynamic in nature

(iii) Which among the following has been the most important factor in connecting the countries of world with India?

(a) Railways (b) Oceanic routes
(c) Traders (d) None of these

Ans. (b) Oceanic routes

2. Read the passage carefully and answer the questions that follows.

In India, Himalayas have acted as great barriers and provided protection but the passes provided routes to the migrants and invaders from Central Asia. The sea coast has encouraged contact with people from East and South-East Asia, Europe and Africa. Navigation technology helped European countries to colonise a number of countries of Asia and Africa, including India as they got accessibility through oceans. The geographical factors have modified the course of history in different parts of the world. Every geographical phenomenon undergoes change through time and can be explained temporally. The changes in landforms, climate, vegetation, economic activities occupations and cultural developments have followed a definite historical course. Many geographical features result from the decision-making process by different institutions at a particular point of time. It is possible to convert time in terms of space and space in terms of time.

(i) Which natural feature in India provided protection from Central Asian invaders but also facilitated their entry through certain passes?

(a) Thar desert (b) Gangetic-plain
(c) Himalayas (d) Islands

Ans. (c) Himalayas

(ii) "Every geographical phenomenon undergoes change through time and can be explained temporally", comes under which type of synthesis?

(a) Spatial synthesis (b) Temporal synthesis
(c) Regional synthesis (d) Local synthesis

Ans. (b) Temporal synthesis

(iii) The geographical factor that helped European countries colonise parts of Asia and Africa is related to

(a) Mountain passes (b) River networks
(c) Navigation technology (d) Desert routes

Ans. (c) Navigation technology

3. Read the passage carefully and answer the questions that follow.

Physical geography includes the study of lithosphere (landforms, drainage, relief and physiography), atmosphere (its composition, structure, elements and controls of weather and climate; temperature, pressure, winds, precipitation, climatic types, etc.), hydrosphere (oceans, seas, lakes and associated features with water realm) and biosphere (life forms including human being and macro-organism and their sustaining mechanism, viz. food chain, ecological parameters and ecological balance). Soils are formed through the process of pedogenesis and depend upon the parent rocks, climate, biological activity and time. Time provides maturity to soils and helps in the development of soil profiles. Each element is important for human beings. Landforms provide the base on which human activities are located. The plains are utilised for agriculture. Plateaus provide forests and minerals. Mountains provide pastures, forests, tourist spots and are sources of rivers providing water to lowlands.

Climate influences our house types, clothing and food habits. The climate has a profound effect on vegetation, cropping pattern, livestock farming and some industries, etc. Human beings have developed technologies which modify climatic elements in a restricted space such as air conditioners and coolers. Temperature and precipitation ensure the density of forests and quality of grassland. In India, monsoonal rainfall sets the agriculture rhythm in motion. Precipitation recharges the groundwater aquifers which later provides water for agriculture and domestic use. We study oceans which are the store house of resources. Besides fish and other sea-food, oceans are rich in mineral resources. India has developed the technology for collecting manganese nodules from oceanic bed. Soils are renewable resources, which influence a number of economic activities such as agriculture.

The fertility of the soil is both naturally determined and culturally induced. Soils also provide the basis for the biosphere accommodating plants, animals and micro-organisms.

(i) What aspects of the Earth does physical geography study?

Ans. Physical geography is the branch of geography that deals with the study of the Earth's natural features and phenomena. It primarily focuses on the lithosphere, which includes the study of landforms, drainage, relief, and physiography, to understand the physical layout of the Earth's surface.

(ii) Why is time important in soil formation?

Ans. Time is an important factor in the process of soil formation because it allows for the gradual development of soil profiles and the maturation of the soil. Initially, soils are not very fertile or structured, but over time, organic matter accumulates, minerals leach and weather and soil horizons begin to form.

(iii) What role do landforms play in human activities?

Ans. Landforms play a crucial role in determining the location, development and nature of human activities. Different types of landforms provide specific benefits for various human needs. For instance, plains are typically flat and fertile, making them ideal for agriculture and settlement.

SELF ASSESSMENT TEST

Objective Type Questions

1. Who considered geography as study of differences of phenomena?
   (a) Erastosthenes (b) Galileo (c) Hettner (d) Richard Hartshorne
2. Geographical phenomena are ....
   (a) Static (b) Dynamic (c) Passive (d) None of these
3. Which of the following is not a method to study geography?
   (a) Cartography (b) Geographical thought
   (c) Quantitative revolution (d) Field survey method
4. Quantitative approach in geography includes fields like
   (i) Sustainable development (ii) GIS and GPS
   (iii) Human Ecology (iv) Field survey methods
   Choose the correct option.
   (a) Only (i) (b) Both (ii) and (iv) (c) Both (i) and (iii) (d) Only (iv)
5. Match the following.

List I		List II	
A.	Geomorphology	1.	Comprises country/ rural and town/ urban planning
B.	Plant geography	2.	Comprises macro, meso and micro regional studies
C.	Regional Studies	3.	Studies landforms and related processes
D.	Regional Planning	4.	Studies natural vegetation in their habitats

Codes

	A	B	C	D		A	B	C	D
(a)	4	3	1	2	(b)	3	4	1	2
(c)	2	3	1	4	(d)	4	2	1	3

Short Answer Type Questions

6. Geographers do not study only the variations in the phenomena over the Earth's surface but also study the associations with the other factors which cause these variations. Justify the statement.
7. Explain how primitive human societies were directly dependent on their immediate environment.
8. Spatial distance has been a very potent factor to alter the course of history of the world. Substantiate the statement.

Long Answer Type Questions

9. Explain the impact of human activities in utilisation of natural resources.
10. Elaborate, how does subject matter and methodology of geography differ from those of other discipline.
11. Discuss the concept of regional approach in geography, how it differs from the systematic approach.

2 CHAPTER

This chapter deals with formation of stars and origin of the Earth. The term 'Earth' comes from the old English word 'ertha' which simply means the ground.

YOUR STUDY GOALS

2.1 Origin of the Earth
2.2 Evolution of the Earth

YOUR PRACTICE GOAL

- Objective Type Questions (22 Qs ; MCQs, Statements, Matching, A-R,)
- Subjective Questions (10 SAs, 3 LAs)
- Source Based Questions (4 Qs)

The Origin and Evolution of the Earth

2.1 Origin of the Earth

- The earth is our home planet[1] which sustains all forms of life on it.
- Many scholars gave theories, concepts and hypothesis (proposed explanations) explaining the origin of the planet Earth.
- There are both early and modern theories that explain the Origin of the Earth.

Early Theories

- Scientists in early period focused more on explaining the origin of the Earth or Planet rather than Origin of the Universe[2].

1. *Nebular Hypothesis*

- This hypothesis was given by **Immanuel Kant**, a German philosopher.
- The hypothesis explains that the planets were formed out of a cloud of material associated with a **Youthful sun**, which was slowly rotating.
- This hypothesis was revised by **Laplace in 1796**. It was further revised by two scholars in 1950 named - **Otto Schmidt (Russia) and Carl Weizascar (Germany)**. They considered that Sun was surrounded by **Solar Nebula** containing mostly **Hydrogen** and **Helium** along with **dust**.

1 Planet It is a celestial body that does not have its own heat and light and is moving in an elliptical orbit around a star.
2. Universe The universe is a large space that includes everything like stars, planets, galaxies, etc.

- The friction and collision of particles led to the formation of a disk-shaped cloud and the planets were formed through the process of accretion[3].

Modern Theories

- Scientists in later period proposed theories regarding the origin of universe, stars[4] and planets.

1. Big Bang Theory

- This theory was given by **Edwin Hubble** in 1920. It is also known as ***Expanding Universe Hypothesis***.
- The theory provides evidence that the universe is expanding. With time, galaxies moved further and further apart.

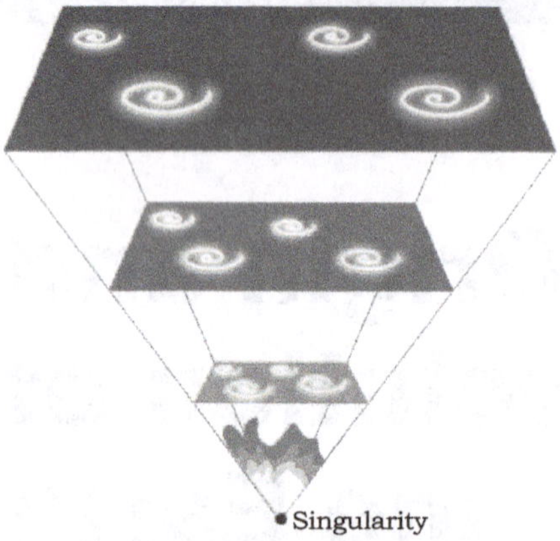

▲ *The Big Bang*

- Big Bang Theory explains following stages in the development of the Universe
  1. In the beginning, all matter forming the universe existed in one place in the form of tiny ball (singular atom) having small volume, infinite temperature and infinite density.
  2. At the Big Bang, the tiny ball exploded violently, leading to huge expansion. It is generally accepted that the event took place **13.7 billion years** before the present. Within the first three minutes from Big Bang event, the first atom began to form.
  3. Within 3,00,000 years from Big Bang Theory, the temperature dropped to 4500K.

     This gave rise to atomic matter and Universe became transparent.

2. Hoyle's Concept of *Steady State*

- According to this concept, the universe is considered to be roughly the same at any point of time.
- Some scientists supported the concept of Steady State but evidences were more in support of Expanding Universe theory.

Formation of The Stars

- The distribution of matter and energy was not equal in the early universe.
- Initially, there was differences in the density of matter which resulted in differences in gravitational force and brought the matters together. These formed the base for the development of galaxies.
- Galaxy contains a large number of stars. The diameters of individual galaxies ranges from 80,000 - 1,50,000 light years.
- There was a large cloud of hydrogen gas that accumulated to form a galaxy called a *Nebula*.
- The growing Nebula develops localised clumps (to gather) of gas. These clumps continue to grow into denser gaseous bodies and forms stars.
- The formation of stars has taken place **5-6 billion years ago**.

LIGHT YEAR

- It is a measurement of astronomical distances which is equal to distance light travels in one year. The Speed of light is 3,00,000 km/second.
- One light year is equal to **9.461×10^{12}** km.
- The means distance between Sun and the Earth is 1,49,598,000 km. In terms of light year, it is 8.311 minutes.

3 **Accretion** It refers to the process of growth or increase by the gradual accumulation of additional layers.

4 **Stars** A natural luminous body in the sky that sends out its own light, generated by nuclear reaction in its centre.

Formation of Planets

There are three stages in the formation of planets.

(i) **First Stage** The stars are localised lumps of gas formed within a Nebula. Presence of Gravitational force within lumps leads to formation of the core of the gas. Huge rotating disc of gas and dust develops around the gas core.

(ii) **Second Stage** The gas clouds start getting condensed and the matter around the core develops into small-rounded objects. These small rounded objects develop into ***Planetesimals***[5] by the process of **cohesion**[6]. Large bodies start forming by collision and gravitation attraction causes the material to stick together.

(iii) **Third Stage** In this stage, the large number of small planetesimals increase to form a fewer large bodies in the form of planets.

Quick Test 1

1 Who revised Nebular Hypothesis?
2 Nebular Hypothesis was revised in which year?
3 Who propounded the Big Bang Theory?
4 What process leads to the formation of planets?
5 What is the distance in One Light Year?

2.2 Evolution of the Earth

- Initially, the Earth was a barren, rocky and hot object with thin atmosphere of **hydrogen** and **helium**. It took 4600 million years to develop in its present form.
- The Earth has different layers from surface towards the deeper depths and each layer has a different physical and chemical characteristics.

Evolution of Lithosphere

- In the beginning stage, the Earth was in an unstable state. With the increasing density, temperature inside the Earth also increased. Materials with different densities started getting separated.
- Heavier material like iron went down towards the Earth's center while the lighter material moved towards the surface.
- Heating up of Earth continued due to great impact during formation of the Moon.
- As time passed, materials **cooled, solidified** and **condensed**[7] into smaller size.
- This solidified layer was termed as **'Crust'** which is the outer layer of the Earth. Different layers of the Earth got separated by the process of differentiation.
- From surface to center of the Earth, we have different layers like - **Crust, Mantle** and **Core**.
- Density of the material increases as we go from **Crust** towards the **Core**.

5 Planetesimal Numerous small celestial bodies that may have existed at an early stage of development of the solar system.
6 Cohesion The act or process of sticking together tightly.
7 Condensed Reduction in volume, area and length.

Evolution of the Atmosphere

- Earth's atmosphere has evolved over time through different physical, biological and chemical processes.
- Stages involved in the formation of Earth's atmosphere are as follows
  - (i) **Loss of existing atmosphere** The loss of early atmosphere which comprised of Hydrogen and Helium.
  - (ii) **Earth's hot interior** Volcanic eruptions released gases like water vapour, carbon dioxide, which resulted in the formation of thick atmosphere.
  - (iii) ***Photosynthesis***[8] Living world like plants, algae, cyanobacteria modified the atmosphere by adding oxygen to the atmosphere.
- As the Earth cooled, it caused release of water vapour and gases from the interior and marked the evolution of the atmosphere.
- **Nitrogen and oxygen** has the maximum contribution in the present atmosphere.
- The process that involved discharging of the gases from interior of the Earth is called as ***degassing***.

Evolution of Hydrosphere

- Water vapour and gases were added to the atmosphere by the activity of volcanic eruption.
- Water vapour condensed as the Earth started cooling.
- Oceans were formed when the condensed water after converting into rain, got collected in **depressions**[9].
- Presence of oxygen in oceans began with the process of photosynthesis around 2500-3000 million years ago.

Origin of Life

- Modern scientists explain the origin of life as a kind of chemical reaction, which first generated complex organic molecules and assembled them.
- This arrangement was designed in a way that they could duplicate themselves by transforming non-living material (matter) into living matter i.e. molecules to human.
- It can be assumed that life began to evolve around 3800 million years ago as fossils found in the rocks provides evidences of life existed on this planet.

Quick Test 2

1 How old is our planet Earth?
2 What are the three different layers of the Earth?
3 Which gas has maximum contribution in the atmosphere?
4 What is the process of outflow of gases from interior of the Earth is known as?

---

8 **Photosynthesis** It is the process by which plants use sunlight to convert carbon-dioxide, water and other minerals to glucose and oxygen.
9 **Depression** It is a landform that is lower than the surrounding area.

Mind Map

ORIGIN AND EVOLUTION OF THE EARTH

1 Theories Related to Origin of the Earth

Early Theories: Nebular Hypothesis
- Given by Immanuel Kant.
- Explains that planets were formed out of a cloud of material associated with youthful Sun.

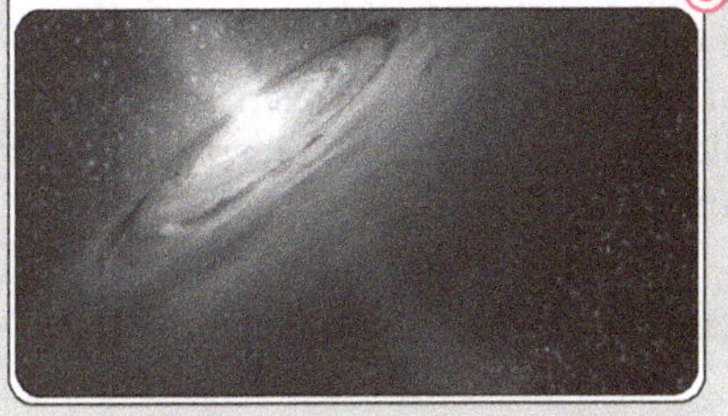

Modern Theories
Big Bang Theory/Expanding Universe Hypothesis
- Given by Edwin Hubble.
- Explains the universe's origin and expansion.
- A tiny, dense and hot ball exploded 13.7 billion years ago.
- Matter formed and the universe expanded, continuing today

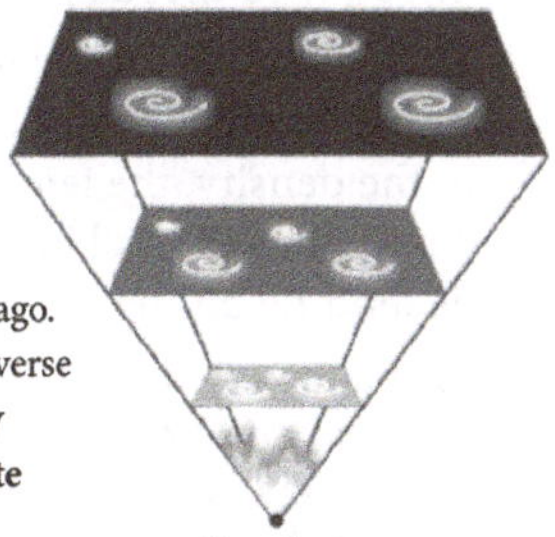

Hoyle's Concept of Steady State
- Given by Fred Hoyle.
- Explains that universe is same at any point of time

2 Formation of Stars and Planets

Formation of Stars
Large cloud of hydrogen gas accumulated to form galaxy which grows denser and formed stars.

Formation of Planets
- **First stage** Huge rotating disc of gas and dust develops around the gas core.
- **Second stage** Large bodies formed by collision.
- **Last stage** Small planetesimals were formed by accretion.

3 Evolutions of the Earth

- **Age of the Earth**-4600 million years. It was a hot, rocky and barren object with hydrogen and helium
- **Present Earth** A planet with ample of water and atmosphere for existence of life.

Evolution of Atmosphere
- Atmosphere evolved in three stages
  (i) Loss of early atmosphere comprising hydrogen and helium.
  (ii) Volcanic eruptions released gases which were added to the atmosphere.
  (iii) Living world like plants, algae added oxygen to the atmosphere.

Evolution of Lithosphere
Different density and temperature inside Earth created different layers like Crust, Mantle and Core.

Evolution of Hydrosphere
- As the Earth cooled, water vapour condensed and rainfall occured which got collected in depressions.
- Nitrogen and oxygen has the maximum contribution in atmosphere.

Origin of Life
- Resulted as a kind of chemical reaction, which first generated complex organic molecules and assembled them.
- Life began to evolve around 3800 million years ago as evidences found from the fossils.

NCERT Folder

Intext Question

1. How was the layered structure of the Earth developed?

Ans. Development of the layered structure of the Earth can be understood through the following points

The Earth was mostly in volatile (unstable) state during its primordial (beginning) stage. Due to gradual increase in the density, the temperature inside has increased. As a result, the material inside started getting separated depending on their density.

This allowed heavier materials (like iron) to sink towards the centre of the Earth and the lighter ones to move towards the surface. With passage of time, it cooled further and solidified and condensed into a smaller size which later led to the development of outer surface in the form of crust.

During the formation of the Moon, due to the giant impact, the Earth was further heated up. It is through the process of differentiation that the Earth forming material got separated into different layers. Starting from the surface to the central parts, it has layers like the crust, mantle, outer core and inner core. From the crust to the core, the density of the material increases.

Multiple Choice Questions

(i) Which one of the following figures represents the age of the Earth?

(a) 4.6 million years
(b) 13.7 billion years
(c) 4.6 billion years
(d) 13.7 trillion years

Ans. (c) 4.6 billion years

(ii) Which one of the following is not related to the formation or modification of the present atmosphere?

(a) Solar winds
(b) Differentiation
(c) Degassing
(d) Photosynthesis

Ans. (b) Differentiation

(iii) Life on the earth appeared around how many years before the present?

(a) 13.7 billion
(b) 3.8 million
(c) 4.6 billion
(d) 3.8 billion

Ans. (d) 3.8 billion

Answer the following questions in about 30 words

(i) What is meant by the process of differentiation?

Ans. Starting from the surface to the central parts, the Earth have layers like the crust, mantle, outer core and inner core. From crust to the core, the density of the material increases. This process of separation is known as differentiation. The Earth forming material got separated into different layers due to difference in density of rock forming material. Lighter materials rose upwards and heavy materials sank downwards.

(ii) What was the nature of the Earth surface initially?

Ans. The planet Earth initially was a barren, rocky and hot object with a thin atmosphere of hydrogen and helium. It took 4600 million years to develop in its present form of a beautiful planet with ample amount of water and existence of life.

(iii) What were the gases which initially formed the Earth's atmosphere?

Ans. The gases which initially formed the Earth's atmosphere were hydrogen and helium. As a result of solar winds, these gases were stripped off and during the cooling of the Earth other gases like nitrogen, carbon dioxide, water vapour, etc were released from the interior solid Earth.

Answer the following questions in about 150 words

(i) Write an explanatory note on the 'Big Bang theory'.

Ans. Big bang theory is the most popular theory about the origin of the universe. It is also called the expanding universe theory. The evidence of expanding universe was provided by Edwin Hubble in 1920.

The big bang theory considers the following stages in the development of the universe:

- In the beginning, all matter forming the universe existed in one place in the form of a 'tiny ball' with an unimaginably small volume, infinite temperature and infinite density.
- At the big bang, the 'tiny ball' exploded violently which led to a huge expansion. It took place 13.7 billion years before the present. The expansion continues even to the present day. The expansion was rapid in first few seconds after the bang but it slowed down during later stage. Within first three minutes from the big bang event, the first atom began to form.
- In the course of process, within 300,000 years, temperature dropped to 4,500K (Kelvin) which gave rise to atomic matter and finally after that, the universe started to come in shape and became transparent.

(ii) List the stages in the evolution of the Earth and explain each stage in brief.

Ans. The following stages define the evolution of the earth

(i) **Stage I** It involves evolution of lithosphere. The existing Earth was unstable. Its density gradually increased with temperature which resulted into the separation of material based on their densities.

With the passage of time, it cooled further and solidified and condensed into a smaller size. This led to differentiation in Earth's structure in the form of crust, mantle, outer core and inner core.

(ii) **Stage II** It involves the evolution of atmosphere and hydrosphere.

Formation of Atmosphere

The stages in the evolution of the present day atmosphere are:

- Loss of existing atmosphere that contained thin layer of hydrogen and helium as a result of stripping off by solar winds.
- The gases were outpoured from the hot interior of the earth during the cooling of the Earth through degassing. This started the evolution of the early atmosphere which largely contained water vapour, and gases.
- Photosynthesis modified the composition of the atmosphere.

Formation of Hydrosphere

As water vapour existed in the atmosphere, it got condensed after cooling of the earth and came down as rainfall. The depressions got filled with rainwater and within 500 billion years from the formation of the earth, oceans came into existence. The process of photosynthesis was initially confined to oceans only and thus ocean started filling up with the oxygen and later the oxygen started to flood the atmosphere.

(iii) **Stage III** In this stage life began to evolve 3800 million years ago. It is considered a kind of chemical reaction which first generated complex organic molecules and assembled them.

This assemblage was such that it could duplicate itself by converting inanimate matter into living substance.

Exam Pattern Questions

Objective Type Questions

Multiple Choice Questions (MCQs)

1. The arguments proposed by Immanuel Kant regarding origin of Earth were revised by .... in 1796.

(a) Laplace (b) Moulton
(c) Chamberlain (d) Otto Schmidt

2. 'The universe is considered to be roughly the same at any point of time' this concept was given by

(a) Einstein (b) Hoyle
(c) Edwin Hubble (d) Galileo

3. Which of the following hypothesis considered the universe roughly the same at any given point? CBSE Diksha

(a) Big Bang Theory (b) Galaxy Expansion Theory
(c) Nebular Hypothesis (d) Steady State Theory

4. Which one of the following represents Hoyle's concept regarding origin of universe?

(a) Universe is in expanding state
(b) Universe is in shrinking state
(c) Universe is almost in same state at any point of time
(d) None of the above

5. 'Expanding Universe' means

(a) distance between galaxies is increasing.
(b) distance between galaxies is decreasing.
(c) distance between galaxies is constant.
(d) None of the above

6. A galaxy contains a large number of ....

(a) Planets (b) Stars
(c) Satellites (d) All of these

7. Light-year is used to measure ....

(a) Years (b) Light
(c) Distance (d) Diameter

8. A galaxy starts to form by accumulation of hydrogen gas in the form of

(a) Nebula (b) Planetesimal
(c) Water vapour (d) Stars

9. There are three stages in the formation of planets. Identify the stage from the description.

The gas cloud starts getting condensed and the matter around the core develops into objects.

These small-rounded objects by the process of cohesion develop into what is called planetesimals. Larger bodies start forming by collision, and gravitational attraction causes the material to stick together. Planetesimals are a large number of smaller bodies.

(a) Beginning stage (b) Middle stage
(c) Final stage (d) None of these

10. Which of the following gases was added to atmosphere during photosynthesis?

(a) Carbon Dioxide (b) Oxygen
(c) Hydrogen (d) Helium

11. Which of the following arrangements of Earth's layer is correct?

(a) Crust, mantle, inner core, outer core
(b) Mantle, crust, outer core, inner core
(c) Mantle, crust, inner core, outer core
(d) Crust, mantle, outer core, inner core

12. Choose the incorrect matching pair from the following.

(a) Primary Atmosphere - Hydrogen and Helium
(b) Accretion of Planetesimals - Formation of Stars
(c) Age of the Earth - 4.6 billion years
(d) Expanding Universe - Big Bang Theory

13. Arrange the following layers of the Earth, according to their increasing density.

(i) Crust (ii) Mantle (iii) Core

Choose the correct sequence

(a) (ii), (iii), (i) (b) (i), (ii), (iii)
(c) (ii), (i), (iii) (d) (iii), (i), (ii)

14. Statement I The stars are localised lumps of gas within a nebula.

Statement II Formation of core of the gas cloud is due to the gravitational pull between lumps.

Consider the following statements and choose the correct one.

(a) Only statement I is correct
(b) Both are correct
(c) Only statement II is correct
(d) Both are incorrect

15. 'Evolution of atmosphere involves three stages'. Choose the correct sequence from the following.

(i) Volcanic eruptions released gases like water vapour, carbon dioxide, which resulted in the formation of thick atmosphere.
(ii) Living world like plants, algae, cyanobacteria modified the atmosphere by adding oxygen to the atmosphere.
(iii) The loss of early atmosphere which comprises of hydrogen and helium.

Options

(a) (iii), (i), (ii) (b) (i), (ii), (iii)
(c) (ii), (i), (iii) (d) (ii), (iii), (i)

16. Consider the following statements. Which of them is/are correct?

I. The process through which gases were outpoured from interior is called degassing.
II. Continuous volcanic eruptions contributed water vapour and gases to atmosphere.

Codes

(a) Only I (b) Only II
(c) Both I and II (d) Neither I nor II

17. Consider the following statements. Which of them is/are correct?

I. A galaxy starts to form by accumulation of hydrogen gas in the form of a very large cloud called Nebula.
II. Eventually, this Nebula develops localised clumps of gas, which continue to grow into even denser gaseous bodies.

Codes

(a) Only I (b) Only II
(c) Both I and II (d) Neither I nor II

Match the Following

18.

	List I (Theory)		List II (Associated Terms)
A.	Steady State	1.	Rocky and Barren
B.	Big Bang	2.	Expanding Universe
C.	Nebular Hypothesis	3.	Non-changing Universe
D	Evolution of the Earth	4.	Solar Nebula

Codes

	A	B	C	D		A	B	C	D
(a)	4	3	1	2	(b)	3	2	4	1
(c)	2	3	1	4	(d)	1	4	3	2

19.

	List I (Spheres)		List II (Component)
A.	Lithosphere	1.	Nitrogen and Oxygen
B.	Hydrosphere	2.	Living Substance
C.	Biosphere	3.	Oceans
D	Atmosphere	4.	Crust

Codes

	A	B	C	D		A	B	C	D
(a)	4	1	3	2	(b)	4	3	1	2
(c)	3	2	4	1	(d)	4	3	2	1

Assertion-Reason

Directions (Q. Nos. 20-22) In the questions given below are two statements labelled as Assertion (A) and other is labelled as Reason (R). In the context of two statements which one of the following is correct?

Codes

(a) Both A and R are true, but R is not the correct explanation of A

(b) Both A and R are true and R is the correct explanation of A

(c) Both A and R are incorrect

(d) A is correct, but R is incorrect

20. **Assertion** (A) The Earth has a layered structure.

Reason (R) Density of material decreases as we move from surface to interior of the Earth.

21. **Assertion** (A) The early Earth had no atmosphere.

Reason (R) The intense solar winds from the young Sun swept away the lighter gases in the early solar system.

22. **Assertion** (A) The Big Bang Theory suggests the universe began from a singularity.

Reason (R) The singularity was an infinitely small and dense point (tiny ball) where all matter and energy were concentrated.

Answers

1. (a) Laplace
2. (b) Hoyle
3. (d) Steady State Theory
4. (c) Universe is almost in same state at any point of time
5. (a) distance between galaxies is increasing.
6. (b) Stars
7. (c) Distance
8. (a) Nebula
9. (b) Middle stage
10. (b) Oxygen
11. (d) Crust, mantle, outer core, inner core
12. (b) Accretion of Planetesimals - Formation of Stars
13. (b) (i), (ii), (iii)
14. (b) Both are correct
15. (a) (iii), (i), (ii)
16. (c) Both I and II
17. (c) Both I and II
18. (b)
19. (d)
20. (d) A is correct, but R is incorrect
21. (b) Both A and R are true and R is the correct explanation of A
22. (b) Both A and R are true and R is the correct explanation of A

Subjective Questions

Short Answer Type Questions

1. Explain the concept of Nebular hypothesis regarding the origin of the Earth.

Ans. The Nebular hypothesis suggests that the Earth and other planets formed around 4.6 billion years ago from a rotating cloud of gas and dust, called a nebula. Gravitational forces caused the nebula to collapse, leading to the formation of a central protostar (the Sun) and a surrounding disk of matter. Over time, particles within the disk collided and fused to form planetesimals, which eventually merged to create planets, including Earth. This occured through the process of accretion with gravity driving the growth of celestial bodies.

2. There were different situations which were responsible for the formation of stars. Explain in brief about the formation of stars.

Ans. The formation of stars took place 5-6 billion years ago. In the early universe, energy and matter were unevenly distributed creating varying gravitational forces. This caused matter to get clumped together to form galaxies and they vary in size from 80000 to 150000 light years in diameters. A galaxy contains a large number of stars.

A galaxy starts to form by the accumulation of hydrogen gas in a large cloud called Nebula and it develops numerous clumps of gas. These clumps continue to grow in size as denser gaseous bodies and turn into stars.

3. What are the three stages of formation of planets?

Ans. The following are considered to be the three stages of formation of planets

(i) **First stage** The stars are localised lumps of gas within a nebula. Presence of gravitational force within the lumps lead to the formation of a core to the gas cloud and a huge rotating disc of gas, and dust develops around the gas core.

(ii) **Second stage** The gas cloud starts getting condensed and the matter around the core develops into small rounded objects. These objects by the process of cohesion develop into planetesimals. Larger bodies start forming by collision and gravitational attraction causes the material to stick together.

(iii) **Third stage** Smaller planetesimals gradually accumulated together to form a fewer large bodies in the form of planets.

4. How did the Earth's lithosphere form?

Ans. The Earth's lithosphere formed as the planet cooled after its molten phase. Initially, the surface was entirely molten, but as heat was released into space, the outer layer solidified into a rigid crust. Over millions of years, the lithosphere thickened and became divided into tectonic plates. These plates float on the semi-fluid asthenosphere beneath them. It is a part of upper mantle located below the crust of the Earth and their movement has shaped Earth's surface through processes like volcanism and mountain formation.

5. Explain the formation of different layers in the lithosphere.

Ans. The formation of different layers of the lithosphere is explained through the process of differentiation as follows

- In the beginning stage, the Earth was in an unstable state and with increasing density, temperature also increased inside the Earth.
- Material with different densities started getting separated.
- Heavier material went down towards centre and lighter material moved towards the surface of the Earth.
- With time, materials cooled, solidified and condensed into smaller size.
- Solidified layer was termed as 'Crust' which is outer layer of the Earth.
- From surface to centre layers are formed as crust, mantle and core.

6. 'Earth's atmosphere has evolved over time through different physical, biological and chemical processes'. Elucidate. Competency Based Que

Ans. Earth's early atmosphere formed primarily through volcanic outgassing during the planet's molten phase. Gases such as water vapor, carbon dioxide, methane and nitrogen were released from the interior. This initial atmosphere lacked oxygen and was primarily composed of heavier gases. Over time, as the planet cooled and early life forms emerged, oxygen was added through photosynthesis, leading to the formation of the present-day atmosphere.

7. Explain different stages in the development of atmosphere.

Ans. The present composition of atmosphere is chiefly contributed by nitrogen and oxygen. There are three stages in the evolution of the present atmosphere

(i) First stage is marked by the loss of primordial atmosphere.

(ii) Secondly, the hot interior of the Earth contributed to the evolution of the atmosphere.

(iii) Finally, the composition of the atmosphere was modified by the living world through the process of photosynthesis.

During the cooling of the Earth, gases and water vapour were released from the interior solid Earth that started the evolution of the present atmosphere.

8. Explain in brief the evolution of oceans.

Ans. The evolution of oceans on the Earth took place as follows

- Water vapour and gases added to the atmosphere due to volcanic eruptions.
- After cooling of the Earth, water vapours released started getting condensed.
- Carbon dioxide in the atmosphere got dissolved in rainwater.
- Temperature further decreased causing more condensation and more rain.
- The rainwater falling onto the surface got collected in the depressions to give rise to oceans.

9. 'Origin and evolution of life began in the last phase of the evolution of the Earth.' Explain the statement in brief. Competency Based Que

Ans. Origin and evolution of life began in the last phase of the evolution of the earth. Early atmosphere was not conducive for the evolution of life on the Earth. According to the modern scientists, life evolved on the Earth due to chemical reactions. The reactions first generated complex organic molecules and assembled them.

This assemblage was capable of duplicating themselves converting inorganic matter into living substance. Records of life in different periods are found in the rocks in the form of fossils. Scientists believe that life began on the Earth sometimes 3800 million years ago.

10. Describe briefly various theories associated with the origin of the Earth. CBSE Diksha

Ans. Several theories explain the formation of Earth, each contributing to our understanding of its origins. Here are some of the most prominent theories

- **Nebular hypothesis** According to this theory, the planets were formed out of a cloud of material associated with youthful Sun which was slowly rotating. It was revised by Laplace in 1796.

- **Big Bang theory** This theory was given by Edwin Hubble. He argued that universe was ever expanding. As time passes, galaxies move further and further apart.
- **Hoyle's Steady State Theory** The concept of steady state considered the universe roughly the same at any point of time and argued the concept of universe to be expanding.

Long Answer Type Questions

1. The Earth has a number of factors which make life possible on our planet. Justify the statement by giving these factors. Competency Based Que

Ans. The Earth has a number of factors which make life possible on our planet. The Earth is a unique planet not only in the solar system, but also in the whole universe. Life exists only on it. Animals, plants, micro-organisms and numerous other living beings live on it.

The factors that have made life possible on our earth are as follows

- **The Distance of the Earth from the Sun** The Earth is at an optimum distance from the Sun as compared to other planets in the solar system. So, the Earth has an average temperature of 15°C. The range of temperature varies so much that water is found in solid, liquid and gaseous state on our Earth.
  Water is a prerequisite for all forms of life. Life originated and developed in the water, then it spread to land. Therefore, plants grow and animals live here.
- **The Existence of Three Realms on the Earth** The Earth is the only known planet in the universe where three realms i.e. atmosphere, hydrosphere and lithosphere exist. These make life possible on the Earth. But other planets do not have these realms.
- **The Right Mixture of Gases in the Earth's Atmosphere** The Earth's atmosphere has an ideal mixture of nitrogen, oxygen, carbon dioxide and ozone. Non-availability of oxygen to our body even for a fraction of second makes us restless. The atmosphere of Venus and Mars mainly consists of carbon dioxide.
- **The Presence of Ozone Layer in the Atmosphere of the Earth** Ozone layer absorbs a large proportion of the Sun's ultraviolet radiation. Without this absorption, the Earth would be subjected to a degree of ultra-violet radiation which is injurious to plants and animals.
- **The Ideal Duration of Day and Night** The average duration of day and night on the Earth is of 12 hours each which is ideal for all living beings.
  A single night on Mercury is as long as 30 Earth nights. On venus, the night is still longer. It is as long as 122 Earth nights. In contrast, on jupiter and saturn, the duration of a night is only of five hours each.

2. Discuss the conditions that contributed to the origin of life on Earth.

Ans. The conditions that contributed to the origin of the Earth are as follows

- The origin of life occurred around 3.5 to 4 billion years ago. The early Earth had a reducing atmosphere mainly composed of methane, ammonia, water vapour, nitrogen, carbon dioxide and very little of free oxygen.
- Abundant energy sources facilitated chemical reactions, including volcanic activity, lightening, ultraviolet radiation from the Sun.
- Large bodies of water on Earth's surface provided a medium for chemical reactions.
- Simple molecules combined over time to form complex organic molecules, such as amino acids, proteins. These complex organic molecules eventually led to the development of self-replicating systems.
- A warm, water-rich environment with essential nutrients and energy sources created ideal conditions for the formation and evolution of the first primitive life forms.

3. "The evolution of present-day atmosphere started with the loss of primordial atmosphere". Justify the statement.

Ans. The statement "The evolution of the present-day atmosphere started with the loss of the primordial atmosphere" is justified through understanding Earth's atmospheric development. Initially, Earth possessed a primordial atmosphere composed mainly of hydrogen and helium, which was lost due to the planet's low gravity and high temperatures. Volcanic outgassing, which released water vapour, carbon dioxide and nitrogen, contributed to the formation of a secondary atmosphere. As Earth cooled, water vapour condensed to form oceans, creating a stable environment.

The advent of photosynthetic organisms, particularly cyanobacteria, played a crucial role by converting carbon dioxide into oxygen, gradually enriching the atmosphere with O_2 significantly transformed the atmosphere, enabling the development of living matters and changing climatic conditions. Thus, the loss of the primordial atmosphere and subsequent geological and biological processes have been pivotal in shaping the present-day atmosphere, which supports diverse life on Earth.

Source Based Questions

1 Read the passage carefully and answer the questions that follow.

The most popular argument regarding the origin of the universe is the Big Bang Theory. It is also called expanding universe hypothesis. Edwin Hubble, in 1920, provided evidence that the universe is expanding. As time passes, galaxies move further and further apart. The distance between the galaxies is also found to be increasing and thereby, the universe is considered to be expanding.

The Big Bang Theory considers the following stages in the development of the universe.

(i) In the beginning, all matter forming the universe existed in one place in the form of a "tiny ball" (singular atom) with an unimaginably small volume, infinite temperature and infinite density.

(ii) At the Big Bang the 'tiny ball' exploded violently. This led to a huge expansion. It is now generally accepted that the event of big bang took place 13.7 billion years before the present. The expansion continues even to the present day. As it grew, some energy was converted into matter. There was particularly rapid expansion within fractions of a second after the bang. Thereafter, the expansion has slowed down. Within first three minutes from the Big Bang event, the first atom began to form.

(iii) Within 300,000 years from the Big Bang, temperature dropped to 4,500K (Kelvin) and gave rise to atomic matter. The universe became transparent.

The expansion of universe means increase in space between the galaxies. An alternative to this was Hoyle's concept of steady state. It considered the universe to be roughly the same at any point of time. However, with greater evidence becoming available about the expanding universe, scientific community at present favours argument of expanding universe.

(i) Who among the following was the first one to give evidence of an expanding state of universe?

(a) Albert Einstein (b) Edwin Hubble
(c) Isaac Newton (d) Hoyle

Ans. (b) Edwin Hubble

(ii) Before the occurrence of Big Bang, the universe was in which of the following state?

(a) Steady state (b) Singular Atom
(c) Expanding state (d) Contracting state

Ans. (b) Singular Atom

(iii) Which of the following can be considered as the age of universe?

(a) 5.4 billion years (b) 13.7 billion years
(c) 9 billion years (d) 2 billion years

Ans. (b) 13.7 billion years

2 Read the passage carefully and answer the questions that follow.

Planet Earth initially was a barren, rocky and hot object with a thin atmosphere of hydrogen and helium. This is far from the present day picture of the earth. Hence, there must have been some events– processes, which may have caused this change from rocky, barren and hot earth to a beautiful planet with ample amount of water and conducive atmosphere favouring the existence of life. How did the period, between the 4,600 million years and the present, led to the evolution of life on the surface of the planet. The earth has a layered structure. From the outermost end of the atmosphere to the centre of the earth, the material that exists is not uniform. The atmospheric matter has the least density. From the surface to deeper depths, the earth's interior has different zones and each of these contains materials with different characteristics.

The earth was mostly in a volatile state during its primordial stage. Due to gradual increase in density the temperature inside has increased. As a result the material inside started getting separated depending on their densities. This allowed heavier materials (like iron) to sink towards the centre of the earth and the lighter ones to move towards the surface. With passage of time it cooled further and solidified and condensed into a smaller size. This later led to the development of the outer surface in the form of a crust. During the formation of the moon, due to the giant impact, the earth was further heated up. It is through the process of differentiation that the earth forming material got separated into different layers. Starting from the surface to the central parts, we have layers like the crust, mantle, outer core and inner core. From the crust to the core, the density of the material increases.

(i) Why the Earth was not habitable in the early periods?

Ans. The Earth was not habitable in the early periods because it was a barren, rocky and hot object with a thin atmosphere of hydrogen and helium. These conditions were not suitable for the survival of organisms.

(ii) Due to which process the heavy material like iron sunk towards the centre of the Earth and the lighter ones to move towards the surface of the Earth?

Ans. Due to gradual increase in density, the temperature inside the Earth has increased. As a result, the material inside started getting separated depending on their densities. This allowed heavier materials like iron to sink towards the centre of the Earth and the lighter ones to move towards the surface.

(iii) The Earth is composed of which how many layers?

Ans. Starting from the surface to the central parts, the earth is composed of three layers like the crust, mantle and the core (outer core and inner core).

3. Read the passage carefully and answer the questions that follow.

The present composition of Earth's atmosphere is chiefly contributed by nitrogen and oxygen. There are three stages in the evolution of the present atmosphere. The first stage is marked by the loss of primordial atmosphere. In the second stage, the hot interior of the Earth contributed to the evolution of the atmosphere. Finally, the composition of the atmosphere was modified by the living world through the process of photosynthesis. The early atmosphere, with hydrogen and helium, is supposed to have been stripped off as a result of the solar winds. This happened not only in case of the earth, but also in all the terrestrial planets, which were supposed to have lost their primordial atmosphere through the impact of solar winds. During the cooling of the earth, gases and water vapour were released from the interior solid earth. This started the evolution of the present atmosphere. The early atmosphere largely contained water vapour, nitrogen, carbon dioxide, methane, ammonia and very little of free oxygen. The process through which the gases were outpoured from the interior is called degassing. Continuous volcanic eruptions contributed water vapour and gases to the atmosphere.

(i) What is the process called by which the living world modified the atmosphere?

(a) Volcanic eruptions
(b) Photosynthesis
(c) Degassing
(d) Primordial stripping

Ans. (b) Photosynthesis

(ii) Which of the following statement(s) is/are true regarding the early atmosphere?

I. It consisted of Hydrogen and Helium.
II. It consisted of water vapour only.
III. It contained water vapour, nitrogen, carbon dioxide, methane, ammonia and very little of free oxygen.
IV. It contained only carbon dioxide.

Options

(a) Only I is correct (b) I and III both
(c) Only II is correct (d) None of these

Ans. (b) I and III both

(iii) What contributed to the release of water vapour and gases during the Earth's cooling?

(a) Degassing and volcanic eruptions
(b) Solar winds
(c) Primordial atmosphere
(d) Hydrogen and helium decay

Ans. (a) Degassing and volcanic eruptions

4. Read the passage carefully and answer the questions that follow.

The stars are localised lumps of gas within a nebula. The gravitational force within the lumps leads to the formation of a core to the gas cloud and a huge rotating disc of gas and dust develops around the gas core. In the next stage, the gas cloud starts getting condensed and the matter around the core develops into small rounded objects. These small-rounded objects by the process of cohesion develop into what is called planetesimals. Larger bodies start forming by collision and gravitational attraction causes the material to stick together. Planetesimals are a large number of smaller bodies. In the final stage, these large number of small planetesimals accrete to form a fewer large bodies in the form of planets.

The earth was mostly in a volatile state during its primordial stage. Due to gradual increase in density the temperature inside has increased. As a result, the material inside started getting separated depending on their densities. This allowed heavier materials (like iron) to sink towards the centre of the earth and the lighter ones to move towards the surface. With passage of time it cooled further and solidified and condensed into a smaller size. This later led to the development of the outer surface in the form of a crust.

(i) Mention the force that lead to the formation of a core to gas cloud.

Ans. The gravitational force within the lumps leads to the formation of a core to the gas cloud and a huge rotating disc of gas and dust developed around the gas core.

(ii) There are different stages in the formation of planets. The final stage involves what activity?

Ans. In the final stage, these large number of small planetesimals accrete to form a fewer large bodies in the form of planets.

(iii) 'The density changes as we go deeper into the earth's surface'. Comment.

Ans. Density increases as we move from surface of the Earth towards the centre. Increase in the density leads to the increase in temperature.

SELF ASSESSMENT TEST

Objective Type Questions

1. The planets are formed through the process of ....
   (a) Photosynthesis (b) Accretion
   (c) Degassing (d) Giant impact
2. Who suggested that the Earth and the Moon formed a single rapidly rotating body?
   (a) Sir George Darwin (b) Edwin Hubble
   (c) Immanuel Kant (d) Otto Schmidt
3. Which of the following was element of early atmosphere?
   (a) Water vapour (b) Ammonia
   (c) Methane (d) All of these
4. Which of the following hypothesis considered universe to be roughly the same at any given point of time?
   (a) Big Bang Theory
   (b) Galaxy Expansion Theory
   (c) Steady State Theory
   (d) Nebular Hypothesis

Short Answer Type Questions

5. 'The origin of the universe is the Big Bang theory'. Justify this statement.
6. 'The universe is considered to be roughly the same at any point of time'. Explain the given statement.
7. 'The Earth was mostly in a volatile state during its primordial stage'. Explain the given statement.

Long Answer Type Questions

8. "Initially the Earth or even the atmospshere of the Earth was not conducive for the development of life'. Justify.
9. 'The planet earth initially was a barren, rocky and hot object with a thin layer of atmosphere'. Explain this visualisation of the Earth.
10. A large number of hypothesis were presented by different philosphers and scientists regarding the origin of the Earth. Explain with the context of early and modern theories.

3 CHAPTER

This chapter deals with the geography of the Earth's surface. It is the result of different processes acting upon it like **Endogenic** (occurring inside) and **Exogenic** (occurring outside) processes.

Interior of the Earth

YOUR STUDY GOALS

3.1 Source of Information about the Interior of the Earth
3.2 Earthquake
3.3 Structure of the Earth
3.4 Volcanoes

YOUR PRACTICE GOAL

- Objective Type Questions (29 Qs ; MCQs, Statements, Matching, A-R)
- Subjective Questions (13 SAs, 7 LAs)
- Source Based Questions (4 Qs)

3.1 Source of Information about the Interior of the Earth

The radius of the Earth is about **6,378 km**, so collecting samples of the material physically is not possible. Thus, scientists mostly depend upon estimates and references.

The two important sources of information about the Earth's interior are as follows

1. Direct Sources
2. Indirect Sources

1. Direct Sources

- These sources include evidences from mining, drilling and volcanic eruptions.
- **Mining** Surface rocks are available easily to study throughout the Earth's crust. Mining activity gives easy access to analyse these rocks, for example, Gold Mines in South Africa.
- **Drilling** Mining beyond 3-4 km is not possible as there is so much heat inside the Earth at this depth. Therefore, scientists are working over projects like - Deep Ocean Drilling and Integrated Ocean Drilling to explore deeper depths.

- The deepest drill that has been done till today is up to 12 km at Kola (Arctic Ocean).
- **Volcanic Eruptions** Magma thrown out during volcanic eruption contains deposits of different chemical composition.Laboratory analysis of these materials provide information about Earth's interior.

2. Indirect Sources

- These sources include analysis of temperature, pressure and density of the material.
- **Temperature, pressure** and **density** increases with increasing depths (from surface towards center).
- Evidences of indirect sources includes - Meteors, Gravitation, Magnetic Field and Seismic activity.
- **Meteors** are solid bodies developed out of materials same as the Earth. So they can be considered as source of information about the interior of the Earth.
- Reading **gravitational value** at different places gives information about the distribution of mass of material in the Earth's crust. Gravitational force near pole is greater than equator because distance from center to the equator is greater than to pole. Gravity[1] value differs according to the mass of the material.
- The reading in gravitational value is influenced by many factors. These readings differ from the expected values. Such a difference is called as **Gravity Anomaly**.
- **Magnetic surveys** provide information about the distribution of magnetic materials (iron rich rocks) in crustal part of the Earth.
- Study of **seismic waves** (earthquake causing waves) provide information about the layered interior of the Earth.

3.2 Earthquake

- Earthquake refers to '**shaking of the Earth**'.
- It is a natural event that occurs because Earth's interior releases energy which generates waves that travel in all directions.

Causes of Earthquake

- Earthquake occurs when the Earth's plates, get locked due to friction and pressure is developed. When the pressure becomes too much, the plates suddenly slip or move, releasing the energy as seismic waves, causing the ground to shake.
- The point where energy is released is called **Focus of an Earthquake** or hypocentre[2].
- The point on the surface nearest to the focus (perpendicular to focus) is called Epicentre[3].

Earthquake Waves

- Earthquake waves are vibrations that travel through the Earth's interior.
- All the natural earthquakes occur in Lithosphere up to 200 km of depth.
- Seismograph[4] is an instrument used to record the waves that reaches to the surface.

Types of Seismic Waves

1. Body Waves
2. Surface Waves

1 Gravity It is the force that attracts the body towards the center of the Earth.
2 Hypocentre It is the point where energy is released. It is also called Focus of Earthquake.
3 Epicentre It is the point on the surface perpendicular to Focus, where earthquake is felt first.
4 Seismograph It is an instrument to detect the magnitude of an earthquake.

Body Waves

- These are formed due to release of energy at the focus and travels in all directions. They are of two types
  1. **P wave** (Primary waves) These waves travels faster and reaches first to the surface. They are similar to sound waves. They travel through solid, liquid and gases. P-waves vibrate parallel to the direction of the wave.
  2. **S wave** (Secondary waves) They arrive at the surface with some time lag. They only travel through solid materials. This characteristic helps scientists to understand the structure of Earth's interior. S waves vibrate perpendicular to direction of the wave.

  Velocity of waves varies as they travel through different densities. Velocity of the wave is higher as it passes through denser material.

  Reflection[5] or Refraction[6] also affects the direction of the waves. Reflection causes waves to bounce back, whereas Refraction causes waves to change direction.

Surface Waves

- These are generated after the body waves interacts with the surface rocks and result in formation of a new set of waves.
- These are the most destructive waves that causes displacement of rocks and collapse of structures.
- These waves are recorded on the seismograph in the last.

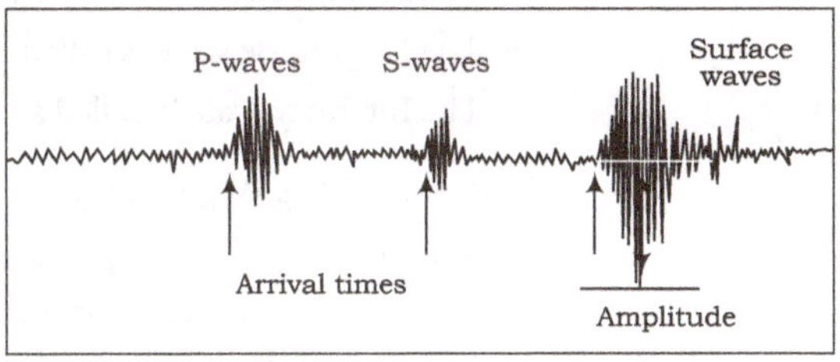

▲ *Earthquake Waves*

Shadow Zone

- There are some specific zones on the Earth surface where earthquake waves are not recorded. These are called **Shadow Zones**.
- In Seismograph up to **105°**, both P and S waves arrives and beyond **145°** only P wave arrives.
- The zone between **105°** to **145°** from the Epicenter is identified as '**The Shadow Zone**'. The shadow zone covered by S wave is large in area about 40% of the Earth surface.
- The entire zone beyond **105°** does not receive S wave.

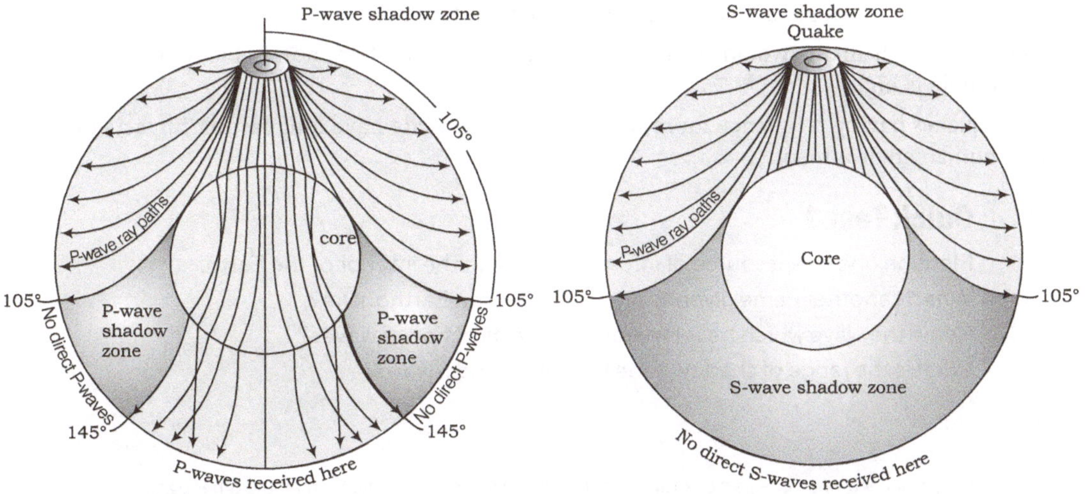

▲ *Earthquake Shadow Zones*

5 Reflection It is a process when light hits the surface and bounces back.

6 Refraction It is a process when light passes through one medium and changes direction.

Types of Earthquakes

There are five types of earthquakes which are as follows

1. **Tectonic Earthquake** These are generated when Earth's tectonic plate moves, causing crust to break.
2. **Volcanic Earthquake** They occurs due to eruption of volcanoes. These are only occured in active volcano zones.
3. **Collapse Earthquake** These occur in areas of intense mining. Tremors are caused when roofs of underground mines collapses.
4. **Explosion earthquake** These occur due to explosion of chemical or nuclear devices.
5. **Reservoir Earthquake** These occur in areas of large reservoirs.

Measurement of Earthquake

- The Earthquake event is measured either by **Magnitude** (energy released) or **Intensity** (damage caused).
- The Magnitude scale is called as **Richter scale** and has numbers from 0 - 10.
- The Intensity scale is called as **Mercalli scale** and has numbers from 1 - 12.

Effects of Earthquake

- The following are the immediate hazardous effects of earthquake. Some has effects on landforms while some has direct effects on life and properties.

1. Ground shaking
2. Differential ground settlement[7]
3. Land and mud slides
4. Soil liquefaction[8]
5. Ground lurching[9]
6. Avalanches[10]
7. Ground displacement
8. Floods from dam and Levee[11] failure
9. Fires
10. Structural collapse
11. Falling objects
12. Tsunami[12]

- **Tsunamis** are waves generated due to underwater earthquakes.
- The effect of tsunami would occur only if the epicenter of tremor is below ocean water and the magnitude is high.
- Earthquakes having frequency more than 5 in **Richter scale** have long lasting impacts on the physical and human environment.

Quick Test 1

1. Mention one direct source of information about the interior of the Earth.
2. What is another name given to Hypocenter of an Earthquake?
3. Name the wave which travels parallel to the direction of waves?
4. What is the range of shadow zone for both P and S wave?

---

7 Differential Ground Settlement It is defined when one part of structure's foundation sinks more or faster than the other part.

8 Soil liquefaction It is a phenomenon in which the strength of soil is reduced by earthquake shaking.

9 Ground lurching It is defined as an earthquake motion at right angle to natural or artificial slopes that results in a series of more or less parallel cracks, separating the ground into rough blocks.

10 Avalanches It is a rapid flow of snow down the slope such as a hill or mountain.

11 Levee It is an embankment built to prevent the overflow of a river. It is also a ridge of sediments deposited naturally alongside a river by overflowing water.

12 Tsunami These are the harbour waves generated in sea water by tremors in sea surface.

3.3 Structure of the Earth

The Earth consists of three layers which are

1. The Crust

- It is the outermost layer of the Earth and is rigid in nature. Crust has two divisions
  - (i) **Oceanic Crust** It is thinner having thickness of 5 km and is made of basalt rocks having density of **$2.7 g/cm^3$**.
  - (ii) **Continental Crust** It is thicker having thickness 30 km and is made of heavier rocks having density of **$3 g/cm^3$**. The continental crust is thicker in area of major mountain regions, as much as 70 km.

2. The Mantle

- It is the second layer beyond the crust. It extends up-to 2900 km from **Moho's** discontinuity.
- The upper portion of the mantle which extends up to 400 km is called as **Asthenosphere**[13] (astheno means weak).
- The crust and the uppermost part of mantle with thickness extending from **10 - 200 km** is called as '**Lithosphere**'.

3. The Core

- The Core-Mantle boundary is located at the depth of **2,900 km**.
- The outer core is in liquid state while the inner core is in solid state. The core is made up of heavy material mostly **nickel** and **iron** (NiFe).

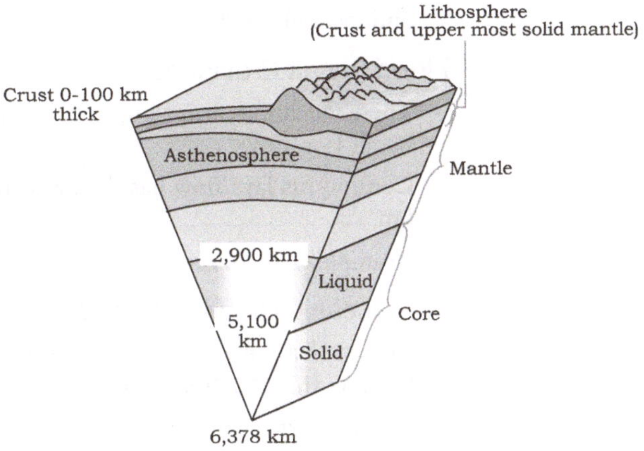

▲ *The Interior of the Earth*

3.4 Volcanoes

- A volcano is an opening on the Earth's surface from which gases, ashes and molten rocks comes out. A volcano is called an active volcano if the material mentioned are being released or have been released out in recent past.
- The molten material comes out to the surface from a weaker zone called as Asthenosphere.
- The material in the upper mantle is called **Magma** and when it reaches the ground, it is called as **Lava**.
- The material reaching the ground includes - lava flows, **pyroclastic debris**[14], volcanic bombs, ash, dust and gases such as nitrogen compounds, sulphur compounds and minor amounts of chlorine, hydrogen and argon.

Types of Volcanoes

Classification of volcanoes are done on the basis of nature of eruption and the form it develops on the surface. Major types of volcanoes are as follows

Shield Volcanoes

- They are the largest of all volcanoes of the Earth. These are made up of basalt (a type of lava which is very fluid when erupted).
- They are generally of **less violent** in nature but could be violent if somehow water gets into the vent (opening).
- Lava comes out of the cone in the form of fountain giving rise to **Cinder Cone**.

---

13 **Asthenosphere** It is the upper portion of the mantle. This shows plastic like properties.

14 **Pyroclastic Debris** It includes fragments blown out by explosive volcanic eruptions.

Composite Volcanoes

- These volcanoes have cooler and more viscous(sticky) lava and are **explosive** in nature. Along with lava, pyroclastic material and ashes are also found.
- Layers of lava are formed on the surrounding of the vent[15] which results in the formation of composite like structure.

Caldera

- These are the most explosive type of volcanoes.
- 'Calderas' are formed when there is collapse of depressions[16].
- The explosive nature of the volcano suggests that the magma chamber providing the lava is both large and located nearby.

Flood Basalt Provinces

- These volcanoes erupt highly fluid lava. In some parts of the world, this volcano covers 1000 sq. km of basalt lava flow.
- Continuous lava flow has thickness of more than 50m and individual flow may extend for hundreds of km.
- Example, The **Deccan Trap** (India)

Mid Oceanic Ridge Volcanoes

- These volcanoes occur in the ocean areas, which results in the formation of a ridge. This ridge extends up to more than **70,000 km** in length.
- Central part of the ridge is characterised by frequent eruptions.

Volcanic Landforms

When lava comes to the surface of the Earth it solidifies and forms different types of landforms. These landforms are called as volcanic landforms.

Intrusive Forms

- The landforms that are formed when lava cools inside the crust, are called '**Intrusive Forms**'.
- Igneous rocks are formed when lava cools after eruption.
- Cooling may occur inside or outside the crustal portion of the Earth. On the basis of this, Igneous Rocks are classified as Volcanic rocks[17] (cooling outside) and Plutonic rocks[18] (cooling inside).

Some of the forms of Intrusive Landforms are

Batholiths

- Cooling and solidification of magma inside the crust forms 'Batholiths'.
- These are large mass of igneous rocks with dome shaped at the base.
- These are cooled part of magma chamber that comes out to the surface after the process of removal of the top surface by the process of denudation.

15 Vent It is an opening in the Earth's crust from which molten lava, rock fragments, ashes, dust and gases are ejected.
16 Depression It is a landform that is lower than the surrounding area.
17 Volcanic Rock It is an Igneous rock formed when magma cools and solidifies near or above the Earth's surface.
18 Plutonic Rock It is an igneous rock formed when magma cools and solidifies beneath the Earth's surface.

Lacoliths

- These are dome-shaped form that is connected by a pipe-like conduit (pipe like structure) from below.
- These are similar to surface volcanic domes of Composite volcano. The only difference is that lacolith is located deeper in depth.

Lapoliths

- These are developed when lava flows in horizontal direction inside crust.
- It has a saucer shaped appearance which is concave to the sky.

Phacolith

- It is a wavy type structure between layers of rocks. It is formed at the base of synclines or at the top of anticlines in areas with folded igneous rocks.
- This is connected to magma chamber by conduit through which magma comes out.

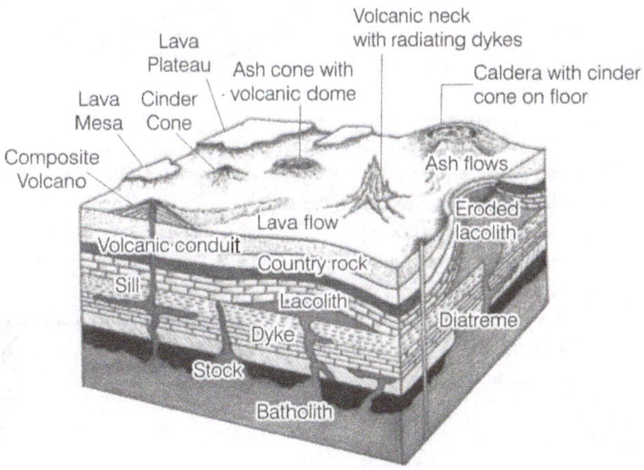

▲ *Volcanic Landforms*

Sills and Dykes

- Sills are the solidified horizontal layer of the lava inside Earth. These are of varying thickness. Thinner one is called as **Sheets** while the thicker one is called as **Sills.**
- When lava flows through cracks, it solidifies in perpendicular position and develops a wall like structure. Such structures are called '**Dykes**'.
- These are common in Western Maharashtra and considered as a supplier for the eruption that developed **the Deccan Trap**.

Quick Test 2

1. What term is given to the upper part of the Mantle?
2. "There exists a discontinuity between crust and mantle", what is the name of that discontinuity?
3. Core is made of which materials?
4. Give an example of the Flood Basalt Province.
5. Which intrusive landform is common in Western Maharashtra ?

Mind Map

INTERIOR OF THE EARTH

1 Sources of Information About the Interior of the Earth

Indirect Sources
Include analysis of temperature, density and pressure of materials.

Evidences of Indirect Sources
- Meteors
- Gravitation
- Magnetic field
- Seismic activity

Direct Sources
These sources include activities like mining, drilling and volcanic eruptions.

2 Earthquake

The shaking of Earth caused by moving Earth's plate.

Earthquake Waves
Vibrations that travel through Earth's interior, e.g., P wave, S wave, Surface wave.

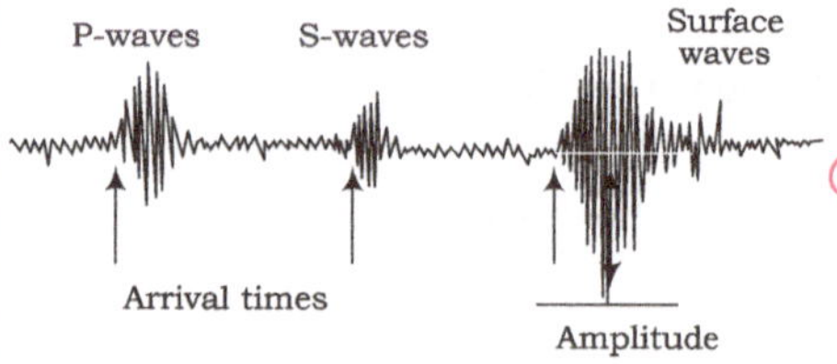

Types of Earthquakes
Tectonic Earthquake, ,Volcanic Earthquake, Collapse Earthquake, Explosion Earthquake, Reservoir Earthquake

Measurement of Earthquake
- Measured either by magnitude or intensity.
- The Richter scale measures magnitude (0-10).
- The Mercalli scale measures intensity (1-12).

Effect of Earthquake
Ground shaking, avalanches, land and mud slides, etc.

3 Structure of Earth's Interior

Crust
- The outermost layer of the Earth and rigid in nature.

Oceanic Crust
- Oceanic crust is thinner as compared to continental crust.

Continental Crust
- The continental crust is thicker in areas of major mountain systems.

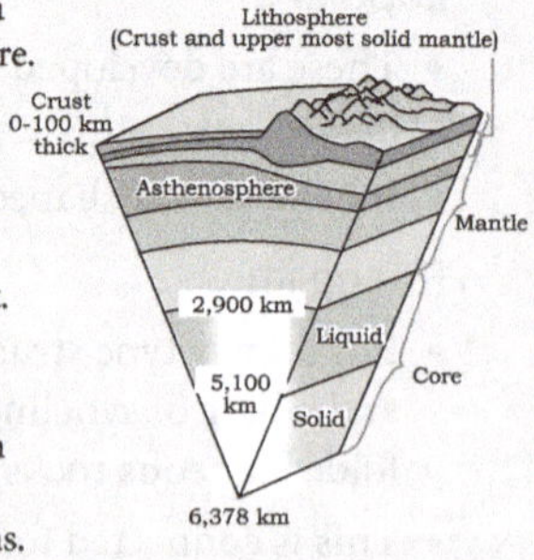

Mantle
- Second layer beyond crust.
- It extends upto 2900 km from Moho's discontinuity.

Core
- Innermost layer of the Earth.
- Made up of iron and nickel.
- **Outer Core** This is in liquid state.
- **Inner Core** This is in solid state.

4 Volcanoes

An opening on the Earth's surface from which gases and molten rocks comes out.

Types of Volcanoes
- Shield volcano
- Composite volcano
- Caldera
- Flood basalt province
- Mid-oceanic ridge volcano

Volcanic Land forms
- Intrusive landforms
- Extrusive landforms

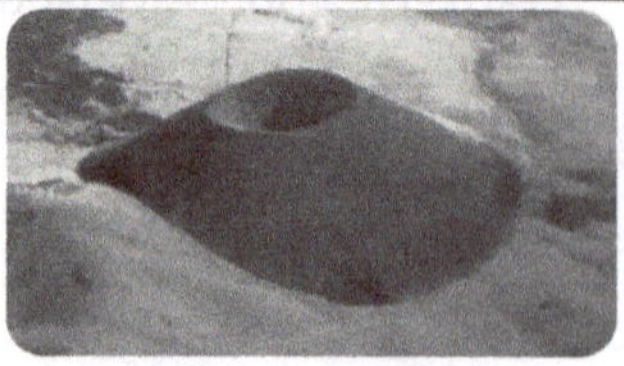

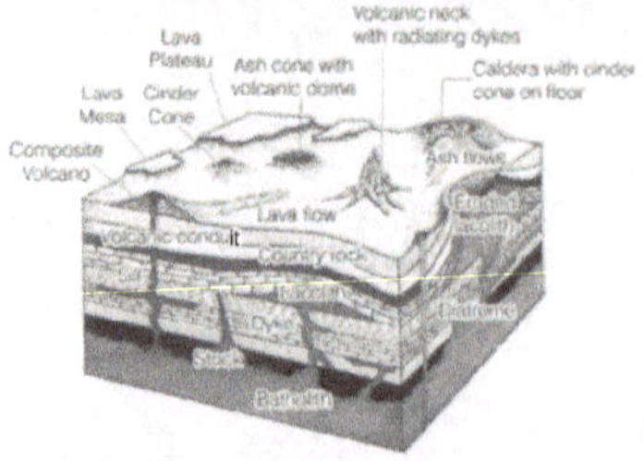

NCERT Folder

Multiple Choice Questions

(i) **Which one of the following earthquake waves is more destructive?**

(a) P-waves
(b) S-waves
(c) Surface waves
(d) None of the above

Ans. (c) Surface waves

(ii) **Which one of the following is a direct source of information about the interior of the Earth?**

(a) Earthquake waves (b) Volcanoes
(c) Gravitational force (d) Earth magnetism

Ans. (b) Volcanoes

(iii) **Which type of volcanic eruptions have caused Deccan trap formations?**

(a) Shield (b) Flood
(c) Composite (d) Caldera

Ans. (b) Flood

(iv) **Which one of the following describes the lithosphere?**

(a) Upper and lower mantle
(b) Crust and upper mantle
(c) Crust and core
(d) Mantle and core

Ans. (b) Crust and upper mantle

Answer the following questions in about 30 words

(i) **What are body waves?**

Ans. Body waves are one of the types of earthquake waves which are generated due to release of energy at the focus. These waves move in all directions travelling through the body of the Earth.

(ii) **Name the direct sources of information about the interior of the Earth.**

Ans. Direct sources of information about the Earth's interior include evidences as follows

- **Deep drilling** Analysis of materials collected at different depths gives information regarding Earth's interior.
- **Volcanic eruptions** Laboratory analysis of magma rocks gives information about Earth's interior.
- **Mining** Rocks obtained through mining gives knowledge of interior of the Earth.

(iii) **Why do earthquake waves develop shadow zone?**

Ans. Earthquake waves develop a shadow zone due to the way seismic waves interact with the Earth's internal layers. When an earthquake occurs, seismic waves, specifically P-waves and S-waves, travel through the Earth. However, these waves do not behave the same way in all areas of the Earth.

P-waves can travel through both solids and liquids, but S-waves can only travel through solids. As seismic waves pass through the Earth, they are refracted or bent when they encounter different layers, such as the Earth's core. The Earth's outer core is liquid, which causes S-waves to be unable to pass through it, creating a 'shadow zone' where S-waves are not detected.

(iv) **Briefly explain the indirect sources of information of the interior of the earth other than those of seismic activity.**

Ans. Following are the indirect sources of information of the interior of the Earth

- Analysis of properties of matter indirectly provides information about the interior.
- Meteors are solid bodies which are similar to material of the Earth and hence, provide a source of information about the interior of the Earth.
- Gravitational force, specially gravity anomaly provides information about the distribution of mass of the material in the crust of the Earth.
- Magnetic surveys also provides information about the distribution of magnetic material in the crustal portion.

Answer the following questions in about 150 words

(i) **What are the effects of propagation of earthquake waves on the rock mass through which they travel?**

Ans. Effects of propagation of earthquake waves on the rock mass are as follows

Effect of Body Waves These are generated due to release of energy at the focus and move in all directions travelling through the body of the Earth. The body waves interact with the surface rocks and generate new set of waves called surface waves. These waves travel in different manners and they cause vibration in the body of the rocks through which they pass.

Body waves are of two types P-waves and S-waves

- P-waves vibrate parallel to the direction of the wave. They exert pressure on the material in the direction of the propogation which creates density differences in the material. This leads to stretching and squeezing of the material.
- The direction of vibration of S-wave is perpendicular to the wave direction in the vertical plane. They create troughs and crests in the material through which they pass.

Effect of Surface Waves These are more destructive. They cause displacement of rocks and hence, leads to collapse of structures.

(ii) What do you understand by intrusive forms? Briefly describe various intrusive forms.

Ans. Instrusive forms are the landforms created by magma that solidifies below the Earth's surface. These are formed when magma faces its way into or between existing rock layers.

Forms of intrusive rocks are as follows

- **Batholiths** These are massive, irregular-shaped bodies of intrusive rocks that are formed deep beneath the surface.
- **Lacoliths** These are Dome-shaped that push overlying rock layers upwards. Lacoliths are smaller than batholiths but still sizable.
- **Sills** These are Horizontal, sheet-like structure that form between layers of sedimentary rock. They solidify parallel to the horizontal planes.
- **Dykes** These are Vertical or steeply inclined that cut across existing rock layers, forming narrow, wall-like structures.
- **Phacoliths** These are wave like structured rocks, which is located near the top of anticline or at the base of syncline.
- **Lapoliths** It is a plate type structure, which is concave to the sky body.

Exam Pattern Questions

Objective Type Questions

Multiple Choice Questions (MCQs)

1. Which of the following is not a direct source of information about the interior of the Earth?

(a) Mining (b) Drilling
(c) Volcanic eruption (d) Magnetic field

2. Which of the given statement regarding gravitational force is correct?

(a) Gravitational force is same at the poles and the equator.
(b) Gravitational force is greater near the poles and less at the equator.
(c) Gravitational force is greater at the equator and less near the poles.
(d) None of the above

3. A sharp break in crustal rocks is known as ....

(a) Focus (b) Epicentre
(c) Fault (d) Hypocentre

4. Which of the following is not a characteristic of S-wave?

(a) They arrive at surface with some time lag.
(b) They travel only through solid materials.
(c) They are the most destructive waves.
(d) All of the above

5. S-waves are also known as ....

(a) surface waves (b) secondary waves
(c) short waves (d) small waves

6. Which zone records arrival of both P and S waves?

(a) Between 105° and 145° from epicentre
(b) Beyond 105° from epicentre
(c) Within 105° from epicentre
(d) Beyond 145° from epicentre

7. .... is an instrument which is used to record the earthquake waves.

(a) Seismograph (b) Richter Scale
(c) Mercalli Scale (d) P-waves Scale

8. Which of the following is an effect of earthquake?

(a) Ground lurching
(b) Fires
(c) Soil liquefaction
(d) All of the above

9. Moho discontinuity is present between

(a) mantle and core
(b) crust and mantle
(c) outer core and inner core
(d) upper mantle and lower mantle

10. **Volcanic earthquakes are special class of .... earthquakes that occur due to eruption of volcanoes.**
(a) Collapse
(b) Tectonic
(c) Explosion
(d) Reservoir induced

11 **Which of the following pairs is correct?**
(a) Lacolith – Horizontal structure
(b) Lapolith – Cone – shaped
(c) Phacolith – Vertical deposits
(d) Sill – Saucer-shaped

12. **"They are characterised by low - explosivity but could be violent if somehow water gets into the vent."**
This statement is defining which type of volcano?
(a) Cinder Cone
(b) Shield Volcano
(c) Flood Basalt
(d) Caldera

13. **Identify the volcanic feature marked as 'k' in the figure given below showing the intrusive landforms.** **CBSE Diksha**

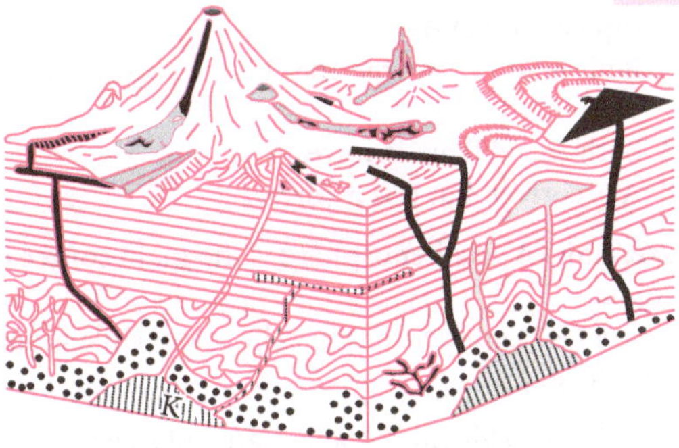

(a) Lapoliths (b) Lacoliths
(c) Batholiths (d) Dykes

14. **Identify the statement that is not true regarding the Mantle.**
(a) It lies beyond the crust.
(b) It has a density of $13 g/cm^3$.
(c) The upper part of the Mantle is termed as 'Asthenosphere'.
(d) Boundary between crust and mantle is called 'Moho's discontinuity'.

15. **"Surface waves are almost entirely responsible for the damage and destruction associated with earthquakes".** **CBSE Diksha**

Which of the following reason support the above statement?
I. They are the first to reach the surface.
II. They are the fastest waves.
III. They are much larger in amplitude.
IV. They roll just under the surface, lifting and dropping the ground leading to displacement of rocks as they pass.

Options
(a) I and II (b) II and III
(c) III and IV (d) IV and I

16. **Consider the following statements regarding 'S Wave'.**
Statement I S waves are recorded after 105°.
Statement II Particle of S waves travel perpendicular to the direction of wave.
Which of the statement is not true about S waves?
(a) Both I and II (b) Only II
(c) Only I (d) None of these

17. **Consider the following statements about P-waves. Which of the given statement is/are incorrect?**
I. They are similar to sound waves.
II. They travel only through solid material.
III. They vibrate perpendicular to wave direction in vertical plane.

Codes
(a) Both I and II (b) Both II and III
(c) Both I and III (d) I, II and III

18. **Consider the following statements about intensity scale. Which of the given statements is/are correct?**
I. It is also known as Richter scale.
II. It refers to energy released during earthquake.

Codes
(a) Only I (b) Only II
(c) Both I and II (d) None of these

Arrange the Following

19. **Arrange the layers of the Earth in sequence from exterior to interior.**
(i) Crust (ii) Outer core
(iii) Inner core (iv) Mantle

Codes
(a) (i), (iv), (iii), (ii)
(b) (i), (iv), (ii), (iii)
(c) (i), (ii), (iii), (iv)
(d) (i), (iii), (ii), (iv)

20. **Arrange the earthquake waves in sequence as per their arrival at the surface of the Earth.**
(i) S-waves (ii) P-waves
(iii) Surface waves

Codes
(a) (i), (ii), (iii) (b) (ii), (i), (iii)
(c) (iii), (ii), (i) (d) (iii), (i), (ii)

21. **"Richter scale measures magnitude of an Earthquake, which is in numbers from 0 - 10".**

Arrange the following in descending order of their magnitude.

(i) 8 (ii) 10
(iii) 3 (iv) 5

Options

(a) (iv), (iii), (ii), (i)
(b) (i), (iv), (ii), (iii)
(c) (ii), (i), (iv), (iii)
(d) (ii), (i), (iv), (iii)

22. **Arrange the following layers of the Earth from "thinnest to thickest".**

Choose the most suitable option:

(a) Core, Crust, Mantle
(b) Mantle, Crust, Core
(c) Crust, Core, Mantle
(d) Core, Mantle, Crust

23. **There are five major types of volcanoes. Identify the type of volcano from the given description.**

These volcanoes are characterised by eruptions of cooler and more viscous lavas than basalt. These volcanoes often result in explosive eruptions. Along with lava, large quantities of pyroclastic material and ashes find their way to the ground. This material accumulates in the vicinity of the vent openings leading to formation of layers.

(a) Composite Volcanoes
(b) Mid-Ocean Ridge Volcanoes
(c) Flood Basalt Provinces
(d) Caldera

Match the Following

24.

List I		List II	
A.	Crust	1.	35-2900 km
B.	Mantle	2.	2900-5100 km
C.	Outer Core	3.	0-35 km
D	Inner Core	4.	5100-6371 km

Codes

	A	B	C	D		A	B	C	D
(a)	1	2	3	4	(b)	3	1	2	4
(c)	4	3	1	2	(d)	2	4	1	3

25.

List I		List II	
A.	Shield Volcano	1.	Volcanoes collapsing on themselves
B.	Composite Volcano	2.	Volcanoes mostly made up of basalt
C.	Caldera	3.	Accumulation of volcanic material in form of layers

Codes

	A	B	C		A	B	C
(a)	3	2	1	(b)	2	3	1
(c)	1	2	3	(d)	2	1	3

Assertion-Reason

Directions (Q. Nos. 26-29) In the questions given below are two statements labelled as Assertion (A) and other is labelled as Reason (R). In the context of two statements which one of the following is correct?

Codes

(a) Both A and R are true, but R is not the correct explanation of A
(b) Both A and R are true and R is the correct explanation of A
(c) Both A and R are incorrect
(d) A is correct, but R is incorrect

26. **Assertion** (A) Asthenosphere is the main source of magma.
Reason (R) Outer core is in solid state while inner core is in liquid state.

27. **Assertion** (A) Shield volcanoes are not steep.
Reason (R) Shield volcanoes are mostly made up of granite.

28. **Assertion** (A) P-waves are the fastest seismic waves and are the first to be recorded by seismographs.
Reason (R) P-waves can travel through both solids and liquids.

29. **Assertion** (A) Earthquake intensity decreases as the distance from the epicenter increases.
Reason (R) Seismic waves lose energy as they travel through the Earth's crust.

Answers

1. (d) Magnetic field
2. (b) Gravitational force is greater near the poles and less at the equator.
3. (c) fault
4. (c) They are the most destructive waves.
5. (b) secondary waves
6. (c) Within 105° from epicentre
7. (a) Seismograph
8. (d) All of the above
9. (b) crust and mantle
10. (b) tectonic
11. (d) Sill - Saucer – shaped
12. (b) Shield Volcano
13. (c) Batholiths
14. (b) It has a density of 13g/cm^3.
15. (c) III and IV
16. (c) Only I
17. (b) Both II and III
18. (d) None of these
19. (b) (i), (iv), (ii), (iii)
20. (b) (ii), (i), (iii)
21. (d) (ii), (i), (iv), (iii)
22. (c) Crust, Core, Mantle
23. (a) Composite Volcanoes
24. (b)
25. (b)
26. (d) A is correct, but R is incorrect
27. (d) A is correct, but R is incorrect.
28. (b) Both A and R are true and R is the correct explanation of A
29. (b) Both A and R are true and R is the correct explanation of A

Subjective Questions

Short Answer Type Questions

1. Discuss why it is important to know about the interior of the Earth.

Ans. It is important to know about the interior of the Earth because the information about interior of the earth helps in understanding of physiographic character of a region which has great influence on human life. This information helps to understand the forces that influence landscape development. Further, it helps to understand the factors responsible for earthquake and generation of tsunami waves. Thus, it is important to know about interior of the Earth.

2. How does the increase in temperature, pressure and density with depth support our understanding of the Earth's layered structure?

Ans. The increase in temperature, pressure and density with depth provides important clues that support the model of the Earth's layered structure.

These properties help scientists infer the nature of materials in the Earth's interior in the following ways

- **Temperature** The gradual increase in temperature with depth supports the idea that the Earth's core is a significant source of heat. As we move down from the Earth's surface to the mantle and core, the temperature rises steadily, suggesting that heat flows from the core to the outer layers..
- **Pressure** Pressure increases with depth because of the overlying mass of rock. The immense pressure at the Earth's core helps explain why the inner core, despite high temperatures, remains solid.
- **Density** As materials become denser with depth, it supports the theory of a differentiated Earth, where heavier elements like iron and nickel are concentrated in the core, while lighter elements form the mantle and crust.

3. How are body waves different from surface waves? Explain in brief.

Ans. Body waves are different from surface waves in the following ways

Body Waves	Surface Waves
These are generated due to the release of energy at the focus.	The body waves interact with the surface rocks and generate new set of waves called surface waves.
They move in all directions travelling through the body of the Earth.	These waves move along the surface.
These are less destructive than the surface waves.	These waves cause more destruction.
These can be detected by Seismographs deep within the Earth.	These can be detected primarily on the Earth's surface.

4. "During an earthquake all the places on the Earth's surface do not record the seismic waves." Justify the statement.

Ans. During an earthquake, all the places on the Earth surface do not record the seismic waves as there are some zones where seismic waves (P and S waves) are not able to reach. Such zones are called shadow zones. The shadow zone of S-waves is much larger than P-waves.

It is observed that seismographs located at any distance within 105° from the epicentre records the arrival of both waves (P and S). While seismographs located beyond 145° from epicentre, record arrival of P-waves, but not that of S-waves.

Thus, zone between 105° and 145° from epicentre is shadow zone of P-wave and entire zone beyond 105° is shadow zone of S-wave.

5. "An earthquake has multiple impact on various aspects of human life and structures." Discuss. **Competency Based Que**

Ans. The impact of earthquake on various aspects of human life and structures are as follows

- Earthquakes can trigger landslides, tsunamis and fires. Recovery from these losses are time taking and expensive. This affects human life by slowing down their daily life activity.
- Buildings, roads, bridges, and infrastructure often collapse or suffer severe damage, leading to homelessness and economic loss.
- Essential services like water supply, electricity, and communication networks are disrupted.

6. "Earthquake is a natural hazard, but some earthquakes are man-made." What are the measures we need to adopt to prevent man-made earthquakes? **Competency Based Que**

Ans. Apart from natural earthquakes, there are some human activities which also cause earthquake such as mining activity, formation of big dam, use of explosive material in geographically sensitive areas etc.

Measures to prevent the earthquakes are

- The building should be made earthquake prone with good quality of design and material.
- Mining activities should be done under effective regulation with all type of precautions.
- Formation of reservoir and dam should be avoided in fault zone.
- Knowledge of disaster management should be promoted in society through education and advertisement.
- Over consumption of ground water should be stopped.
- Nuclear test should be ignored on ground, it may only permitted in laboratory.

7. What are the features of outermost solid part of the Earth?

Ans. Features of the outermost solid part of the Earth are as follows

- Crust is the outer most solid part of the earth which is fragile in nature.
- The thickness of the crust varies under the oceanic and continental areas from 5 km to 30 km, respectively.
- The density of crust also varies in continent and oceanic part from 3 g/cm^3 to 2.7 g/cm^3 respectively.
- The oceanic crust is made up of basalt rock which is different from continental crust.

8. How do we know that the outer core of the Earth is in liquid state?

Ans. The earthquake waves have different types of paths and velocities. Both P and S-waves are reflected and refracted while passing through different layers. S-waves can travel only through solid materials. No S-waves have been recorded in the core region, thus, outer core of the Earth is in liquid state.

9. Discuss the densities of the Earth's core, mantle and crust. Why does core have the highest density?

Ans. The earth's interior does not have uniform density from the outer surface to the centre. The average density of Earth as a whole is 5.53 g/cm^3. But its upper layer i.e. crust has density of 2.75 to 3 g/cm^3. Density of mantle is 3.4 g/cm^3. The average material density of the core at mantle core boundary is 5 g/cm^3 and at centre of Earth is 13 g/cm^3.

The core has the highest density because of two reasons

(i) Core is made up of iron and nickel which are very dense in comparison to other materials.

(ii) The density of the core is also high due to increasing pressure from overlying layers.

10. "Earth has different layers that vary in their characteristics", discuss about the layers beyond the crust. **Competency Based Que**

Ans. The interior of the Earth beyond the crust is classified into Mantle and Core.

The Mantle

- It is the second layer from the top of the Earth.
- The Mantle extends from Moho's Discontinuity to a depth of 2900 km.
- The Upper part of the Mantle is called as 'asthenosphere'. This extends up to 400 km and considered to be the main source of magma.
- It has a density of 3.4g/cm^3.
- The lower mantle extends beyond asthenosphere.

The Core

- The Core-Mantle boundary is located at the depth of 2900 km.
- The outer core is in liquid state, while the inner core is in solid state.
- The density of the material at mantle-core boundary is 5g/cm^3 and at the center it is 13g/cm^3.
- The core is made up of heavy metals like iron and nickel.

11. "Tsunami waves are more devastating than earthquake waves." Give your argument in support of the statement. Also discuss the impact of Tsunami on human life. Competency Based Que

Ans. Tsunami waves are more devastating than earthquake as first, the Tsunami waves continue to move within ocean and second, these cause more fatal impact on the coastal region. These waves negatively affect the coastal vegetation and biodiversity.

The impact of tsunami on human life is as follows

- **Loss of Life** Tsunamis with their immense power can result in thousands of deaths. People living in coastal areas are particularly vulnerable.
- **Displacement of People** Tsunamis often destroy homes, infrastructure and livelihoods, forcing survivors to become displaced. People may have to flee their homes, living in temporary shelters for months or even years.
- **Destruction of Infrastructure** Tsunamis destroy important infrastructure such as roads, bridges, hospitals, schools and communication networks.
- **Economic Impact** The economic toll of a tsunami can be devastating. Coastal economies reliant on tourism, fishing, or agriculture are often hit hard, leading to job losses and economic instability.
- **Environmental Impact** Tsunamis can cause severe environmental damage, including the destruction of ecosystems like coral reefs, mangroves and wetlands.

12. What materials are released during a volcanic eruption?

Ans. The material released during volcanic eruption include lava flows, pyroclastic debris, volcanic bombs, ash and dust and gases such as nitrogen compounds, sulphur compounds, chlorine, hydrogen and argon. Solid materials coming out of the volcanic eruptions include volcanic ash and rocks varying from small particles to huge rocks. When the volcanic eruption is explosive, the rocks are blown high into the sky and cool down very rapidly. They fall on the surface and cause huge damage on it.

13. Write a short note on 'Mid-oceanic Ridge volcanoes'.

Ans. Mid-oceanic ridge volcanoes are underwater volcanic features located along divergent plate boundaries, where tectonic plates are moving apart. These ridges form the longest volcanic mountain chain on Earth, such as the Mid-Atlantic Ridge. As the plates separate, magma from the mantle rises to fill the gap, creating new oceanic crust. This process results in frequent volcanic activity, but eruptions are generally less explosive due to the thin, basaltic magma. Mid-oceanic ridge volcanoes play a crucial role in seafloor spreading and contribute to the creation of new ocean basins, driving the dynamic nature of Earth's crust.

Long Answer Type Questions

1. "The interior of the Earth can be understood by different sources of information". Justify the statement with suitable examples. Competency Based Que

Ans. Evidences about interior of the Earth can be understood by different sources which have been divided into direct sources and indirect sources.

Direct sources are those that are accessible for direct observation. These include following activities

- **Deep Drilling** Analysis of materials collected at different depths gives information regarding interior of the Earth.
- **Volcanic Eruptions** Eruptions bring magma from deep within the Earth to the surface, giving clues about the composition of the mantle and lower crust.
- **Mining** Surface rocks are available easily to study the Earth's crust. Mining activity gives easy access to analyse these rocks, for example, Gold Mines in South Africa.

Indirect sources are those that are not accessible for direct observation. These include following activities

- **Seismic Waves** The study of earthquake-generated seismic waves is one of the most important tools. These waves change speed and direction when passing through different layers, allowing scientists to infer the Earth's internal structure, density and composition.
- **Gravity and Magnetic Field** Variations in Earth's gravitational and magnetic fields provide insights into the distribution of materials within the Earth.
- **Meteorites** Since meteorites are believed to have formed from the same material as Earth, their composition helps understand the Earth's internal layers, especially the core.

2. Define earthquake and also write its types. What is the reason behind earthquake occurence?

Ans. Earthquake refers to the shaking of the Earth. It is a natural event which is caused due to release of energy, which generates waves that travel in all directions.

There are various types of earthquakes which are as follows

Tectonic Earthquakes These are generated due to sliding of rocks along a fault line.

Volcanic Earthquakes These are the part of tectonic earthquakes which occurs due to eruption of volcanoes and are confined to areas of active volcanoes.

Collapse Earthquakes These are originated in the area of intense mining activity when the roofs collapse causing minor tremors.

Explosion Earthquakes These occur due to explosion of chemical and nuclear devices.

Reservoir Induced Earthquakes The earthquake that occurs in the area of large reservoirs are referred to as reservoir induced earthquakes.

Reason behind the Occurrence of Earthquake The release of energy occurs along a fault which is a sharp break in the crustal rocks. Rocks along a fault tend to move in opposite directions. As overlying rock strata press them, the friction locks them together. However, their tendency to move apart at some point of time overcomes the friction. As a result, the blocks become deformed and suddenly slide past each other. This causes a release of energy and energy waves travel in all directions causing earthquakes.

3. "Earthquake is a natural hazard that has impacts on physical environment, life and property". Elucidate.

Competency Based Que

Ans. Earthquakes are natural hazards that arise due to the sudden release of energy from the Earth's crust, causing ground shaking and tremors. These events have profound impacts on the physical environment, life and property as discussed below

- **Physical environment** Earthquakes can lead to drastic changes in landscapes. Ground shaking can cause the collapse of buildings, roads and bridges, while fault lines may shift, creating cracks in the ground. Earthquakes often trigger secondary hazards like landslides, tsunamis and soil liquefaction, further altering the environment and causing widespread destruction.
- **Life and property** Earthquakes pose a direct threat to human life. The collapse of buildings and infrastructure can result in significant casualties and injuries, especially in densely populated areas with poor construction standards. Moreover, earthquakes displace communities, destroy homes and disrupt basic services such as water, electricity and communication. Economic losses can be severe as industries, businesses and agriculture suffer from the destruction of assets and infrastructure.

In summary, earthquakes have wide-ranging impacts on the natural environment, human life and property, making them one of the most destructive natural hazards.

4. "Different types of earthquake waves travel in different manners, as they move or propagate." Explain.

Competency Based Que

Ans. Earthquake waves are categorised into two main types: body waves and surface waves. Each type travels differently through the Earth's layers.

(i) **Body waves** These are formed due to release of energy at the focus and travels in all directions. It consists of P-waves (primary) and S-waves (secondary).

- **P-waves** These are compression waves that move by shrinking and expanding the rock they travel through. They can propagate through both solid and liquid materials, making them the fastest seismic waves.
- **S-waves** They can only move through solid materials and are slower than P-waves.

(ii) **Surface waves** They travel along the Earth's surface and are responsible for most of the damage during earthquakes. The direction of vibration of particles in S wave is perpendicular to the wave direction in the vertical plane. Hence, they create crests in material through which they pass.

The different travel patterns of these waves are crucial for seismologists. P-waves arrive first, followed by S-waves and finally surface waves. This sequence helps scientists determine the earthquake's epicenter and magnitude.

5. How do P-waves and S-waves help scientists understand the structure of the Earth's interior?

Ans. P-waves (Primary waves) and S-waves (Secondary waves) provide essential clues about the Earth's internal structure by how they travel through different layers. Their behaviour and movement through various materials allow scientists to infer details about the composition, state, and density of the Earth's interior layers.

P-waves are the fastest seismic waves and they are the first to be detected by a seismograph. They can travel through solids, liquids and gases, which makes them useful in determining the nature of materials in the Earth's interior. The fact that P-waves can pass through both solid and liquid layers suggests that the Earth's outer core is molten, which was confirmed when scientists observed that P-waves do not travel through the outer core.

S-waves are slower than P-waves and can only travel through solid materials. The inability of S-waves to pass through the outer core of the Earth provides important evidence that the outer core is liquid. The shadow zone for S-waves, where no S-waves are detected, occurs at angles greater than 105° from the earthquake's epicenter. This shadow zone provides indirect evidence for the existence of a liquid outer core beneath the Earth's solid mantle.

6. Classify volcanoes on the basis of nature of eruption and the form developed at the surface. Also state their examples.

Ans. Volcanoes can be classified based on the nature of their eruption and the form they develop on the Earth's surface. These forms are

Shield Volcanoes

- They are the largest of all volcanoes of the Earth.
- These are made up of basalt (a type of lava which is very fluid when erupted)
- They are generally of low - explosivity in nature.

Composite Volcanoes

- These volcanoes have cooler and more viscous(sticky) lava and are explosive in nature.
- Along with lava, pyroclastic material and ashes are also found.
- Layers of lava are formed on the neck of the vent which results in formation of composite structure.

Caldera

- These are the most explosive type of volcanoes.
- There is a formation of 'Calderas' which are collapsed depressions formed during eruption.
- These are explosive in nature.

Flood Basalt Province

- These are highly fluid and flows lava to long distances.
- They form a series of flow with some flows having thickness of 50 m.

Mid Ocean Ridge Volcano

- These occur in oceanic area and are less explosive in nature.
- There is a system of mid oceanic ridge which is more than 70,000 km long.
- The central part of the ridge experiences frequent eruptions.

7. What do you understand about plutonic rocks? Also discuss about the various forms developed by these rocks.

Ans. Plutonic rocks are also known as intrusive igneous rocks. These rocks are formed when magma cools and solidifies deep beneath the Earth's surface. Granite is one of the most common examples of plutonic rocks.

Various forms of plutonic rocks are

- **Batholiths** These are large, irregularly shaped masses of plutonic rock that form deep in the Earth. Batholiths often span hundreds of kilometres and become exposed over time due to erosion.
- **Lacoliths** Lacoliths form when magma pushes the overlying rock upwards, creating a dome-like structure. They are smaller and deeper than batholiths.
- **Sills** Sills are horizontal, sheet-like intrusions that form between layers of sedimentary rock. They solidify parallel to the existing rock layers.
- **Dykes** Dykes are vertical or steeply inclined rock formations that cut across existing rock layers, forming when magma fills fractures.
- **Phacoliths** Phacoliths form when magma solidifies into the crests (anticlines) or troughs (synclines) of folded sedimentary rock layers, filling the curved spaces.
- **Lapoliths** Lapoliths form when magma intrudes into the Earth's crust, spreading out between pre-existing rock layers. Due to the weight of the overlying rock, the magma forces the layers below, giving it a concave, basin-like shape.

Source Based Questions

1. Read the passage carefully and answer the questions that follow.

Most of our knowledge about the interior of the earth is largely based on estimates and inferences. The most easily available solid earth material is surface rock or the rocks we get from mining areas. Gold mines in South Africa are as deep as 3 - 4 km. Going beyond this depth is not possible as it is very hot at this depth. Besides mining, scientists have taken up a number of projects to penetrate deeper depths to explore the conditions in the crustal portions. Scientists world over are working on two major projects such as "Deep Ocean Drilling Project" and "Integrated Ocean Drilling Project". The deepest drill at Kola, in Arctic Ocean, has so far reached a depth of 12 km. This and many deep drilling projects have provided large volume of information through the analysis of materials collected at different depths. Volcanic eruption forms another source of obtaining direct information. As and when the molten material (magma) is thrown onto the surface of the earth, during volcanic eruption it becomes available for laboratory analysis. However, it is difficult to ascertain the depth of the source of such magma.

(i) "The value of gravity is different at different places on the Earth".
Which among the following is the prime reason for these differences?
(a) Uneven distribution of mass
(b) Magnetic field of Earth
(c) Tilt of Earth
(d) Attraction of Moon

Ans. (a) Uneven distribution of mass

(ii) **Why is it difficult to mine deeper than 3–4 km in gold mines in South Africa?**
(a) Lack of advanced mining technology
(b) High temperature at deeper depths
(c) Economic reasons
(d) Lack of valuable minerals beyond this depth

Ans. (b) High temperature at deeper depths

(iii) **What additional type of survey compliments gravity survey by providing information about magnetic material distribution?**
(a) Seismic Survey (b) Electromagnetic spectrum
(c) Magnetic Surveys (d) Radiometric Surveys

Ans. (c) Magnetic Surveys

2. Study the following diagram and answer the questions that follow.

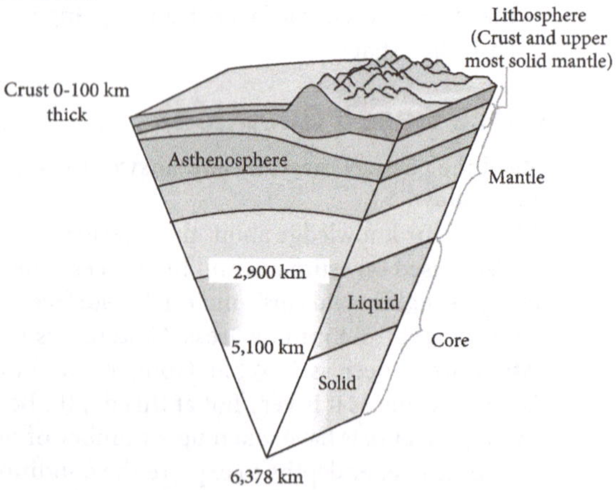

The Interior of the Earth

(i) **Which of the following is the thinnest part of Earth's interior?**
(a) Core (b) Oceanic Crust
(c) Continental Crust (d) Mantle

Ans. (b) Oceanic Crust

(ii) **What is the main source of magma inside Earth's surface?**
(a) Core
(b) Crust
(c) Asthenosphere
(d) Magnetosphere

Ans. (c) Asthenosphere

(iii) **Which of the following layers is known as NiFe?**
(a) Mantle (b) Continental Crust
(c) Oceanic Crust (d) Core

Ans. (d) Core

3. Read the passage carefully and answer the questions that follow.

The study of seismic waves provides a complete picture of the layered interior. An earthquake in simple words is shaking of the Earth. It is a natural event. It is caused due to release of energy, which generates waves that travel in all directions. As the overlying rock strata press them, the friction locks them together. However, their tendency to move apart at some point of time overcomes the friction. As a result, the blocks get deformed and eventually, they slide past one another abruptly. This causes a release of energy, and the energy wave's travel in all directions. The point where the energy is released is called the focus of an earthquake, alternatively, it is called the hypocenter. The energy waves travelling in different directions reach the surface. The point on the surface, nearest to the focus, is called epicenter. It is the first one to experience the waves. It is a point directly above the focus. All natural earthquakes take place in the lithosphere. It is sufficient to note here that the lithosphere refers to the portion of depth up to 200 km from the surface of the Earth. An instrument called 'seismograph' records the waves reaching the surface.

(i) **"Earthquake is a natural event", explain how it happens naturally?**

Ans. An earthquake in simple words is shaking of the Earth. It is caused due to release of energy, which generates waves that travel in all directions. This creates tension and friction among rocks which ultimately results in release of energy waves.

(ii) **How does the location of Epicenter relate to the Focus of an earthquake?**

Ans. The point where energy is released is called Focus of an earthquake which is located below the Earth surface, perpendicular to focus on the surface lies a point where the waves are first experienced is called an Epicenter.

(iii) **In which layer of the Earth do natural earthquakes typically occurs?**

Ans. All the natural earthquakes take place in Lithosphere, which lies at a depth of 200 km from the surface of the Earth.

4. Read the passage carefully and answer the questions that follow.

A volcano is a place where gases, ashes and/or molten rock material - lava - escape to the ground. A volcano is called an active volcano if the materials mentioned are

Mind Map

DISTRIBUTION OF OCEANS AND CONTINENTS

1 Continental Drift Theory

- Given by Alfred Wegner in 1912.
- This explained the distribution of oceans and continents.
- Super continent was named as Pangaea and super ocean was called Panthalassa.

Evidences in Support of Theory

- Jig-saw fits of continents.
- Similar aged rocks were found.
- Glacial tillites found in India, Africa and others.
- Distribution of fossils, e.g, Mesosaurus found in South America and Africa.
- Occurence of rich placer deposits of gold in Ghana coast.

Forces Responsible for Drifting

- **Pole Fleeing Force** It is related to rotation of the Earth.
- **Tidal Force** It is due to the attraction of the Moon and the Sun.

2 Post-Drift Studies

Convectional Current Theory

- Given by Arthur Holmes in 1930's.
- This explains that convection currents are generated in mantle that causes movement of plates.

Mapping of Oceans

- Discovery of mid-oceanic ridges, abyssal plains, trenches took place.
- Rocks from the oceanic areas are much younger then those in continental areas.

3 Ocean-Floor Configuration

Ocean floor has three parts: Continental margins, deep sea basins and mid-ocean ridges.

- Continental margins like land to deep sea basins
- Abyssal plains collect sediments.
- Mid-ocean ridges are submerged mountain chains with volcanic activity.

4 Sea-Floor Spreading

Evidences

- Occurence of shallow earthquakes near ridges.
- Magnetic stripping on sea-floor.

Concept

- Given by Harry Hess in 1961.
- This explains the spreading of sea-floor near mid-oceanic ridge.

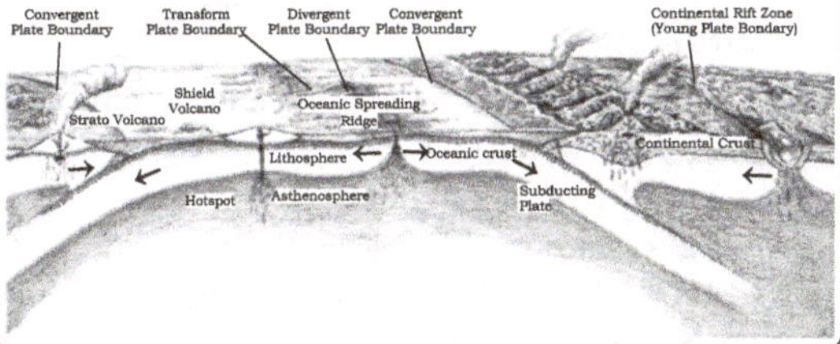

Movement of Indian plates

- **225 million years ago** India was a large island and part of Australian coast.
- **200 million years ago** India started to move Northward.
- **140 million years ago** India was located as South as 50° latitude.
- 60 million years ago Formation of Deccan Trap took place.
- **40-50 million years ago** Upliftment of Himalaya took place.

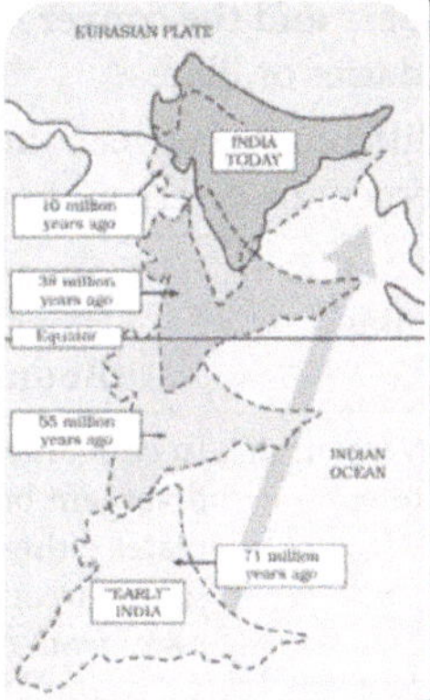

5 Plate-Tectonics Theory

Major Plates

- Antarctica and surrounding oceanic plate, North American, South American, Pacific, India-Australia-New Zealand, Africa with Eastern Atlantic and Eurasian plate.

Minor Plates

- Cocos plate, Naca plate, Arabian plate, Philippine plate.

Types of Plate Boundary

- **Divergent** Plates move away from each other.
- **Convergent** Plates move towards each other.
- **Transform** Plates move side by side of each other.

Concept

Given by Mckenzie, Parker and Morgan in 1967 and explained the movement of lithospheric plates.

Force For the Plate Movement

The slow movement of hot, softened mantle that lies below the rigid plates is the driving force behind the plate movement.

NCERT Folder

Intext Question

1. How do you think the rate of plate movement is determined?

Ans. The rate of plate movement is determined with the help of the strips of normal and reverse magnetic field that are parallel to the mid-oceanic ridges. These rates vary considerably.

The Arctic Ridge has the slowest rate (less than 2.5 cm/yr). The East Pacific Rise near Eastern Island, in the South Pacific about 3,400 km West of Chile, has the fastest rate (more than 15 cm/yr).

Multiple Choice Questions

(i) Who amongst the following was the first to consider the possibility of Europe, Africa and America having located side by side?

(a) Alfred Wegener (b) Antonio Pellegrini
(c) Abraham Ortelius (d) Edmond Hess

Ans. (c) Abraham Ortelius

(ii) Polar fleeing force relates to

(a) Revolution of earth (b) Gravitation
(c) Rotation of the earth (d) Tides

Ans. (c) Rotation of the earth

(iii) Which one of the following is not a minor plate?

(a) Nazca (b) Arabia
(c) Philippines (d) Antarctica

Ans. (d) Antarctica

(iv) Which one of the following facts was not considered by those while discussing the concept of sea floor spreading?

(a) Volcanic activity along the mid-oceanic ridges.
(b) Stripes of normal and reverse magnetic field observed in rocks of ocean floor.
(c) Distribution of fossils in different continents.
(d) Age of rocks from the ocean floor.

Ans. (c) Distribution of fossils in different continents.

(v) Which one of the following is the type of plate boundary of the Indian plate along the Himalayan mountains?

(a) Ocean-continent convergence
(b) Divergent boundary
(c) Transform boundary
(d) Continent-continent convergence

Ans. (d) Continent-continent convergence

Answer the following questions in about 30 words

(i) What were the forces suggested by Wegener for the movement of the continents?

Ans. For the movement of the continents Wegener suggested two types of forces

(i) **Pole-Fleeing Force** It is the force related to the rotation of the Earth. The bulge at the equator is also due to rotation of the Earth.

(ii) **Tidal Force** Force due to the attraction of the Moon and the Sun is known as tidal force. Wegener suggested that these forces would become effective when applied over many million years.

(ii) How are the convectional currents in the mantle initiated and maintained?

Ans. Arthur Holmes, in 1930s discussed the possibility of convectional currents operating in the mantle portion.

The initiation and maintenance of convectional currents in the mantle is due to radioactive elements causing thermal difference. The system of such current exists in the entire portion of the mantle.

(iii) What is the major difference between the transform boundary and the convergent boundary or divergent boundaries of Plates?

Ans. The differences between the transform boundary and the convergent or divergent boundary of plates are as follows

Basis	Convergent or Divergent Boundaries	Transform Boundaries
Movement of Plate	In convergent or divergent boundaries, plates either move in same direction or move away from each other.	In transform boundaries, there is a parallel movement of plates.
Formation of Landforms	In convergent or divergent boundaries, there is either destruction or construction of crust.	In transform boundaries, the crust is neither produced nor destroyed.

(iv) What was the location of the Indian landmass during the formation of Deccan Traps?

Ans. About 140 million years before the present, India was located at 50° S latitude. At the time of formation of Deccan Traps around 60 million years ago, India was moving towards the Eurasian plate.

Answer the following questions in about 150 words

(i) What are the evidences in support of continental drift theory?

Ans. The theory of continental drift is supported by a number of pieces of evidence, which includes

- **Matching coastlines** The shorelines of Africa and South America are a notable match.
- **Similar geological formations** Rocks of the same age have been found across oceans, such as the 2,000-million-year-old rocks in Brazil and Western Africa.
- **Distribution of Fossils** Identical fossils of plants and animals have been found on continents that are now separated by oceans. For example, the extinct reptile Mesosaurus has been found in both South America and Africa.
- **Tillite** The Gondwana system of sediments from India has counterparts in other landmasses of the Southern Hemisphere, including Africa, Madagascar, Antarctica and Australia.
- **Placer deposits** The gold deposits in Ghana are derived from the Brazil plateau, as there is no source rock in the Ghana region.
- **Seafloor spreading** This natural geologic process separates large tectonic plates from the Earth's lithosphere. Evidence for seafloor spreading comes from magnetic stripes and molten material.

(ii) Bring about the difference between drift theory and plate tectonics.

Ans. Differences between drift theory and plate tectonics are as follows

Basis	Drift Theory	Plate Tectonics
Origin	The theory of drifting continent is known as continental drift theory which was given by Alfred Wegener in 1912.	The theory of drifting plate is called plate tectonics theory which was initiated by Mckenzie, Parker and Morgan in 1967.
Concept	According to drift theory, Pangaea, the supercontinent was surrounded by Panthalassa, the mega ocean.	The earth is divided into several huge masses of land which are called plates. A tectonic plate is massive, irregular slab of solid rocks.
Force	Behind drift, pole-fleeing and tidal force are responsible.	Radioactive decay and residual heat within the interior of the earth are the main forces.
Motion	Continental drift theory only considers the horizontal motion.	Plate tectonics takes into account the subduction of plates too.
Evidence	Drift theory mostly relies on circumstantial evidences of Jig-saw fit, fossils, placer deposit, etc.	Plate tectonics is based on scientific analysis of the processes inside the Earth's surface.
Outcome	Due to drift, seven continents and five oceans came into being and continents are still drifting.	Due to plate tectonic, there are 7 big plates and 17 small plates which are always in motion.

(iii) What were the major post-drift discoveries that rejuvenated the interest of scientists in the study of distribution of ocean and continents?

Ans. Post-drift theories that renewed the interest of scientists in the distribution of oceans and continents, particularly through the development of plate tectonics were

- The concept of plate tectonic says that lithospheric plates are moving on the semi-fluid asthenosphere which are driven by convection currents. This mechanism explained the formation of mountain ranges, ocean trenches and earthquakes, linking geological activity directly to continental drift.
- Additionally, the discovery of sea-floor spreading provided evidence for the movement of tectonic plates. As new crust formed at mid-ocean ridges and older crust was pushed away, it gave an idea about the understanding of how continents shifted over geological time.
- The theory of plate tectonics also took view from Palaeomagnetism, showing how continents have changed position relative to the magnetic poles.

Collectively, these advancements promoted a renewed scientific focus on continental and oceanic distribution.

Exam Pattern Questions

Objective Type Questions

Multiple Choice Questions (MCQs)

1. Alfred Wegener was a .... meteorologist.
(a) American (b) German (c) French (d) Greek

2. Who proposed Continental Drift Theory?
(a) Cess (b) Alfred Wegener
(c) Mckenzie (d) Morgan

3. In which year, Alfred Wegener, a German meteorologist proposed the 'Continental Drift Theory'?
(a) 1910 (b)1912 (c) 1914 (d) 1950

4. The Mega Ocean was called ....
(a) Pangaea (b) Laurasia
(c) Panthalassa (d) Gondwanaland

5. Southern component of Pangaea was known as ....
(a) Laurasia (b) Lemuria
(c) Panthalassa (d) Gondwanaland

6. As evidence of Continental Drift Theory, the shoreline of which two specific continents fit together most remarkable and unmistakably? **CBSE Diksha**
(a) Africa and North America
(b) South America and Europe
(c) South America and Africa
(d) Antarctica and Africa

7. Which of the following places is not included in Lemuria?
(a) India (b) Madagascar
(c) Falkland Island (d) Africa

8. According to Continental Drift Theory, the earliest marine deposits were found along the coastline of South America and ....
(a) North America (b) Africa
(c) Europe (d) Antarctica

9. "The theory of Plate tectonic proposes that there are seven major and some minor plates". Identify the minor plates.
(a) Antarctica and Cocos (b) Pacific and Nazca
(c) Nazca and Philippine (d) Africa and Indo-Australian

10. Which one of the following is a type of plate boundary along Mid-Atlantic Ridge?
(a) Oceanic-Oceanic Convergence
(b) Transform Boundary
(c) Oceanic Continent Convergence
(d) Divergent Boundary

11. The boundary between India and Antarctic Plate is marked by
(a) Continent-Continent Convergence
(b) Divergent Boundary
(c) Continent Oceanic Convergence
(d) Transform Boundary

12. How many years ago did the formation of Deccan Trap start?
(a) 40 million (b) 200 million
(c) 60 million (d) 225 million

13. A variety of evidences was offered in support of the Continental Drift. Identify the evidence from the given description.
It is a sedimentary rock formed out of deposits of glaciers. The Gondwana system of sediments from India is known to have its counterparts in six different landmasses of the Southern Hemisphere. Counterparts of this succession are found in Africa, Falkland Island, Madagascar, Antarctica and Australia besides India.
(a) Placer Deposits
(b) Glacial Deposits
(c) Tillites
(d) Sedimentary Deposits

14. Identify the statement that is not correct regarding 'Continental Drift Theory'.
i. This theory was postulated by Alfred Wegener, A German Meteorologist in 1912.
ii. This theory talks about different plates of the lithosphere
iii. Supercontinent was named as Panthalassa and mega ocean was named as Pangaea.
iv. Laurasia formed the Northern component while Gondwanaland formed the Southern component.

Options
(a) Only (i) (b) Statements (ii) and (iii)
(c) Only (iii) (d) Only (iv)

15. Consider the following statements.
I. Mid-oceanic ridges are active in terms of volcanic eruptions.
II. Oceanic crust is younger than continental areas.
III. Rocks on either side of crests of oceanic ridges having equi-distant location from crest are dissimilar in their constituents and age.

Which of the above statements is/are correct?

(a) I, II and III (b) I and III
(c) I and II (d) II and III

16. Consider the following statements. Which of the given statement(s) is/are incorrect?

I. Continental margin forms transition between continental shores and deep sea basins.
II. Extensive plains between continental shelf and continental slope is Abyssal Plain.
III. Inter-connected chain of mountain system within the ocean is Mid-oceanic Ridge.

Codes
(a) Only I (b) Only II
(c) Only III (d) I, II and III

Arrange the Following

17. Arrange the following according to increasing depth.

(i) Mountains (ii) Abyssal plains
(iii) Continental shelf (iv) Ocean trenches

Options
(a) (i), (ii), (iii), (iv) (b) (i), (iii), (iv), (ii)
(c) (i), (iii), (ii), (iv) (d) (iv), (ii), (iii), (i)

18. Arrange the following statements according to the period (Past to recent).

(i) The Indian plate split from Madagascar and formed peninsular India.
(ii) The Indian plate collided with the Eurasian plate, forming the Himalayas.
(iii) The Indian plate was a large island off the coast of Australia.
(iv) The Indian plate was part of the supercontinent Gondwana.

Options
(a) (i), (ii), (iii), (iv) (b) (ii), (i), (iv), (iii)
(c) (iv), (iii), (ii), (i) (d) (iii), (iv), (i), (ii)

19. Arrange the following theories in sequence according to the period of development.

(i) Sea Floor Spreading
(ii) Convectional Current Theory
(iii) Plate Tectonic Theory
(iv) Continental Drift Theory

Codes
(a) (ii), (i), (iii), (iv)
(b) (ii), (iv), (i), (iii)
(c) (iv), (ii), (i), (iii)
(d) (iv), (iii), (i), (ii)

20. Arrange the following personalities in sequence according to the period of their theories.

(i) Wegener (ii) Arthur Holmes
(iii) McKenzie (iv) Hess

Codes
(a) (ii), (i), (iii), (iv) (b) (iv), (iii), (ii), (i)
(c) (i), (ii), (iv), (iii) (d) (iii), (i), (ii), (iv)

Match the Following

21.

	List I		List II
A.	Cocos plate	1.	Between South America and Pacific plate
B.	Arabian plate	2.	Between the Philippine and Indian plate
C.	Caroline plate	3.	Mostly the Saudi Arabian landmass
D.	Nazca plate	4.	Between Central America and Pacific plate

Codes

	A	B	C	D		A	B	C	D
(a)	1	2	3	4	(b)	2	3	4	1
(c)	4	3	2	1	(d)	3	1	2	4

22.

	List I (Events)		List II (Period)
A.	India started its Northward journey towards Asian continent	1.	200 million years ago
B.	Upliftment of the Himalayas	2.	40-50 million years ago
C.	India's location at 50°S latitude	3.	140 million years ago
D.	Formation of the Deccan Traps	4.	Around 60 million years ago

Codes

	A	B	C	D		A	B	C	D
(a)	1	2	3	4	(b)	4	3	2	1
(c)	3	2	1	4	(d)	4	1	2	3

23.

	List I		List II
A.	Jig-saw fit	1.	Gold deposits in the Ghana
B.	Placer deposits	2.	Shorelines of Africa and South America
C.	Distribution of fossils	3.	Brazil coast matches with Western Africa
D.	Rocks of same age across the oceans	4.	Lemuria landmass

Codes

	A	B	C	D		A	B	C	D
(a)	1	2	3	4	(b)	2	1	4	3
(c)	2	4	3	1	(d)	4	3	2	1

Assertion-Reason

Directions (Q. Nos. 24-27) In the questions given below are two statements labelled as Assertion (A) and other is labelled as Reason (R). In the context of two statements which one of the following is correct?

Codes

(a) Both A and R are true, but R is not the correct explanation of A
(b) Both A and R are true and R is the correct explanation of A
(c) Both A and R are incorrect
(d) A is correct, but R is incorrect

24. **Assertion** (A) The sediments on ocean floor are very thin.
Reason (R) Continental crust rocks are younger than ocean crust rocks.

25. **Assertion** (A) Along transform boundaries, crust is neither produced nor destroyed.
Reason (R) Along transform boundaries, the plates horizontally pass each other.

26. **Assertion**(A) Continental drift theory suggests that continents were once part of a single landmass called Pangaea.
Reason (R) Fossil evidence of similar species has been found on widely separated continents.

27. **Assertion** (A) The theory of plate tectonics accounts for the occurrence of earthquakes.
Reason (R) Earthquakes primarily occur along plate boundaries where stress builds up and is released.

Answers

1. (b) German
2. (b) Alfred Wegner
3. (b)1912
4. (c) Panthalassa
5. (d) Gondwanaland
6. (c) South America and Africa
7. (c) Falkland Island
8. (b) Africa
9. (c) Nazca and Philippine
10. (d) Divergent Boundary
11. (b) Divergent Boundary
12. (c) 60 million
13. (c) Tillites
14. (b) Statements ii and iii
15. (c) I and II
16. (b) Only II
17. (c) (i), (iii), (ii), (iv)
18. (d) (iii), (iv), (i), (ii)
19. (c) (iv), (ii), (i), (iii)
20. (c) (i), (ii), (iv), (iii)
21. (c)
22. (a)
23. (b)
24. (d) A is correct, but R is incorrect
25. (b) Both A and R are true and R is the correct explanation of A
26. (b) Both A and R are true and R is the correct explanation of A
27. (d) A is correct, but R is incorrect

Subjective Questions

Short Answer Type Questions

1. Discuss the Continental Drift Theory regarding the distribution of continents and oceans. **CBSE Diksha**

Ans. The Continental Drift Theory explains that continents were once part of a single landmass called Pangaea, this supercontinent Pangaea gradually broke into two parts. This explains the current distribution of continents and oceans.

To explain this phenomenon there were some evidences that seems to be in support of the theory. Evidences in support of the theory includes-matching geological formations, fossil evidence and coastlines suggest that landmasses have shifted over time, influencing oceanic patterns and climates.

2. **Define the development of continent as per Continental Drift Theory.**

Ans. The development of continent as per the Continental Drift Theory can be explained in following stages

- In the first stage, there was a supercontinent Pangaea surrounded by Mega Ocean Panthalassa.
- In the second stage, around 200 million years ago, there was a splitting of Pangaea. The Northern part was called as 'Laurasia' while the Southern part was called as 'Gondwanaland', between them, there was an origination of new water body named 'Tethys sea'.
- In the last stage, there was splitting of Laurasia which gave birth to two continents namely Eurasia and North America and the new water body was named as Atlantic Ocean. Later on, Gondwanaland splitted into several smaller continents.

3. What was the condition of India immediately before and after when Pangaea broke?

Ans. Before Pangaea broke, India was a large island situated off the Australian coast, in a vast ocean. The Tethys sea separated it from the Asian continent till about 225 million years ago.

India is supposed to have started its journey Northward about 200 million years ago at the time when Pangaea broke. India collided with Asia about 40-50 million years ago causing rapid uplift of the Himalayas.

4. "Volcanoes and earthquake activity often occur in similar belts of the world". Discuss. **Competency Based Que**

Ans. Most of the earthquake and volcanic zones occur near convergent plate boundaries.

There are two popular belts of earthquake and volcano where frequency of occurrence is very high. These are

- **Rim of the Pacific** This area is the convergence of Pacific plate with other minor and major plates which causes frequent earthquake and volcanoes. For example, Japan lies on same belt faces maximum earthquake in the world. The Rim of Pacific is also called Rim of Fire due to the existence of active volcanoes in this areas.
- **Alpine-Himalayan Belt** This area is the convergence of Indo-Australian plate with Eurasian plate which causes earthquake in the area of Myanmar, India, Africa and Europe. Volcanoes near Italy are the outcomes of subduction zone near the continental margin.

5. What are the evidences that helped in the study of plate movement?

Ans. Following are the evidences that helped for the study of plate movement:

- Continuous eruption of lava in main oceanic area which created large oceanic ridge.
- Change in the property of rock from ridge areas to shoreline.
- In mid of ocean area, there is a thin layer of sediments and in coastal areas, there is a thick sediment.
- The oceanic crust rocks are much younger than the continental rocks.

Hence, these facts and evidences were further analysed and concept of sea floor spreading and plate tectonics were proposed.

6. "Different mechanisms help in the movement of plates." Analyse the statement. **Competency Based Que**

Ans. It is true, that there are different mechanisms which help in the movement of plates. In 1930, Arthur Holmes, advocated that subcrustal convention currents form the mechanism of thermal convention. It causes the movement of plates. Hot currents rise and later, they cool down as they reach the surface.

Cooler currents sink down and this convectional movement moves the crustal plates. The rigid plates of lithosphere, which float on more mobile asthenosphere, are in constant motion. Such mechanism does not exist below the crust. Small centres of past volcanic activity and often located far from any active plate boundary reveals the effect of convection currents on the lithosphere.

7. Tectonic plates are known for their different characteristic features. Explain in brief. **Competency Based Que**

Ans. Different characteristic features of tectonic plates are as follows

- Tectonic plates or simply lithospheric plates are the slab of solid rock which move horizontally over the asthenosphere.
- These are the massive rigid units which include upper part of mantle and the crust.
- The plate have both continental and oceanic crust but it is referred as continental or oceanic plate based on which type occupies a greater area of the plate.
- The size of the plate varies as well as density of oceanic and continental plate also vary.
- The composition of oceanic plate is also different from continental plate as upper layer of oceanic plate has basalt rock, whereas upper layer of continental plate is granite.

8. Plate movement is the result of different forces. Elucidate.

Ans. Before plate tectonic theory, the convectional current principle was developed by Arthur Holmes in 1930s. In plate tectonic theory, it was defined that the movement of plate is due to convectional currents and this movement of plates by convectional current is responsible for the formation of landforms. It is believed that the mobile rock beneath the rigid plates is moving in a circular manner.

Heat within the Earth comes from two main sources i.e. radioactive decay and residual heat which causes a convectional cell or convectional flow. The slow movement of hot, softened mantle that lies below the rigid plates is the driving force behind the plate movement.

9. How does plate tectonics explain earthquakes?

Ans. Earthquakes occur due to the stress built up along faults at plate boundaries. As the tectonic plates are in constant motion, earthquakes are generated when stress is released. The initiation of earthquakes happens in three ways

(i) **Convergent Boundaries** Plates move towards each other and one plate is under subduction. This builds intense pressure and its release causes powerful earthquake.

(ii) **Divergent Boundaries** Plates move apart, creating gaps and magma rises to fill these gaps. It results into formation of new crust. Earthquake also generates here but it is less intense.

(iii) **Transform Boundaries** Plates slide past each other horizontally. The friction between them results in earthquake with medium magnitude.

Convergent boundaries generally cause strong earthquakes as compared to other boundaries.

10. How does continental drift relate to plate tectonics?

Ans. Continental drift is a pioneer to the modern theory of plate tectonics. Plate tectonic is a concept that describes the movement of large tectonic plates which are massive rigid slabs on the Earth's surface. Plate tectonic contains ideas of continental drift theory ideas and explains the forces that are responsible for the continental movement, such as convection currents. These currents are driven by the forces that comes from hot and softened mantle that lies below the lithosphere.

11. Explain the oceanic and continental plate collision in convergence boundaries.

Ans. The convergence of plates happens in three ways which are: continental-continental, continental-oceanic and oceanic-oceanic. Continental and oceanic plates are made of different material which has different density.

Oceanic plate is heavier and continental plate is lighter in density. When there is collision between these two plates, the heavier plate gets subducted (submerged) under the lighter plate and the plate gets destroyed in Mantle. It results into the formation of trench and volcanoes.

12. "Divergent plate boundary results in the formation of new crust". Explain how? Competency Based Que

Ans. Divergent plate boundaries occur when tectonic plates move away from each other. This creates a gap between them. This movement allows magma from the Earth's mantle to rise and solidify on the surface. Hence, formation of new crust takes place. This process primarily occurs at mid-ocean ridges where oceanic plates are moving apart and over time due to continuous flow and solidification of magma, new oceanic crust pushes the older crust at spreading centers. This process is called sea-floor spreading which helps in maintaining the Earth's crust.

13. How do lithospheric plate behave along the transform faults?

Ans. Transform faults are the plane of separation generally perpendicular to the mid-oceanic ridges. The lithospheric plates slide horizontally past each other in the region of these faults and the crust is neither produced nor destroyed.

As the eruption do not take all along the entire crest at the same time, there is a differential movement of a portion of the plate away from the axis of the Earth. Also, the rotation of the Earth has its effect on the separated blocks of the plate portions.

Long Answer Type Questions

1. "The Continental Drift Theory is a very important theory which provides evidences from the past." Discuss the theory in brief. Competency Based Que

Ans. In 1912, Alfred Wegener propounded his hypothesis of continental drift. According to him, all the continents formed a single continental mass surrounded by mega ocean. The super continent was Pangaea which was surrounded by Panthalassa, a mega ocean.
Wegner described the continental drift theory as follows

- **Beginning of Split** Around 200 million years ago, the super continent Pangaea began to split into two large continental masses and had a sea in their middle part which was called Tethys sea.
  The two continental masses i.e. Laurasia landmass situated to the North of Tethys sea and Gondwana was on the Southern side.
- **Drifting of Continents** According to Wegener, the Pangaea broke up in Carboniferrous period and began to drift. The continents had two directions of drift i.e. towards the equator and towards the West.
  The movement towards the equator is considered to be caused by the effect of the forces of gravitation and buoyancy and the movement towards the West is considered to be caused by the tidal forces of the Sun and the Moon affecting the Earth.
  The drift in these ways caused the redistribution of continents and ocean basin resulting in the present form and shape of the Earth.

Evidences in Support of Continental Drift

- The matching of coastal configuration of continents in the form of Jig-Saw Fit.
- Rocks of same age are found across the ocean.
- The glacial tillite available in six different landmasses of the Southern hemisphere.
- The occurrence of rich placer deposits in the coast of Ghana in the absence of source rocks.
- Distribution of similar fossils in different continents. e.g. Lemur occur in India, Madagascar and Africa.

2. **"Plate tectonic theory is considered an important theory". Explain why?** **Competency Based Que**

Ans. In 1967, Mckenzie, Parker and Morgan explained the theory of plate tectonics. This theory is considered an important theory because it has revealed that the lithosphere is broken into a number of moderately rigid plates. These plates move continuously and have relative direction of motion.

A plate may be referred to as the continental plate or an oceanic plate depending on which of the two occupy a larger portion of the plate. Relative motion of plates forms three kind of plate boundaries or marginal zones which are

(i) **Zone of Divergence** These are boundaries along which plate separates. In this process of separation, molten material upwells which is clearly observed along linear ocean ridges where new lithosphere is created in the form of new ocean floors. Active volcanism and shallow focus earthquakes mark such boundaries.

(ii) **Zone of Convergence** These are boundries along which the edge of one plate overrides the other. This over ridden plate sinks down into the mantle and is absorbed. This process is known as subduction. Besides volcanism and shallow to deep focus earthquakes, these boundaries also produce deep trenches and folded mountain chains.

(iii) **Transform Boundaries** The transform fault has neither creation nor destruction. These are the plane of separation generally perpendicular to the mid-oceanic ridges.

3. **What is a tectonic plate? Describe the major and minor plates.**

Ans. Tectonic plates are large slabs of Earth's lithosphere (the outermost layer) that move over the semi-fluid asthenosphere beneath them. These plates are responsible for many geological processes, including earthquakes, volcanic activity and the formation of mountains. Their movements are driven by the heat from Earth's interior, causing them to diverge, converge, or slide past one another.

There are seven major tectonic plates-the African, Antarctic, Eurasian, Indo-Australian, North American, Pacific, and South American plates. These plates cover significant portions of Earth's surface and are involved in large-scale tectonic activity.

Some of the important minor plates include-the Arabian, Caribbean, Cocos, Nazca, Philippine, and Fuji plates. These plates often interact with major plates at their boundaries, resulting in dynamic geological phenomena such as subduction zones, mountain building and oceanic trench formation.

4. **It took many years to India to come in the present position. Explain in brief.** **Competency Based Que**

Ans. India's current position on the globe is a result of millions of years of tectonic plate movements. These periods are as follows

- About 225 million years ago, India was a large island situated off the Australian coast in a vast ocean.
- Around 200 million years ago, the Indian plate broke away from Gondwana and began moving northward.
- During 60 million years ago, a major event that occurred was the formation of Deccan Trap.
- Driven by the forces of plate tectonics, this northward journey continued for about 50 million years, during which India moved across the Tethys Ocean, which once separated the Indian subcontinent from Eurasia.
- Around 40-50 million years ago, the Indian plate collided with the Eurasian plate, leading to the uplift of the Himalayan mountain range and the Tibetan Plateau. This collision is still ongoing, causing frequent seismic activity in the region.

5. **"It is not the continent but the plate that moves". Justify this statement.** **Competency Based Que**

Ans. The idea that "It is not the continent but the plate that moves" aligns with the different theories and methodologies. Initially, in the Continental Drift Theory, Alfred Wegener described the movement of continent with some natural forces. A variety of evidences were offered in support of this argument.

Later, post drift studies discarded continental drift theory on the basis of convectional current theory and the mapping of the ocean floor. This combined with palaeomagnetic studies of rocks from oceanic region revealed the fact of sea floor spreading. These studies revived the interest in the problem of distribution of oceans and continents.

In 1967, Mckenzie, Parker and Morgan collected the available ideas and came out with another concept named 'plate tectonics'.

As per this theory, lithosphere is divided into various plates and these plates as a rigid unit move horizontally over asthenosphere.

There are seven major and some minor plates and these plates have been constantly moving over the globe throughout the history of the earth. Hence, it is proved that it is not the continent that moves as believed by Wegener. Continents are the part of the plate and it is the plate that moves.

6. **"It is now a well accepted fact that oceans and continents will not continue to enjoy their present positions in time to come". Give your argument in support of this statement.** Competency Based Que

Ans. The positions of the continents and the ocean bodies, as we see them in the map, have not been the same as in the past. The continental drift theory widely explained the previous condition of continents and oceans.

According to this, initially there was a super continent Pangaea and mega ocean Panthalassa, which further broke into various smaller continents. Evidence like Jig-Saw-Fit were given in support of this argument.

Later, convectional current theory proved that there exist convectional current in mantle portion due to presence of radioactive elements. Hence, a drifting force had been found. Later, mapping of ocean floor and palaeomagnetic studies proved the spreading of floor.

Finally, after the analysis of Mckenzie, Parker and Morgan, plate tectonic theory was revealed which showed the movement of plate in asthenosphere due to presence of heated materials. This theory proved that these plates have been constantly moving over the globe throughout the history of the earth and it was proved that all the plates have moved in the geological past and shall continue to move in the future. So, the continents and oceans will not continue to enjoy their present position in time to come.

7. **What facts and studies encouraged Harry Hess to postulate the concept of Sea Floor Spreading?**

Ans. Harry Hess postulated the concept of Sea Floor Spreading in the early 1960s based on several key observations and studies.

- During World War II, Hess mapped the ocean floor and discovered mid-ocean ridges, underwater mountain ranges with deep valleys at their centres. He also observed that the oceanic crust was much thinner than continental crust and lacked the thick sediment layers that would be expected if the seafloor were ancient.
- Hess connected these findings to earlier work on continental drift by Alfred Wegener and he discovered the symmetrical patterns of magnetic strips on the ocean floor, which showed the formation of new crust along the Mid Oceanic Ridge.
- This crust spreads outward, pushing older crust away. Hess theorized that magma from Earth's mantle rises at the ridges, creating new seafloor, which is then recycled back into the mantle at subduction zones.

Source Based Questions

1. **Read the passage carefully and answer the questions that follow.**

It was Alfred Wegener—a German meteorologist who put forth a comprehensive argument in the form of "The Continental Drift Distribution of Oceans and Continents Chapter Theory" in 1912. This was regarding the distribution of the oceans and the continents. According to Wegener, all the continents formed a single continental mass and mega-ocean surrounded the same. The super continent was named PANGAEA, which meant all earth. The mega-ocean was called PANTHALASSA, meaning all water. He argued that, around 200 million years ago, the super continent, Pangaea, began to split. Pangaea first broke into two large continental masses as Laurasia and Gondwanaland forming the Northern and Southern components respectively. Subsequently, Laurasia and Gondwanaland continued to break into various smaller continents that exist today.

Wegener suggested that the movement responsible for the drifting of the continents was caused by pole-fleeing force and tidal force. The polar-fleeing force relates to the rotation of the earth. The earth is not a perfect sphere; it has a bulge at the equator. This bulge is due to the rotation of the earth. The second force that was suggested by Wegener — the tidal force — is due to the attraction of the moon and the sun that develops tides in oceanic waters. Wegener believed that these forces would become effective when applied over many million years. However, most of scholars considered these forces to be totally inadequate. It is interesting to note that for continental drift, most of the evidence was collected from the continental areas in the form of distribution of flora and fauna or deposits, like tillite.

(i) **What revolutionary concept would a scientist studying Earth's geological history in 1912 have encountered in Wegener's work?**
(a) The idea of stationary
(b) The concept of a single landmass called Pangaea
(c) The theory of multiple original continents
(d) The notion of permanent ocean basins

Ans. (b) The concept of a single landmass called Pangaea

(ii) **How would a geologist studying the Earth's equatorial region explain its distinctive shape according to Wegener's understanding?**
(a) Due to meteorite impacts
(b) Due to the Earth's rotation
(c) Due to tectonic activity (d) Due to lunar gravity

Ans. (b) Due to the Earth's rotation

(iii) "Wegener suggested that some forces were responsible for the drifting of the continents", which forces would a researcher examining Wegener's theory find cited as the drivers of continental movement?

(a) Volcanic and seismic forces
(b) Gravitational and magnetic forces
(c) Pole-fleeing and tidal forces
(d) Wind and water erosion

Ans. (c) Pole-fleeing and tidal forces

2. Study the following graph and answer the questions that follow.

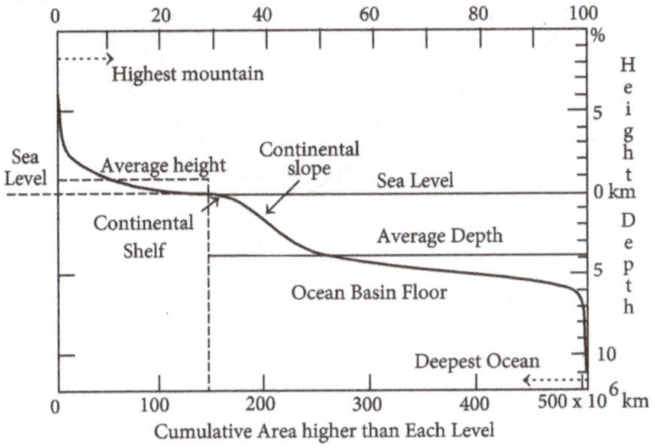

Ocean Floor

(i) Which of the following feature constitute the deepest part of the ocean?

(a) Continental shelf
(b) Continental slope
(c) Trenches
(d) Basin floors

Ans. (c) Trenches

(ii) What is the average depth of continental slope from mean sea level?

(a) 0-5 km (b) 5-10km
(c) 3-10km (d) 2-5 km

Ans. (a) 0-5 km

(iii) Arrange the following in decreasing depth from mean sea level.

(i) Ocean basin floor (ii) Continental slope
(iii) Continental shelf (iv) Mountains

Options

(a) (iv), (iii), (ii), (i) (b) (i), (ii), (iii), (iv)
(c) (i), (iv), (iii), (ii) (d) (iv), (iii), (i), (ii)

Ans. (b) (i), (ii), (iii), (iv)

3. Read the passage carefully and answer the questions that follow.

The boundary between India and the Antarctic plate is also marked by oceanic ridge (divergent boundary) running in roughly W-E direction and merging into the spreading site, a little South of New Zealand. India was a large island situated off the Australian coast, in a vast ocean.

The Tethys Sea separated it from the Asian continent till about 225 million years ago. India is supposed to have started her northward journey about 200 million years ago at the time when Pangaea broke. India collided with Asia about 40-50 million years ago causing rapid uplift of the Himalayas. About 140 million years before the present, the subcontinent was located as South as 50°S latitude. The two major plates were separated by the Tethys Sea and the Tibetan block was closer to the Asiatic landmass. During the movement of the Indian plate towards the Eurasian plate, a major event that occurred was the outpouring of lava and formation of the Deccan Traps. This started somewhere around 60 million years ago and continued for a long period of time. From 40 million years ago and thereafter, the event of formation of the Himalayas took place. Scientists believe that the process is still continuing and the height of the Himalayas is rising even to this date.

(i) Which body of water would a time traveller encounter if they visited the space between India and Asia 225 million years ago?

Ans. If a time traveller visited the space between India and Asia 225 million years ago, they would encounter the Tethys Sea, which separated India from the Asian continent.

(ii) What remarkable event would someone observe if they could go back 40-50 million years in Earth's history?

Ans. If someone goes back to 40-50 million years in Earth's history, they would witness the collision between India and Asia, which led to the rapid uplift of the Himalayas.

(iii) "The boundary between India and the Antarctic plate is also marked by oceanic ridge" Explain.

Ans. The boundary between India and the Antarctic plate is also marked by oceanic ridge which is a divergent boundary where both the plates move away from each other giving rise to formation of a ridge.

4. **Study the following map and answer the questions that follow.**

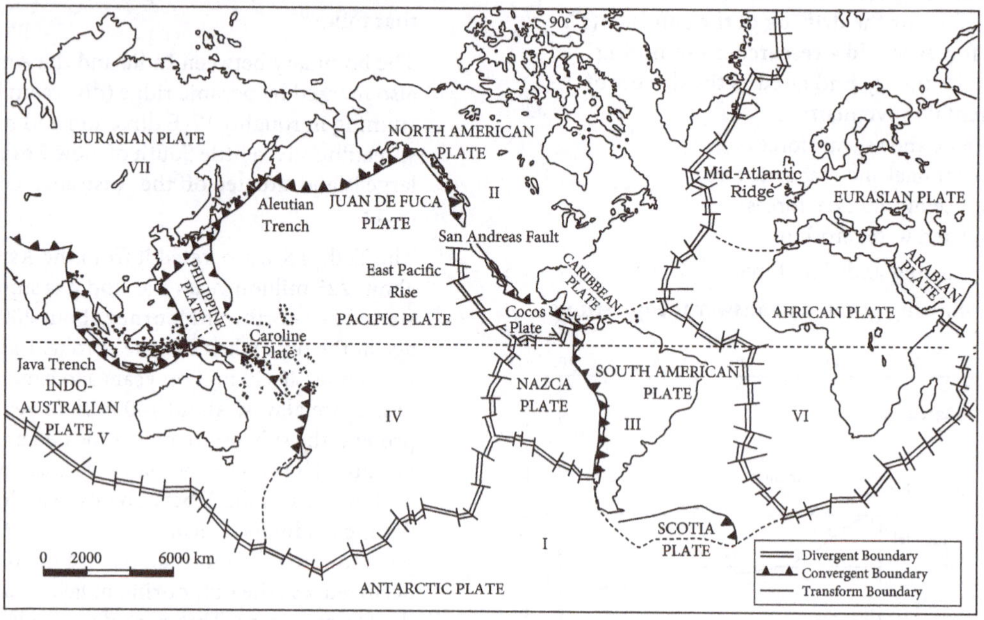

(i) Name the plate that is getting converged with South American Plate.

Ans. There is convergence of Nazca Plate with the South American Plate.

(ii) Why there is formation of new crust near Mid-Atlantic ridge?

Ans. There is divergence of two plates near Atlantic Ridge which results in the upwelling of magma which solidifies and forms new crust.

(iii) Write one physical feature formed due to convergence of plates.

Ans. Convergence of two plates may lead to formation of mountains. For example, Himalayas.

Map Based Questions

1. **Identify the major plates in the given map.**

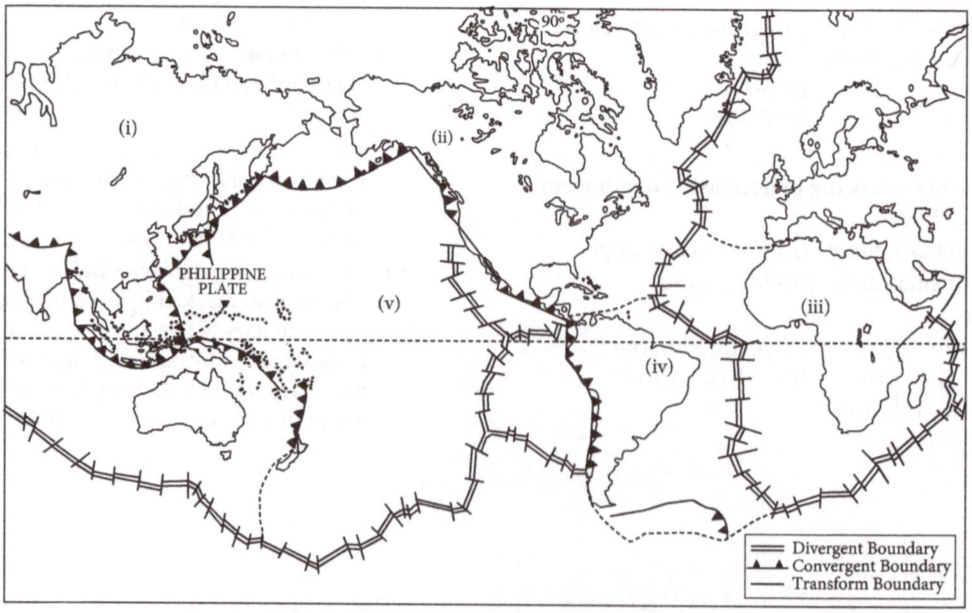

Ans.

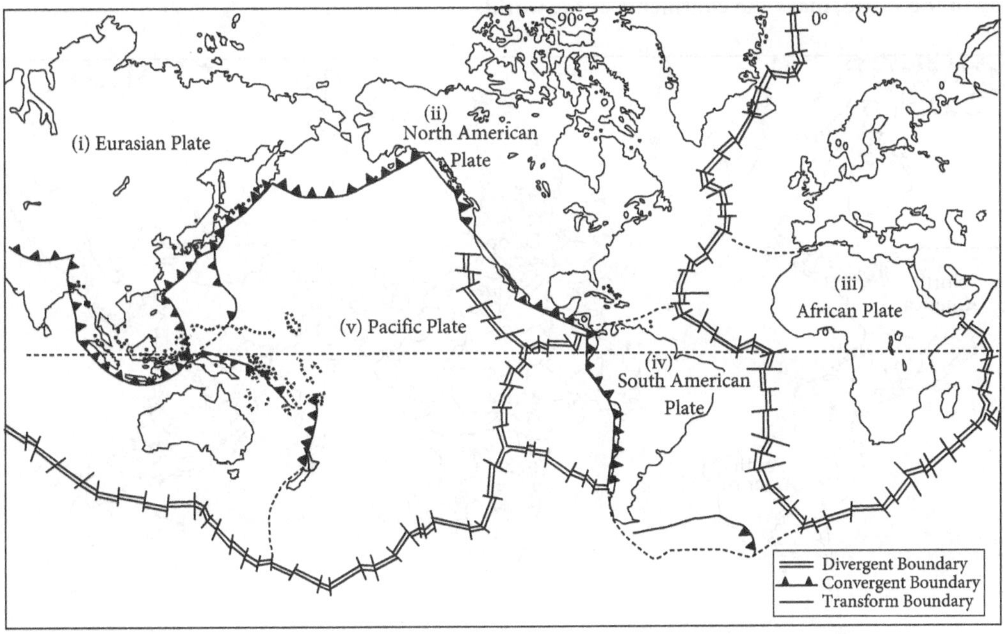

2. Mark the following on a map.

(i) **Cocos Plate** (ii) **Nazca Plate** (iii) **Arabian Plate**
(iv) **Philippine Plate** (v) **Caroline Plate** (vi) **Ring of Fire**
(vii) **Mid-Atlantic Ridge**

Ans.

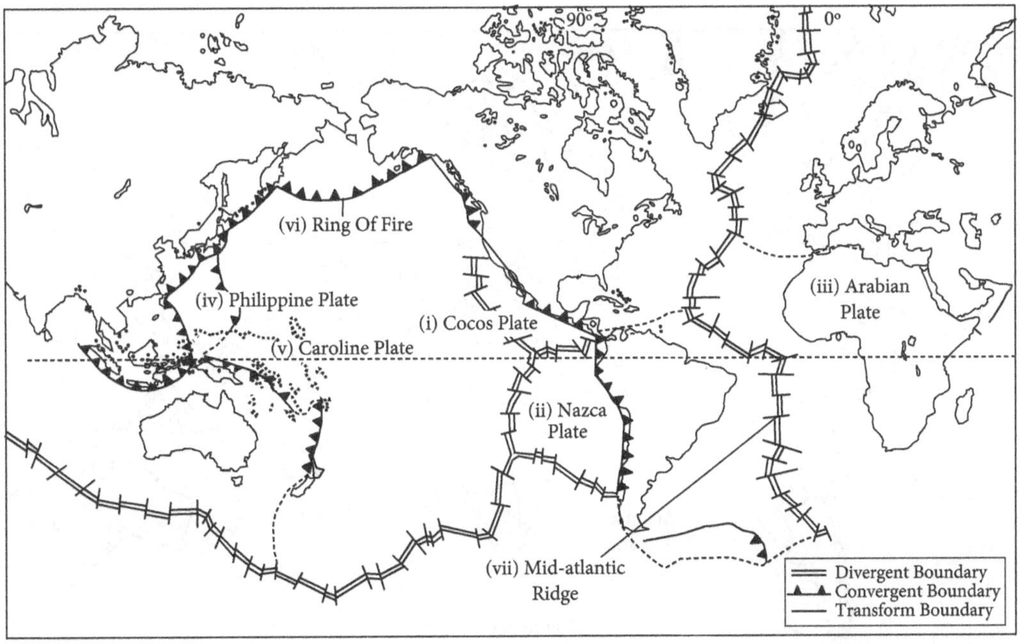

3. On the map of the world, mark the continents of the world.

Ans.

4. On the map of the world, mark the major oceans of the world.

Ans.

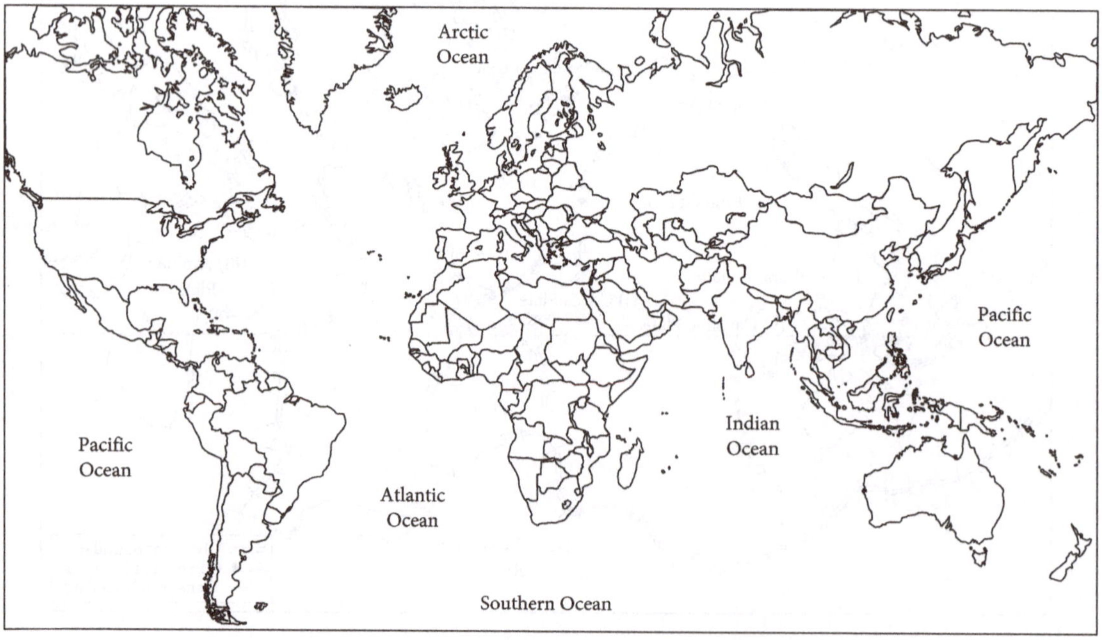

SELF ASSESSMENT TEST

Objective Type Questions

1 Antonio Pellegrini is related with
(a) Sea Floor Spreading
(b) Continental Drift
(c) Plate Tectonics
(d) Convectional Current Theory

2 Where are placer deposits of gold found in Africa?
(a) Madagascar
(b) South Africa
(c) Ghana
(d) Western Sahara

3 Which of the given arrangements of Ocean Floor Configuration is correct?
(a) Continental Margin, Mid-Oceanic Ridge, Abyssal Plain
(b) Abyssal Plain, Continental Margin, Mid-Oceanic Ridge
(c) Continental Margin, Abyssal Plain, Mid-Oceanic Ridge
(d) Mid-Oceanic Ridge, Continental Margin, Abyssal Plain

4 Which of the following is known as Rim of Fire?
(a) Alpine-Himalayan Belt
(b) Rim of Atlantic
(c) Rim of Pacific
(d) Both (b) and (c)

5 Which of the following is a minor plate?
(a) Antarctica Plate
(b) Arabian Plate
(c) South American Plate
(d) India-Australia New Zealand Plate

6 Where was Indian sub-continent located about 140 million years before present?
(a) 50°N latitude
(b) 50°S latitude
(c) 0° latitude
(d) $66\frac{1}{2}$°S latitude

Short Answer Type Questions

7. What is palaeomagnetism? How is it used for oceanic study?
8. How does Laurasia and Gondwanaland differ from each other in terms of their geographic characteristics?
9. 'There are certain zones all over the world where earthquake occurs'. Explain.
10. 'The theory of plate tectonic proposes that lithosphere is made of major and minor plates'. Elucidate the statement.
11. What are the different types of interactions that occur between tectonic plates at their boundaries and how do these interactions shape the Earth's surface?

Long Answer Type Questions

12. "India was a large island situated off the Australian coast, in a vast ocean." Give reasons to explain this statement.
13. 'There are a series of discoveries that took place after World War II and added new information to the concept of Continental Drift Theory'. Justify the statement with suitable examples.
14. Explain plate tectonics and also provide information about major and minor plates.
15. 'Position of the continents was not same in the past as it is today'. Explain the given statement.

UNIT 3

5
CHAPTER

Geomorphic Processes

This chapter deals with the surface of the Earth and its various features. Humans rely on it for survival and use it heavily. Therefore, it is important to understand its dynamic nature to use it wisely without harming its balance for the future.

YOUR STUDY GOALS

YOUR PRACTICE GOAL

- Objective Type Questions (32 Qs ; MCQs, A-R, Statements, Matching)
- Subjective Questions (12 SAs, 8 LAs)
- Source Based Questions (3 Qs)

- The Earth's crust is dynamic as it has moved vertically and horizontally and it is still moving.
- The uneven nature of Earth's surface is the result of **Endogenic** and **Exogenic forces.**
- Endogenic forces are land building forces whereas Exogenic forces are land wearing (wash out) forces.

5.1 Meaning of Geomorphic Process

- Geomorphic processes are the natural mechanism that shapes and changes the Earth's surface with the help of Endogenic and Exogenic forces.
- The Endogenic forces are the internal forces that comes from interior of the Earth and the Exogenic forces are the external forces that comes from Earth's atmosphere.

Geomorphic Agent

- Any exogenic element of nature which is capable to remove the materials, transport and deposit Earth's material from one place to another is called Geomorphic Agent. These agents include running water, groundwater, wind, glaciers, waves and currents, etc.
- When these agents become active due to gradients (slope), they remove and transport the material over slope and deposit them in low level areas.

Role of Gravity and Gradient

- **Gravity** is a directional force that activates all downslope movement of materials.
- Gradient[1] affects the geomorphic process as all the movement either within the Earth or on the surface of the Earth is from 'high level to low level' and 'high pressure to low pressure'.
- Without gravity or gradient there would be no movement and hence, no erosion, transportation and deposition.

5.2 Endogenic Processes

- These are processes that brings physical and chemical changes to the Earth's surface due to the energy released from within the Earth.
- These processes are generated by energy sources such as: Radioactivity[2], Rotational and Tidal friction[3], and Primordial heat[4].
- The action of endogenic forces is not uniform because there is variation in geothermal gradient[5] and heat flow from crustal thickness and strength.
- **Diastrophism** and **Volcanism** are caused by the endogenic processes.

Diastrophism

- It includes the processes of deformation of earth's crust by natural processes such as movement, elevation or building up of Earth's crust. They include
  - **Orogenic processes** These involve mountain building through folding[6] and affecting long and narrow belt of Earth's crust.
  - **Epeirogenic processes** They involve uplifting or warping[7] of large parts of Earth's crust i.e. continental building.
  - **Earthquakes** They involve local, relatively minor movements. Earthquake occurs when there is sudden release of stress from the rocks (interior of the Earth).
  - **Plate tectonics** They involve horizonal movement of tectonic plates (major and minor plates).
- The above processes may result in the folding and fracturing (breaking) of the crust and also causes change in Temperature, Pressure and Volume (PVT) of rocks. These changes results in the formation of **Metamorphic rocks.**

Volcanism

- It is the process by which molten rocks (magma) moves towards the surface of the Earth from interior and results in the formation of different intrusive[8] and extrusive[9] landforms.

Quick Test 1

1. What is the force that keeps us in contact with the Earth's surface?
2. Which process involves the uplift or warping of large parts of the Earth's crust?
3. What is the result of pressure, volume and temperature changes in the Earth's crust?

1 Gradient It refers to the slope of a land.
2 Radioactivity It is the process by which there is release of radiation.
3 Rotational and tidal friction These are frictions that slows down Earth's rotation.
4 Primordial heat This is the heat lost by the Earth as it continues to cool from its original formation.
5 Geothermal gradient It is the rate of change in temperature with respect to increasing depth in Earth's interior.
6 Folding An Earth movement resulting from the horizontal compression of rock layers by internal forces of the Earth.
7 Warping It is the downward movement of crustal rocks.
8 Intrusive These are formed when magma cools and solidifies within the Earth's crust.
9 Extrusive These are formed when magma cools and solidifies outside the Earth's surface.

5.3 Exogenic Processes

- Exogenic processes are process that occurs on the Earth's surface by obtaining their energy from Earth's atmosphere. Sun and tectonic factors are the sources of energy for these processes.
- Exogenic forces results in **degradation** (wearing down or erosion) of relief/elevation and **aggradation** (filling up or deposition) of basins or depression on the surface of the Earth.
- The phenomena of wearing down of relief through erosion is known as **Gradation**.
- Forces acting upon Earth's material are shear stresses (separating forces) which break rocks and result in angular displacement[10] or slippage.
- Force applied per unit area is called 'stress'. Stress is produced in a solid body by pushing or pulling which results in deformation. Earth materials experiences two types of stresses
  - (i) **Gravitational stress** It includes gravitational force that causes the downslope movement of Earth's materials.
  - (ii) **Molecular stress** It is a type of stress that occurs in Earth material due to change in temperature, crystallisation[11] and melting. For example, chemical processes lead to loosening of grains, which results in dissolving or cementation.

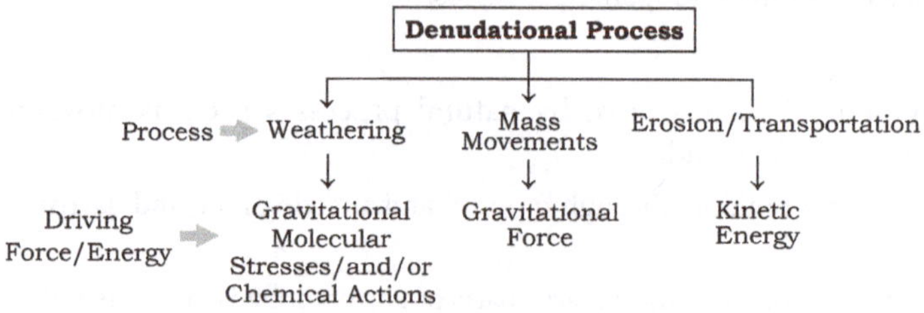

▲ *Denudational Processes and their Driving Forces*

Denudation

- The word denude means 'strip off or to uncover'. All the exogenic geomorphic processes are covered under denudation.
- Examples of denudational processes are weathering, mass movement, erosion and transportation. Each process is carried out by different forces.

Factors Affecting Exogenic Processes

1. Climate

- There is climatic variation all over the Earth's surface which result in variation in Geomorphic processes.
- Climatic variations are affected by several factors which are of global and local level. They are as follows
  - At **Global** level, variations occurs due to temperature differences which are created by latitudinal, seasonal, land-water distribution all over the globe.
  - At **Local** level, variation in climate occur due to altitudinal difference and variation in amount of insolation(sunlight) received by North-South facing slopes as compared to West-East facing slopes.
- The differences in wind velocity and direction, precipitation (amount, kind and intensity), relation between precipitation and evaporation, daily range of temperature, freezing and thawing (melt) frequency and depth of frost penetration[12], all these influences Geomorphic processes within a climatic region.

2. Vegetation

- The density, type and distribution of vegetation affects the exogenic geomorphic processes indirectly.
- Density, distribution and type of vegetation depends upon temperature and precipitation of a place.

10 Angular displacement It is a vector quantity which has both magnitude and direction.
11 Crystallisation It is defined as a process by which a chemical is converted from a liquid solution into a solid crystalline state.
12 Frost Penetration It is the process by which cold temperatures cause the ground to freeze from the surface downward.

3. Types and Structure of Rocks

- Structure of rocks include - folds, faults, arrangement and inclination of beds, presence and absence of joints(cracks), **bedding planes**[13], hardness or softness of minerals, **chemical susceptibility**[14], **permeability**[15] or impermeability.
- Rocks with different resistant property affects the Geomorphic Processes. For example - a particular rock may be resistant to one geomorphic process but can be non-resistant to another, hence they react at different rates and give rise to different **topography**[16].
- The effects of geomorphic processes on rocks for short period of time are invisible but when applied for long period of time, it can affect the rock severely.

Types of Exogenic Geomorphic Processes

Weathering

- Weathering is defined as breaking down and dissolving of rocks through the actions of various elements of weather and climate.
- Weathering is an **in-situ** or on - **site** process. In- situ means there is no movement of material from its place of origin.
- The process of weathering is affected by many factors such as geology, climate, topography and vegetation. Weathering process is also affected by the depth of the **weathering mantle**[17].

Types of Weathering Processes

There are three types of weathering processes which are as follows

1. Physical or Mechanical Weathering

Physical weathering is a process that breaks down rocks into smaller pieces without changing its chemical composition. There are some applied forces that results in the process of physical weathering. These are as follows

- **Gravitational forces** These forces include **overburden pressure**[18], load and **shearing stress**[19].
- **Expansion forces** These forces occur due to temperature change, **crustal growth** or animal activity.
- **Water pressure** It plays an important role in weathering as minerals swell up when they are wet and cause cracks when they dry. This helps in breaking down of rocks.
- Temperature and pressure change are the major cause of physical weathering. These are slow and small processes but can cause large damage to rocks when applied for long duration.

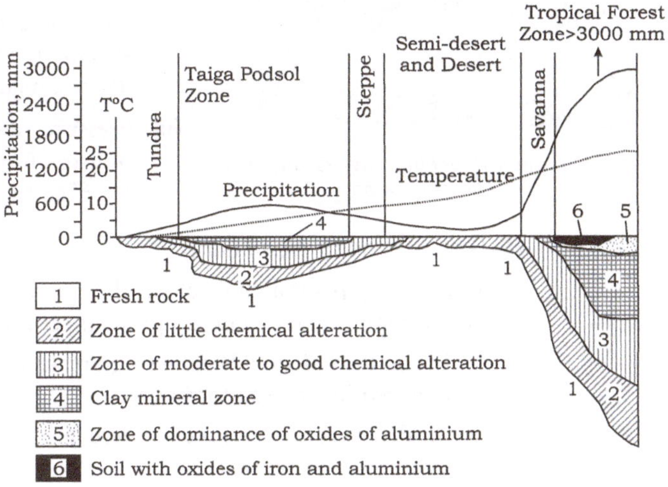

▲ *Climatic regimes and depth of weathering mantles (adapted and modified from Strakhov, 1967)*

2. Chemical Weathering

- Chemical weathering is a process that occurs when mineral in a rock reacts with chemicals in environment such as water, oxygen, carbon dioxide, which results in change in the composition of rocks.

---

13 **Bedding plane** The surface that separates each successive layer of a layered rock from its preceding rock.
14 **Chemical susceptibility** It is the capacity of a substance to take part in chemical reaction.
15 **Permeability** It is the ability of a material to allow fluids to pass through it.
16 **Topography** It is the physical characteristics of an area of land, especially the position of its rivers, mountains, etc.
17 **Weathering mantle** It is the layer of loose, broken-down material on Earth's surface that forms as a result of weathering.
18 **Overburden pressure** It refers to the pressure caused by the weight of the overlying layers of material at a specific depth under the Earth's, surface.
19 **Shear stress** It is a type of force that tries to cause one part of a material to slide or move sideways past another part.

- Weathering processes such as carbonation[20], oxidation[21], hydration[22] and reduction[23], act on rocks to decompose, dissolve or reduce them.
- Presence of water, air (oxygen and carbon dioxide) and heat increases the rate of chemical reactions.

3. Biological Weathering

- It is a process that occurs when living organisms such as plants and animals break down rocks or dissolve them into smaller pieces.
- The agents of biological weathering are as follows
  - **Animals** Animals such as earthworms, ants, rodents physically disturb the soil and rock by burrowing[24] and wedging[25]. This activity exposes fresh rock surfaces to the atmosphere and water, and thus the process of weathering starts.
  - **Humans** Humans acts as an agent by mixing and creating contact between air, water and minerals through activities like ploughing, deforestation and soil cultivation.
  - **Plant roots** Plant roots help in weathering process by exerting pressure on the rock, which causes breaking of rocks.
  - **Organic acids** When plants and animals die, they releases organic acids, like humic and carbonic acids. These acids chemically react with minerals in the rock and break them into simpler forms.

▲ *Exfoliation (Flacking) and Granular Disintegration*

Exfoliation

- It is a **special effect of weathering** in which the outer layer of the curved rock surface is removed.
- Exfoliation occurs mostly due to two reasons; they are as follows
  - (i) **Thermal expansion and contraction** Exfoliation may occur due to expansion and contraction in rocks because of temperature change in day and night.
  - (ii) **Pressure release** (unloading) Exfoliation may occur due to release of pressure from overlying rocks. Formation of exfoliation domes[26] and tors[27] occurs when this phenomenon happens.

Significance of Weathering

Weathering plays a vital role in shaping the Earth's surface and it has significant geological, ecological and human impacts. These significances are listed below

- **Formation of soils** Weathering breaks down rocks into smaller particles and provide the raw material required for the soil formation.
- **Biodiversity and Biomes** These are mainly the result of forests which depend on the depth of weathering in the soil.
- **Landforms** Weathering helps in bringing changes to the landforms by mass wasting[28] and reduction of relief. Weathering starts after the process of erosion takes place.
- **Mineral resources** Weathering of rocks exposes ore deposits that remain hidden under the Earth's surface. For example, ores of iron, manganese, aluminium and copper. These minerals are important for nation's economy.

---

20 **Carbonation** It refers to the process of adding carbon dioxide (CO_2) to a substance, often resulting in the formation of carbonic acid.
21 **Oxidation** It is a chemical process in which a substance loses electrons, often involving the reaction of the substance with oxygen.
22 **Hydration** In this the chemical bond of the minerals are changed as it interacts with water.
23 **Reduction** It is a chemical process in which a substance gains electrons or decreasing its oxidation state.
24 **Burrowing** To dig a hole in the ground.
25 **Wedging** The process by which rocks break apart due to water freezing and expansion in cracks.
26 **Exfoliation Domes** These are large, smooth rounded domes.
27 **Tors** It is smooth surfaced and rounded small to big boulders form due to exfoliation.
28 **Mass wasting** It refers to the movement of soil, rock and other materials down a slope under the influence of gravity.

Enrichment

- Enrichment in weathering is the process by which groundwater physically or chemically leaches (dilutes) material from rocks and this leaching[29] increases the concentration of materials that are left in the rocks.
- This process can make valuable materials easier and more cost-effective to extract, process and refine.

Quick Test 2

1. What is another name for physical weathering?
2. List two major causes of physical weathering.
3. Name one agent of biological weathering.

5.4 Mass Movement

- Mass movement is the process in which the transfer of mass of rocks, debris[30] and soil happens down the slope because of gravity. Gravitational force is exerted on both the bedrock and the products of weathering.
- The speed of movement of these debris may range between slow to rapid, which are called as creep[31], flow, slide and fall.
- The process of weathering is not pre-required for mass movement but it helps in the process of mass movement. Mass movement is easy over weathered rocks as compared to unweathered rocks.
- Mass movement does not come under erosion because no Geomorphic agents like water, wind, wave, etc are involved in the process of moving the material from one place to another.
- There are three forms of mass movement which include heave[32], flow and slide. These are related to each other.

Pre-conditions for Mass Movement

- **Removal of support** Removing support from below a slope can cause mass movement of the materials.
- **Slope steepness** Increasing the steepness (gradient and height) of a slope can cause mass movement.
- **Overloading** Overloading is the addition of materials to a slope; it can be natural or artificial filling. It causes mass movement of the material. Presence of too much water in a slope makes it heavier, more slippery and less stable.
- **Removal of load or material** The removal of load from over the original slope surfaces may cause mass movement.
- **Earthquakes** Earthquake tremors can affect the balance of a slope and increase the chances of mass movement.
- **Excessive natural seepage** This include flow of water from lakes, reservoirs and rivers which results in the slow outflow of water from under the slopes or river banks.
- **Indiscriminate removal of vegetation** Decrease in the vegetation cover may increase the chances of mass movement.

29 Leaching It is a natural process by which water-soluble substances are washed away from soil due to flood or rainfall.
30 Debris It refers to scattered fragments or pieces of material that result from the breaking down or destruction of larger objects.
31 Creep It is the slow and steady downward movement of materials.
32 Heave It is a slow mass movement. It is caused by freezing, thawing or wetting and drying of the soil.

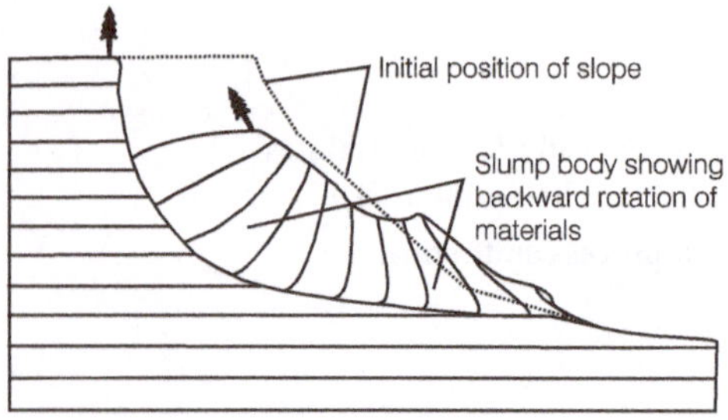

Slumping of debris with backward rotation

Landslide scars in Shivalik Himalayan ranges near river Sarada at India-Nepal border, Uttar Pradesh

Landslide

- It is a type of mass movement of materials such as rocks and debris which are dry in nature. The movement of materials in landslides are visible and rapid.
- The size and shape of the materials that move depends upon the nature of discontinuity (breaks) in the rock, amount of weathering and the steepness of slope.
- Depending upon the type of movement of materials, there are four types of landslides. These are as follows
  1. **Slump** It is a type of landslide in which several units of rocks move down a slope with backward rotation.
  2. **Debris Slide** It is a type of landslide in which Earth materials moves rapidly by rolling or sliding without backward rotation. It is free fall of Earth material from vertical face.
  3. **Rockslide** It is a type of landslide in which there is sliding of single rock masses down on bedding, joint or fault surface. In this type, the rock falls down, breaking other rocks and anything in their path.
  4. **Rock Fall** It is a type of fast-moving landslide that happens when there is free falling of rocks down a steep slope without being in touch with the slope. It occurs from the superficial layers of rock face.

Factors Responsible for Landslides and Debris Avalanches in Various Regions of India

- In India, Debris Avalanches and landslides are very common and frequent in Himalayan Region and Western Ghats.
- The factors for landslides and debris avalanches in Himalayas are
  - **Himalayas** Himalayas are tectonically active. Rocks of Himalayas are made up of sedimentary rocks. They also contain loose and semi loose particles of rocks which slides easily.
  - Steepness of the slope is also very high in this region, which increases the chances of landslides and debris avalanches in this region.
  - **The Western Ghats** is less tectonically active and contains hard rocks. Despite this, landslides and debris avalanches occur here because of the following reasons
    - In Western Ghats and Nilgiris, there is presence of steep slopes with vertical cliffs and escarpments[33].
    - Mechanical weathering is very common in this region because of temperature changes. This helps in the breaking down of rock fragments.
    - Rock falls are very common along with landslide and debris avalanches[34] because this region receives heavy rainfall for short period.

Erosion and Deposition

Erosion and deposition are natural processes that changes the surface of the Earth over time.

Erosion

- Erosion is the removal and transportation of broken pieces of rocks by the action of running water, wind, groundwater and waves. Amount of erosion increases when there is process of abrasion[35] by rock fragments.

33 **Escarpments** It is a steep slope or cliff that separates two relatively flat areas of land.
34 **Avalanches** An avalanche is a rapid flow of snow down a slope, such as a hill or mountain.
35 **Abrasion** It is a process in which rocks and sediment collide against each other and results in more smaller fragments.

- Erosion is a degradational process as it degrades (reduces) the relief features of the Earth. Weathering is not pre-required for erosion but it may increase the intensity of erosion.
- Weathering, erosion and mass wasting are degradational processes.
- Denudational processes like erosion and transportation are controlled by **kinetic energy**.
- Geomorphic agents that results in erosion and transportation of Earth materials are - wind, running water, glaciers, wave and ground water. Out of these, only wind, running water and glaciers are controlled by the climatic conditions.
- The work of wave depends upon its location along the coastal region and the work of groundwater depends upon the **lithology**[36] of the region. For example, Karst topography develops only in the region where the rocks are soluble and water is available.

Deposition

- Deposition is the process by which the eroded materials gets deposited to another location. Deposition is the result of erosion.
- The process of deposition starts when the erosional agents lose their velocity and energy, they start to settle down the materials brought with them. The coarser material gets deposited first and the fine materials are deposited later.
- Agents that perform the process of deposition are called Aggradational or Depositional agents. These agents are running water, waves, wind, groundwater and glaciers.

Quick Test 3

1 What causes materials on slopes to yield in mass movements?
2 Where do debris avalanches and landslides occur most frequently in India?
3 Which type of rocks make up the Himalayas?
4 How does abrasion contribute to erosion?
5 What determines the work of waves as an erosional agent?

5.5 Soil Formation

- Soil is a natural material that covers the surface of the Earth. It is a mixture of organic matter, minerals, gases, liquids and organisms.
- Soil is a medium in which chemical, physical and biological activities occurs constantly. It acts as a platform where the process of decay (break down) and growth, both takes place.
- The characteristics of soil changes with season. When the soil is too cold and too dry, biological activities occurs at slow rate.
- **Pedology** is the science related with the study of soil. A scientist who studies soil is called a **pedologist**.

Process of Soil formation

- The process of soil formation or pedogenesis is a slow process that occurs through weathering and decay of plants and animals. The basic input materials for soil formation comes from weathering mantle.
- Process of soil formation includes several steps which are as follows
  - First, when rocks break down into smaller pieces, tiny organisms like **bacteria, mosses** and **lichens** start to live on them.
  - When plants and small organisms die, their remains are converted into **humus**[37]. As the humus builds up, small plants like grasses and ferns start to grow in the soil. Seeds carried by the birds helps in growing bushes and trees.

36 Lithology It is the study of the general physical characteristics of a rock.
37 Humus It is the dark organic matter in soil that is formed by the decomposition of plant and animal matter.

- As plant roots grow deeper into the ground and burrowing animals like worms dig through the soil, they help break it up and mix it. This process makes the soil porous (full of tiny holes),
- Over time, this turns the soil into a rich, healthy mixture of minerals and organic material, creating a mature soil.

Factors Affecting Soil Formation

There are five major factors that influence the soil formation process. These are as follows:

1. Parent Material

- Parent material is a passive control factor in soil formation. It can be ***in-situ*** or **on-site**.
- Soil formation depends upon the texture (size of debris), structure and mineral and chemical composition of the rocks.
- Soil formation depends upon the nature and rate of weathering and depth of weathering mantle.
- Similar bedrock may form soil of different type and same soil may be found over different bedrocks.
- The link between soil and parent rock can be seen when weathering patterns are different for different parent material like limestone areas.

2. Topography

- Topography is another passive factor that control the soil formation. Soils found on steep slopes are thin as compared to soils found on gentle slope.
- Soil formation takes place over flat upland (high above sea level) because the rate of erosion is slow and **percolation**[38] of water is good.
- In flat areas, soils are dark in colour and develop a thick layer of clay because of good accumulation of organic matter.

3.Climate

- Climate is an important active factor in soil formation. The major climatic elements that affects the soil development are as follows

(i) Moisture

- It includes intensity, frequency and duration of precipitation.
- Precipitation provides moisture to the soil which helps in the chemical and biological activities.
- Water carries soil particles from the top layers (**eluviation**) and deposit those particles in the lower layers (**illuviation**).
- In areas with heavy rainfall, calcium, magnesium, sodium, potassium and major parts of silica are removed. This process of removal of silica is called as *desilication*.
- In dry climates, evaporation is more than precipitation. The groundwater comes to surface by **capillary action**[39] and in this process the water evaporates and salt is left behind. Such salts form a layer in the soil called as **'hardpans'**.
- There is formation of calcium carbonate nodules (*kanker*) in the tropical area where medium amount of precipitation occurs.

(ii) Temperature

- It includes seasonal and diurnal (daily) variations in temperature.
- Rate of chemical and biological activity changes with temperature. In high temperature, the rate of chemical activity increases while in low temperature the rate is reduced or it stops.

---

38 **Percolation** It is a process of passing liquid slowly through a filter.

39 **Capillary action** It is the ability of a liquid, like water, to move up or through narrow spaces without help of gravity.

Mind Map

GEOMORPHIC PROCESS

1 Endogenic Processes (Internal Forces)

- These forces gain energy from within the Earth, e.g., diastrophism and volcanism.
- **Diastrophism** Includes all the process that move, elevate or build up Earth's portion.
- **Volcanism** Includes the movement of magma onto or towards the Earth's surface.

2 Exogenic Processes (External Forces)

These forces are powered by energy from sunlight and gradients, e.g., gravity atmospheric energy.

Weathering

Breaking down of rock through mechanical and chemical process.

Types of Weathering

- **Chemical Weathering** Involves process like carbonation, solution, oxidation.
- **Physical Weathering** Involves process like thermal expansion and contraction.
- **Biological Weathering** Involves breakdown of rock through physical and chemical actions of plants and animals.

Effects and significance of weathering

- **Exfoliation** Rock layers pull due to temperature changes and unloading.
- Weathering breaks rocks, forms soil, helps in erosion and shapes landforms.
- It enriches ores like iron and manganese.

Erosion

- Removal and transportation of broken rocks by different agents.
- Geomorphic agents responsible for erosion are wind, water, glaciers, groundwater/waves

Mass Movement

Movement of Earth's material down slope because of gravity.

Landslides These are rapid and perceptible movements

Types of Landslides

Slump, debris slide, rock slide, rock fall

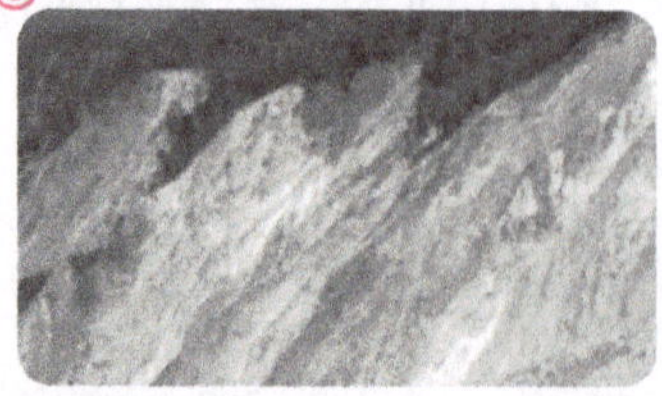

Deposition

- Accumulation of eroded materials
- Agents that perform the process of deposition are called aggradational or depositional agents.
- These agents are running water, waves, winds, glaciers and groundwater.

3 Soil Formation

Factors Affecting Soil Formation

- **Parent Material** e.g., texture, structure, chemical composition of rocks
- **Topography** e.g., slope of the area
- **Biological Activity** e.g., remains of plants and animals, bacterias
- **Time** Duration of time decides the maturity of soil
- **Climate** e.g., moisture and temperature

Process of Soil Formation (Pedogenesis)

Following steps are involved in pedogenesis

- Weathering of rock materials formed the basic input for soil formation.
- After weathering, decay of plant and animal provided base for humus formation.
- A mature soil with complex mixture of mineral and organic products are formed.

NCERT Folder

Intext Questions

1. Why is the surface of the Earth uneven?

Ans. The Earth crust is dynamic. There exist different exogenic and endogenic forces which are responsible for continuous change in the configuration of the Earth surface. The action of both endogenic processes and exogenic processes is not uniform and hence, the crustal surface of the Earth is uneven.

2. Do you think it is essential to distinguish geomorphic agents and geomorphic processes?

Ans. Geomorphic processes comprise of endogenic processes and exogenic processes which bring about the change in the configuration of the surface of the Earth. Whereas, geomorphic agents are the medium to execute the processes like water, moving ice, wind, waves and current. So, first one is processes and second is its medium. Hence, it is essential to distinguish both for clear understanding.

3. Cite the differences between epeirogeny and orogeny.

Ans. In the process of orogeny, the crust is severely deformed into folds. It is a mountain building process. Whereas, epeirogeny results in simple deformation. It is a continental building process.

4. What do the words volcanism and volcanoes indicate?

Ans. Volcanism is the process in which the movement of molten rock occurs toward the Earth's surface. It also includes formation of many intrusive and extrusive volcanic forms. On the other hand, volcanoes are the activities of explosion of lava from the interior of the Earth.

5. Why do you think that the slopes or gradients are created by tectonic factors?

Ans. Tectonic factors help to create topography and maintain relief through rock upliftment and deformation. This is mainly due to radioactive energy and pressure generated beneath the Earth's surface. This leads to the creation of slopes or gradients due to tectonic factors.

6. What is the sole driving force behind all the exogenic processes?

Ans. Stress or gravitational force is the sole driving force behind all exogenic processes.

7. Is the little motion which can occur sometimes due to weathering synonymous with transportation? If not, why?

Ans. No, the little motion which can occur sometimes due to weathering is not synonymous with transportation. This is because weathering is in-situ mechanical disintegration and chemical decomposition of rocks. While, transportation is movement of material across the Earth's surface by water, wind, ice or gravity.

8. Between mass wasting and mass movement, which term do you feel is most appropriate? Why? Can solifluction be included under rapid flow movements? Why it can be and why can't be?

Ans. Between mass wasting and mass movement, mass movement is more appropriate to use because it is the movement of mass which includes wasting and transportion both and not just wasting.

Solifluction is a slow mass movement which occurs in moist temperate region. Whereas, rapid movement occurs in humid climatic regions. Hence, solifluction can't be included under rapid movement.

9. Can you compare the three climatically controlled agents?

Ans. The climatically controlled agents of erosion are wind, water (running water) and glaciers (ice).

The comparison between these agents is discussed below

- **Wind Erosion** Erosion by wind is known as aeolian erosion and it occurs almost always in deserts and arid regions. This erosion of sand in the desert is partially responsible for the formation of sand dunes. The power of wind erodes rocks and sand.
- **Water Erosion** Water is the most important erosional agent and erodes most commonly as running water in streams. Raindrops in dry regions create splash erosion, that moves tiny particles of soil. Water collecting on the surface of the soil collect as it moves towards tiny rivulets and streams and creates sheet erosion.
- **Glacial Erosion/Ice Erosion** Glaciers also perform erosive functions i.e. they pluck and abrade. Plucking takes place by water entering cracks under the glacier, freezing and breaking off pieces of rock that are then transported by the glacier. Abrasion cuts into the rock under the glacier, scooping rockup like a bulldozer and smoothing and polishing the rock surface.

10. There is a shift of material in mass movements as well as in erosion from one place to the other. So, why can't both be treated as one and the same? Can there be appreciable erosion without rocks undergoing weathering?

Ans. Weathering, mass movement and erosion are the degradational processes but there is a significant difference between all. Although, there is a shift of material in both erosion and mass movement but mass movement only occurs due to gravitational force as a agent where there are various agents like wind, water, and glacier for erosion. Although weathering aids erosion but it is not a pre-condition for erosion to take place.

11. Is weathering solely responsible for soil formation? If not, why?

Ans. Weathering is not solely responsible for soil formation as it is the first stage which provides basic input to soil . But other factors like formation of humus, plant and organism also play a significant role in soil formation.

12. Is it necessary to separate the process of soil formation and the soil forming control factors?

Ans. Yes, it is necessary to separate the process of soil formation and soil forming control factors. It is because soil forming process like weathering, provides only the basic input for soil formation.

Whereas there are five soil forming factors which include parent materials, topography, climate, biological activity and also time. These provide much needed mechanical, chemical as well as biological inputs for soil formation. These are very important not only for its formation but also for soil fertility and age.

13. Why are time, topography and parent material considered as passive control factors in soil formation?

Ans. Parent material determines the mineral and chemical composition of soil. Topography determines the thickness of layer and availability of organic material in the soil. Time or length of soil formation process determine the maturation of soil and profile development.

Hence, all three factors are considered as passive control factor in the soil formation.

Multiple Choice Questions

(i) Which one of the following processes is a gradational process?

(a) Deposition (b) Volcanism
(c) Diastrophism (d) Erosion

Ans. (d) Erosion

(ii) Which one of the following materials is affected by hydration process?

(a) Granite (b) Quartz
(c) Clay (d) Salts

Ans. (d) Salts

(iii) Debris avalanche can be included in the category of

(a) landslides
(b) slow flow mass movements
(c) rapid flow mass movements
(d) subsidence

Ans. (c) rapid flow mass movements

Answer the following questions in about 30 words

(i) "It is weathering that is responsible for biodiversity on the Earth." How?

Ans. Weathering processes are responsible for disintegration of rocks into smaller fragments which further develop as a soil. Soil is the basic source for the development of flora in any region. Hence, biomes and biodiversity are basically the result of weathering and weathered rocks.

(ii) What are mass movements that are real rapid and perceptible? List.

Ans. The mass movements that occurs in humid climatic regions mainly in gentle to steep slopes are rapid movements. Some real rapid and perceptible mass movements are

- Earth flow
- Mud flow
- Debris avalanche
- Debris flow
- Landslides

(iii) What are the various mobile and mighty exogenic geomorphic agents and what is the prime job they perform?

Ans. The mobile exogenic geomorphic agents are

- Running water
- Moving ice masses
- Wind
- Waves
- Currents

The prime job of these mobile mediums is to remove, transport and deposit the Earth material.

(iv) Is weathering essential as a pre-requisite in the formation of soils? Why?

Ans. Soil formation depends upon weathering. It is the weathering mantle which is the basic input for soil to form. Hence, weathering is essential as a pre-requisite in the soil formation.

Answer the following questions in about 150 words

(i) 'Our Earth is a playfield for two opposing groups of geomorphic processes'. Discuss.

Ans. Geomorphic processes comprise of endogenic processes and exogenic processes which are responsible to bring the change in configuration of the Earth's surface. But both endogenic and exogenic processes exert opposing actions which cause variations in the Earth's surface. endogenic processes are mainly land building processes, whereas the exogenic processes are land wearing processes. The two opposing groups of geomorphic processes are as follows

- **Endogenic Processes** These include mainly volcanoes, earthquakes which are caused by plate tectonics. They bring abrupt changes on the surface of the Earth. These processes continuously elevate or build up parts of the Earth's surface.

- **Exogenic Processes** These generate within the Earth's atmosphere and cause changes in the surface. Weathering, mass movement, erosion and deposition are the main processes through which the surface of the Earth undergoes changes.
  As a result of exogenic geomorphic processes, elevated land masses are lowered and lowlands are uplifted or elevated which help to level the Earth's surface. But due to endogenic processes, exogenic processes fail to even out the relief variations on the surface of the Earth.

Hence, both endogenic and exogenic geomorphic processes play an important role in changing the configuration of Earth's surface.

(ii) **"Exogenic geomorphic processes derive their ultimate energy from the Sun's heat." Explain.**

Ans. Exogenic geomorphic processes derive their ultimate energy from the Sun's heat in the following ways

- **Solar Heating and Atmospheric Circulation** The Sun heats the Earth's surface unevenly, which creates temperature differences. This difference leads to atmospheric movements such as winds and ocean currents. Winds, in turn, cause erosion, transportation and deposition of materials by processes like abrasion, which are key exogenic processes.
- **Water Cycle** The Sun heats water in oceans, lakes and rivers, causing evaporation. The moisture in the atmosphere condenses to form clouds, which eventually precipitate as rain. The flowing water leads to processes such as erosion, transportation and sediment deposition.
- **Wind Action** Solar energy warms the Earth's surface, causing air to rise and creating wind currents. Winds can carry sand and dust, leading to erosion, particularly in arid regions and also to deposition that forms dunes and other wind-driven landforms.
- **Glacial Movements** In polar and high-altitude regions, solar energy melts ice and snow, causing glaciers to move. These glaciers transport and deposit material, creating various landforms.
- **Evaporation and Transpiration** Plants take up water from the soil and through the process of transpiration, moisture is released into the atmosphere. This contributes to weathering and soil formation, which are exogenic processes that shape the landscape.

(iii) **Are physical and chemical weathering processes independent of each other? If not, why? Explain with examples.**

Ans. No, physical and chemical weathering are not independent of each other. Because, physical or mechanical weathering processes depend on some applied forces, namely; gravitational forces such as overburden pressure, load and shearing stress; expansion forces due to temperature changes, crystal growth or animal activity and water pressures controlled by wetting and drying cycles.

Whereas, chemical weathering depends on a group of weathering processes such as; solution, carbonation, hydration, oxidation and reduction act on the rocks to decompose, dissolve or reduce them to a fine classic state through chemical reactions by oxygen, surface and/or soil water and other acids.

Water and air (oxygen and carbon dioxide) alongwith heat must be present to speed up all chemical reactions. Both the weatherings are seemed to be different but they are still interdependent.

For example, availability of water and heat depends on physical factors which are further necessary in chemical reactions. Therefore, it can be said that physical and chemical weathering are not independent of each other.

(iv) **How do you distinguish between the process of soil formation and soil forming factors? What is the role of climate and biological activity as two important control factors in the formation of soils?**

Ans. Differences between the process of soil formation and soil forming factors are as follows:

- **Process of Soil Formation** Weathering is the first stage from where process starts and weathered material is the basic input for soil formation. Then the weathered material transported and colonised by bacteria and other bodies like mosses and lichens. Dead remains of organisms and plants help in humus accumulation. After sometime when mass of material becomes porous and sponge like, a mature soil and a complex mixture form.
- **Soil Formation Factors** Soil forming factors are responsible to form soil and create differences in the soil of various regions. There are five factors which are majorly responsible in soil formation. These are parent material, climate, topography, biological activity and time. All these factors act in union and affect the action of one another.

Role of climate and biological activity in soil formation

- **Climate** Climate plays a critical role in soil formation by influencing the temperature and precipitation. In wetter climates, leaching occurs, while in drier climates, evaporation leads to salt accumulation in the soil.
- **Biological activity** Organisms, especially plants and microorganisms, greatly influence soil formation. Additionally, animals like earthworms and termites help in mixing the soil. Biological activity also plays a role in nitrogen fixation, converting atmospheric nitrogen into a usable form for plants.

Exam Pattern Questions

Objective Type Questions

Multiple Choice Questions (MCQs)

1. Which of the geomorphic agents of erosion is not controlled by climate?
(a) Wind (b) Running water
(c) Wave (d) Glacier

2. The natural elements like wind, water, ice is capable of transporting the Earth's material from one place to another, these elements are known as CBSE Diksha
(a) Exfoliation (b) Geomorphic Agents
(c) Geological Agent (d) Diastrophic Agents

3. Which of the following is the source of energy for endogenic geomorphic processes?
(a) Radioactivity
(b) Rotational and tidal friction
(c) Primordial heat from origin of Earth
(d) All of the above

4. Which of the following is not correct with respect to epeirogenic processes?
(a) Uplifting or warping of earth's crust
(b) Involved in continental building
(c) Crust is severely deformed into folds
(d) It is a form of diastrophism

5. Which of the factors influences geomorphic process?
(a) Climate (b) Vegetation
(c) Structure of rocks (d) All of these

6. Weathering is an .... process.
(a) Ex situ (b) On-site
(c) In-situ (d) Both (b) and (c)

7. Exfoliation tors form due to ....
(a) Unloading (b) Thermal contraction
(c) Thermal expansion (d) Erosion

8. Which of the following factors favours mass movement?
(a) Weak unconsolidated material
(b) Thinly bedded rocks
(c) Scarcity of vegetation
(d) All of the above

9. Which of the following is not a reason for landslide in Western Ghat and Nilgiri region?
(a) Steeper slopes
(b) Mechanical weathering due to temperature changes
(c) Heavy rainfall
(d) Tectonic instability

10. Removal of silica from soil is known as ....
(a) Illuviation (b) Eluviation
(c) Desilication (d) Pedogenesis

11. Which of the following is not a passive control factor of soil formation?
(a) Parent material
(b) Topography
(c) Time
(d) Biological activity

12. Which one of the following cause physical stresses and chemical actions on the Earth material and bring changes in configuration of the Earth? CBSE Diksha
(a) Tidal force and convection force
(b) Polar fleeing force and tidal force
(c) Exogenic and endogenic force
(d) Polar fleeing and convection force

13. "There is a relation between humus and the bacterial activity", choose the incorrect statement from below.
(a) Low bacterial activity leads to low humus content.
(b) High bacterial activity leads to high humus content.
(c) There is direct relation between humus and bacterial activity.
(d) Low bacterial activity leads to high humus content.

14. There are several factors responsible for the formation of soil, identify the factor from the given description.
'It is a passive control factor in soil formation. It can be **in-situ** or **on-site**'.
(a) Parent rock (b) Topography
(c) Climate (d) Time

15. Choose the incorrect statement about deposition.
(a) It is a consequence of erosion.
(b) Finer material gets deposited first and then coarser material.
(c) It is an endogenic process.
(d) Both (b) and (c)

16. 'Exfoliation is the removal of outer layer of the rocks. Exfoliation occurs mostly due to two reasons', what are those reasons.
(i) Mass wasting (ii) Thermal differences
(iii) Unloading (iv) Overloading
Choose the correct options from the following.
(a) Only (i) (b) Both (ii) and (iii)
(c) Only (iv) (d) None of these

17. There are several types of weathering. Identify the type of weathering from the given description.

It is a contribution to or removal of minerals and ions from the weathering environment and physical changes due to growth or movement of organisms. Burrowing and wedging by organisms like earthworms, termites, rodents etc., help in exposing the new surfaces to chemical attack and assists in the penetration of moisture and air.

(a) Chemical Weathering
(b) Physical Weathering
(c) Biological weathering
(d) Exfoliation

18. Identify the statement that is not true regarding factors affecting 'exogenic processes'.

(i) Temperature and precipitation determine density, type and distribution of vegetation.
(ii) The variations in thermal gradients lead to different climatic regions.
(iii) Rocks with differences in their structure under similar climatic conditions offer similar resistance to various geomorphic processes.

Codes
(a) (i) and (ii) (b) Only (ii)
(c) Only (iii) (d) (i) and (iii)

19. Consider the following statements. Which of the given statements is correct?

I. Earth materials experience only gravitational stress.
II. Shear stress results in angular displacement of rocks.

Codes
(a) Only I (b) Only II
(c) Both I and II (d) None of these

20. Consider the following statements. Which of the given statements is correct?

I. Weathering is a pre-requisite for mass movement.
II. Mass movement is transfer of mass of rock, debris, soil down the slopes under direct influence of gravity.

Codes
(a) Only I
(b) Only II
(c) Both II and II
(d) None of the above

21. Consider the following statements. Which of the given statements is correct?

I. Soil is a static medium.
II. Biological activity is slowed if soil becomes too cold or too dry.

Codes
(a) Only I (b) Only II
(c) Both I and II (d) None of these

Arrange the Following

22. Arrange the following steps of soil formation in sequence.

(i) Formation of mature soil.
(ii) Growth of minor grasses and fern.
(iii) Mass of material becomes porous.
(iv) Penetration of plant roots.
(v) Colonisation of weathered material by bacteria.
(vi) Humus accumulation due to dead remains of organisms and plants.

Codes
(a) (v), (vi), (iv), (iii), (ii), (i) (b) (v), (vi), (ii), (iv), (iii), (i)
(c) (vi) (v), (ii), (iv), (iii), (i) (d) (v), (vi), (iii), (ii), (iv), (i)

23. Arrange the following according to the increasing speed of the movement.

(i) Creep (ii) Flow (iii) Slide (iv) Rock fall

Options
(a) (i), (iv), (iii), (ii) (b) (i), (ii), (iii), (iv)
(c) (i), (iii), (ii), (iv) (d) (i), (iv), (ii), (iii)

24. Arrange the following factors influencing soil formation in the order of their direct impact on the soil's physical properties

(i) Parent Material (ii) Climate
(iii) Topography (iv) Time

Options
(a) (i), (ii), (iii), (iv) (b) (i), (iii), (ii), (iv)
(c) (i), (iii), (iv), (ii) (d) (i), (iv), (ii), (iii)

Match the Following

25.

	List I		List II
A.	Physical	1.	Carbonation
B.	Chemical	2.	Overburden pressure
C.	Biological	3.	Organic acids
D	Exfoliation	4.	Tors

Codes

	A	B	C	D		A	B	C	D
(a)	2	1	3	4	(b)	3	2	1	4
(c)	1	4	2	3	(d)	2	3	4	1

26.

	List I		List II
A.	Climate	1.	Provides maturity to soil
B.	Parent material	2.	Impacts rate of weathering and organic matter
C.	Micro-organisms	3.	Contributes to organic content through decay
D.	Time	4.	Provides minerals and texture to soil

Codes

	A	B	C	D		A	B	C	D
(a)	4	1	3	2	(b)	1	2	3	4
(c)	2	4	3	1	(d)	3	4	1	2

27.

List I		List II	
A.	Desilication	1.	Downward movement of dissolved nutrients
B.	Leaching	2.	Removal of silica
C.	Humification	3.	Breaking down of rocks into fine particles
D	Weathering	4.	Formation of organic-rich top-soil layer

Codes

	A	B	C	D		A	B	C	D
(a)	2	4	3	1	(b)	2	1	4	3
(c)	3	2	1	4	(d)	2	1	3	4

Assertion-Reason

Directions (Q. Nos. 28-32) In the questions given below are two statements labelled as Assertion (A) and other is labelled as Reason (R). In the context of two statements which one of the following is correct?

Codes

(a) Both A and R are true, but R is not the correct explanation of A

(b) Both A and R are true and R is the correct explanation of A

(c) Both A and R are incorrect

(d) A is correct, but R is incorrect

28. **Assertion** (A) Physical weathering process cause great damage to rocks.
Reason (R) The rocks suffer from continued fatigue due to repetition of contraction and expansion.

29. **Assertion** (A) Human beings play a role in biological weathering.
Reason (R) Human beings help in creating new contacts between air, water and minerals in earth materials by disturbing vegetation and ploughing soils.

30. **Assertion** (A) Lichens and mosses contribute to biological weathering of rocks.
Reason (R) Lichens and mosses releases acids that chemically break down the minerals in rocks.

31. **Assertion** (A) Chemical weathering processes are less effective in deserts.
Reason (R) Deserts have low moisture levels, which slows down the chemical reactions needed for weathering.

32. **Assertion** (A) Time is an important factor in soil formation.
Reason (R) Length of time of soil formation process determines maturation of soil and profile development.

Answers

1. (c) Wave
2. (c) Geological Agent
3. (d) All of the above
4. (c) Crust is severely deformed into folds
5. (d) All of these
6. (d) Both (b) and (c)
7. (c) thermal expansion
8. (d) All of the above
9. (d) Tectonic instability
10. (c) Desilication
11. (d) Biological activity
12. (c) Exogenic and endogenic force
13. (d) Low bacterial activity leads to high humus content.
14. (a) Parent rock
15. (d) Both (b) and (c)
16. (b) Both (ii) and (iii)
17. (c) Biological weathering
18. (c) Only (iii)
19. (b) Only II
20. (b) Only II
21. (b) Only II
22. (b) (v), (vi), (ii), (iv), (iii), (i)
23. (c) (i), (iii), (ii), (iv)
24. (a) (i), (ii), (iii), (iv)
25. (a)
26. (c)
27. (b)
28. (b) Both A and R are true and R is the correct explanation of A
29. (b) Both A and R are true and R is the correct explanation of A
30. (b) Both A and R are true and R is the correct explanation of A
31. (b) Both A and R are true and R is the correct explanation of A
32. (b) Both A and R are true and R is the correct explanation of A

- In tropical areas, the soil profiles are deep and in tundra (cold) areas, soil is poorly developed, because of difference in temperature.

4. Biological Activity

- Biological activity plays a key role in soil development. Plants, animals and micro-organisms all contribute to this process in different ways

Plants

- Dead plant material (like leaves and roots) adds organic matter to the soil. This improves the soil structure and quality of the soil.
- Some organic acids are also released by plants during **humification**[40], which helps in the decomposition of soil's parent material.

Large Animals

- Large animals like ants, earthworms, rodents play an important role in the soil development process.
- Earthworms, ants and other soil organisms helps in mixing of the soil which allows air and water to pass through the soil.
- Earthworms helps in breakdown of organic material which helps in making a soil full of nutrients.

Micro-organisms

- Intensity of bacterial activity affects the process of soil development. Bacterial activity happens at different rates in cold and warm climate.
- In cold climate, like sub-arctic and tundra there is low bacterial activity due to which decomposition is slow resulting in the development of **peat**[41].
- In humid climate like tropical and equatorial climates, bacterial activity is high. This intense bacterial action helps in fast break down of dead vegetation resulting in less humus accumulation in the soil.
- There is presence of some bacteria like Rhizobium in the roots of leguminous plants. These bacteria take gaseous nitrogen from air and convert it into chemical form that is used by plants. This process is called as **nitrogen fixation.**

5. Time

- The duration of time decides the maturity of soil and development of soil profile. A soil profile becomes mature when all soil forming factors acts for sufficient amount of time.
- Soils formed from **recently deposited alluvium** (materials left by rivers) and **glacial till** (materials left by glaciers) are considered **young**. They have poorly developed soil profile.

Quick Test 4

1. What causes an increase in organic matter in soil?
2. After the weathered material or transported deposits, which organisms are the first to colonise the area?
3. Which topographic feature tends to have thicker soils?
4. What term refers to the removal of silica from the soil, typically in wet equatorial climates?
5. Due to slow bacterial activity in cold climates, what accumulates in the soil?

40 **Humification** It is the process of decomposing organic matter, such as dead plants and animals, into humus.

41 **Peat** It is the surface organic layer of the soil that consists of partially decomposed organic matter.

Subjective Questions

Short Answer Type Questions

1. Discuss the reason for variations in the outer surface of the crust.

Ans. The reasons for variations in the Earth's crust are as follows

- **Tectonic Activity** The movements of crustal plates, results in uplift, folding and faulting on Earth's crust.
- **Endogenic Forces** Internal forces like diastrophism and volcanism build and elevate landforms on the crust.
- **Exogenic Forces** Weathering, erosion and depositions changes the structure of landforms.
- **Gradation** The processes of degradation and aggradation reshapes the surface.
- **Dynamic Processes** The continuous interaction of internal and external forces prevents complete leveling of the crust.

Thus, Earth's crust is constantly changing.

2. Explain the role of gravity in geomorphic processes.

Ans. Gravity causes stress on the Earth's material, indirect gravitational stresses activate waves and tides, induced currents and winds. Without gravity and gradients, there would be no mobility and hence no erosion, transportation and deposition are possible. Gravitational stresses are as important as the other geomorphic process.

Gravity is the force that is keeping us in contact with the surface and it is the force that switches on the movement of all surface materials on earth.

Thus, the basic reason that leads to geomorphic processes is the development of gravitational stress in the body of Earth materials.

3. What are exogenic processes? Define the driving forces behind the exogenic processes.

Ans. Exogenic processes are external geomorphic processes which derive their energy from within the atmosphere.

Driving forces behind the exogenic processes are as follows

- The ultimate source of energy is Sun and the gradient created by tectonic forces. Gravitational force acts upon all earth materials which has a sloping surface.
- Force applied per unit area is called as stress which is produced in a solid by pushing or pulling. Shear stresses are forces acting along faces of the earth material and results in angular displacement of materials.
- Beside, gravitational stress, Earth materials became subjected to molecular stresses that may be caused by a number of factors like temperature changes, crystallisation and melting.

4. "Physical weathering depends on various forces". Explain.

Ans. Physical weathering or mechanical weathering processes depends on some applied forces; these forces are as follows

- **Gravitational forces** On slopes, gravity pulls rocks and soil downwards. This force can lead to landslides or rockfalls.
- **Expansion forces** When rocks heat up during the day, they expand and when they cool down at night, they contract. This repetition cause cracks to form and eventually break the rock apart.

Water pressure plays an important role in weathering as minerals swell up when they are wet and cause cracks when they dry, this helps in breaking down of rocks.

5. Give an account of physical weathering process.

Ans. The physical weathering process occurs through the following ways

Unloading and Expansion It is the removal of overlying rocks due to continuous erosion which causes vertical pressure release. Consequently, upper layer of the rock expands by producing disintegration of rock masses.

Temperature Changes and Expansion It occurs in dry climate where diurnal temperature changes are drastic. The differential heating results in expansion and contraction of rocks which cause breaking of rocks.

Freezing, Thawing and Frost Wedging These occur due to growth of ice within pores and cracks of the rocks during repeated cycle of freezing and melting.

Salt Weathering It is an important agent of rock disintegration in the dry climatic region. Salt in rock expand due to thermal action, hydration and crystallisation.

6. 'Weathering is an important part of exogenic process'. Explain.

Ans. Weathering is essentially the breakdown of rocks due to physical and chemical processes at their places.

Following are the significances of weathering

- Weathering is a critical base to our ecology and our existence depends on it.
- Biomes and biodiversity are basically a result of vegetation which are developed on the weathering mantle.

- Weathering prepare the way for formation of soil.
- Agriculture depends on the weathering, as it produces soil.
- Weathering aids mass movement and erosion which result in change in landform.
- Weathering of rock helps in the enrichment and concentrations of certain valuable ores of iron, manganese, aluminium, copper, etc.

7. Distinguish between biological and mechanical weathering.

Ans. Differences between biological and mechanical weathering are as follows

	Biological Weathering	Mechanical Weathering
Definition	The process of rock breakdown caused by living organisms.	The physical breakdown of rocks into smaller pieces without changing their chemical composition.
Causes	These are caused by plants, animals, fungi, and bacteria.	These are caused by physical forces like temperature changes, freeze-thaw cycles, pressure and wind.
Mechanism	It involves processes such as root growth, acid production and organic decay.	It involves processes like freezing and thawing, thermal expansion and abrasion.
Impact on Rock	It changes the chemical structure of the rock and can lead to soil formation.	It changes the physical structure of the rock but not its chemical features.
Rate of Weathering	It is generally slower, as it depends on the growth rates of organisms.	It is faster, as it can occur rapidly with environmental changes.
Examples	• Roots of plants growing into rock cracks. • Lichens releasing acids to dissolve rock minerals.	• Frost wedging where water freezes and expands in rock cracks. • Expansion and contraction due to temperature changes.

8. What is meant by mass movement? Explain factors that result in mass movement. CBSE Diksha

Ans. The transfer of the mass of rock debris down the slopes under the direct influence of gravity is called mass movement.

The factors resulting in mass movements are as follows

- The main factor behind the movement of the rock debris down the slope is the gravity. Gravity exerts its force on all matter, both bedrock and the products of weathering.
- Weathering is not a pre-requisite for mass movement though it aids mass movements. Mass movements are very active over weathered slopes rather than over unweathered materials.
- Weak unconsolidated materials, thinly bedded rocks, faults, steeply dipping beds, vertical cliffs or steep slopes, abundant precipitation and torrential rains and scarcity of vegetation etc., favour mass movements.

9. What is meant by landslide? How many types are identified in landslide category?

Ans. A landslide is the movement of rock, soil and debris down a slope due to gravity. They are relatively rapid and perceptible movements.

Types identified in landslide category are as follows

- **Slump** is slipping of one or several units of rock debris with a backward rotation with respect to the slope over which the movement takes place
- **Debris slide** is rapid rolling or sliding of earth debris without backward rotation of mass. Debris fall is nearly a free fall of Earth debris from a vertical or overhanging face.
- **Rockslide** is sliding of individual rock masses down bedding, joint or fault surfaces. Over steep slopes, rock sliding is very fast and destructive.
- **Slides** occur as planar failures along discontinuities like bedding planes that dip steeply.
- **Rock fall** is free falling of rock blocks over any steep slope keeping itself away from the slope. Rock falls occur from the superficial layers of the rock face, an occurrence that distinguishes it from rockslide which affects materials up to a substantial depth.

10. Despite being tectonically stable, debris avalanches and landslides do occur in Western Ghats and Nilgiri. Justify. Competency Based Que

Ans. In India, debris avalanches and landslides occur in the Nilgiri bordering Tamil Nadu, Karnataka, Kerala and the Western Ghats along the West coast though it is relatively tectonically stable region and mostly made up of very hard rocks. The reasons for this are as follows:

(i) Many slopes are steeper with almost vertical cliffs and escarpments in the Western Ghats and Nilgiri.

(ii) Mechanical weathering due to temperature changes and ranges is pronounced.

(iii) They receive heavy amount of rainfall over a short period.

So, there is almost direct rock fall quite frequently in these places alongwith landslides and debris avalanches.

11. Explain in brief the process of erosion.

Ans. Erosion is the process by which rocks and soil are broken down and moved from one place to another by natural agents like wind, water, glaciers and waves. The process begins when massive rocks break into smaller fragments through weathering or other processes. These small pieces are then carried away by erosional agents such as running water, groundwater, glaciers, wind and waves, which transport the debris to new locations.

Abrasion, which occurs when rock debris carried by these agents scrapes against surfaces, helps further in the breakdown of materials. Through erosion, the Earth's surface is worn down and the landscape is gradually degraded.

12. Describe how micro-organisms and plant growth contribute to the development of soil.

Ans. Micro-organisms and plant growth contribute to the development of soil in many ways such as

- Once the weathered material has been broken down into smaller particles, it is colonised by various micro-organisms like bacteria, fungi and other plants such as mosses and lichens. These organisms are crucial in the soil formation process because they decompose the weathered material, breaking it down into even smaller particles and creating organic matter.
- The decomposition of plant and animal remains by these micro-organisms leads to the formation of humus, which is a dark, nutrient-rich material that enhances soil fertility and structure.
- Additionally, the growth of plants such as grasses and ferns, followed by bushes and trees, contributes to soil formation by adding organic material through root systems and decaying plant matter.
- Plant roots penetrate the weathered material, breaking it up further, which helps to create a porous structure that allows water and air to pass through. This process leads to the creation of soil that can support further plant growth.

Long Answer Type Questions

1. Explain the term weathering. Define the contribution of biological activities in weathering.

Ans. Weathering is the natural process by which rocks and minerals on the Earth's surface are broken down into smaller particles through physical, chemical, or biological means. It is a crucial part of soil formation and landscape shaping, leading to the disintegration of rocks into finer material.

Contribution of Biological Activities in Weathering

- **Plant Roots** Roots from plants, trees, grow into rock joints in search of nutrients and water. As they grow, these roots exert pressure on the rock, gradually making cracks wider and breaking pieces of rock apart.
- **Micro-organisms** Fungi, bacteria and algae produce organic acids that chemically react with minerals in the rock, slowly dissolving and weakening it. For example, lichens grow on rock surfaces, releasing acids that break down minerals over time.
- **Animal Activity** Burrowing animals like earthworms, ants, and rodents disturb the soil and rock by digging. This activity exposes more rock surfaces to weathering agents like air and moisture, which accelerates the weathering process.
- **Organic Acids** Decaying plants and animals release organic acids that can chemically changes rocks, they dissolve minerals that bind the rock structure. This weakens rocks and aids in their breakdown.

2. Describe the chemical weathering processes and its various types.

Ans. Chemical weathering is brought about by the action of substance dissolved in rain water. They are usually acidic in character. It particularly occurs in the hot and humid climates of the equatorial, monsoon and other sub-tropical wet regions. It is more pronounced in the regions of Karst topography and limestone regions. Water and air (oxygen and carbon dioxide) along with heat must be present to speed up all chemical reactions.

Types of Chemical Weathering

- **Oxidation** Chemical combination of oxygen with another substance is known as oxidation. The most familiar is the 'rusting' of iron-ore in rocks or soil that produces a reddish-brown stain of oxide. Thus, the iron bearing rocks become weak by the process of oxidation.
- **Carbonation** This is a process of chemical weathering by a weak carbonic acid (water and carbon dioxide) that reacts with many minerals, especially limestone containing calcium, magnesium, potassium and sodium transforming them into carbonates.
- **Hydrolysis** When minerals chemically combine with water, the process is called hydrolysis.
- **Solution** When something is dissolved in water or acid, the water or acid with dissolved content is called solution. For example, the change of limestone from the solid state to the liquid state is by combination with water.

3. 'Weathering plays a significant role on our biodiversity and also on our economy'. Discuss CBSE Diksha

Ans. Weathering is essential to both biodiversity and the economy in the following ways

- It breaks down rocks into soil, creating a base for plant growth, which is vital for land ecosystems. This process supports biodiversity by providing nutrients and habitats for various organisms, from microbes to large mammals.

- Landforms created by weathering, such as cliffs and caves, offer habitats that sustain a wide range of species, fostering ecosystem diversity.
- Economically, weathering contributes significantly through agriculture, as fertile soils formed from weathered rocks support crop production, which is crucial for food security and rural income.
- Additionally, weathered rock materials like sand, clay and gravel are vital for the construction industry.
- Weathering also forms aquifers that store groundwater, providing essential water resources for drinking, irrigation, and industrial use. Finally, landscapes shaped by weathering attract tourism, benefiting local economies.

Thus, weathering is fundamental to ecological health and economic sustainability.

4. Briefly describe the various classes of mass movement.

Ans. Mass movement is the transfer of the mass of rocks deposits down to the slopes under the effect of gravity. It is classified on the basis of speed of flow and type of material it carries. There are three forms of Mass Movements-Heave, Flow and Slide which are related to each other.

The various classes of mass movements are discussed below

- **Slump** It is a type of landslide in which several units of rocks move down a slope with backward rotation.
- **Debris Slide** It is a type of landslide in which Earth materials moves rapidly by rolling or sliding without backward rotation. It is free fall of Earth material from vertical face.
- **Rock Slide** It is a type of landslide in which there is sliding of single rock masses down on bedding, joint or fault surface. In this type, the rocks fall and break other rocks or anything in their way.
- **Rock Fall** It is a type of fast-moving landslide that happens when there is free falling of rocks down a steep slope without being in touch with the slope.

5. 'In India, Debris Avalanches and landslides are very common and frequent in Himalayan Region and Western Ghats', substantiate the statement with suitable reasons. Competency Based Que

Ans. In India, Debris Avalanches and landslides are very common and frequent in Himalayan Region and Western Ghats. This could be explained with the following factors

(i) **Himalayas** Himalayas are marked with active plate movements.

- Rocks of Himalayas are made up of sedimentary rocks. They also contain loose and semi loose particles of rocks which slides easily.
- Steepness of the slope is also very high in this region, which increases the chances of landslides and debris avalanches in this region.

(ii) **The Western Ghats** This region is less tectonically active and contains hard rocks. Despite this, landslides and debris avalanches occur here because of the following reasons

- In Western Ghats and Nigiris, there is presence of steep slopes with vertical cliffs and steep slopes.
- Mechanical weathering is very common in this region because of temperature changes. This helps in the breaking down of rock fragments.
- Rock falls are very common along with landslide and Debris Avalanches because this region receives heavy rainfall of short period.

6. How do climatic conditions affect the erosion process and the work of different geomorphic agents?

Ans. Climatic conditions affect the erosion process and the work of different geomorphic agents involved in erosion and transportation. Wind, water and glaciers, the main causes of erosion, are directly affected by climate.

- **Wind erosion** is most active in dry, arid climates, such as deserts, where there is less vegetation to hold soil in place. High winds in these areas can pick up loose sand and dust, causing significant erosion of rock and soil.
- **Running water** is affected by precipitation and temperature. In regions with heavy rainfall, running water from rivers and streams will have a greater volume and power to erode landscapes. Whereas in areas with low rainfall, rivers may not have enough water to transport material, resulting in less erosion.
- **Glaciers** are primarily found in colder climates. In areas where temperatures are low enough for ice to accumulate, glaciers can form and begin to erode the land. In warmer climates, glaciers may melt, reducing their ability to erode the landscape.
- **Waves** are influenced by oceanic conditions, which are themselves affected by climate patterns. Strong winds, for example, generate large waves that can cause significant coastal erosion.

7. 'Climate is one of the factors that contribute to the variation in exogenic processes from region to region'. Explain. Competency Based Que

Ans. Climate is a key factor contributing to variations in exogenic processes from one region to another in the following ways

- The different climatic conditions, created by factors such as latitude, seasonal changes and the distribution of land and water, affect the intensity and type of geomorphic processes.

- The density, type and distribution of vegetation, which depend largely on temperature and precipitation, also influence exogenic processes indirectly. For example, regions with dense vegetation may experience less erosion because plants help hold the soil in place, while areas with little vegetation may face more erosion.
- Within a specific climatic region, local variations can occur due to factors like altitude, slope direction and the amount of sunlight different areas receive. For instance, North-facing slopes receive less sunlight than South-facing slopes, which can lead to different weathering and erosion rates.
- Additionally, factors like wind speed and direction, precipitation (including its amount, type and intensity), the relationship between precipitation and evaporation, temperature variations and freezing/thawing cycles all influence the intensity and nature of geomorphic processes in any given region. These factors can lead to significant local variations in how processes like erosion, sediment transport and weathering occur within a broader climatic zone.

8. "Soil forming factors act in union and affect the action of one another." Discuss. **Competency Based Que**

Ans. Soil formation is influenced by five main factors, which work together and affect each other in the following ways

- **Parent Material** This refers to the rock or material from which the soil forms. It can be either weathered rock debris or transported soil. The type of parent material affects the soil's texture, structure and mineral composition.
- **Topography** The shape and slope of the land influence soil formation. On steep slopes, soils tend to be thin, while on flat areas, soils are thicker. Gentle slopes allow for slow erosion and better water drainage, which favours soil formation. In flat areas, clay layers often develop, and organic matter accumulates, giving the soil a dark colour.
- **Climate** Climate is a key active factor. Elements like moisture, temperature, precipitation and evaporation directly impact soil development. In wet climates, high rainfall can leach out minerals like calcium and potassium, while in dry climates, evaporation can bring salts to the surface, forming hardpans. Temperature affects chemical and biological processes: higher temperatures increase activity, while cooler temperatures slow it down.
- **Biological Activity** Plants, animals and micro-organisms contribute to soil formation by adding organic matter, retaining moisture and promoting nutrient cycles. Bacteria help decompose parent materials and fix nitrogen, making it available to plants. Animals like earthworms and termites also affect soil by burrowing and mixing the soil.
- **Time** Soil formation takes time. Over long periods, soil develops distinct layers (horizons) and the soil-forming processes lead to a more mature profile. Soils that form from recently deposited materials, like alluvium or glacial till, are considered young and may not yet have well-defined horizons.

Source Based Questions

1 Read the following passage and answer the questions that follow.

The energy emanating from within the Earth is the main force behind endogenic geomorphic processes. This energy is mostly generated by radioactivity, rotational and tidal friction and primordial heat from the origin of the earth. This energy due to geothermal gradients and heat flow from within induces diastrophism and volcanism in the lithosphere.
Due to variations in geothermal gradients and heat flow from within, crustal thickness and strength, the action of endogenic forces are not uniform and hence the tectonically controlled original crustal surface is uneven.

In the process of orogeny, the crust is severely deformed into folds. Due to epeirogeny, there may be simple deformation. Orogeny is a mountain building process whereas epeirogeny is continental building process. Through the processes of orogeny, epeirogeny, earthquakes and plate tectonics, there can be faulting and fracturing of the crust. All these processes cause Pressure, Volume and Temperature (PVT) changes which in turn induce metamorphism of rocks.

Volcanism includes the movement of molten rock (magma) onto or toward the Earth's surface and also formation of many intrusive and extrusive volcanic forms.

(i) Endogenetic forces originate from which of the following elements?

(a) Winds (b) Surface water
(c) Radioactivity (d) All of these

Ans. (c) Radioactivity

(ii) Diastrophic forces are involved in which of the following processes?

(a) Plantation of Earth's surface
(b) Destruction of physical features
(c) Uplifting of features on surface
(d) Weathering of old features

Ans. (c) Uplifting of features on surface

(iii) **Which of the following process leads to the formation of mountains on Earth's surface?**
(a) Epeirogenic processes (b) Exogenic processes
(c) Orogenic processes (d) Metamorphic processes

Ans. (c) Orogenic processes

2. Read the following passage and answer the questions that follow.

The exogenic processes derive their energy from atmosphere determined by the ultimate energy from the Sun and also the gradients created by tectonic factors. Gravitational force acts upon all Earth materials having a sloping surface and tend to produce movement of matter in down slope direction. Besides the gravitational stress Earth materials become subjected to molecular stresses that may be caused by a number of factors amongst which temperature changes, crystallisation and melting are the most common. Chemical processes normally lead to loosening of bonds between grains, dissolving of soluble minerals or cementing materials. Thus, the basic reason that leads to weathering, mass movements, and erosion is development of stresses in the body of the Earth materials. Temperature and precipitation are the two important climatic elements that control various processes. All the exogenic geomorphic processes are covered under a general term, denudation. The word 'denude' means to strip off or to uncover. Weathering, mass wasting/movements, erosion and transportation are included in denudation.

As there are different climatic regions owing to variations in thermal gradients created by latitudinal, seasonal, and land and water spread on the surface of the Earth, the exogenic geomorphic processes vary from region to region. The density, type and distribution of vegetation which largely

(i) **'Sun and tectonic plates are the ultimate source of energy for exogenic processes'. Explain.**

Ans. The Sun and tectonic plates are the ultimate sources of energy for exogenic processes. The Sun's energy heats the Earth's surface, creating weather patterns, winds and water cycles that contribute to these surface processes. Tectonic plates create gradients in the Earth's surface, such as mountains, valleys and ocean basins. These gradients influence how wind, water and ice move, shaping the landscape.

(ii) **'Temperature and precipitation play a crucial role in denudation processes'. Justify the statement.**

Ans. Temperature and precipitation affects denudation processes as the distribution of vegetation of a region depends on temperature and precipitation patterns, it also indirectly influences the geomorphic processes. This variation creates diverse landscapes across different climatic regions.

(iii) **How do chemical processes contribute to the breakdown of Earth materials?**

Ans. Chemical processes play a crucial role by weakening the bonds between mineral grains and dissolving soluble materials within rocks. These processes, along with factors like crystallisation and temperature changes, create stresses within Earth materials and breaks them.

3 Read the following passage and answer the questions that follow.

Landslides are relatively rapid and perceptible movements. Depending upon the type of movement of materials several types are identified in this category. Slump is slipping of one or several units of rock debris with a backward rotation with respect to the slope over which the movement takes place. Rapid rolling or sliding of earth debris without backward rotation of mass is known as debris slide. Debris fall is nearly a free fall of earth debris from a vertical or overhanging face. Sliding of individual rock masses down bedding, joint or fault surfaces is rockslide. Over steep slopes, rock sliding is very fast and destructive.

In our country, debris avalanches and landslides occur very frequently in the Himalayas. Himalayas, the Nilgiris bordering Tamil Nadu, Karnataka, Kerala and the Western Ghats along the West coast are relatively tectonically stable and are mostly made up of very hard rocks; but, still, debris avalanches and landslides occur though not as frequently as in the Himalayas, in these hills.

(i) **What is the most important and primary force behind occurrence of landslides?**
(a) Corialis force (b) Tidal force
(c) Gravity (d) Radioactivity

Ans. (c) Gravity

(ii) **Landslides are most frequent in Himalayas because of which of the following factor?**
(a) Tectonic instability
(b) High precipitation
(c) Unconsolidated rock material
(d) All of the above

Ans. (d) All of the above

(iii) **Which among the following element will lead to an increase in landslides?**
(a) Consolidated soil
(b) Rock faults
(c) Low rainfall
(d) Hard rock material

Ans. (b) Rock faults

SELF ASSESSMENT TEST

Objective Type Questions

1. The internal forces which are applied within Earth are ....
   (a) exogenic forces
   (b) endogenic forces
   (c) land grading forces
   (d) land wearing forces
2. Orogenic processes are involved in ....
   (a) continental building
   (b) weathering
   (c) mountain building
   (d) erosion
3. Which of the following is not included in denudation?
   (a) Weathering
   (b) Mass movement
   (c) Erosion
   (d) Deposition
4. Consider the following statements.
   I. Mass movements are active over unweathered material rather than weathered slopes.
   II. Mass movement is aided by gravity.

   Which of the given statements is/are correct?
   (a) Only I (b) Only II (c) Both I and II (d) None of these
5. The work of which geomorphic agent is determined by location along interface of lithosphere and hydrosphere?
   (a) Groundwater (b) Wave (c) Wind (d) Running water
6. Hardpans are formed due to
   (a) Illuviation (b) Capillary action (c) Eluviation (d) Desilication

Short Answer Type Questions

7. How does gravity, besides being a directional force, activate downslope movements of matter?
8. All processes that move, elevate or build up portions of the Earth's crust come under diastrophism. Justify the statement.
9. Assess the importance of shear stresses in breaking rocks and other Earth materials.
10. Different types of rocks with differences in their structure offer varying resistances to various geomorphic processes. Justify the statement with relevant arguments.
11. Explain how oxygen, surface and soil water and other acids play a role in the chemical reactions that cause weathering.

Long Answer Type Questions

12. Evaluate the differences in wind velocities, precipitation and temperature which affect geomorphic processes in different climatic regions.
13. Explain how weathering leads to the reduction of relief and changes in landforms as a consequence of erosion.
14. Mass movements do not come under erosion though there is a shift of materials from one place to another. Justify the statement.

6

CHAPTER

This chapter is about the landforms that are created by the different geomorphic agents like running water, glacier, wind and waves.

Weathering is the first process, after which erosion and deposition takes place. All these processes altogether result in the development of landforms.

▼ **YOUR STUDY GOALS**

▼ **YOUR PRACTICE GOAL**

- Objective Type Questions (34 Qs ; MCQs, Statements, Matching, A-R,)
- Subjective Questions (15 SAs, 6 LAs)
- Source Based Questions (4 Qs)

Landforms and their Evolution

6.1 Landforms

- Landforms are the natural features of the Earth surface that include mountains, hills, plains and plateaus.
- Landforms are the result of different geomorphic processes that occurs on the Earth surface by the help of geomorphic agents. These have their own shape, size and composition of materials.
- Landforms once formed may change their shape, size and nature. This change may be slow or fast due to geomorphic processes and agents.
- Changes in landforms may be affected by the change in climatic condition and vertical and horizontal movements of landmasses.

Evolution of Landforms

- Evolution[1] of landforms refers to the different processes of transformation of one landform to another or an individual landform.
- Stages of landform development are similar to the stages of human life which include three stages i.e. **Youth**, **Mature** and **Old**.

1 Evolution It the gradual development of something.

6.2 Running Water Landforms

- Running water is an active and most important agent that shapes the landform by **degradation**[2]. In humid regions, which receives heavy rainfall, running water as an agent is very active.
- There are two components of running water, which are as follows
  - (i) **Overland Flow** In this water flows on general land as a sheet.
  - (ii) **Linear Flow** In this water flows as stream and rivers in valleys.

Process of Formation of Running Water Landforms

- Most of the running water landforms are made during the young age of a river and along steep slopes. During this period, there is an active erosion of the slope by the fast-moving streams.
- After sometimes, the slope becomes gentle and streams lose their velocity and then the process of deposition starts.
- Deposition of material depends on the steepness of the slope. Deposition is more on the gentle slopes as compared to the steep slopes.
- Continued erosion results in the development of gentle stream bed due to which, downcutting by the stream becomes less active and sidewise erosion of banks starts.
- Overflow results in the **sheet erosion**[3]. Depending upon the irregularity in the landform, overflow may occur through narrow or wide paths.
- Flowing water may develop a **sheer friction**[4] because of which minor or major quantities of materials from the surface are removed in the direction of flow. This results in the formation of a **rills**[5].
- The rills develop into long and wide **gullies**[6]. Further increase in the depth, width and length of gullies results in the formation of a valley.

Stages of Development of Running Water Landforms

Youth Stage

- In this stage, downcutting by the river is more dominant. There are few poorly connected streams flowing over old slopes. The valley is deep, narrow and V-shaped, with little to no floodplains.
- Marshes, swamps and lakes are formed on the flat areas between streams.
- There is development of meanders over the broad upland surfaces. Waterfalls and **rapids**[7] are formed where hard rocks are present on the bed of the river.

Mature stage

- At this stage, there are many well-connected streams. Streams start cutting the beds slowly and erosion along the sides of the valley becomes active. This gradually leads to reduction in slope of the valley.
- The valleys are still V-shaped but wider and deeper due to side erosion. The main streams have wide floodplains where rivers flow in meanders.
- Young marshes and swamps disappear, and the streams gets divided suddenly. Rapids and waterfalls also disappear.

---

2 Degradation It is the process of lowering of surface.
3 Sheet Erosion This is the uniform removal of soil layer by the raindrops and overland flow.
4 Sheer Friction It is a force that acts parallel to the surface in direction of deformation.
5 Rills These are small, narrow channels carved by the flow of water, typically found on slopes where erosion has occurred.
6 Gullies These are deep, steep-sided channels or trenches formed by the erosion of running water, typically on slopes.
7 Rapids These are sections of a river where the water flows quickly and forcibly over a rocky bed creating fast-moving, foamy water.

Old Stage

- At this stage, smaller tributaries are few and they have gentle slopes. The divide between drainage basins are lowered until they become almost flat.
- Streams meander freely over wide floodplains, ox bow lakes, natural levees, etc.
- The landscape is mostly at or just above sea level.

Erosional Landforms of Running Water

Valleys

▲ *The Valley of Kaveri river near Hogenekal, Dharmapuri district, Tamil Nadu in the form of gorge*

- Formation of a valley starts as small and narrow rills. These rills gradually develop into long and wide gullies and these gullies become deeper and wider which results in the formation of valleys.
- Valleys are divided into different types on the basis of dimension and shape, they are V-shaped valley, gorge, canyon, etc.
- A **gorge** is characterised by deep valley whose sides may be steep to straight. Width of a Gorge at its bottom and top is almost equal.
- A **canyon** is characterised by slopes that are steep and step-like and can be deep just like a gorge. Width of canyon is wider at the top as compared to its bottom.
- Types of valley depends upon the type and structure of rocks in which they are formed. For example, canyons are formed where sedimentary rocks are present in horizontal bed, while gorges are formed where hard rocks are present.

Potholes and Plunge Pools

▲ *An entrenched meander loop Colorado in USA showing step-like side slopes of its valley typical of a canyon*

- *Pothole* is a depression like structure which is more or less circular in shape. These are formed over streams of hilly area with rocky beds.
- Potholes are formed during stream erosion when the process of **abrasion**[8] takes place between rock fragments.
- When a shallow depression is created, pebbles and **boulders**[9] get collected in those depressions and rotates by flowing water and as a result the depression grows bigger.
- A series of potholes when joined together results in the deepening of a valley.
- Large potholes also develop at the foot of waterfalls, which are deep and wide because of powerful impact of water and rotation of boulders. These large and deep holes formed at the base of waterfalls, are called ***plunge pools***.

Incised or Entrenched Meanders

- A meander is formed when the water flows in a curvy, bendy paths like a snake. This is formed because of active lateral (side) erosion by streams.
- Lateral erosion happens when streams flow on low and gentle slopes. In this condition stream flowing over gentle slope develops **sinuous**[10] or meandering pattern over floodplains and **delta plains**.
- **Meanders** can also be formed over hard rocks where they are very deep and wide. Such meanders are called **incised** or **entrenched meanders**.

River Terraces

- River terraces are areas that are formed where old floodplains or valley floors are present. River terraces form mainly due to erosion, when a stream vertically erode its own floodplain.

---

8 **Abrasion** The river carries rock particles like gravel, sand and pebbles, which rub against the rocks on the riverbed and along the riverbanks. This causes the rocks to wear down, a process called abrasion.

9 **Boulders** It is a large rock fragment rounded or angular formed through weathering, erosion or glacial processes.

10 **Sinuous** It refers to the curving shape of a feature, like river.

- They can be of **stream deposits** (alluvial terraces) or **bare rocks** (bed rock without alluvial cover).
- There can be number of river terraces at different heights which shows the existence of earlier river bed level. River terraces formed at same elevation are called **paired terraces**.

Depositional Landforms of Running Water

Alluvial Fans

- Alluvial fans are formed when stream flowing from higher level break into foot slope plains of low gradient.
- When a stream flows from the mountains to the plains, coarser load is carried by the streams over mountain slope. This load can not be carried to gentle slopes. Therefore, these materials are dumped near the foothill as a broad cone shaped feature known as **alluvial fan**.
- When channels flow over fans, they get distributed into many channels, which are called as **distributaries**.
- Alluvial fans formed in humid areas have low cones with gentle slope (foothill to top) while alluvial fans formed in arid and semi-arid areas have high cones with steep slope.

▲ *An alluvial fan deposited by a hill stream on the way to Amarnath, Jammu and Kashmir*

Deltas

- A delta is an area which is like alluvial fans but develop at different locations. They are formed near the mouth of a river.
- Delta is formed when the load carried by rivers is not carried away far into the sea; the load gets spread and accumulate as a low cone.
- Deposits are well arranged in layers in a delta. The coarser materials are settled first and the finer materials like silt and clay are carried out into the sea.
- As the delta grows, there is increase in length of river distributaries and delta continues to build up.

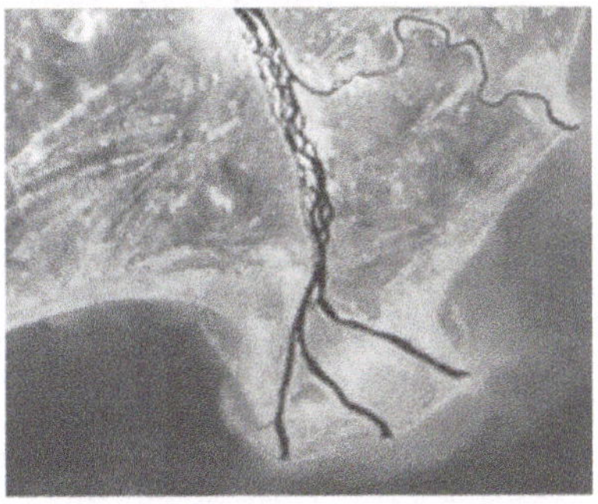

▲ *A satellite view of part of Krishna river delta, Andhra Pradesh*

Floodplains

- A floodplain is a landform which is created by river deposits. When a river flows from a flat area towards a slope, larger materials are deposited first.
- Streams with low velocity in plains carry fine particles like sand, silt and clay, which are deposited on the riverbed during floods.
- There are two types of floodplains

  (i) **Active** This type of floodplain contains river deposits.

  (ii) **Inactive** This type of floodplain contains two types of deposits - flood deposits and channel deposits.

- Sometimes, river channels change its direction, leaving behind cut-off areas that gets filled later. Coarse materials are found in these abandoned channels, while silt and clay come from flood deposits.
- Floodplains in a delta are known as **delta plains.**

Natural Levees

- These are important landforms associated with floodplains. These are found along the banks of large rivers.
- Natural levees are linear, low and parallel ridges formed of coarse materials along the banks of river.

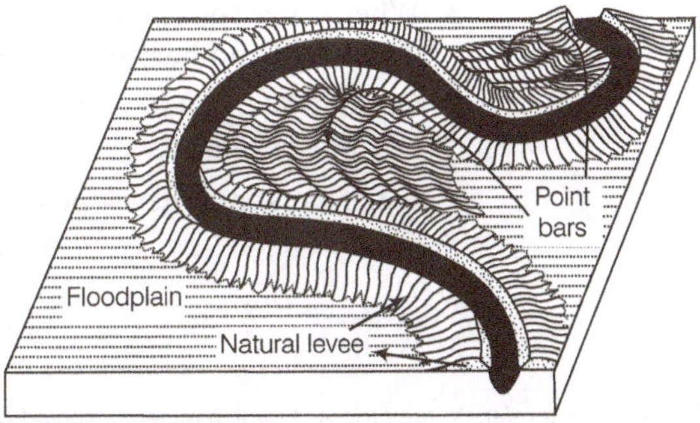

▲ *Natural Levee and Point Bars*

Point Bars

- Point bars are also called as **meander bars**. They are found on the concave side of meanders of large rivers. These are sediments that are deposited in a linear pattern by a stream.
- Point bars have uniform profile and width. Point bar contains sediments of mixed size.

Meanders

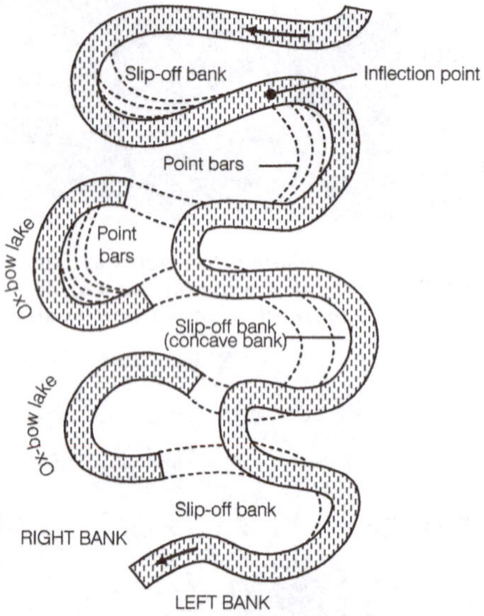

▲ *Meander growth and cut-off loops and slip-off and undercut banks*

- Meander is a type of channel pattern in which river flows in a loop- like pattern. In flood and delta plains, rivers do not follow a straight path.
- Meandering of river happens because of the following reasons
  - Nature of the water to do more lateral erosion when it is flowing over a gentle gradient.
  - The uneven and loose nature of the alluvial deposits on the banks, allows water to exert lateral pressure, leading to erosion.
  - Coriolis force which deflects water in the same way it deflects wind.
- Little irregularities along the river bank gets converted into small curvatures. Inside the curvature materials gets deposited while outside the curvature erosion takes place.
- If there is no erosion and deposition along the banks, the tendency of a river to meander reduces. In large rivers, there is active deposition along the concave side while active erosion along the convex side.
- The concave side is known as '**cut-off**' bank which is steep slope and the convex side is gentle in slope.
- When meanders grow in size, it may get cut-off due to deep erosion, and **ox-bow lakes** are formed.

Quick Test 1

1. Mention two landforms formed at the young age of river.
2. What is another name for Point Bars?
3. River terraces are formed due to which type of physical processes?
4. What is the concave side of a bank of river called?

6.3 Groundwater Landforms

- Groundwater plays an important role in eroding and shaping landforms. This is an active agent for areas where rocks are permeable, thinly bedded and there is presence of joints and cracks.
- When water enters the surface vertically, it goes to some depth and then starts flowing horizontally. This downward and horizontal movement of water results in the erosion of rocks.
- Groundwater landforms are found in the areas of rocks like limestone, dolomites which are rich in calcium carbonate.
- Landforms are developed over these rocks by the chemical process such as **solution**[11] and **precipitation**[12].

11 **Solution** It refers to the process in which minerals and other soluble substances dissolve in water.

12 **Precipitation** It refers to the process in which a subtance dissolved in water separates out as a solid such as, the formation of crystals or sediment as a result of a chemical reaction.

- Landforms developed by the process of solution and deposition are called as **Karst Topography**. This is named after the topography developed in limestone rocks of Karst region in Balkans which is situated adjacent to Adriatic sea.

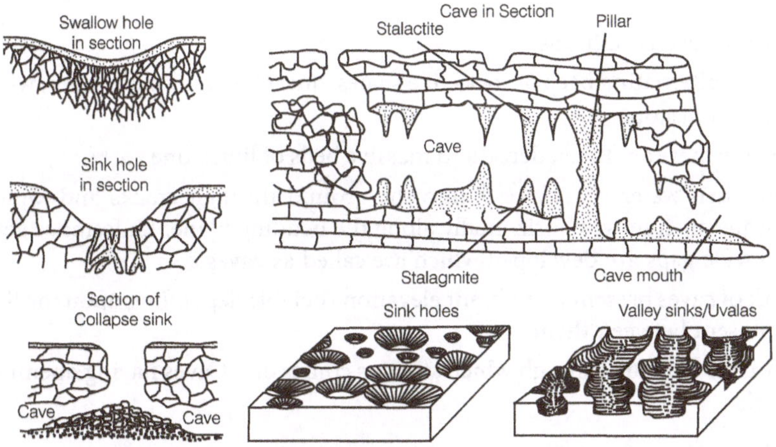

▲ *Various Karst Features*

Erosional Landform of Groundwater

Sinkholes

- On the surface of limestone, there is a shallow depression of small to medium size which is called as **swallow hole**. When swallow hole differs in size and area it is called as **sinkhole**.
- Sinkhole is an opening of circular shape at the top and funnel-shape towards the bottom. It is very common in limestone areas.
- Sinkholes are formed in two ways
  - **Solution Action** Solution Sinks are formed through the process of solution where limestones dissolve and form depressions.
  - **Collapse Sinks** These are formed when the roof of a void or underground cave collapse after going through the process of solution, leaving a large hole. Solution sinks are more common than collapse sinks.
- The surface water disappears through swallow hole or sinkhole from the surface and reappears at some distance through a cave.

Pools and Dolines

- Pools are formed when sinkholes are covered with soil mantle. They appear as water pools.
- Dolines are formed by the collapse of overlying rock or material into an underground cave.

Valley Sinks or Uvalas

- Valley sinks or Uvalas are formed when the sinkholes and dolines joins together. This happens because of the **slumping**[13] of material along the margin or because of collapse of roof of caves.
- Uvalas are generally long, narrow to wide trench like features.

Lapies

- Lapies are formed when most of the surface of limestone is removed by solution. This results in a development of irregular surface which has points, ridges and **grooves**[14].
- They are rough surface characterised by low ridges and pinnacles.

---

13 **Slumping** It refers to a type of mass wasting in which there is downward movement of a cohesive block of material along a curved surface.

14 **Grooves** It refers to narrow, elongated channels or depressions formed in various surfaces.

- Lapies field sometimes turns into smooth surface when process of solution is applied at different rate to the surface. It is known as **limestone pavements.**

Caves

- Caves are formed in two conditions
  (i) When there is alternating beds of rocks like shales, quartzites and sandstones, with the presence of dolomite and limestone.
  (ii) In areas where there are thick, dense and massive beds of limestone rocks.
- Cave is formed when water percolates[15] into the ground through cracks and joints or through the material. This water then moves horizontally along the bedding plane. Limestones gets dissolved and a long, narrow to wide gaps are developed which are called as **caves.**
- There is network of caves present at different elevation (height) depending upon the limestone beds and rocks that are present between them.
- Caves generally have opening through which streams comes out. Caves having opening at both the ends are called **tunnels.**

Depositional Landforms of Groundwater

- There is development of many depositional landforms by groundwater which are developed within the limestone caves.
- The main chemical in limestone is calcium carbonate which gets easily dissolved in carbonated water[16]. This calcium carbonate is deposited when water gets evaporated and it starts to get deposited by dripping on the surface of the rocks.

▲ *Stalactites and stalagmites in limestone caves.*

Stalactite

- Stalactite is a column of pure limestone, which is of different diameters hanging from roof of a cave like an icicle[17] towards the ground.
- They are broad at their base and pointed at the tips.

Stalagmite

- Stalagmite is an upward growing deposits of minerals.
- Stalagmites rises from the floor of a cave due to the accumulation of material deposited on the floor from ceiling drippings.
- Stalagmites look like a column. Sometimes it also looks like a disc which is smooth, rounded with bulging ends. It sometimes takes the shape of a crater like depression.

Pillars and Columns

- Pillars and columns are a depositional landform which is formed when stalactites and stalagmites after growing towards each other gets merged at a point.

Quick Test 2

1 Groundwater landforms are found in which type of areas?
2 Name the two processes by which landforms are developed over limestone rocks.
3 How are dolines formed?
4 Stalagmites look like which type of structure?

15 Percolate It refers to the process by which water moves through soil or porous rock layers.
16 Carbonated water It is water that has been infused with carbon dioxide gas under pressure.
17 Icicle These are pointed, hanging formations of ice that form when water drips or flows from a surface and freezes as it cools in the air.

6.4 Glaciers

- Glaciers are the masses of ice that moves as a sheet over the land. For example, **continental glacier** or **piedmont glaciers** is a sheet of ice which is spread over the plains at the foot of mountains. It may also be a linear flow when the sheet of ice moves down a slope of mountains in trough like valley.

▲ *A glacier in its valley*

- Glaciers moves basically because of force of gravity. Movement of glaciers is slow. Glaciers may move to a distance of few centimeters to a few meters in a day.
- Erosional work of a glacier is so powerful because of friction caused by huge weight of ice sheets.
- The process of erosion by glacier starts when the material removed from the land by glaciers is dragged along the floors or sides of valleys and it causes great impact by the process of **abrasion**[18] and **plucking**[19].
- Glacier have impact on both weathered and unweathered rocks and they are capable of reducing a height of mountain to low hills and plains.
- As glaciers continue to move, material gets removed by erosion and slope starts becoming gentle. Gentle slopes do not allow glaciers to move further and hence it stops.
- A mass of low hills and vast outwash plains are left at the end. Depositional landforms are also formed at the end of the process.

Glaciers in India

- India has many glaciers moving down the slopes and valleys in the Himalayas. States like Uttarakhand, Jammu and Kashmir, Himachal Pradesh also have some glaciers.
- Bhagirathi river get its water from Gangotri glacier and Alaknanda river get its water from Alkapuri glacier.
- River Alaknanda and Bhagirathi join together to make river Ganga near Devprayag.

Erosional Landforms by Glaciers

Cirque

- Cirques are deep, long and wide basins with steep sides. These are the most common landforms in the glaciated mountains.
- Cirques are found at the head of the glacial valleys.
- After the glacier disappears, a lake of water is formed within the cirque, which is known as **cirque lake** or **tarn lake**.
- There can be multiple cirques which are present in a stepped sequence one after another.

Horns and Serrated Ridges

- Horns are formed when there is headward erosion of the cirques. They are high, pointed and steep sided peaks.
- When the divide between two cirque walls becomes narrow because of continued erosion, it turns into a saw-toothed ridge which is called as an **arete**.
- Aretes have very sharp crest and zig-zag kind of outline.

---

18 **Abrasion** It refers to the process of mechanical erosion that occurs as glaciers move over the underlying bedrock or sediment.

19 **Plucking** It is a glacial erosion process that occurs when a glacier moves over bedrock and removes (or "plucks") pieces of rock from the layer.

- The highest peak in the Alps, Matterhorn and the highest peak in the Himalayas, Everest are examples of horns formed by the headward erosion of radiating cirques.

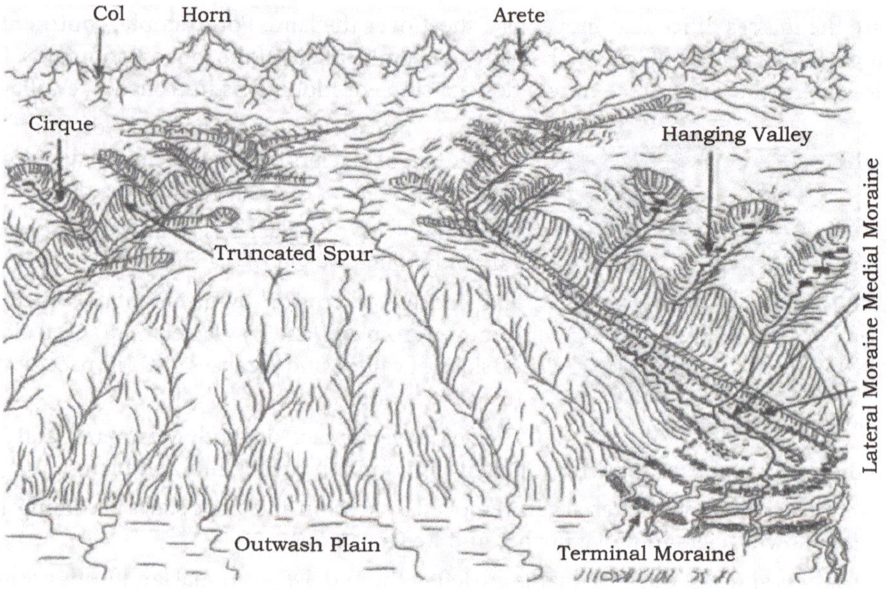

▲ *Some glacial erosional and depositional forms (adapted and modified from Spencer, 1962)*

Glacial Valleys/Troughs

- Glacial valleys are formed by the glacial erosions in the shape of letter 'U' and hence these are called as U-shaped valleys. They have broad floors and are also smooth.
- Glacial valleys contain debris which are swampy in nature.
- There is a formation of lake which is cut out of rocky floor or formed by debris within the valley.
- There can be hanging valleys at an elevation on one or both sides of the main glacial valleys. The divides of such valleys have triangular surface.
- Very deep glacial troughs(basins) filled with sea water and having shoreline (in high latitude) are called as **fjords/fiords.**

Depositional Landforms by Glaciers

- The materials brought by the glaciers during erosion are deposited after travelling some distance.
- Glacial deposits are of two types
  (i) **Glacial Till** This consists of unassorted[20] coarse and fine deposits. The rock fragments in till are angular and sub-angular in form.
  (ii) **Outwash Plain** This consists of assorted and layered deposits. Outwash plains are formed when the streams carry rock fragments/debris with them and deposit them. Such glacio-fluvial deposits are called **outwash deposits.**

Moraines

- These are formed when the glacial till is deposited in the form of a long ridge.
- Moraines are deposited in three ways
  (i) **Terminal Moraine** This is formed when the till is deposited at the end of a glacier.
  (ii) **Lateral Moraine** This is formed when the till is deposited on both the sides of a glacier.

20 Unassorted It refers to sediments or debris that have not been sorted or classified according to size, shape or composition.

(iii) **Medial Moraine** This is formed when the lateral moraines of two glaciers is joined together.

- When terminal moraine and lateral moraine are joined, they form a **horse-shoe shaped ridge**.
- There are number of lateral moraines present on either side of a valley. Lateral moraines are the result of glacio-fluvial deposits.
- When valley glaciers melt and retreat (shrink), they leave behind a messy layer of rock and soil on the valley floor. This layer is called a **ground moraine**.

Eskers

- When glaciers melt in summer, the water which formed as a result of melting get collected under the glacier and flows like streams in channels beneath the ice.
- Very coarse material like boulders, blocks and some minor pieces of rock debris are carried away by these streams.
- They later get deposited in the valleys itself and once the ice melts completely, they are visible to the surface as **sinuous ridges**[21]. These ridges are called **eskers**.

Outwash Plains

- These are plains formed at the foot of the glacial mountains. These are covered with glacio-fluvial deposits in the form of broad and flat alluvial fans like structure.
- Outwash plains consist of particles like gravel, sand and silt.

Drumlins

- They are smooth oval-shaped ridge-like structures composed mainly of glacial till. The long axes of drumlins are parallel to the direction of ice movement.
- Drumlins may measure up to 1 km in length and 30m in height.
- One end of the drumlins which is facing the glacier is called **stoss** and the other end is called **tail**. Stoss has steep slopes than tail.
- Drumlins are formed as a result of glacial movement over some minor obstacles like small surface rocks. The glacial till gets deposited in those obstacles and the movement of glacier shapes these deposits like an inverted spoon.
- Drumlins shows the direction of movement of a glacier.

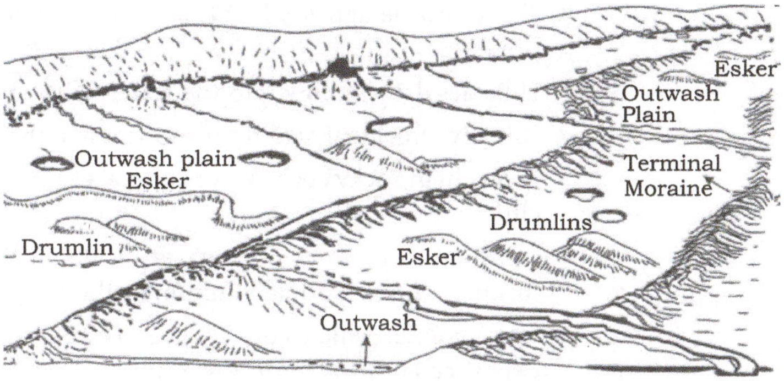

▲ *A panoramic diagram of glacial landscape with various depositional landforms*

Quick Test 3

1. Give an example of an erosional landform of glaciers.
2. Which landform has a very sharp crest and zig-zag type of outline?
3. Moraines are deposited in how many ways and also name them?
4. Mention one feature of the stoss and tail.

21 **Sinuous Ridge** It is a geographic feature characterised by a long, narrow elevation that has a winding or curving shape.

6.5 Waves and Currents

- Waves and currents are an active agent that plays an important role in shaping the coastal areas.
- Coastal processes are most dynamic and they are most destructive in nature, so it is important to know about the coastal processes and their forms.
- The changes along coasts are fast, at one place there can be erosion in one season and deposition in another season. Waves are the most powerful agent for these changes taking place over the coast.
- When waves break, the water is thrown with great force to the shores with a lot of sediments.
- Constant impact of breaking waves affects the coast. Strong waves like tsunami and storm waves may have powerful impact in short period of time than regular waves.
- Coastal landform development also depends on
  - the configuration of land and sea floor.
  - the nature of coast if it is advancing seaward[22] or retreating landward.
- There are basically two types of coasts
  (i) High rocky coasts (submerged coasts)
  (ii) Low, smooth and gentle sloping sedimentary coasts (emerged coasts)

High Rocky Coasts

There are some characteristics of high rocky coasts, which are mentioned below

- Along the high rocky coast, the river appears to have been flooded and the coastlines are highly irregular in shape.
- The coastline appears highly indented[23] with water extending into the land where glacial valleys are present.
- Hillsides drop steeply into the water, with few deposits like sand or gravel on the shore at first.
- Initially, erosional activity is more active therefore no depositional landforms is formed at the shores.
- Along high rocky coast, waves interact with the land with great force, which convert the hill sides into a cliff.
- Constant force applied by waves results in the receding (decreasing) cliffs and a wave-cut platform is formed. Waves gradually minimise the irregularity along the shore.
- The material which fall off, and are removed from sea cliff, break into smaller pieces and they are deposited at the offshore. Over time, as cliffs erode and retreat, a wave-built terrace[24] is formed in front of the wave-cut terrace from these deposits.
- Beaches are formed by the materials deposited by waves and currents.
- In shallow water, **bars** are formed which are long underwater ridges of sand or gravel that run parallel to the coast. When bars rise above the water, they are called **barrier bars.**
- When a barrier bar extends from the shore and connects to a headland across a bay, it results in the formation of a spit.
- When spits or barrier bars stretches out from the shore and blocks off the entrance to a bay, a lagoon is formed.
- The Western coast of India is a high rocky retreating coast. Erosional forms are more active in the West coast.

---

22 Advancing Seaward It refers to a process in which a geographic feature, such as a shoreline, landform or sediment deposit, is moving or extending outward towards the sea.

23 Indented It refers to a feature that has an uneven outline or shape.

24 Wave-built Terrace It is a gently sloping coastal feature at the seaward or lakeward edge of a wave cut platform.

Low Sedimentary Coasts

- River on low sediment-rich coasts often extend their reach by **creating coastal plains** and **deltas**. The coastline is generally smooth, with some shallow water areas like ***lagoons*** and *tidal creeks*[25].
- The land gradually slopes down into the water, which leads to the development of **marshes** and **swamps**.
- Depositional features are more common at this coast as compared to erosional features.
- When waves hit these gently sloping coasts, they bring up bottom sediments, forming **bars, barrier bars, spits** and **lagoons**.
- Over time, lagoons are filled with sediment, they become swampy and eventually coastal plains are formed.
- These coastal features need a continuous supply of sand, mud and other sediments to maintain their shape and size.
- **Storms** and **tsunamis** can reshape these coasts, regardless of sediment supply.
- Large rivers which carry high sediment loads builds up **deltas** along these low sedimentary coastlines.
- The East coast of India is a low sedimentary coast. Depositional forms are more active in the East.

Erosional Landforms of Waves and Currents

Cliffs and Terraces

- They are usually found where erosion is more dominant. All the cliffs are steep sided, and height of the slope ranges from 30m or more.
- At the foot of such cliffs, there is a flat or gentle sloping platform which is covered by rock materials/debris. Such platform that occurs at elevation above the average height of the wave is called **Wave-cut terrace.**
- Coastal hills and cliffs erode over time, leading to the formation of narrow coastal plains made up of **alluvium**[26] or sandy deposits. This deposition results in the development of beaches.

Caves

- A cave is a large natural hollow in the cliff along the coast of horizontal opening. Sea caves are formed when the waves hit against the base of cliff and the rock debris gets hit against the cliff.
- The roof of cave collapse after continued erosion, which results in the reducing of sea cliff towards the shore.

Stacks

- Stacks are a mass of rock, which is originally a part of cliff. These are formed when the receding cliff leave some remains of hard rock. Sea stacks are temporary feature.

Depositional Landforms by Wave and Currents

Beaches and Dunes

- Beaches are found along shorelines that are formed by deposition, but they can also be found in patches along the shoreline that have rocky surface.
- The sediment that give rise to beaches comes from land that is carried by streams and rivers or from erosion by waves.
- The beaches are temporary feature. The sandy beach that appears permanent may be reduced to a very narrow strip of coarse pebbles in some other season.

---

25 **Tidal Creeks** These are narrow, winding waterways that are influenced by the tidal fluctuations of nearby bodies of water, such as oceans.

26 **Alluvium** It refers to sediment that has been deposited by flowing water, typically in riverbeds, floodplains and deltas.

- Most of the beaches are made up of materials that are of same size as sand. **Shingle beaches** contain excessively small pebbles and even cobbles[27].
- Behind the beach, sand dunes are formed by the deposition of sands from beaches. Sand dunes are long ridges that are parallel to the coastline.

Bars and Barrier Bar

- Bar is a ridge like structure made of sand and shingle in the sea in an **offshore zone.**
- Bars which lie parallel to the coast are called as *off-shore bars*[28].
- **Barrier bars** are the offshore bars that are formed due to more addition of sand to the bars.
- The coastal off-shore bars can act as natural barriers by reducing the intensity of storms and tsunamis.

Spits

- Spits are depositional landforms that have one end attached to land (bay) and the other end extends into the sea.
- These are formed when waves and currents carry sand along the shoreline, depositing it in one area.

Lagoon

- When the bars, barriers and spits at the mouth of the bay gradually extends towards the sea, they leave only a small opening of the bay into the sea and the bay develops into a lagoon.
- The lagoon gets filled up by sediments coming from land or from beach. This sedimentation results in the formation of a coastal plain replacing a lagoon.

Quick Test 4

1 What are barrier bars on high rocky coasts?
2 Which coast of India is a high rocky retreating coast?
3 Beaches are formed by which type of landform?
4 Name any two types of deposition landforms by waves and currents.

6.6 Wind

- Wind is one of the dominant geomorphic agent in hot deserts area. The powerful impact of wind starts, when the desert floor gets heated up too much and too quickly because they are dry and barren.
- The heated floor starts heating the air above the ground and results in the upward movement of the hot lighter air with turbulence.
- While the air travels upward, any obstructions in between the path creates eddies[29], whirlwinds, updraft and downdraft of air.
- Winds also move along the desert floor with great speed and the obstructions in their path creates disturbance.
- There are storm winds which are very destructive in nature. Winds causes deflation, abrasion and impacts
  - **Deflation** It includes lifting and removal of dust and small particles from the surface of rocks.
  - **Abrasion** It is active during transportation process in which the sand and silt act as an effective agent in wearing out of the materials.

27 Cobbles These are rounded, larger-sized stones or gravel that typically range in diameter from about 2.5 to 10 inches.
28 Offshore It refers to areas that are located away from the shore or coastline of a body of water, typically the ocean.
29 Eddies These are circular or spiral movements of water or air that occur in fluids, often resulting in localised currents.

- **Impact** This is simply the sheer force of momentum[30] that occurs when the sand is blown into or against a rock surface. It is similar to sand blasting[31] operation.

- Wind actions create variety of erosional and depositional landforms in the desert.
- Mass wasting and running water as sheet flood[32] are responsible for the formation of many features. Water in desert comes from torrential rain[33].
- Since, there is less vegetation cover in desert areas, the rocks can easily be broken down into fragments by mechanical and chemical weathering. The diurnal temperature changes also affect the intensity of the weathering. These processes lead to fast breakdown of rocks and the weathered material are transported by the torrential rain.
- In deserts, the weathered material is transported by both wind and rain/sheet wash. The wind carries the finer particles and the mass erosion is done by the sheet wash.
- Stream channels in desert areas are broad, smooth and not defined. They flow for a short period of time after rain.

Erosional Landforms by Wind

Pediments

- These are gently inclined rocky floors which are close to the foot of a mountain. These may have thin cover of debris.
- Pediments are formed by the erosion of front of a mountain through two processes which are lateral erosion by streams and by sheet flooding.

Pediplains

- After the formation of pediments, erosion starts along the steep sides of the pediments, this results in the retreat of the cliffs and slope. This method is called parallel retreat of the slopes.
- As the process of parallel retreat continues, pediments extend backward reducing the slope of the mountain. Mountains get reduced leaving behind an inselberg, which is a residu of the original mountain.
- This is how the high relief in desert areas is reduced to down to low featureless plains known as **pediplains**.

Playas

- These are shallow lakes that cover the plain area of the deserts. In desert, plains are the most important landforms that are formed.
- These plains have some basins that are surrounded by the mountains and hills and the direction of drainage is towards the basin.
- There is gradual deposition of sediments from basin margins, and a low-level plain is developed at the centre of the basin. When there is sufficient water available this plain is converted into shallow water body called as **Playa**.
- In playas, the water is present for short duration due to evaporation. The playa plain that contains good deposition of salts is called as **alkali flats**.

30 Sheer Force of Momentum It describes the powerful impact or effect resulting from the momentum of an object.
31 Sand Blasting It refers to the natural process of erosion caused by wind, particularly in arid and semi-arid environments.
32 Sheet Flood It refers to a type of flooding characterised by a broad, shallow flow of water across a large, relatively flat area.
33 Torrential Rain It refers to a very heavy and intense downpour of rain that occurs over a short period of time.

Deflation Hollow and Caves

- Deflation hollow is a depression-like structure which is formed when there is continued movement of wind in one direction.
- Deflation results in the formation of pits and small cavities in rock surface.
- The wind blowing in desert area affects the rock by abrasion. Firstly, a shallow depression is created which is called as **blow-out**.
- When blow-outs become deeper and wider, it results in the formation of **caves**.

Mushroom, Table and Pedestal Rocks

- Mushroom rocks are unique rock formations found in desert regions, formed by wind erosion.
- These rocks have a shape similar to a mushroom, with a narrow base and a wider top.
- The softer layers of rock are eroded quickly while the harder layers are resistant, which leads to the formation of a broad top and narrow base.
- The top surface of these rocks is broad-like table while the hard rocks stands-like a pedestal[34].

Depositional Landforms of Wind

- Wind carries grains and sands of different sizes with them and deposit them on the surface forming depositional landforms.
- Grains of large size are transported by the process of saltation[35] while grains of finer particles are transported by the process of suspension[36].
- When the speed of wind is slowed down, it starts depositing the material. In depositional landforms made by wind, good sorting of grains is found.
- Depositional features in arid regions can develop anywhere where good source of sand and constant wind direction is available.

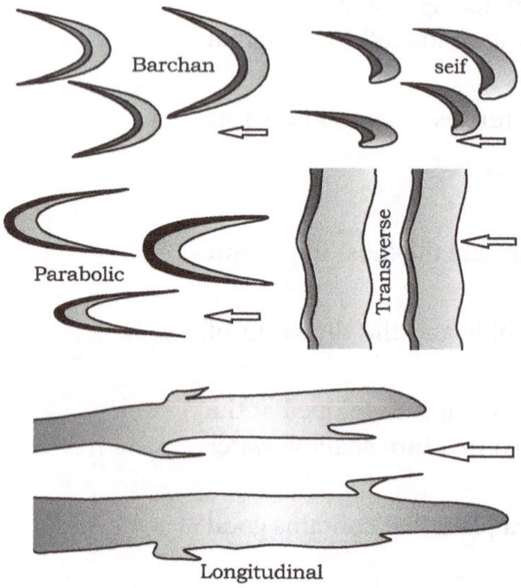

▲ *Various types of sand dunes (Arrows indicate wind direction)*

Sand Dunes

- In hot and dry deserts, sand dunes are very common depositional feature. For the formation of sand dunes there must be some obstacles on the surface of the desert.
- There are different types of sand dunes formed on the surface of the desert. These are as follows

Crescent Shaped Dunes

- These are called as **Barchans**. They are formed like a pointed dune in direction away from the wind direction.
- They are found in desert areas where the wind blows constantly in one direction and where sand is uniformly available.

Parabolic Dunes

- They are formed in those areas where the surface is covered with vegetation.
- They are reverse of barchans as they are formed in the direction of the wind.

---

34 Pedestal A base or foundation to support statue or column.

35 Saltation It is the movement of sediment particles, such as sand or small gravel, by bouncing or hopping along the surface rather than being suspended in the air or water.

36 Suspension It refers to the process by which fine sediment particles are lifted and carried within a fluid, such as air or water, without settling to the bottom.

Seif

- These are similar to barchans, the only difference is that it has a single point that can grow very long and high.
- These are formed in areas where there is change in wind directions.

Longitudinal Dunes

- These dunes are formed when there is poor supply of sand and wind direction is constant.
- They are formed like a long ridge, which is good in length but height is low.

Transverse Dunes

- These are formed perpendicular to wind direction. The source of sand in this type of dune is arranged in a line which is perpendicular to the direction of wind.
- They are very long in length and low in height.
- When there is good amount of sand in the desert, dunes are joined together and individual dunes almost disappears.
- Most of the dunes in desert change their position and few of them are stabilised near human habitations

Quick Test 5

1 Water in the desert comes from which type of rain?
2 Define playas in erosional landforms by wind.
3 Mushroom rocks are unique rock formations found in which regions?
4 Which dunes are called barchans?

Mind Map

LANDFORMS AND THEIR EVOLUTION

1 Running Water Landforms

Running water is an active agent which shapes the landforms.

Stages of development of landforms are youth stage, mature and old stage.

Process Involved

- Sheet erosion, down cutting by river water, lateral erosion.

Erosional Landforms

- Valleys
- Potholes and plunge pool
- Incised and entrenched meander
- River terraces

Valley

Depositional Landforms

- Alluvial fans
- Deltas
- Flood plains
- Natural levee
- Point bars

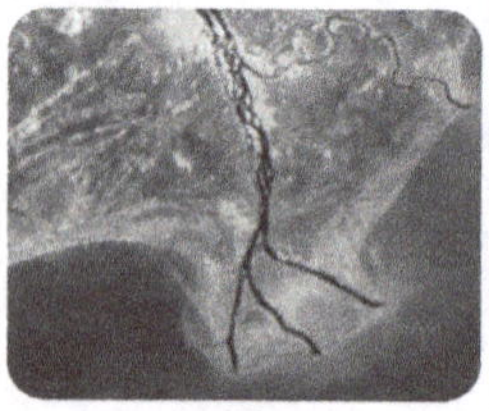

Delta

2 Ground Water Landforms

Ground water is an active agent which is effective in areas with permeable rocks.

Process Involved

Chemical processes like carbonation, solution, precipitation

Erosional Landforms

- Sink holes
- Pools
- Dolines
- Valley sinks/uvalas
- Lapies
- Caves

Depositional Landforms

- Stalagmite
- Stalactite
- Pillars and Columns

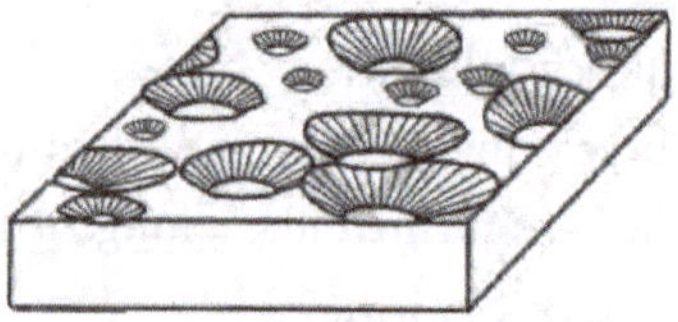

Sinkholes

Stalagmite

3 Glaciers

In this, the moving mass of ice shapes the landform.

Process Involved

- Mechanical processes like abrasion and plucking.

Erosional Landforms

- Cirque
- Horns and serrated ridge
- Glacial valleys and Troughs

Depositional Landforms

- Moraines
- Eskers
- Outwash plain
- Drumlins

4 Waves and Currents

Active agents which are most destructive for coastal regions.

Process Involved

- Hydraulic force, weathering and wave energy.

Erosional Landforms

- Cliff and terraces
- Caves
- Stacks

Depositional Landforms

- Beaches and dunes
- Bars
- Barrier bar
- Spits
- Lagoon

5 Wind

An active agent in hot desert areas.

Process Involved

- Deflation, abrasion and impacts

Erosional Landforms

- Pediments
- Pediplain
- Playas
- Deflation hollow
- Mushroom rocks

Depositional Landforms

- Crescent shaped sand dunes
- Transverse sand dunes
- Parabolic sand dunes
- Seif sand dunes
- Longitudinal sand dunes

NCERT Folder

Intext Questions

1. If landform is a small to medium sized part of the surface of the Earth, what is a landscape?

Ans. Landform is a small to medium tracts of the Earth's surface, whereas landscape are the large tracts of Earth's surface. Several related landforms together makeup landscape.

2. What are the two important aspects of the evolution of landforms?

Ans. Changes in climatic conditions and movement of landmass either vertically or horizontally are the important aspects of the evolution of landforms.

Evolution implies two stages of transformation

(i) Transformation of a part of the Earth's surface from one landform into another.

(ii) Transformation of individual landforms after they are once formed.

3. Is complete reduction of relief of a highland mass possible?

Ans. When the stream bed turn gentler due to continued erosion, downward cutting becomes less dominant and lateral erosion of banks increases and as a consequence the hills and valleys are reduced to plains. Therefore, the complete reduction of relief of a highland mass is possible.

4. In what way do natural levees differ from point bars?

Ans. Natural levees differ from point bars in the following ways

Natural Levees	Point Bars
These are formed by sediment deposition during flooding, creating raised ridges along riverbanks.	These are formed by sediment deposition on the inside curve of a riverbend.
These are found on the banks of rivers, parallel to the river channel.	These are found on the inner curve of meanders or riverbends.

5. What are the basic differences between glacial valleys and river valleys?

Ans. The differences beween glacial valleys and river valleys are

Glacial Valleys	River Valleys
Glacial valleys are U-shaped valleys that are formed by the erosion and movement of glaciers and are characterised by smooth and steep sides.	On the other hand, river valleys are formed by flowing water and are usually V-shaped.
These contains U-shaped valleys, hanging, valleys, fjords, cirque, etc.	Depending upon dimensions and shape there are many types of valleys like V-shaped valley, gorge, canyon, etc.

6. Distinguish between river alluvial plains and glacial outwash plains.

Ans. River alluvial plains are the major landforms of river deposition which are developed by normally fine sized materials like sand, silt which are carried by relatively slow moving water. On the other hand, outwash plains at the foot of glacial mountains are covered with glacio-fluvial deposits in the form of broad flat alluvial fans.

7. What is the difference between till and alluvium?

Ans. The difference between till and alluvium are

Till	Alluvium
Till is used to describe a coarse, rocky soil.	Alluvium or alluvial deposits are depositional landforms of river.
It is deposited directly by the action of a glacier.	These are found in the form of colluvial deposits, alluvial fans, etc.

8. What are the various differences between high rocky coast and a low sedimentary coast in terms of processes and landforms?

Ans. Differences between high rocky coast and a low sedimentary coast in terms of processes and landforms are as follows

Basis	High Rocky Coast	Low Sedimentary Coast
Process	In such coast, erosional processes are involved. Constant pounding of waves breaking with great force, shape the hill sides into cliffs.	It is dominated by depositional features. Rivers appear to extend their length by building coastal plains and deltas.
Landform	Cliffs, caves, stacks, wave cut ridges.	Lagoon, spits, bars, barrier bars

9. List the erosional features carved out by wind action and action of sheet floods.

Ans. Erosional features carved out by wind action and action of sheet floods are as follows

- Pediments
- Pediplains
- Playas
- Mushroom rocks
- Deflation hollows caves

Multiple Choice Questions

(i) **In which of the following stages of landform development, downward cutting is dominated?**

(a) Youth stage (b) Late mature stage
(c) Early mature stage (d) Old stage

Ans. (a) Youth stage

(ii) **A deep valley characterised by steep-like side slopes is known as**

(a) U-shaped valley (b) Gorge
(c) Blind valley (d) Canyon

Ans. (d) Canyon

(iii) **In which one of the following regions, the chemical weathering process is more dominant than the mechanical process?**

(a) Humid region (b) Limestone region
(c) Arid region (d) Glacier region

Ans. (a) Humid region

(iv) **Which one of the following sentences best defines the term 'lapies'?**

(a) A small to medium sized shallow depression.
(b) A landform whose opening is more or less circular at the top and funnel shaped toward bottom.
(c) A landform formed due to dripping water from surface.
(d) An irregular surface with sharp pinnacles, grooves and ridges.

Ans. (d) An irregular surface with sharp pinnacles, grooves and ridges.

(v) **A deep, long and wide trough or basin with very steep concave high walls at its head as well as in sides is known as**

(a) Cirque (b) Glacial valley
(c) Lateral moraine (d) Eskers

Ans. (a) Cirque

Answer the following questions in about 30 words

(i) **What do incised meanders in rocks and meanders in plains of alluvium indicate?**

Ans. In large flood and delta plains, loop-like channel pattern are called meanders. They indicate depositional landform of running water. On the other hand, deep and wide meanders found cut in hard rocky terrains are known as incised meanders. They indicate erosional landform of running water.

(ii) **Explain the evolution of valley sinks or uvalas.**

Ans. When sinkhole and dolines join together because of sinking of materials along their margins or due to roof collapse of caves, valley sinks or uvalas form.

(iii) **Underground flow of water is more common than surface run-off in limestone areas. Why?**

Ans. In limestone regions, underground water flow predominates over surface runoff due to the active processes of precipitation and solution, which results in formations that are only limestone or inter-bedded with various other types of rock.

(iv) **Glacial valleys show up many linear depositional forms. Give their locations and names.**

Ans. Glacial valleys are U-shaped valleys with broad floors and relatively smooth and steep sides. These valleys at depositional stage show many linear depositional forms which are called moraines.

Their locations and names are

- **Terminal Moraines** at the end of glacier.
- **Lateral Moraines** join the terminal moraine of either side in glacial valley.
- **Medial Moraine** in the centre of glacial valley.
- **Ground Moraine** at the surface.

(v) **How does wind perform its task in desert areas? Is it only agent responsible for the erosional feature in the desert?**

Ans. Winds move along the desert floors with great speed and the obstructions in their path create disturbance.

Storm winds are very destructive which cause deflation, abrasion and impact. Wind action creates a number of interesting erosional and depositional features in the desert.

Wind is the dominant agent in hot desert but is not the only agent responsible for the erosional features. Other agents like rain/river, etc are also responsible for erosional landforms.

Answer the following questions in about 150 words

(i) **Running water is by far the most dominating, geomorphic agent in shaping the Earth's surface in humid as well as arid climates. Explain.**

Ans. In humid as well as arid climates, running water is considered as the most important of the geomorphic agent in bringing about the erosional and depositional landforms.

There are two components of running water

(i) **Overland Flow on General Land Surface as a Sheet** Overland flow concentrates into narrow to wide paths depending upon the irregularities of the land surface. Continuous over land flow on the surface develops rills of small size. These rills in course of time develop into gullies leading to gully erosion.

(ii) **Linear Flow as Streams and Rivers in Valleys** Most of the erosional landforms made by running water are associated with vigorous and youthful rivers flowing along gradients. With the passage of time, stream channels over steep gradients turn gentler due to continuous erosion and as a consequence, lose their velocity, and facilitate active deposition. The gentler the river channels in gradient, the greater is the deposition.

When the stream bed turn gentler due to continued erosion, downward cutting becomes less dominant and lateral erosion of banks increases and as a consequence the hill and valleys are reduced to plain.

(ii) Limestones behave differently in humid and arid climate. Why? What is the dominant and almost exclusive gemorphic process in limestone areas and what are its results?

Ans. Limestone is a soft sedimentary rock which is rich in calcium carbonate. These rocks perform chemical reaction with groundwater. This incident is often seen in humid regions. And the result of the work of groundwater cannot be seen in all type of rocks. Hence, humid region provide favourable conditions to limestone for erosion and deposition, whereas in arid region the condition is different. In arid regions, limestone harden due to heat and temperature. Sometimes limestone turn into marble due to heat and pressure of rock. Thus, limestones behave differently in humid and arid climate.

Dominant Geomorphic Processes

The most dominant and almost exclusive type of geomorphic processes in limestone areas are the erosion and deposition by the action of the groundwater.

Result of geomorphic processes in limestone areas

- The erosional landforms produced by the action of the groundwater are pools, sinkholes, lapies and limestone pavements.
- In areas of alternating beds of rocks, limestone caves are also formed.
- The depositional landforms in limestone areas by the action of groundwater are stalactites, stalagmites and pillars.

(iii) How do glaciers accomplish the work of reducing high mountains into low hills and plains?

Ans. The movement of glaciers is slow unlike water flow. They move from high mountains to the lower parts under the force of gravity. Erosion of glaciers is tremendous because of friction caused by sheer weight of ice. The material plucked from the land by glaciers, cause great damage through abrasion and plucking.

Glacier can cause significant damage to even unweathered rocks and can reduce high mountains into low hills and plains. Continuous movement of glacier removes the debris and lower the divides and eventually, the slope is reduced to such an extent that glaciers will stop moving leaving only a mass of low hills and vast outwash plains along with other depositional features.

Exam Pattern Questions

Objective Type Questions

Multiple Choice Questions (MCQs)

1. Which of the following is not an erosional landform of running water?

(a) Valleys (b) Plunge pools
(c) Point bars (d) Entrenched meander

2. Waterfalls and rapids are formed during which stage of landform development?

(a) Youth (b) Mature
(c) Old (d) None of these

3. What is the main process responsible for the formation of V-shaped valleys in river systems?

(a) Lateral erosion (b) Vertical erosion
(c) Deposition (d) Solution

4. Which of the following landform is formed due to receding water after a peak flow?

(a) Entrenched meanders (b) River terraces
(c) Meander bars (d) Potholes

5. An alluvial fan is typically found where a river

(a) meets the sea
(b) flows through a plain
(c) flows from a mountain onto a flat valley floor
(d) flows through a canyon

6. Which landform is formed when deep loops formed in meander get cut-off due to erosion at inflection points.

(a) Meander bars (b) River terraces
(c) Natural levee (d) Ox-bow lakes

7. **The repeated flooding of a river on a floodplain often results in the build-up of ridges along the river banks called**

(a) ox-bow lakes (b) levees
(c) canyons (d) rapids

8. **'The streams flowing over gentle slopes develop sinuous or meandering course.'**

Which type of erosion results in meandering of a river?

(a) Sheet erosion (b) Lateral erosion
(c) Vertical erosion (d) Abrasion

9. **'Karst Topography is effective in areas where such rocks are present which can be dissolved in water and are affected by the chemical process easily'. Identify the type of rock.**

(a) Limestone (b) Granite
(c) Dolomite (d) Both (a) and (c)

10. **Which of the following is known as collapse sinks?**

(a) Uvala
(b) Doline
(c) Lapies
(d) Limestone pavement

11. **Which of the following is true about medial moraine?**

(a) Moraine at end of glacier
(b) Moraine at end of valley floor
(c) Moraine along side parallel to glacial valley
(d) Moraine in centre of glacial valley flanked by lateral moraine

12. **Which statement accurately describes an *eskers* formation?**

(a) It is a ridge of sand and gravel deposited by streams flowing underneath a glacier.
(b) It is a ridge formed by wind erosion in an arid region.
(c) It is a rounded hill formed in glacial till.
(d) It is a flat, low-lying area left by melting glacier ice.

13. **Which of the following statements correctly describes a fiord?**

(a) It is a large glacial lake formed by the melting of a glacier.
(b) It is a narrow, deep coastal valley that has been flooded by the sea after glacial retreat.
(c) It is a bowl-shaped depression in a mountainous region formed by glacial erosion.
(d) It is a steep ridge separating two glacial valleys.

14. **Which of the following correctly defines sea stack?**

(a) Large natural hollow in cliff.
(b) Resistant masses of rock which were originally part of cliff
(c) Ridge of sand and shingle in off-shore zone of sea
(d) Off-shore bar exposed due to addition of sand

15. **'On this coast depositional feature is more common than the erosional feature'. This statement is related to which coast. Choose the correct option from the following**

(a) Highly Rocky coast (b) Emerged coast
(c) Submerged coast (d) Both (a) and (b)

16. **Which of the following is a depositional landform of wind?**

(a) Pediment (b) Barchan (c) Playa (d) Pediplain

17. **Consider the following statements regarding depositional landform of running water and choose the correct option.**

Statement I Alluvial fans formed in humid areas have low cone with gentle slope.

Statement II A floodplain is a landform which is not created by river deposits.

Codes

(a) Only I (b) Both I and II
(c) Only II (d) None of these

18. **Which of the following statements is incorrect regarding the wind?**

Statement I The wind carries the finer particles and the mass erosion is done by the sheet wash.

Statement II Winds do not move along the desert floor, it only blows at higher elevations.

Options

(a) Both I and II (b) Only II
(c) Only I (d) None of these

19. **Consider the following statements.**

I. The small to medium tracts or parcel of Earth surface are called landscapes.
II. The large tracts of Earth's surface are called landforms.

Which of the given statements is/are correct?

(a) Only I (b) Only II
(c) Both I and II (d) None of these

20. **Consider the following statements.**

I. Canyons form in horizontal bedded sedimentary rock.
II. Gorge form in hard rocks.

Which of the given statements is/are incorrect?

(a) Only I (b) Only II
(c) Both I and II (d) None of these

21. **Consider the following statements.**

I. Alluvial fans in humid areas show low cones with gentle slope from head to toe.
II. Alluvial fans appear as high cones with steep slope in arid and semi-arid climates.

Which of the given statements is/are correct?

(a) Only I (b) Only II
(c) Both I and II (d) None of these

22. How many of the following is incorrectly matched?

Erosional landform	–	Features
1. Cliffs	–	Narrow at base and broad at top
2. Caves	–	A natural hollow
3. Deflation hollow	–	Forms pits and small cavities
4. Mushroom rock	–	Steep slopes ranging from 30m or more

Codes

(a) Only one (b) More than two
(c) Only two (d) All of these

23. There are number of depositional landforms formed by the action of running water. The materials that are carried by the streams from the mountains are dumped when they reach the flat plain.

Identify the depositional landform by the given description.

It is also called as 'meander bars. They are found on the concave side of meanders of large rivers. These are sediments that are deposited in a linear pattern by a stream. They have uniform profile and width. They contain sediments of mixed sizes.

Options

(a) Delta plains (b) Natural levee
(c) Point bars (d) Ox-bow lake

24. Identify the type of landform from given description.

It rises from the floor of a cave due to the accumulation of material deposited on the floor from ceiling drippings. Sometimes it also looks like a disc which is smooth, rounded with bulging ends.

Options

(a) Stalactite (b) Pillars
(c) Stalagmite (d) Lapies

25. Identify the type of sand dune from the given statement.

'They are formed in those areas where the surface is covered with vegetation. They are reverse of barchans'.

Options

(a) Seif (b) Parabolic dune
(c) Crescent dune (d) Transverse dune

Match the Following

26.

List I	List II
A. Plunge pool	1. Wave and current
B. Lapies	2. Glacier
C. Esker	3. Running water
D. Spits	4. Groundwater

Codes

	A	B	C	D		A	B	C	D
(a)	4	3	1	2	(b)	3	4	2	1
(c)	2	1	4	3	(d)	3	2	4	1

27.

List I	List II
A. Esker	1. Smooth oval shaped ridge
B. Outwash plains	2. Sinuous ridges
C. Drumlins	3. Saw-toothed ridges
D. Aretes	4. Plains of gravel, silt, sand, clay

Codes

	A	B	C	D		A	B	C	D
(a)	2	1	4	3	(b)	2	1	3	4
(c)	2	4	1	3	(d)	1	2	4	3

28.

List I	List II
A. V- shaped valley	1. Solution
B. Monadnocks	2. Vertical erosion
C. Potholes	3. Lowland feature
D. Swallow hole	4. Rotation of boulders

Codes

	A	B	C	D		A	B	C	D
(a)	1	3	2	4	(b)	2	3	4	1
(c)	3	1	4	2	(d)	1	2	3	4

Assertion-Reason

Directions (Q. Nos. 29-34) In the questions given below are two statements labelled as Assertion (A) and other is labelled as Reason (R). In the context of two statements which one of the following is correct?

Codes

(a) Both A and R are true, but R is not the correct explanation of A
(b) Both A and R are true and R is the correct explanation of A
(c) Both A and R are incorrect
(d) A is correct, but R is incorrect

29. Assertion (A) Meander is a type of channel pattern.
Reason (R) Meander is formed due to unconsolidated nature of alluvial deposits which make up the bank with many irregularities.

30. Assertion (A) The work of groundwater cannot be seen in all types of rocks.
Reason (R) Physical or mechanical removal of materials by moving groundwater is insignificant in developing landforms.

31. **Assertion** (A) The divide between cirque side walls turn into aretes.
Reason (R) The divide between cirque side walls undergo progressive erosion and become narrow.

32. **Assertion** (A) Stoss end of drumlin is blunter.
Reason (R) Stoss end is formed due to push by moving ice.

33. **Assertion** (A) A river delta is formed at the mouth of a river.
Reason (R) Deltas are formed due to the deposition of sediments as river velocity decreases upon entering a standing body of water.

34. **Assertion** (A) Stalactites and stalagmites are common features in limestone caves.
Reason (R) Stalactites form when minerals deposit as water drips from the ceiling of the cave, while stalagmites form from deposits building up from the floor.

Answers

1. (c) Point bars
2. (a) Youth
3. (b) Vertical erosion
4. (b) River terraces
5. (c) flows from a mountain onto a flat valley floor
6. (d) Ox-bow lakes
7. (b) levees
8. (b) Lateral erosion
9. (d) Both (a) and (c)
10. (b) Doline
11. (d) Moraine in centre of glacial valley flanked by lateral moraine
12. (a) It is a ridge of sand and gravel deposited by streams flowing underneath a glacier.
13. (b) It is a narrow, deep coastal valley that has been flooded by the sea after glacial retreat.
14. (b) Resistant masses of rock which were originally part of cliff
15. (c) Submerged coast
16. (b) Barchan
17. (a) Only I
18. (b) Only II
19. (d) None of these
20. (c) Both I and II
21. (b) Only II
22. (c) Only two
23. (c) Point bars
24. (c) Stalagmite
25. (b) Parabolic dune
26. (b)
27. (c)
28. (b)
29. (b) Both A and R are true and R is the correct explanation of A
30. (b) Both A and R are true and R is the correct explanation of A
31. (b) Both A and R are true and R is the correct explanation of A
32. (a) Both A and R are true, but R is not the correct explanation of A
33. (b) Both A and R are true and R is the correct explanation of A
34. (b) Both A and R are true and R is the correct explanation of A

Subjective Questions

Short Answer Type Questions

1. 'Erosional landforms made by running water are associated with three stages.' Explain these in brief. Competency Based

Ans. Erosional landforms made by running water are associated with three stages namely, youth, mature and old stage.

The characteristic of each of the stages of landscapes developing by running water are

(i) **Youth Stage** Streams are few during this stage with poor integration and flow over original slopes showing V-shaped valleys with no floodplains. Waterfall and rapids exist where local hard rock bodies are exposed.

(ii) **Mature Stage** Streams are plenty with good integration. The valleys are still V-shaped but deep streams are broad enough to have wider floodplains within which streams may flow in meanders confined within the valley.

(iii) **Old Stage** Smaller tributaries during old age are few with gentle gradients. Streams meander freely over vast flood plains showing different landforms like natural levees, ox-bow lakes, etc.

2. 'River valleys develop through various phases.' Explain in brief. Competency Based Que

Ans. River valleys develop through various phases. These phases are as follows

- Valley starts as small and narrow rills. The rills will gradually develop into long and wide gullies.
- The gullies will further deepen, widen and lengthen to give rise to valleys.
- Depending upon the dimension and shape, valley can be recognised as V-shaped valley, gorge, canyon, etc.
- Gorge is a deep valley with very steep sides. It is almost equal in width at its top as well as its bottom.
- Canyon is characterised by steep step like side slopes and may be as deep as gorge. It is wider at its top than at its bottom.
- Types of valleys depend upon the type and structure of rocks in which they form. For example, canyon form in sedimentary rocks and gorge form in hard rocks.

3 What are the river terraces? Explain its various forms.

Ans. River terrace are surfaces which are a site of old valley floor or floodplain levels. They are the bedrock surfaces without any alluvial covers. River terraces are basically product erosion as they result due to vertical erosion by the stream into its own depositional floodplain. There can be a number of such terraces at different heights indicating former river bed levels.

There are two forms of river terraces

(i) **Paired Terraces** Such river terraces may occur at the same elevation on either sides of the rivers.

(ii) **Non-paired Terraces** When a terrace is present only on one side of the stream or at different elevation on the other side.

4. Floodplains are a major landforms of river deposition. Explain. Competency Based Que

Ans. Floodplains are a major landforms of river deposition. These are the flat alluvial landform, formed largely by the flow regime of present river and subject to flooding. A river bed made of river deposits is the active floodplains. The floodplains above the bank are inactive floodplains.

Inactive floodplains above the banks basically contain two types of deposits—flood deposits and channel deposits. The flood deposits of spilled waters carry relatively finer materials like silt and clay. The floodplains in a delta are called delta plains.

5. What are the causes behind the formation of meanders?

Ans. Meanders form in rivers when water flows over a gently sloping area with soft soil or sediment. The water moves faster on the outer side of bends, causing erosion, while it moves slower on the inner side, depositing sediment.

The causes behind the formation of a meander can be as follows

- Nature of the water to do more lateral erosion when it is flowing over a gentle gradient.
- Alluvial deposits are more prone to lateral erosion due to their loose particles, which can be easily carried away by water.
- Coriolis force which deflects water in the same way it deflects wind.

6. "Cave is an erosional landform of groundwater." Analyse the statement in the light of its formation. Competency Based Que

Ans. Cave is an erosional landform of groundwater. It is a naturally formed sub-terranean open area where there are alternating beds of rocks with limestone in between or areas where there are dense, massive and thick beds of limestone is present.

Water percolates down either through the material or through cracks and joints and move horizontally along the bedding plan.

7. Discuss the conditions which are responsible for the formation of eskers landforms.

Ans. The works of depositional glacial activities give birth to eskers. Conditions which are responsible for its formation are

- When glaciers melt in summer, the water flows on the surface of the ice or seeps down along the margins or even moves through holes in the ice.
- These waters accumulate beneath the glacier and flow like streams in a channel beneath the ice.

Such streams flow over the ground (not in a valley cut in the ground) with ice forming its banks. Very coarse materials like boulders and blocks along with some minor fractions of rock debris carried into this stream settle in the valley of ice beneath the glacier and after the ice melts can be found as a sinuous ridge called eskers.

8. Drumlins are the deposional landforms of glaciers. Explain.

Ans. Drumlins are smooth, elongated hills formed by glaciers as they move over the land. They are made up of materials like clay, sand, gravel and rocks, which were carried and deposited by the glacier. When a glacier moves, it reshapes and molds the sediments beneath it, creating these hills. The steep, rounded end of a drumlin faces the direction from which the glacier came, while the gently sloping end points in the direction the glacier moved. They show the direction of glacier movement, giving clues about the past behaviour of ice sheets.

9. There are different types of landforms formed by the erosion of coastal area. Explain.

Ans. Coastal erosional landforms are shaped by the action of waves, tides and currents eroding the shoreline. Key types of landforms include cliffs and terraces, wave-cut platforms, sea stacks and caves. These are as follows

- Cliffs are steep rock faces formed when waves continuously erode the base of the land.
- Wave-cut platforms are flat, rocky surfaces left behind as cliffs retreat.
- Caves develop when waves erode softer rock in headlands.
- Stacks are a mass of rock, which is originally a part of cliff. These are formed when the receding cliff leave some remains of hard rock.

10. Explain the formation of different varieties of sand dunes.

Ans. Sand dunes have various shapes, formed by wind direction and sand supply. These are as follows

- **Crescent Shaped Dunes** These are called as 'barchans'. They are formed like a pointed dune in direction away from the wind direction.
- **Parabolic Dunes** They are formed in those areas where the surface is covered with vegetation.
- **Seif** These are similar to barchans, but they have single point that can grow very long and high.
- **Longitudinal Dunes** These dunes are formed when there is poor supply of sand and wind direction is constant.
- **Transverse Dunes** These are formed perpendicular to wind direction.

11. What is the role of geomorphic process and agents in the evolution of landforms?

Ans. Each geomorphic agent produce its own type of landforms and leave their distinct imprints on the landforms they produce. Running water, wind, wave, glacier, groundwater are the powerful erosional and depositional agents shaping and changing the surface of the Earth aided by weathering and mass wasting processes. Geomorphic process can be seen and measured through their result i.e. landforms and characteristics.

Many varieties of landforms develop by the action of each of geomorphic agents which depend upon especially the type and structure of rock i.e. folds, faults, joints, fractures, hardness and softness permeability and impermeability, etc.

12. Differentiate between gorge and canyon.

Ans. Differences between gorge and canyon are as follows

Gorge	Canyon
A gorge is a narrow deep opening of the river across the mountain.	Canyons are formed in dry areas.
Side cutting are absent due to hard rocks.	It has high vertical walls for long distance.
The river's down cutting leads to the formation of deep gorge.	The upper part of the canyon is wide due to weathering.
It is almost equal in width at its top as well as its bottom.	The lower part is deeper due to rapid down cutting.

13. Differentiate between stalactites and stalagmites.

Ans. Differences between stalactites and stalagmites are as follows

Stalactites	Stalagmites
These are a column of pure limestone hanging from the roof of a cave.	These are the columns of pure limestone formed on the floor of a cave.
They are broad at their base and taper towards the free ends.	They take the shape of a column or a disc, with either a smooth, rounded bulging end.
Stalactites developed by sinking of water with lime from the roof of the surface.	Stalagmites form due to dripping water from the surface.

14. Discuss the significance of off-shore zone for the life and livelihood of human being.

Ans. Significance of off-shore zone for life and livelihood of human being are as follows

- The coastal off-shore bars offer the first buffer or defence against storms.
- Off-shore zones are capable to absorb the destructive force of Tsunami.
- The mangroves vegetation developed as barriers in beach not only protects from storm but also provides sufficient resources for livelihood.
- Mangroves vegetation is the habitat of huge biodiversity. It provides food, fibre, fuel to the native people and also gives economically important goods.
- Lagoon develops in off-shore region provides opportunity for fishery and other economic activities.

Thus, in this way, off-shore zone is highly valuable for the human and society.

15. **What is Karst Topography? Explain the process of formation of Karst landforms.**

Ans. **Karst Topography** Any limestone or dolomitic region showing typical landforms produced by action of groundwater through the processes of solution and deposition is called Karst Topography.

Process of Formation

Karst regions are formed by the dominant erosional process of solution, the lack of surface water and the development of stream sink cave system.

All the various landforms formed in karst regions are primarily influenced by the process of stream sinking. However, karst topography is characterised by the absence of a well integrated drainage system.

Long Answer Type Questions

1. **Give an account of fluvial depositional or running water landforms.**

Ans. Fluvial depositional landforms are created by the deposition of sediments carried by rivers as they lose energy. Key landforms include floodplains, levees, alluvial fans, deltas, and point bars.

- Floodplains are flat areas alongside rivers that get covered with nutrient-rich silt during floods, making them ideal for agriculture.
- Levees are natural embankments formed by sediment deposition along river banks during floods.
- Alluvial fans occur when rivers flow out of steep areas onto flat plains, depositing sediment in a fan shape.
- Deltas form at river mouths where the river slows and deposits its load, creating fertile land with multiple distributaries.
- Point bars develop on the inner bends of river meanders, where slower water deposits sand and gravel.
- These landforms play a significant role in shaping landscapes and supporting ecosystems and human activities, like farming and settlement, due to their fertile soil and access to water.

2. **Explain the erosional landforms of Karst Topography.**

Ans. Erosional landforms of Karst Topography are created by the dissolution of soluble rocks, like limestone, by water. Landforms that are developed by the erosional action of groundwater on rocks are as follows

- Sinkhole is an opening of circular shape at the top and funnel shaped towards bottom. It is very common in limestone areas.
- Caves are formed when water seeps through cracks, gradually dissolving the rock and creating underground passages and chambers.
- Pools are formed when sinkholes are covered with soil mantle. They appear as water pools.
- Lapies are sharp, jagged rock features formed by chemical weathering on limestone surfaces.
- Valley sinks or uvalas are formed when the sinkholes and dolines joins together.
- These landforms give Karst regions a distinctive and rugged landscape, often containing complex underground water systems that are vital for ecosystems and human water resources.

3. **The movement of glacier creates both erosional as well as depositional landforms. Discuss about these landforms in brief.**

Ans. The movement of glaciers create both erosional and depositional landforms which are as follows

(i) **Erosional landforms** Glaciers erode mountains and other landforms by creating

- **Glacial valleys** Glaciers create large depressions in the ground, which can eventually turn into valleys.
- **Cirques** They are deep, long and wide basins with very steep concave to vertically drop high walls at its head as well as sides. These are the most common landforms in glaciers.
- **Horns** Formed due to headward erosion of the cirque walls.
- **Aretes** When two neighbouring glaciers erode opposite sides of a rock, they create a steep ridge called an arete.

(ii) **Depositional landforms** Glaciers deposit eroded materials to create landforms by creating

- **Moraines** Glaciers and ice sheets deposited in the form of ridges.
- **Drumlins** These are smooth oval shaped ridge-like features composed mainly of glacial till with some masses of gravel and sand.
- **Eskers** They are created when glacial meltwater deposits sediment in tunnels or channels within or below the glacier.
- **Outwash plains** Formed at the foot of the glacial mountain and covers with glacio-fluvial deposits.

4. **'Wind as a geomorphic agent has powerful impact in shaping landforms, there are different type of erosional landforms developed by the action of wind'. Elucidate.**

Ans. Wind erosion creates various landforms in arid and semi-arid regions. Following are the erosional landforms developed by the action of winds

- **Pediments** These are gently inclined rocky floors which are close to the foot of a mountain. These may have thin cover of debris.
- **Pediplain** These are extensive, gently sloping plains formed in arid and semi-arid regions through prolonged erosion processes.

- **Playas** These are shallow lake that covers the plain area of the deserts.
- **Deflation Hollow** It is a depression-like structure which is formed when there is continued movement of wind in one direction.
- **Mushroom, Table and Pedestal Rocks** These rocks have a characteristic shape similar to a mushroom, with a narrow base and a wider top.

5. 'Stages of landform development are similar to the stages of human life'. Justify the statement.

Ans. The statement "Stages of landform development are similar to the stages of human life" can be justified by comparing the processes and transformations that both landforms and humans undergo. Just as humans experience childhood, adolescence, adulthood and old age, landforms also evolve through distinct stages.

Initially, newly formed landforms, like mountains, represent the "childhood" stage, characterised by rapid growth and dynamic changes due to tectonic activities. As they mature, they undergo processes like erosion and weathering, similar to the challenges faced in adolescence, leading to the development of more complex features like valleys and plateaus.

In adulthood, landforms stabilise, reaching a state of equilibrium, while old age can be compared to erosion and degradation, where features degrade over time. Just as human experiences shape individual lives, geological processes and environmental factors shape the evolution of landforms.

6. 'Groundwater is an active agent for shaping areas where rocks are permeable, thinly bedded and there is presence of joints and cracks'. Discuss. Competency Based Que

Ans. Groundwater plays a crucial role in shaping landscapes, especially in regions where rocks are permeable, thinly bedded, and where joints and cracks are present. In such areas, water seeps through the soil and into the sub-surface through the cracks and joints in the rock. This movement of water helps in the process of chemical weathering, where minerals in the rock dissolve and are transported away, gradually enlarging the openings and forming features such as caves and sinkholes.

As groundwater continues to flow, it can also lead to the formation of Karst topography, characterised by unique landforms like limestone pavements, caves and dolines. The presence of permeable rocks allows for efficient water drainage and storage and creates aquifers that are essential for human consumption and agriculture. Overall, groundwater acts as an active agent in erosion and landscape evolution, significantly influencing the geological features and ecological balance of an area.

Source Based Questions

1. Read the passage carefully and answer the questions that follow.

Coastal processes are the most dynamic and hence most destructive. At one place, there can be erosion in one season and deposition in another. Most of the changes along the coasts are accomplished by waves. When waves break, the water is thrown with great force onto the shore, and there is a great churning of sediments on the sea bottom. Storm waves and tsunami waves can cause far-reaching changes in a short period of time than normal breaking waves.

Other than the action of waves, the coastal landforms depend upon (i) the configuration of land and sea floor; (ii) whether the coast is advancing (emerging) seaward or retreating (submerging) landward. Assuming sea level to be constant, two types of coasts are considered to explain the concept of evolution of coastal landforms: (i) high, rocky coasts (submerged coasts); (ii) low, smooth and gently sloping sedimentary coasts (emerged coasts).

Along high rocky coasts, waves break with great force against the land shaping the hill sides into cliffs. With constant pounding by waves, the cliffs recede leaving a wave-cut platform in front of the sea cliff. Waves gradually minimise the irregularities along the shore.

Along low sedimentary coasts the rivers appear to extend their length by building coastal plains and deltas. The land slopes gently into the water. Marshes and swamps may abound along the coasts. Depositional features dominate. When waves break over a gently sloping sedimentary coast, the bottom sediments get churned and move readily building bars, barrier bars, spits and lagoons.

(i) Which of the following is a depositional feature of sea waves?

(a) Wave-cut platform (b) Cave
(c) Stack (d) Beach

Ans. (d) Beach

(ii) Which among the following is the most important factor that influences coastal landforms?

(a) Climate (b) Rocks
(c) Sea waves (d) Magma

Ans. (c) Sea waves

(iii) Which of the following is an erosional feature formed due to effects of sea waves?

(a) Wave-cut terrace
(b) Barrier bar
(c) Stalagmite
(d) Mushroom rock

Ans. (a) Wave-cut terrace

2. Read the passage carefully and answer the questions that follow.

Wind is one of the two dominant agents in hot deserts. The desert floors get heated up too much and too quickly because of being dry and barren. Winds also move along the desert floors with great speed and the obstructions in their path create turbulence. Of course, there are storm winds which are very destructive. Winds cause deflation, abrasion and impact. Deflation includes lifting and removal of dust and smaller particles from the surface of rocks. The wind action creates a number of interesting erosional and depositional features in the deserts. In fact, many features of deserts owe their formation to mass wasting and running water as sheet floods.

The wind moves fine materials and general mass erosion is accomplished mainly through sheet floods or sheet wash. Stream channels in desert areas are broad, smooth and indefinite and flow for a brief time after rains.

Wind is a good sorting agent. Depending upon the velocity of wind, different sizes of grains are moved along the floors by rolling or saltation and carried in suspension and in this process of transportation itself, the materials get sorted. When the wind slows or begins to die down, depending upon sizes of grains and their critical velocities, the grains will begin to settle. So, in depositional landforms made by wind, good sorting of grains can be found. Since wind is there everywhere and wherever there is good source of sand and with constant wind directions, depositional features in arid regions can develop anywhere.

(i) Wind erosion is most dominant in which of the following region?

(a) Himalayan Mountains
(b) North Indian Alluvial Plains
(c) Sahara Desert
(d) Sunderban Delta

Ans. (c) Sahara Desert

(ii) Which of the following is a depositional agent of winds?

(a) Pediment (b) Pediplain
(c) Deflation Hollow (d) Barchan

Ans. (d) Barchan

(iii) Which among the following process influences the formation of landforms in desert regions?

(a) Wind erosion (b) Fluvial erosion
(c) Wind deposition (d) All of these

Ans. (d) All of these

3. Read the passage carefully and answer the questions that follow.

In humid regions, which receive heavy rainfall running water is considered the most important of the geomorphic agents in bringing about the degradation of the land surface. There are two components of running water. One is overland flow on general land surface as a sheet. Another is linear flow as streams and rivers in valleys. Most of the erosional landforms made by running water are associated with vigorous and youthful rivers flowing over steep gradients. With time, stream channels over steep gradients turn gentler due to continued erosion, and as a consequence, lose their velocity, facilitating active deposition. There may be depositional forms associated with streams flowing over steep slopes. But these phenomena will be on a small scale compared to those associated with rivers flowing over medium to gentle slopes. The gentler the river channels in gradient or slope, the greater is the deposition. When the stream beds turn gentler due to continued erosion, downward cutting becomes less dominant and lateral erosion of banks increases and as a consequence the hills and valleys are reduced to plains. Overland flow causes sheet erosion. Depending upon irregularities of the land surface, the overland flow may concentrate into narrow to wide paths. Because of the sheer friction of the column of flowing water, minor or major quantities of materials from the surface of the land are removed in the direction of flow and gradually small and narrow rills will form.

(i) How does the transformation of stream beds affect the erosional pattern of rivers?

Ans. As stream beds become gentler, downward cutting decreases while lateral erosion increases, leading to the transformation of hills and valleys into plains.

(ii) Compare the significance of depositional forms in different slope conditions.

Ans. Depositional forms on steep slopes are small-scale phenomena, whereas rivers flowing over medium to gentle slopes create more significant depositional features.

(iii) Explain how the velocity of rivers influences the process of deposition in different gradient zones.

Ans. Rate of deposition is more when the rivers flow with less velocity on gentle slopes, while steep slope with high velocity shows minimal deposition due to active erosional activity.

4. Read the passage carefully and answer the questions that follow.

Masses of ice moving as sheets over the land (continental glacier or piedmont glacier if a vast sheet of ice is spread over the plains at the foot of mountains) or as linear flows down the slopes of mountains in broad trough-like valleys (mountain and valley glaciers) are called glaciers. The movement of glaciers is slow unlike water flow. The movement could be a few centimetres to a few metres a day or even less or more. Glaciers move basically because of the force of gravity.

Erosion by glaciers is tremendous because of friction caused by sheer weight of the ice. The material plucked from the land by glaciers (usually large-sized angular blocks and fragments) get dragged along the floors or sides of the valleys and cause great damage through abrasion and plucking. Glaciers can cause significant damage to even unweathered rocks and can reduce high mountains into low hills and plains. As glaciers continue to move, debris gets removed, divides get lowered and eventually the slope is reduced to such an extent that glaciers will stop moving leaving only a mass of low hills and vast outwash plains along with other depositional features.

We have many glaciers in our country moving down the slopes and valleys in Himalayas. Higher reaches of Uttaranchal, Himachal Pradesh and Jammu and Kashmir, are places to see some of them. River Bhagirathi is basically fed by meltwaters from under the snout (Gaumukh) of the Gangotri glacier. In fact, Alkapuri glacier feeds waters to Alakananda river. Rivers Alkananda and Bhagirathi join to make river Ganga near Deoprayag.

(i) **What distinguishes the movement pattern of glaciers compared to water flow?**

Ans. Glaciers move slowly, ranging from a few centimetres to meters per day or less, unlike water's rapid flow.

(ii) **Continental and mountain glaciers differ in their formation patterns. Comment.**

Ans. Continental glaciers spread as sheets over land, while mountain glaciers flow linearly down slopes through valley troughs.

(iii) **How do glaciers manage to cause such significant erosion?**

Ans. The tremendous friction caused by the sheer weight of ice enables glaciers to cause significant erosion.

SELF ASSESSMENT TEST

Objective Type Questions

1. What is the name given to caves with openings at both ends ?
   (a) Uvala (b) Lapies
   (c) Swallow hole (d) Tunnel
2. What are the unassorted coarse and fine debris dropped by melting glaciers known as?
   (a) Outwashed deposits (b) Glacial till
   (c) Aretes (d) Fjord
3. When barrier bars are keyed up to one end of bay it is known as
   (a) beaches (b) spits
   (c) lagoon (d) sea stack
4. Consider the following statements.
   (i) Valleys are formed from rills.
   (ii) Type and structure of rocks determine the type of valley formed.
   Which of the given statements is/are correct?
   (a) Only (i) (b) Only (ii)
   (c) Both (i) and (ii) (d) None of these

Short Answer Type Questions

5. Differentiate between erosional landforms and depositional landforms.
6. What is the importance of alluvial fans as a landforms?
7. The wind action creates a number of interesting erosional and depositional features in the deserts. Explain.
8. Elucidate the depositional landforms of Karst topography.
9. The load carried by the rivers is dumped and spread into the sea.Explain this statement with respect to the formation of deltas.

Long Answer Type Questions

10. Explain the different stages of the rivers and also explain their impact in making landforms.
11. 'Most of the dunes in the deserts shift and a few of them will get stabilised especially near human habitations.' Justify this statement with suitable examples.
12. 'Erosion by glaciers is tremendous because of friction caused by sheer weight of the ice'. Explain this statement in the context of various erosional and depositional works of glaciers.
13. Analyse the role of river system in the development of landforms through process of erosion and deposition.
14. 'Glacial processes like plucking and abrasion contribue to the formation of glacial landforms.' Elucidate.

7

CHAPTER

This chapter deals with the atmosphere, its composition and structure. Atmosphere is like an envelope of gases and other elements around the Earth.

Composition and Structure of Atmosphere

YOUR STUDY GOALS

7.1 Composition of the Atmosphere
7.2 Structure of the Atmosphere
7.3 Elements of Weather and Climate

YOUR PRACTICE GOAL

- Objective Type Questions (24 Qs ; MCQs, Statements, Matching, A-R)
- Subjective Questions (8 SAs, 3 LAs)
- Source Based Questions (3 Qs)

- The air is colourless and odourless. It can only be felt when it blows in the form of a wind.
- Air or atmosphere is an essential part of the Earth. It is necessary for the survival of all organisms.
- 99% of the total mass of the air is limited to the height of 32 km from Earth's surface.

7.1 Composition of the Atmosphere

- The atmosphere is composed of gases, water vapour and dust particles.
- The proportion of gases varies with height. The quantity of oxygen is very less at the height of 120 km.
- Similarly, gases like carbon dioxide and water vapour are found only up to 90 km from the surface of the Earth.

Gases

- Carbon dioxide, ozone and water vapour are some of the important gases in the atmosphere.

Carbon Dioxide (CO_2)

- Carbon dioxide is transparent and allows the incoming solar radiation of the Sun but it is opaque to the outgoing **terrestrial radiation**.

1 Terrestrial Radiation These are the radiation that comes back from the earth's surface.

- Carbon dioxide absorbs some of the terrestrial radiation and reflects back a part of it towards the earth's surface.
- CO_2 is largely responsible for the greenhouse effect[2].
- The volume of carbon dioxide has been rising in the atmosphere in the past few decades because of the burning of fossil fuels and this has resulted in the increase of earth's temperature.

Ozone

- It is found between 10-50 km above the earth's surface.
- This gas acts as a filter and absorbs the ultraviolet rays or radiations coming from the Sun. It prevents these radiations from reaching the earth's surface.

Water Vapour

- It is a variable gas in the atmosphere. Its concentration decreases as we go to higher altitude.
- The amount of water vapour present in the warm and wet areas is about 4% while in the dry and cold areas of desert and polar regions, it is less than 1%.
- The content of water vapour in the atmosphere also varies from equator[3] towards the pole.
- Water vapour absorbs parts of the insolation[4] from the Sun and helps in retaining the Earth's heat.
- Water vapour acts as a blanket for the earth as it helps the earth neither to become too cold nor too hot. It also helps in maintaining the **stability** and **instability** of the air.

Dust Particles

- These are small solid particles that originate from different sources. These are present in the atmosphere that originate in the form of sea salts, fine soil, smoke-soot, ash, pollen, dust and disintegrated particles of meteors.
- Dust particles are present generally in the lower layers of the atmosphere but sometimes they are transported to the greater heights due to convectional air currents[5].
- The concentration of these particles is higher in the sub-tropical and temperate region due to dry winds while in equatorial and polar areas, they are present in less amount.
- Dust particles helps in the formation of clouds as the dust and salt particles act as a hygroscopic nuclei[6] around which the water vapour condenses.

7.2 Structure of the Atmosphere

- The atmosphere consists of different layers and each layer has different density and temperature.
- Density of the air is highest near the surface of the earth and it decreases with increasing altitude.
- The column of atmosphere is divided into **five different layers** on the basis of temperature conditions. These are **troposphere, stratosphere, mesosphere, thermosphere** and **exosphere**.

Troposphere

- It is the **lowermost** layer of the atmosphere. It has an average height of 13 km. The height of troposphere varies at poles and equator. It lies at 8 km near poles and 18 km near equator.
- Thickness of troposphere is more at the equator because the rising warm air pushes the upper boundary of the troposphere higher.

2 Greenhouse Effect It is the process by which certain gases in the atmosphere trap heat from the sun, keeping the earth warm enough to support life.
3 Equator It is an imaginary line around the middle of the earth at an equal distance from the north pole and the South pole.
4 Insolation It refers to the incoming solar radiation from the Sun.
5 Convectional Air Currents These are vertical movements of air caused by the heating of the earth's surface.
6 Hygroscopic Nuclei These are small particles, typically found in the atmosphere, that have the ability to absorb water vapour from the surrounding air.

- Temperature in this layer decreases at the rate of 1°C for every 165m of height. This layer contains dust particles and water vapours.

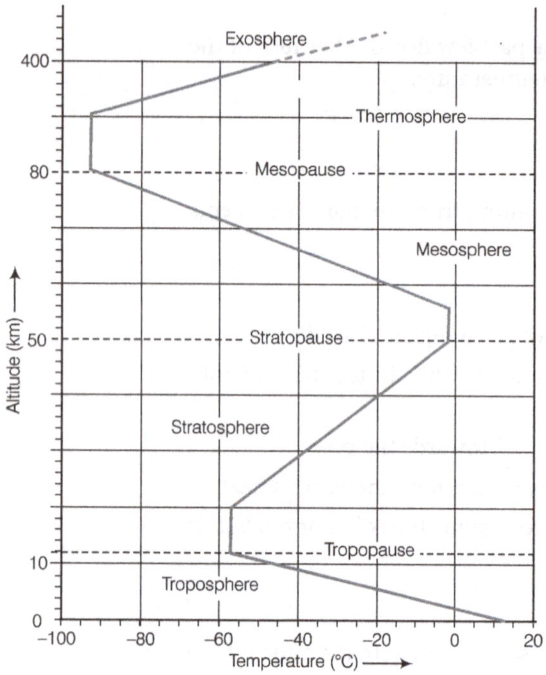

▲ *Structure of the Atmosphere*

- All the climatic and weather phenomena occur in this layer and it is an important layer for biological activities.
- There is a zone that separates the troposphere and stratosphere, which is called **tropopause**. Temperature in tropopause is almost constant.
- The air temperature at tropopause is about minus 80°C near equator and minus 45°C over the poles.

Stratosphere

- This layer lies above the troposphere. This layer extends up to height of 50 km from tropopause.
- It contains **ozone layer**. This layer acts as a shield for life on the earth by giving protection from intense, harmful form of energy i.e. ultra-violet radiation.

Mesosphere

- This layer lies above the stratosphere. It extends up to a height of 80 km.
- In this layer, temperature starts decreasing with increasing altitude. The temperature reaches up to minus 100°C at 80 km. The upper limit of this layer is known as **Mesopause**[7].

Ionosphere

- This layer is located between 80 and 400 km above from the mesopause. Temperature in this layer starts decreasing with height.
- This layer consists of electrically charged particles which is known as **ions**, and hence it is called as ionosphere.
- This layer helps in reflecting back of **radio waves**[8] transmitted by the earth.

Exosphere

- This is the **uppermost** layer of the earth's atmosphere.
- The content present in this layer gradually merges with the outer space.

7.3 Elements of Weather and Climate

- The main elements of the atmosphere that keeps on changing and which affects the human life and surroundings are as follows
  - Temperature
  - Pressure
  - Winds
  - Clouds
  - Humidity
  - Precipitation

7 **Mesopause** It is the boundary in the earth's atmosphere lies between the mesosphere and the thermosphere.
8 **Radio Waves** These are long wave radiations that are used for telecommunication.

Mind Map

COMPOSITION AND STRUCTURE OF ATMOSPHERE

1 Composition of the Atmosphere

Ozone
- It is found between 10-50 km above Earth's surface.
- It absorbs ultraviolet rays coming from the sun.

Carbon-dioxide
- It is transparent to incoming solar radiation.
- It absorbs terrestrial radiation
- It is responsible for the greenhouse effect.

Water Vapour
- It is a variable gas in the atmosphere.
- Its concentration decreases with height.
- It acts as a blanket, regulating Earth's temperature.
- It helps in maintaining stability and instability in the air.

Dust Particles
- They include ashes, pollens, sea salts, fine soil.
- They help in the formation of clouds.

2 Structure of the Atmosphere

The atmosphere consists of different layers and each layer has different density and temperature.

Exosphere
- This is the uppermost layer of the atmosphere.
- Content present in this layer gradually merges with the outer surface.

Ionosphere
- This layer is located between 80-400 km.
- It helps in reflecting back of radio waves transmitted by Earth.

Mesosphere
- It extends upto 80 km and lies above stratosphere.
- Temperature decreases with increasing altitude.

Troposphere
- It is the lowermost layer of the atmosphere.
- It has an average height of 13 km.
- All climate and weather phenomenon occurs here.

Stratosphere
- This layer lies above troposphere and contains ozone.
- It extends upto height of 50 km from tropopause.

3 Elements of Weather and Climate

- Temperature
- Humidity
- Precipitation
- Clouds
- Winds
- Pressure

NCERT Folder

Multiple Choice Questions

(i) Which one of the following gases constitutes the major portion of the atmosphere?

(a) Oxygen (b) Nitrogen
(c) Argon (d) Carbon dioxide

Ans (b) Nitrogen

(ii) Atmospheric layer important for human being is

(a) Stratosphere (b) Mesosphere
(c) Troposphere (d) Ionosphere

Ans (c) Troposphere

(iii) Sea salt, pollen, ash, smoke-soot, fine oil– these are associated with

(a) Gases (b) Dust particles
(c) Water vapour (d) Meteors

Ans (b) dust particles

(iv) Oxygen gas is in negligible quantity at the height of atmosphere

(a) 90 km (b) 120 km (c) 100 km (d) 150 km

Ans (b) 120 km

(v) Which one of the following gases is transparent to incoming solar radiation and opaque to outgoing terrestrial radiation?

(a) Oxygen (b) Nitrogen
(c) Helium (d) Carbon dioxide

Ans (d) Carbon dioxide

Answer the following questions in about 30 words

(i) What do you understand by atmosphere?

Ans Atmosphere is the mixture of different gases and it envelopes the earth all round. It contains life giving gases like oxygen for humans and animals and carbon dioxide for plants. 99% of total mass of the atmosphere is confined to the height of 32 km from the earth's surface.

(ii) What are the elements of weather and climate?

Ans The elements of weather and climate include temperature, pressure, winds, humidity, clouds and precipitation. These elements constantly changes and have a significant impact on human life on Earth.

(iii) Describe the composition of atmosphere.

Ans The atmosphere consists of gases, water vapour, dust particles, etc. The proportion of gases varies layer to layer. Nitrogen, Oxygen, Argon, Carbon dioxide, etc., are the prominent gases of atmosphere. Atmosphere is divided into different layers depending upon the temperature conditions.

(iv) Why is the troposphere the most important of all the layer of the atmosphere?

Ans Troposphere is the lowermost layer of the atmosphere. Its features are

- Its average height is 13 km.
- Troposphere contains dust particles and water vapours.
- All changes in climate and weather take place in this layer.
- Temperature in this layer decreases at the rate of 1°C for every 165 m of height.
- All phenomena which are important for existence of life like precipitation, clouds, etc. occur only in this layer.

Hence, this is the most important layer for all biological activity.

Answer the following questions in about 150 words

(i) Describe the composition of the atmosphere.

Ans The atmosphere is a mixture of different gases and it envelopes the earth all round. It contains life-giving gases like oxygen for humans and animals and carbon dioxide for plants.

The atmosphere is composed of gases, water vapour and dust particles.

The proportion of gases changes in the higher layers of the atmosphere in such a way that oxygen will be almost in negligible quantity at the height of 120 km. Similarly, carbon dioxide and water vapour are found only up to 90 km from the surface of the earth. Carbon dioxide is meteorologically a very important gas, as it is transparent to the incoming solar radiation but opaque to the outgoing terrestrial radiation and reflects back some part of it towards the earth's surface. It is largely responsible for the greenhouse effect. Ozone is another important component of the atmosphere. It is found between 10 and 50 km above the earth's surface and acts as a filter. It absorbs the ultra-violet rays, radiating from the sun. It prevents them from reaching the surface of the earth.

(ii) Draw a suitable diagram for the structure of the atmosphere and label it and describe it.

Ans On the basis of composition of gases, the atmosphere can be divided into following parts

(i) **Troposphere** It is the lowermost layer of the atmosphere. Its average height is 13 km. The thickness of the troposphere is greatest at the equator because heat is transported to great heights by strong convectional currents. All weather and climate related prominent incidents occur in this layer.

(ii) **Stratosphere** It is found above the tropopause and extends up to a height of 50 km. This layer is characterised by the presence of ozone layer which protects us from the ultraviolet rays coming from the sun.

(iii) **Mesosphere** It lies above the stratosphere which extends up to a height of 80 km. Temperature decreases with increase in altitude and reaches upto minus 100°C at the height of 80 km.

(iv) **Ionosphere** It is located in between 80 km and 400 km. It contains electrically charged particles known as ions, that is why it is called Ionosphere. The temperature here starts increasing with height that is the reason, it is also known as thermosphere.

(v) **Exosphere** The uppermost layer of the atmosphere above the thermosphere is known as the exosphere. It is the highest layer and gradually merges with the outer space.

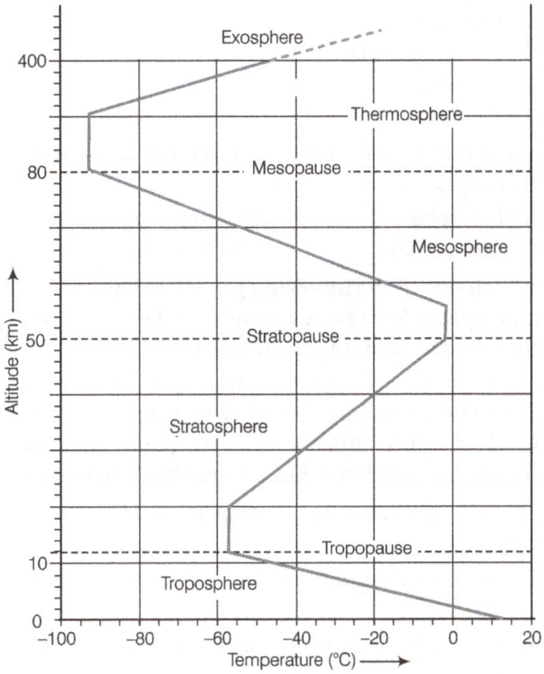

Exam Pattern Questions

Objective Type Questions

Multiple Choice Questions (MCQs)

1. There are two gases in the atmosphere which are found only up to 90 km from the surface of the earth.

Identify the gases from the options.

(a) Carbon dioxide and water vapour
(b) Water and argon
(c) Helium and neon
(d) Nitrogen and water vapour

2. Which gas is meteorologically a very important gas as it is transparent to the incoming solar radiation but opaque to outgoing terrestrial radiation? CBSE Diksha

(a) Oxygen (b) Methane
(c) Carbon dioxide (d) Nitrogen

3. Which of the following gases is essential for plants?

(a) Oxygen (b) Carbon dioxide
(c) Helium (b) Argon

4. Which of the following gases is largely responsible for the greenhouse effect?

(a) Oxygen (b) CO_2 (c) Xenon (d) Krypton

5. What is the primary function of the ozone layer in the atmosphere?

(a) To absorb infrared radiation
(b) To protect against ultraviolet (UV) radiation
(c) To support cloud formation
(d) To regulate earth's temperature

6. Which of the following is the lowermost layer of the atmosphere?

(a) Stratosphere (b) Troposphere
(c) Mesosphere (d) Ionosphere

7. Identify the layer of the atmosphere that has high concentration of water vapour and dust particles.

(a) Tropopause (b) Stratosphere
(c) Troposphere (d) Mesosphere

8. **How the temperature changes as we ascend from troposphere?**

(a) Increases
(b) Remains constant
(c) Decreases
(d) Fluctuates randomly

9. **What is the name of the layer that lies above the stratosphere?**

(a) Ionosphere (b) Exosphere
(c) Troposphere (d) Mesosphere

10. **Which one of the following groups of layers of atmosphere have been arranged in the sequence as per their height from the earth's surface?**

(a) Mesosphere, troposphere, stratosphere, ionosphere
(b) Stratosphere, troposphere, mesosphere, ionosphere
(c) Troposphere, stratosphere, mesosphere, ionosphere
(d) Mesosphere, ionosphere, troposphere, stratosphere

11. **Consider the following statements and choose the correct one.**

Statement I Oxygen is found in abundance at the height of 120 km.

Statement II Almost zero amount of oxygen is found at the height of 120 km.

Options

(a) Only I (b) Both I and II
(c) None of these (d) Only II

12. **Atmosphere contains which of the following elements?**

(i) Gases (ii) Dust particles (iii) Water vapour

Codes

(a) (i) and (ii) (b) (ii) and (iii)
(c) (i) and (iii) (d) All of these

13. **Dust particles are a mixture of which of the following matters?**

(i) Sea salts (ii) Smoke-soot
(iii) Ash (iv) Pollen, dust

Codes

(a) (i), (ii) and (iii) (b) (i), (iii) and (iv)
(c) (i), (ii) and (iv) (d) All of these

14. **Which of the following statements is correct regarding the earth's atmosphere?**

(i) The air is an integral part of earth's mass.
(ii) 99 per cent of the total mass of atmosphere is confined to the height of 32 km.
(iii) The atmosphere consists of gases only.

Options

(a) (i), (ii), (iii)
(b) (ii) and (iii)
(c) Only (i)
(d) (i) and (ii)

15. **Consider the following statements and choose how many statements are correct.**

(i) The ozone layer is found above the tropopause.
(ii) The radio waves transmitted from the earth are reflected back by ionosphere.
(iii) The ozone layer is located between 15 km and 70 km above the earth's surface.
(iv) The ozone layer absorbs X rays radiating from the sun.

Options

(a) Only two (b) All are correct
(c) Three are correct (d) None of these

Arrange the Following

16. **Identify the type of layer from the description given below.**

This layer acts as a shield for life on earth by giving protection from intense, harmful form of energy i.e. Ultraviolet radiation.

Options

(a) Tropopause (b) Stratosphere
(c) Thermosphere (d) Mesopause

17. **Arrange the following components of the atmosphere based on their location (from nearest to farthest) in relation to the earth's surface.**

(i) Ozone layer (ii) Troposphere
(iii) Stratosphere (iv) Ionosphere

Options

(a) (ii), (iii), (i), (iv) (b) (i), (ii), (iii), (iv)
(c) (iv), (iii), (i), (ii) (d) (ii), (iv), (i), (iii)

18. **Arrange the following atmospheric layers according to their main characteristics from least dense to most dense.**

(i) Troposphere (ii) Stratosphere
(iii) Mesosphere (iv) Thermosphere

Options

(a) (iv), (ii), (iii), (i) (b) (i), (ii), (iii), (iv)
(c) (iii), (iv), (ii), (i) (d) (iv), (iii), (ii), (i)

Match the following

19.

	List I		List II
A.	Troposphere	1.	Contains the ozone layer
B.	Stratosphere	2.	Where weather phenomena occur
C.	Mesosphere	3.	Layer where meteors burn up
D	Thermosphere	4.	Highest layer with very low density

Codes

	A	B	C	D		A	B	C	D
(a)	2	1	3	4	(b)	3	4	1	2
(c)	2	3	1	4	(d)	4	3	2	1

20.

	List I		List II
A.	Troposphere	1.	Extends from 10 km to 50 km above sea level
B.	Stratosphere	2.	Extends from the surface to about 13 km
C.	Mesosphere	3.	Extends from about 50 km to 80 km
D	Thermosphere	4.	Extends from about 80 km to 400 km

Codes

	A	B	C	D		A	B	C	D
(a)	2	1	3	4	(b)	3	4	1	2
(c)	2	3	1	4	(d)	4	3	2	1

Assertion-Reason

Directions (Q. Nos. 21-24) In the questions given below are two statements labelled as Assertion (A) and other is labelled as Reason (R). In the context of two statements which one of the following is correct?

Codes

(a) Both A and R are true, but R is not the correct explanation of A
(b) Both A and R are true and R is the correct explanation of A
(c) Both A and R are incorrect
(d) A is correct, but R is incorrect

21. **Assertion** (A) Atmosphere is a very essential part for human beings as well as for other living organisms.
Reason (R) Atmosphere contains life-giving gases like oxygen for humans and animals.

22. **Assertion** (A) In sub-tropical and temperate regions, concentration of dust particles is high.
Reason (R) It is due to dry winds.

23. **Assertion** (A) The troposphere is the layer of the atmosphere where weather activities occur.
Reason (R) The troposphere contains the majority of the atmosphere's water vapour and aerosols.

24. **Assertion** (A) The stratosphere contains the ozone layer, which protects life on earth from harmful ultraviolet radiation.
Reason (R) Ozone is a greenhouse gas that contributes to global warming.

Answers

1. (a) Carbon dioxide and water vapour
2. (c) Carbon dioxide
3. (b) Carbon dioxide
4. (b) CO_2
5. (b) To protect against ultraviolet (UV) radiation
6. (b) Troposphere
7. (c) Troposphere
8. (c) It decreases
9. (d) Mesosphere
10. (c) Troposphere, stratosphere, mesosphere, ionosphere
11. (d) Only II
12. (d) All of these
13. (d) All of these
14. (d) (i) and (ii)
15. (a) Only two
16. (b) Stratosphere
17. (a) (ii), (iii), (i), (iv)
18. (d) (iv), (iii), (ii), (i)
19. (a)
20. (a)
21. (b) Both A and R are true and R is the correct explanation of A
22. (b) Both A and R are true and R is the correct explanation of A
23. (b) Both A and R are true and R is the correct explanation of A
24. (d) A is correct, but R is incorrect

Subjective Questions

Short Answer Type Questions

1. 'Carbon dioxide is meteorologically a very imporant gas.' Justify the statement. Competency Based Que

Ans The carbon dioxide is meteorologically a very important gas as it is transparent to the incoming solar radiation but opaque to the outgoing terrestrial radiation. Carbon dioxide absorbs a part of terrestrial radiation and reflects back some part of it towards the earth's surface.

In meteorology, CO_2 plays a vital role in predicting weather patterns, climate shifts and the impact of human activity on the environment. By monitoring and controlling CO_2 emissions, we can mitigate the adverse effects of climate change and maintain a balanced, sustainable climate.

2. 'Water vapour contributes to the stability and instability in the air'. Explain. Competency Based Que

Ans Water vapour is a variable gas in the atmosphere. It decreases with altitude. In the warm and humid region, it accounts for 4% of the air by volume but only 1% in dry and polar regions.

Water vapour also decreases from the equator toward the poles. It absorbs part of the insolation from the Sun and preserves the earth's radiated heat. The most significant aspect of water vapour is that it acts like a blanket allowing the earth neither to become too cold nor too hot. In this way, water vapour contributes to the stability and instability in the air.

3. "Water vapour and dust particles are important variable of weather and climate." Explain why.

Ans Water vapour and dust particles are important elements of weather and climate, as they affect the atmosphere and contribute to the water cycle.

Both water vapour and dust particles are the source of all forms of condensation and main absorbers of heat received from the sun or radiated from the earth. Dust particles and salt particles act as hygroscopic nuclei around which water vapour condenses to produce cloud. Hence, water vapour and dust particles are important variables of weather and climate.

4. How does the temperature change with altitude in the different layers of the atmosphere?

Ans In the atmosphere, temperature varies with altitude in distinct patterns across its layers. In the troposphere, temperature decreases as we go at higher altitudes. In this layer most of the weather events occur. In the stratosphere, temperature increases with altitude due to the absorption of UV radiation by the ozone layer, which warms this layer. The mesosphere experiences a decrease in temperature with altitude again, leading to the coldest temperatures ranging in minus in the atmosphere. In the thermosphere, temperatures rise sharply with altitude as solar radiation is absorbed, resulting in very high temperatures.

5. 'Stratosphere acts as a shield for life on earth by giving protection from harmful UV rays'. Elucidate with suitable reason. Competency Based Que

Ans. Stratosphere is one of the layers of atmosphere, this layer lies above the troposphere. This layer extends up to height of 50 km from tropopause. One important feature of stratosphere is that it contains ozone layer. Ozone as a gas has the property to absorb the ultraviolet rays that is released by the Sun. So the presence of ozone in stratosphere acts as a shield for the earth from incoming UV rays and give protection to the earth.

6. Differentiate between mesosphere and ionosphere.

Ans Differences between mesosphere and ionosphere are as follows

Mesosphere	Ionosphere
The mesosphere lies above the stratosphere.	Ionosphere lies above the mesosphere.
It extends upto the 80 km.	It is the thinner layer which starts at a height of 80 km.
In this layer, the temperature starts decreasing with increase in height.	The temperature increases with increase in height.
It is the coldest portion of the atmosphere.	It contains ions that acquire electrical charges when they absorb cosmic rays.
The upper limit of mesosphere is mesopause.	In this layer, radio waves transmitted from the earth are reflected back to the earth.

7. **"Humans may survive for sometimes without food and water but can't survive even a few minutes without breathing air". Point out the factors which are responsible for polluting air. Also discuss the ways which need to be adopted for making the air breathable.** Competency Based Que

Ans Atmosphere contains life-giving gases like oxygen for humans and animals and carbon dioxide for plants. Air which consists of oxygen is the integral part of human life. But due to increasing human activities and using modern medium for comfortability, air is being polluted day by day.

Responsible factors for air pollution are

- Consumption of fossil fuels in the form of coal, petroleum, etc.
- Growing industrialisation without any safety measures for environment.
- Burning of agriculture residue in the farms.

The ways which we need to adopt for making the air breathable are

- We should shift towards renewable source of energy which is eco-friendly and cheap for consumption.
- Appropriate technology should be developed to absorb carbon and other harmful gases from industries.
- Proper guidelines and strict regulations are required to prevent air pollution.
- Sufficient carbon sink should be developed in the form of forestation.

8. **Why is air important and why we should understand the atmosphere in detail?** CBSE Diksha

Ans. Air is essential for life on earth which provides the oxygen necessary for respiration and plays a critical role in regulating temperature through the greenhouse effect. It facilitates weather patterns and climate, influencing ecosystems and agriculture. Understanding the atmosphere in detail is vital for addressing environmental issues such as air pollution, climate change and ozone depletion. Knowledge of atmospheric processes aids in predicting weather, mitigating natural disasters and enhancing human health. Moreover, as global challenges arise, a comprehensive understanding of the atmosphere fosters informed decision-making and sustainable practices to protect the planet for future generations.

Long Answer Type Questions

1. **'Along with gases present in the atmosphere, dust particles also play a crucial role for the earth's atmosphere'. Justify the statement.** Competency Based Que

Ans. Along with the gases, atmosphere has a sufficient capacity to keep small solid particles known as dust particles. Dust particles originate from different sources like sea salts, fine soil, smoke-soot, ash, pollen, dust and disintegrated particles of meteors. These particles are present generally in the lower layers of the atmosphere but sometimes they are transported to the greater heights due to convectional air currents. Dust particles play a significant role in the earth's atmosphere, influencing climate, weather patterns and air quality. These tiny particles, composed of soil, salt and pollutants, serve as nuclei for cloud condensation which helps in the formation of clouds and precipitation. However, excessive dust can degrade air quality, leading to respiratory issues and other health problems.

2. **Give an account of atmosphere and also explain its characteristics.**

Ans The atmosphere is the thin envelop of gases surrounding the earth that forms a protective boundary between the outer space and the biosphere. The atmosphere of the earth is formed by gases from the crust and interior and the exhalations of all life over the time.

Characteristics of Atmosphere

- The uniqueness of earth's atmosphere is that it supports life.
- Atmosphere is composed of balanced amount of life-giving gases such as oxygen for humans and animals and carbon dioxide for plants.
- The composition is so unique that it doesn't cause any combustion in the atmosphere.
- Atmosphere works as a protective boundary between the outer space and the biosphere.
- It also has water vapour and dust particles. Water vapour absorbs parts of the insolation from the sun and preserves the earth's radiated heat. Thus, it acts like a blanket allowing the earth neither to become too hot nor too cold.

3. Differentiate between troposphere and thermosphere.

Ans. The difference between troposphere and thermosphere are given below

	Troposphere	Thermosphere
Location	It is the lowest layer of the atmosphere, extending from the earth's surface up to about 18 km above the earth's surface.	It is located above the mesosphere and below the exosphere between 80 km to 400 km above the earth's surface.
Temperature Trend	The temperature decreases with altitude in this layer.	In this layer temperature increases significantly with increasing altitude
Weather Phenomena	It contains clouds, storms, and all-weather phenomena. This layer is well-mixed due to convection.	In this layer, weather phenomena are absent. However, it contains the auroras (Northern and Southern Lights)
Function	It supports life on earth, regulates climate and is critical for weather systems.	It plays an important role in earth's ionosphere, which is crucial for radio communication and satellite operations.

Source Based Questions

1 Read the passage carefully and answer the questions that follow.

The atmosphere is composed of gases, water vapour and dust particles. The proportion of gases changes in the higher layers of the atmosphere in such a way that oxygen will be almost in negligible quantity at the height of 120 km. Similarly, carbon dioxide and water vapour are found only up to 90 km from the surface of the earth. Carbon dioxide is meteorologically a very important gas as it is transparent to the incoming solar radiation but opaque to the outgoing terrestrial radiation. It absorbs a part of terrestrial radiation and reflects back some part of it towards the earth's surface. It is largely responsible for the greenhouse effect. The volume of other gases is constant but the volume of carbon dioxide has been rising in the past few decades mainly because of the burning of fossil fuels. This has also increased the temperature of the air. Ozone is another important component of the atmosphere found between 10 and 50 km above the earth's surface and acts as a filter and absorbs the ultraviolet rays radiating from the sun and prevents them from reaching the surface of the earth.

Water vapour is also a variable gas in the atmosphere, which decreases with altitude. In the warm and wet tropics, it may account for four per cent of the air by volume, while in the dry and cold areas of desert and polar regions, it may be less than one per cent of the air. Water vapour also decreases from the equator towards the poles.

It also absorbs parts of the insolation from the sun and preserves the earth's radiated heat. It thus, acts like a blanket allowing the earth neither to become too cold nor too hot. Dust particles are generally concentrated in the lower layers of the atmosphere; yet, convectional air currents may transport them to great heights. The higher concentration of dust particles is found in sub-tropical and temperate regions due to dry winds in comparison to equatorial and polar regions. Dust and salt particles act as hygroscopic nuclei around which water vapour condenses to produce clouds.

(i) Which of the following gas is primarily responsible for the heating of atmosphere?

(a) Oxygen
(b) Water vapour
(c) Carbon dioxide
(d) Both (b) and (c)

Ans (d) Both (b) and (c)

(ii) Dust particles are found in large quantities in which of the following regions?

(a) Polar region (b) Rainforests
(c) Tropical Region (d) Tundra region

Ans (c) Tropical Region

(iii) Which of the following helps in maintaining the balance of earth's temperature?

(a) Rivers (b) Ozone
(c) Water vapour (d) Ocean

Ans (c) Water vapour

2. Read the passage carefully and answer the questions that follow.

The atmosphere consists of different layers with varying density and temperature. Density is highest near the surface of the earth and decreases with increasing altitude. The column of atmosphere is divided into five different layers depending upon the temperature condition. They are: troposphere, stratosphere, mesosphere, thermosphere and exosphere. The troposphere is the lowermost layer of the atmosphere. Its average height is 13 km and extends roughly to a height of 8 km near the poles and about 18 km at the equator. Thickness of the troposphere is greatest at the equator because heat is transported to great heights by strong convectional currents. This layer contains dust particles and water vapour. All changes in climate and weather take place in this layer. The temperature in this layer decreases at the rate of 1°C for every 165 m of height. This is the most important layer for all biological activity. The zone separating the troposphere from stratosphere is known as the tropopause. The air temperature at the tropopause is about minus 80°C over the equator and about minus 45°C over the poles. The temperature here is nearly constant, and hence, it is called the tropopause. The stratosphere is found above the tropopause and extends up to a height of 50 km. One important feature of the stratosphere is that it contains the ozone layer. This layer absorbs ultraviolet radiation and shields life on the earth from intense, harmful form of energy.

(i) What is the reason behind the greater thickness of the troposphere at the equator compared to the poles?

Ans. The troposphere is thicker around the equator as compared to poles due to presence of strong convectional currents at equator that moves heat at higher altitudes and allows the layer to extend further upward.

(ii) How might life on earth be different without the ozone layer in the stratosphere?

Ans. In the absence of ozone, life could be severely damaged or impossible due to exposure to harmful ultraviolet radiation reaching earth's surface.

(iii) Why could the troposphere be considered the most crucial atmospheric layer for earth's inhabitants?

Ans. Troposphere contains essential elements like water vapour and is responsible for all weather phenomena and supports all biological activity.

3. Study the following graph and answer the questions that follow.

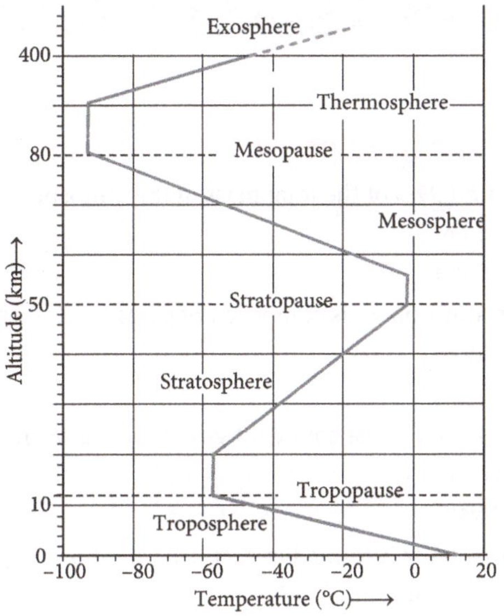

(i) What do you mean by the tropopause zone and also mention its significance ?

Ans. The tropopause is the boundary between the troposphere and the stratosphere, where the temperature is nearly constant.This layer marks the transition to the next atmospheric layer, the stratosphere.

(ii) What is the main feature of the exosphere?

Ans The exosphere is the outermost layer of the atmosphere, and it gradually merges with outer space.

(iii) What happens to the temperature as we go higher in the troposphere?

Ans. The temperature decreases by 1°C for every 165 meters of height in the troposphere.

SELF ASSESSMENT TEST

Objective Type Questions

1. Around 99% of the total mass of the atmosphere is confined at what height?
   (a) 15 km (b) 13 km
   (c) 25 km (d) 32 km
2. The atmosphere is composed of gases .... and dust particles.
   (a) clouds (b) precipitation
   (c) sun (d) water vapour
3. The second most abundant gas in the atmosphere is ....
   (a) Oxygen (b) CO_2
   (c) Neon (d) Krypton
4. Ozone layer is found between .... above the earth's surface.
   (a) 3 to 5 km (b) 10 to 50 km
   (c) 12 to 30 km (d) 30 to 60 km
5. Water vapour contributes to which of the following in the atmosphere?
   (a) Temperature regulation only
   (b) Stability and instability in the air
   (c) Only the cooling of the earth
   (d) Only the heating of the earth
6. What is the role of the ionosphere in communication?
   (i) It absorbs radio waves.
   (ii) It reflects radio waves back to earth.
   (iii) It allows radio waves to pass through to space.
   Choose the correct option
   (a) Only one (b) Only two (c) All of these (d) None of these

Short Answer Type Questions

7. The proportion of gases changes in the higher layers of the atmosphere. Write a short note on this statement.
8. How does the amount of water vapour differ in tropical regions compared to desert and polar regions?
9. Carbon dioxide is meteorologically a very important gas. Briefly explain the importance of carbon dioxide on earth.

Long Answer Type Questions

10. Discuss the composition of the Earth's atmosphere and explain how the proportion of gases, water vapour and dust particles change with increasing altitude.
11. What are the main differences between the troposphere and stratosphere in terms of temperature variation, composition and the occurrence of weather phenomena?
12. What are the main elements of the atmosphere?Discuss their role in influencing daily weather and long-term climate patterns.

8

CHAPTER

This chapter deals with the study of solar radiation[1], its distribution and its impact on Earth's temperature and heat balance. It examines hour energy coming from the sun influences global temperature patterns, climate and atmospheric conditions.

The Earth is surrounded by atmosphere which contains different gases. It receives most of its energy from the Sun through the incoming solar radiation. It maintains its temperature by reflecting back the energy received from the Sun.

YOUR STUDY GOALS

8.1 Insolation

8.2 Heating and Cooling of the Atmosphere

8.3 Temperature

YOUR PRACTICE GOAL

- Objective Type Questions (29 Qs ; MCQs, Statements, Matching, A-R)
- Subjective Questions (11 SAs, 7 LAs)
- Source/Graph Based Questions (4 Qs)

Solar Radiation, Heat Balance and Temperature

- Different surfaces and features on the Earth radiate heat in varying amount. This variation creates pressure difference in the atmosphere. As there is pressure difference, this results in the transfer of heat from one region to another by winds.

8.1 Insolation

- The Earth is Geoid in shape which is similar to a sphere. The Sun rays fall sidewise at the top of the atmosphere.
- Earth receives very small amount of solar energy. On an average, Earth receives 1.94 calorie per sq. cm per minute at the top of the atmosphere.
- The energy received by Earth is in the form of incoming solar radiation, which is also called **insolation**. This radiation is in the form of short-wave length.
- The Sun's radiation received at the top of atmosphere varies yearly because of change in the distance between the Earth and the Sun.
- On 4th July, the Earth is farthest from the Sun (152 million km) during its revolution and this position is known as **aphelion**.
- On 3rd January, the Earth is closest to the Sun (147 million km) and this position is known as **perihelion**.

1 Radiation It is the emission of energy in the forms of rays or waves.

- Therefore, the annual insolation received on 3rd January is more than the amount of insolation received on 4th July.
- These small variations in solar output don't have a major impact on our daily weather. This is because factors like land and water distribution and atmospheric circulation play a much bigger role in influencing daily weather patterns.

Variability of Insolation at the Surface of the Earth

- The amount and intensity of insolation received by the Earth is different during a day, in a season and in a year.
- There are certain factors that influence the insolation received by the Earth. These are as follows
    (i) The rotation of Earth on its axis
    (ii) The angle of inclination of the Sun's rays
    (iii) The length of the day
    (iv) The transparency of the atmosphere.
    (v) The variation of physical features on the land including their direction.

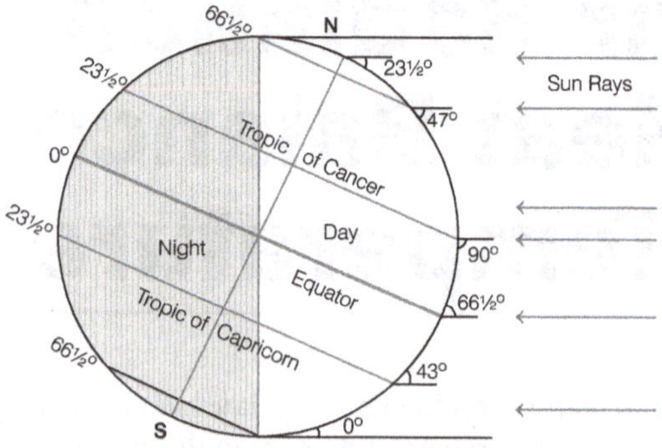

▲ *Summer Solstice*

- Earth makes an angle of **66½ degrees** with the plane of its orbit. This inclination has a great influence on the amount of insolation received at different latitudes.
- The angle of inclination of the Sun's rays depends upon the latitude of a place. The higher latitude areas receive slanting sun rays as they make less angle with the surface of the Earth.
- Slanting rays covers more area than the vertical rays. If more area is covered, the energy received by that area is less.
- Slanting rays passes through the layers of atmosphere and hence they go through the process of absorption, scattering and diffusion.

The Passage of Solar Radiation through the Atmosphere

- The incoming solar radiation passes through the layers of atmosphere before reaching the surface of the Earth.
- The particles present in the troposphere like water vapour, ozone and other gases absorb the near **infrared radiations**[2].
- Dust particles present in the atmosphere in the form of small solid particles also scatters the **visible spectrum**[3] towards the Earth and to the outer space.
- The red colour during sunrise and sunset and the blue colour of the sky is because of this process of scattering.

Spatial Distribution of Insolation at the Earth's Surface

- The insolation received at the surface of the tropical area is about **320Watt/m^2** while polar area receives insolation of about **70Watt/m^2**.
- The subtropical area receives maximum amount of insolation because of less cloudiness in the area. Equatorial area receives less insolation as compared to tropical area.
- At the same latitude, amount of insolation received over the continents is more than insolation received over the oceans.
- Insolation received by different latitudes is also different. During winters, high and middle latitude's receive less insolation than in summer.

---

2 **Near infrared Radiation** It is a type of electromagnetic radiation that is visible to human eyes and has wavelength of 750-2500 nanometer.
3 **Visible Spectrum** It is a part of electromagnetic spectrum which is visible to human eyes and has wavelength of 400-700 nanometer.

Quick Test 1

1 What is the name of the position when the Earth is closest to the Sun?
2 At what angle the Earth inclined to the plane of its orbit?
3 On which date the Earth is farthest to the Sun?
4 Name one factor that influences the insolation received by the Earth.
5 What amount of insolation is received by polar and equatorial area?

8.2 Heating and Cooling of the Atmosphere

There are different ways by which the heating and cooling of the Earth's atmosphere takes place. These ways are discussed below

Conduction

- This is the process in which there is transfer of heat from lower layer of the atmosphere to the upper layers.
- This process starts when the Earth gets heated up and transmits heat to the atmospheric layers in the form of long wave radiations.
- The air in contact with the land starts heating slowly and upper layer which is in contact with the lower layer also gets heated up.
- Conduction takes place when two bodies of different temperature are in contact with one another and the energy flows from warmer to the cooler body.
- The process continues until the temperature of both bodies become equal or the process stops only when the contact between bodies is broken.

Convection

- The air after getting heated up rises vertically in the form of currents and then it transmits heat to the atmosphere.
- This vertical heating of the atmosphere is known as 'Convection'. This process of transfer of heat only takes place in the troposphere.

Advection

- In this process, the heat is transferred by the horizontal movement of the air.
- The effect of advection can be seen in the diurnal (day and night) weather variations taking place in the middle latitudes.
- In tropical areas, specially in Northern India during summer season, a local wind blows known as 'Loo[4]'. It is also the result of advection.

Terrestrial Radiation

- The Earth after being heated up by short wave radiations from Sun becomes a radiating body. It radiates energy to the atmosphere in the form of long wave radiations. This radiation helps in heating the atmosphere and this process is called as 'Terrestrial Radiation'.
- The long wave radiation is absorbed by the gases present in the atmosphere specially carbon dioxide and other greenhouse gases[5].
- The absorbed heat is transmitted back to the space by the atmosphere. By this process, the heat is balanced on the Earth which helps in maintaining its temperature.

4 Loo This is a hot dry and dusty wind that blows during summers in Northern plains of India.
5 Greenhouse gases These are some gases that trap the heat in the atmosphere and raises the temperature of Earth.

Heat Budget of the Earth

- The Heat budget is defined as the balance between the incoming solar radiation and the outgoing terrestrial radiation. If this balance is not maintained the Earth would become either too cold or too hot.
- The Earth maintains its temperature through terrestrial radiation. This happens when the amount of received radiation is equal to the amount of radiation lost by the Earth.
- Different features on the Earth radiates different amount of energy. The amount of radiation reflected back by various sources is known as **albedo of the Earth.**

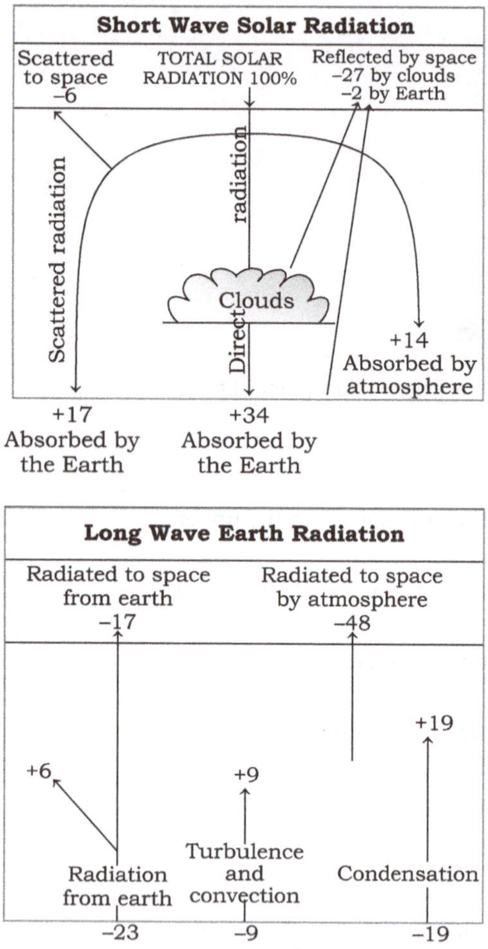

▲ *Heat Budget of the Earth*

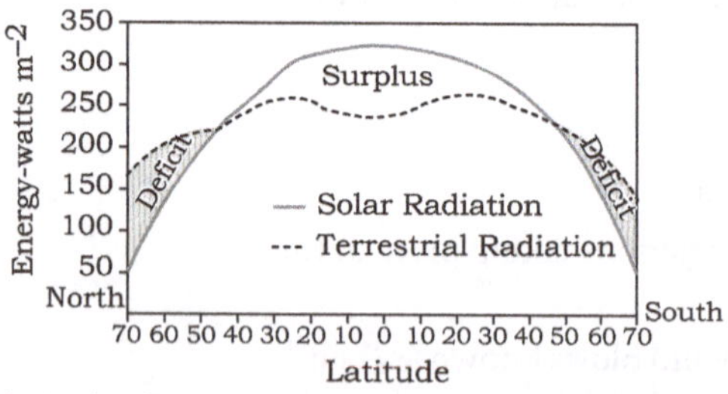

▲ *Latitudinal variation in net radiation balance*

Estimation of Radiation

- The insolation received at the top of the atmosphere is **100 units**, while passing through the atmosphere some amount of energy is scattered, absorbed and reflected.
- Only 35 units are reflected back to the space before reaching the Earth surface. Out of these, 27 units are reflected from the top of the clouds and 2 units are reflected from the snow and ice-covered area.
- Remaining 65 units reaches the Earth, out of which 14 units are absorbed within the atmosphere and 51 units are absorbed by the Earth's surface.
- The Earth radiates back 51 units in the form of terrestrial radiation. Out of these, 17 units are radiated to space directly and 34 units are absorbed by the atmosphere.
- Within this 34 units of the atmosphere, 6 units are absorbed directly by atmosphere, 9 units is absorbed through convection and turbulence[6] and 19 units through latent heat of condensation[7].
- 48 units absorbed by the atmosphere (14 units from insolation +34 units by terrestrial radiation) is also radiated back to the space. Thus, the total radiation returning from the Earth and the atmosphere is 17+ 48 = 65 units. This balances the 65 units received from the Sun.

Variation in the Net Heat Budget at the Earth's Surface

- There are variations in the amount of radiation received at the Earth's surface. Some part of Earth has excess radiation balance while other part has deficit balance.
- There are latitudinal variations in the net radiation balance, for example 40°N and S latitude receives surplus net radiation while region near the poles have a deficit net radiation.
- The surplus heat energy from the tropics is distributed towards the poles. This protects the tropical region from becoming too hot and polar region from becoming permanently frozen.

Quick Test 2

1. Which process involves the vertical movement of heated air in the atmosphere?
2. Where is the local wind 'loo' primarily found during the summer season?
3. What phenomenon causes the Earth's atmosphere to be indirectly heated?
4. How much heat does the Earth radiate back into space through terrestrial radiation?

6 **Turbulence** Chaotic flow of air inthe Earth's atmosphere.
7 **Condensation** It is the process by which a vapour or gas is converted into a liquid.

8.3 Temperature

- The temperature is the measurement of how hot or cold a thing or a place is. This is measured in degrees.
- The interaction of insolation with the atmosphere and Earth surface creates heat and this heat is measured in temperature. Heat represents how molecules in a substance is moving.

Factors affecting temperature Distribution

The Latitude

- The temperature of a place depends upon the insolation received at that place.
- Since, insolation varies according to the latitudes, therefore temperature also varies latitudinally.

The Altitude

- As the atmosphere is indirectly heated by the terrestrial radiation, there is temperature difference between places situated at sea level and at high altitudes.
- The places near the sea-level have higher temperature than the places situated at high altitude.
- The temperature decreases as one goes from low height to high height. The rate of decrease of temperature with height is termed as **Normal Lapse Rate** and this is equal to **6.5°C/km**.

Distance from the Sea

- Sea water gets heated up and cools down slowly while land heats up and cools down quickly. This creates variation in temperature over sea and land.
- The places situated near the sea experiences moderate temperature. This is because of the presence of land and sea breezes which moderates the temperature.

Air Mass and Ocean Currents

- The places which comes under the influence of warm air mass experiences higher temperature and the place under the influence of cold air mass experiences low temperature.
- Ocean currents[8] also affects the temperature of a place. Places located near the coast where warm currents flow have higher temperature while the places located on coast where cold currents flow have lower temperature.

Distribution of Temperature

- The temperature pattern of January and July shows the global distribution of temperature.
- The distribution of temperature is shown through **isotherms**. *Isotherms* are the lines joining places having equal value of temperature. Isotherms runs parallel to the latitude.
- In Northern hemisphere, January month shows more differences in the general trend of isotherm as compared to July month.
- Effects of landmass and ocean currents on temperature pattern is more noticeable in Northern hemisphere because of large land surface area as compared to Southern hemisphere.

Temporal Distribution

- In January, the isotherms shift to the North over the oceans and to the South over the continents. This shift can be noticed in the North Atlantic oceans.
- The North Atlantic ocean becomes warmer because of the presence of warm currents like Gulf Stream and North Atlantic drift. Hence, the isotherms bend towards the North.
- Over the land area, there is Southward bend of isotherm in Europe. This is much noticeable in Siberian plain.

---

8 Ocean Currents It is a continuous and directed movement of ocean water generated by number of forces.

- The mean **January** temperature along 60°E longitude and 80°N and 50°N latitude is -20°C.
- The mean monthly January temperature is over 27°C in oceans near equators. In tropical area it is 24°C, in middle latitudes the temperature is around 2°C to 0°C and in Eurasian continent interior it is -18°C to -48°C.
- In Southern hemisphere, the isotherms are more or less parallel to the latitudes and there is less variation in temperature as compared to Northern hemisphere.
- In Southern hemisphere, temperature near 35°S latitude is 20°C, near 45°S latitude is 10°C and near 60°S latitude is 0°C.
- In **July**, the isotherms are parallel to the latitude. The oceans in the equatorial region are warmer having temperature of 27°C.
- Temperature over the land area in the sub-tropical continental region of Asia is more than 30°C. Along 40°N and 40°S, the temperature value is same that is 10°C.
- The **highest range of temperature** between January and July is observed to be more than 60°C. This is near North-Eastern part of Eurasia and this is due to the factor of Continentality[9].
- The least range of temperature is 3°C and this is found between 20°S and 15°N latitudes.

Inversion of Temperature

- When the temperature increases as we go to higher elevation, it is called as inversion of temperature.
- Inversion of temperature usually happens for a short period of time. Favourable conditions that are required for inversion of temperature are
  - Long winter nights when the sky is clear.
  - The air present in the region should be calm and stable.
- Smoke and dust particles are trapped under the inversion layer and they spread horizontally and fill the gap in the lower layer of the atmosphere.
- Inversion of temperature causes dense fogs in mornings specially during winters. This inversion last for few hours until the Sun rises.
- Over polar areas, temperature inversion occurs throughout the year.
- Another type of inversion called **surface inversion** helps in maintaining the stability of the lower layer of the atmosphere.
- The inversion of temperature in hills and mountains occurs due to air drainage. In hilly areas, cold air is produced during night. These heavy and dense air flows downslope under the influence of gravity.
- These cold air moves down the slope like water to fill the deep valley bottoms. Warm air lies above this cold air in the valley. This is called **Air drainage** which protects plants from frost[10] damages.

Terms to Know

- **Plank's Law** States that a hot body radiates more energy and this energy is in the form of short-wave radiation.
- **Specific heat** It is the energy needed to increase the temperature of one gram of substance by one degree Celsius.

Quick Test 3

1. Which process is responsible for the vertical heating of the atmosphere?
2. Which part of the Earth gets surplus heat energy?
3. What is the value of normal lapse rate?
4. Mention one ideal condition for the occurrence of inversion of temperature.

---

9 Continentality This is a measure of how a place's climate is affected by its distance from the ocean and ocean air.
10 Frost It is a thin layer of ice forms on the ground and other surfaces, especially at night when the temperature falls below 0 degrees.

Mind Map

SOLAR RADIATION, HEAT BALANCE AND TEMPERATURE

1 Insolation

- The energy received by Earth is called insolation.
- When the Earth is farthest from Sun during its revolution, it is known as aphelion.
- When it is closest to the Sun, it is known as perihelion.

Factors affecting Variability of Insolation

- Angle of inclination
- Length of day
- Angle of Sun's rays
- Transparency of atmosphere
- Configuration of land

2 Heating and Cooling of Atmosphere

- Earth's atmosphere is heated by different processes
- **Convection** This is vertical air movement (heat transfer). The process of transfer of heat only takes place in troposphere.
- **Advection** This is horizontal heat transfer by wind. Its effect can be seen in the diurnal when weather variation takes place in the middle latitude.
- **Conduction** This is direct transfer of heat from Earth's surface to air. It takes place when two bodies of different temperature are in contact with one another and energy flows from warmer to cooler body.
- **Terrestrial Radiation** Radiation by Earth's surface in the form of long wave. It helps in heating the atmosphere.

3 Heat Budget of the Earth

It is defined as the balance between incoming solar radiation and outgoing terrestrial radiation.

Latitudinal Variation in Net Radiation Balance

- **Tropics** These areas receive surplus of insolation.
- **Poles** These areas are deficit of insolation.

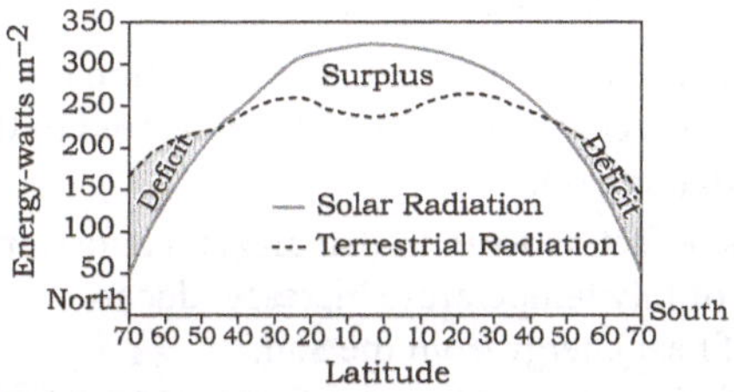

4 Temperature

Distribution of Temperature

- **Normal Lapse Rate** Temperature decreases at the rate of 6.5°C/km above Earth's surface
- **Inversion of Temperature** Temperature increases with height.

Factor Influencing Temperature Distribution

- **Latitude** Temperature of a place depends upon the insolation received at that place as insolation varies according to the latitudes.
- **Altitude** Temperature decreases from low height to high height.
- **Proximity to Water** Places situated near the sea experience moderate temperature.
- **Ocean Currents** Places located near the coast have higher temperature while places located on coast have lower temperature.

NCERT Folder

Multiple Choice Questions

(i) The Sun is directly overhead at noon on 21st June at

(a) the equator (b) 23.5° S (c) 23.5° N (d) 66.5° N

Ans (c) 23.5° N

(ii) In which one of the following cities, are the days the longest?

(a) Thiruvananthapuram (b) Chandigarh
(c) Hyderabad (d) Nagpur

Ans (b) Chandigarh

(iii) The atmosphere is mainly heated by the

(a) Short wave solar radiation
(b) Reflected solar radiation
(c) Long wave terrestrial radiation
(d) Scattered solar radiation

Ans (c) Long wave terrestrial radiation.

(iv) Make correct pairs from the following columns.

(i)	Insolation	(a)	The difference between the mean temperature of the warmest and the coldest month.
(ii)	Albedo	(b)	The lines joining the places of equal temperature.
(iii)	Isotherm	(c)	The incoming solar radiation.
(iv)	Annual range	(d)	The percentage of visible light reflected by an object.

Ans (i) → (c), (ii) → (d), (iii) → (b), (iv) → (a)

(v) The main reason that the earth experiences highest temperature in the subtropics in the Northern Hemisphere rather than at the equator is

(a) Sub-tropical areas tend to have less cloud cover than equatorial areas.
(b) Sub-tropical areas have longer day hours in the summer than the equatorial.
(c) Sub-tropical areas have an enhanced 'green house effect' compared to equatorial areas.
(d) Sub-tropical areas are nearer to the oceanic areas than the equatorial locations.

Ans (a) Sub-tropical areas tend to have less cloud cover than equatorial areas.

Answer the following questions in about 30 words

(i) How does the unequal distribution of heat over the planet earth in space and time cause variations in weather and climate?

Ans The amount of heat received by different parts of the Earth is not the same. In equatorial region, the heat is received more and hence, more evaporation occurs. Therefore, these areas have hot and humid climate.

In same way, in temperate region the heat is received less and hence, these regions have cold and dry climate.

(ii) What are the factors that control temperature distribution on the surface of the Earth?

Ans The factors controlling temperature distribution are

- **Latitude** The temperature of a place depends on the insolation received.
- **Altitude** The temperature generally decreases with increasing height.
- **Distance from Sea** The temperature is influenced by the location of a place with respect to the sea.
- **Airmass and Ocean Currents** The passage of air masses also affects the temperature.

(iii) In India, why is the day temperature maximum in May and why not after the summer solstice?

Ans In India, the Sun reaches on the Tropic of Cancer on 21st June but May is accounted as the hottest month because of the following reasons

- Before summer solstice, the Sun covers a large portion of Indian peninsula and the sunrays are perpendicular to that region.
- At that time due to high amount of heat, evaporation is very high.
- Atmost of the places, condensation does not occur which causes high temperature in many parts of India.
- From 1st June onwards, monsoon reaches to Indian sub- continent with sufficient amount of rainfall and cloud, temperature is not able to increase.

(iv) Why is the annual range of temperature high in the Siberian plains?

Ans Annual range of temperature is high in the Siberian plains due to the following reasons

- Siberia is located at 60° E longitude and around 60° N latitude. Hence, continental effect could be seen in the climate of that region.
- There is less effect of ocean in that area, therefore, in the month of July temperature increases due to presence of heat energy from the Sun.
- In January, when the sun is at the Tropic of Capricorn, temperature falls to minus 20° C and there is no advection due to its latitudinal and longitudinal position and hence, annual range of temperature is high.

Answer the following questions in about 150 words

(i) How do the latitude and the tilt in the axis of rotation of the Earth affect the amount of radiation received at the Earth's surface?

Ans The rotation of the Earth on the tilted axis and the angle of inclination of the Sun rays i.e. latitudinal difference affect the amount of radiation received at the Earth's surface in the following ways

- **Latitude** The angle of inclination of the Sun's rays depends on the latitude of a place. The higher the latitude, the less is the angle they make with the surface of the Earth. This results in slant Sun rays. Slant sun rays cover more area hence, the energy gets distributed and the net energy received per unit area decreases. Since angle of incidence is always higher between the Tropic of Cancer and Capricorn, hence temperature is high.
- **Rotation of the Earth** The earth rotates on the tilted axis and the earth's axis makes an angle of $66\frac{1^\circ}{2}$ with the plane of its orbit round the sun. It has a greater influence on the amount of insolation received at different latitudes. This tilted axis causes movement of the sun from the Tropic of Cancer to the Tropic of Capricorn. When the Sun comes at the Tropic of Cancer on 21st June, it is called summer solstice. At this situation, Sun rays cover maximum area of the Northern Hemisphere hence, the Northern Hemisphere is warm in comparision to the Southern Hemisphere. In same way, when the Sun reaches on the Tropic of Capricorn, it is known as winter solstice. At this situation, the Southern Hemisphere is more warm than the Northern Hemisphere.

(ii) Discuss the processes through which the Earth atmospheric system maintains heat balance.

Ans There are variations in the amount of radiation received at the earth's surface due to different factors. Some part of the earth has surplus radiation balance and some part has deficit radiation balance in the surface atmosphere.

Inspite of all these facts, the Earth's atmosphere succeed to maintain the heat balance.

Factors behind maintaining heat balance are

- **Terrestrial Radiation** The insolation received by the earth is in short wave form and heats up its surface. Later, earth radiates its energy to the atmosphere in long wave form which heats up the atmosphere from below.
  The long wave radiation is absorbed by the atmospheric gases particularly by carbon dioxide. The atmosphere in turn radiates and transmits heat to the space i.e. the amount of heat received from the Sun is returned to space. This process is responsible for maintaining constant temperature at the Earth and in the atmosphere.
- **Process of Conduction** The Earth transmits the heat to the atmospheric layers near to the earth in long wave form. The air in contact with the land gets heated slowly and the upper layers in contact with the lower layers also get heated. This process of conduction is important in heating the lower layers of the atmosphere.
- **Process of Convection** The air in contact with the earth rises vertically on heating in the form of currents and further transmits the heat of the atmosphere through the process of convection.
- **Process of Advection** Advection is the transfer of heat through horizontal movement of air.

Through these processes, the Earth's surface and the atmosphere maintain the heat balance.

(iii) Compare the global distribution of temperature in January over the Northern and the Southern hemisphere of the Earth.

Ans The global distribution of temperature can be understood with the study of isotherm lines which are the lines joining places having equal temperature.

The comparison of the global distribution of temperature in January over the Northern and Southern Hemisphere of the earth can be seen through the following points

Northern Hemisphere	Southern Hemisphere
The effect of land is well observed in this region.	The effect of ocean is well observed in this region. Isotherms are more or less parallel to the latitudes.
In the month of January, the deviation in isotherm line is more. Due to larger land surface area, the isotherms deviate to the North over the ocean and to the South over the continent.	Since, continental part is less in the Southern Hemisphere, so deviation of isotherm line is less.
In the month of January, temperature decreases sharply over the continental part of the Northern Hemisphere. Although in North Atlantic ocean, the presence of warm ocean currents, Gulf Stream, North Atlantic drift make the oceans warmer.	The variation of temperature is less in comparison to the Northern Hemisphere.
In the Siberian region, the mean January temperature is minus 20°C due to continental temperate climate. Whereas the mean monthly temperature for Januray over tropics is 24°C and 2°C-0°C in middle latitudes.	In the month of January, the isotherms of 20°C, 10°C and 0°C runs parallel to 35°S 45°S and 60°S latitude, respectively.

Exam Pattern Questions

Objective Type Questions

Multiple Choice Questions (MCQs)

1. Choose the incorrect statement regarding insolation.
(a) The Sun rays fall sidewise at the top of the atmosphere.
(b) Earth receives 3.0 calorie per sq cm per minute at the top of the atmosphere.
(c) This radiation is in the form of short-wave length.
(d) Insolation received on the Earth is not uniform.

2. On which of the following days Aphelion is observed?
(a) 31st December (b) 30th June
(c) 4th July (d) 1st August

3. Which of the following factors does not significantly influence the amount of solar energy received at the Earth's surface?
(a) Angle of incidence of solar rays
(b) Distance from the Earth to the Sun
(c) Composition of the atmosphere
(d) Lunar gravitational pull

4. Within the troposphere which of the following absorbs much of the near infrared radiation?
(a) Water Vapour (b) Ozone
(c) Gases (d) All of these

5. Which of the following phenomenon takes place when two bodies of unequal temperature are in contact with one another?
(a) Convection (b) Advection
(c) Conduction (d) None of these

6. Consider the following statement regarding conduction and choose the correct statements.
(a) In this process, there is transfer of heat from upper layer of the atmosphere to the lower layers.
(b) Conduction takes place when two bodies of different temperature are in contact.
(c) The energy flows from the cooler body to warmer body.
(d) the process continues even after the bodies are not in contact with each other.

7. Convection only occurs in which of the following layers of the atmosphere?
(a) Stratosphere (b) Troposphere
(c) Mesosphere (d) Thermosphere

8. The transfer of heat through horizontal movement of air called **CBSE Diksha**
(a) Conduction (b) Convection
(c) Advection (d) Heat budget

9. Which of the following is the perfect balance between incoming heat absorbed by the earth and outgoing heat escaping it in the form of radiation?
(a) Conduction (b) Convection
(c) Advection (d) Heat Budget

10. There are latitudinal variations in the net radiation balance. Which region receives surplus amount of heat energy?
(a) 40° N and S latitude (b) 90° N and S latitude
(c) 0° N and S latitude (d) 10° N and S latitude

11. What happens to solar energy as it enters the Earth's atmosphere?
(a) It is entirely absorbed by land and water surfaces.
(b) It is evenly distributed between the troposphere and stratosphere.
(c) It is partly reflected, absorbed and scattered.
(d) It passes through without any interaction.

12. Which of the following statement is incorrect? **CBSE Diksha**
(a) The process of vertical heating of the atmosphere is known as convection.
(b) the reflected amount of radiation is known as Albedo of the Earth.
(c) The long wave radiation is absorbed by the atmospheric gases particularly by carbon dioxide and other greenhouse gases.
(d) The insolation received by the Earth is in the form of long wave and heats up the surface.

13. Which of the following best explains why the heat distribution varies between land and water bodies?
(a) Water has a higher albedo than land.
(b) Land absorbs and releases heat more slowly than water.
(c) Water has a higher heat capacity and can store more energy.
(d) Land surfaces reflect more solar radiation than water bodies.

14. Identify the type of process of heat transfer from the given description.
In this process, the heat is transferred by the horizontal movement of the air. The effects can be seen in the diurnal (day and night) weather variations taking place in the middle latitudes. Local level wind in Northern India called Loo is the result of this type of process of heat transfer to the atmosphere.
(a) Terrestrial radiation (b) Conduction
(c) Advection (d) Convection

15. **Which of the following is incorrectly matched?**

(a) 4th July – Aphelion
(b) 3rd January – Perihelion
(c) 66½ degrees _ Earth's inclination
(d) 40° N and S _ Minimum insolation

16. **Which of the following is/are the factors responsible for variation in insolation?**

I. The rotation of the Earth on its Axis.
II. The length of the Day.
III. Transparency of the Atmosphere.

Codes

(a) I and II (b) I and III
(c) II and III (d) All of these

17. **The Heat budget is defined as the balance between the incoming solar radiation and the outgoing terrestrial radiation. Choose the incorrect statement about the heat budget of the Earth.**

(i) Different features on the Earth radiates same amount of energy.
(ii) 35 units are reflected back to the space before reaching the Earth surface.
(iii) The Earth radiates back 51 units in the form of terrestrial radiation.
(iv) 48 units absorbed by the atmosphere (14 units from insolation +34 units by terrestrial radiation).

Options

(a) Statements (i) and (ii) (b) Only (i)
(c) Only ii (d) Statements (ii) and (iii)

18. **Identify the statement that is not true with regard to factors affecting the temperature distribution.**

(i) The temperature of a place depends upon the insolation received at that place.
(ii) The temperature increases as we go from lower height to higher height.
(iii) The difference in the temperature of air masses does not affects the temperature of a place.
(iv) Places located near the coast where warm currents flow have higher temperature.

Options

(a) Statements (i) and (ii)
(b) Only (iv)
(c) Only (ii)
(d) Statements (ii) and (iii)

19. **Which of the following phenomena are arranged in the sequence as per their date of occurrence?**

(a) Aphelion, Perihelion, Summer Solstice, Winter Solstice
(b) Perihelion, Summer Solstice, Aphelion, Winter Solstice
(c) Perihelion, Aphelion, Winter Solstice, Summer Solstice
(d) Winter Solstice, Summer Solstice, Perihelion, Aphelion

Arrange the Following

20. **Arrange the following processes involved in the solar radiation pathway from the Sun to the Earth's surface.**

(i) Reflection by clouds
(ii) Absorption by the atmosphere
(iii) Transmission through the atmosphere
(iv) Scattering by atmospheric particles

Codes

(a) (iii), (iv), (ii), (i) (b) (i), (ii), (iii), (iv)
(c) (iv), (iii), (ii), (i) (d) (iii), (ii), (iv), (i)

21. **Arrange the following components of the Earth's heat budget in order of the energy flow:**

(i) Solar energy absorbed by the surface
(ii) Longwave radiation emitted by the Earth
(iii) Solar energy absorbed by the atmosphere
(iv) Solar energy reflected by the Earth's surface

Codes

(a) (iv), (i), (ii), (iii) (b) (i), (iii), (ii), (iv)
(c) (iii), (i), (ii), (iv) (d) (ii), (i), (iv), (iii)

Match the Following

22.

	List I (Terms)		List II (Meaning)
A.	Convection	1.	Transfer of heat through horizontal movement of air.
B.	Advection	2.	Vertical heating of the atmosphere.
C.	Aphelion	3.	Shortest distance between the Sun and the Earth.
D.	Perihelion	4.	Longest distance between the Sun and Earth.

Codes

	A	B	C	D		A	B	C	D
(a)	2	1	4	3	(b)	1	2	3	4
(c)	3	2	1	4	(d)	4	2	1	3

23.

	List I		List II
A.	Latitude	1.	Distance from North and South of the equator measured in degrees upto 90 degree.
B.	Radiation	2.	The emission of energy in the form of rays or waves.
C.	Scattering	3.	The process in which radiation or particles are deflected or diffused.
D.	Isotherm	4.	The line which joins the places having equal temperature.

Codes

	A	B	C	D		A	B	C	D
(a)	1	2	3	4	(b)	2	3	1	4
(c)	3	2	1	4	(d)	2	4	3	1

24.

	List I		List II
A.	Short wave radiation	1.	Heat emitted by the Earth surface
B.	Long wave radiation	2.	Diffusion of solar radiation by particles
C.	Scattering	3.	Heat energy from the Sun
D.	Absorption	4.	Taking in and converting energy

Codes

	A	B	C	D		A	B	C	D
(a)	3	1	2	4	(b)	1	2	3	4
(c)	2	3	4	1	(d)	4	1	2	3

25.

	List I		List II
A.	Latitude	1.	Causes difference in temperature over land and sea
B.	Altitude	2.	Higher elevations are cooler
C.	Ocean current	3.	Affects the intensity of solar energy
D.	Land-water distribution	4.	Warm or cold current modify the temperature

Codes

	A	B	C	D		A	B	C	D
(a)	3	2	4	1	(b)	1	2	3	4
(c)	3	2	1	4	(d)	2	1	3	4

Assertion-Reason

Directions (Q. Nos. 26-29) In the questions given below are two statements labelled as Assertion (A) and other is labelled as Reason (R). In the context of two statements which one of the following is correct?

Codes

(a) Both A and R are true, but R is not the correct explanation of A
(b) Both A and R are true and R is the correct explanation of A
(c) Both A and R are incorrect
(d) A is correct, but R is incorrect

26. **Assertion** (A) Maximum insolation is received over the sub-tropical deserts.
Reason (R) Cloudiness is the least in the sub-tropical deserts.

27. **Assertion** (A) The amount of heat causes pressure differences in the atmosphere.
Reason (R) The amount of heat received by different parts of the Earth is not same.

28. **Assertion** (A) The polar regions experience extreme cold weather compared to the equatorial regions.
Reason (R) The Sun's rays strike the polar regions at a much lower angle, spreading the solar energy over a larger area.

29. **Assertion** (A) Areas near the ocean have a more moderate climate compared to inland areas.
Reason (R) Water bodies regulate temperature by absorbing and releasing heat more slowly than land.

Answers

1. (b) Earth receives 3.0 calorie per sq cm per minute at the top of the atmosphere.
2. (c) 4th July
3. (d) Lunar gravitational pull
4. (d) All of these
5. (c) Conduction
6. (b) Conduction takes place when two bodies of different temperature are in contact.
7. (b) Troposphere
8. (c) Advection
9. (d) Heat Budget
10. (a) 40° N and S latitude
11. (c) It is partly reflected, absorbed and scattered.
12. (d) The insolation received by the Earth is in the form of long wave and heats up the surface.
13. (c) Water has a higher heat capacity and can store more energy.
14. (c) Advection
15. (d) 40° N and S-Minimum insolation
16. (d) All of these
17. (b) Only (i)
18. (d) Statements (ii) and (iii)
19. (b) Perihelion, Summer Solstice, Aphelion, Winter Solstice
20. (c) (iv), (iii), (ii), (i)
21. (b) (i), (iii), (ii), (iv)
22. (a)
23. (a)
24. (a)
25. (a)
26. (b) Both A and R are true and R is the correct explanation of A
27. (b) Both A and R are true and R is the correct explanation of A
28. (b) Both A and R are true and R is the correct explanation of A
29. (b) Both A and R are true and R is the correct explanation of A

Subjective Questions

Short Answer Type Questions

1. List the factors which are responsible for the variability of insolation at the Earth's surface.

Ans The amount and the intensity of insolation vary during a day, in a season and in a year because of the following reasons

- The rotation of the Earth on its axis.
- The angle of inclination of the sun's rays.
- The length of the day.
- Transparency of the atmosphere.
- The configuration of land in terms of its aspect.

2. How scattering takes place? Explain.

Ans Scattering takes place due to the dispersion of incident radiation by various particles in the atmosphere. Very small suspended particles in the troposphere scatter the visible spectrum of light both towards space and back to the Earth's surface. This scattering process is responsible for the colours observed in the sky. The blue colour of the sky and the red hues of the rising and setting Sun are the result of the scattering of light within the atmosphere. Shorter wavelengths, like blue, scatter more than longer wavelengths, like red, creating these distinctive visual effects.

3. The spatial distribution of insolation at the Earth's surface is not uniform. Explain. Competency Based Que

Ans The insolation received at the surface of the Earth varies from 320 watt/m^2 in the tropics to about 70 watt/m^2 in the poles. The maximum insolation is received by the subtropical deserts where the formation of cloud is least.

Equatorial regions receive comparatively less insolation than the tropics as in equatorial region, there is more evaporation and more condensation. Generally, at the same latitude the insolation is more over the continents than over the oceans. In winter, the middle and higher latitudes receive less radiation than in summer.

4. The terrestrial radiation is important to maintain constant temperature on the Earth's surface. Explain in brief. Competency Based Que

Ans The insolation received by the Earth is in short wave form which heats up the surface. The Earth after being heated itself becomes a radiating body and it radiates energy to the atmosphere in long wave form which heats up the atmosphere from below. This process is known as terrestrial radiation.

The long wave radiation is absorbed by the atmospheric gases and thus, the atmosphere is indirectly heated by the Earth's radiation.

The atmosphere in turn radiates and transmits heat into the space. Finally, the amount of heat received from the Sun is returned to space which maintains constant temperature on the Earth's surface.

5. Describe the variation in the net heat budget of the earth surface.

Ans The net heat budget of the Earth's surface varies geographically and temporally. The equatorial regions receive more incoming solar energy due to the direct angle of the Sun's rays, leading to a heat surplus.

In contrast, polar regions experience a heat deficit as solar radiation is spread over a larger area and more energy is lost to space. Seasonal variations also influence the heat budget as earth receives more heat during perihelion and less heat during aphelion. This imbalance creates atmospheric and oceanic circulation to redistribute heat globally.

6. There is influence of continentality on the temperature distribution. Explain. Competency Based Que

Ans The influence of continentality on the temperature distribution is given below

- As compared to land, the sea gets heated slowly and loses heat slowly.
- Land heats up and cools down quickly.
- Therefore, the variation in temperature over the sea is less in comparison to land.
- The place situated near the sea comes under the moderating influence of the sea and land breezes which moderate the temperature.

7. Distinguish between conduction and convection.

Ans Differences between conduction and convection are as follows

Conduction	Convection
Conduction takes place when bodies of different temperature are in contact with one another.	In convection, there is transfer of heat vertically in the form of current.
In conduction, the air in contact with the land gets heated slowly and further heat is transferred to another layer.	In convection, the heat is transmitted layer by layer in atmosphere through air.
The transfer of heat continues until both the bodies attain the same temperature.	In convection the transfer of energy is confined only to the lower layer i.e., troposhere.

8. Differentiate between insolation and terrestrial radiation.

Ans Differences between insolation and terrestrial radiation are as follows

Insolation	Terrestrial Radiation
Insolation is the incoming solar radiation.	It is the radiation of energy from the Earth's surface into the atmosphere.
The earth surface receives insolation in short wave length.	It radiates energy to the atmosphere in long wave form.
It does not cause heating up of the atmosphere.	The atmosphere is heated by the Earth's radiation.
The main source of insolation is the sun rays.	Solar radiation is the source of terrestrial radiation.
It is only received in day time.	Terrestrial radiation continues to radiate both during day as well as at night.

9. Over polar areas, temperature inversion is normal throughout the year. Discuss. **Competency Based Que**

Ans If there is increase of air temperature with increase in height, it is known as inversion of temperature.

This situation is found in polar areas throughout the year because of following reasons

- The area has cold climate, sky often clear without cloud throughout the year and hence, it provides condition of ground surface inversion.
- The earth has curved geoid shape because of which the sun rays can't reach on the surface of the poles and it makes solar vertex which is above the surface. Due to this circumstance, temperature increases with increase in height.

10. There is differential heating of land and sea at the same latitude. Elucidate with examples. **Competency Based Que**

Ans Land and sea experience differential heating at the same latitude due to differences in their physical properties. Land heats up and cools down faster because it has a lower heat capacity and does not mix heat vertically. In contrast, water has a higher heat capacity, it absorbs more energy and distributes heat through mixing and currents. This causes it to warm and cool more slowly. As a result, coastal areas typically have more moderate temperatures, while inland regions experience greater variations in temperature variations.

11. Define inversion of temperature and mention ideal condition for development of this phenomenon.

Ans. As we go from lower elevation to higher elevation temperature decreases, this happens in normal condition and this is called as normal lapse rate. Sometimes, in certain conditions the situation is reversed and the temperature increases as we go to higher elevation. This is called as 'inversion of temperature'.

The conditions required for the development of inversion of temperature are as follows

(i) Inversion of temperature takes place during long winter night when the sky is clear.

(ii) Another condition required for the development of inversion of temperature is the presence of stable air.

Long Answer Type Questions

1 Explain the variability of insolation at the surface of the earth.

Ans The amount of insolation, or incoming solar radiation, at the Earth's surface varies due to several factors. These are as follows

- Latitude is a key factor: equatorial regions receive more insolation as the Sun's rays are direct, while higher latitudes get less due to the oblique angle of sunlight.
- Seasonal variations which is caused by the Earth's inclination of the axis, this results in change in sun angles and length of the day throughout the year. This affects the amount of insolation received at any place.
- Atmospheric conditions, such as cloud cover, dust, and pollution, further influence insolation by scattering and absorbing solar radiation.
- Lastly, the Earth's surface features, including elevation and albedo, also impact how much energy is absorbed or reflected.

2. 'There is a balance maintained between the incoming solar radiation and outgoing terrestrial radiation, which helps in maintaining the Earth's temperature'. Elucidate the statement. **Competency Based Que**

Ans The balance between incoming solar radiation and outgoing terrestrial radiation is maintained by Earth's heat budget. The Sun emits shortwave radiation, some of which is absorbed by the atmosphere and Earth's surface, warming the planet. The Earth, in turn, radiates heat back as longwave terrestrial radiation. While some of this energy escapes into space. Some portion of radiation is trapped by greenhouse gases which warms the atmosphere and helps in maintaining temperatures that is suitable for life. This balance is essential for thermal equilibrium, where energy received is equal to energy lost. If this balance shifts, it can lead to global temperature changes. Human activities, like burning fossil fuels, disrupt this budget by increasing greenhouse gas concentrations, contributing to global warming and climate change.

3. Explain the distribution of temperature and its controlling factors with reference to July and January condition.

Or 'The angle of inclination of the Sun rays determines the insolation at the surface of the Earth.' Justify the statement. CBSE Diksha

Ans The global distribution of temperature varies significantly between July and January due to the Earth's inclined axis and revolution around the Sun.

The reasons behind this are as follows

- In July, the Northern Hemisphere experiences summer, with higher temperatures as it tilts toward the Sun, this results in longer days and more direct solar rays. Landmasses, like Asia and North America, heat up rapidly which causes large temperature differences. The Southern Hemisphere, in contrast, has winter, with cooler temperatures and shorter days.
- In January, the situation reverses: The Southern Hemisphere tilts toward the Sun, experiencing summer, while the Northern Hemisphere has winter. Controlling factors include latitude, altitude, closeness to oceans, ocean currents, and prevailing winds, all of these influence temperature variations across regions during these months.

Or It is true to say that the angle of inclination of the sun rays determines the insolation at the surface of the earth. This can be understood by following points

- This depends on the latitude of a place. The higher the latitude the less is the angle they make with the surface of the earth resulting in slant Sun rays.
- The area covered by vertical rays is always less than the slant rays. If more area is covered, the energy gets distributed and the net energy received per unit area decreases.
- Moreover, the slant rays are required to pass through greater depth of the atmosphere resulting in more absorption, scattering and diffusion.

4. 'Normally, temperature decreases with increase in elevation. But sometimes the situations are reversed and the normal lapse rate is inverted.' Substantiate the statement CBSE Diksha

Ans. Normally, temperature decreases with an increase in elevation because the atmosphere becomes thin as we go upward and air pressure also decreases. This is called as the Normal lapse rate. However, under certain conditions, the normal lapse rate can be inverted and this phenomenon is called as Temperature inversion. This occurs when a layer of warm air locks cooler air near the surface. Factors contributing to inversion include clear skies at night, which allow the ground to cool rapidly, cooling the air near the surface, while the air above remains warmer. In coastal areas, sea breezes can also cause inversion, as cooler air from the ocean is trapped beneath warmer land air. Temperature inversion often leads to static weather conditions and may affect weather patterns like fog.

5. "The inversion of temperature affects adversely the society and the economy of the region". Give your arguments in support of this statement. Competency Based Que

Ans Sometimes the effect of inversion of temperature becomes so adverse for the society and region. Some of the important consequences of inversion are

Occurrence of Fog In the urban areas, the fog gets mixed with the smoke and formed smog. While fog is harmful to crops, the smog is a health hazard. Lung diseases, breathing problems, etc are common in urban areas of North India especially during the winter season when the smog occurs.

Accidents At the occurrence of inversion, fog is a common phenomenon which causes poor visibility due to which the frequency of road, railway, air, sea-route accidents increases.

Damage to Crops The winter crops, e.g. wheat, barley, gram, etc are seriously damaged.

Impact on Human Settlements In the Mediterranean region, the human settlements and location of orchards are closely influenced by the inversion of temperature. The lower parts of valleys of the Alps mountain are almost without settlements. The upper slopes of the valleys are characterised by fruit orchards, hotels, etc.

Inversion of Temperature and Atmospheric Stability Inversion of temperature causes atmospheric stability which stops upward and downward movement of air. The atmospheric stability is less conducive to rainfall.

6. Give an account of the distribution of incoming solar radiation and outgoing terrestrial radiation.

Ans. The insolation received at the top of the atmosphere is **100 units**. The incoming solar radiation and outgoing terrestrial radiation is distributed in the following ways

- Approximately 35 units are reflected to space even before reaching the Earth's surface.
- Of these, 27 units are reflected from the top of the clouds and 2 units from the snow and ice-covered areas of the Earth.
- The remaining **65 units** are absorbed, in which 14 units by the atmosphere and 51 units by the Earth's surface. The Earth radiates back 51 units in the form of terrestrial radiation.
- Of these, 17 units are radiated to space directly and the remaining 34 units are absorbed by the atmosphere.

- The 48 units absorbed by the atmosphere (14 units from insolation + 34 units from terrestrial radiation) are also radiated back into space.
- Thus, the total radiation returning from the earth and the atmosphere respectively is 17+48=65 units which balance the total of 65 units received from the Sun.

7. 'The Earth's tilted axis influence seasonal temperature variations'. Explain how.

Ans. The inclination of the Earth's axis has a great influence on the amount of insolation received at different latitudes. The Earth's axial tilt of approximately 23.5° causes seasonal temperature variations. During summer, the hemisphere that is closer to the Sun, experiences longer days and more direct sunlight, which results in increase of temperatures.

Conversely, during winter, the hemisphere tilted away from the Sun has shorter days and less direct sunlight received, this results in lower temperatures in that region\hemisphere.

This tilt is responsible for the changing seasons. This change in season creates significant temperature differences between summer and winter, especially at higher latitudes. In higher latitudes the angle of the Sun's rays varies more dramatically.

Source Based Questions

1. Read the passage carefully and answer the questions that follow.

There are different ways of heating and cooling of the atmosphere. The earth after being heated by insolation transmits the heat to the atmospheric layers near to the earth in long wave form. The air in contact with the land gets heated slowly and the upper layers in contact with the lower layers also get heated. This process is called conduction. Conduction takes place when two bodies of unequal temperature are in contact with one another, there is a flow of energy from the warmer to cooler body. The transfer of heat continues until both the bodies attain the same temperature or the contact is broken. The air in contact with the earth rises vertically on heating in the form of currents and further transmits the heat of the Atmosphere.

This process of vertical heating of the atmosphere is known as convection. The convective transfer of energy is confined only to the troposphere. The transfer of heat through horizontal movement of air is called advection. Horizontal movement of the air is relatively more important than the vertical movement. In tropical regions particularly in Northern India during summer season local winds called 'loo' is the outcome of advection process.

The insolation received by the Earth is in short waves forms and heats up its surface. The Earth after being heated itself becomes a radiating body and it radiates energy to the atmosphere in long wave form. This energy heats up the atmosphere from below. This process is known as terrestrial radiation. The long wave radiation is absorbed by the atmospheric gases particularly by carbon dioxide and the other greenhouse gases. Finally the amount of heat received from the Sun is returned to space, thereby maintaining constant temperature at the Earth's surface and in the atmosphere.

(i) Earth's atmosphere is mainly heated by which of the following?

(a) Shortwave insolation (b) Terrestrial radiation
(c) Ultraviolet rays (d) X rays

Ans. (b) Terrestrial radiation

(ii) Advection results in which of the following phenomenon?

(a) Tidal waves (b) Surface winds
(c) Greenhouse effect (d) Ozone layer depletion

Ans. (b) Surface winds

(iii) Which process allows solar radiation to reach the Earth's surface in short wavelengths?

(a) Reflection (b) Refraction
(c) Transmission (d) Absorption

Ans. (c) Transmission

2. Study the following diagrams and answer the questions that follow.

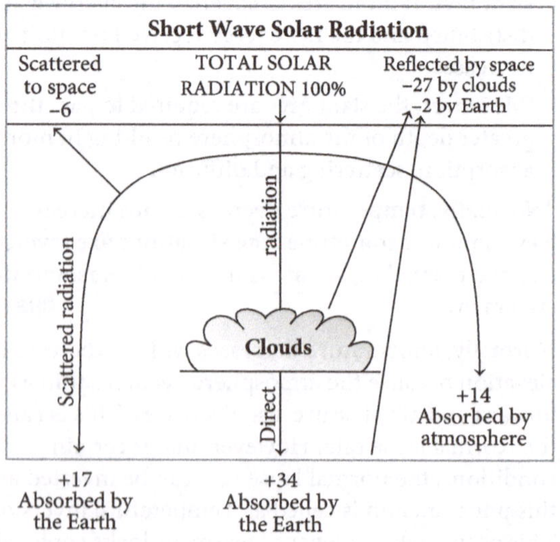

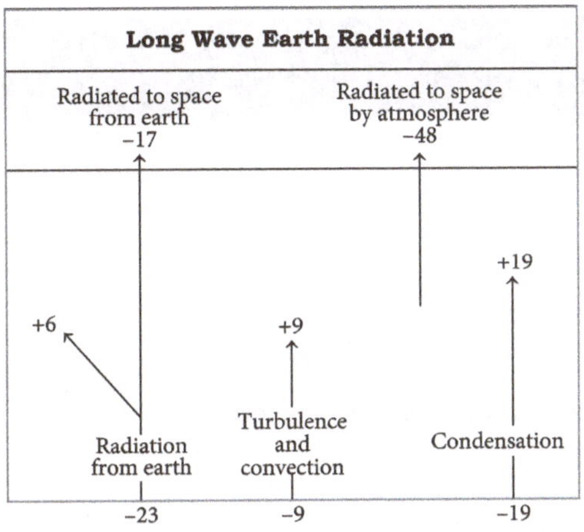

(i) **What amount of radiation is reflected back to Outer space directly without reaching the surface?**

(a) 50 units (b) 35 units
(c) 22 units (d) 10 units

Ans (b) 35 units

(ii) **What is the total amount of terrestrial radiation originating from the surface of earth?**

(a) 51 units (b) 22 units (c) 19 units (d) 9 units

Ans (a) 51 units

(iii) **What is the total amount of energy that passes through the earth's atmosphere?**

(a) 35 units (b) 100 units (c) 65 units (d) 51 units

Ans (c) 65 units

3. Read the passage carefully and answer the questions that follow.

The Earth's surface receives most of its energy in short wavelengths. The energy received by the Earth is known as incoming solar radiation which in short is termed as insolation. As the earth is a geoid resembling a sphere, the Sun's rays fall obliquely at the top of the atmosphere and the Earth intercepts a very small portion of the sun's energy. The solar output received at the top of the atmosphere varies slightly in a year due to the variations in the distance between the Earth and the Sun. During its revolution around the sun, the Earth is farthest from the Sun (152 million km) on 4th July. This position of the Earth is called aphelion.

On 3rd January, the Earth is the nearest to the Sun (147 million km). This position is called perihelion. Therefore, the annual insolation received by the Earth on 3rd January is slightly more than the amount received on 4th July. However, the effect of this variation in the solar output is masked by other factors like the distribution of land and sea and the atmospheric circulation. Hence, this variation in the solar output does not have great effect on daily weather changes on the surface of the Earth. The amount and the intensity of insolation vary during a day, in a season and in a year.

(i) **The variation in solar output between perihelion and aphelion doesn't significantly impact Earth's daily weather patterns. Explain why?**

Ans. The slight variation in solar output between perihelion and aphelion has little impact on our daily weather patterns, as other factors, such as the distribution of land and sea and atmospheric circulation, play a much larger role in influencing the weather. These factors effectively mask any minor changes in solar radiation.

(ii) **How does Earth's spherical shape influence the reception of solar radiation at its surface?**

Ans Due to Earth's geoid shape, sun's rays fall obliquely at the atmosphere's top which causes the planet to receive only a small portion of total solar energy.

(iii) **How do Earth's positions of aphelion and perihelion relate to annual insolation patterns?**

Ans. During perihelion on January 3rd, Earth is closest to the sun and receives more insolation while during aphelion on July 4th, Earth is farthest to the Sun and receives less insolation.

4. Study the diagram and answer the questions that follow.

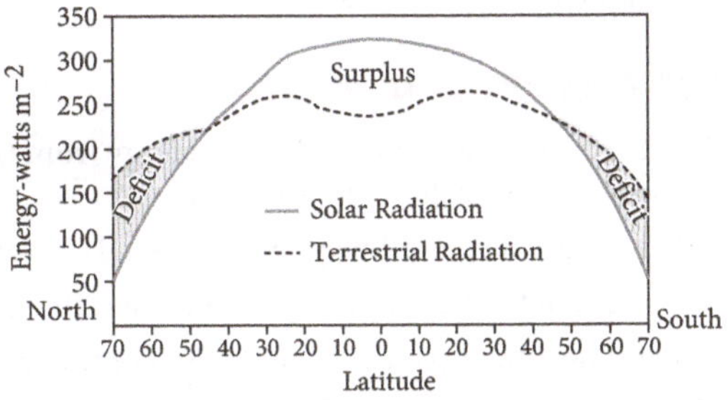

(i) **Identify the latitudinal range where the energy received is deficit.**

Ans. Latitude between: 50° N – 70°N and 50°S – 70°S receives less amount of heat energy.

(ii) **How surplus and deficit heat received is balanced latitudinally?**

Ans. The surplus heat received at the tropics and equators are redistributed to the polar areas by currents.

(iii) **Mention one factor that affects the distribution of temperature.**

Ans. The distribution of temperature is affected by the altitude. The places near the sea-level have higher temperature than the places situated at high altitude. The temperature decreases as we go from lower height to higher height.

SELF ASSESSMENT TEST

Objective Answer Type Questions

1. Incoming solar radiation is also known as
   (a) Conduction (b) Convection
   (c) Advection (d) Insolation
2. Out of 100 units of heat received, roughly how many units are reflected back to space even before reaching the earth's surface?
   (a) 15 Units (b) 30 Units
   (c) 35 Units (d) 50 Units
3. The Earth is farthest from the sun on which date?
   (a) 1st August (b) 2nd October
   (c) 4th July (d) 3rd January
4. What type of waves easily passes through the atmosphere?
   (a) Long waves (b) Short waves
   (c) Medium waves (d) Micro waves
5. Which local wind is the result of Advection.
   (a) Loo (b) Blizzard
   (c) Chinook (d) Heat wave

Short Answer Type Questions

6. The Earth receives almost all of its energy from the Sun. Discuss this with the variation in the distribution of insolation over the Earth's surface.
7. What is the role played by prevailing winds in temperature modification?
8. The angle of the Sun rays fall variably on different latitudes. Explain why?
9. Explain how the ocean currents influence the temperature distribution over the Earth's surface.
10. There are different ways of heating and cooling of the atmosphere.Explain these processes in the context of this statement.

Long Answer Type Questions

11. Isotherm bend polewards on continents and the equator towards on oceans. Explain why?
12. Inversion is usually of short duration but quite a common phenomenon. Justify this with the various conditions for inversion of temperature.
13. How is atmosphere heated? Discuss the role of terrestrial radiation in this process.
14. 'There are different factors that controls the distribution of temperature'. Justify.
15. The isotherms are lines joining places having equal temperature. Explain the distribution of surface air temperature in winter and summer season.
16. Explain the heat budget of the Earth and why the Earth neither warms up nor cools down despite the huge transfer of heat that takes place.

9 CHAPTER

This chapter deals with the concept of atmospheric pressure, characteristics of air, turbulent pattern of wind and the formation of air masses. Air expands when it is heated and compressed when it is cooled. This property brings variation in atmospheric pressure.

YOUR STUDY GOALS

YOUR PRACTICE GOALS

- Objective Type Questions (28 Qs.; MCQs, statements, Matching, A-R)
- Subjective Questions (14 SAs, 9 LAs)
- Source/Diagram Based Questions (5 Qs)
- Map Based Question (1 Qs)

Atmospheric Circulation and Weather System

- Pressure difference in air masses results in the movement of air from high pressure area to low pressure area.
- Wind created as a result of pressure differences plays a great role in maintaining a constant temperature of the Earth by redistributing the heat and moisture.

9.1 Atmospheric Pressure

- Atmospheric pressure is defined as the force exerted by the weight of column of air above the Earth's surface per unit area.
- It is expressed in units of **milibar**. At sea level, the average atmospheric pressure is 1,013.2 milibar.
- Atmospheric pressure near the surface of the Earth is high because of presence of dense (heavy) air near the surface.
- It is measured with the help of an instrument called as **mercury barometer**. It is not uniform everywhere and varies from place to place.

Vertical Variation in Pressure

- Air pressure changes vertically when we move from lower atmosphere to upper atmosphere.
- In the lower atmosphere, the pressure decreases rapidly as we go to higher elevation. The rate of decrease of pressure is about 1mb per 10 meters.

- The given table shows the average pressure and temperature at a particular elevation for a standard atmosphere.

Level	Pressure in mb	Temperature °C
Sea Level	1,013. 25	15.2
1 km	898.76	8.7
5 km	540.48	-17.3
10 km	265.00	-49.7

- The vertical **pressure gradient**[1] is much stronger than the horizontal pressure gradient. But we do not experience strong upward winds because of the balancing gravitational force.

Horizontal Distribution of Pressure

- Small differences in pressure are significant for determining the wind direction and velocity.
- Horizontal distribution of pressure is determined by drawing 'Isobars' at constant levels.
- Isobars are the lines that connects places having equal value of air pressure.
- To understand air pressure differences accurately across different locations, air pressure is reduced to mean sea level.
- Low pressure system is surrounded by one or more isobars with lowest pressure in the center.
- High-pressure system is surrounded by one or more isobars with highest pressure in the center.

World Distribution of Sea Level Pressure

- There is distribution of low pressure and high-pressure system all over the globe. This pressure system is divided into four pressure belts which are as follows
  - (i) **Equatorial lows** This is a low-pressure system belt that lies near the equator.
  - (ii) **Subtropical Highs** This is a high-pressure system area that lies between 30°N and 30°S latitude.
  - (iii) **Subpolar Lows** This is a low-pressure system area that lies between 60°N and 60°S latitude.
  - (iv) **Polar Highs** This is a high-pressure system area that lies near the poles.
- These pressure belts are not permanent in nature. They shift with the movement of Sun in the Northern and Southern hemisphere.

Pressure Belts

These are the regions on the Earth with higher or lower pressure cells or systems. The high and low-pressure belts are arranged alternatively on the Earth's surface.

9.2 Factors Affecting the Velocity and Direction of Wind

- Wind is the result of pressure difference between two places and the direction of wind is from high pressure to low pressure area.
- Wind blows with different velocity and direction. The horizontal wind near the Earth's surface is affected by three forces - the pressure gradient force, Coriolis force and the frictional force.

1 **Pressure gradient** It is the rate of change of atmospheric pressure with regard to horizontal distance at a point.

(i) Pressure Gradient Force

- It is a force generated when there are differences in atmospheric pressure. The rate of change of pressure with respect to distance is called pressure gradient.
- The pressure gradient is strong where the isobars are close to each other and it is weak where the isobars are placed apart.

(ii) Frictional Force

- The winds blowing at the surface of the Earth experience Friction[2]. This friction affects the speed of the wind.
- Frictional force is greatest at the surface and its effects are seen up to an elevation of 1-3 km. Frictional force is minimal over the sea surface.

(iii) Coriolis Force

- It is the force generated by the rotation of the Earth about its axis which affects the direction of the wind. This is named after a French Physicist who described it in 1844.
- The wind blowing in the Northern Hemisphere deflects to its right and in the Southern hemisphere deflects to its left because of Coriolis force. The deflection of wind is more when the wind velocity is high.
- Coriolis force is also directly proportional to the angle of latitude fronts. It is maximum at the poles and is absent at the equator and is perpendicular to the pressure gradient force. The pressure gradient force is perpendicular to an isobar.
- There is close relation between Coriolis force, wind velocity and pressure gradient as greater the pressure difference, the faster the wind blows and the more it is deflected.
- At the equator, the Coriolis force is zero and the wind blows perpendicular to the isobars due to which the low pressure gets filled instead of getting intensified. This is the reason due to which tropical cyclones are not formed near the equator.

(iv) Pressure and Wind

- The velocity and direction of wind are the net result of wind generating forces.
- The winds in the upper atmosphere around 2-3 km above the surface are free from frictional forces and are mainly affected by Coriolis force and pressure gradient.
- When the isobars are straight and there is no friction, the pressure gradient force is balanced by the Coriolis force and as a result the wind blows parallel to the isobars. This wind is known as **Geostrophic Wind.**

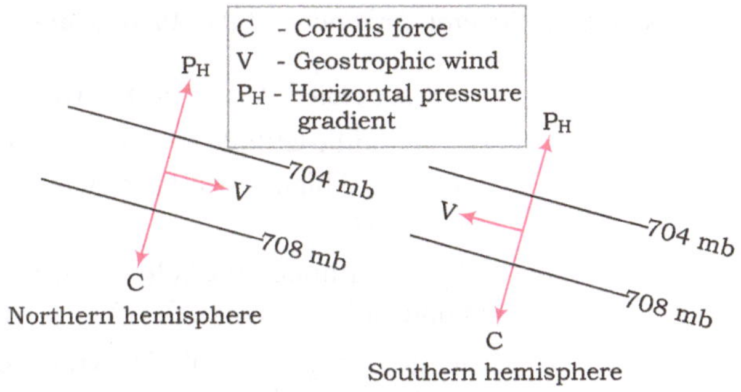

▲ *Geostrophic Wind*

Quick Test 1

1. Which instrument is used to measure the air pressure?
2. What is the value of Coriolis force at Equator?
3. Why tropical cyclones are not found near the equator?
4. Name the wind that blows parallel to the isobars.

---

2 Friction It is the force which resist the relative motion of the solid surfaces, fluid layers and material elements sliding against each other.

9.2 General Circulation of the Atmosphere

- The pattern of movement of planetary winds is called as general circulation of the atmosphere.
- The pattern of Planetary Winds[3] depends on various factors as follows
  (i) Differential heating of atmosphere at different latitudes
  (ii) Emergence of pressure belts
  (iii) Shift in the pressure belts due to movement of Sun
  (iv) The distribution of continents and oceans
  (v) The rotation of the Earth

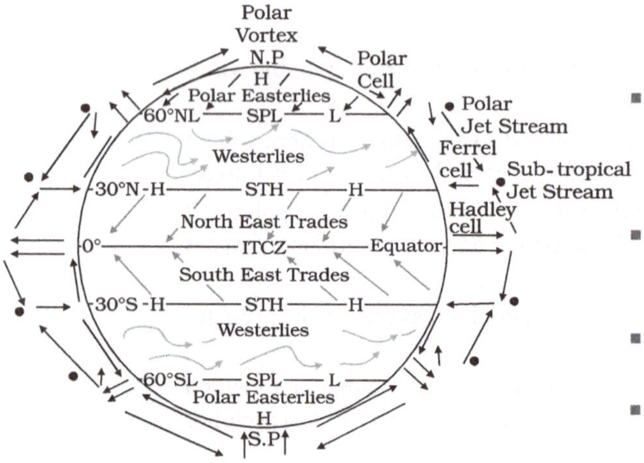

▲ *Simplified General Circulation of the Atmosphere*

- The general circulation of atmosphere leads to the formation of ocean water circulation which influences the climate of the Earth.
- Because of convection generated by high insolation, the air in the Inter-Tropical Convergence Zone[4] (ITCZ) rises and develops a low pressure. The winds coming from tropics converge in this low-pressure zone.
- The rising air moves with the convective cell, reaching up to 14 km in the troposphere. It then travels towards the poles, causing air to accumulate around 30°N and 30°S.
- When some of the collected air sinks to the ground, it leads to the formation of subtropical high-pressure zone.
- Near the land surface, the air flows towards the equator as easterlies[5]. The easterlies coming from both sides of the equator converge at the ITCZ.
- The circulations taking place from surface upwards and vice versa are called **Cells.** In the tropics, such a cell is called **Hadley Cell.**
- In the middle latitudes the cold air that comes from the poles, sinks and the warm air that blows from the subtropical high, rises. These winds are known as westerlies[6] at the surface and the cell is known as the **Ferrel Cell.**
- At polar latitudes, the cold and dense air sinks near the poles and blows as **polar easterlies** towards the middle latitude. This cell is known as the **Polar Cell.**
- The general pattern of circulation of atmosphere is decided by these three cells. This circulation is maintained by the transfer of heat energy from lower latitude to the higher latitude.

General Atmospheric Circulation and its Effects on Oceans

- Warming and cooling of the Pacific Ocean is most important in terms of general atmospheric circulation. The warm water of the central Pacific Ocean slowly moves towards South American coast and replaces the cool Peruvian current. Such appearance of warm water off the coast of Peru is known as the **El Nino.**
- The El Nino event is closely associated with the pressure changes in the Central Pacific and Australia. This change in pressure condition over Pacific is known as the Southern oscillation. The combined phenomenon of Southern oscillation and El Nino is known as **ENSO.**
- When the ENSO is strong, large-scale variations in weather occur over the world. The arid West coast of South America receives heavy rainfall, drought occurs in Australia and sometimes in India and floods in China.

3 Planetary Winds These are permanent winds that blows from high pressure to low pressure belts throughout the year.
4 Inter Tropical Convergence Zone It is a belt of low pressure near the equator where trade winds cause frequent thunderstorms or rainfall.
5 Easterlies These are the winds that flow from the East to the West in tropical areas.
6 Westerlies These are permanent winds that blows in middle latitudes from high pressure to low pressure area.

Seasonal Wind

- The pattern of wind circulation changes in different seasons due to the shifting of regions of maximum heating, pressure and wind belts.
- The effect of this shift is much noticed in the Monsoons, especially over South-East Asia.

Local Winds

- Several local, common and regional winds are formed due to differences in heating and cooling of the Earth surfaces.

Land and Sea breeze

- These type of local winds are created due to the differences in the heating and cooling property of land and water.
- During day, the land gets heated up quickly as compared to the sea. Therefore, the air rises over the land resulting in the development of low-pressure area.
- At the same time, the sea develops high pressure area because they are cooler as compared to the land. Thus, wind blows from sea to land because of the development of pressure gradient from sea towards land. This is called as **Sea Breeze.**
- During night this process is reversed as land loses heat faster and cools down rapidly as compared to sea. The wind blows from land to sea because the pressure gradient is developed from land to sea. This is called as **Land Breeze.**

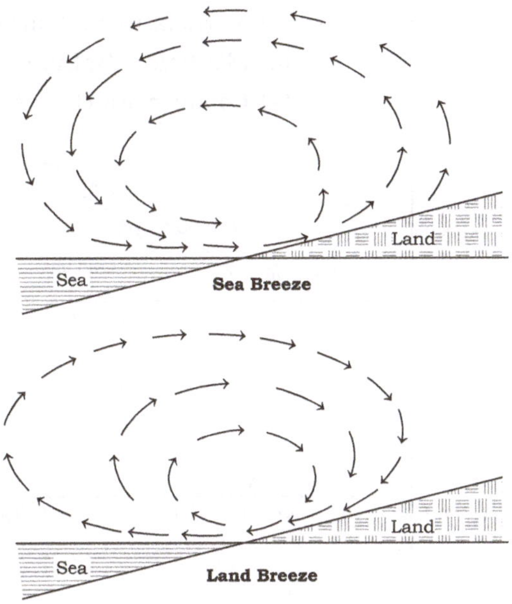

▲ *Land and Sea Breezes*

Mountain and Valley Winds

- The type of local winds are created due to differences in the heating and cooling of the mountainous regions and valleys.
- During day, the slopes in the mountainous regions are heated up quickly and the air moves upward along the slope.
- Air from the surrounding valleys moves down the slope to fill the gap created by upward moving air. This is called as **Valley Breeze.**
- During the night, the slopes of the mountain is cooled down quickly and the dense air move downwards into the valley. The direction of wind is from mountain towards valley. This is called as **Mountain Breeze.**
- When the cold and dense air from the plateaus and ice fields falls down the slope into the valley, it is called as **Katabatic wind.**
- Another type of warm wind originates on the leeward side of the mountain range. The moisture present in these winds condenses and results in to precipitation. When these warm winds moves down the slope, the dry air gets warmed up by a process called as **Adiabatic Process.** This dry air may melt the snow in cold areas in a short time.

Air Mass

- The air with distinctive characteristics in terms of temperature and humidity is called as **Air Mass.** It is defined as a large body of air which has horizontal variation in temperature and moisture.
- Air masses are formed over homogenous surfaces which are called **source regions.** These can be the vast ocean surface or vast plains.

- The air masses are classified according to the source regions. There are five major source regions which are as follows
  - (i) Warm tropical and subtropical oceans
  - (ii) The subtropical hot deserts
  - (iii) The relatively cold high latitude oceans
  - (iv) The very cold snow-covered continents in high latitudes
  - (v) Permanently ice-covered continents in the Arctic and Antarctica
- On the basis of these source regions, following types of air masses are identified
  - (i) Maritime tropical (mT)
  - (ii) Continental tropical (cT)
  - (iii) Maritime polar (mP)
  - (iv) Continental polar (cP)
  - (v) Continental arctic (cA)

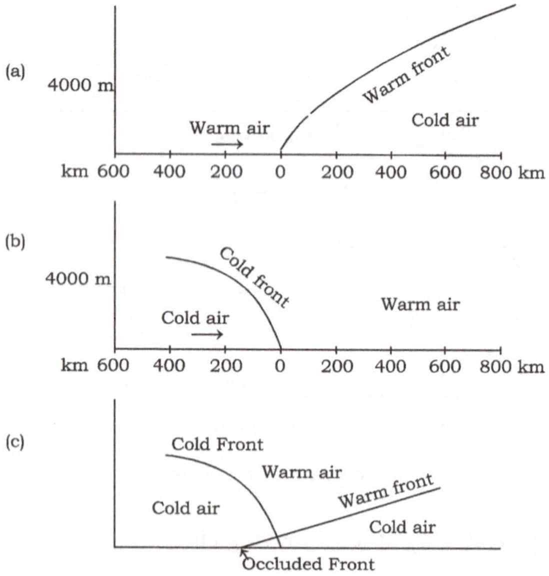

▲ *Vertical Sections of: (a) Warm Front, (b) Cold Front, (c) Occluded Front*

Fronts

- A front is a boundary zone where two different air masses meet. The process of formation of front is known as **Frontogenesis.**
- There are four types of fronts:
  - (i) **Cold Front** It is formed when cold air moves towards the warm air.
  - (ii) **Warm Front** It is formed when warm air mass moves towards the cold air.
  - (iii) **Stationary Front** It is formed when the two air masses remain stationary.
  - (iv) **Occluded Front** It is formed when one air mass is fully lifted above the land surface.
- Fronts are mostly common in middle latitudes. They are characterised by steep temperature and pressure gradient.
- When there is a formation of front in a region, there is sharp change in the temperature and this results in the formation of clouds and causes precipitation.

Quick Test 2

1. What is the full form of ITCZ?
2. How many pressure belts are found on the Earth?
3. Which type of air mass is formed ever warm tropical and subtropical oceans?
4. What is frontogenesis?

9.3 Cyclones and Anticyclones

- The wind circulation around a low-pressure system is called as '**Cyclonic Circulation**' and when it is around a high-pressure system it is called as '**Anticyclonic Circulation**'.
- Direction of winds in Cyclonic and Anticyclonic circulations changes according to their location in different hemispheres.

- The movement of wind near the Earth's surface is linked to how wind moves in higher atmosphere. In low pressure, the air converges and rises up while in high-pressure areas, air sinks toward the ground and it spreads outward at the surface.
- Other factors also lead to the rising of air like eddies, convection currents, orographic uplift[7] and uplift along fronts. These are essential for the formation of clouds and precipitation.

Pattern of Wind Direction in Cyclones and Anticyclones

Pressure System	Pressure Condition at the Centre	Pattern of Wind Direction	
		Northern Hemisphere	Southern Hemisphere
Cyclone	Low	Anti-clockwise	Clockwise
Anti-cyclone	High	Clockwise	Anti-clockwise

Extra Tropical Cyclones

- The pressure system that develops in the middle and higher latitude region, beyond the tropical area are called **Extra Tropical Cyclones.**
- In the middle and higher latitudes, the development of front causes sudden change in the weather conditions and these fronts intensify the cyclone.

Formation of Extra Tropical Cyclones

- Extra tropical cyclones are formed along the polar front. Initially, the front is in stationary stage.
- In the Northern hemisphere, warm air blows from the South and cold air from the North of the front.
- When the pressure drops along the front, the warm air moves Northwards and the cold air move towards South giving rise to an anticlockwise cyclonic circulation.
- The cyclonic circulation leads to a well-developed extra tropical cyclone, with a warm front and a cold front.
- There are pockets of warm air mass between cold air mass. The warm air slides over the cold air and a sequence of clouds develops in the sky in front of the warm front and this causes precipitation.
- The cold front approaches the warm air from behind and pushes the warm air up. As a result, cumulus clouds[8] develop along the cold front.
- The cold front moves faster than the warm front ultimately overtaking the warm front. The warm air is completely lifted up and **occluded front** is formed and the cyclone disappears.

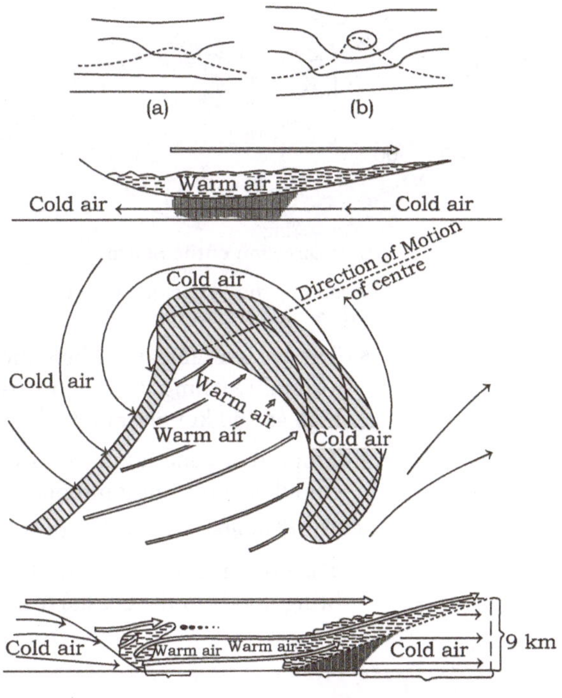

▲ *Extra tropical Cyclones*

7 Orographic uplift This uplift of wind takes place when wind hits the mountain and it is forced to move upward the slopes of the mountain.
8 Cumulus clouds These are the clouds that have flat bases and are often characterised by their fluffy, white appearance.

Tropical Cyclones

- Tropical cyclones are violent storms that originate over oceans in tropical areas. These storms move over to the coastal areas and bring about large-scale destruction caused by violent winds, very heavy rainfall and storm surges.
- They are known by different names in different countries like ***Cyclones*** in the Indian Ocean, ***Hurricanes*** in the Atlantic, ***Typhoons*** in the Western Pacific and South China Sea and ***Willy-willies*** in the Western Australia.

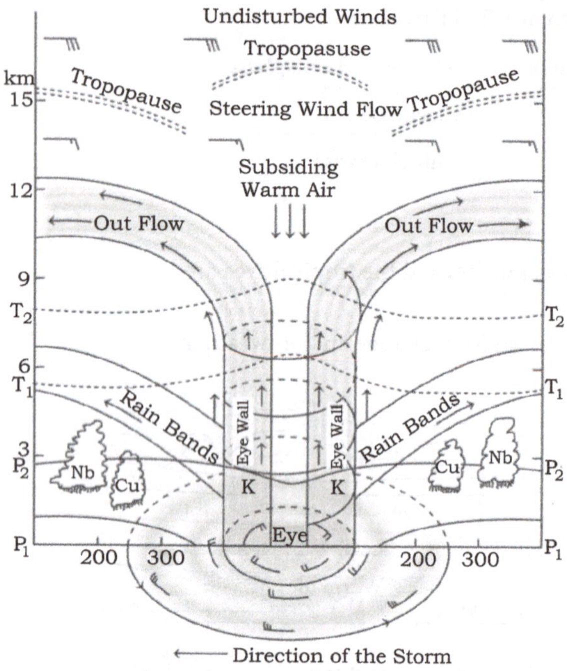

▲ *Vertical Section of the Tropical Cyclone (after Rama Sastry)*

- Tropical cyclones originate and intensify over warm tropical oceans. The conditions favourable for the formation and intensification of tropical storms are
  - (i) Presence of large sea surface with temperature of 27° C or more.
  - (ii) Presence of the Coriolis force.
  - (iii) Presence of small difference in the vertical wind speed.
  - (iv) Pre-existing weak low-pressure area or low-level-cyclonic circulation.
  - (v) Presence of upper divergence above the sea level system.
- The intensity of cyclone increases as it gains energy from the condensation process in the **cumulonimbus clouds**[9] that are present around the center of the storm.
- The place where a tropical cyclone crosses the coast is called the **landfall of the cyclone**. The cyclones which cross 20° N latitude generally change their direction and they are more destructive.

Characteristics of Tropical Cyclone

- A fully developed tropical cyclone has strong spirally circulating wind around the centre which is called the eye of the cyclone.
- The diameter of the circulating system varies between 150 and 250 km.
- The eye is a calm area where the air is sinking. There is eye wall around the eye where air rises sharply in a spiral reaching the tropopause. The wind reaches maximum velocity in this region having speed as high as 250 km per hour.
- Tropical cyclone results in torrential rain. From the **eye wall**[10] rain bands moves outward and groups of cumulus and cumulonimbus clouds also moves towards the outer region.
- The diameter of the storm over the Bay of Bengal, Arabian sea and Indian ocean is between 600-1200 km.
- The cyclone moves slowly about 300 - 500 km per day. The cyclone creates **storm surges**[11] and they bring floods to the coastal low lands.

---

9 **Cumulonimbus clouds** These are tall huge clouds that brings storms, heavy rain, lightning and sometimes tornadoes.

10 **Eye Wall** It is the most dangerous and destructive part of a tropical cyclone. Here winds are strongest, rainfall is heaviest, and deep convective clouds rise.

11 **Storm Surges** It is the rise in sea water level due to storms like cyclone and thunderstorm.

Difference between Extra Tropical Cyclones and Tropical Cyclones

Extra Tropical Cyclones	Tropical Cyclones
The extra tropical cyclones have a clear frontal system.	A clear frontal system is not present in the tropical cyclones.
They cover a larger area and can originate over the land and sea.	They originate only over the seas and on reaching the land they dissipate.
They affect a large area.	They affect a smaller area as compared to extra tropical cyclones.
The wind velocity in an extra tropical cyclone is high and destructive.	The wind velocity in a tropical cyclone is much higher and it is more destructive.
They move from West to East.	They move from East to West.

Thunderstorms and Tornadoes

- They are other local storms of short duration, occurring over a small area but are violent.
- *Thunderstorms* are caused by intense process of convection on hot and humid days. A thunderstorm is a well-developed cumulonimbus cloud producing thunder and lightening.
- When the clouds extend to heights where sub-zero temperature is present, hails are formed and they come down as **hailstorm**.
- If there is insufficient moisture, a thunderstorm can generate dust storms.
- A thunderstorm is characterised by intense upward movement of rising warm air which causes the clouds to grow bigger and rises to greater height. This causes precipitation. Later, the cool air and the rain comes down to the Earth.
- Severe thunderstorms can produce spiralling winds that descend with great force, creating a low-pressure centre and causing massive destruction. Such a phenomenon is called a ***tornado***.
- Tornadoes generally occur in middle latitudes. The tornado developed over the sea is called ***water spouts***.
- In these storms, the potential and heat energies are converted into kinetic energy and the unstable atmosphere again becomes stable.

Quick Test 3

1. Which type of cloud develop along the cold front?
2. What is a cyclone called in Philippines?
3. Mention one condition required for the development of tropical cyclone.
4. Give one example of local storm.

Mind Map

ATMOSPHERIC CIRCULATION AND WEATHER SYSTEM

1 Atmospheric Pressure

- Weight of air per unit area
- Measured in millibars

Horizontal Variation in Atmospheric Pressure
It is studied by drawing isobars at constant level at different latitudes.

Vertical Variation in Atmospheric Pressure
In the lower atmosphere, the pressure decreases rapidly with height with 1 mb for each 10 m.

2 Factors Affecting Velocity and Direction of Wind

- **Pressure Gradient** It is a force generated when there are differences in atmospheric pressure.
- **Coriolis Force** It is generated by the rotation of the Earth. At the equator, it is zero because the Earth rotation is directly overhead.
- **Frictional Force** Its effects are seen upto an elevation of 1-3 km and is minimal over the sea surface.

Types of Winds

Geostrophic Wind These blows parallel to the isobars.

3 General Circulation of the Atmosphere

Pressure Belts

- A belt of high and low pressure distributed all over the globe.

Global Pressure Belts

- Equatorial Low Pressure Belt
- Sub-tropical High Pressure Belt
- Sub-Polar Low Pressure Belt
- Polar-High Pressure Belt

Air Mass

- A large volume of air in the atmosphere of similar temperature and moisture propensity, e.g., tropical, polar, maritime.
- Formed over homogenous surfaces (source regions).

Fronts

- The boundary between two contrasting air masses, e.g., warm, cold, occluded.
- Mostly common in middle latitudes
- Four types of fronts: cold, warm, stationary, occluded

Wind System

- **Planetary Winds** These winds originate at global level, e.g., trade winds, westerlies, easterlies.
- **Local winds** These winds originate at local level, e.g., land and sea breeze, mountain-valley breeze.

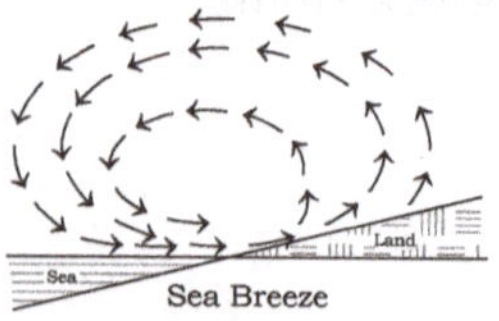

Sea Breeze

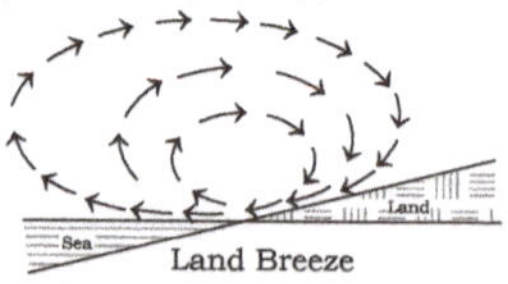

Land Breeze

4 Cyclone and Anti-cyclones

- **Cyclone** Low pressure at centre
- **Anti-cyclone** High pressure at centre

Types of Cyclone

- **Tropical Cyclone** It is formed along warm tropical oceans. Conditions favourable for these cyclone are high temperature, coriolis force, differences in wind speed and low pressure area..
- **Extra-Tropical Cyclones** It is formed along polar fronts. This moves from West to East.

NCERT Folder

Multiple Choice Questions

(i) **If the surface air pressure is 1,000 mb, the air pressure at 1 km above the surface will be**

(a) 700 mb (b) 1,100 mb
(c) 900 mb (d) 1,300 mb

Ans (c) 900 mb

(ii) **The Inter Tropical Convergence Zone normally occurs**

(a) Near the Equator
(b) Near the Tropic of Capricorn
(c) Near the Tropic of Cancer
(d) Near the Arctic Circle

Ans (a) near the Equator

(iii) **The direction of wind around a low pressure area in the Northern hemisphere is**

(a) Clockwise
(b) Anti-clockwise
(c) Perpendicular to isobars
(d) Parallel to isobars

Ans (b) Anti-clockwise

(iv) **Which one of the following is the source region for the formation of air?**

(a) The Equatorial forest (b) The Himalayas
(c) The Siberian Plain (d) The Deccan Plateau

Ans (c) The Siberian Plain

Answer the following questions in about 30 words

(i) **What is the unit in measuring pressure? Why is the pressure measured at station level reduced to the sea level in preparation of weather maps?**

Ans The pressure is measured in units of mb (milibar) and Pascals.
In order to eliminate the effect of altitude on pressure, it is measured at any station level after being reduced to the sea level.

(ii) **While the pressure gradient force is from North to South i.e. from the sub-tropical high pressure to the equator in the Northern hemisphere, why are the winds North Easterlies in the tropics?**

Ans In the Northern hemisphere, the wind between the 0° to 30° N latitude flows North Easterlies i.e. from North-East to South-West because of two reasons

(i) According to Ferrel's law, the direction of wind in tropics is toward the equator.
(ii) As per the Coriolis force, in the Northern hemisphere, the wind deflects rightward.

(iii) **What are the geostrophic winds?**

Ans Geostrophic winds are the winds moving between pressure areas along the paths that are parallel to the isobars. Geostrophic winds are characteristics of upper tropospheric circulation.

(iv) **Explain the land and sea breezes.**

Ans **Land Breeze** In the night, the land loses heat faster and is cooler than the sea. The pressure gradient is from the land to the sea which causes movement of wind from land to sea. This is known as land breeze.

Sea Breeze During day, the land heats up faster and becomes warmer than sea. The pressure gradient from sea to land is created and the wind blows from the sea to land. This is known as sea breeze.

Answer the following questions in about 150 words

(i) **Discuss the factors affecting the speed and direction of wind.**

Ans The horizontal winds near the Earth's surface respond to the combined effect of three forces:

(a) **The Pressure Gradient Force** The pressure gradient is the driving force as wind moves from high pressure to low pressure. The greater thte difference in pressure, the faster the wind will blow.

(b) **Frictional Force** It affects the speed of wind. It is the greatest at the surface and its influence generally extends upto an elevation of 1-3 km. Over the sea surface, the friction is minimal.

(c) **Coriolis Force** The force exerted by the rotation of the Earth is known as the Coriolis force. It is named after the French physicist who described it in 1844. Coriolis force deflects the wind to the right direction in the Northern hemisphere and to the left in the Southern hemisphere. Coriolis force is directly proportional to the angle of latitude. It is maximum at the poles and is absent at the equator.

(ii) **Draw a simplified diagram to show the general circulation of the atmosphere over the globe. What are the possible reasons for the formation of sub-tropical high pressure over 30° N and S latitudes?**

Ans The general circulation of the atmosphere over the globe is given below

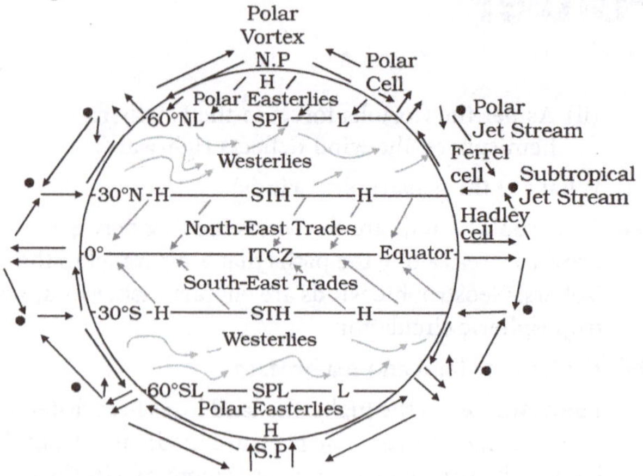

Following are the reasons for the formation of sub-tropical high pressure over 30° N and S latitudes

- Occurrence of low pressure zone due to upward movement of air at ITCZ.
- The winds from the tropic converge over the low pressure area and due to accumulation, they rise along the convection cell and reaches the top of the troposphere at 14 km height. These winds move towards the tropics and begin to cool down.
- The cooled air becomes dense and descends over the 30° N and S latitude causing high pressure areas on these latitudes.

(iii) Why does the tropical cyclone originate over the seas? In which part of the tropical cyclones do torrential rain and high velocity winds blow and why?

Ans A tropical cyclone usually develops from a small tropical depression. Condensation begins in the ascending air and the tropical cyclone takes shape. The tropical cyclone originates over the seas because latent heat of condensation is the main source of energy for tropical cyclones. This condition is available in the tropical oceanic part.

Thus, the tropical cyclones form within one warm, humid air mass between 10° and 25° in both the hemispheres.

Torrential rains and high velocity wind blows in the area of eyewall. The area around the eye is eyewall. There is a strong spiralling ascent of air to greater height reaching the tropopause. The central part of the tropical cyclone is surrounded by the walls of cumulonimbus clouds.

The maximum wind velocity are always recorded adjacent to the centre of tropical cyclone. The winds slow down at uniform rate from the eye wall to the centre, where rain practically ceases.

Exam Pattern Questions

Objective Type Questions

Multiple Choice Questions (MCQs)

1. At sea level the average atmospheric pressure is

(a) 1013.2 mb (b) 1000.2 mb
(c) 1021.4 mb (d) 1006.7 mb

2. Along 30° N and 30° S are found the high-pressure areas known as CBSE Diksha

(a) Equatorial low (b) Subtropical high
(c) Polar high (d) Tropical high

3. Which of the following is not a type of cell?

(a) Hadley cell (b) Ferrel cell
(c) Polar cell (d) Deadly cell

4. Which of the following best describes the "monsoon" phenomenon?

(a) Seasonal reversal of wind direction due to temperature differences
(b) Formation of tornadoes in tropical regions
(c) Permanent high-pressure system over the equator
(d) Movement of cold currents towards the equator

5. In a weather map, if two air masses are shown as meeting but not moving significantly, which type of front does this indicate?

(a) Occluded front (b) Warm front
(c) Stationary front (d) Cold front

6. When a warm air mass is trapped between two cold air masses, what type of front forms?

(a) Cold front (b) Warm front
(c) Stationary front (d) Occluded front

7. A tropical cyclone is named differently in different countries. Where it is called as Willy-Willies?

(a) Atlantic Ocean (b) West Pacific Ocean
(c) Indian Ocean (d) Western Australia

8. Which part of a tropical cyclone is characterised by calm weather and low pressure?

(a) Eye wall (b) Spiral bands
(c) Eye (d) Rain bands

9. Consider the following statements regarding thunderstorms and choose the incorrect one.

(a) They are of long duration, occurring over a small area but are violent.
(b) A thunderstorm is a well-developed cumulonimbus cloud producing thunder and lightning.
(c) A thunderstorm is characterised by intense upward movement of rising warm air.
(d) Hails are also formed during a thunderstorm.

10. Pressure difference in air masses results in the movement of air. Choose the correct option.

(i) It moves from low pressure area to high pressure area.
(ii) It moves from high pressure area to low pressure area.
(iii) The difference in pressure results in the formation of winds.
(iv) There is no difference between density of the contrasting air masses.

Options

(a) Only (i)	(b) Both (ii) and (iv)
(c) (i), (ii) and (iii)	(d) All of these

11. The Intertropical Convergence Zone (ITCZ) is characterised by

I. High pressure and dry conditions
II. Low pressure and heavy rainfall
III. High winds and cold temperatures
IV. Clear skies and calm weather

Options

(a) Only I	(b) Only II
(c) II and III	(d) None of these

12. Choose the correct statement regarding Coriolis force.

I. This is the force generated by the revolution of the Earth.
II. It affects the direction of the wind.
III. It is directly proportional to the angle of latitude.
IV. It is maximum at the poles and minimum at equator.

Options

(a) Only I	(b) Both III and IV
(c) II, III and IV	(d) All of these

13. Identify the type of cyclone from given description.

These are violent storms that originate over oceans in tropical areas. These storms move over to the coastal areas and bring about large-scale destruction caused by violent winds, very heavy rainfall. This is one of the most devastating natural calamities. They are known by different names in different countries.

(a) Temperate cyclone
(b) Tropical cyclone
(c) Extra tropical cyclone
(d) Polar cyclone

14. 'Airmasses are formed over homogeneous surfaces known as source regions'. Identify the correct source regions from the following options.

(i) Warm tropical and subtropical oceans.
(ii) The subtropical cold deserts.
(iii) The relatively cold high latitude oceans.
(iv) The very cold snow-covered continents in high latitudes.

Options

(a) (i), (ii) and (iv)	(b) (ii) and (iv)
(c) Only (i)	(d) (iii) and (iv)

15. There are different pressure belts all over the globe. Choose the high-pressure zones from the given options.

(i) Equatorial region	(ii) Subtropical region
(iii) Sub-polar region	(iv) Polar region

Options

(a) (i) and (ii)	(b) (i), (iv), and (iii)
(c) (ii) and (iv)	(d) (i) and (iii)

16. Identify the type of local wind from the given description.

During night, the slopes of the mountain is cooled down quickly and the dense air move downward into the valley. The direction of wind is from mountain towards valley.

(a) Valley breeze	(b) Land breeze
(c) Loo	(d) Mountain breeze

17. Consider the following statements regarding atmospheric pressure and choose the incorrect one.

(i) It is defined as the force exerted by the weight of column of air above the Earth's surface per unit area.
(ii) It is expressed in units of 'milibar'.
(iii) At sea level the average atmospheric pressure is 1.055 milibar.
(iv) It is measured with the help of an instrument called as 'Mercury Barometer'.

Options

(a) Only (i)	(b) Both (i) and (iv)
(c) Only (iii)	(d) All are correct

18. The pattern of planetary winds largely depends on which of the following aspects?

I. Latitudinal variation of atmospheric heating.
II. Emergence of pressure belts.
III. The migration of belts following apparent path of the Sun.

Codes

(a) I and II	(b) II and III
(c) I and III	(d) All of these

Arrange the Following

19. **Arrange the following steps in the formation of a Hadley cell from the equator to higher latitudes**

(i) Warm air rises at the equator
(ii) Rising air moves poleward at high altitudes
(iii) Air cools and sinks around 30° latitude
(iv) Sinking air moves back toward the equator as trade winds

Codes

(a) (i), (iii), (ii), (iv) (b) (i), (ii), (iii), (iv)
(c) (iii), (iv), (i), (ii) (d) (ii), (i), (iv), (iii)

20. **Arrange the following zones in order zones from the equator to the poles.**

(i) Hadley Cell (ii) Polar Cell
(iii) Ferrel Cell
(iv) Intertropical Convergence Zone (ITCZ)

Codes

(a) (i), (iii), (ii), (iv) (b) (i), (ii), (iii), (iv)
(c) (iii), (iv), (i), (ii) (d) (iv), (i), (iii), (ii)

21. **Arrange the following regions of pressure zones from the equator to the poles**

(i) Equatorial Low (ii) Subtropical High
(iii) Subpolar Low (iv) Polar High

Codes

(a) (i), (iii), (ii), (iv) (b) (ii), (i), (iii), (iv)
(c) (ii), (i), (iv), (iii) (d) (i), (ii), (iii), (iv)

Match the Following

22.

List I		List II	
A.	Maritime tropical	1.	mP
B.	Continental tropical	2.	mT
C.	Maritime polar	3.	cT
D	Continental polar	4.	cP

Codes

	A	B	C	D		A	B	C	D
(a)	1	2	3	4	(b)	2	3	1	4
(c)	3	2	1	4	(d)	4	2	1	3

23.

List I (Types of Front)	List II (Characteristics)
A. Cold front	1. Forms when a warm air mass meets a cold air mass and stalls
B. Warm front	2. Cold air advances and pushes warm air upward
C. Occluded front	3. Warm air moves over a cold air mass
D. Stationary front	4. When the air do not move

Codes

	A	B	C	D		A	B	C	D
(a)	1	2	3	4	(b)	2	1	3	4
(c)	4	1	3	2	(d)	1	4	3	2

24.

List I		List II	
A.	Pressure gradient	1.	Wind blows parallel to the Isobars
B.	Frictional force	2.	Wind blows perpendicular to the isobars
C.	Coriolis force	3.	Its effects are seen up to an elevation of 1-3 km
D	Geostrophic winds	4.	It is strong where the isobars are close to each other

Codes

	A	B	C	D		A	B	C	D
(a)	4	3	2	1	(b)	1	2	3	4
(c)	3	2	1	4	(d)	2	4	1	3

Assertion-Reason

Directions (Q. Nos. 25-28) In the questions given below are two statements labelled as Assertion (A) and other is labelled as Reason (R). In the context of two statements which one of the following is correct?

Codes

(a) Both A and R are true, but R is not the correct explanation of A
(b) Both A and R are true and R is the correct explanation of A
(c) Both A and R are incorrect
(d) A is correct, but R is incorrect

25. **Assertion** (A) The pressure decreases with height.
Reason (R) The air at the surface is denser and hence, has higher pressure.

26. **Assertion** (A) Wind moves from high pressure areas to low pressure areas.
Reason (R) At any elevation pressure varies from place to place and its variation is the primary cause of air motion.

27. **Assertion** (A) The Intertropical Convergence Zone (ITCZ) is a zone of low pressure and is characterised by heavy rainfall.
Reason (R) The ITCZ forms where the winds from the Northern and Southern Hemispheres meet and rise.

28. **Assertion** (A) Tropical cyclones are more likely to form over warm ocean waters.
Reason (R) Warm ocean waters provide the necessary heat and moisture for the development of tropical cyclones.

Answers

1. (a) 1013.2 mb
2. (b) Subtropical high
3. (d) Deadly cell
4. (a) Seasonal reversal of wind direction due to temperature differences
5. (c) Stationary front
6. (d) Occluded front
7. (d) Western Australia
8. (c) Eye
9. (a) They are of long duration, occurring over a small area but are violent.
10. (c) (i), (ii) and (iii)
11. (b) Only (ii)
12. (c) II, III and IV
13. (b) Tropical cyclone
14. (a) (i), (ii) and (iv)
15. (c) (ii) and (iv)
16. (d) Mountain breeze
17. (c) Only (iii)
18. (d) All of these
19. (b) (i), (ii), (iii), (iv)
20. (d) (iv), (i), (iii), (ii)
21. (d) (i), (ii), (iii), (iv)
22. (b)
23. (b)
24. (a)
25. (b) Both A and R are true and R is the correct explanation of A
26. (b) Both A and R are true and R is the correct explanation of A
27. (b) Both A and R are true and R is the correct explanation of A
28. (b) Both A and R are true and R is the correct explanation of A

Subjective Questions

Short Answer Type Questions

1. 'Pressure is distributed horizontally'. Explain in brief.
Competency Based Que

Ans The distribution of atmospheric pressure over the globe is known as horizontal distribution of pressure. Horizontal distribution of pressure is studied by drawing isobars at constant levels.

Isobars are lines connecting places having equal pressure. In order to eliminate the effect of altitude on pressure, it is measured at any station after being reduced to sea level for purposes of comparison.

2. Explain the pressure belts on the globe and world distribution of sea level pressure.

Ans On the basis of mode of genesis, pressure belts are divided into two broad categories i.e. low pressure belts and high pressure belts. A brief description of the pressure belts is given below

Equatorial Low Pressure Belt Located either side of geographical equator.

Sub-tropical High Pressure Belt This belt is located 30°N and 30°S latitude in both the hemispheres.

Sub-polar Low Pressure Belt The belt of sub-polar low pressure is located between 60°N and 60°S latitude in both the hemispheres.

Polar High Pressure Belt High pressure is found at the poles throughout the year in both the hemispheres due to less energy received from the Sun.

3. There are certain factors that determines the pattern of planetary wind. Substantiate the statement.

Ans The pattern of planetary wind largely depends upon following aspects

- Latitudinal variation of atmospheric heating.
- Emergence of pressure belt.
- The migration of belts following apparent path of the Sun.
- The distribution of continents and oceans.
- The rotation of the Earth.

4. Air masses are classified according to the source regions. Explain the source region. Also mention major source regions.
Competency Based Que

Ans The air masses are formed on the homogenous surfaces that can be vast ocean surface or vast plains. The homogenous surface are called the source regions.

The five major source regions are

(i) Warm tropical and sub-tropical oceans.
(ii) The sub-tropical hot deserts.
(iii) The relatively cold high latitude ocean.

(iv) The very cold snow covered continents in high latitude.

(v) Permanently ice covered continents in the Arctic and Antarctica.

5. 'Front is the boundary zone between two air masses.' Discuss its various types. Competency Based Que

Ans When two different air masses meet, the boundary zone between them is called a front.

Fronts may be classified into four types

(i) **Stationary Front** When the front remain stationary, it is called stationary front.

(ii) **Cold Front** When the cold air mass moves towards the warm air mass, its contact zone is called the cold front.

(iii) **Warm Front** If the warm air mass moves towards the cold air mass, the contact zone is called warm front.

(iv) **Occluded Front** If an air mass is fully lifted above the land surface, it is called the occluded front.

6. Describe the process of formation of Extra-tropical cyclone.

Ans Extra-tropical cyclones are formed when contrasting air masses, typically warm and moist from lower latitudes and cold and dry from polar regions, meet at a frontal boundary in mid to high latitudes. This creates temperature gradient with rotation of air due to the Coriolis effect. The cyclone develops a warm and cold front which causes spiralling of winds and diverse weather. Eventually, the faster-moving cold front captures the warm front and occluded front is formed. This stage marks the cyclone's peak after which the cyclone dies or disappears.

7. Extra-tropical cyclones have many important characteristics. Identify them.

Ans The important characteristics of extra-tropical cyclones are as follows

- These cyclones have a clear frontal system.
- They cover a large area and can originate over the land and sea.
- They affect a much larger area as compared to tropical cyclone.
- The extra-tropical cyclone moves from West to East but tropical cyclones move from East to West.
- They are less destructive and causes light showers.

8. Tropical cyclones have many important features. Identify them.

Ans Important features of tropical cyclones are as follows

- A mature tropical cyclone is characterised by the strong, spirally circulating wind around the centre called the eye.
- The diameter of the circulating system can vary between 150 and 250 km.
- The eye is a region of calm with subsiding air.
- Around the eye is the eyewall, where there is a strong spiralling ascent of air to greater height, reaching the tropopause. The wind reaches maximum velocity in this region reaching as high as 250 km per hour.
- They give torrential rainfall.
- They are destructive causing great damage to life and property.

9. Thunderstorms are local storms which are of short duration but are violent. Elucidate. Competency Based Que

Ans Thunderstorms are local storms that are of short duration, occuring over a small area but are violent. Thunderstorms are caused by intense convection on moist hot days. A thunderstorm is a well- grown cumulonimbus clouds producing thunder and lightening. When the clouds extend to heights where sub-zero temperature prevails, hails are formed and they come down as hail storm.

A thunderstorm is characterised by intense updraft of rising warm air, which causes the clouds to grow bigger and rise to greater height which cause precipitation.

10. The tropical cyclones are more destructive than temperate. Discuss. Competency Based Que

Ans Tropical cyclones are generally more destructive than temperate cyclones due to their intense wind speeds, heavy rainfall and large storm surges. They gain energy by warm ocean waters. Tropical cyclones can reach higher intensities with winds often exceeding 150 km/h. These are capable of causing severe structural damage and widespread flooding. The storm surges bring floods to the coastal areas which leads to significant property damage and loss of life. In contrast, temperate cyclones formed due to temperature difference in mid-latitudes. This cyclone brings milder winds and less intense flooding.

11. The wind redistribute the heat and moisture across the planet. Discuss. Competency Based Que

Ans The wind is the horizontal movement of air. Air moves from high pressure to low pressure. When the heat or temperature of any area increases, it causes low pressure zone and air starts to move from high pressure to low pressure. The Earth's atmospheric circulation is an important transfer mechanism for both energy and mass.

The transfer of heat energy from lower latitude to higher latitude is done in general circulation. It reduces the imbalance between equatorial energy surplus and polar energy deficit. In this way, the wind redistribute the heat and moisture across the planet.

12. The Eastern part of India is mostly affected by tropical cyclone which causes loss of life and property. Discuss the possible ways to reduce the calamity which are helpful to prevent destruction of life and property of region. **Competency Based Que**

Ans The Eastern part of India is one of the most affected regions for the tropical cyclone. Thousands of lives and valuable properties lost every year. Although, the origin of tropical cyclone is natural but through human efforts, we could decrease its bad impact on the society.

Possible measures to adopt are as follows

- The coastal regions should be well strengthened with the protection and plantation of mangrove vegetation.
- Construction of resorts, hotels should be restricted near coastal area which are more sensitive.
- Awareness related to protection and reaction against the cyclone should be provided to society with the channel of media, TV, advertisement, street dramas, etc.
- Preparedness related to disaster should be done effectively to tackle any challenge.
- The suspected area for cyclone should be vacated before time to prevent any big loss.

In this way, the impact of cyclone could be reduced over society and life and property could be saved.

13. "Tornadoes are the violent storms which cause massive destruction on its way". Discuss its impact on human life. Also suggest some important measures to mitigate this disaster. **Competency Based Que**

Ans Tornadoes are the strong circular moving storms which generally occur in middle latitudes. Hence, this region, especially Eastern parts of continent are highly vulnerable to tornadoes. Tornado occurs on landmass, therefore, it causes huge loss of mass, man and money and affect the whole human life i.e. education, bussiness, hospital facilities, etc.

To mitigate its effect on the human life, following are the measures which should be adopted

- The tornado sensitive areas should be identified.
- Regional based planning must be adopted for mitigation on particular region.
- Proper alternatives should be developed to assist the human life.
- Fundamental services should be well protected from any storms and calamities.

14. Explain the forces affecting the velocity and direction of wind near the Earth surface. **CBSE Diksha**

Ans. Factors that affects the velocity and direction of wind near the Earth surface are discussed below

(i) **Pressure Gradient Force** The differences in atmospheric pressure produces a force. The rate of change of pressure with respect to distance is the pressure gradient. The pressure gradient is strong where the isobars are close to each other and is weak where the isobars are apart.

(ii) **Frictional Force** It affects the speed of the wind. It is greatest at the surface and its influence generally extends up to an elevation of 1-3 km. Over the sea surface the friction is minimal.

(iii) **Coriolis Force** The rotation of the Earth about its axis affects the direction of the wind. This force is called the Coriolis force. It deflects the wind to the right direction in the Northern hemisphere and to the left in the Southern hemisphere.

Long Answer Type Questions

1. The winds are the horizontal movement of air which are classified into major groups. Explain. **Competency Based Que**

Ans. The winds are the horizontal movement of air. They are classified into four major groups

(i) **Permanent Winds** The trade winds, anti-trade winds and polar winds are known as the permanent winds. These winds follow a definite track throughout the year.

- **Trade Winds** They are categorised in easterlies and westerlies. Easterlies blow from sub-tropical high pressure areas around 30° latitude towards the equator. Trade winds are a major components of general circulation of the atmosphere, as they are most constant wind system on the Earth. Trade winds blow with great regularity over the oceans throughout the year.
- **Anti-trade Winds or Westerlies** They blow in the region lying on the polarward sides of the sub-tropical high pressure areas.
- **Polar Easterlies** They blow between the latitude (60°and 90°) in the polar regions. From the polar areas cold air tends to move towards the equator. The polar easterlies are quite pronounced in the Southern hemisphere.

(ii) **Periodic or Seasonal Winds** Seasonal winds change their direction with change in season. Monsoon is a seasonal wind. In the monsoon climate, there is a complete reversal of wind direction after every six months.

The monsoon is the product of many factors working together. One is the migration of the Inter Tropical Convergence Zone between 25°and 30° and second is the landmass interior records a large change in pressure.

(iii) **Local Winds** Daily variations in atmospheric pressure develop in many parts of the world lead to distinctive local wind patterns. These variations in pressure result from moving air caused by changing surface temperature through out the day. They result in daily changes in wind direction and velocity. There are many locally named winds such as sea breeze, land breeze, valley breeze, mountain breeze, *chinook*, etc.

(iv) **Variable Winds** The winds which change their direction after every few hours are known as variable winds. These include cyclones and anti-cyclones.

2. Tropical cyclones are violent storms that originate over oceans in tropical areas and move over to the coastal areas. Give an account about its process of development and characteristics in detail. Competency Based Que

Ans. Tropical cyclones are violent storms that originate over tropical oceans and move toward coastal areas, bringing large-scale destruction due to strong winds, heavy rainfall and storm surges.

The development of tropical cyclones require specific conditions to form and intensify. These are

- The presence of a large sea surface with the ocean temperature must be 27°C or more.
- The presence of Coriolis force.
- There should be minimal difference in wind speeds at different altitudes to allow the storm to develop without disruption.
- A weak low-pressure area or a low-level cyclonic circulation must already be present for the storm to intensify.
- The presence of upper divergence above the sea level system.

The key characteristics of tropical cyclones are as follows

- The strong spirally circulating wind around the centre is called the eye. The eye is a region of calm with sinking of air.
- The diameter of the circulating system can vary between 150 and 250 km.
- The region around the eye with strong winds and heavy rainfall, where the storm's intensity is highest, is called the eye wall.
- Winds can reach speeds up to 250 km/h or more, with maximum intensity near the eye wall.
- Torrential rainfall occurs, particularly around the eye wall. From the eyewall rain bands move outward and groups of cumulus, and cumulonimbus clouds also move towards the outer region.
- The diameter of the storm over the Bay of Bengal, Arabian sea and Indian ocean is between 600 -1200 km.
- Cyclones move at a speed of 300 to 500 km per day and create storm surges with floods to the coastal lowlands.

3. Discuss the effect of general circulation of atmosphere.

Ans. The movement of air is known as atmospheric circulation and when the average of the entire globe is considered, the motion is referred to as the general circulation of the atmosphere.

The effects of this circulation are as follows

- Earth's atmospheric circulation is an important transfer mechanism for both energy and mass. In this process, the imbalances between equatorial energy surplus and polar energy deficit is partly resolved, Earth's weather patterns are generated and ocean currents are produced.
- The general circulation of the atmosphere also affects the oceans. The large scale winds of the atmosphere initiate large and slow moving currents on the ocean. Ocean in turn provides input of energy and water vapours into the air.

  For example, warming and cooling of the Pacific Ocean is the most important in terms of general atmospheric circulation. The warm water of the central Pacific ocean slowly drift towards South American coast and replaces the cold Perunian current which is known as El-Nino.

  The El-Nino event is closely associated with the pressure changes in the central Pacific and Australia which is called Southern Oscillation.

  The combination of both El-Nino and Southern Oscillation is known as ENSO. In the years where the ENSO is strong, the large scale variations in weather occur over the world.

4. "The temperate cyclone has greater significance in the region it occurs." Give your argument in support of this statement. Competency Based Que

Ans The temperate cyclone occurs in mid-latitude of Southern hemisphere which are born along the polar front. The temperate cyclone may covers 1000 km wide area. These cyclones move at a gentle pace of 5 to 25 km per hour. The weather condition in different parts of the cyclone varies significantly. Temperature increases suddenly when the cyclone comes very close to the observation point.

Significance of temperate cyclones for the region are

- Temperate cyclone gives light shower which are highly beneficial for the agriculture.
- It causes snowfall in the region which causes attraction for tourism.
- The snowfall becomes the fresh source of water for rivers.
- Since the movement of wind is low, it does not cause any harm to life and property.
- These temperate cyclones do not require, so much disaster management machinery due to their less violent nature.

Thus, this way temperate cyclones has greater significance to the region it occurs.

5. Distinguish between tropical and extra-tropical cyclone.

Ans Differences between tropical and extra-tropical cyclone are as follows

Basis	Tropical Cyclone	Extra-tropical Cyclone
Formation	Tropical cyclones originate entirely within tropical air mass, due to circular movement of air.	These originate along the polar front due to cyclonic circulation of air masses.
Location	Tropical cyclone occurs from 8°-25° N and S latitudes in Eastern part of continent.	These are formed in the mid-latitudes (35°-65° N and S).
Structure	It has an eye in inner part and eyewall in the central part.	There are cold fronts and warm fronts which finally form occluded front.
Frontal system	No clear frontal system.	Clear frontal system.
Area under influence	The diameter of the circulating system can vary between 150 km to 200 km.	It covers huge area approx 1000 km.
Nature	Violent in nature, heavy rainfall and thunderstorm.	Less destructive, low rainfall.
Duration	It is a short period process.	It is a long period process. Extra-tropical cyclones remain for 10-15 days.
Pressure gradient	It is maximum in tropical cyclone.	It is comparatively low.
Significance	These are destructive and cause harm to life and property.	These are economically and ecologically useful as these cause snowfall to attract tourists and low rainfall which is good for agriculture.

6. 'Air masses are distinct in its nature and source'. Examine the statement. **CBSE Diksha**

Ans The air with different characteristics in terms of temperature and humidity is called an air mass. It is defined as a large body of air having little horizontal variation in temperature and moisture. The homogenous surfaces, over which air masses form, are called the source regions. Tropical air masses are warm and polar air masses are cold.

The air masses are classified according to the source regions. There are five major source regions and accordingly different types of air masses are recognised. These are

(i) Warm tropical and subtropical oceans - Maritime tropical (mT)

(ii) The subtropical hot deserts-Continental tropical (cT)

(iii) The relatively cold high latitude oceans - Maritime polar (mP)

(iv) The very cold snow-covered continents in high latitudes - Continental polar (cP)

(v) Permanently ice-covered continents in the Arctic and Antarctica - Continental arctic (cA).

7. There are different types of fronts formed on the basis of contrasting property of air masses. Give a detailed diagrammatic explanation of the different types of fronts.

Ans. When two different air masses meet, the boundary zone between them is called a front. The fronts occur in middle latitudes and are characterised by steep gradient in temperature and pressure. They bring abrupt changes in temperature and cause the air to rise to form clouds and cause precipitation. The process of formation of the fronts is known as frontogenesis.

There are four types of fronts

(i) **Cold Front** When the cold air moves towards the warm air mass, its contact zone is called the cold front.

(ii) **Warm Front** If the warm air mass moves towards the cold air mass, the contact zone is a warm front.

(iii) **Stationary Front** When the front remains stationary, it is called a stationary front.

(iv) **Occluded Front** If an air mass is fully lifted above the land surface, it is called the occluded front.

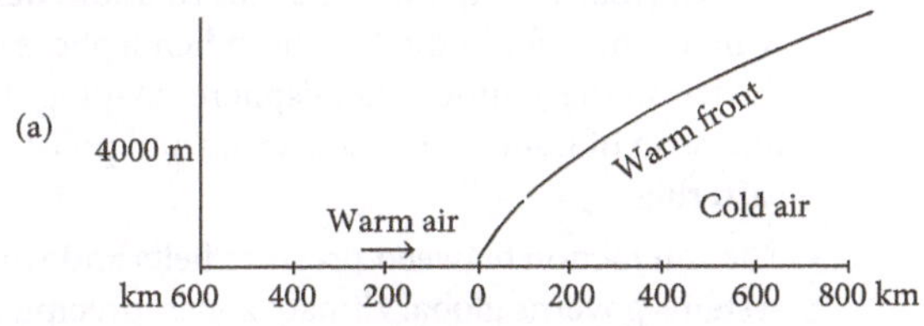

(b)

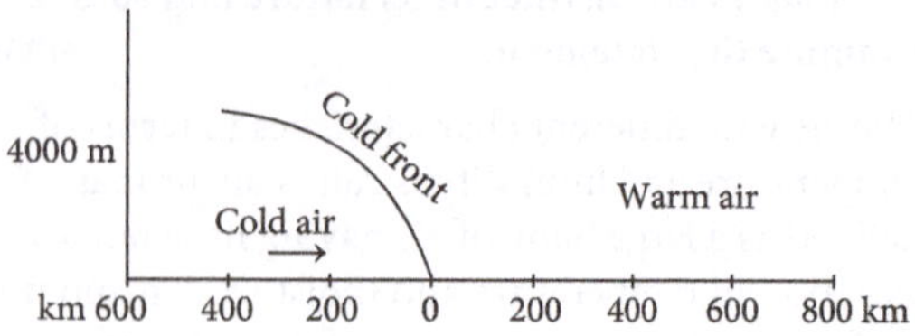

(c)

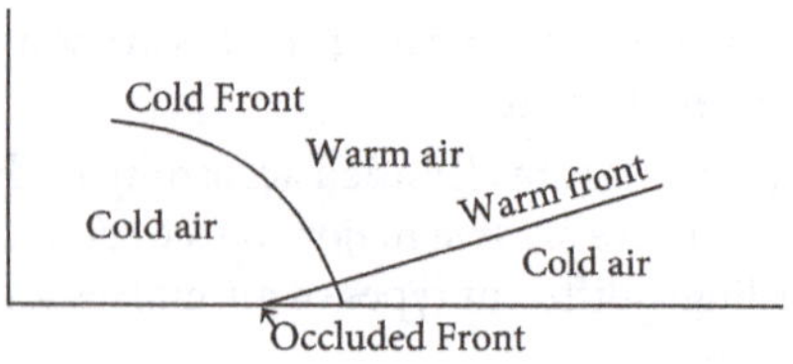

8. Analyse the relationship between atmospheric pressure belts and global wind patterns.

Ans. Atmospheric pressure belts and global wind patterns are very much linked. The movement of air between these belts (influenced by the Coriolis Effect), establishes the global wind systems that regulate Earth's weather and climate as follows

- These pressure zones are created by the Earth's rotation and uneven solar heating, which generate distinct belts of high and low pressure across latitudes. At the equator, intense solar heating causes warm, moist air to rise, creating the equatorial low-pressure belt (Inter-Tropical Convergence Zone or ITCZ). This rising air moves poleward in the upper atmosphere, cools, and sinks around 30° N and S, forming the subtropical high-pressure zones. Air moves from high-pressure to low-pressure areas due to pressure gradients, forming global wind systems as
  (i) **Trade Winds** Air from the subtropical highs flows towards the equatorial low, forming steady winds called trade winds. These are deflected westward by the Coriolis Effect.
  (ii) **Westerlies** Air flowing poleward from the subtropical highs is deflected eastward, forming westerlies.
  (iii) **Polar Easterlies** At polar regions, sinking cold air forms high-pressure areas, and winds blow towards the subpolar lows, deflected westward.
- The Coriolis Effect, due to Earth's rotation, deflects wind to the right in the Northern hemisphere and to the left in the Southern hemisphere, shaping the direction of trade winds, westerlies and polar easterlies.
- The interaction between pressure belts and wind systems governs global climate zones, precipitation patterns and oceanic currents.

9. Isobars plays crucial role in understanding the weather patterns. Elucidate.

Ans. Isobars are lines drawn on weather maps that connect points of equal atmospheric pressure. They play a critical role in the following ways

- Isobars helps in understanding weather patterns, as they reveal pressure differences across regions.
- The spacing between isobars indicates the pressure gradient; closely spaced isobars represent a steep gradient which shows strong winds in the area. While widely spaced isobars indicate a gentle gradient and calm condition.
- Isobars also helps in identifying high and low-pressure systems. Closed isobars forming a circle around a high-pressure area indicate an anticyclone. Conversely, closed isobars around a low-pressure area form a cyclone, this brings clouds, precipitation, and stormy weather.
- By analysing isobar patterns, meteorologists can predict wind direction (which moves from high to low pressure) and forecast changes in weather, such as approaching fronts or shifts in temperature and humidity.

Source Based Questions

1. Read the passage carefully and answer the questions that follow.

Tropical cyclones are violent storms that originate over oceans in tropical areas and move over to the coastal areas bringing about large scale destruction caused by violent winds, very heavy rainfall and storm surges. This is one of the most devastating natural calamities.

They are known as Cyclones in the Indian Ocean, Hurricanes in the Atlantic, Typhoons in the Western Pacific and South China Sea, and Willy-willies in the Western Australia. Tropical cyclones originate and intensify over warm tropical oceans. The conditions favourable for the formation and intensification of tropical storms are: (i) Large sea surface with temperature higher than 27°C; (ii) Presence of the Coriolis force; (iii) Small variations in the vertical wind speed; (iv) A pre-existing weak low-pressure area or low-level-cyclonic circulation; (v) Upper divergence above the sea level system. The energy that intensifies the storm, comes from the condensation process in the towering cumulonimbus clouds, surrounding the centre of the storm. With continuous supply of moisture from the sea, the storm is further strengthened. On reaching the land the moisture supply is cut off and the storm dissipates. The place where a tropical cyclone crosses the coast is called the landfall of the cyclone. The cyclones, which cross 20° N latitude generally, recurve and they are more destructive.

A mature tropical cyclone is characterised by the strong spirally circulating wind around the centre, called the eye.

The diameter of the circulating system can vary between 150 and 250 km. The eye is a region of calm with subsiding air. Around the eye is the eye wall, where there is a strong spiralling ascent of air to greater height reaching the tropopause. The wind reaches maximum velocity in this region, reaching as high as 250 km per hour. Torrential rain occurs here. From the eye wall rain bands may radiate and trains of cumulus and cumulonimbus clouds may drift into the outer region.

(i) Which of the following is not a characteristic of a mature tropical cyclone?

(a) Calm winds in the center
(b) Strong spirally circulating winds around the eye
(c) Torrential rain in the eye wall
(d) No rain in the outer region

Ans. (d) No rain in the outer region

(ii) In the vertical structure of a mature tropical cyclone, the strongest wind speeds are typically found in which region?

(a) The center of the eye
(b) The outer rain bands
(c) The eye wall
(d) The upper layers of the troposphere

Ans. (c) The eye wall

(iii) Which of the following is correct according to the name of the cyclones in different regions?

(a) Atlantic - Cyclones
(b) Indian Ocean - Hurricanes
(c) Western Australia - Willy-willies
(d) Eastern Pacific -Typhoons

Ans. (c) Western Australia - Willy-willies

2. Read the passage carefully and answer the questions that follow.

The systems developing in the mid and high latitude, beyond the tropics are called the middle latitude or extra tropical cyclones. The passage of front causes abrupt changes in the weather conditions over the area in the middle and high latitudes. Extra tropical cyclones form along the polar front. Initially, the front is stationary. In the Northern hemisphere, warm air blows from the South and cold air from the North of the front.

When the pressure drops along the front, the warm air moves northwards and the cold air move towards, south setting in motion an anticlockwise cyclonic circulation. The cyclonic circulation leads to a well-developed extra tropical cyclone, with a warm front and a cold front. There are pockets of warm air or warm sector wedged between the forward and the rear cold air or cold sector. The warm air glides over the cold air and a sequence of clouds appear over the sky ahead of the warm front and cause precipitation. The cold front approaches the warm air from behind and pushes the warm air up. As a result, cumulus clouds develop along the cold front. The cold front moves faster than the warm front ultimately overtaking the warm front. The warm air is completely lifted up and the front is occluded and the cyclone dissipates. The processes of wind circulation both at the surface and aloft are closely interlinked. The extra tropical cyclone differs from the tropical cyclone in number of ways.

The extra tropical cyclones have a clear frontal system which is not present in the tropical cyclones. They cover a larger area and can originate over the land and sea. Whereas the tropical cyclones originate only over the seas and on reaching the land they dissipate. The extra tropical cyclone affects a much larger area as compared to the tropical cyclone. The wind velocity in a tropical cyclone is much higher and it is more destructive. The extra tropical cyclones move from West to East but tropical cyclones, move from East to West.

(i) Which of the following is the most important factor that leads to the origin of Extra-tropical cyclones?

(a) Contrasting winds (b) Surface temperature
(c) Presence of Mountain (d) Warm ocean

Ans (a) Contrasting winds

(ii) Which of the following front is formed at the death of an extra tropical cyclone?

(a) Warm front (b) Cold front
(c) Occluded front (d) Both (a) and (b)

Ans (c) Occluded front

(iii) Extra tropical cyclones are formed mainly in which of the following areas?

(a) Equatorial regions
(b) Polar regions
(c) Temperate regions
(d) Tropical regions

Ans (c) Temperate regions

3. Study the given diagram and answer the questions that follow

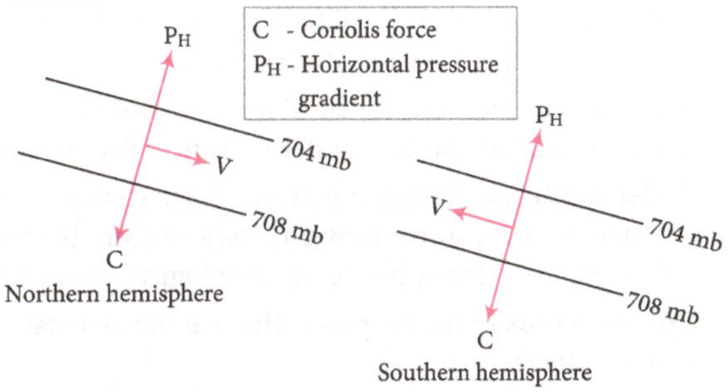

(i) What type of wind is shown by the Symbol V?

(a) Easterly wind (b) Sea breeze
(c) Geostrophic wind (d) Jet stream

Ans. (c) Geostrophic wind

(ii) **Which of the following force determines the velocity of a wind?**

(a) Corialis force (b) Pressure Gradient force
(c) Gravitational force (d) Magnetic force

Ans. (b) Pressure Gradient force

(iii) **The Corialis force is zero in which of the following regions?**

(a) Polar region (b) Mountains
(c) Equatorial regions (d) Temperate region

Ans. (c) Equatorial regions

4. Read the passage carefully and answer the questions that follow.

The pattern of the movement of the planetary winds is called the general circulation of the atmosphere. The general circulation of the atmosphere also sets in motion the ocean water circulation which influences the Earth's climate. The air at the Inter Tropical Convergence Zone (ITCZ) rises because of convection caused by high insolation and a low pressure is created. The winds from the tropics converge at this low-pressure zone. The converged air rises along with the convective cell. It reaches the top of the troposphere up to an altitude of 14 km and moves towards the poles. This causes accumulation of air at about 30° N and S. Part of the accumulated air sinks to the ground and forms a subtropical high. Another reason for sinking is the cooling of air when it reaches 30° N and S latitudes. Down below near the land surface the air flows towards the equator as the easterlies. The easterlies from either side of the equator converge in the Inter Tropical Convergence Zone (ITCZ). Such circulations from the surface upwards and vice-versa are called cells. Such a cell in the tropics is called Hadley Cell. In the middle latitudes the circulation is that of sinking cold air that comes from the poles and the rising warm air that blows from the subtropical high. At the surface these winds are called westerlies and the cell is known as the Ferrel cell. At polar latitudes the cold dense air subsides near the poles and blows towards middle latitudes as the polar easterlies. This cell is called the polar cell.

(i) **Why do you think understanding atmospheric circulation is crucial for modern weather forecasting?**

Ans. Understanding circulation patterns helps in predicting weather changes, storm movements, and climate trends. This is essential for accurate meteorological predictions.

(ii) **How do winds in the tropics influence the circulation of ocean waters?**

Ans. Winds in the tropics drive surface ocean currents by distributing warm water across the oceans. This influence the global climate patterns and helps in regulating temperatures worldwide.

(iii) **The process of air circulation that leads to the formation of subtropical high-pressure zones around 30° N and S latitudes. Comment.**

Ans. Warm air rises at the equatorial ITCZ and moves poleward in the upper atmosphere, it cools and sinks around 30° N and S. This forms subtropical high-pressure zones.

5. Study the given diagram and answer the questions that follows .

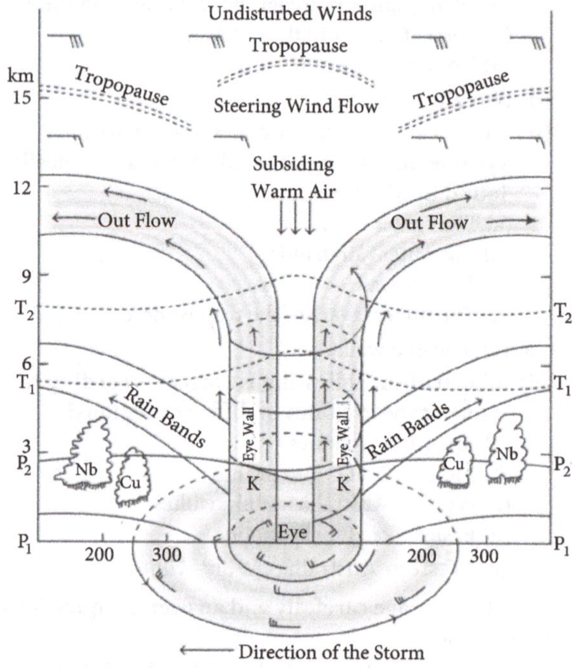

(i) **Name the part of the cyclone where subsidence of air takes place.**

Ans. Eye of the cyclone is the part where subsidence of air takes place.

(ii) **Write one favourable condition required for the formation of tropical cyclone.**

Ans. There must be continuous supply of moisture from the oceans for the formation of a cyclone.

(iii) **Write one feature of tropical cyclone that makes it different from extratropical cyclone.**

Ans. Tropical cyclones develop in tropical areas whereas extratropical cyclones develop in middle latitudes. Tropical cyclones are more destructive as compared to the extratropical cyclone.

Map Based Question

1. Mark the following major hot deserts of the world on a world map.

(i) Mojave Desert
(ii) Patagonian Desert
(iii) Sahara Desert
(iv) Gobi Desert
(v) Thar Desert
(vi) Great Victoria Desert

Ans

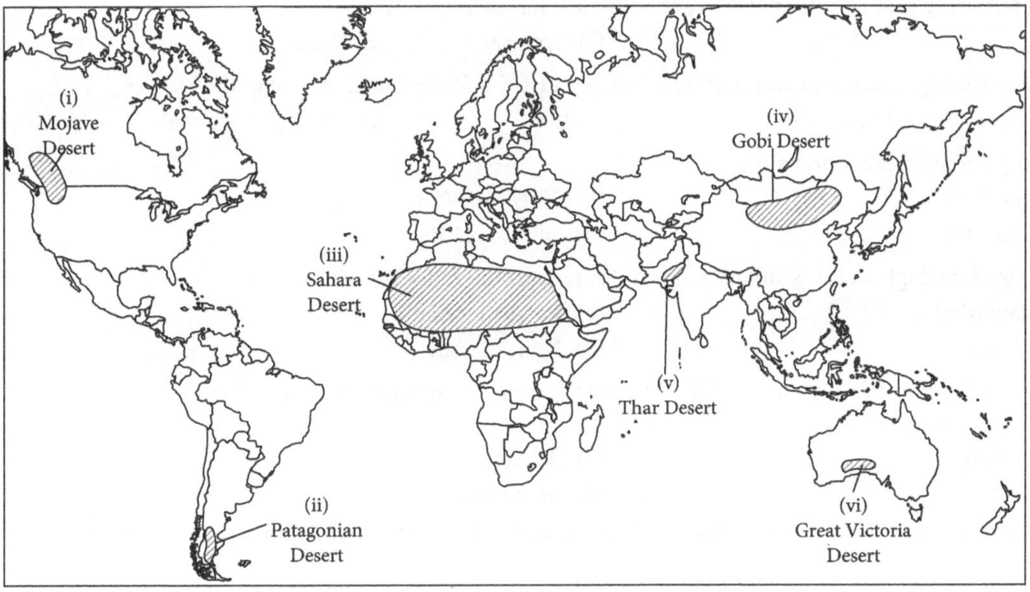

SELF ASSESSMENT TEST

Objective Answer Type Questions

1. Which of following redistributes the heat and moisture across the Planet?
   (a) Wind (b) Cloud (c) Cyclones (d) Tornadoes
2. In the lower atmosphere, the pressure decreases to about 1 mb for each .... height.
   (a) 5m (b) 10 m (c) 15m (d) 20m
3. The subtropical highs are found along
   (a) 10°N and 10°S (b) 20°N and 20°S
   (c) 30°N and 30°S (d) 50°N and 50°S
4. The cool air of the high plateaus and ice fields draining into the valley is called ....
   (a) Mountain wind (b) Katabatic wind
   (c) Valley breeze (d) None of these
5. Warming and Cooling of which of the following oceans is most important in terms of general atmospheric circulation?
   (a) Arctic ocean (b) Atlantic ocean
   (c) Pacific ocean (d) Indian ocean
6. What is the tropical circulation called that involves rising air at the ITCZ and sinking air at 30° N and S latitudes?
   (a) Ferrel cell (b) Polar cell
   (c) Hadley cell (d) Equatorial cell

Short Answer Type Questions

7. How do air pressure and wind influence the weather?
8. What is Coriolis force and who discovered it first?
9. Describe the characteristics of the Hadley cell and Ferrel cell in the Earth's atmospheric circulation.
10. Explain the significance of the Intertropical Convergence Zone (ITCZ) in global weather patterns.
11. What are Isobars? Explain its characteristics.
12. What is an air mass ? Also,discuss the different types of air masses based on their source regions.

Long Answer Type Questions

13. Explain the world distribution of sea level pressure and describe the different pressure belts found across the globe.
14. There is seasonal variations in the pressure distribution over the Earth's surface. Discuss.
15. Discuss the formation, characteristics and impact of thunderstorms and tornadoes.
16. Write about the formation and development of extra tropical cyclones. How do these cyclones differ from tropical cyclones?
17. What do you mean by the process of frontogenesis ? Explain the four types of fronts: cold, warm, stationary and occluded.

10 CHAPTER

This chapter deals with the concept of forms of water present in the atmosphere and its importance. There is a continuous exchange of water between atmosphere, ocean and the continents through the process of evaporation, condensation and precipitation.

▼ **YOUR STUDY GOALS**

10.1 Water Vapour and Humidity
10.2 Precipitation
10.3 World Distribution of Rainfall
10.4 Rainfall Regions of the World

▼ **YOUR PRACTICE GOAL**

- Objective Type Questions (27 Qs ; MCQs, Statements, Matching, A-R)
- Subjective Questions (13 SAs, 6 LAs)
- Source Based Questions (2 Qs)

Water in the Atmosphere

10.1 Water Vapour and Humidity

- Air contains water vapour and the amount of water vapour in the atmosphere ranges between 0 - 4 % by volume.
- Water is present in the atmosphere mainly in three forms which are gaseous, solid and liquid form.
- The moisture in the atmosphere comes from water bodies through evaporation and transpiration[1] from plants.
- Water vapour present in the air is known as **humidity**. Humidity is expressed in terms of quantity in different ways.

Absolute Humidity

- The actual amount of water vapour present in the atmosphere is known as **absolute humidity**.
- It is measured by the weight of water per unit volume of air. It is expressed in **grams per cubic metres**.
- The absolute humidity is not uniform everywhere, it differs from place to place on the earth's surface.
- Temperature of a place plays an important role in deciding the ability of the air to hold water vapour.

1 Transpiration It is the process by which plants release water vapour into the air through tiny pores, mainly on their leaves called stomata.

Relative Humidity

- Relative humidity is the actual percentage of humidity present in the atmosphere as compared to the capacity the atmosphere can hold. It is measured in percentage.
- It is affected by the change in air temperature as the capacity to hold moisture increases or decreases with temperature.
- It is greater over the oceans and least over the continents.
- When air present in the atmosphere contains maximum amount of water vapour/humidity at a given temperature and pressure it is called **saturated air**.
- Relative humidity of this type of air is 100%. This means that air can no longer hold any more moisture.
- The temperature at which the saturation occurs in a given sample of air is known as the **dew point.**

Evaporation

- It is the process by which water is converted from liquid to gaseous state. This process adds more moisture to the atmosphere.
- Evaporation occurs whenever there is presence of heat in the atmosphere. The temperature at which water starts evaporating is known as **latent heat of vaporisation**.
- Water is absorbed more by the air when there is increase in temperature and the capacity of air to hold moisture also increases.
- Movement of air replaces the saturated layer of air with the unsaturated layers. Hence, the movement of air affects the rate of evaporation.

Condensation

- Condensation is the process by which water in gaseous form is converted into liquid form. This process removes the water vapour from the atmosphere.
- When moist air is cooled, it reaches to a level when its capacity to hold water vapour stops. Then, the excess water vapour is converted into liquid form.
- Condensation takes place around small solid particles of dust, smoke and salt from the ocean. These are called as **hygroscopic condensation nuclei**.
- Condensation also takes place when the moist air comes in contact with some colder object. It may also take place when the temperature is close to the dew point.
- The process of condensation is influenced by certain factors like volume of air, temperature, pressure and humidity.
- Condensation depends upon the amount of cooling and the relative humidity of the air.

Conditions for Condensation

- Condensation happens when the temperature of the air is equal to or lower than the dew point. Volume should remain constant.
- Condensation happens when the temperature and volume of air is reduced.
  - The third condition for the process of condensation is the addition of moisture to the air through evaporation.
  - Among all the conditions, the most favourable is the decrease in air temperature.

Forms of Condensation

- After condensation, the water vapour or the moisture in the atmosphere changes into different forms.
- Forms of condensation can be classified on the basis of temperature and location. These forms are dew, frost, fog and clouds.

Dew

- When the moisture is deposited in the form of water droplets on cooler surfaces of solid objects such as stones, grass blades and plant leaves, it is known as **dew**.
- The ideal conditions for the formation of dew are clear sky, calm air, high relative humidity and cold and long nights.
- For the formation of dew, it is necessary that the dew point is above the freezing point.

Frost

- It is formed on cold surfaces when condensation takes place below freezing point (0°C), i.e. the dew point is equal to or below the freezing point.
- The excess moisture is deposited in the form of little ice crystals instead of water droplets.
- The ideal conditions for the formation of white frost are the same as those for the formation of dew, but the air temperature must be equal to or below the freezing point.

Fog and Mist

- The **fog** is similar to a cloud which has its base at or very near to the ground.
- When the temperature of an air mass that has a large quantity of water vapour falls suddenly, the process of condensation takes place on small dust particles. This condensation results in the formation of fogs.
- Fogs are like mini clouds in which condensation takes place around nuclei such as dust, smoke and the salt particles.
- Formation of fog and mist affects the visibility of the area, the visibility becomes poor to zero.
- In urban and industrial centres, smoke provides plenty of dust particles which helps in the formation of fog and mist. Such a condition when fog is mixed with smoke, is described as **smog**.
- The difference between the mist and fog is that mist contains more moisture than the fog. In mist, each particle contains a thick layer of moisture.
- Mists are common in mountains because the rising warm air from the surface moves up the slopes meets a cold surface.
- Fogs contain less moisture than mist and they occur where warm currents of air come in contact with cold currents.

Clouds

- Cloud is a mass of small water droplets or tiny crystals of ice, formed by the condensation of the water vapour in free air at a certain height.
- As the clouds are formed at some height over the surface of the earth, they take various shapes.
- The expanse, density and transparency or opaqueness clouds are grouped under four types according to their height : cirrus, cumulus, stratus and nimbus clouds.

1. Cirrus Clouds

- These clouds are formed at high altitudes of 8,000-12,000 m.
- They are thin clouds. They appear as an individual cloud which is not attached to any other clouds. They are always white in colour.

2. Cumulus Clouds

- These clouds look like cotton wool. They are generally formed at a height of 4,000-7,000 m.
- They exist in patches and can be seen scattered here and there. They have a flat base.

3. Stratus Clouds

- These clouds are layered clouds and spreaded in large portions of the sky.

▲ *Stratus Clouds*

- These clouds are generally formed either due to loss of heat or the mixing of air masses of different temperatures.

4. Nimbus Clouds

- These clouds are black or dark grey in colour. They are formed at middle levels or very close to the surface of the earth.
- These are extremely dense and opaque to the rays of the sun.
- Sometimes, the clouds are so low that they seem to touch the ground. Nimbus clouds have no defined shape and they contain thick vapour.

Categories of Clouds

- When these four basic types of clouds combine in certain conditions they give rise to variety of clouds. These are mentioned below
- **High Clouds** They are formed at high elevations and include clouds like cirrus, cirrostratus, cirrocumulus.
- **Middle Clouds** They are formed in middle heights and includes clouds like altostratus and altocumulus.
- **Low Clouds** They are formed at low heights and includes clouds like- stratocumulus and nimbostratus.
- **Cumulus and Cumulonimbus** These are the clouds that have extensive vertical development.

Quick Test 1

1. In how many forms water vapour is present in the atmosphere?
2. Which is the lowest cloud in terms of elevation?
3. Mention one difference between fog and mist.
4. What is the height of the cumulus clouds?

10.2 Precipitation

- The condensed particles grow bigger in size when the process of condensation continues for long period of time.
- The air reaches to a stage where it can no longer hold the moisture against the force of gravity, so they start falling on to the ground. This is known as precipitation.

Forms of Precipitation

- The moisture falls on the ground in different forms. This may take place in solid or liquid form.
- When the precipitation is in the form of water, it is called **rainfall** and when the temperature is lower than the 0°C, the precipitation takes place in the form of fine flakes of snow and it is called **snowfall**.
- Snow flakes are formed when the moisture is released in the form of hexagonal crystals.
- Besides rain and snow, other forms of precipitation are **sleet** and **hail**[2]. But they don't happen everywhere or all the time. They are usually limited to certain weather events.
- Sleet is formed when raindrops freeze into small ice pellets before reaching the ground.
- This usually occurs when there's a warm layer of air above a colder layer near the ground. This causes the rain to partially freeze as it falls through the cold layer.

2 Hail It is a type of precipitation received in the form of ice pellets. The size of the hail can be between 5 to 190 mm in diameter.

- Sometimes, raindrops after being released by the clouds, become solidified into small rounded solid pieces of ice. These are called as **hailstones**.
- These are formed when the rainwater passes through the layers of cold air. Hailstones have several concentric layers of ice one over the other.

Types of Rainfall

On the basis of origin, rainfall may be classified into three main types. These types are discussed below

1. Convectional Rainfall

- When the air is heated, it becomes light and rises up in form of convection currents. As it rises, it expands and loses heat and consequently, condensation takes place.
- Cumulous clouds are formed with thunder and lightning. Heavy rainfall also takes place but this is for a short duration of time.
- Convection rains are common in summer in the hotter part of the day. This occurs in equatorial regions and in interior part of the continents, mainly in **Northern hemisphere**.

2. Orographic Rainfall

- When the saturated air mass comes in contact with a mountain, it is forced to move upward the slopes and as air rises, it expands.
- When the air moves to a higher elevation, the temperature starts decreasing and it causes condensation of the air. This results in the formation of orographic rainfall.
- One of the important characteristics of this type of rain is that the windward side of the mountain receives more rainfall, while the leeward side remains dry and rainless as the air descends.
- The area which is situated in the leeward side is called as **rain-shadow area**. It is also known as the **relief rain.**

3. Cyclonic Rainfall

- It occurs when temperate and tropical cyclones are formed in an area.

10.3 World Distribution of Rainfall

- Different places on the earth's surface receive different amounts of rainfall in a year and in different seasons.
- In general, as we go from the equator towards the poles, the amount of rainfall decreases.
- The **coastal areas** of the world receive greater amounts of rainfall than the interior of the continents.
- The rainfall is more over the oceans than on the landmasses of the world because oceans provide great source of moisture for condensation.
- Between the latitudes 35° and 40°N and S of the equator, the rain received is more on the Eastern coasts and it decreases when we go towards the West. But, between 45° and 65° N and S of equator, because of the westerlies, the rainfall is **first received on the Western margins** of the continents and it goes on decreasing towards the East margin.
- Another variation in rainfall can be seen where mountains run parallel to the coast. In this condition, the rain is greater on the coastal plain on the windward side and it decreases towards the leeward side.
- In areas like the **equatorial belt** and some cool temperate regions, rain is spread more evenly throughout the year.

10.4 Rainfall Regions of the World

On the basis of the total amount of annual precipitation received in an area. Major precipitation regions of the world are

High Rainfall Region

- The region that receives annual rainfall of 200 cm or more comes under this category.
- The equatorial belt, the windward slopes of the mountains along the Western coasts in the cool temperate zone and the coastal areas of the monsoon land, comes under this category.

Moderate Rainfall Region

- The regions that receives annual rainfall between 100-200 cm comes under this category.
- Interior part of the continents and the coastal areas of the continents comes under this category.

Low Rainfall Region

- The region that receives annual rainfall between 50-100 cm comes under this category.
- The central parts of the tropical land and the Eastern and interior parts of the temperate lands comes under this category.

Very Low Rainfall Region

- The region that receives annual rainfall less than 50 cm comes under this category.
- Areas situated in the rain shadow zone of the interior of the continents and high latitudes areas comes under this category.

Quick Test 2

1. Name any two forms of precipitation.
2. Which areas of the world receive greater amount of rainfall?
3. What is the range of rainfall received in high rainfall region?
4. Which margin of the continent receives heavy rainfall?

Mind Map

WATER IN ATMOSPHERE

1 Water Vapour and Humidity

- Humidity it is defined as water present in the atmosphere, e.g., relative humidity and absolute humidity.
- It is expressed in terms of quantity.

Forms of Condensation

- **Dew** Formed during clear sky, calm air and high relative humidity.
- **Frost** Formed when temperature is below freezing point 10° C
- **Fog/Mist** Similar to cloud which has base near the ground.
- **Clouds** Mass of minute water droplets

Categories of Clouds

- **High Clouds** (e.g., Cirrus, Cirrostratus, Cummulonimbus)
- **Middle Clouds** (e.g., Altostratus and Altocumulus)
- **Low Clouds** (e.g., Stratocumulus and Nimbostratus)

2 Evaporation

- Process by which water is converted from liquid to gaseous state.
- Occurs when heat is present in the atmosphere.
- Movement of air affects the rate of evaporation.

Forms of Precipitation

- **Sleet** Frozen raindrops.
- **Snowfall** These are in the form of flakes of snow.
- **Rainfall** When the precipitation is in liquid form.

3 Condensation

- A process by which gaseous form of water is converted into liquid form.
- Depends upon the amount of cooling and the relative humidity of the air.

4 Precipitation

It is the water that falls to the ground in liquid or frozen state.

Types of Rainfall

- **Convection Rainfall** Caused because of heating of the Earth's surface. Occurs in equatorial regions and interior part of the continent.
- **Orographic Rainfall** Caused when the warm air moves upward the mountain slope. Windward side of the mountain receives more rainfall, while leeward side remains dry.
- **Cyclonic Rainfall** Caused during cyclonic storms.

5 World Distribution of Rainfall

- **High Rainfall Regions**
  e.g., Equatorial region, coastal areas, between latitude and 35° and 40° N and S of Equator, windward side of mountain.
- **Low Rainfall Regions**
  e.g., Polar areas, interior of continent, Western coasts, leeward side of mountains.

NCERT Folder

Multiple Choice Questions

(i) **Which one of the following is the most important constituent of the atmosphere for human being?**

(a) Water vapour (b) Nitrogen
(c) Dust particle (d) Oxygen

Ans (d) Oxygen

(ii) **Which one of the following process is responsible for transforming liquid into vapour?**

(a) Condensation (b) Transpiration
(c) Evaporation (d) Precipitation

Ans (c) Evaporation

(iii) **The air that contains moisture to its full capacity**

(a) Relative humidity (b) Specific humidity
(c) Absolute humidity (d) Saturated air

Ans (d) Saturated air

(iv) **Which one of the following is the highest cloud in the sky?**

(a) Cirrus (b) Stratus (c) Nimbus (d) Cumulus

Ans (a) Cirrus

Answer the following questions in about 30 words

(i) **Name the three type of precipitation.**

Ans The three types of precipitation are

(i) **Rain** The precipitation which is in the form of water.

(ii) **Snow** When the temperature is lower than the 0°C, precipitation takes place in the form of fine flakes of snow.

(iii) **Hail** When drops of rain after being released by the clouds become solidified into small rounded solid pieces of ice and reach to the surface of the Earth.

(ii) **Explain relative humidity.**

Ans The percentage of moisture present in the atmosphere as compared to its full capacity at a given temperature is known as relative humidity. It is higher over oceans and lower over continents because oceans hold more moisture than land.

(iii) **Why does the amount of water vapour decrease rapidly with altitude?**

Ans Since, water vapours are heavy molecules as compared to other gases and after a definite height the water vapour condenses into cloud, hence the amount of water vapour dsecreases rapidly with altitude.

(iv) **How are clouds formed? Classify them.**

Ans **Formation of Clouds** Cloud is a mass of tiny droplets which is formed by the condensation of the water vapour in free air at considerable elevations.

Classification of Clouds According to their height, expanse and density, clouds are grouped under four categories

(i) Cirrus (ii) Cumulus (iii) Stratus (iv) Nimbus

Answer the following questions in about 150 words

(i) **Discuss the salient features of the world distribution of precipitation.**

Ans The release of moisture after the condensation is known as precipitation. It may take place in liquid or solid forms. Snowfall, rainfall, hailstone are the popular types of precipitation. Different places on the earth's surface receive different types and amount of precipitation.

The salient features of the world distribution of precipitation are as follows

- Snowfall is found in the region of higher latitude and higher altitude. The areas like Antarctica, Siberia, Arctic ocean have permanent snowfall precipitation.
- Precipitation in the form of water, i.e. rainfall is seen throughout the globe with different amount and in different seasons.
- The equatorial region has daily precipitation in the form of convectional rainfall. In the same way, coastal areas of the world receive greater amount of rainfall in comparsion to interior continents.
- Rainfall as a whole is more over the oceans than on landmasses.
- Between the latitudes 35° and 40° N and S of the equator, the rain is heavier on the Eastern coast.
- Between 45° and 65° N and S of the equator due to the westerlies, the rainfall is heavier on the Western margins of the continent.

(ii) **What are the forms of condensation? Describe the process of dew and frost formation.**

Ans Forms of condensation can be classified on the basis of temperature and location. These forms are dew, frost, fog and clouds.

Dew

- When the moisture is deposited in the form of water droplets on cooler surfaces of solid objects such as stones, grass blades and plant leaves, it is known as dew.
- For the formation of dew, it is necessary that the dew point is above the freezing point.

Frost

- It is formed on cold surfaces when condensation takes place below freezing point (0°C), i.e. the dew point is equal to or below the freezing point.
- The ideal conditions for the formation of white frost are the same as those for the formation of dew, but the condition is that the air temperature must be equal to or below the freezing point.

Exam Pattern Questions

Objective Type Questions

Multiple Choice Questions (MCQs)

1. The moisture in the atmosphere is derived from which of the following?

(a) Water bodies (b) Plants
(c) Human beings (d) Both (a) and (b)

2. Which of the following best describes humidity?

(a) The amount of liquid water in the atmosphere
(b) The amount of water vapour in the air
(c) The temperature of the air
(d) The amount of clouds in the sky

3. Consider the following statements regarding humidity and choose the correct option.

(i) Humidity is expressed in terms of quantity in different ways.
(ii) The actual amount of water vapour present in the atmosphere is known as 'absolute humidity'.
(iii) The absolute humidity is uniform everywhere.
(iv) Relative humidity is greater over the continents and least over the oceans.

Options

(a) Only (i) and (ii) (b) (i), (ii) and (iv)
(c) Only (iii) and (iv) (d) All of these

4. Which of the following conditions decreases relative humidity?

(a) Increasing air temperature
(b) Decreasing air temperature
(c) Increasing water vapour content
(d) Decreasing water vapour content

5. If the air temperature and dew point are the same, what is the relative humidity?

(a) 50% (b) 75%
(c) 0% (d) 100%

6. What term refers to the temperature at which air becomes saturated and water vapour begins to condense?

(a) Boiling point (b) Freezing point
(c) Dew point (d) Humidity index

7. Which of the following is the process by which water is transformed from liquid to gaseous state?

(a) Evaporation (b) Dew point
(c) Relative humidity (d) Condensation

8. Water is continuously exchanged through which of the following processes?

(i) Evaporation (ii) Condensation
(iii) Precipitation (iv) Conduction

Codes

(a) (i) and (ii) (b) (i), (ii) and (iii)
(c) (ii), (iii) and (iv) (d) All of these

9. Which of the following are the favourable conditions for condensation?

(i) When the temperature of the air is reduced to dew point with its volume remaining constant.
(ii) When both the volume and temperature are reduced.
(iii) When moisture is added to the air through evaporation.

Codes

(a) (i) and (ii) (b) (ii) and (iii)
(c) (i) and (iii) (d) All of these

10. How is the change in air temperature is related to moisture holding capacity?

(a) They are directly proportional.
(b) They are inversely proportional.
(c) No change
(d) None of the above

11. There are certain atmospheric condition which is necessary for the formation of clouds.
Identify that condition.

(a) Low humidity
(b) High humidity and cooling of air
(c) High air pressure
(d) Strong winds

12. This type of precipitation occurs when warm, moist air rises and cools rapidly, often leading to thunderstorms. Identify the type of precipitation.

(a) Convectional precipitation
(b) Orographic precipitation
(c) Frontal precipitation
(d) Snowfall

13. Consider the following statements regarding the types of rainfall and choose the incorrect option.

(i) Convectional rains are common in summer or when the day temperature is high.
(ii) Convectional rain occurs when the air is forced to move upward the slopes of the mountains.

(iii) Cumulous clouds are formed with thunder and lightning during orographic rainfall.
(iv) These are the rainfalls that occurs when temperate and tropical cyclones are formed in any area.

Options

(a) Only (i) (b) Both (ii) and (iii)
(c) both (i) and (iv) (d) None of these

14. Consider the following statements regarding world distribution of rainfall. Choose the correct option.

(i) Different places on the earth's surface receive same amounts of rainfall in a year.
(ii) As we go from the equator towards the poles, the amount of rainfall decreases.
(iii) The rainfall is more over the oceans than on the landmasses of the world.
(iv) The rain is greater on the leeward side and it decreases towards the windward side.

Options

(a) Only (iv) (b) Both (ii) and (iii)
(c) (i),(iii) and (iv) (d) All of these

15. Identify the process based on the given description.

This is the process by which water in gaseous form is converted into liquid form. This process removes the water vapour from the atmosphere. When moist air is cooled, it reaches to a level when its capacity to hold water vapour stops.

Option

(a) Sublimation (b) Condensation
(c) Evaporation (d) Precipitation

16. Read the given statement and identify the type of cloud.

They are black or dark grey. They form at middle levels or very near to the surface of the earth. They are dense and opaque. They are shapeless masses of thick vapour. **CBSE Diksha**

Options

(a) Stratus Clouds (b) Cumulus Clouds
(c) Nimbus Clouds (d) Cirrus Clouds

17. Identify the type of rainfall region according to the following description.

The region that receives annual rainfall between 50 - 100 cm comes under this category. The central parts of the tropical land and the Eastern and interior parts of the temperate lands comes under this type of region.

Options

(a) High rainfall region
(b) Low rainfall region
(c) Very low rainfall region
(d) Moderate rainfall region

Arrange the Following

18. Arrange the steps in the process of convectional precipitation in the correct order

(i) Rising warm air cools
(ii) Sun heats the earth's surface
(iii) Air reaches dew point and condenses
(iv) Rainfall occurs

Codes

(a) (i), (ii), (iii), (iv) (b) (ii), (i), (iii),(iv)
(c) (i), (iii), (ii), (i) (d) (ii), (i), (iv), (iii)

19. Arrange the following steps in the cloud formation process that leads to precipitation.

(i) Cooling of moist air
(ii) Formation of water droplets
(iii) Rising of warm air
(iv) Clouds become heavy and release precipitation

Codes

(a) (iii), (i), (ii), (iv) (b) (ii), (i), (iii), (iv)
(c) (i), (ii), (iii), (iv) (d) (iv), (iii), (ii), (i)

Match the Following

20.

List I (Amount of Annual Rainfall)	List II (Regions)
A. More than 200 cm	1. The equatorial belt
B. 100-200 cm	2. Interior continental areas
C. 50-100 cm	3. Central part of the tropical land
D. Less than 50 cm	4. Area of high latitudes

Codes

	A	B	C	D		A	B	C	D
(a)	1	2	3	4	(b)	2	3	1	4
(c)	4	3	2	1	(d)	1	4	3	2

21.

List I (Phenomena)	List II (Meaning)
A. Humidity	1. Water vapour present in the atmosphere
B. Source of atmospheric moisture	2. Oceans
C. Dew point	3. The temperature at which saturation occurs in a given sample of air
D. Condensation	4. The transformation of water vapour into water

Codes

	A	B	C	D		A	B	C	D
(a)	1	2	3	4	(b)	2	3	4	1
(c)	4	3	2	1	(d)	3	2	4	1

22.

List I (Phenomena)		List II (Meaning)	
A.	Frost	1.	Moisture deposited in the form of water droplets on cooler surfaces like stones, grass blades
B.	Dew	2.	Frozen droplets and refrozen melted snow
C.	Sleet	3.	Rain drops turning into ice pellets and coming down on the surface
D.	Hailstones	4.	Condensation takes place below freezing point on cold surfaces

Codes

	A	B	C	D		A	B	C	D
(a)	4	1	2	3	(b)	1	3	2	4
(c)	4	3	2	1	(d)	3	2	1	4

23.

List I (Phenomena)		List II (Meaning)	
A.	Convectional Rainfall	1.	Receives annual rainfall of 200 cm or more
B.	Rain shadow area	2.	Occurs in leeward side of the mountain
C.	Orographic Rainfall	3.	It is the result of uplift of air along the slope.
D.	Equatorial Belt	4.	These are common in summer

Codes

	A	B	C	D		A	B	C	D
(a)	3	2	4	1	(b)	4	3	2	1
(c)	4	2	3	1	(d)	1	2	3	4

Assertion-Reason

Directions (Q. Nos. 24-27) In the questions given below are two statements labelled as Assertion (A) and other labelled as Reason (R). In the context of two statements which one of the following is correct?

Codes

(a) Both A and R are true, but R is not the correct explanation of A

(b) Both A and R are true and R is the correct explanation of A

(c) Both A and R are incorrect

(d) A is correct, but R is incorrect

24. Assertion (A) The amount of water vapour in the atmosphere is added or withdrawn.

Reason (R) Evaporation and condensation are responsible for this change.

25. Assertion (A) The evaporated water is transformed into water.

Reason (R) It is due to the process of condensation.

26. Assertion (A) The amount of moisture in the atmosphere is associated with latitude.

Reason (R) The ability to keep the moisture in the form of water vapour is related to temperature. **CBSE Diksha**

27. Assertion (A) The rainfall is more over the oceans than on the landmasses of the world.

Reason (R) The oceans provide great source of moisture for condensation.

Answers

1. (d) Both (a) and (b)
2. (b) The amount of water vapour in the air
3. (a) Only (i) and (ii)
4. (a) Increasing air temperature
5. (d) 100%
6. (c) Dew point
7. (a) Evaporation
8. (b) (i), (ii) and (iii)
9. (d) All of these
10. (a) They are directly proportional.
11. (b) High humidity and cooling of air
12. (a) Convectional precipitation
13. (b) Both (ii) and (iii)
14. (b) Both (ii) and (iii)
15. (b) Condensation
16. (c) Nimbus Clouds
17. (b) Low rainfall region
18. (b) (ii), (i), (iii), (iv)
19. (a) (iii), (i), (ii), (iv)
20. (a)
21. (a)
22. (a)
23. (c)
24. (b) Both A and R are true and R is the correct explanation of A
25. (b) Both A and R are true and R is the correct explanation of A
26. (b) Both A and R are true and R is the correct explanation of A
27. (b) Both A and R are true and R is the correct explanation of A

Subjective Questions

Short Answer Type Questions

1. Humidity play an important role in the atmosphere. Explain how? Competency Based Que

Ans. Humidity is the amount of water vapour present in the air. It makes us feel warmer or cooler. High humidity can make temperatures feel warmer, while low humidity feels cooler. Humidity is crucial for weather patterns and the water cycle, as it develops important conditions for cloud formation and results in precipitation. It also impacts ecosystems, human comfort and health.

Relative humidity, specifically, shows the percentage of moisture in the air compared to its maximum capacity at that temperature.

2. Point out the favourable conditions for condensation.

Ans Condensation depends upon the amount of cooling and the relative humidity of air. It is influenced by volume of air, temperature, pressure and humidity. Following are the favourable conditions for condensation to take place

- When the temperature of the air is reduced to dew point with its volume remaining constant.
- When both the volume and temperature are reduced.
- When moisture is added to the air through evapouration.

3. What is fog? How it affects the normal life of people?

Ans Fog is a kind of cloud that touches the ground. Fog forms when the air near the ground is cold enough to turn its water vapour into liquid water or ice.

Effects of Fog

Fog becomes harmful for human life when it mixes with smoke and forms smog. Its effects are as follows

- Fog reduces the visibility due to which road and train accidents occurs.
- Smog is made up of a combination of air pollutants that can compromise human health, harm the environment and even cause property damage.
- Smog can cause or aggravate health problems such as asthma, emphysenra, chronic bronchitis and other respiratory problems.
- It also causes eye irritation and reduces resistence to colds and lung infections.
- The ozone present in smog can impact the plant growth and can cause widespread damage to crops and forests.

4. How is relative humidity affected by temperature changes?

Ans. Relative humidity changes with temperature because warmer air can hold more moisture. As temperature increases, relative humidity decreases if no additional moisture is added. Decrease in temperature leads to increase in relative humidity.

For example, when warm air cools, it can reach its dew point this makes relative humidity reach 100%. This may lead to condensation or precipitation. This relationship between temperature and relative humidity is crucial for understanding cloud formation, dew and other weather phenomena.

5. Sleet is frozen raindrops and refrozen melted snow water. Explain how does it occur? Competency Based Que

Ans Sleet is frozen raindrops and refrozen melted snow-water. When a layer of air with the temperature above freezing point overlies a sub-freezing layer near the ground, precipitation takes place in the form of sleet.

Raindrops. which leave the warmer air, encounter the colder air below. As a result, they solidify and reach the ground as small pellets of ice not bigger than the raindrops from which they are formed.

6. Different conditions leads to different types of rainfall'. Discuss about convectional type of rainfall. Competency Based Que

Ans The air on being heated becomes light and rises up in convection currents. As it rises, it expands and loses heat and consequently, condensation takes place and cumulus clouds are formed which causes convectional rainfall.

With thunder and lightening, heavy rainfall takes place but this does not last long. Such rain is common in the summer or in the hotter part of the day. This type of rainfall is very common in equatorial regions, where rainfall occurs daily. In the interior part of the continents particularly in the Northern hemisphere, convectional rainfall occurs prior to monsoon.

7. Temperature affects the moisture carrying capacity of the air. Elucidate the statement. Competency Based Que

Ans. Warm air can hold more moisture than cool air because higher temperatures increase the energy available for water molecules to stay in a gaseous state. As temperature rises, the air's capacity to hold water vapour increases and this results in higher humidity levels without saturation.

Conversely, cooler air holds less moisture and hence, air reaches to its saturation level quickly. This led to condensation. This relationship between temperature and moisture capacity is essential for understanding humidity, dew point and precipitation.

8. **"Dew is not formed on the cloudy nights". Give reason for the specification of statement.** Competency Based Que

Ans Dew is not formed on the cloudy nights. The reason for this are as follows

- The ideal conditions for the formation of dew are clear sky, calm air, cold and long night and high relative humidity.
- Dew is formed when objects radiate heat thoroughly so that the moist air coming into contact with them may be sufficiently cooled down and the water vapour condenses into water droplets.
- The cloud acts as a blanket for the earth's surface. In the condition of cloudy night, cloud checks the radiation of heat, so it does not radiate heat thoroughly. Hence, dew is not formed on the cloudy nights.

9. **Differentiate between absolute and relative humidity.**

Ans. Differences between absolute and relative humidity are as follows

Absolute Humidity	Relative Humidity
It is the actual amount of water vapour present in the atmosphere.	It is the percentage of moisture present in the atmosphere as compared to its full capacity.
It is the weight of water vapour per unit volume of air.	It is the ratio between actual amount of water vapour and the capacity to hold moisture.
It is expressed in gram per cubic metre.	It is expressed in percentage by hygrometer.
It remains constant with the increase or decrease of temperature of the air.	It is the amount of heat required to raise the temperature.

10. **Why does the amount of water vapour decreases rapidly with altitude?** CBSE Diksha

Ans. The amount of water vapour decreases rapidly with altitude because temperatures decrease as altitude increases. This reduces the air's capacity to hold moisture. Near the earth's surface, warmer temperatures allow more water to evapourate and stay as vapour in the air.

At high altitudes, colder temperatures cause water vapour to condense into liquid or ice. This leads to cloud formation and precipitation. Additionally, most water vapour originates from surface-level evapouration, so it's more concentrated in the lower atmosphere and diminishes at greater heights.

11. **"Excess evaporation and less precipitation is the main reason behind the dry climate". Discuss the economic activities which are important for human being in such climate.** Competency Based Que

Ans. Some parts of the world experience less precipitation in comparison to evaporation. Due to excess evaporation, desertification or dry zones are developed. In such regions, due to scarcity of water and fertile land, agriculture is not a good option for livelihood. Therefore, human beings depend on trade and transport activity.

Merchants and sellers are prominent professionals of dry areas. Apart from that with the help of dry farming, some adaptable crops could be cultivated. Date palm is a famous product in these regions which could be easily grown.

12. **"Smog severely harms the health of human beings". Discuss the measures to mitigate this hazard.** Competency Based Que

Ans. Smog is a form of air pollution that is particularly hazardous. According to experts, it can be dangerous to breathe in too much smog. Smog is mainly a mixture of smoke and fog but it also contains some harmful gases which affect the health of human beings.

Measures to mitigate the effect of smog are follows

- Avoid exercising near places with heavy traffic, especially during peak hours.
- Avoid outdoor activities when smog level is high.
- Ride bicycle or use public transportation system instead of car, whenever possible to reduce smoke.

13. **How does precipitation in the form of dew form?**

Ans. Dew forms when moisture in the air condenses on cool surfaces like grass, leaves, or car windows. It happens during calm, clear nights when the ground cools rapidly. It happens on reaching the dew point, which is the temperature at which air becomes fully saturated.

Dew is not a form of precipitation falling from clouds. But it's a result of direct condensation near the surface. A necessary condition for the formation of dew is that the dew point must be above the freezing point.

Long Answer Type Questions

1. **Define the term humidity. Also elaborate the various types of humidity.**

Ans The amount of water vapour in the air is called humidity. Humidity is a significant term in the atmospheric contents.

There are three types of humidity

(i) **Absolute Humidity** It is the actual amount of water vapour present in a volume of air at a given temperature. It is the density of water vapour present in a mixture of air which is the ratio of the mass of water vapour to the volume occupied by the mixture. It is usually measured in grams per cubic metre. Cold air cannot contain as much water vapour as warm air, so cold air has a low absolute humidity than warm air.

(ii) **Specific Humidity** It is the mass of water vapour (in grams) per unit mass of air (in kilograms) at any specific temperature. Specific humidity has no relation with pressure or temperature as it is measured in units of weight.

(iii) **Relative Humidity** It is a widely used measure of water vapour in the atmosphere. The calculation of relative humidity depends on the maximum amount of moisture that air can hold i.e. saturation level. The relative humidity is the percentage of saturation. Humidity is generally calculated in relation to saturated vapour density. Relative humidity is expressed in percentage. When relative humidity is 100 per cent, the atmosphere is said to be saturated.

2. 'Different places on the earth's surface receive different amounts of rainfall in a year and that too in different seasons'. Support the statement with five examples. CBSE Diksha

Ans. Different places on the earth's surface receive different amounts of rainfall in a year and in different seasons in the following ways

- In general, as we go from the equator towards the poles, the amount of rainfall decreases.
- The coastal areas of the world receive greater amounts of rainfall than the interior of the continents. The rainfall is more over the oceans than on the landmasses of the world.
- Between the latitudes 35° and 40° N and S of the equator, the rain received is more on the Eastern coasts and it decreases when we go towards the West.
- But, between 45° and 65° N and S of equator, because of the westerlies, the rainfall is first received on the Western margins of the continents and it goes on decreasing towards the East margin.
- Another variation in rainfall can be seen where mountains run parallel to the coast. In this condition the rain is greater on the coastal plain on the windward side and it decreases towards the leeward side.

3. 'Orographic rainfall leads to the development of rain-shadow region'. Substantiate the statement. Competency Based Que

Ans. Orographic rainfall leads to the development of a rain-shadow region due to the interaction between moist air and mountain ranges. When moist air from a body of water, such as an ocean moves towards a mountain range, it is forced to move upward the slope. As the air rises, it cools and loses moisture and starts forming clouds and precipitation on the windward side of the mountain. This side receives heavy rainfall.

However, as the air moves over the mountain and descends on the leeward side, it warms up and becomes drier. This warming effect reduces the air's ability to hold moisture and this makes the air dry. As a result, the leeward side experiences significantly reduced rainfall, creating a dry, often desert-like region called the rain shadow.

4. "In India all three types of rainfall are responsible for the precipitation". Give your argument in support of the statement. Competency Based Que

Ans. The precipitation in the form of water is rainfall. India has monsoon climate and more than 50 per cent rainfall occurs in the four months of monsoon. But there is a significant role of convectional and cyclonic rainfall in the climatic conditions of India. Rainfall is classified in three categories

(i) **Convectional Rainfall** This rain is caused by the convection process in the atmosphere. Mostly pre-monsoonous rainfall are of convectional type. It largely occurs in the month of April and May.

(ii) **Orographic Rainfall** This is also known as relief rainfall. It occurs where the saturated air mass comes across a mountain. In India, due to the Himalayas, monsoon winds cause sufficient amount of rainfall in the whole part of India.

(iii) **Cyclonic Rainfall** Rain associated with the passage of cyclone is known as cyclonic rainfall. It is also known as frontal rainfall. Winter rainfall in the Northern part of India is also the result of cyclonic rainfall. It not only causes rainfall but also a sufficient amount of snowfall.

5. 'Condensation takes place in certain conditions and the process is influenced by certain factors'. Justify the statement. Competency Based Que

Ans. The process of condensation takes place in certain conditions and the process is influenced by certain factors like volume of air, temperature, pressure and humidity. Following are the favorable conditions for the process of condensation

- Condensation happens when the temperature of the air is equal to or lower than the dew point. Volume should remain constant.
- Condensation happens when the temperature and volume of air is reduced.
- The third condition for the process of condensation is the addition of moisture to the air through evaporation.
- The process of condensation also depends upon the amount of cooling and the relative humidity present in the air. Condensation takes place when the dew point is lower than the freezing point as well as higher than the freezing point.

6. How clouds are formed? Classify clouds according to their height, expanse, density and transparency or opaqueness. CBSE Diksha

Ans. Cloud is a mass of minute water droplets or tiny crystals of ice formed by the condensation of the water vapour in free air at a certain height. According to their height, expanse, density and transparency or opaqueness clouds are grouped under four types. These types are discussed below

- **Cirrus** These clouds are formed at high altitudes of 8,000 - 12,000 m. They are thin clouds. They appear as an individual cloud which is not attached to any other clouds. They are always white in colour.
- **Cumulus** These clouds look like cotton wool. They are formed at a height of 4,000 - 7,000 m. They exist in patches and they are scattered here and there. They have a flat base.
- **Stratus** These clouds are layered clouds covering large portions of the sky. These clouds are generally formed either due to loss of heat or the mixing of air masses with different temperatures.
- **Nimbus** These clouds are black or dark grey. They form at middle levels or very close to the surface. These are extremely dense or opaque to the rays of the Sun.

Source Based Questions

1 Read the passage carefully and answer the questions that follow.

Water vapour present in the air is known as humidity. It is expressed quantitatively in different ways. The actual amount of the water vapour present in the atmosphere is known as the absolute humidity. It is the weight of water vapour per unit volume of air and is expressed in terms of grams per cubic metre. The ability of the air to hold water vapour depends entirely on its temperature. The absolute humidity differs from place to place on the surface of the earth. The percentage of moisture present in the atmosphere as compared to its full capacity at a given temperature is known as the relative humidity. With the change of air temperature, the capacity to retain moisture increases or decreases and the relative humidity is also affected. The air containing moisture to its full capacity at a given temperature is said to be saturated. It means that the air at the given temperature is incapable of holding any additional amount of moisture at that stage. The temperature at which saturation occurs in a given sample of air is known as dew point.

The amount of water vapour in the atmosphere is added or withdrawn due to evaporation and condensation respectively. Evaporation is a process by which water is transformed from liquid to gaseous state. Heat is the main cause for evaporation. The temperature at which the water starts evaporating is referred to as the latent heat of vapourisation. Increase in temperature increases water absorption and retention capacity of the given parcel of air. Movement of air replaces the saturated layer with the unsaturated layer. Hence, the greater the movement of air, the greater is the evaporation. The transformation of water vapour into water is called condensation. Condensation is caused by the loss of heat. When moist air is cooled, it may reach a level when its capacity to hold water vapour ceases. Then, the excess water vapour condenses into liquid form. If it directly condenses into solid form, it is known as sublimation.

(i) Relative humidity is greatest in which of the following regions?

(a) Mountains (b) Deserts
(c) Rainforests (d) Plateaus

Ans (c) Rainforests

(ii) Which of the following process will add moisture in the atmosphere?

(a) Radiation (b) Evapouration
(c) Condensation (d) Sublimation

Ans (b) Evaporation

(iii) Saturation of air occurs at a particular temperature. This temperature is known as

(a) condensation point (b) dew point
(c) triple point (d) boiling point

Ans (b) dew point

2. Read the passage carefully and answer the questions that follow.

The process of continuous condensation in free air helps the condensed particles to grow in size. When the resistance of the air fails to hold them against the force of gravity, they fall on to the earth's surface. So after the condensation of water vapour, the release of moisture is known as precipitation. This may take place in liquid or solid form. The precipitation in the form of water is called rainfall. When the temperature is lower than the 0°C, precipitation takes place in the form of fine flakes of snow and is called snowfall. Besides rain and snow, other forms of precipitation are sleet and hail. Sleet is frozen raindrops and refrozen melted snow-water. When a layer of air with the temperature above freezing point overlies a subfreezing layer near the ground. precipitation takes place in the form of sleet. Raindrops, which leave the warmer air, encounter the colder air below. Sometimes, drops of rain after being released by the clouds become solidified into small rounded solid pieces of ice and which reach the surface of the earth are called hailstones. Different places on the earth's surface receive different amounts of rainfall in a year and that too in different seasons. In general, as we proceed from the equator towards the poles, rainfall goes on decreasing steadily. The coastal areas of the world receive greater amounts of rainfall than the interior of the continents.

(i) How does the layering of different temperature air masses contribute to the formation of unique precipitation?

Ans. When warm air lies over cold air, it creates conditions for the formation of sleet. As raindrops freeze while passing through temperature variations.

(ii) There exist a relationship between latitude and rainfall patterns. Comment.

Ans. There exist a relationship between latitude and rainfall as when we move to higher latitudes the amount of rainfall decreases.

(iii) The coastal areas experience more rainfall than inland regions. Explain why?

Ans. Coastal areas is close to water bodies and this provides more moisture for evaporation and condensation. This results in increased precipitation opportunities.

SELF ASSESSMENT TEST

Objective Type Questions

1. It is greater over the oceans and least over the continents. Which type of humidity is indicated in this statement?
   (a) Absolute humidity (b) Normal humidity
   (c) Relative humidity (d) Specific humidity
2. The temperature at which saturation occurs in a given sample of air is known as ....
   (a) saturation (b) relative humidity
   (c) absolute humidity (d) dew point
3. If the excess water vapour directly condenses into solid form, it is known as
   (a) condensation (b) evapouration
   (c) dew point (d) sublimation
4. In free air, condensation which results from cooling around very small particles is termed as ....
   (a) condensation (b) hygroscopic condensation nuclei
   (c) evapouration (d) None of these
5. Which of the following forms on cold surface when condensation takes place below freezing point (0°C) i.e. dew point is at or below the freezing point?
   (a) Dew (b) Frost (c) Fog (d) Mist

Short Answer Type Questions

6. There is a continuous exchange of water between the atmosphere, the oceans and the continents. Explain this statement with the different processes involved in this briefly.
7. Differentiate between specific humidity and absolute humidity.
8. What are the conditions for the formation of frost? Also, mention the ideal condition for white frost formation.
9. Explain the process of condensation.
10. 'In urban and industrial centres smoke provides plenty of nuclei which help in the formation of fog and mist'. Distinguish between fog and mist in the context of this statement.
11. How does rainfall occur in cyclone?

Long Answer Type Questions

12. 'Cloud is a mass of minute water droplets or tiny crystals of ice'. Describe the various forms of clouds in the context of this statement.
13. Explain the different types of rainfall and their effects on different regions.
14. Describe the region where precipitation is received throughout the year.
15. Hygroscopic condensation nuclei plays a great role in condensation process. Explain.
16. 'Different places on the Earth's surface receive different amounts of rainfall in a year and that too in different seasons'. Justify this statement.

11

CHAPTER

This chapter deals with the concept of climate change, its causes and the impacts of global warming, highlighting the importance of reducing pollution and adapting to environmental changes.

World Climate and Climate Change

▼ **YOUR STUDY GOALS**

11.1 Koeppen's Scheme of Classification of Climate
11.2 Climate Change
11.3 Global Warming

▼ **YOUR PRACTICE GOALS**

- Objective Type Questions (26 Qs ; MCQs, Statements, A-R, Matching)
- Subjective Questions (14 SAs, 6 LAs)
- Source Based Questions (3 Qs)

- The world climate can be studied by organising climate data into smaller, simpler units to make it easier to understand, describe and analyse.
- **Empirical**[1], **genetic**[2] and **applied**[3] approaches have been adopted for classifying climate.

11.1 Koeppen's Scheme of Classification of Climate

- The most widely used classification of climate is the empirical climate classification scheme developed by **V. Koeppen** in 1918.
- Koeppen identified a close relationship between the distribution of vegetation and climate.
- Koeppen's classification is based on mean annual and mean monthly temperature and precipitation data.
- He used capital and small letters to designate climatic groups and types. The capital letters: A, C, D and E represent humid climates and B dry climate.

1 **Empirical** It refers to the knowledge based on experiment and observation rather than theory.

2. **Genetic** The method of studying geographical features and landscapes by examining their origins, development and processes.

3. **Applied** It is an approach in geography that refers to using geographical knowledge and methods to address real-world problems and practical issues.

Climatic Groups According to Koeppen

Group	Characteristics
A. Tropical	Average temperature of the coldest month is 18° C or higher.
B. Dry Climates	Potential evaporation exceeds precipitation.
C. Warm Temperate	The average temperature of the coldest month of the (Mid-latitude) climates years is higher than minus 3°C but below 18°C.
D. Cold Snow Forest Climates	The average temperature of the coldest month is minus 3° C or below.
E. Cold Climates	Average temperature for all months is below 10° C.
H. Highland	Cold due to elevation.

Classification of Climatic Groups

- Climatic groups are divided into various types, which are named using small letters based on the patterns of precipitation and temperature.
- The **seasons of dryness** are indicated by the small letters: f, m, w and s, where f corresponds to **no dry season**, m to **monsoon climate**, w to **winter dry season** and s to **summer dry season.**
- The small letters a, b, c and d refer to the **degree of severity of temperature.**
- The B- Dry Climates are subdivided using the capital letters 'S' for **steppe** or semi-arid and 'W' for **deserts.**

Climatic Types According to Koeppen

Group	Type	Letter Code	Characteristics
A-Tropical Humid Climate	Tropical wet	Af	No dry season
	Tropical monsoon	Am	Monsoonal, short dry season
	Tropical wet and dry	Aw	Winter dry season
B-Dry Climate	Sub-tropical steppe	BSh	Low-latitude semi-arid or dry
	Sub-tropical desert	BWh	Low-latitude arid or dry
	Mid-latitude steppe	BSk	Mid-latitude semi-arid or dry
	Mid-latitude desert	BWk	Mid-latitude arid or dry
C-Warm Temperate (Mid-latitude) Climates	Humid subtropical	Cfa	No dry season, warm summer
	Mediterranean	Cs	Dry hot summer
	Marine West coast	Cfb	No dry season, warm and cool summer
D-Cold Snowforest Climates	Humid continental	Df	No dry season, severe winter
	Subarctic	Dw	Winter dry and very severe
E-Cold Climates	Tundra	ET	No true summer
	Polar ice cap	EF	Perennial ice
H-Highland	Highland	H	Highland with snow cover

Group A: Tropical Humid Climates

- Tropical humid climates exist between Tropic of Cancer and Tropic of Capricorn.
- The climate is hot and humid because the Sun is overhead all year and the **Inter Tropical Convergence Zone** (ITCZ) is present.
- Annual range of temperature is very low and annual rainfall is high.
- This group is divided into three types : Af-Tropical wet climate, Am-Tropical monsoon climate and Aw-Tropical wet and dry climate.

(i) **Af- Tropical Wet Climate**

- Tropical wet climate is found near the equator. The major areas are the Amazon Basin in South America, Western equatorial Africa and the islands of East Indies.

- There is heavy rainfall every month, usually in the form of afternoon thunderstorms.
- The temperature is uniformly high and the annual range of temperature is negligible. The maximum temperature on any day is around 30°C while the minimum temperature is around 20°C.
- This climate has tropical evergreen forests[4] with thick canopy cover and a large biodiversity.

(ii) **Am - Tropical Monsoon Climate**

- This climate is found in the Indian subcontinent, North-Eastern part of South America and Northern Australia.
- It has heavy rainfall in summer and dry winters.

(iii) **Aw- Tropical Wet and Dry Climate**

- This climate occurs North and South of Af type climate regions.
- It borders with dry climate on the Western part of the continent and Cf or Cw on the Eastern part.
- Extensive Aw climate is found to the North and South of the Amazon forest in Brazil and adjoining parts of Bolivia and Paraguay in South America, Sudan and South of Central Africa.
- The annual rainfall is much lower and more variable than in the Af and Am climates.
- The wet season is shorter and the dry season is longer, with more severe droughts.
- Temperature is high throughout the year, with the biggest daily temperature changes occurring during the dry season.
- Deciduous forest[5] and tree-shredded grasslands are found in this climate.

Group B: Dry Climates

- These climates have very low rainfall that is not enough for the growth of plants. These climates cover a vast area, stretching from 15° to 60° North and South of the equator.
- At low latitudes, from 15° - 30°, they occur in the area of subtropical high where subsidence and inversion of temperature do not produce rainfall.
- On the Western edges of continents, near cold ocean currents, these climates extend closer to the equator, especially along the West coast of South America.
- In middle latitudes, between 35° and 60° North and South of the equator, these climates are found in the interior of continents, where oceanic winds don't reach and in areas often surrounded by mountains.
- Dry climates are divided into **steppe** or **semi-arid climate** (BS) and **desert climate** (BW). They are further subdivided as
  - Subtropical steppe (BSh) and subtropical desert (BWh) at latitudes from 15°-35°.
  - Mid-latitude steppe (BSk) and mid-latitude desert (BWk) at latitudes between 35°-60°.

Subtropical Steppe (BSh) and Subtropical Desert (BWh) Climates

- Subtropical steppe (BSh) and subtropical desert (BWh) have common precipitation and temperature characteristics.
- The subtropical steppe is located between humid and dry climates. It gets slightly more rainfall than the desert, enough for the growth of sparse grasslands.
- The rainfall in both the climates is highly variable. This variability affects the life in the steppe more than in the desert, often causing famine.
- Rain occurs in short intense thunderstorms in deserts and is ineffective in building soil moisture.
- Fog is common in coastal deserts bordering cold currents.

4 Evergreen forest These are dense, multilayered and are usually found in areas receiving more than 200 cm of rainfall.
5 Deciduous forest These are the forests in which trees shed their leaves annually or in a particular season.

- Maximum temperature in the summer is very high. The highest shade temperature of 58° C was recorded at ***Al Aziziyah, Libya*** on 13th September, 1922.
- The annual and diurnal ranges of temperature are also high.

Quick Test 1

1 Who developed the empirical climate classification scheme?
2 Koeppen's climate classification is primarily based on which two factors?
3 What causes the consistently hot and humid conditions in tropical climates?
4 The Tropical Wet and Dry (Aw) climate borders with dry climates on which part of the continent?
5 The subtropical steppe climate is located between which two types of climates?

Group C: Warm Temperate (Mid-Latitude) Climates

- These climates extend from 30° - 50° of latitude mainly on the Eastern and Western margins of continents.
- These climates generally have warm summers with mild winters. They are grouped into four types-Humid subtropical (Cwa), Mediterranean (Cs), Humid subtropical (Cfa) and Marine West coast (Cfb) climate.

(i) Humid Subtropical Climate (Cwa)

- This climate is dry in winter and hot in summer. It occurs poleward of Tropic of Cancer and Capricorn, mainly in North Indian plains and South China interior plains.
- This climate is like the Aw climate, but with warmer winters.

(ii) Mediterranean Climate (Cs)

- This climate occurs around the Mediterranean sea, along the West coast of continents in subtropical latitudes between 30° - 40° latitudes. For example, Central California, Central Chile, along the coast in South Eastern and South Western Australia.
- These areas come under the influence of subtropical high in summer and Westerly wind in winter. Hence, the climate is characterised by hot, dry summers and mild, rainy winters.
- Monthly average temperature in summer is around 25° C and in winter below 10°C. The annual precipitation ranges between 35 - 90 cm.

(iii) Humid Subtropical Climate (Cfa)

- This climate has no dry season and mild winter. It lies on the Eastern parts of the continent in subtropical latitudes.
- In this region, the air masses are generally unstable and cause rainfall throughout the year. They occur in the Eastern United States of America, Southern and Eastern China, Southern Japan, North-Eastern Argentina, coastal South Africa and Eastern coast of Australia.
- The annual averages of precipitation vary from 75-150cm. Thunderstorms in summer and frontal precipitation in winter are common.
- The average monthly temperature in summer is about 27°C, while winter temperature ranges from 5°C to 12°C. The daily temperature variation is small.

(iv) Marine West Coast Climate (Cfb)

- This climate is found poleward from the Mediterranean climate on the West coast of the continents.
- The main areas are North-Western Europe, West coast of North America, North of California, Southern Chile, South-Eastern Australia and New Zealand.
- Due to marine influence, the temperature is moderate and in winter, it is warmer than for its latitude.
- The mean temperature in summer ranges from 15°-20°C and in winter 4°-10°C. The annual and daily ranges of temperature are low.
- Precipitation occurs throughout the year with variation from 50-250 cm.

Group D- Cold Snow Forest Climates

- These climates occur in the large continental area in the Northern hemisphere between 40°-70° North latitudes in Europe, Asia and North America. Winter is more severe at higher latitudes.
- They are divided into two types: Cold climate with humid winter (Df) and cold climate with dry winter (DW).

(i) Df- Cold Climate with Humid Winters

- It occurs poleward of marine West coast climate and mid latitude steppe.
- Winters are cold and snowy, with a short frost-free season. The winters are more severe towards the pole.
- The annual ranges of temperature are large. There are abrupt and short weather changes.

(ii) Dw-Cold Climate with Dry Winters

- It occurs mainly over North-Eastern Asia. The strong winter anticyclone weakens in summer, causing a monsoon-like reversal of winds in this region.
- Summer temperatures decrease poleward and winter temperatures become extremely cold with some places staying below freezing for up to seven months a year.
- Precipitation occurs in summer and the annual rainfall is low between 12-15 cm.

Group E- Polar Climates

- Polar climates exist poleward beyond 70° latitude. They are of two types : Tundra (ET) and Ice Cap (EF) climate.

(i) Tundra (ET)

- This climate is named after the vegetation found there, such as mosses, lichens and flowering plants.
- This is the region of permafrost[6] where the subsoil is permanently frozen. The short growing season and waterlogged soil only support low-growing plants.
- In summer, tundra regions experience very long days.

(ii) Ice Cap (EF)

- This climate occurs over interior Greenland and Antarctica. This area receives very little precipitation. The temperature is below freezing point even in summer.
- Snow and ice build up the pressure which causes the ice sheets to break. These break into icebergs that float in the Arctic and Antarctic waters.
- Example of this climate is **Plateau Station** situated in Antarctica, 79°S.

Group H- Highland Climates

- These climates are influenced by topography. In high mountains, mean temperatures can change significantly over short distances.
- Precipitation types and intensity vary across highlands. In mountains, different climate types are found at different heights.

Quick Test 2

1. Which climate is like the Aw climate with a warmer winter?
2. What is the average summer temperature in Humid Subtropical Climate?
3. Group- D climate is divided into how many subtypes?
4. Given an example of Ice Cap(EF) climate present on the Earth.

6 Permafrost A layer of soil which is permanently frozen.

11.2 Climate Change

- The planet Earth has seen many variations in climate since the beginning.
- Geological records show changes between glacial and inter-glacial periods.
- The geomorphological features, especially in high altitudes and latitudes, show signs of glaciers advancing and retreating.
- The sediment deposits in glacial lakes also show the occurrence of warm and cold periods.
- The rings in the trees provide clues about wet and dry periods.
- All these evidences indicate that change in climate is a natural and continuous process.
- India also witnessed alternate wet and dry periods. Archaeological findings show that the Rajasthan desert had a wet and cool climate around 8,000 B.C. The period 3,000-1,700 B.C. had higher rainfall. From about 2,000-1,700 B.C., this region was the center of the Harappan civilisation. Since then, the climate has become drier.
- During the geological past, specifically between 500 and 300 million years ago, the Earth experienced a warm climate throughout the Cambrian, Ordovician and Silurian periods.
- During the Pleistocene era/period, there were glacial and inter-glacial periods, with the last major ice age occurring about 18,000 years ago. The present inter-glacial period started 10,000 years ago.

Climate in the Recent Past

- The present climate has likely existed for the past 10,000 years with minor and occasional changes.
- Variability in climate occurs all the time. The nineties decade of the last century witnessed extreme weather events such as
  - The 1990s recorded the warmest temperature of the century and some of the worst floods around the world.
  - The Sahel region, located South of the Sahara Desert witnessed the worst devastating drought from 1967-77.
  - During the 1930s, severe drought occurred in South-Western Great Plains of the United States, described as the **dust bowl**.
- The effects of climate change could be observed by the historical records of crop yield or crop failures of floods and migration of people.
- Europe had warm, wet, cold and dry periods. It also faced '**Little Ice Age**' from 1550 to about 1850.
- The 10th and 11th centuries were marked by warm and dry conditions, during which the Vikings settled in Greenland.
- From about 1885-1940, world temperature started to increase. After 1940, the rate of increase in temperature slowed down.

Causes of Climate Change

There are many causes for climate change which can be grouped into astronomical and terrestrial causes.

Astronomical Causes

The astronomical causes are the changes in solar output associated with sunspot activities.

- Sunspots are dark and cooler patches on the Sun which increase and decrease in a cyclical manner.
- Some meteorologists believe that more sunspots lead to cooler, wetter weather and more storms, whereas a decrease in sunspot numbers results in warm and drier conditions.

- **Milankovitch Oscillations** refer to cycles in Earth's orbit, its wobble[7] and changes in its axial[8] tilt.
- All these change the amount of insolation received from the Sun, which in turn, might influence the climate.

Terrestrial Causes

- **Volcanism** is considered as the cause of climate change as volcanic eruption throws up aerosols[9] which remain in the atmosphere reducing the Sun's radiation reaching the Earth's surface.
- The recent **Pinatoba** and **El Cion** volcanic eruptions led to a fall in the average temperature of the Earth to some extent for some years.

11.3 Global Warming

- The increasing trend in the concentration of greenhouse gases in the atmosphere causes global warming, which is the most important anthropogenic[10] effect on climate change.
- Due to the presence of greenhouse gases, the atmosphere is behaving like a *greenhouse*.
- The atmosphere also transmits the incoming solar radiation but absorbs most of the long-wave radiation emitted by Earth's surface. The gases that absorb long wave radiation are called **greenhouse gases**.
- The processes that warm the atmosphere are often collectively known as the greenhouse effect.

Greenhouse

- The term greenhouse is derived from the idea of greenhouse structure used in cold areas for preserving heat.
- A greenhouse is made up of glass. The glass is transparent to incoming shortwave solar radiation and opaque to outgoing long wave radiation. The glass, therefore, allows in more sunlight and traps heat inside, keeping the temperature in the greenhouse warmer than outside.
- For example, in summer, a car or bus with closed windows feels hotter inside than outside. Similarly, in winter, closed vehicles stay warmer than the outside temperature.

Greenhouse Gases (GHGs)

- Carbon dioxide (CO_2), Chlorofluorocarbons[11] (CFCs), Methane (CH_4), Nitrous oxide (N_2O) and Ozone (O_3) are the main GHGs.
- Some other gases such as Nitric oxide (NO) and Carbon monoxide (CO) easily react with GHGs and affect their concentration in the atmosphere.
- The effectiveness of any GHGs molecule depends on its concentration, how long it stays in the atmosphere and the type of radiation it absorbs.
- The **CFCs** and **ozone** are highly effective in absorbing terrestrial radiation. *Ozone* absorbs ultraviolet radiation in the stratosphere. It is very effective in absorbing terrestrial radiation when it is present in the lower troposphere.
- The longer a greenhouse gas stays in the atmosphere, the longer it takes for the Earth's atmosphere to recover from any changes it causes.

---

7 Wobble To move side by side in an unbalanced form.
8 Axial Invisible line or plane around which an object rotates.
9 Aerosols These are tiny particles suspended in the atmosphere. They may be solid or liquid form.
10 Anthropogenic Any environmental changes caused by humans.
11 Chlorofluorocarbons It is an artificially created gas that has become concentrated in the earth's atmosphere.

Role of Carbon Dioxide (CO)

- The largest concentration of GHGs in the atmosphere is carbon dioxide which comes mainly from fossil fuel combustion (oil, gas and coal).
- Forests and oceans are the sinks for carbon dioxide. Forests use CO_2 in their growth and deforestation due to changes in land use increases the concentration of CO_2.
- It takes 20-50 years for atmospheric CO_2 to adjust to changes in its sources and sinks and hence its level is rising by about 0.5% each year.
- Doubling of concentration of CO_2 over pre-industrial level is used as an index for estimating the changes in climate in climatic models.
- Chlorofluorocarbons are the products of human activities. The CFCs moves to the stratosphere and destroys the ozone layer, which protects us from ultraviolet rays.

Chlorofluorocarbons and Ozone

- Ozone occurs in the stratosphere where ultraviolet rays convert oxygen into ozone.
- The large depletion of ozone concentration in the stratosphere is called the ozone hole which allows the UV rays to pass through the troposphere.
- There is large depletion of ozone over **Antarctica**.

Effects of Global Warming

- The rising levels of greenhouse gases in the atmosphere may eventually warm the Earth.
- Rise in the sea level due to melting of glaciers and ice-caps and thermal expansion of the sea, could lead to flooding in large coastal areas and islands. These incidents will definitely lead to social problems.

Global Warming as a Major Concern

Today, global warming is one of the major concerns of the world. The following temperature records show how much the planet Earth has warmed up since past

- The annual average near-surface air temperature of the world is approximately **14°C.**
- Global temperatures steadily increased in the 20th century, with the biggest warming occurring in two periods: **1901-1944** and **1977-1999**, when temperatures rose by about 0.4°C each time. There was a slight cooling in between, especially in the Northern Hemisphere.
- The globally averaged annual mean temperature at the end of the 20th century was about 0.6°C above that was recorded at the end of the 19th century.
- The seven warmest years during the **1856-2000** were recorded in the last decade.
- **1998** was the warmest year for the whole millennium.

Efforts to Control the Emission of GHGs

- There have been international efforts for reducing the emission of GHGs into the atmosphere. The most important among them is **Kyoto protocol**, which was introduced in 1997.
- Kyoto protocol came into effect in 2005. It was signed by 141 nations. It bounds the 35 industrialised countries to reduce their emissions by the year 2012 to 5 per cent less than the levels in the year 1990.

Quick Test 3

1. Which region was described as dust bowl in 1930s?
2. Mention the terrestrial causes of climate.
3. Where does ozone occur in the Earth's atmosphere?
4. Name any four primary GHGs.
5. What is the aim of Kyoto protocol?

Mind Map

WORLD CLIMATE AND CLIMATE CHANGE

1 Classification of Climate

Approaches for Climatic Classification
- **Empirical** Based on observed data.
- **Genetic** Focuses on causes of climate.
- **Applied** Designed for specific uses.

Koppen's Scheme of Classification of Climate
This classification was based on the values of temperature, precipitation and distribution of vegetation

Classification of Climatic Groups
- **Group A (Tropical)** e.g., Af (tropical wet)
- **Group B (Dry)** e.g., Bwh (Sub-tropical desert)
- **Group C (Warm Temperature)** e.g., Cs (Mediterranean)
- **Group D (Cold Snow-forest)** e.g., Df (No dry season, severe winter)
- **Group E (Cold Climate)** e.g., Et (Tundra)
- **Group H (Highland)** e.g., Highland with snow cover

2 Climate Change

Global Warming
Rising global temperatures due to greenhouse gas.

Key Greenhouse Gases
Carbon dioxide (CO_2), Methane (CH_4), Nitrous Oxide (N_2O), Ozone (O_3) and Chlorofluorocarbons (CFCs).

Effects
- Melting ice-caps
- Rising sea level

Causes of Climate Change
- **Astronomical Causes** The changes in solar output associated with sunspot activities.
- **Terrestrial Causes** Volcanic eruption throws up aerosols which remain in the atmosphere reducing the Sun's radiation reaching the Earth's surface.

Climate change it is a continuous and natural process.

Evidences
- Traces of advances and retreats of glaciers.
- Rings in the tree provides clues about wet and dry periods.

Climate in the Recent Past
- The present climate has likely existed for the past 10,000 years with minor and occasional changes.
- The 1990s recorded the warmest temperature of the century and some of the worst floods around the world.
- The Sahel region, located South of the Sahara Desert witnessed the worst devastating drought from 1967-77.
- Europe faced 'Little Ice Age' from 1550 to about 1850.
- From about 1885-1940, world temperature started to increase and slowed down after 1940.

NCERT Folder

Multiple Choice Questions

(i) **Which one of the following is suitable for Koeppen's 'A' type of climate?**

(a) High rainfall in all the months.
(b) Mean monthly temperature of the coldest month more than freezing point.
(c) Mean monthly temperature of all the months more than 18° C.
(d) Average temperature for all the months below 10° C.

Ans. (a) High rainfall in all the months.

(ii) **Koeppen's system of classification of climates can be termed as**

(a) Applied (b) Systematic
(c) Genetic (d) Empirical

Ans. (d) Empirical

(iii) **Most of the Indian Peninsula will be grouped according to Koeppen's system under**

(a) 'Af' (b) 'BSh'
(c) 'Cfb' (d) 'Am'

Ans. (d) 'Am'

(iv) **Which one of the following years is supposed to have recorded the warmest temperature the world over?**

(a) 1990 (b) 1998
(c) 1885 (d) 1950

Ans. (b) 1998

(v) **Which one of the following groups of four climates represents humid condition?**

(a) A - B - C - E
(b) A - C - D - E
(c) B - C - D - E
(d) A - C - D - F

Ans. (b) A - C - D - E

Answer the following questions in about 30 words

(i) **Which two climatic variables are used by Koeppen for classification of the climate?**

Ans. For the classification of climate, Koeppen used the following climatic variable and related them to the distribution of vegetation

(i) Temperature
(ii) Precipitation

(ii) **How is the 'genetic' system of classification different from the 'empirical' one?**

Ans. The differences between genetic and empirical classification are as follows

Genetic Classification	Empirical Classification
Genetic classification attempts to organise climates according to their causes.	Empirical classification is based on observed data, particularly on temperature and precipitation.
These causes are related to the weather processes.	These are responsible for climate differentiation.

(iii) **What type of climates have very low range of temperature?**

Ans. Tropical humid climates which exist between the Tropic of Cancer and Capricorn have low annual range of temperature. These comprise of Tropical wet climate (Af), Tropical monsoon climate (Am) and Tropical wet and dry climate (Aw).

(iv) **What type of climatic conditions would prevail if the sunspots increase?**

Ans. Sunspots are dark and cooler patches on the Sun which increase and decrease in cyclical manner. When the number of sunspots increase, cooler and wetter weather and greater storminess occur.

Answer the following questions in about 150 words

(i) **Make a comparison of the climatic conditions between the 'A' and 'B' types of climate.**

Ans. Comparison of the climatic conditions between the 'A' and 'B' types of climate are as follows

Group A	Group B
It exists between the Tropic of Cancer and the Tropic of Capricorn.	It covers a large area from 15°-60° N and S of the equator.
The presence of perpendicular Sun rays.	Sun rays are not perpendicular throughout the year.
Annual range of temperature is very low.	Annual range of temperature is very high.

Group A	Group B
Annual rainfall is high.	Area of sub-tropical high causes less rainfall.
These are tropical humid climates.	These are dry climates.
It comprises of tropical wet, tropic monsoon and wet and dry climates.	It includes sub-tropical steppe and sub-tropical desert type climate.
Presence of ITCZ makes the climate hot and humid.	Areas of high pressure and inversion of temperature do not produce rainfall but temperature remains high.

(ii) What type of vegetation would you find in the 'C' and 'A' types of climate?

Ans. Vegetation of any region depends upon the temperature and precipitation. Hence, vegetation of every climatic region varies. Koeppen identified the following types of vegetation in Group 'A' and 'C' types of climate

Vegetation of Group 'A' type of Climate

- In tropical wet climate, evergreen forest with dense canopy cover are found.
- In tropical monsoon climate, dry and wet deciduous forests are found.
- In tropical wet and dry climate, deciduous forest and tree- shredded grasslands are found.

Vegetation of Group 'C' type of Climate

- Group C has warm humid climate, thus, they have wet deciduous forest.
- Humid sub-tropical climate have broad leaved evergreen trees.
- Mediterranean climate is famous for citrus fruits, so plantation is often found with evergreen trees.
- In humid sub-tropical climate, coastal vegetation dominates in some parts and Mangroves are also found in these areas.
- In Marine West coast climate, precipitation occurs throughout the year but marine ecology is in sufficient quantity and tall evergreen trees are absent here.

(iii) What do you understand by the term 'Green house' gases? Make a list of greenhouse gases.

Ans. The gases that absorb long wave radiation are called greenhouse gases and the processes that warm the atmosphere are often collectively referred to as the greenhouse effect.

These gases are responsible for the increase in temperature of the atmosphere. The effectiveness of GHGs molecule depends on the magnitude of the increase in its concentration, its life time in the atmosphere and the wavelength of the radiation that it absorbs.

The more time the GHG molecule remains in the atmosphere, the longer it will take for Earth's atmosphere system to recover from any change brought about by the latter.

List of GHGs

- Carbon dioxide (CO_2)
- Chlorofluorocarbons (CFC)
- Methane (CH_4)
- Nitrous Oxide (N_2O)
- Ozone (O_3)

Exam Pattern Questions

Objective Type Questions

Multiple Choice Questions (MCQs)

1. V Koeppen developed which of the following types of classification of climate?

(a) Empirical (b) Applied
(c) Genetic (d) None of these

2. Koeppen identified a close relationship between distribution of

(a) Vegetation and soil (b) Soil and climate
(c) Vegetation and climate (d) None of these

3. Which of the following is the primary criterion used in Koeppen's climatic classification system?

(a) Soil type
(b) Temperature and precipitation
(c) Vegetation types
(d) Topography

4. In which year V Koeppen developed empirical climate classification scheme?

(a) 1901 (b) 1910
(c) 1918 (d) 1925

5. **The seasons of dryness are indicated by the letter**

(a) f (b) m
(c) w (d) All of these

6. **Group 'A' stands in the Koeppen's climatic classification for**

(a) Dry climates (b) Tropical climates
(c) Warm climates (d) Cold climates

7. **Choose from the following that makes the tropical humid climates hot and humid.**

(a) Terrestrial radiation
(b) Presence of ITCZ
(c) Perpendicular sunrays
(d) All of the above

8. **Which type of climate occurs in the North and South of the 'Af' type climate regions?**

(a) Am (b) Group-B
(c) Bwh (d) Aw

9. **Identify the type of climate from given description. These climates extend from 30° - 50° of latitude mainly on the Eastern and Western margins of continents. These climates generally have warm summers with mild winters.**

(a) Group A (b) Group B
(c) Group E (d) Group C

10. **Which Koeppen climate type is characterised by hot, dry summers and mild, wet winters?**

(a) Cs (Mediterranean)
(b) Dfa (Humid Continental)
(c) Af (Tropical Rainforest)
(d) ET (Tundra)

11. **In which type of climate low growing mosses, lichens, and flowering plants are found?** **CBSE Diksha**

(a) Tropical Humid Climates
(b) Mediterranean Climate (Cs)
(c) Polar Climates (E)
(d) Dry Climates: B

12. **What do the dark and cooler patches on the Sun known as, which increase and decrease in a cyclical manner?** **CBSE Diksha**

(a) Sun holes (b) Sunspots
(c) Solar winds (d) Solar gases

13. **Choose from the following the approaches for classifying climate.**

I. Empirical II. Genetic
III. Applied

Codes

(a) I and II (b) II and III
(c) Only III (d) All of these

14. **Consider the following statement regarding climate change and choose the incorrect one.**

I. The effects of climate change could be observed by the historical records of crop yield or crop failures, of floods and migration of people.
II. Change in climate is a natural and continuous process.
III. Volcanism is not considered as the cause of climate change.

Options

(a) I, II and III (b) I and III
(c) Only I (d) Only III

15. **Consider the following statement and choose the correct one.**

I. The atmosphere also transmits the incoming solar radiation but absorbs most of the long-wave radiation emitted by Earth's surface.
II. The gases that do not absorb long wave radiation are called greenhouse gases.
III. A greenhouse is made up of glass. The glass is transparent to incoming shortwave solar radiation.
IV. The effects of global warming is uniform everywhere on the Earth surface.

Options

(a) I, II and IV (b) II and IV
(c) I and III (d) III and IV

16. **Consider the following statement regarding Kyoto Protocol and choose the incorrect one.**

I. Kyoto Protocol was introduced in 1996.
II. Kyoto Protocol came into effect in 2005.
III. Kyoto Protocol was signed by 141 nations.
IV. It bounds the 35 industrialised countries to reduce their emissions by 2012 to 5 per cent less than the levels in the year 2000.

Options

(a) I and IV (b) II and IV
(c) I, II and IV (d) III and IV

Arrange the Following

17. **Arrange the following Koeppen climate types in order from the hottest to the coldest average annual temperatures.**

(i) ET (Tundra)
(ii) Af (Tropical Rainforest)
(iii) Dfa (Humid Continental)
(iv) Cs (Mediterranean)

Codes

(a) (ii), (iv), (iii), (i) (b) (i), (ii), (iii), (iv)
(c) (iv), (iii), (ii), (i) (d) (iii), (iv), (i), (ii)

18. **Arrange the following groups of climates as per the alphabetical sequence.**

(i) Dry climate (ii) Tropical climate
(iii) Warm climate (iv) Tundra climate

Options

(a) (i), (ii), (iii), (iv) (b) (ii), (i), (iii), (iv)
(c) (iv), (i), (iii), (ii) (d) (iv), (iii), (ii), (i)

19. **Arrange the following groups of climate as per their alphabetic series.**

(i) Cold snow forest climate
(ii) Highland
(iii) Cold climates

Codes

(a) (i), (ii), (iii) (b) (iii), (ii), (i)
(c) (ii), (i), (iii) (d) (i), (iii), (ii)

Match the Following

20.

List-I (Climatic Groups Letters)		List-II (Climatic Groups)	
A.	A	1.	Cold snow forest climates
B.	B	2.	Warm temperate climate
C.	C	3.	Tropical climates
D.	D	4.	Dry climates

Codes

	A	B	C	D		A	B	C	D
(a)	3	4	2	1	(b)	2	4	3	1
(c)	4	3	2	1	(d)	1	2	3	4

21.

List-I (Climatic Groups Letters)		List-II (Climatic Types)	
A.	Af	1.	Tropical wet
B.	Am	2.	Tropical monsoon
C.	Aw	3.	Tropical wet and dry
D.	Cfa	4.	Humid sub-tropical

Codes

	A	B	C	D		A	B	C	D
(a)	1	2	3	4	(b)	2	3	1	4
(c)	4	1	2	3	(d)	3	2	1	4

22.

List-I		List-II	
A.	Carbon dioxide	1.	Fossil fuel combustion
B.	Ozone	2.	Antarctica
C.	Ozone hole	3.	UV rays
D.	CFCs	4.	Artificially created gases

Codes

	A	B	C	D		A	B	C	D
(a)	1	3	2	4	(b)	1	2	3	4
(c)	4	3	2	1	(d)	1	4	3	2

Assertion-Reason

Directions (Q. Nos. 23-26) In the questions given below are two statements labelled as Assertion (A) and other is labelled as Reason (R). In the context of two statements, which one of the following is correct?

Codes

(a) Both A and R are true, but R is not the correct explanation of A
(b) Both A and R are true and R is the correct explanation of A
(c) Both A and R are incorrect
(d) A is correct, but R is incorrect

23. **Assertion** (A) At low latitudes, from 15°-30° rainfall does not occur.

Reason (R) It is the result of subsidence and inversion of temperature.

24. **Assertion** (A) In humid sub-tropical climatic regions, rainfall occurs throughout the year.

Reason (R) In this region, the air masses are generally unstable.

25. **Assertion** (A) Koeppen's classification system uses letters to represent different climate types.

Reason (R) The system categorises climates primarily based on temperature and precipitation patterns.

26. **Assertion** (A) The increased concentration of carbon dioxide in the atmosphere is a significant driver of global warming.

Reason (R) Carbon dioxide traps heat in the atmosphere, leading to an enhanced greenhouse effect.

Answers

1. (a) Empirical
2. (c) Vegetation and climate
3. (b) Temperature and precipitation
4. (c) 1918
5. (d) All of these
6. (b) Tropical climates
7. (d) All of the above
8. (d) Aw
9. (d) Group C

10. (a) Cs (Mediterranean)
11. (c) Polar Climates (E)
12. (b) Sunspots
13. (d) All of these
14. (d) Only III
15. (c) I and III
16. (a) I and IV
17. (a) (ii), (iv), (iii), (i)
18. (b) (ii), (i), (iii), (iv)
19. (d) (i), (iii), (ii)
20. (a)
21. (a)
22. (a)
23. (b) Both A and R are true and R is the correct explanation of A
24. (b) Both A and R are true and R is the correct explanation of A
25. (b) Both A and R are true and R is the correct explanation of A
26. (b) Both A and R are true and R is the correct explanation of A

Subjective Questions

Short Answer Type Questions

1. Explain the three broad approaches that have been adopted for classifying climate. CBSE Diksha

Ans. Three broad approaches have been adopted for classifying climate. They are empirical, genetic and applied.

(i) Empirical classification is based on observed climate data like temperature and precipitation, an example being Koeppen's system which uses vegetation patterns.

(ii) Genetic classification attempts to organise climates according to their causes. Focuses on the causative factors of climate, such as air masses and circulation patterns, helping to explain climate origins.

(iii) Applied classification focuses on specific applications, like agriculture or tourism, using criteria important for those fields.

2. "Koeppen classified climate into many groups, one was Group B". Discuss about this classification.

Ans. Koeppen classified Group B, as a type of climate which specifically includes dry conditions. Dry climate is characterised by very low rainfall that is not adequate for the growth of plants. This climate covers a very large area extending 15°-60° North and South of the equator.

At low latitudes from 15°-30° they occur in the area of sub-tropical high where subsistence and inversion of temperature do not produce rainfall. In the middle latitudes from 35°-60° North and South of the equator, they are confined to the interior of continents where maritime humid winds do not reach and to areas often surrounded by mountain.

Dry climates are divided into steppe or semi-arid climate (BS) and desert climate (Bw). They are further sub-divided as sub-tropical steppe (BSh) and sub-tropical desert (BWh) at latitudes from 15°-35° and mid-latitude steppe (BSk) and mid-latitude desert (BWk) at the latitudes between 35°-60°.

3. Give a brief description about Humid Subtropical Climate (CfA).

Ans. This is one of the climatic classifications of Koeppen and it is described as below

- This climate has no dry season and mild winter. It lies on the Eastern parts of the continent in subtropical latitudes.
- In this region, the air masses are generally unstable and cause rainfall throughout the year. The annual averages of precipitation vary from 75-150 cm.
- Thunderstorms in summer and frontal precipitation in winter are common.
- The average summer temperature is about 27°C, while winter temperatures range from 5°C to 12°C. The daily temperature variation is small.

4. What type of climatic conditions characterise cold climate with dry winter?

Ans. Dw is the type of climate which characterises with cold climate with dry winter. It occurs mainly over North Eastern Asia.

The main feature of such climate is the development of anti-cyclonic conditions in winter and monsoon in summer. Poleward summer temperatures are lower and winter temperature is extremely low.

Many locations experience below freezing point temperatures for upto seven months in a year. Precipitation occurs only in summer with low annual amount ranging from 12-15 cm.

5. Describe briefly the characteristics of Polar type of climate according to Koeppen's classification.

Ans. In Koeppen's classification, the Polar climate (E) is defined by very low temperatures and limited seasonal variation, resulting in two subtypes: ET (Tundra) and EF (Ice Cap).

In ET (Tundra) climates, temperatures rise slightly above freezing during brief summers, allowing sparse vegetation like mosses, lichens, and low shrubs to grow. Winters are long, dark, and extremely cold.

EF (Ice Cap) climates are even colder, with temperatures rarely rising above 0°C throughout the year, which restricts any vegetation growth. The land is permanently covered in ice and snow, as seen in Greenland and Antarctica. Polar climates are also dry due to minimal precipitation.

6. 'The planet/Earth has seen many variations in climate since the beginning. Justify the statement. Competency Based Que

Ans. The planet/Earth has witnessed many variations in climate since the beginning which are as follows

- Geological records show alteration of glacial and inter-glacial periods.
- The geomorphological features especially in high altitudes and high latitudes exhibit traces of advances and retreats of glaciers.
- The sediment deposits in glacial lakes also reveal the occurrence of warm and cold periods.
- The ring in the trees provide clues about wet and dry periods.

All these evidences indicate that change in climate is a natural and continuous process.

7. The present climate has likely existed for the past 10,000 years with minor and occasional changes. Discuss the climate of recent past. Competency Based Que

Ans. The present climate might be prevailing over the last 10,000 years with minor and occasionally wide fluctuations. The decade of nineties of the last century witnessed extreme weather events. 1990s recorded the warmest temperature of the century and some of the worst flood around the world.

The effects of climate change could be observed by the historical records of crop yield or crop failure, flood and migration of people. From about 1885-1940, world temperature showed an upward trend. After 1940, the rate of increase in temperature slowed down.

8. There are many causes for climate change. Discuss about the astronomical causes. Competency Based Que

Ans. The astronomical causes are the changes in solar output associated with sunspot activities. These are discussed below

(i) Sunspots

- They are dark and cooler patches on the Sun which increase and decrease in a cyclical manner.
- Some meteorologists believe that more sunspots lead to cooler, wetter weather and more storms. Whereas a decrease in sunspot numbers results in warm and drier conditions.

(ii) Milankovitch Oscillations

- It refers to cycles in Earth's orbit, its wobble and changes in its axial tilt.
- All these change the amount of insolation received from the Sun, which in turn, might influence the climate.

9. Briefly describe the term 'greenhouse'.

Ans. Greenhouse gases (GHGs) are atmospheric gases that trap heat, contributing to the greenhouse effect and global warming. Major GHGs include carbon dioxide (CO_2), methane, (CH_4), nitrous oxide (N_2O), water vapour and ozone (O_3).

Human activities, such as burning fossil fuels, deforestation, and industrial processes, have increased GHG concentrations in the atmosphere. CO_2 is the most abundant GHG released, largely from fossil fuels, while methane comes from livestock and landfills, and N_2O from fertilisers. These gases absorb and emit infrared radiation, warming the Earth's surface. Without GHGs, Earth would be too cold, but excessive levels lead to climate change.

10. Today, global warming is one of the major concerns of the world. Discuss the effect of global warming. Competency Based Que

Ans. The effect of global warming may not be uniform everywhere. Following are the major effects of global warming

- Global warming will harm ecosystems and the systems that support life, which are crucial for human survival.
- Global warming results in melting of ice caps due to which the sea levels are rising.
- Flooding of coastal regions may cause people to lose their homes and jobs, leading to more social tensions.
- Global warming also affects the change in crop pattern.

11. "Global warming is a serious concern for the world community". Discuss the efforts in this regards. Competency Based Que

Ans. The adverse effect of global warming is on the life supporting system mainly water and air. Increasing global temperature and melting glacier will lead to social problems.

Although, efforts have already been initiated to control the emission of GHGs and to arrest the trend towards global warming.

Initiatives by World Community

- International efforts have been started to reduce the GHGs emission into the atmosphere.

- Kyoto protocol proclaimed in 1997 is the most important initiative in this regard.
- It went into effect in 2005 ratified by 141 countries and bounds the 35 industrialised countries to reduce their emission by the year 2012 to 5 per cent less than the level prevalent in the year 1990.

12. Discuss the possible consequences of continued addition of greenhouse gases in the atmosphere.

Ans. The increasing trend in the concentration of GHGs in the atmosphere may, in the long run warm up the Earth. It will increase the atmospheric temperature up to an extent that it will cause ice to melt in the Arctic Ocean and in Antarctica.

The melting of ice will rise the sea level causing drowning of central lowlands and islands, altering rainfall and evaporation patterns, creating new plant diseases and health problems.

Increasing concentration of CFC will enlarge the ozone hole. Enlargement of the ozone hole, in turn will cause more and more ultraviolet radiations to reach the earth's surface, leading to further rise in temperature of the lower layers of the atmosphere.

13. "Himalayan glaciers are receding at very fast rate in the world due to global warming". Discuss the measures to mitigate this challenge. Competency Based Que

Ans. Himalayan glaciers are the biggest source of Northern rivers in India which are known as lifeline for the people. But due to increasing global warming these glaciers are melting faster which will cause big challenge for the existence of human beings.

Measures to Mitigate

- Major cause of glacier melting is aerosols which contain black carbon, dust and water vapour. These aerosols should be reduced to form cleaner atmospheric conditions, thereby slowing down glacier melting.
- Use of fossil fuel for energy in the Himalayan region should be restricted.
- Global warming is a worldwide phenomenon, hence, global efforts are required to mitigate the challenge.

14. Emission of greenhouse gases have been increased drastically in last decades. Discuss how it adversely affects the human life.

Ans. The primary GHGs are carbon dioxide (CO_2) methane (CH_4), chlorofluorocarbons (CFCs), nitrous oxide (N_2O). Out of these, CFCs are most harmful for human being and it is most reacting among GHGs. The main component of CFCs are chlorine, fluorine and carbon. These are frequently used in spray, refrigerators and other coolent devices. The increasing demand of fuel and energy and emission of CFCs are contributing in global warming.

Effects on Human Beings

- Increasing global warming will cause irregular weather and frequent floods and droughts which will affect human life.
- Excess GHGs will cause severe health problems like asthma, respiratory diseases, cancer, etc.
- Rising temperature on the Earth will disturb the food chain and crop cycle.

Long Answer Type Questions

1. Mention the characteristics of Dry climates: B. CBSE Diksha

Ans. Following are the characteristics of Dry climate : B

- Dry climates are characterised by very low rainfall that is not adequate for the growth of plants.
- These climates cover a very large area of the planet extending over large latitudes from 15° - 60° North and South of the equator.
- At low latitudes, from 15° - 30°, they occur in subtropical high.
- On the Western margin of the continents, adjoining the cold current, particularly over the West coast of South America, they extend more equatorward and occur on the coastland.
- In middle latitudes, from 35° - 60° North and South of the equator, they are confined to the interior of continents where maritime-humid winds do not reach.
- Dry climates are divided into steppe or semi-arid climate (BS) and desert climate (BW). They are further subdivided as subtropical steppe (BSh) and subtropical desert (BWh) at latitudes from 15°-35° and mid-latitude steppe (BSk) and mid-latitude desert (BWk) at latitudes between 35°-60°.

2. Carbon dioxide is an important gas as a greenhouse gas. Justify the statement. Competency Based Que

Ans. Carbon dioxide (CO_2) is a crucial greenhouse gas because it plays a significant role in regulating Earth's temperature as follows

- It absorbs infrared radiation emitted from the Earth's surface, trapping heat in the atmosphere, which is essential for maintaining the planet's habitable temperature.
- Without CO_2, Earth's average temperature would be much colder, making life as we know it unsustainable.
- Human activities, such as burning fossil fuels (coal, oil, and natural gas), deforestation, and industrial processes, have significantly increased CO_2 levels, intensifying the greenhouse effect and contributing to global warming.

- CO_2 remains in the atmosphere for long periods, making it a key driver of long-term climate change. Thus, controlling CO_2 emissions is critical in mitigating climate change and maintaining environmental stability.

3. What are the causes of climate change? CBSE DIksha

Ans. The causes of climate change are many. They can be grouped into astronomical and terrestrial causes.

The Astronomical Causes

- They are the changes in solar output associated with sunspot activities. Sunspots are dark and cooler patches on the sun which increase and decrease in a certain manner. When the number of sunspots increases, cooler and wetter weather and greater storm occur. A decrease in sunspot numbers is associated with warm and drier conditions.
- Another astronomical theory is Milankovitch oscillations, which is the variations in the Earth's orbital characteristics around the sun, the wobbling of the earth, and the changes in the Earth's axial tilt.

Terrestrial Causes

- Volcanism is considered as the cause of climate change as volcanic eruption throws up aerosols which remain in the atmosphere reducing the Sun's radiation reaching the Earth's surface.
- The anthropogenic effects are very significant nowadays. The increasing trend in the concentration of greenhouse gases in the atmosphere causes global warming, which has the most anthropogenic effect on climate change.

4. Write a detailed note on greenhouse gases.

Ans. The gases that absorb long wave radiations are called greenhouse gases (GHGs), Carbon dioxide, Chlorofluorocarbon, Methane, Nitrous Oxide and Ozone are the primary GHGs.

Some other gases such as Nitric oxide (NO) and Carbon monoxide (CO) easily react with GHGs and affect their concentration in the atmosphere.

Effect of GHGs The effectiveness of GHGs molecule depends on the magnitude of the increase in its concentration, its life time in the atmosphere and the wavelength of the radiation that it absorbs.

The CFCs and ozone are highly effective in absorbing terrestrial radiation. The more time the GHG molecule remains in the atmosphere, the longer it will take for the earth's atmosphere system to recover from any change brought about by latter.

Role of Some Prominent Gases The largest concentration of GHGs in the atmosphere is carbon dioxide which comes mainly from fossil fuel combustion. Forests use CO_2 in their growth and deforestation increases the concentration of CO_2 which is rising at about 0.5 percent annually.

Doubling of concentration of CO_2 over pre-industrial level is used as an index for estimating the changes in climatic model. Chloroflurocarbons are the product of human activities. It drifts into the stratosphere and destroys the ozone which protects us from UV rays.

Ozone occurs in the stratosphere where ultraviolet rays convert oxygen into ozone. The depletion of ozone concentration in the stratosphere is called the ozone hole which allows the UV rays to pass through the troposphere.

5. "The Earth has witnessed many variations in climate since the beginning". Illustrate this statement with suitable examples. Competency Based Que

Ans. In the geological past, the Earth was warm some 500-300 million years ago, through the cambrian, ordovician and silurian periods.

During the pleistocene epoch, glacial and inter-glacial periods occurred. Geological records show alteration of glacial and inter-glacial periods. The last major peak of glacial period was about 18,000 years ago.

The geomorphological features, especially in high altitudes, and high latitudes, exhibit traces of advances and retreats of glaciers.

Some examples of these variations that the earth has witnessed are discussed below

- The sediment deposits in glacial lakes also reveal the occurrence of warm and cold periods.
- The rings in the trees provide clues about wet and dry periods.
- Historical records describe the vagaries in climate. All these evidences indicate that change in climate is a natural and continuous process.
- The type of climate we experience now might be prevailing over the last 10,000 years with minor and occasionally wide fluctuations.
- An increasing trend in temperature was discernible in the 20th century. The greatest warming of the 20th century was during the two periods, 1901-44 and 1977-99. Over each of these two periods global temperature rose by about 0.4°C. In between, there was a slight cooling which was more marked in the Northern hemisphere.

6. "One of the major concerns of world today is global warming". Discuss the ways and lifestyle we need to adopt that will help to leave behind a livable world for the coming generation. Competency Based Que

Ans. The global warming is adversely affecting the life support system. Neither water nor air is pure now. The increasing global temperature and concentration of GHGs will lead to serious social problems. The changing pattern of rainfall and melting glaciers will lead to flood and drought frequently. Increasing emission of CFC will harm ozone layer more and ultraviolet rays that will come direct to surface will cause skin diseases and cancer.

Reason behind Global Warming Apart from some geographical reasons, there are some human activities which are highly responsible for the fast pace of climate change.

The superfluous use of fossil fuels, use of CFCs in refrigerators and other domestic products contributing in the concentration of green house gases.

Possible Way Out To make the earth a livable planet and to ensure the future of coming generation, we need to adopt a sustainable approach:

- We need to increase the dependency over renewable sources of energy.
- Consumption of fossil fuels should be demotivated and alternative means should be evolved.
- Sustainable pattern of development should be adopted on country and world level. The 17 goals of sustainable development should be implemented by every nation.
- Deforestation should be avoided as possible as it can, and afforestation should be done to create more carbon sink.
- Lifestyle should be changed according to demand of environment. Eco-friendly things should be adopted for daily use. Use of bicycle should be promoted for local transportation.

Source Based Questions

1. Read the passage carefully and answer the questions that follow.

Tropical wet climate is found near the equator. The major areas are the Amazon Basin in South America, Western equatorial Africa and the islands of East Indies. Significant amount of rainfall occurs in every month of the year as thunder showers in the afternoon. The temperature is uniformly high and the annual range of temperature is negligible. The maximum temperature on any day is around 30°C while the minimum temperature is around 20°C. Tropical evergreen forests with dense canopy cover and large biodiversity are found in this climate. Tropical monsoon climate (Am) is found over the Indian sub-continent, North-Eastern part of South America and Northern Australia. Heavy rainfall occurs mostly in summer. Winter is dry.

Tropical wet and dry climate occurs North and South of Af type climate regions. It borders with dry climate on the Western part of the continent and Cf or Cw on the Eastern part. Extensive Aw climate is found to the North and South of the Amazon forest in Brazil and adjoining parts of Bolivia and Paraguay in South America, Sudan and South of Central Africa. The annual rainfall in this climate is considerably less than that in Af and Am climate types and is variable also. The wet season is shorter and the dry season is longer with the drought being more severe. Temperature is high throughout the year and diurnal ranges of temperature are the greatest in the dry season. Deciduous forest and tree-shredded grasslands occur in this climate.

Sub-tropical steppe (BSh) and sub-tropical desert (BWh) have common precipitation and temperature characteristics. Located in the transition zone between humid and dry climates, sub-tropical steppe receives slightly more rainfall than the desert, adequate enough for the growth of sparse grasslands.

(i) In which of the following climate, the annual range of temperature is almost zero?

(a) Stepee climate (b) Desert climate
(c) Tropical wet climate (d) Mediterranean climate

Ans. (c) Tropical wet climate

(ii) Deciduous forests and tropical grasslands are commonly found in which of the following climate?

(a) Tropical wet climate
(b) Sub-tropical desert climate
(c) Tropical wet and dry climate
(d) Tropical monsoon climate

Ans. (c) Tropical wet and dry climate

(iii) Which climate experience daily thunderstorms in the afternoon?

(a) Sub-tropical stepee climate
(b) Sub-tropical desert climate
(c) Tropical wet climate
(d) All of the above

Ans. (c) Tropical wet climate

2. Read the passage carefully and answer the questions that follow.

The type of climate we experience now might be prevailing over the last 10,000 years with minor and occasionally wide fluctuations. The planet earth has witnessed many variations in climate since the beginning. Geological records show alteration of glacial and inter-glacial periods. The geomorphological features, especially in high altitudes and high latitudes, exhibit traces of advances and retreats of glaciers. The sediment deposits in glacial lakes also reveal the occurrence of warm and cold periods. The rings in the trees provide clues about wet and dry periods. Historical records describe the vagaries in climate. All these evidences indicate that change in climate is a natural and continuous process.

The causes for climate change are many. They can be grouped into astronomical and terrestrial causes. The astronomical causes are the changes in solar output associated with sunspot activities. Sunspots are dark and cooler patches on the sun which increase and decrease in a cyclical manner. According to some meteorologists, when the number of sunspots increase, cooler and wetter weather and greater storminess occur. A decrease in sunspot numbers is associated with warm and drier conditions.

An another astronomical theory is Millankovitch oscillations, which infer cycles in the variations in the earth's orbital characteristics around the sun, the wobbling of the earth and the changes in the earth's axial tilt. All these alter the amount of insolation received from the sun, which in turn, might have a bearing on the climate. Volcanism is considered as another cause for climate change.

(i) What evidence suggests that climate change is a natural and ongoing process?

Ans. Geological records, sediment deposits, tree rings and historical documentation collectively demonstrate that climate change has occurred continuously throughout Earth's history.

(ii) Explain how sunspot activities potentially influence Earth's weather patterns?

Ans. Increased sunspot activity correlates with cooler, wetter weather, and more storms, while decreased sunspot numbers relate to warmer and drier conditions.

(iii) Geomorphological features assist scientists in understanding historical climate patterns. Comment.

Ans. Geomorphological features in high altitudes and latitudes show evidence of glacier advances and retreats and this indicates past climate changes.

3. Read the passage carefully and answer the questions that follow.

Due to the presence of greenhouse gases, the atmosphere is behaving like a greenhouse. The atmosphere also transmits the incoming solar radiation but absorbs the vast majority of long wave radiation emitted upwards by the earth's surface. The gases that absorb long wave radiation are called greenhouse gases. The processes that warm the atmosphere are often collectively referred to as the greenhouse effect.

The primary GHGs of concern today are carbon dioxide (CO_2), Chlorofluorocarbons (CFCs), methane (CH_4), nitrous oxide (N_2O) and ozone (O_3). Some other gases such as nitric oxide (NO) and carbon monoxide (CO) easily react with GHGs and affect their concentration in the atmosphere. The effectiveness of any given GHG molecule will depend on the magnitude of the increase in its concentration, its life time in the atmosphere and the wavelength of radiation that it absorbs.

The chlorofluorocarbons (CFCs) are highly effective. Ozone which absorbs ultra violet radiation in the stratosphere is very effective in absorbing terrestrial radiation when it is present in the lower troposphere. Another important point to be noted is that the more time the GHG molecule remains in the atmosphere, the longer it will take for earth's atmospheric system to recover from any change brought about by the latter. The largest concentration of GHGs in the atmosphere is carbon dioxide. The emission of CO_2 comes mainly from fossil fuel combustion (oil, gas and coal). Forests and oceans are the sinks for the carbon dioxide.

Chlorofluorocarbons (CFCs) are products of human activity. Ozone occurs in the stratosphere where ultra-violet rays convert oxygen into ozone. Thus, ultra violet rays do not reach the earth's surface. The CFCs which drift into the stratosphere destroy the ozone. Large depletion of ozone occurs over Antarctica. The depletion of ozone concentration in the stratosphere is called the ozone hole. This allows the ultra violet rays to pass through the troposphere.

(i) What is the main source of carbon dioxide emissions?

Ans. Carbon dioxide mainly comes from combustion of fossil fuels like oil, gas and coal .

(ii) How does ozone get affected by CFCs in the stratosphere?

Ans. The CFCs drift into the stratosphere and destroy the ozone which results in depletion of ozone over Antarctica region.

(iii) What process leads to atmospheric warming through greenhouse gases?

Ans. Greenhouse gases absorb long wave radiation emitted by the Earth and prevent it from escape. This process is called the greenhouse effect.

SELF ASSESSMENT TEST

Objective Type Questions

1. Koeppen's climatic classification is based on

(a) Mean annual and mean monthly temperature (b) Mean annual and mean monthly precipitation
(c) Soil types (d) Both (a) and (b)

2. Koeppen recognised how many climatic groups?

(a) 3 (b) 5 (c) 7 (d) 10

3. The average temperature for all months is below 10° C in this climate.Which climate group this?

(a) A (b) H (c) E (d) D

4. Group 'F' stands in the Koeppen's climatic classification for

(a) Dry climates (b) Tropical climates
(c) Warm Temperature (d) Highlands

5. Tropical humid climates are divided into how many types?

(a) 1 (b) 3 (c) 5 (d) 7

6. Which climate is characterised by heavy rainfall in summer and dry winters?

(a) Tropical Wet and Dry Climate (Aw) (b) Tropical Wet Climate (Af)
(c) Tropical Monsoon Climate (Am) (d) Desert Climate

7. Which of the following is the characteristic of Group 'E' climatic classification?

I. Average temperature of the coldest month is 18°C or higher.
II. Potential evaporation exceeds precipitation.
III. Average temperature for all months is below 10°C.

Codes

(a) Only I (b) I and III (c) Only III (d) All of these

Short Answer Type Questions

8. Discuss the characteristics of tropical wet and dry climate.

9. What type of climatic conditions are characterised by sub-Arctic climate?

10. Due to the presence of greenhouse gases, the atmosphere is behaving like a greenhouse.Justify this statement in the context of greenhouse effect.

11. Explain the conditions for C-group climate and also explain the subtypes of this group.

Long Answer Type Questions

12. International efforts have been initiated for reducing the emission of GHGs into the atmosphere. Explain the measures to prevent global warming in context of this statement.

13. Koeppen identified a close relationship between the distribution of vegetation and climate. Write in brief about Koeppen's climate classification.

14. Explain the geographical distribution of the Group D climate. Where are these climates typically found?

15. 'Volcanism is considered as the cause of climate change'. Elucidate the statement.

UNIT 5

12 CHAPTER

Water (Oceans)

The Earth is called the Blue Planet as it has a huge supply of water on its surface. Water is an essential component for all life forms that exist over the surface of the Earth. Water is a rare commodity in our solar system and is not present in the Sun or anywhere else in the solar system.

YOUR STUDY GOALS

12.1 Hydrological or Water Cycle
12.2 Relief of the Ocean Floor
12.3 Temperature Of Ocean Waters
12.4 Salinity of Ocean Waters

YOUR PRACTICE GOALS

- Objective Type Questions (32 Qs ; MCQs, Statements, Matching, A-R)
- Subjective Questions (14 SAs, 9 LAs)
- Source/Graph Based Questions (3 Qs)
- Map Based Question (1 Qs)

12.1 Hydrological Cycle

- Hydrological or water cycle describes the movement of water on, in and above the Earth.
- It is the **circulation of water** within the Earth's hydrosphere in different forms like **solid**, **liquid** and **gaseous phase** which results in exchange of water between ocean, atmosphere and land surface.

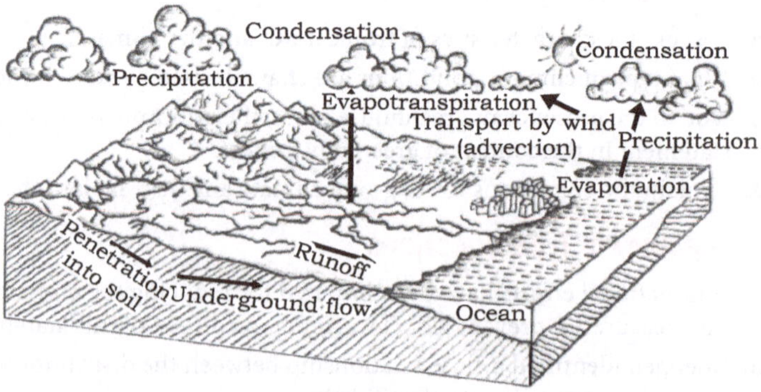

▲ *Hydrological Cycle*

- About 71% of Earth's water is found in the ocean and remaining is found as freshwater in glaciers, groundwater, rivers, etc.
- About 59% of water that falls on land returns to the atmosphere through the process of evaporation and the rest of the water flows on the surface or goes down to the Earth.

Components and Processes of the Water Cycle

Components	Processes
Water storage in oceans	Evaporation, Evapotranspiration, Sublimation
Water in the atmosphere	Condensation, Precipitation
Water storage in ice and snow	Snowmelt runoff to streams
Surface runoff	Stream flow freshwater storage infiltration
Groundwater storage	Groundwater discharge springs

12.2 Relief of the Ocean Floor

- The oceanic part of the Earth is divided into five **oceans** by the geographers namely- the **Pacific**, the **Atlantic**, the **Arctic**, the **Indian** and the **Southern** ocean.
- The various seas, bays, gulfs and other inlets are parts of these oceans.
- A major portion of the ocean floor is found between 3-6 km below the sea level.
- Various complex features are found in the floor of the oceans such as world's largest mountain ranges, deepest trenches and the plains. These features are formed due to various tectonic, volcanic and depositional processes.

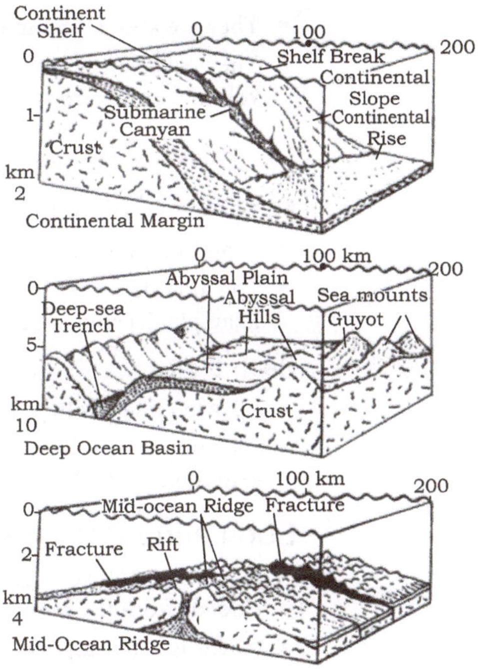

▲ *Relief Features of Ocean Floors*

Divisions of the Ocean Floors

- The ocean floors can be divided into four major divisions
  - (i) The Continental Shelf (ii) The Continental Slope
  - (iii) The Deep Sea Plain (iv) The Oceanic Deeps or Trenches

Continental Shelf

- The continental shelf is the extended margin of each continent covered by shallow seas and **gulfs**[1].
- It is the shallowest part of the ocean having an **average gradient of 1°** or even less.
- The shelf typically ends at a very steep slope, called the **shelf break**[2].
- The width of the continental shelves vary from one ocean to another.
- The average width of continental shelves is about 80 km.
- These shelves are almost absent or very narrow along some of the margins like the coasts of Chile, the West coast of Sumatra, etc. On the other hand, the **Siberian shelf in the Arctic Ocean**, which is the largest in the world, stretches to 1,500 km in width.
- The depth of the shelves also varies. It may be as shallow as 30 m in some areas while in some areas it is as deep as 600 m.
- The continental shelves are covered by the sediments brought and deposited by the rivers, glaciers, etc. These sedimentary deposits over a long period of time become the source of fossil fuels.

1 **Gulf** The Gulf is a large body of water (part of sea or ocean) that extend towards the land.

2 **Shelf break** It is the submerged edge of a continental shelf where the seafloor's slope increases significantly, marking the transition to the continental slope.

Continental Slope

- The continental slope connects the continental shelf and the ocean basins.
- It begins where the bottom of the continental shelf sharply ends into a steep slope.
- The gradient of the slope varies between 2-5°. The depth of the slope varies between 200 and 3,000 m. The slope boundary indicates the end of the continents. Canyons[3] and trenches are found in this region.

Deep Sea Plain

- Deep sea plains are low sloping areas of the ocean basins. These are the flattest and smoothest regions of the world.
- The depths of the sea plain range between 3,000 and 6,000 m. These plains are covered with fine sediments like clay[4] and silt[5].

Oceanic Deeps or Trenches

- Trenches are the deepest parts of the oceans. They are relatively steep sloped and narrow basins.
- They are about 3-5 km deeper than the surrounding ocean floor.
- They occur at the bases of continental slopes and along island areas. They are associated with active volcanoes and strong earthquakes.

Minor Relief Features

Mid-Oceanic Ridges

- A mid-oceanic ridge comprises two chains of mountains separated by a large depression.
- The mountain ranges can have peaks as high as 2,500 m and some even reach above the ocean's surface. Example, Iceland, a part of the mid-Atlantic Ridge.

Seamount

- It is a mountain with pointed summits. It rises from the seafloor but does not reach the surface of the ocean.
- Seamounts are volcanic in origin. These can be 3,000-4,500 m tall. Example, the Emperor seamount, an extension of the Hawaiian Islands in the Pacific Ocean.

Submarine Canyons, Guyots and Atolls

- Submarine Canyons are the deep valleys, found cutting across the continental shelves and slopes. It extends from the mouths of large rivers. Example of submarine canyon, is The Hudson Canyon.
- Guyot is a flat topped seamount which became submerged mountains after degradation. More than 10,000 seamounts and guyots exist in the Pacific Ocean.
- Atolls are low islands found in the tropical oceans. Atoll consists of coral reefs[6] surrounding a central depression. It may be a part of the sea water or fresh water.

Quick Test 1

1. What percentage of planetary water is found in the ocean?
2. What is the gradient of continental shelf?
3. Define shelf break.
4. In which part of the oceans, fossil fuels are found?

---

3 **Canyons** It refers to a deep valley with very steep sides
4 **Clay** It is a type of soil that is soft and sticky when it is wet and becomes hard when it is baked or dried up.
5 **Silt** Sand, soil or mud that collects at the sides or on the bottom of a river.
6 **Coral reefs** It refers to structure made of living marine organisms.

12.3 Temperature of Ocean Waters

- This section deals with the spatial and vertical changes of temperature in various oceans.
- Ocean waters are heated by solar energy just as land. The process of heating and cooling of the oceanic water is slower than land.

Factors Affecting Temperature Distribution

- **Latitude** The temperature of surface water decreases from the equator towards the poles because the amount of insolation[7] decreases polewards.
- **Unequal distribution of land and water** The oceans in the Northern hemisphere receive more heat due to their contact with larger amounts of land than the oceans in the Southern hemisphere.
- **Prevailing wind** The winds blowing from the land towards the oceans take warm surface water away from the coast, resulting in the upwelling(coming up) of cold water from below. It results in a change in the temperature. On the other hand, the onshore winds bring warm water near the coast and this raises the temperature.
- **Ocean currents** Warm ocean currents raise the temperature in cold areas while the cold currents decrease the temperature in warm ocean areas. For example, the **Gulf stream** (warm current) raises the temperature near the Eastern coast of North America while the **Labrador current** (cold current) lowers the temperature near the North-East coast of North America.

Horizontal and Vertical Distribution of Temperature

- The temperature-depth profile for the ocean water shows how the temperature decreases with the increasing depth. It shows a boundary region between the surface waters of the ocean and the deeper layers.
- The boundary usually begins around 100-400 m below the sea surface and extends several hundred of meters downward. This boundary region where there is a rapid decrease of temperature is called the **thermocline.**
- The average temperature of surface water of the oceans is about 27°C and it gradually decreases from the equator towards the poles.
- The rate of decrease of temperature with increasing latitude is generally **0.5°C** per latitude.
- The oceans in the Northern hemisphere record comparatively higher temperature than in the Southern hemisphere. This is due to the unequal distribution of land and water in the Northern and Southern hemispheres.
- The highest temperature is not recorded at the equator but slightly towards North of it.
- The temperature structure of oceans over middle and low latitudes can be described as a three-layer system from surface to the bottom.

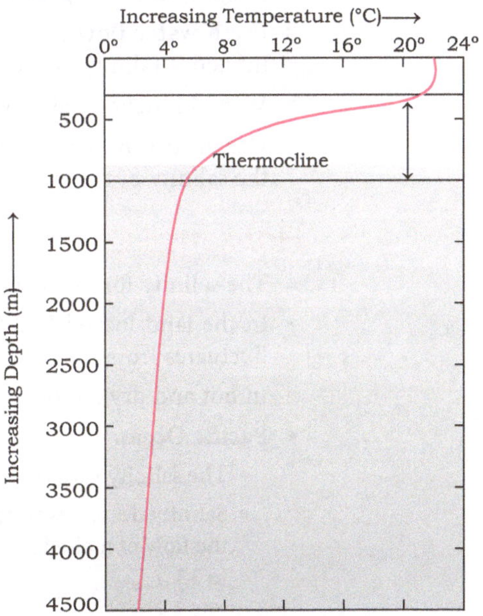

▲ *Thermocline*

- **First layer**
    - The first layer represents the top layer of warm oceanic water.
    - It is about 500 m thick with temperatures ranging between 20° and 25° C.
    - In the tropical region, this layer is present throughout the year but in mid latitudes it is present only during summer.

---

7 **Insolation** It refers to the incoming solar radiation from the Sun, which is received on Earth in short waves.

- **Second Layer**
  - It is also called the **Thermocline layer** and is present below the first layer. It is 500 -1,000 m thick.
  - It is characterised by rapid decrease in temperature with increasing depth.
  - About 90 per cent of the total volume of water is found below the thermocline in the deep ocean. In this zone, temperatures approach 0°C.
- **Third layer**
  - It is very cold and extends up to the deep ocean floor.
  - In the Arctic and Antarctic circles, the surface water temperatures are close to 0°C and so the temperature change with the depth is very less.

12.4 Salinity of Ocean Waters

- Salinity is defined as the total content of dissolved salts in the sea water.
- It is calculated as the **amount of salt** (in gm) dissolved in 1,000 gm (1 kg) of seawater.
- It is usually expressed as parts per thousand ($^{\circ}/_{oo}$) or ppt.
- Salinity of 24.7$^{\circ}/_{oo}$ has been considered as the upper limit to define **brackish water.**
- Water bodies with **highest salinity** are Lake Van in Turkey (330$^{\circ}/_{oo}$), Dead Sea (238$^{\circ}/_{oo}$) and Great Salt Lake (220$^{\circ}/_{oo}$).

Factors affecting Ocean Salinity

- **Evaporation** and **precipitation** influence the salinity of water in the surface layer of oceans.
- **Fresh water flow** from rivers and the processes of **freezing and** thawing[8] **of ice** in the polar regions influence salinity of the ocean
- **Wind** influences salinity of an area by transferring water to other areas.
- **Ocean currents** contribute to the salinity variations as any change in temperature and density influences the salinity of the water in an area.

Horizontal Distribution of Salinity

- The salinity for normal open ocean ranges between 33$^{\circ}/_{oo}$ and 37$^{\circ}/_{oo}$.
- In the land-locked Red Sea, it is as high as 41$^{\circ}/_{oo}$, while in the estuaries and the Arctic, the salinity fluctuates from 0 - 35$^{\circ}/_{oo}$, seasonally.
- In hot and dry regions, where evaporation is high, the salinity reaches 70$^{\circ}/_{oo}$.
- **Pacific Ocean**
  - The salinity variation in the Pacific Ocean is mainly due to its shape and larger areal extent.
  - Salinity decreases from 35$^{\circ}/_{oo}$ - 31$^{\circ}/_{oo}$ in the Western parts of the Northern hemisphere because of the flow of melted ice water from the Arctic region. In the same way, after 15°- 20° South, it decreases to 33 $^{\circ}/_{oo}$.

8 Thawing It refers to change of state from solid to liquid due to increase in temperature.

- **Atlantic Ocean**
  - The average salinity of the Atlantic Ocean is around $36^\circ/_{oo}$. The highest salinity is recorded between 15° and 20° latitudes.
  - Maximum salinity ($37^\circ/_{oo}$) is observed between 20°N and 30°N and 20°W - 60°W. It gradually decreases towards the North.
  - The **North Sea**, in spite of its location in higher latitudes, records higher salinity due to more saline water brought by the North Atlantic Drift.
  - **The Baltic Sea** records low salinity due to the addition of river waters in large quantities.
  - **The Mediterranean** Sea records higher salinity due to high evaporation.
  - Salinity is very low in **Black Sea** due to enormous freshwater added by rivers.
- **Indian Ocean**
  - The average salinity of the Indian Ocean is $35^\circ/_{oo}$.
  - The low salinity trend is observed in the Bay of Bengal due to addition of river water.
  - The Arabian Sea shows higher salinity due to high evaporation and low addition of fresh water.

Vertical Distribution of Salinity

- Salinity at the surface increases by the loss of water to ice or evaporation, or decreased by the input of fresh waters, such as from the rivers.
- Salinity at depth is very much fixed, because there is no way that water is 'lost', or the salt is 'added.'
- The lower salinity water rests above the higher salinity heavy water.
- Salinity increases with depth and there is a distinct zone called the **halocline**, where salinity increases sharply.
- Increasing salinity of seawater causes its density to increase. High salinity seawater, generally sinks below the lower salinity water. This leads to **stratification**[9] by salinity.

Quick Test 2

1. What is the average temperature of surface water of the ocean?
2. Salinity is measured in which unit?
3. What is the average salinity of the Indian Ocean?
4. Mention the depth of the Halocline layer.

9 **Stratification** It is a process of separation of a water body into different layers based on salinity differences.

Mind Map

1 Hydrological Cycle

The continuous exchange of water between the oceans, atmosphere, land surface and sub-surface and organisms.

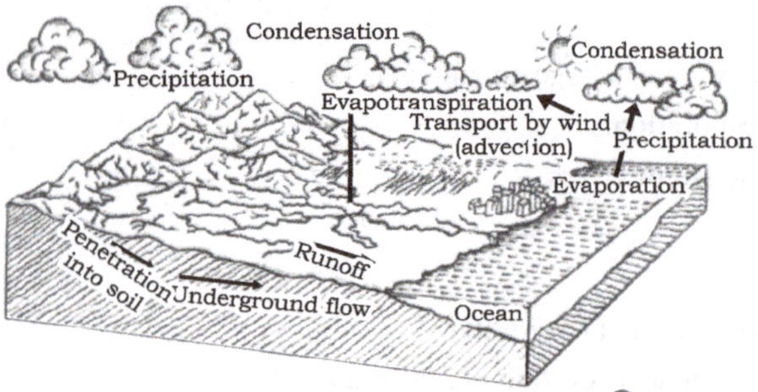

Minor Relief Division

- **Mid Oceanic Ridge** It comprises two chains of mountains separated by a large depression.
- **Seamount** It is a mountain with a pointed summits, rising from the seafloor that does not reach the surface of the ocean. It is volcanic in nature and can be 3,000-4,500 m tall.
- **Submarine Canyon** These are deep valleys, found cutting across the continental shelves and slope.
- **Guyots** It is a flat topped seamount which became submerged mountains after degradation.
- **Atoll** These are low islands found in the tropical oceans. It may be a part of the sea water or fresh water.

WATER (OCEANS)

2 Division of Ocean Floor

Major Relief Division

- **Continental Shelf** Shallowest part of the ocean having an average gradient of 1° (average width 80 km.) These are covered by the sediments brought and deposited by the rivers, glaciers, etc. These sedimentary deposits over a long period of time become the source of fossil fuels.
- **Continental Slope** Connects the continental shelf and the ocean basins(depth between 200 and 3,000 m) Canyons and trenches are found in this region.
- **Deep Sea Plains** These are the flattest and smoothest regions of the world (depth 3,000 and 6,000 m) and covered with fine sediments like clay and silt.
- **Oceanic Deeps and Trenches** Deepest parts of the oceans (3-5 km deeper) occur at the bases of continental slopes and along island areas and are associated with active volcanoes and strong earthquakes.

3 Temperature of the Ocean Water

Factors Affecting Temperature Distribution

- **Latitude** Temperature decreases from the equator towards the pole.
- **Unequal distribution of land and water** Oceans in the Northern hemisphere receive more heat than those in the Southern hemisphere.
- **Prevailing Winds** Winds blowing from the land towards the oceans takes warm surface water away, resulting in decrease in temperature. On the other hand, the onshore winds bring warm water near the coast, resulting in increase in temperature.
- **Ocean Currents** Warm ocean currents raise the temperature in cold areas while the cold currents decrease the temperature in warm ocean areas.

Horizontal and Vertical Distribution of Temperature

- **Horizontal** Temperature decreases from equator towards the pole.
- **Vertical** Temperature decreases as we go from surface towards the deep ocean.

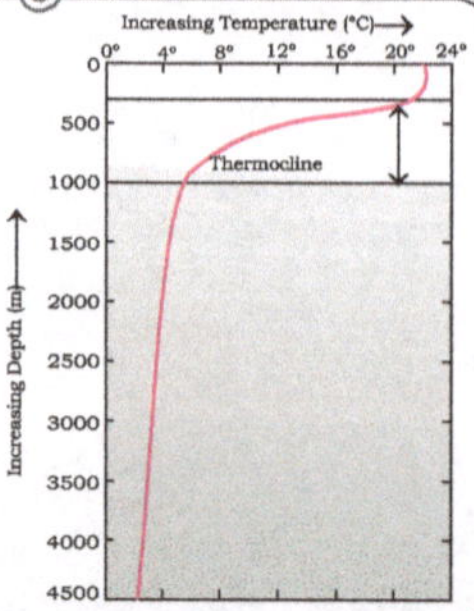

4 Salinity of Ocean Waters

Factors Affecting Ocean Salinity

- Rate of evaporation and precipitation
- Inflow of fresh river water
- Prevailing wind
- Ocean currents

Horizontal and Vertical Distribution of Salinity

- **Horizontal** High salinity is found between 15°-20° latitudes and low salinity is found in polar regions and estuaries.
- **Vertical** Salinity increases with depth. High salinity water generally sinks below the lower salinity water.

NCERT Folder

Multiple Choice Questions

(i) **Identify the element which is not a part of hydrological cycle.**

(a) Evaporation (b) Hydration
(c) Precipitation (d) Condensation

Ans (b) Hydration

(ii) **The average depth of continental slope varies between:**

(a) 2-20 m (b) 200-2,000 m
(c) 20-200 m (d) 2,000-20,000 m

Ans (b) 200-2000 m

(iii) **Which one of the following is not a minor relief feature in the oceans?**

(a) Seamount (b) Atoll (c) Oceanic deep (d) Guyot

Ans (c) Oceanic deep

(iv) **Salinity is expressed as the amount of salt in grams dissolved in sea water per**

(a) 10 gm (b) 1,000 gm (c) 100 gm (d) 10,000 gm

Ans (b) 1,000 gm

(v) **Which one of the following is the smallest ocean?**

(a) Indian Ocean (b) Arctic Ocean
(c) Atlantic Ocean (d) Pacific Ocean

Ans (b) Arctic Ocean

Answer the following questions in about 30 words

(i) **Why do we call the Earth a blue planet?**

Ans The Earth is called a blue planet because of the abundant supply of water on its surface. Water is an essential compnent of all life form that exist over the surface of the Earth. We all would have no existence if our Earth was not a water planet.

(ii) **What is a continental margin?**

Ans Continental margin is the transition between continental shore and deep sea basin. It can be understand as the region of transition from the land to deep sea floor i.e. between continent and crust of ocean. It includes continental shelf, continental slope, continental rise and deep oceanic trenches.

(iii) **List out the deepest trenches of various oceans.**

Ans There are 57 deep trenches which have been explored so for, out of which 32 are in the Pacific Ocean, 19 in the Atlantic Ocean and 6 in the Indian Ocean.

The deepest trenches of various oceans are as follows
Pacific ocean- Mariana trench
Atlantic ocean- Puerto Rico trench
Indian ocean- Sunda trench

(iv) **What is a thermocline?**

Ans Thermocline is a boundary region from where there is a rapid decrease of temperature between the surface waters of the ocean and the deeper layers. This boundary usually begins around 100-400 m below the sea surface and extends several hundred of meters downward.

(v) **When you move into the ocean what thermal layers would you encounter? Why the temperature varies with depth?**

Ans As we move into the ocean, we would encounter three layers from surface to the bottom which are

(i) **First Layer** It is the top layer of 500 m thickness.
(ii) **Second Layer** It is the thermocline layer.
(iii) **Third Layer** It is very cold and extends upto the deep ocean floor.

Temperature varies with depth because the source of temperature is the Sun rays which are not able to penetrate upto lower surface as most of insolation are absorbed by upper surface.

(vi) **What is salinity of sea water?**

Ans Salinity is the total content of dissolved salt in sea water. It is calculated as the amount of salt (in gm) dissolved in 1,000 gm (1 kg) of sea water. It is an important property of sea water. It mainly depends on evaporation and precipitation.

Answer the following questions in about 150 words

(i) **How are various elements of the hydrological cycle interrelated?**

Ans Hydrological cycle describes the movement of water in various stages. It is one of the most significant cycles that maintains life on the Earth.

The various elements of the hydrological cycle are

- The hydrological cycle depends basically on the inter-relationship between the circulation of ocean water and that in atmosphere.
- Due to temperature, water withdrawn from the oceans into the atmosphere by process of evaporation.
- Evaporation depends upon the air, sea, temperature, wind strength and the humidity.
- The minute particles of salt and other minerals from the sea help for the condensation.
- Water vapour is condensed in the atmosphere and is returned back to the Earth's surface in the form of precipitation like rain, snow, etc.

- The water on the surface run off merge in the ocean through rivers.
- Some part of the water infiltrates into the ground which later turn into water vapour through evaporation and reach to the ocean.

Hence, this circulation of water forms the water cycle which explains the movement of water within the earth's hydrosphere in different forms.

(ii) **Examine the factors that influence the temperature distribution of the oceans.**

Ans The temperature distribution of ocean water is influenced by several factors

(i) **Latitude** The temperature of surface water decreases from the equator to the poles because the amount of sunlight, or insolation, diminishes as one moves towards the poles.

(ii) **Unequal distribution of land and water** Oceans in the Northern hemisphere receive more heat due to their proximity to large landmasses, unlike those in the Southern hemisphere, which have more water-covered areas.

(iii) **Prevailing winds** Winds blowing from land to sea can drive warm surface waters away from the coast, causing cold water to rise in a process called upwelling, lowering the temperature. Onshore winds, however, cause warm water to accumulate near the coast, raising the temperature.

(iv) **Ocean currents** Warm currents, like the Gulf Stream, raise the temperature of nearby regions, while cold currents, like the Labrador Current, lower temperatures in the areas they pass through. These factors together contribute to both local and regional variations in ocean temperature.

Exam Pattern Questions

Objective Type Questions

Multiple Choice Questions (MCQs)

1. It is also referred to as the continuous exchange of water between the oceans, atmosphere, land surface, subsurface and the organisms.Which of the following is being referred to in the above statement?

(a) Oxygen cycle (b) Hydrogen cycle
(c) Hydrological cycle (d) Geochemical cycle

2. The component 'water storage in oceans' is associated with which of the following processes of the water cycle?

(a) Evaporation (b) Evapotranspiration
(c) Sublimation (d) All of these

3. The continental shelf is the extended margin of each continent occupied by which type of seas and gulfs?

(a) Shallow seas and gulfs.
(b) Deep sea trenches and gulfs.
(c) High mountain ranges and gulfs.
(d) Large plains and gulfs.

4. The deep sea plains are

(a) Steep slopes and deep trenches.
(b) Gently sloping areas of the ocean floor covered with fine-grained sediments.
(c) High mountain ranges and volcanic activity.
(d) Shallow waters and coral reefs.

5. A group of scientists is investigating the structure of the ocean floor. Which feature would they study if they are examining the narrow, steep-sided depressions at the base of continental slopes?

(a) Mid-oceanic ridges (b) Continental shelves
(c) Oceanic trenches (d) Seamounts

6. Which of the following is the minor relief feature of the ocean floor?

(a) Mid-oceanic ridges (b) Seamount
(c) Guyot (d) All of these

7. Which of the following minor relief features of the ocean is composed of two chains of mountains separated by a large depression?

(a) Atoll (b) Seamount
(c) Guyot (d) Mid-Oceanic ridges

8. A group of scientists is studying the temperature variations in the ocean. Which of the following is the main factor affecting the temperature distribution in the ocean waters?

(a) Latitude
(b) Ocean currents
(c) Unequal distribution of land and water
(d) All of the above

9. Which of the following statements is true about the temperature distribution in the oceans?
(a) The temperature decreases uniformly with increasing latitude.
(b) The highest ocean temperature is recorded slightly towards North of the equator.
(c) The temperature decreases rapidly to a depth of 500 meters.
(d) Oceans in the Southern hemisphere are warmer than those in the Northern hemisphere.

10. Which of the following is mainly responsible for lowering the temperature near the North-East coast of North America?
(a) North East trade winds (b) Coriolis force
(c) Labrador current (d) Pressure Gradient

11. In the vertical distribution of ocean water the layer which is characterised by rapid decrease in temperature with increasing depth is known as
(a) Halocline (b) Thermocline
(c) Ionosphere (d) Stratosphere

12. A team of researchers is studying the variations in ocean salinity across different regions. Which factor among the following most directly impacts ocean salinity?
(a) Ocean currents
(b) Location of mid-oceanic ridges
(c) Types of marine life in the area
(d) Presence of submarine canyons

13. Which of the following is not a factor affecting ocean salinity?
(a) Wind (b) Evaporation
(c) Ocean currents (d) Tidal waves

14. In which of the following regions would you find the highest salinity levels due to high evaporation and low influx of fresh water?
(a) Bay of Bengal (b) Red Sea
(c) Baltic Sea (d) Black Sea

15. What is a primary factor influencing the high salinity observed in the Mediterranean Sea?
(a) High influx of fresh river water
(b) Low evaporation rates
(c) High evaporation and low freshwater influx
(d) Cold temperatures limiting water circulation

16. Which of the following statements best describes the factors affecting ocean salinity and the regions with high or low salinity?
(a) High salinity is found in coastal regions with abundant freshwater inflow, while low salinity is seen in central oceans with high evaporation.
(b) High salinity is common in polar regions due to cold temperatures, while tropical regions have low salinity due to heavy rainfall.
(c) Salinity is high in areas with low evaporation and significant freshwater influx, while low salinity is found in high evaporation areas with minimal freshwater input.
(d) High salinity is found in areas with high evaporation, like the Mediterranean and Red Seas, while low salinity is observed in regions like the Bay of Bengal with significant freshwater input.

17. Which of the following statements are correct related to the divisions of the ocean floors?
I. The continental shelf is the shallowest part of the ocean, with a gradient of 1°or less.
II. The continental slope connects the ocean basins and typically has a depth of 3,000 to 5,000 m.
III. The deep sea plains are the flattest and smoothest regions of the ocean, with depths ranging from 3,000 to 6,000 m.
IV. Oceanic deeps are the shallowest parts of the ocean and are associated with active volcanoes and earthquakes.

Choose the correct option.
(a) I, III, IV (b) I, II, III
(c) II, III, IV (d) I, II, IV

18. Which of the following statements are correct?
I. The distribution of water on Earth is quite uneven.
II. About 71 per cent of the planetary water is found in the oceans.
III. Nearly 89 per cent of the water that falls on land returns to the atmosphere through evaporation from over the oceans as well as from other places.
IV. The geographers have divided the oceanic part of the Earth into eight oceans.

Options
(a) I and II (b) Only IV
(c) Only III (d) I and IV

19. Which of the following factors mainly affect the salinity of ocean water in coastal regions?
I. Evaporation and precipitation
II. Freshwater flow from rivers
III. Freezing and thawing of ice in polar regions
IV. Wind

Codes
(a) Both I and II (b) Only II
(c) Both III and IV (d) Only I

20. **Which of the following statements are correct related to the ocean's relief features?**

I. The continental slope connects the continental shelf and ocean basins.

II. Oceanic deeps or trenches are the shallowest parts of the ocean.

III. Seamounts are volcanic mountains that rise from the ocean floor.

IV The mid-oceanic ridges are composed of two chains of mountains separated by a large depression.

Options

(a) I, III, IV (b) I, II, IV
(c) II, III, IV (d) I, II, III

21. **Hydrological cycle is the continuous exchange of water between the**

I. Oceans II. Atmosphere
III. Land surface IV. Organisms

Codes

(a) Both I and II (b) II and III
(c) I and IV (d) All of these

22. **Identify the statement that is not true with regard to minor relief features of the ocean floor**

(i) Mid-oceanic ridges are composed of two chains of mountains separated by a large depression, with peaks reaching up to 2,500 m.

(ii) Seamounts are volcanic mountains that reach above the ocean's surface.

(iii) Submarine canyons are deep valleys that sometimes cut across the continental shelves and slopes.

(iv) Atolls are low islands found in the tropical oceans consisting of coral reefs surrounding a central depression.

Options

(a) (i) and (ii) (b) Only (ii)
(c) Only (iii) (d) (ii) and (iii)

23. **Identify the feature from the information given below.**

This feature connects the continental shelf and the ocean basins. It begins where the bottom of the continental shelf sharply drops off into a steep slope. The gradient of the slope region varies between 2-5°. The depth of the slope region varies between 200 and 3,000 m. The slope boundary indicates the end of the continents. Canyons and trenches are observed in this region.

Options

(a) Atoll
(b) Continental slope
(c) Seamount
(d) Oceanic Deeps

Arrange the Following

24. **Arrange the following water bodies as per their salinity from highest to lowest.**

(i) Lake Van (ii) Great Salt lake
(iii) Dead sea (iv) Red sea

Codes

(a) (i), (ii), (iii), (iv) (b) (i), (iii), (ii), (iv)
(c) (iii), (ii), (i), (iv) (d) (iv), (iii), (ii), (i)

Match the Following

25.

List I	List II
A. Water storage in oceans	1. Evaporation, Evapotranspiration, Sublimation
B. Water in the atmosphere	2. Condensation, 'Precipitation'
C. Water storage in ice and snow	3. Snowmelt runoff to streams
D. Surface runoff	4. Stream flow freshwater storage, infiltration

Codes

	A	B	C	D		A	B	C	D
(a)	1	2	3	4	(b)	2	3	4	1
(c)	3	2	1	4	(d)	4	3	2	1

26.

List I (Layers of Ocean Temperature)	List II (Feature)
A. First layer	1. Warm oceanic water
B. Second layer	2. Thermocline layer
C. Third layer	3. Very cold oceanic water

Codes

	A	B	C		A	B	C
(a)	1	2	3	(b)	2	3	1
(c)	3	2	1	(d)	2	1	3

27.

List I	List II
A. Continental Slope	1. The flattest and smoothest regions of the ocean floor.
B. Deep Sea Plain	2. A region where two chains of mountains are separated by a depression.
C. Mid-Oceanic Ridges	3. Connects the continental shelf and the ocean basins, often with canyons

Codes

	A	B	C		A	B	C
(a)	3	1	2	(b)	2	3	1
(c)	3	2	1	(d)	2	1	3

Assertion-Reason

Directions (Q. Nos. 28-32) In the questions given below are two statements labelled as Assertion (A) and other is labelled as Reason (R). In the context of two statements, which one of the following is correct?

Codes

(a) Both A and R are true, but R is not the correct explanation of A
(b) Both A and R are true and R is the correct explanation of A
(c) Both A and R are incorrect.
(d) A is correct, but R is incorrect

28. **Assertion** (A) Salinity at depth is very much fixed.

Reason (R) There is no way that water is 'lost' or the salt is added at depth.

29. **Assertion** (A) In temperate latitudes salinity is lower.

Reason (R) In temperate latitudes, evaporation is less and rains are more abundant.

30. **Assertion** (A) There is huge water crisis in different parts of the world.

Reason (R) The renewable water on the earth is constant while the demand is increasing tremendously.

31. **Assertion** (A) The continental slope connects the continental shelf to the ocean basins and is characterised by steep gradients and varying depths.

Reason (R) The continental slope begins where the continental shelf drops sharply and is often associated with deep ocean features like canyons and trenches.

32. **Assertion** (A) The temperature of ocean waters decreases as one moves from the equator towards the poles.

Reason (R) The amount of solar insolation decreases poleward, causing a reduction in surface water temperature towards the poles.

Answers

1. (c) Hydrological cycle
2. (d) All of these
3. (a) Shallow seas and gulfs
4. (b) gently sloping areas of the ocean floor covered with fine-grained sediments.
5. (c) Oceanic trenches
6. (d) All of these
7. (d) Mid-Oceanic ridges
8. (d) All of the above
9. (b) The highest ocean temperature is recorded slightly towards North of the equator.
10. (c) Labrador current
11. (b) Thermocline
12. (a) Ocean currents
13. (d) Tidal waves
14. (b) Red Sea
15. (c) High evaporation and low freshwater influx
16. (d) High salinity is found in areas with high evaporation, like the Mediterranean and Red Seas, while low salinity is observed in regions like the Bay of Bengal with significant freshwater input.
17. (a) I, III, IV
18. (a) I and II
19. (a) Both I and II
20. (a) I, III, IV
21. (d) All of these
22. (b) Only (ii)
23. (b) Continental slope
24. (b) (i), (iii), (ii), (iv)
25. (a)
26. (a)
27. (a)
28. (b) Both A and R are true and R is the correct explanation of A
29. (b) Both A and R are true and R is the correct explanation of A
30. (b) Both A and R are true and R is the correct explanation of A
31. (b) Both A and R are true and R is the correct explanation of A
32. (b) Both A and R are true and R is the correct explanation of A

Subjective Questions

Short Answer Type Questions

1. Define the distribution of water on the Earth's surface.

Ans Out of 100, about 71 per cent of planetary water is found in the oceans. The remaining 29 per cent is found as freshwater in glaciers and ice caps, groundwater sources, lakes, soil moisture, atmosphere, streams and within life.

Nearly 59 per cent of the water that falls on land return to the atmosphere through evaporation from over the oceans as well as from other places. Remaining part run off on the surface, infiltrates into the ground or a part of it becomes glacier.

2. Continental shelf is a major division of the ocean floor. Explain the statement.

Ans Continental shelf is a major division of ocean floor. It is the submerged margin of continental mass extending from the shore to the first prominent break in slope.

Some shelves reach a depth of over 500 m but 200 m is often conveniently used as a depth limit. The mean width is about 70 km, but there is a marked variation between different coasts. It is estimated that the continental shelves cover approximately 5 per cent of the Earth's surface. The vast majority of sea exploitation occurs on the continental shelf such as fishing and gas and oil drilling.

3. Explain the main storage areas of water on Earth and the cycle that maintains its distribution.

Ans The main storage areas of water on Earth are oceans, glaciers, groundwater, lakes, rivers, and the atmosphere. Almost 71% of water is found in oceans and remaining found as freshwater in glaciers, icecaps, lakes, soil moisture, streams, etc. The water cycle maintains water distribution through processes like evaporation, condensation, precipitation, and runoff. Water moves between these areas, ensuring a balanced system of storage and circulation across the planet and it managed 59% of water that falls on land.

4. The horizontal distribution of temperature of ocean water is different at different latitudes. Explain.

Ans The average temperature of surface water of ocean is about 27° C and it gradually decreases from the equator towards poles. Temperature decreases with the rate of 0.5° C per latitude. The average temperature is around 22° C at 20° latitude, 14° C at 40° latitude and 0°C at the poles. The oceans of the Northern hemisphere record relatively higher temperature than in the Southern hemisphere. Highest temperature is not recorded at the equator but slightly toward North of it. Average annual temperature of the Northern and the Southern hemisphere is around 19° C and 16° C, respectively, due to unequal distribution of land and water.

5. "Enclosed seas such as the Mediterranean and Baltic show unique salinity patterns". Analyse this statement with examples of the factors that lead to these distinct salinity variations. **Competency Based Que**

Ans. Enclosed seas like the Mediterranean and Baltic have unique salinity patterns due to limited water exchange with the open ocean, high evaporation rates and freshwater inputs. For example, the Mediterranean's high salinity results from intense evaporation, while the Baltic Sea's low salinity stems from significant river inflow and low evaporation.

The other important factors that affects the salinity are

(i) Wind redistribute the water in an area which also affects the salinity

(ii) Salinity also gets affected by mixing of sea water from one origin to another due to the ocean currents.

(iii) Also, any change in the temperature or density influences the salinity of water in an area.

6. Salinity changes with depth according to the location of the sea. Explain.

Ans Salinity changes with depth according to the location of the sea. Salinity at the surface increases or decreases due to evaporation and influx of water but at depth, it is very much fixed because there is no way for the salt to be added. There is a marked difference in the salinity between the surface zones and the deep zones of the oceans. The lower salinity water rests above the higher salinity dense water. Salinity generally increases with depth and there is a distinct zone called the halocline where salinity increases sharply. Salinity increases the density of water. High salinity sea water, generally sinks below the lower salinity water which leads to stratification by salinity.

7. Which reasons are significant behind the salinity in sea water? Explain.

Ans The following reasons are significant behind the salinity of sea water

- The sea water is saline because a number of salts are dissolved in it.
- The total weight of salts dissolved in the sea is 4800 million tonnes.
- Of these, sodium chloride or common salt accounts for 3800 million tonnes, sulphate for 3000 million tonnes, magnesium for 1600 million tonnes, potassium for 480 million tonnes and bromide for 83 million tonnes.

- The salinity of sea water depends upon the extent of evaporation, river discharge and precipitation but composition of salt remains invariable.

8. Discuss the latitudinal variation in the salinity of ocean water.

Ans Salinity of sea water varies from place to place. At the equator, the salinity is somewhat lower due to abundant rains, greater cloudiness and low rate of evaporation. In latitudes about 20° in both the hemispheres, where evaporation is more intense and precipitation is lower, salinity is greater. In temperate latitudes, evaporation is less and rains are more abundant, salinity is lower. In Red sea where no river flows, the salinity is 40 to 41 part per thousand. In the Black sea, in which numerous rivers discharge, the salinity is 17 to 18 part per thousand. In the White sea, it is between 25 and 26 part per thousand, while in Baltic sea, it is 3 to 4 part per thousand on an average.

9. Differentiate between continental shelf and continental slope.

Ans Differences between continental shelf and continental slope are as follows

Continental Shelf	Continental Slope
It is the extended margin of each continent.	It is the connecting link between continental shelf and ocean basin.
The average depth is 200 m.	Depth varies between 200 m and 3000 m.
The mean width is about 70 km.	It begins where the bottom of continental shelf drops off.
The average gradient is 1° or even less.	The average gradient is 2-5°.
Continental shelf covers approximately 5 per cent of the Earth's surface.	It covers 6.4 per cent of the Earth's surface.

10. "Land is the actual source of salinity in ocean water". Justify the statement.

Ans Land is the actual source of salinity in ocean water because land contributes dissolved salts through processes like weathering. Rivers and streams transport minerals and salts, such as sodium chloride, from the land to the ocean. This runoff significantly affects the ocean's salinity levels. Also due to the volcanic activity on land, ashes and other mineral rich chemicals added into the ocean water which results in increase in salinity.

11. "Oceans in the world have become dumping spots for all the waste". Explain the possible harms due to ocean waste and also suggest some possible measures. **Competency Based Que**

Ans The possible harms due to ocean wastes are as follows

- Now-a-days oceans are used as a dumping centre for the biological and chemical waste.
- Apart from it, nuclear and electronic waste in ocean causes huge loss of biodiversity in the region.
- The increasing waste in the ocean probably harms the human life too.
- The disease may spread through food cycle i.e. through eating fishes and sea foods by human being.
- It may also cause environmental harm.

Possible Measures

- The awareness and prevention are the best possible measures for this hazard.
- Along with it effective policies and proper regulation should be available to manage waste.
- Proper disposal of harmful waste should be done.

12 "Continental shelves are the most significant relief features of ocean for the human being". Give your argument in support of this statement. **Competency Based Que**

Ans The continental shelves have strong ties to geological evolution and even exobiology in following ways

- For the prediction of earthquake.
- For understanding the history of the earth.
- For expanding our knowledge of geology and the ocean.

Apart from these, continental shelves are ecologically and economically significant to human being.

From ecological point of view, continental shelves are much shallower than the rest of the ocean, hence it has enough light for primary production and therefore, most of our major fish species are found in the continental shelves.

Availability of fishes is a big economic resources for the coastal regions and their people. Continental shelves have massive sedimentary deposists received over a long time and hence, these are the huge source of fossil fuels. Continental shelves are also known as bank for stones, jems and other sea products.

13. Why does the temperature distribution of the ocean water vary? **CBSE Diksha**

Ans. Factors responsible for variation in the temperature distribution of water in the ocean are

- **Latitude** The temperature of surface water decreases from the equator towards the poles because the amount of insolation decreases poleward. Temperature of the ocean water in lower latitudes is higher than the temperature in the higher latitudes.
- **Unequal distribution of land and water** Variation in the expanse of land in the Northern and Southern hemisphere has effects on the temperature of the ocean water. The oceans in the Northern hemisphere receive more heat due to their contact with larger extent of land than the oceans in the Southern hemisphere.

- **Prevailing wind** The winds blowing from the land towards the oceans drive warm surface water away from the coast resulting in the upwelling of cold water from below. It results into the longitudinal variation in the temperature. Contrary to this, the onshore winds pile up warm water near the coast and this raises the temperature.

14. Give three suitable reasons to examine the spatial variation in the salinity of the ocean water.

Ans. The salinity of the ocean water varies because of the following reasons

- **Evaporation and precipitation** The salinity of water in the surface layer of oceans depends mainly on evaporation and precipitation. Higher the evaporation, more the salinity. Higher the precipitation lower the salinity.
- **Inflow of fresh water** Surface salinity is greatly influenced in coastal regions by the fresh-water flow from rivers, and in polar regions by the processes of freezing and thawing of ice.
- **Wind and the ocean currents** Salinity of an area is affected by transferring water to other areas by winds. Ocean currents contribute to the salinity variations by mixing of ocean currents with varying salinity. Salinity, temperature and density of water are interrelated. Hence, any change in the temperature or density influences the salinity of water in an area.

Long Answer Type Questions

1 'The ocean floor is divided into major divisions'. Justify the statement.

Ans The statement "The ocean floor is divided into major divisions" can be justified by recognising that the ocean floor is classified into distinct regions based on depth, topography and geological features. These divisions play a crucial role in understanding the structure and dynamics of the Earth's oceanic crust.

The major ocean floor divisions are as follows

- **Continental Shelf** This is the submerged extension of the continents, forming shallow waters along coastlines. It slopes gently and is rich in marine life due to abundant nutrients.
- **Continental Slope** The steep drop-off that occurs beyond the continental shelf, where the ocean floor descends rapidly towards deeper regions. It marks the boundary between the continental crust and the oceanic crust.
- **Abyssal Plain** Located at depths of about 3,000 to 5,000 meters, this vast, flat area covers a large portion of the ocean floor. It consists of fine sediments and is sparsely populated by marine life.
- **Mid-Ocean Ridges** Underwater mountain ranges formed by tectonic activity, where oceanic plates are moving apart, allowing magma to rise and create new crust.
- **Ocean Trenches** Deep, narrow valleys formed at convergent plate boundaries, such as the Mariana Trench, where oceanic plates subduct beneath each other.

These divisions are fundamental to the study of oceanography and help explain oceanic processes, biodiversity, and plate tectonics.

2. Explain the minor relief features of ocean floor.

Ans The minor relief features of the ocean floor refer to smaller, yet significant, geological formations that shape the ocean's topography. These features play an important role in oceanic processes, such as circulation, marine life distribution and sediment deposition.

The key minor relief features of ocean floor are discussed below

Seamounts Underwater mountains formed by volcanic activity, typically rising several thousand meters from the ocean floor. Seamounts are often hotspots for marine biodiversity due to nutrient upwelling, attracting various marine species.

Guyots Flat-topped seamounts that were once above sea level but have since been submerged due to erosion and tectonic activity. The flat tops of guyots disrupt ocean currents, creating isolated ecosystems.

Atolls These are low islands found in the tropical oceans consisting of coral reefs surrounding a central depression.

Submarine Canyons Steep, deep valleys carved into the continental slope by underwater currents. These canyons often serve as conduits for the movement of sediments and nutrients.

3. Vertical distribution of temperature can be understood by different layers. Explain.

Ans The vertical distribution of temperature in the ocean is influenced by depth and the interaction between sunlight, water currents, and heat exchange. This can be understood through the following layers

- **Surface Layer** (Epipelagic Zone) The uppermost layer, which extends up to about 200 meters, is directly heated by the sun. This layer experiences the highest temperatures, often ranging between 20°C to 30°C in tropical regions, and varies with seasons.
- **Thermocline Layer** Below the surface layer, the thermocline is found between 200 and 1,000 meters. In this layer, the temperature drops rapidly as depth increases. The depth of the thermocline varies with latitude, being more shallow in tropical regions and deeper in polar regions.

- **Deep Ocean Layer** Below the thermocline, the temperature remains constant, usually just above freezing, around 2°C. This cold water is relatively unaffected by seasonal changes and is typically influenced by cold water from polar regions, which slowly mixes downward.

4. What are the determinants of the salinity of the oceans? Discuss in brief.

Ans The distribution of salinity of the oceans depends on the rate of evaporation, temperature, precipitation, cloudiness, influx of freshwater, winds and ocean currents. These are discussed below

Evaporation In general, higher the rate of evaporation, higher the salinity of oceans. The highest rate of evaporation is recorded along the Tropic of Cancer, especially in the Red sea and the Persian gulf.

Temperature There is a direct relationship between temperature and salinity of the oceans. In general, the higher the temperature, the higher the salinity of the oceans.

Precipitation The amount of precipitation is inversely related to salinity. In general, the higher the precipitation, the lower the proportion of salinity.

Ocean Currents Ocean currents also affect the spatial distribution of salinity in the ocean bodies of the world. The equatorial warm water current drive away salts from the Eastern coastal areas and accumulate them along the Western coastal areas of the oceans.

Influx of Freshwater Comparatively low salinity is found along the mouth of the Amazon, Congo and Ganga deltas mainly due to influx of freshwater.

5. "The pollution of river water has aggravated the crisis for human life". What are the possible measures to adopt for improving the water quality?

Ans The pollution of river water significantly worsened the water crisis. Possible measures that are adopted to improve the water quality is to promote the cleanliness in the river, and both preventive and curative measures should be taken. Apart from these, promotive measures to raise the awareness are also significant for the sustainable development. These are as follows

- Sewage treatment plant should be established.
- Industrial waste should be treated well before draining into river.
- Open defecation should be stopped for which awareness should be created alongwith giving facilities.
- Religious items and idols should be avoided to throw in river water.
- Electronic cremation should be promoted.
- River should be considered as living object and it should be treated like so.

6. "The thermocline layer acts as a thermal boundary within the ocean". Analyse this statement by explaining the function and significance of the thermocline with examples. Competency Based Que

Ans. The thermocline layer, located between the warm surface layer and the colder deep ocean, serves as a thermal boundary within the ocean. This layer is marked by a sharp temperature gradient where temperature drops significantly with increasing depth.

The thermocline acts as a barrier that limits the mixing of surface and deep waters, which impacts heat transfer, nutrient flow, and marine life distribution. For instance, in tropical oceans, a strong thermocline prevents the warmer, nutrient-poor surface water from mixing with the nutrient-rich cold water below, affecting marine ecosystems. In temperate regions, the thermocline weakens seasonally, allowing nutrients to rise to the surface, supporting plankton growth and marine food chains.

Furthermore, the thermocline is crucial in regulating global climate patterns, as it influences the storage and release of heat in ocean currents. Thus, the thermocline's role as a thermal boundary is essential for both ocean ecology and climate stability.

7. "The temperature of ocean water is a dynamic system that changes across latitudes and depths." Explain this statement by discussing the factors that affect ocean temperature and its impact on marine life. Competency Based Que

Ans. The factors affecting temperature of ocean are as follows

- **Latitudes** At different latitudes, ocean temperature varies because the equator receives direct sunlight, warming the surface waters, while the poles receive sunlight at an angle, keeping the waters cooler. As a result, tropical regions are warmer and polar regions are colder.
- **Depth** The depth of the ocean also impacts temperature, with the surface waters being warmer due to sunlight absorption, and deeper waters becoming colder. The thermocline layer separates the warm surface water from the cold water below.
- **Ocean currents** Ocean currents further influence temperature by redistributing heat across vast distances, moving warm water from the equator toward the poles and cold water from the poles to the equator.

These temperature variations impact marine life, as different species are adapted to specific temperature ranges, affecting their distribution and ecosystem dynamics.

8. 'Apart from the major relief features of the ocean floor, some minor but significant features predominate in different parts of the oceans'. Substantiate the statement by describing any five minor relief features of oceans. CBSE Diksha

Ans. Some of the minor relief features are

(i) **Mid-Oceanic Ridges** A mid-oceanic ridge is composed of two chains of mountains separated by a large depression. The mountain ranges can have peaks as high as 2,500 m and some even reach above the ocean's surface. Iceland, a part of the mid Atlantic Ridge, is an example.

(ii) **Seamount** It is a mountain with pointed summits, rising from the seafloor that does not reach the surface of the ocean. Seamounts are volcanic in origin. These can be 3,000-4,500 m tall. The Emperor seamount, an extension of the Hawaiian Islands in the Pacific Ocean, is a good example.

(iii) **Submarine Canyons** These are deep valleys, some comparable to the Grand Canyon of the Colorado river. They are sometimes found cutting across the continental shelves and slopes, often extending from the mouths of large rivers. The Hudson Canyon is the best-known submarine canyon in the world.

(iv) **Guyots** It is a flat-topped seamount. They show evidences of gradual subsidence through stages to become flat topped submerged mountains. It is estimated that more than 10,000 seamounts and guyots exist in the Pacific Ocean alone.

(v) **Atoll** These are low islands found in the tropical oceans consisting of coral reefs surrounding a central depression. It may be a part of the sea (lagoon), or sometimes form enclosing a body of fresh, brackish, or highly saline water.

9. Giving suitable reasons examine the variation in the horizontal distribution of salinity in the ocean water. CBSE Diksha

Ans. Amount of salinity of ocean water varies significantly horizontally. Some areas have high salinity whereas other areas have low.

Some of the examples of variations in salinity of ocean water are

- The average salinity of the Indian Ocean is 35°/₀₀ The low salinity trend is observed in the Bay of Bengal due to influx of river water. On the contrary, the Arabian Sea shows higher salinity due to high evaporation and low influx of fresh water.
- The North Sea, despite its location in higher latitudes, records higher salinity due to more saline water brought by the North Atlantic Drift.
- Baltic Sea records low salinity due to influx of river waters in large quantity.
- The salinity variation in the Pacific Ocean is mainly due to its shape and larger areal extent. Salinity decreases from 35°/₀₀ - 31°/₀₀ on the Western parts of the Northern hemisphere because of the influx of melted water from the Arctic region.
- The Mediterranean Sea records higher salinity due to high evaporation.

Source/Graph Based Questions

1. Read the following passage and answer the questions that follow.

Ocean waters get heated up by the solar energy just as land. The process of heating and cooling of the oceanic water is slower than land.

The factors which affect the distribution of temperature of ocean water are

Latitude The temperature of surface water decreases from the equator towards the poles because the amount of insolation decreases poleward.

Unequal Distribution of Land and Water The oceans in the Northern Hemisphere receive more heat due to their contact with larger extent of land than the oceans in the Southern Hemisphere.

Prevailing Winds The winds blowing from the land towards the oceans drive warm surface water away form the coast resulting in the upwelling of cold water from below. It results into the longitudinal variation in the temperature. Contrary to this, the onshore winds pile up warm water near the coast and this raises the temperature.

Ocean Currents Warm ocean currents raise the temperature in cold areas while the cold currents decrease the temperature in warm ocean areas. Gulf stream (warm current) raises the temperature near the Eastern coast of North America and the West Coast of Europe while the Labrador current (cold current) lowers the temperature near the North-East coast of North America. All these factors influence the temperature of the ocean currents locally. The enclosed seas in the low latitudes record relatively higher temperature than the open seas; whereas the enclosed seas in the high latitudes have lower temperature than the open seas.

(i) **Which of the following region has the least ocean surface temperature?**

(a) Equatorial Region
(b) Polar regions
(c) Mediterranean region
(d) Tropical regions

Ans (b) Polar regions

(ii) **Oceans of Northern Hemisphere receive more heat because of which of the following factors?**

(a) Warm current (b) Direct rays of Sun

(c) Larger area of land (d) Less clouds

Ans (c) Larger area of land

(iii) **Which among the following regions are under the influence of cold oceanic currents?**

(a) North-East USA (b) Eastern-North America

(c) East Australia (d) Mozambique

Ans (b) Eastern-North America

2. Read the passage carefully and answer the questions that follow.

The continental shelf is the extended margin of each continent occupied by relatively shallow seas and gulfs. It is the shallowest part of the ocean showing an average gradient of 1° or even less. The shelf typically ends at a very steep slope, called the shelf break. The width of the continental shelves vary from one ocean to another. The average width of continental shelves is about 80 km. The shelves are almost absent or very narrow along some of the margins like the coasts of Chile, the West coast of Sumatra, etc. On the contrary, the Siberian shelf in the Arctic Ocean, the largest in the world, stretches to 1,500 km in width. The depth of the shelves also varies. It may be as shallow as 30 m in some areas while in some areas it is as deep as 600 m. The continental shelves are covered with variable thicknesses of sediments brought down by rivers, glaciers, wind, from the land and distributed by waves and currents. Massive sedimentary deposits received over a long time by the continental shelves, become the source of fossil fuels.

The continental slope connects the continental shelf and the ocean basins. It begins where the bottom of the continental shelf sharply drops off into a steep slope. The gradient of the slope region varies between 2-5°. The depth of the slope region varies between 200 and 3,000 m. The slope boundary indicates the end of the continents. Canyons and trenches are observed in this region.

Deep sea plains are gently sloping areas of the ocean basins. These are the flattest and smoothest regions of the world. The depths vary between 3,000 and 6,000m. These plains are covered with fine-grained sediments like clay and silt.

(i) **What are the major differences between the continental shelf and the continental slope?**

Ans. The continental shelf is a shallow, flat area with a gentle slope, while the continental slope is steeper, connecting the shelf to the deeper ocean basins, with a greater depth range.

(ii) **How do the continental slope and the deep sea plains differ in terms of features and depth?**

Ans. The continental slope connects the shelf to the ocean basin, with depths between 200-3,000m, while the deep ocean basin features flatter, smoother areas with depths ranging from 3,000 to 6,000m.

(iii) **Name the largest continental shelf in the world.**

Ans. The Siberian shelf in the Arctic Ocean is the largest shelf in the world. It stretches to 1500 km in width.

3. Study the following graph and answer the questions that follow.

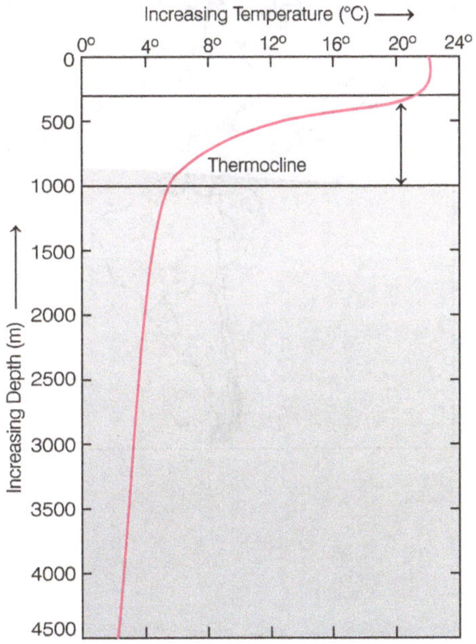

(i) **What are the characteristics of the first layer?**

Ans The first layer is the top layer of warm oceanic water. The temperature is in the range of 20°- 25° C and it is about 500 m thick.This is present throughout the year in tropical areas, and in mid latitudes it develops only in summer.

(ii) **Why does the temperature fall very rapidly up to the depth of 200 m?**

Ans The temperature fall very rapidly up to the depth of 200 m because the sunlight is being only capable of reaching up to 200 meters deep in the ocean.

(iii) **Name the circles where the surface water temperatures are close to 0° C.**

Ans The circles where the temperature is close to 0° C of surface water are Arctic and Antarctic circles.

Map Based Question

1. On the map of the world, mark the following major seas of the world.

(i) Black Sea (ii) Baltic Sea (iii) Caspian Sea (iv) Mediterranean Sea
(v) North Sea (vi) Red Sea (vii) Bay of Fundy

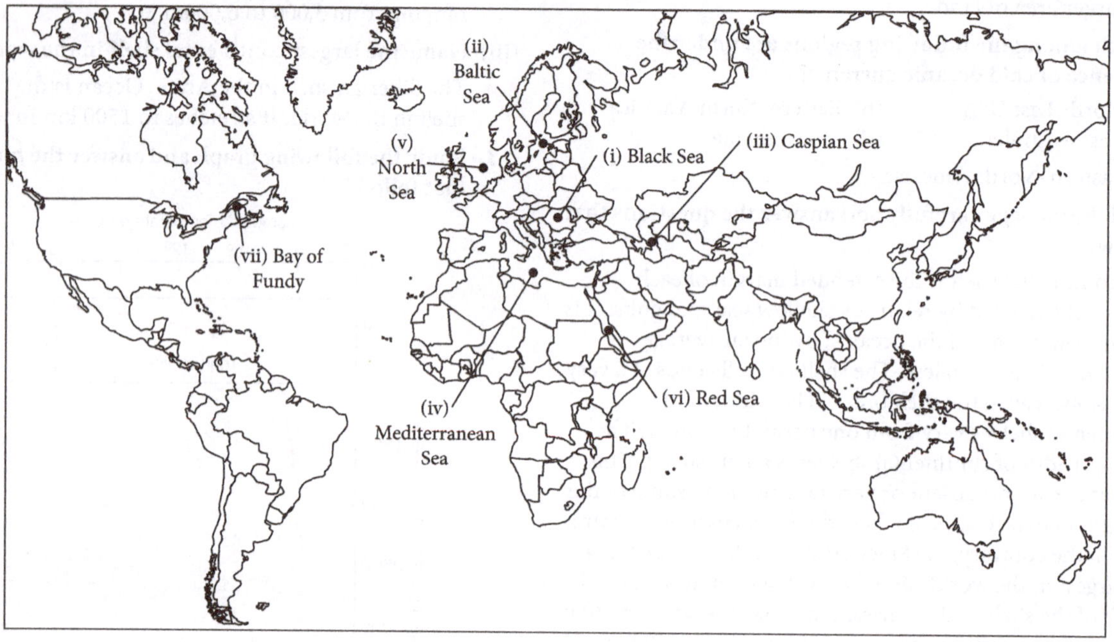

SELF ASSESSMENT TEST

Objective Type Questions

1. What percentage of the total water is found in the glaciers and groundwater?
   (a) 97.25% (b) 2.05%
   (c) 0.68% (d) 0.01%
2. The component 'water in the atmosphere' is associated with which of the following components of water cycle?
   (a) Evaporation (b) Condensation
   (c) Precipitation (d) Both (b) and (c)
3. Which of the following is the largest continental shelf in the world?
   (a) South-East Florida Continental Shelf (b) Siberian Shelf
   (c) Both (a) and (b) (d) None of the above
4. The depth of the continental slope region varies from
   (a) 100-300 m (b) 200-1000 m
   (c) 200-3000 m (d) 3000-6000 m
5. The shallowest part of the ocean is
   (a) continental slope (b) continental shelf
   (c) oceanic trenches (d) None of these

Short Answer Type Questions

6. Explain the Mid-Oceanic Ridges and its characteristics. How they are different from Atolls?
7. What do you mean by salinity and also name the highest salinity water body in the world?
8. Explain Submarine Canyons , also write one example for this.
9. Differentiate between the Deep Sea Plain and the Oceanic Deeps.
10. How is the continental shelf useful for man?
11. What are the direct and indirect uses of oceans to man?

Long Answer Type Questions

12. "The floors of the oceans are rugged with the world's largest mountain ranges, deepest trenches and the largest plains". Explain the different features in the context of the statement.
13. Explain the different factors which affect the distribution of temperature of the ocean water.
14. What do you mean by thermocline? Also explain the vertical distribution of temperature in oceans.
15. "All waters in nature, whether rainwater or ocean water, contain dissolved mineral salts". Justify the statement in relation to oceanic salinity and also mention the factors affecting the salinity.
16. "Water is a cyclic resource. It can be used and reused". Explain the process of hydrological cycle in the context of this statement.

13

CHAPTER

Ocean water is always in a state of motion. Movement of the ocean water is affected by physical characteristics like temperature, salinity, density, etc. Movements of ocean water are also affected by some external forces exerted by the sun, moon and winds.

Movements of Ocean Water

YOUR STUDY GOALS

YOUR PRACTICE GOAL

- Objective Type Questions (27 Qs; MCQs, Statements, Matching, A-R,)
- Subjective Questions (11 SAs, 5 LAs) Source Based Questions (2 Qs)
- Map based Questions (2 Qs)

13.1 Horizontal and Vertical Movement of Ocean Water

- Movement of ocean water takes place both horizontally and vertically. Horizontal movement of ocean water results in the formation of **ocean currents** and **waves**. When there is vertical movement of ocean water, there is formation of a **tide.**
- Ocean currents are the continuous flow of huge amount of water in one direction. Ocean currents leads to the movement of volume of water from one place to another.
- The waves are the horizontal motion of water in which the water does not move, but the wave trains (group of waves) move ahead.
- The vertical motion of ocean water refers to the rise and fall of water in the oceans and seas.
- The ocean water rises up and falls down due to the attraction of the Sun and the Moon. This happens twice in a day.
- Vertical motion of ocean water is caused due to the upwelling[1] of cold water from below and the sinking of surface water.

1 **Upwelling** It is defined when the cold water comes up at the surface of the oceans from the deep bottom.

13.2 Types of Ocean Water Movement

The movement of ocean water occurs through three ways. These are waves, tides and ocean currents.

Waves

- Waves are the energy moving across the surface of water, rather than the water itself moving forward.
- The water molecules in a wave just move in small circles. This allows the energy to pass through them.
- Wind provides energy to the waves to travel in the ocean and the energy is released on shorelines.
- The motion of the surface water rarely affects the still or motionless deep bottom water of the oceans.

Features of Waves

- As a wave moves towards the beach, its speed decreases. This is due to the friction between the water and the sea floor.
- When the depth of water is less than half the wavelength of the wave, the wave becomes unstable and it finally breaks.
- The largest waves are found in the open oceans. Waves continue to grow larger as they move and absorb energy from the wind.
- When a gentle breeze (moving at around two knots or less) blows over calm water, it starts to create small ripples on the surface of water.
- Waves may travel thousands of kilometres before reaching the **shoreline**[2], breaking and dissolving as **surf**[3].

Components of Waves

- **Wave Crest and Wave Trough** The highest point of a wave is called as a 'crest' and the lowest point is called as a 'trough'.
- **Wave Height** It is the vertical distance measured from the bottom of the trough to the top of the crest.
- **Wave Amplitude** When wave height is reduced to half, it is called as wave amplitude.
- **Wave Period** It is measured as the time interval between two successive wave crests or troughs that passes through a fixed point.
- **Wavelength** It is the horizontal distance between two successive crests.
- **Wave Speed** It is the distance a wave travels in a given interval of time. It is measured in **knots**.
- **Wave Frequency** It is the number of waves passing through a point in one second time interval.

Origin of Waves

- The origin of a wave can be understood by observing its shape and size.
- Waves having steep sides are young in nature and they are formed by local wind.
- Waves that are slow and steady have their origin from far away places. They travel through a long distance like another hemisphere.
- The maximum height of the wave is determined by the strength of the wind, i.e. how long it blows and the area over which it blows in a single direction.

---

2 **Shorelines** It is the line of contact between land surface and ocean surface.

3 **Surf** It is the foam, splash created by breaking waves, on the ocean when the wave reaches near the shore.

Motion of Wave

- Waves move across the ocean because of two main forces: wind and gravity.

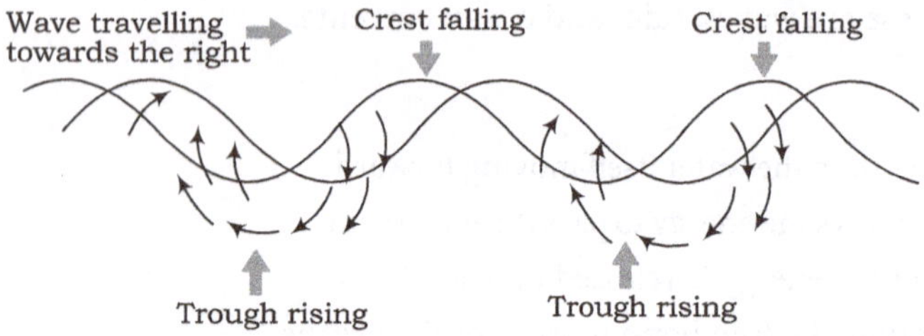

▲ *Motion of Waves and Water Molecules*

- Wind pushes the water body in its course while gravity pulls the crests of the waves downward.
- The falling water pushes the trough upward and the wave moves to a new position.
- The actual motion of the water beneath the waves is circular. It indicates that water particles are carried up and forward as the wave moves ahead, and down and back as it moves back.

Quick Test 1

1. What is ocean current and waves?
2. What is the name given to the vertical movement of ocean water?
3. Mention one important feature of a wave.
4. Mention one force that drives the wave.

Tides

- The periodical rise and fall of the sea level, once or twice a day, mainly due to the attraction of the sun and the moon, is called as tide.
- There is another movement of water which is caused by meteorological effects like winds and atmospheric pressure changes, these are called as **surges**. Surges are not regular like tides.

Causes of Tides

- The tides occur due gravitational pull of the moon and the sun. Gravitational pull of the moon is stronger than that of sun.
- The **centrifugal force**[4] is another cause of tides. This is the force that acts to counter balance the gravity.

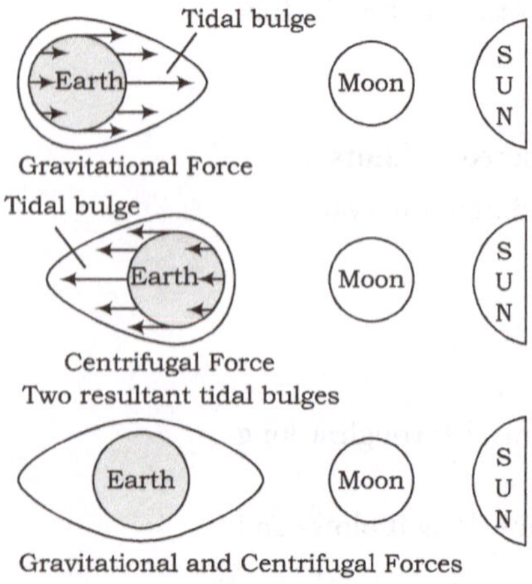

▲ *Relation between Gravitational Forces and Tides*

- The gravitational pull and the centrifugal force together are responsible for creating the two major **tidal bulges**[5] on the earth.
  - (i) **On the Side Facing the Moon** On this side a tidal bulge is caused because the gravitational pull of moon is stronger than the centrifugal force.
  - (ii) **Opposite Side** On the opposite side, the moon's gravity is weaker because it's farther away. Here, centrifugal force is stronger and it causes tidal bulge.
- On the surface of the earth, the horizontal tide generating forces are more important than the vertical forces in generating the tidal bulges.
- The tidal bulges are of greater heights near the continental shelves, while they are of low height near the mid-oceanic islands.
- Shape of the bays and **estuaries**[6] also influences the magnitude of the tides. For example, the magnitude of tide is changed when the bay is funnel shaped.
- When the tide is channelled between islands or into bays and estuaries, they are called **tidal currents**.

---

4 **Centrifugal Force** It is the force that is created in the outward direction, when a body is rotating.
5 **Tidal Bulge** It is the highest point of ocean water on the Earth which is raised up due to the gravitational pull of moon.
6 **Estuaries** It is an area where a freshwater river or stream meets the ocean.

Tides of Bay of Fundy, Canada

- The highest tides in the world occur in the Bay of Fundy in Nova Scotia, Canada. The tidal bulge is 15-16 m. Because there are two high tides and two low tides every day (roughly a 24-hour period), then a tide must come in within about a six-hour period. As a rough estimate, the tide rises about 240 cm an hour (1,440 cm divided by 6 hours).

Types of Tides

- Tides are grouped into different types according to their frequency, direction and movement from place to place and also from time to time.

Tides Based on Frequency

- **Semi-diurnal tides** This tide has two high tides and two low tides each day. The successive high or low tides are approximately of the same height.
- **Diurnal tide** In this type of tide, there is only one high tide and one low tide, that occurs in a day. The height of each high and low tides is same.
- **Mixed tide** These tides have variations in their height. These tides generally occur along the West coast of North America and on many islands of the Pacific Ocean.

Tides Based on the Sun, Moon and Earth's Positions

Spring Tide

- This tide occurs when the sun, the moon and the earth are in a straight line. The height of the tide becomes higher.
- These tides occur twice a month. Once during full moon period and another during new moon period.

Neap Tide

- This tide occurs when the sun and moon are at right angles to each other and the forces of the sun and moon tend to counter balance each other.
- Though, the moon's force is twice than that of sun, but sun's attractional force reduces the power of moon's force.
- Neap tide occurs at seven-day interval, after the spring tide has occurred.

Perigee and Apogee

- Once in a month, moon is closest to the earth and this is called as **perigee**. At this time high and low tides occurs. During this time, the tidal range is greater than the usual.
- Two weeks after the perigee, the moon is farthest from the earth and this position is known as **apogee**.
- During apogee, the moon's tidal force is weak and limited and hence, the tidal range are less than their average heights.
- On 3rd January every year, the earth is closest to the sun (perihelion). During this time, tidal ranges are also much greater, with unusually high and unusually low tides.
- On 4th July every year, the earth is farthest from the sun (aphelion). During this period, tidal ranges are much less than average.
- The time between the high tide and low tide, when the water level is falling, is called the **ebb**.
- The time between the low tide and high tide, when the water level is rising, is called the **flow** or **flood**.

Importance of Tides

- The prediction of tides helps navigators and fishermen to plan their activities in the open oceans, as tides help in navigation.

- The shallow bars at the mouth of rivers and estuaries prevents the entrance of ships and boats from entering into the harbour during tides.
- The tides also help in desilting[7] of sediments and removal of pollutants from the estuaries.
- The tides are also used for generating electricity. For example, in countries like France, Canada, Russia and China, a 3MW power project process which is located at Durgaduani in Sundarbans of West Bengal.

Quick Test 2

1 Name the two forces which are responsible for tides.
2 Where are the highest tides in the world found?
3 What is the difference between perigee and apogee?
4 Write any two importance of tides.

Ocean Currents

- A regular volume of water flowing in an ocean in a definite path and direction is called **ocean current**.
- The forces that influence the ocean currents are of two types : primary and secondary forces.

Primary Forces

These are the forces that helps in initiating the movement of water in an ocean. Some of the important primary forces are given as under

- **Heating by Solar Energy** It causes the water to expand because of thermal expansion. Because of this expansion the water level rises about 8 cm near equator than middle latitudes.
- **Wind** It helps in pushing the surface ocean water to move in the direction of the wind. The movement of water starts because of the friction created between wind and the ocean surface, when they come in contact.
- **Gravity** It causes the denser water to go down the surface of the ocean and pushes away the less dense water. Less dense water comes on the surface. This helps in the movement of ocean water.
- **Coriolis force** It causes the water to move towards the right direction in Northern hemisphere and towards left in the Southern hemisphere. The water gets collected and starts moving in circulating manner. This is called **Gyre**. Gyres produces large circular ocean currents in all ocean basins.

Secondary Forces

- These are the forces that affects the flow of currents after the water has started moving.
- Differences in water density affect vertical movement of ocean currents.
- Water with high salinity is denser than the water with low salinity. In the same way cold water is dense as compared to warm water.
- Denser water tends to sink, while relatively lighter water tends to rise.
- Cold ocean currents occur when the cold water at the poles sinks and slowly moves towards the equator.
- Warm ocean currents from the equator flows towards the poles to replace the sinking cold water. This gives rise to warm ocean currents.

Characteristics of Ocean Currents

- Speed of a current is referred to as **drift**. The speed of a current is measured in terms of **knots.**
- The power of an ocean current depends upon its speed. A current with high speed is considered as a strong current.

---

7 Desilting It is the process of removal of silt from a body of water

- Currents are strongest at the surface of the ocean and their speed decreases as we go to some depth under the water.
- Generally, the ocean currents move at a speed less than or equal to 5 knots. At some depth under the water, the speed of the current is around 0.5 knots.

Types of Ocean Currents

Ocean currents are classified according to their depth and temperature.

On the Basis of Depth

1. **Surface Currents** These currents move on the surface of the ocean up to a depth of 400 metres. They constitute about 10% of all the water in the ocean.
2. **Deep Water Currents** These currents are originated in deep water. They constitute about 90% of the total ocean water. These currents are originated because of density and gravity differences in the water of high latitude region.

   At high latitude, due to low temperature, water is of high density and cold. This cold water sinks into the ocean basin. This difference makes the currents to flow in high latitudes.

On the Basis of Temperature

Cold Ocean Currents

- The ocean current that carries the cold water from cold region to the warm region is called as 'cold ocean currents'.
- These cold currents are found on the West coast of continents in low and middle latitudes, and in the East coast of continents in the higher latitudes (only in Northern hemisphere).

Warm Ocean Currents

- The ocean current that brings the warm water from warm region to the cold region is called as 'warm ocean current'.
- These currents are generally found on the East coast of the continents in the low and middle latitudes (in both the hemispheres).
- In Northern hemisphere, these currents are found in West coast of the continents in the high latitude regions.

Major Ocean Currents

Major ocean currents are greatly affected by the forces exerted by the winds and coriolis force. The ocean currents movement around the earth is similar to the wind movement in the atmosphere. This can be explained by the given points:

- In the middle latitudes, the air circulation over the ocean is mainly anti-cyclonic in nature i.e. they move in anticlockwise direction (more effective in Southern hemisphere); the ocean circulation follows the same pattern.
- At high latitudes, winds flow in cyclonic pattern, the ocean circulation also follows the same pattern in the Southern hemisphere.
- In the regions where monsoon winds blow, the movement of ocean currents is influenced by such winds.
- Due to coriolis force, the warm currents move from the low latitudes deflects to their right in the Northern hemisphere and to their left in Southern hemisphere, in the same way as air deflects.
- Ocean currents transports heat from one latitude to another latitude in the same way as the general air circulation.
- The cold water of the Arctic and Antarctic circles moves towards warmer region in the tropical and equatorial regions, while the warm waters of lower latitudes moves towards pole (colder region).

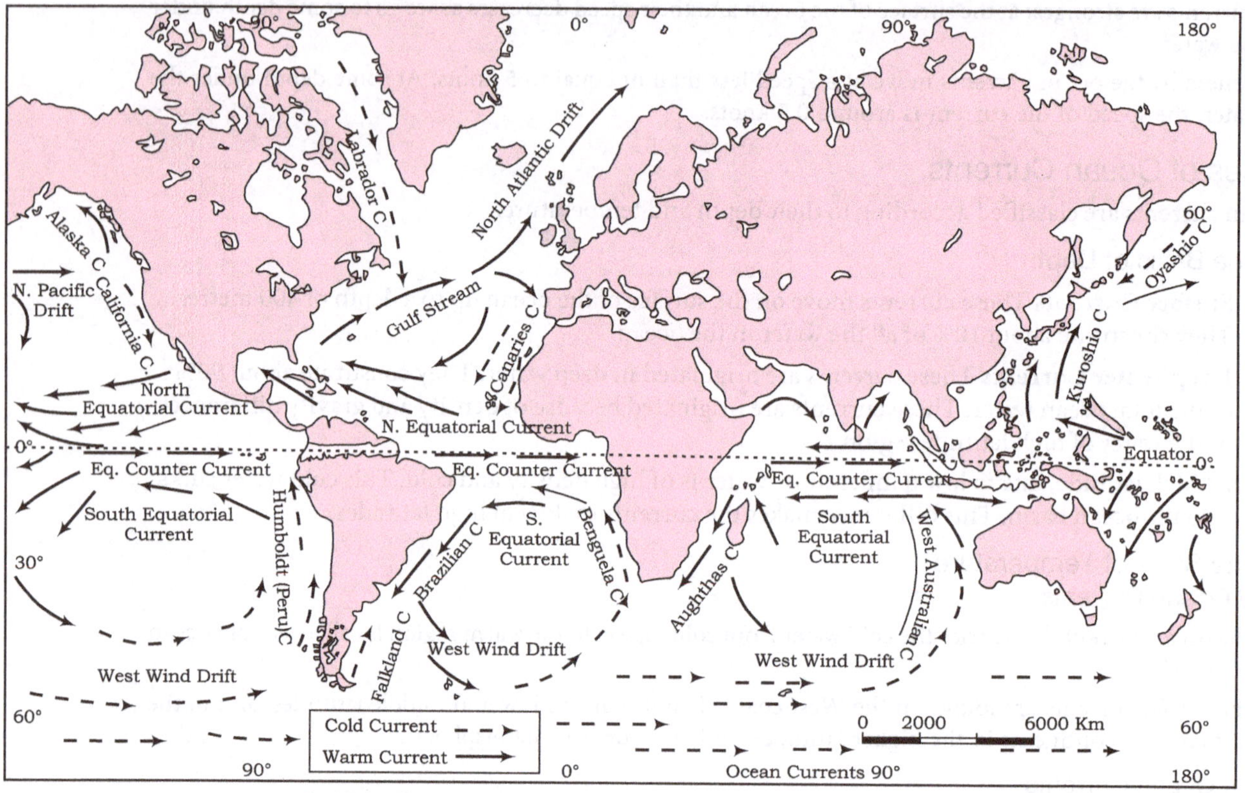

▲ *Major Currents in the Pacific, Atlantic and Indian Oceans*

Effects of Ocean Currents

- On the Western coasts of the continents in tropical and sub-tropical region, the cold currents are found which bring fog and make the area arid/dry. These currents have low average temperature.
- On the Western coasts of continents in the middle and higher latitude, warm currents are found. They develop a marine type of climate. They bring cool summers and mild winters and keep annual range of temperature is low.
- In tropical and sub-tropical latitudes, the warm currents flow parallel to the Eastern coasts of the continents. They bring warm and rainy climate to the region. The areas with warm and rainy climate are located on the Western margins of sub-tropical anti-cyclones.
- In the regions where warm and cold water meets, there is high growth of **phytoplankton**[8] as currents help them to derive oxygen. These regions are world's best fishing grounds as large volume of fishes comes to eat the phytoplankton.

Quick Test 3

1. What are the forces which influences the ocean currents?
2. What is the unit of measurement of speed of ocean current?
3. Where are warm currents found?
4. Mention one primary factor that affects the movement of ocean water.

8 **Phytoplankton** These are a diverse group of photosynthetic microorganisms that float in the upper layers of water, where sunlight pass through them.

Mind Map

MOVEMENTS OF OCEAN WATER

1 Waves

- Horizontal motion of water is called a wave.
- Origin of a wave can be understood by observing its shape and size.

Characteristics of Waves

- **Wave Crest and Wave Troughs** Highest and lowest point of wave.
- **Wave Length** Horizontal distance between two successive crests.
- **Wave Frequency** Number of waves passing through a point in one second time interval.
- **Wave Heights** Vertical distance measured from the bottom of the trough to the top of the crest.
- **Wave Speed** The distance a wave travels in a given interval of time(measured in 'knots).
- **Wave Amplitude** When wave height is reduced to half, it is called as wave amplitude.

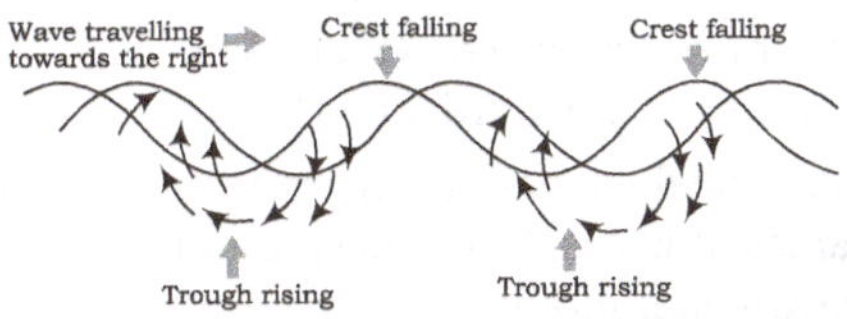

2 Tides

- Periodic rise and fall in the sea level is called tide.
- Occur due to gravitational pull of the moon and the sun.

Types of Tide

Based on Frequency

- **Semi-diurnal Tide** It has two high tides and two low tides each day.
- **Diurnal Tide** Only one high tide and one low tide, that occurs in a day.
- **Mixed Tide** These have variations in their height.

Based on Sun, Moon and Earth's Position

- **Spring Tide** Occurs when the sun, the moon and the Earth are in a straight line.
- **Neap Tide** Occurs when the sun and moon are at right angles to each other and the forces of the sun and moon tend to counter balance each other.
- **Perigee and Apogee** When the moon is closest to the Earth it is called as 'perigee' and when the moon is farthest from the Earth it is known as 'apogee'.

3 Ocean Currents

Large volume of water travelling in a definite path and direction.

Forcses influencing the Ocean Current

Primary Force

- Heating by solar energy
- Wind
- Coriolis force
- Gravity

Secondary Force

- Temperature difference
- Salinity difference

Types of Ocean Currents

Based on Depth

- **Surface Ocean Current** It constitute about 10% of all the water in the ocean.
- **Deep Water Ocean Current** It constitute about 90% of all water in the ocean.

Based on Temperature

- **Cold Ocean Current** It is found on the West coast of continents in low and middle latitudes, and in the East coast of continents in the higher latitudes, e.g., Benguela current, Labrador current.
- **Warm Ocean Current** It is found on the East coast of continents in the low and middle latitudes, e.g., Gulf Stream, Kuroshio Current.

Effects of Ocean Currents

- Cold currents found on Western coast of the continents in tropical and sub-tropical region bring fog and make the area arid/dry.
- Warm currents found on the Western coasts of continents in the middle and higher latitude bring cool summers and mild winters.
- When warm currents flow parallel to the Eastern coasts of the continent in tropical or sub-tropical latitudes they bring warm and rainy climate to the region.
- There is high growth of phytoplankton in the regions where warm and cold water meets, as currents help them to derive oxygen.

NCERT Folder

Multiple Choice Questions

(i) **Upward and downward movement of ocean water is known as the**

(a) Tide (b) Current (c) Wave (d) None of these

Ans (a) Tide

(ii) **Spring tides are caused**

(a) As result of the moon and the sun pulling the earth gravitationally in the same direction.
(b) As result of the moon and the sun pulling the earth gravitationally.
(c) Indention in the coastline.
(d) None of the above

Ans (a) As result of the moon and the sun pulling the earth gravitationally in the same direction.

(iii) **The distance between the earth and the moon is minimum when the moon is in**

(a) Aphelion (b) Perigee (c) Perihelion (d) Apogee

Ans (b) Perigee

(iv) **The earth reaches its perihelion in**

(a) October (b) September (c) July (d) January

Ans (d) January

Answer the following questions in about 30 words

(i) **What are waves?**

Ans. The movement of ocean water caused by the wind blowing over it is known as wave. Waves are the energy which moves across the surface of the ocean.

(ii) **Where do waves in the ocean get their energy from?**

Ans. The primary source of energy for the generation of wave is the wind. Waves are generated when wind passes over the ocean surface.

(iii) **What are tides?**

Ans. Tides are the periodical rise and fall of the sea level due to the attraction of the sun and the moon. Tides occurs once or twice a day.

(iv) **How are tides caused?**

Ans. Tides are generated because of the difference between gravitational force of moon and the centrifugal force of the earth. It acts on the earth's side facing the moon and on opposite side of the earth.

(v) **How are tides related to navigation?**

Ans. Tides are caused by the earth-moon-sun position which are already accurate. Due to which tides can be predicted in advance which helps the navigators and fisherman to plan this journey. Tidal heights also helps the ships to prevent entering into the shallow harbours.

Answer the following questions in about 150 words

(i) **How do currents affect the temperature? How does it affect the temperature of coastal areas in the North-Western Europe?**

Ans The ocean currents bring large number of direct and indirect influences on the surrounding areas. They affect the temperature of their neighbouring regions. The ocean currents affect the temperature in the following manner

- The cold currents bring down the temperature of the region through which they pass. As winds blow over cold currents and move towards land these further bring the temperature down.
- The warm currents act in an opposite manner. The warm currents increase the temperature of the surrounding regions. As winds blow over warm currents, they bring warm and rainy climates to the surrounding region.

The currents of coastal areas affect the temperature of North-Western Europe in the following manner

- The Gulf stream moves in the coastal areas of North-West Europe as North Atlantic Drift.
- It is a warm current which has higher temperature than surrounding areas. It keeps the coastal areas and parts frost-free during winter months.

(ii) **What are the causes of currents?**

Ans The major causes of ocean currents are classified into two broad groups. These are

(a) Primary forces (b) Secondary forces

(a) **Primary Forces** These are those forces which initiate the movement of ocean currents. The primary forces are further classified as under

Heating by Solar Energy It creates slope gradient between equatorial and middle latitudes. This causes currents to move towards higher latitudes from lower latitudes.

Wind It pushes the ocean water to move. Under the influence of easterlies, the ocean water moves westwards.

Gravity It pulls the water down and creates gradient variation.

Coriolis Force This force makes ocean currents to move towards right in the Northern hemisphere and towards left in the Southern hemisphere. This deflected motion creates a circular motion known as gyre.

(b) **Secondary Forces** The other forces which are small but do affect the ocean current to flow are known as secondary forces. Factors like temperature, pressure, density difference, local topography, ocean basin relief, etc are some of the important secondary forces which cause ocean currents.

Exam Pattern Questions

Objective Type Questions

Multiple Choice Questions (MCQs)

1. The movement of ocean water are primarily studied through
(a) Waves (b) Tides
(c) Ocean currents (d) All of these

2. Which of the following causes wave to travel in the ocean?
(a) Temperature (b) Precipitation
(c) Winds (d) None of these

3. The maximum wave height is determined by the strength of the
(a) Evaporation (b) Wind
(c) Temperature conditions (d) Precipitation

4. The crests of waves move in which direction due to gravity?
(a) Forward (b) Downward
(c) Upward (d) None of these

5. The highest point of a wave is called as
(a) Crest (b) Trough
(c) Gyre (d) Surge

6. Which of the following is the vertical movement of ocean water?
(a) Tides (b) Ocean currents
(c) Waves (d) All of these

7. Periodically rise and fall of the sea level, once in a day due to the attraction of the sun and the moon is called a
(a) Current (b) Waves
(c) Tide (d) All of these

8. Neap tides in the ocean are the result of which of the following ? **CBSE Diksha**
(a) Earth is between the sun and the moon.
(b) Moon is between the earth and the sun.
(c) Sun is between the earth and the moon.
(d) Earth is at right angle to the sun and the moon

9. Which factor does not influence the movement of ocean currents?
(a) Earth's rotation (b) Wind patterns
(c) Location of deserts (d) Temperature differences

10. How many types of ocean currents are found on the basis of temperature?
(a) 1 (b) 2
(c) 4 (d) 6

11. Consider the following statements and choose the correct option.
(i) Movement of the ocean water is affected by physical characteristics like temperature, salinity, density, etc.
(ii) Ocean water is not always in a state of motion.
Options
(a) Both (i) and (ii) (b) Only (i)
(c) Only (ii) (d) None of these

12. Choose the incorrect statements from the following.
(i) Gravitational pull of the moon is stronger than that of sun.
(ii) The tidal bulges are of greater heights near the continental shelves.
(iii) The tidal bulges are of greater height near the mid-oceanic islands.
(iv) Shape of the bays and estuaries does not influence the tides in any way.
Options
(a) (i), (ii) and (iii) (b) (ii) and (iv)
(c) (iii) and (iv) (d) only (iv)

13. The movement of ocean water is influenced by which of the following features?
(i) Temperature (ii) Salinity (iii) Density
Codes
(a) (i) and (ii) (b) (ii) and (iii)
(c) (i) and (iii) (d) All of these

14. Which of the following geographical phenomenon is/are horizontal motions of ocean water? **CBSE Diksha**
(i) Waves
(ii) Tides
(iii) Upwelling
(iv) Ocean Currents
Select the correct answer using codes given below
(a) (i) and (iv) (b) (ii) and (iii)
(c) (i) and (iii) (d) All of these

15. Identify the cold currents from the following
(i) Humboldt current (ii) Oyashio Current
(iii) Brazilian current (iv) Benguela current
Options
(a) (i), (ii) and (iv)
(b) (i), (iii), (iv)
(c) (i) and (iv)
(d) (i) and (ii)

16. **Consider the following statements and choose the incorrect statements from the following.**

(i) Gravity causes the denser water to go down the surface of the ocean.
(ii) Coriolis force causes the water to move towards the left direction in Northern hemisphere.
(iii) Differences in water density affect horizontal movement of ocean currents.
(iv) Warm ocean currents from the equator flows towards the poles to replace the sinking cold water.

Options

(a) (i), (ii) and (iii) (b) (ii) and (iii)
(c) (iii) and (iv) (d) (i), (iii) and (iv)

17. **Which of the following is/are the advantage(s) of tides?**

(i) Navigation of ships towards coasts with shallow ocean depth.
(ii) Desiltation of sediments from river estuaries.

Select the correct answer using codes below **CBSE Diksha**

(a) Only (i) (b) Only (ii)
(c) Both (i) and (ii) (d) Neither (i) nor (ii)

18. Arrange the following ocean currents from West to East across the Atlantic Ocean.

I. Gulf Stream II. Canary Current
III. North Equatorial Current IV. North Atlantic Drift

Codes

(a) I, II, III, IV (b) III, I, IV, II
(c) II, I, III, IV (d) I, II, III, IV

19. **Arrange the following ocean currents in the correct sequence as they form a part of the North Pacific gyre:**

I. North Pacific Current II. California Current
III. Kuroshio Current IV. North Equatorial Current

Codes

(a) I, II, III, IV (b) III, I, II, IV
(c) IV, III, II, I (d) I, IV, III, IV

20. **Identify the type of tide from the description given below.**

It is the most common type of tide. This tide has two high tides and two low tides each day. The successive high or low tides are approximately of the same height.

Options

(a) Spring Tide (b) Semi-diurnal Tide
(c) Neap Tide (d) Mixed Tide

Match the Following

21.

	List I		List II
A.	Labrador current	1.	East coast of North America
B.	California current	2.	East coast of South America
C.	Benguela current	3.	West side of South Africa
D.	Agulhas current	4.	West coast of North Africa

Codes

	A	B	C	D		A	B	C	D
(a)	1	2	3	4	(b)	1	4	3	2
(c)	4	3	2	1	(d)	1	3	4	2

22.

	List I		List II
A.	Surface Currents	1.	10% of all the waters in the oceans
B.	Cold Ocean Currents	2.	Speed of the current
C.	Warm Ocean Currents	3.	Found on the East coasts of the continents
D.	Knots	4.	Found on the West coasts of continents

Codes

	A	B	C	D		A	B	C	D
(a)	1	2	3	4	(b)	1	4	3	2
(c)	1	4	2	3	(d)	3	2	4	1

23.

	List I (Natural Phenomena)		List II (Meaning)
A.	Perigee	1.	When moon's orbit closest to the earth
B.	Apogee	2.	When moon is farthest from the earth
C.	Perihelion	3.	When the earth is closest to the sun.
D.	Aphelion	4.	When the earth is farthest from the sun

Codes

	A	B	C	D		A	B	C	D
(a)	1	2	3	4	(b)	4	3	2	1
(c)	3	1	4	2	(d)	2	1	4	3

Assertion-Reason

Directions (Q. Nos. 24-27) In the questions given below are two statements labelled as Assertion (A) and other is labelled as Reason (R). In the context of two statements, which one of the following is correct?

Codes

(a) Both A and R are true but R is not the correct explanation of A
(b) Both A and R are true and R is the correct explanation of A
(c) Both A and R are incorrect.
(d) A is correct, but R is incorrect

24. **Assertion** (A) At higher latitudes, the density of water increases.

Reason (R) At higher latitudes, the temperature is high.

25. Assertion (A) Deep bottom water remains stagnant.

Reason (R) The horizontal movement of surface water is continued to top surface layer of ocean water.

26. Assertion (A) Ocean currents play a significant role in regulating the climate of coastal areas.

Reason (R) Ocean currents transfer warm and cold water across different regions, affecting local temperatures and weather patterns.

27. Assertion (A) Waves travel because wind pushes the water body in its course.

Reason (R) Gravity pulls the crests of the waves downward. The falling water pushes the former troughs upward, and the wave moves to a new position.

Answers

1. (d) All of these
2. (c) Winds
3. (b) Wind
4. (b) Downward
5. (a) Crest
6. (a) Tides
7. (c) Tide
8. (d) Earth is at right angle to the sun and the moon.
9. (c) Location of deserts
10. (b) 2
11. (b) Only (i)
12. (c) (iii) and (iv)
13. (d) All of these
14. (a) (i) and (iv)
15. (a) (i), (ii) and (iv)
16. (b) (ii) and (iii)
17. (c) Both (i) and (ii)
18. (b) III, I, IV, II
19. (b) III, I, II, IV
20. (b) Semi-diurnal Tide
21. (b)
22. (b)
23. (a)
24. (d) A is correct, but R is incorrect
25. (b) Both A and R are true and R is the correct explanation of A
26. (b) Both A and R are true and R is the correct explanation of A
27. (b) Both A and R are true and R is the correct explanation of A

Subjective Questions

Short Answer Type Questions

1. What are the horizontal and vertical movements of ocean water? Explain.

Ans. The ocean water is highly dynamic. It keeps moving all the time both vertically as well as horizontally. The horizontal motion of the ocean surface occurs across the latitudes. It occurs mainly in the form of ocean currents and waves.

The ocean currents are definite flow of huge volume of water along a definite path and direction. Whereas, the waves are movement of energy through the ocean water.

The vertical movement of ocean water occurs in the form of tides. The tides are periodical rise and fall of sea water under the gravitational force of the sun and the moon.

2. Define waves. What are the major characteristics of waves?

Ans. Waves are energy which move across the surfaces of the oceans.

Major characteristics of waves are

- Waves are flow of energy through water.
- The energy for waves is given by winds.
- The shape and size of waves reveal their origin.
- The waves break when depth of water is less than half the wavelength of the wave.
- Circular water movements are found beneath the waves.

3. 'Tides have great variation with respect to frequency, magnitude and height?' Explain why?

Competency Based Que

Ans. Primarily, the tides are produced by gravitational force of the sun and the moon alongwith centrifugal force. Besides these, there are other marginal factors which play their roles in the occurrence of tides. A combination of all these primary and marginal factors bring great variations in tide with respect to frequency, magnitude and height. For example,

- The coastal areas having narrow outlets have larger tidal range.
- The atmospheric factors like cyclones further affects the tides.

- Shape of bay and estuary affects the intensity of tides.
- On wide continental shelves, the tidal bulges are of greater heights.

4. Define tide-generating force. Also explain how tides are generated.

Ans. The tide-generating force is the net difference between gravitational and centrifugal force of the moon. On the earth's side facing moon, gravitational force is dominant, whereas on the opposite side, the centrifugal force dominates over gravitational force.

Tides are generated in the following ways

- The tides generate in the form of bulge, on the earth's side facing the moon.
- Similar bulge occurs on the opposite side because of centrifugal force.
- The tides occur primarily because of gravitational force of the moon, as it is stronger than gravitational force of the sun.

5. Tide can be predicted by observing the position of moon and sun with respect to earth. This prediction helps us in many ways. Elucidate the statement. **Competency Based Que**

Ans. Tides can be predict by the position of moon and sun. Due to this tides play important role in many aspects which are as follows

- The prediction of tides helps navigators and fishermen to plan their activities in the open oceans, as tides help in navigation.
- Secondly, tidal heights which are located near the mouth of river and estuaries, which has shallow bars at the entrance prevent the ships and boats from entering into the harbour.
- The tides also help in desilting of sediments and removal of pollutants from the estuaries.
- The tides are also used for generating electricity. For example, in countries like France, Canada, Russia and China, a 3MW power project is under way which is located at Durgaduani in Sundarbans of West Bengal.

6. The moon's gravitational force has more influence over tides in comparison with the sun's gravitational force. Discuss. **Competency Based Que**

Ans. The effect of gravitational force depends upon the distance between the objects. Although, the sun has more gravitational energy as compared to the moon, yet moon's gravitational force has more influence over tides in comparison with the sun's gravitational force.

The distance between the earth and the moon is 3.6 lakh km, whereas the distance between the earth and the sun is 14.5 crore kms. Therefore, the moon exerts more gravitational attraction over the earth than the sun.

7. How are ocean currents affected by the prevailing winds and the coriolis force? Give examples.

Ans. Some of the major influences of prevailing winds and coriolis force over ocean currents are given as under

- The oceanic circulation pattern roughly corresponds with atmospheric circulation pattern.
- Over middle latitude, the atmospheric circulation is anti-cyclonic, the oceanic pattern also becomes anti-cyclonic.
- Similarly in higher latitudes, the oceanic circulation is cyclonic and atmospheric circulation is anti-cyclonic.
- In the North Indian Ocean, the ocean currents reverse their direction seasonally with winds.
- According to coriolis force, the ocean currents move towards their right in the Northern hemisphere and towards their left in the Southern hemisphere.

8. "Horizontal movement of ocean water has great significance for human beings". Elucidate. **Competency Based Que**

Ans. The ocean water moves horizontally in the form of ocean currents and waves. Ocean currents are continuous flow of huge amount of water in a definite direction over long distances. This continuous flow helped the human beings for voyage and establish connectivity with all continents. Hence, horizontal movement of ocean water is responsible for all trade and transport activities across the globe.

9. Explain how do heating by solar energy, wind, gravitation and coriolis force affect the ocean currents? **CBSE Diksha**

Ans. Heating by solar energy, wind, gravitation and coriolis force affect the ocean currents in the following ways

- **Heating by Solar Energy** This factor causes the water to expand because of thermal expansion. This results in rise of water by 8 cm near equator.
- **Wind** Wind pushes the water to move. Friction between the wind and the water surface affects the movement of the water body in its course
- **Gravity** Gravity tends to pull the water down the pile and create gradient variation.
- **The Coriolis Force** This force causes the water to move towards the right direction in Northern hemisphere and towards left in the Southern hemisphere.

10. Explain the importance of gravitational force in creating tidal bulge over the oceans.

Ans. The gravitational pull and the centrifugal force together are responsible for creating the two major tidal bulges on the earth.

There are two types of bulges created on the earth.

(i) **On the Side Facing the Moon** On this side, a tidal bulge is caused because the gravitational pull of moon is stronger than the centrifugal force.

(ii) **Opposite Side** On the opposite side, the moon's gravity is weaker because it is farther away. Here, centrifugal force is stronger and it causes tidal bulge.

11. Study the following map and answer the following questions.

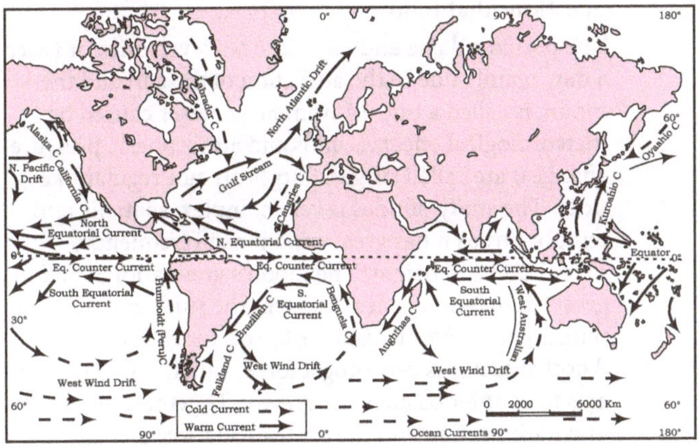

(i) Name the cold ocean current that passes through the West and East coast of South America.

Ans. Humboldt current passes through the West coast of South America and Falkland current passes through the East Coast of South America.

(ii) Mention one characteristic of cold current.

Ans. Cold currents are found on the West coast of continents in low and middle latitudes and in the East coast of continents in the higher latitudes (only in Northern hemisphere).

(iii) Discuss one effect of ocean current on climate and human life.

Ans. In the regions where warm and cold water meets, there is high growth of phytoplankton as currents help them to derive oxygen from water. This region is world's best fishing ground as large volume of fishes comes to eat the phytoplankton.

Long Answer Type Questions

1. A wave has different components which results in its varying shape and size. Elucidate the statement.

Ans. There are some important components of waves. These are mentioned below

- **Wave Crest and Wave Troughs** The highest point of a wave is called as a 'crest' and the lowest point is called as a 'trough'.
- **Wave Heights** It is the vertical distance measured from the bottom of the trough to the top of the crest.
- **Wave Amplitude** When wave height is reduced to half, it is called as wave amplitude.
- **Wave Period** It is measured as the time interval between two successive wave crests or troughs that passes through a fixed point.
- **Wavelength** It is the horizontal distance between two successive crests.
- **Wave Speed** It is the distance travelled by a given point on a wave in a given interval of time.
- **Wave Frequency** It is the number of waves passing through a point in one second time interval.

2. 'Ocean currents are divided into different types based on the temperature and depth'. Justify the statement.

Ans. Following are the divisions of ocean currents on the basis of temperature and depth.

On the Basis of Temperature

(i) **Cold Ocean Currents** The ocean currents that carries the cold water from cold region to the warm region is called as 'cold ocean currents'.

(ii) **Warm Ocean Currents** The ocean current that brings the warm water from warm region to the cold region is called as 'warm ocean current'.

On the Basis of Depth

(i) **Surface Currents** These currents move on the surface of the ocean up to a depth of 400 metres. They constitute about 10% of all the water in the oceans.

(ii) **Deep Water Currents** These currents are originated in deep water. They constitute about 90% of the total ocean water. These currents are originated because of density and gravity differences in the water of high latitude region.

3. The ocean currents have large numbers of direct and indirect effects on the areas through which they pass. Elucidate the statement.

Ans. Following are the direct and indirect effects of ocean currents

- On the Western coasts of the continents in tropical and sub-tropical region, the cold currents are found this bring fog and make the area arid/dry. These currents have low average temperature.
- On the Western coasts of continents in the middle and higher latitude, warm currents are found. This develops a marine type of climate. They bring cool summers and mild winters and the annual range of temperature is low.

- In tropical and sub-tropical latitudes, the warm currents flow parallel to the Eastern coasts of the continents. They bring warm and rainy climate to the region. These are located on the Western margins of sub-tropical anti-cyclones.
- In the regions where warm and cold water meets, there is high growth of phytoplankton as currents help them to derive oxygen. This region is world's best fishing ground as large volume of fishes comes to eat the phytoplankton.

4. In how many categories can tides be classified on the basis of their height and frequency? Explain each category in brief.

Ans. Following are the division of tides on the basis of height and frequency

(i) Semi-diurnal Tide

- It is the most common type of tide. This tide has two high tides and two low tides each day.
- The successive high or low tides are approximately of the same height.

(ii) Diurnal Tide

- In this type of tide, there is only one high tide and one low tide, that occurs in a day.
- The height of successive high and low tides is almost similar.

(iii) Mixed Tide

- These tides have variations in their height.
- These tides generally occur along the West coast of North America and on many islands of the Pacific Ocean.

5. 'The way the ocean currents move around the earth is similar to how the wind moves in the atmosphere'. Justify the statement. Competency Based Que

Ans. This statement can be explained by following points

- In the middle latitude, the air circulation over the ocean is mainly anti-cyclonic in nature, i.e. they move in anticlockwise direction (more effective in Southern hemisphere), the ocean circulation follows the same pattern.
- At high latitudes, winds flow in cyclonic pattern, ocean circulation also follows the same pattern in the Southern hemisphere.
- In the regions affected by monsoonal winds. The monsoon winds affects the ocean current movement.
- Due to coriolis force, the warm currents move from the low latitudes deflects to it right in the Northern hemisphere and to their left in Southern hemisphere, in the same way as air if affected.
- Ocean currents transports heat from one latitude to another latitude in the same way as the general air circulation.
- The cold water of the Arctic and Antarctic circles moves towards warmer region in the tropical and equatorial regions, while the warm water moves towards the colder regions.

Source Based Questions

1. Read the following paragraph and answer the questions that follow.

The periodical rise and fall of the sea level, once or twice a day, mainly due to the attraction of the sun and the moon, is called a tide. Movement of water caused by meteorological effects (winds and atmospheric pressure changes) are called surges. Surges are not regular like tides. The study of tides is very complex, spatially and temporally, as it has great variations in frequency, magnitude and height. The moon's gravitational pull to a great extent and to a lesser extent the sun's gravitational pull, are the major causes for the occurrence of tides. Another factor is centrifugal force, which is the force that acts to counter balance the gravity. Together, the gravitational pull and the centrifugal force are responsible for creating the two major tidal bulges on the earth. On the side of the earth facing the moon, a tidal bulge occurs while on the opposite side though the gravitational attraction of the moon is less as it is farther away, the centrifugal force causes tidal bulge on the other side.

The tidal bulges on wide continental shelves, have greater height. When tidal bulges hit the mid-oceanic islands they become low. The shape of bays and estuaries along a coastline can also magnify the intensity of tides. Funnel-shaped bays greatly change tidal magnitudes. When the tide is channelled between islands or into bays and estuaries they are called tidal currents.

(i) Which is the most important force behind the origin of tides on earth?

(a) Sun's gravitational pull
(b) Moon's gravitational pull
(c) Rotation of earth
(d) Earth's gravity

Ans. (b) Moon's gravitational pull

(ii) When the tide is channelled between islands or into bays and estuaries, they are called ....

(a) Tidal Bulge (b) Surges
(c) Tidal currents (d) Mixed tide

Ans. (c) Tidal currents

(iii) Which forces are responsible for creating tidal bulges on the Earth?

(a) Gravitational pull (b) Coriolis force
(c) Centrifugal force (d) Both (a) and (c)

Ans. (d) Both (a) and (c)

2. Read the following passage and answer the questions that follow.

Heating by solar energy causes the water to expand. That is why, near the equator the ocean water is about 8 cm higher in level than in the middle latitudes. This causes a very slight gradient and water tends to flow down the slope. Wind blowing on the surface of the ocean pushes the water to move. Friction between the wind and the water surface affects the movement of the water body in its course. Gravity tends to pull the water down the pile and create gradient variation. The coriolis force intervenes and causes the water to move to the right in the Northern hemisphere and to the left in the Southern hemisphere. These large accumulations of water and the flow around them are called Gyres.

These produce large circular currents in all the ocean basins. Differences in water density affect vertical mobility of ocean currents. Water with high salinity is denser than water with low salinity and in the same way cold water is denser than warm water. Denser water tends to sink, while relatively lighter water tends to rise. Cold water ocean currents occur when the cold water at the poles sinks and slowly moves towards the equator. Warm water currents travel out from the equator along the surface, flowing towards the poles to replace the sinking cold water.

(i) What makes ocean water near the equator higher in level compared to middle latitudes?

Ans. The ocean water near the equator is higher due to the solar heating which expands the water almost by 8 cm than the middle latitudes.

(ii) 'Coriolis force deflect ocean water in both the hemisphere'. Comment.

Ans. The coriolis force deflects water to the right in the Northern hemisphere and to the left in the Southern hemisphere.

(iii) What role does water density play in ocean current movement?

Ans. Differences in water density affect vertical movement of ocean current and the difference is due to the salinity and temperature. The denser water sinks while lighter water rises to the surface of the ocean.

Map Based Questions

1. Identify the following currents marked on the map of the world given below.

(i) Alaska Current (ii) Humboldt Current (iii) Labrador Current
(iv) Oyashio Current (v) Brazilian Current (vi) Agulhas Current

Ans.

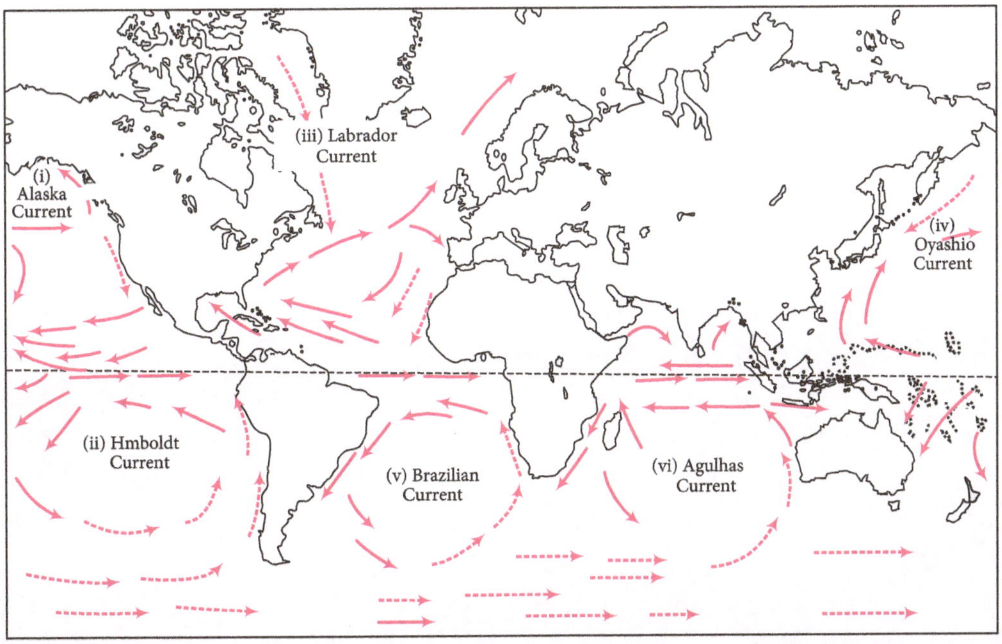

2. On the map of the world, mark the following ocean currents.

(i) California Current (ii) Falkland Current (iii) Canaries Current
(iv) West Australian Current (v) Kuroshio Current (vi) Gulf Stream Current

Ans.

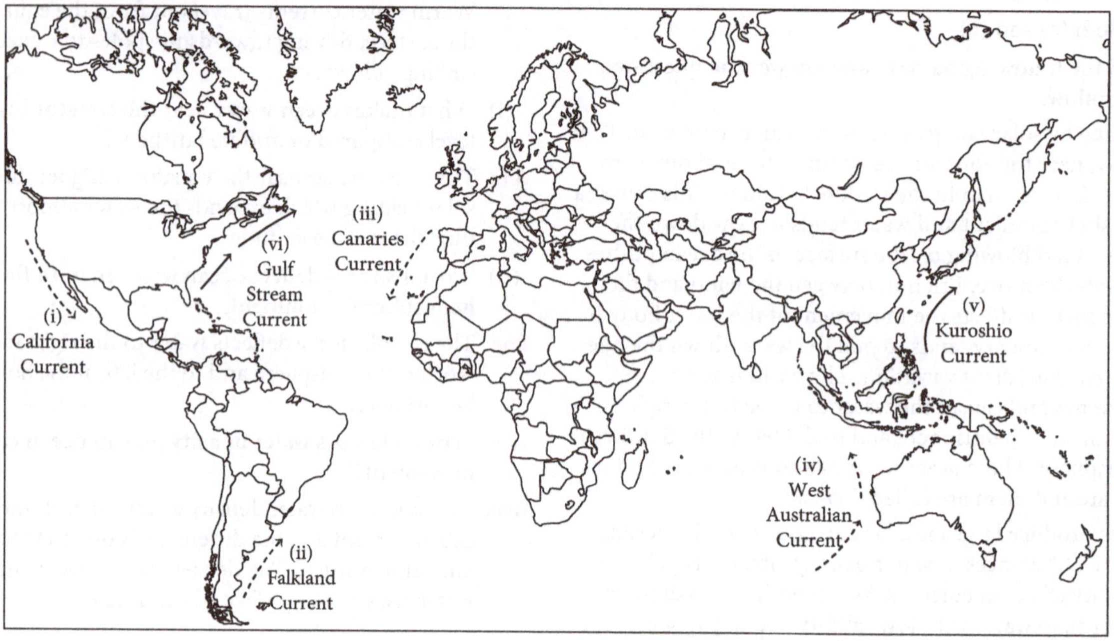

SELF ASSESSMENT TEST

Objective Type Questions

1. Which of the following is the horizontal movement of ocean water?
   (a) Tides
   (b) Ocean currents
   (c) Waves
   (d) Both (a) and (b)
2. Which of the following is the important feature of the waves?
   (a) When wave approaches to the beach, it slows down due to the friction occurring between the dynamic water and sea floor.
   (b) When the depth of water is less than half the wavelength of wave, the wave breaks.
   (c) The largest waves are found in the open oceans.
   (d) All of the above
3. The actual motion of the water beneath the waves is
   (a) Horizontal
   (b) Vertical
   (c) Circular
   (d) Diagonal
4. Which of the motions is found in a wave?
   (a) Upward
   (b) Forward
   (c) Downward
   (d) All of these
5. Wave amplitude is
   (a) Time interval between two successive wave crests.
   (b) One-half of the wave's height.
   (c) Horizontal distance between two successive crests.
   (d) Rate of wave movements.

Short Answer Type Questions

6. The periodic rise and fall of the sea level, once or twice a day, mainly due to the attraction of the sun and the moon, is called a tide. Explain the major causes of tide formation in the context of this statement.
7. What do you mean by upwelling of ocean water? How does it help in the movement of ocean water?
8. How waves break upon reaching the shoreline? Explain.
9. Together, the gravitational pull and the centrifugal force are responsible for creating the two major tidal bulges on the earth. Elucidate the statement.
10. 'Ocean currents have some important characteristics'. Explain.

Long Answer Type Questions

11. 'Spring tide occurs only on new moon or full moon day.' Explain in detail. Why?
12. Describe the major ocean currents of the Pacific, Atlantic and Indian Oceans taking one cold current and one warm current from every ocean.
13. The horizontal and vertical motions are common in ocean water bodies. Write the difference between waves and tides.
14. Tides may be grouped into various types. Describe all the types of tides based on different parameters.
15. Ocean currents have a number of direct and indirect influences on human activities. Justify the statement with valid reasons.

14
CHAPTER

Biodiversity and Conservation

Biodiversity is not found evenly on the Earth. It is rich in the tropics. Weathering mantle is the basis for the diversity of vegetation and hence, the biodiversity. The basic cause for such weathering variations and resultant biodiversity is the input of solar energy and water. Areas that are rich in these inputs are the areas of wide range of biodiversity.

YOUR STUDY GOALS

14.1 Biodiversity
14.2 Loss of Biodiversity
14.3 Conservation of Biodiversity

YOUR PRACTICE GOALS

- Objective Type Questions (23 Qs ; MCQs, Statements, Matching, A-R,)
- Subjective Questions (15 SAs, 7 LAs)
- Source Based Questions (2 Qs)
- Map Based Question (1 Q)

14.1 Biodiversity

- Biodiversity is a combination of two words - **Bio** (life) and **diversity** (variety).
- Biodiversity is the number and variety of organisms found within a specified geographic region.
- It refers to the varieties of plants, animals and micro-organisms, the **genes**[1] they contain and the ecosystems they form.
- It relates to the variability (variety) among living organisms on the Earth, including the variability within and between the species and, that within and between the ecosystems.
- Biodiversity is classified in three levels i.e. **Genetic**, **Species** and **Ecosystem**.

Genetic Diversity

- Genetic biodiversity refers to the variation of genes within **species**. Genes are the basic building blocks of various life forms.
- A species is a group of individual organisms having some similarities in their **physical characteristics**.
- Human beings genetically belong to the **homo sapiens**[2] group. They differ in characteristics such as height, colour, physical appearance, etc. This is due to genetic diversity.
- This genetic diversity is essential for a healthy multiplying of the population of species.

1 **Genes** A unit of information inside a cell which controls what a living thing will be like.
2 **Homo sapiens** Homo is the Latin word for 'human' or 'man' and sapiens is derived from a Latin word that means 'wise'. It is the species to which all wise human belongs.

Species Diversity

- Species diversity means number of species in a defined area.
- This diversity of species can be measured through its richness, wide presence and types of species.
- Areas rich in species diversity are called **hotspots of diversity**.

Ecosystem Diversity

- The differences between ecosystem types and the diversity of **habitats**[3] and ecological processes occurring within each ecosystem type constitute the ecosystem diversity.

Importance of Biodiversity

- Biodiversity contributes to the development of human culture and in turn, human communities have played a major role in shaping the diversity of nature.
- Biodiversity plays the following roles: **Ecological, Economic and Scientific.**

Ecological role of Biodiversity

Species play an important role in ecosystem functions and human survival as follows

- They capture and store energy.
- They produce and decompose organic materials.
- They help to cycle water and nutrients throughout the ecosystem.
- They fix atmospheric gases and help regulate the climate.
- The loss of species would decrease the ability of the system to maintain itself.
- An ecosystem with high biodiversity has a greater chance of adapting to environmental change. In other words, more variety of species in ecosystem results in more stable ecosystem.

Economic role of Biodiversity

- Biodiversity provides numerous resources that can be used for manufacturing of food, pharmaceutical and cosmetic products.
- Some of the important economic commodities that biodiversity supplies to humankind are: food crops, livestock, forests, fish, medicinal resources, etc.
- **Crop diversity** also known as **agro diversity**[4] is an important part of biodiversity.

Scientific Role of Biodiversity

- Biodiversity is important as each species gives us evidence of how life evolved.
- Biodiversity also helps in understanding how life functions and the role of each species in sustaining ecosystems.

Quick Test 1

1. What are the input resources of biodiversity?
2. In how many levels biodiversity is divided?
3. What is the basis of genetic diversity?
4. Mention one function of species in an ecosystem.

14.2 Loss of Biodiversity

Since the emergence of humans, biodiversity has seen a rapid decline, with one species after another bearing the brunt of **extinction**[5]. This loss of species is caused due to following reasons

- **Growth in the human population** has increased the rate of consumption of natural resources. It has accelerated the loss of species and habitation in different parts of the world.

3 **Habitat** The place or environment where a plant or animal naturally or normally lives and grows.
4 **Agro diversity** It is a sub-set of general biodiversity that deals with the agricultural ecosystem.
5 **Extinction** It means when all members of a particular group die.

- **Overexploitation of resources** and deforestation[6] have increased to fulfill the needs of a large population. This causes loss of habitat of species.
- Destruction of natural habitats in tropical regions have proved disastrous for the entire biosphere. Tropical regions which occupy only about one-fourth of the total area of the world, contain about three-fourth of the world human population and contain 50 per cent of the species on the Earth.
- **Natural calamities** such as earthquakes, floods, volcanic eruptions, forest fires, droughts, etc cause damage to the flora and fauna of the Earth.
- **Pesticides** and other **pollutants** such as hydrocarbons and toxic heavy metals destroy the weak and sensitive species.
- Introduction of exotic species[7] causes extensive damage to the natural biotic community of the ecosystem.
- Some animals like tigers, elephants, rhinoceros, crocodiles, minks and birds are hunted mercilessly by **poachers** for their horn, tusks, hides, etc.

Classification of Threatened Species

The International Union of Conservation of Nature and Natural Resources (IUCN) has classified the threatened species of plants and animals into three categories for the purpose of their conservation. These are

▲ *Red Panda-An Endangered Species*

(i) **Endangered Species** It includes those species which are in danger of extinction. Information about endangered species is published as the ***Red List*** of threatened species by IUCN.

(ii) **Vulnerable Species** This includes the species which are likely to be in danger of extinction in near future, if the factors threatening to their extinction continue. Survival of these species is not assured as their population has reduced greatly.

(iii) **Rare Species** Population of these species is very small in the world. They are confined to limited areas or have small population over a wider area.

14.3 Conservation of Biodiversity

- Conservation of Biodiversity refers to the protection of different species plants, animals and their habitats to maintain the balance of nature and ensure the survival of ecosystems for future generations.
- It involves educating people to adopt environment friendly practices.
- There is a need to modify our activities in such a way that development process is sustainable[8] and harmonious with other life forms.
- There is need for involvement and cooperation of local communities and individuals in the process of conservation of biodiversity.
- The process of conservation should be continued along with conservation of species and their habitat.

Earth Summit

- The Convention on Biodiversity was signed at the Earth Summit held at Rio de Janeiro, Brazil in June 1992. It was signed by the 155 countries including India.
- The world conservation strategy has suggested following steps for biodiversity conservation
  - Efforts should be made to preserve the species that are endangered.
  - Prevention of extinction requires proper planning and management.

6 Deforestation It refers to clearing of forest for land.
7 Exotic species Species which are not the natural inhabitants of the local habitat but are introduced into the system.
8 Sustainable The place or environment where a plant or animal naturally or normally lives and grows.

- Varieties of food crops, forage plants[9], timber trees, livestock, animals and their wild relatives should be preserved.
- Each country should identify habitats of wild relatives and ensure their protection.
- Habitats where species feed, breed, rest and nurse their young ones, should be safeguarded and protected.
- International trade in wild plants and animals be regulated.

Wildlife Protection Act, 1972

- It aims to protect, preserve and propagate the variety of species within natural boundaries.
- Under this Act, **national parks** and **sanctuaries** were established and **biosphere reserves** were declared.

Mega Diversity Centres

- Some countries in the tropical region possess a large number of the world's species diversity. These are called *mega diversity centers*.
- There are 12 countries, namely Mexico, Columbia, Ecuador, Peru, Brazil, Democratic Republic of Congo, Madagascar, China, India, Malaysia, Indonesia and Australia in which mega diversity centers are located.

Hotspots

- The **International Union** for the **Conservation of Nature** and **Natural Resources** (IUCN) has identified certain areas as biodiversity hotspots, to concentrate resources on the areas that are most vulnerable.
- Hotspots are defined on the basis of **vegetation**. Plants determine the primary productivity of an ecosystem. For example, about 85% of plants and animals in Madagascar are found nowhere else in the world.
- The hotspots of rich and wealthy countries are facing threats. For example, Hawaii islands which have unique plants and animals are threatened by the introduction of new species and land development.

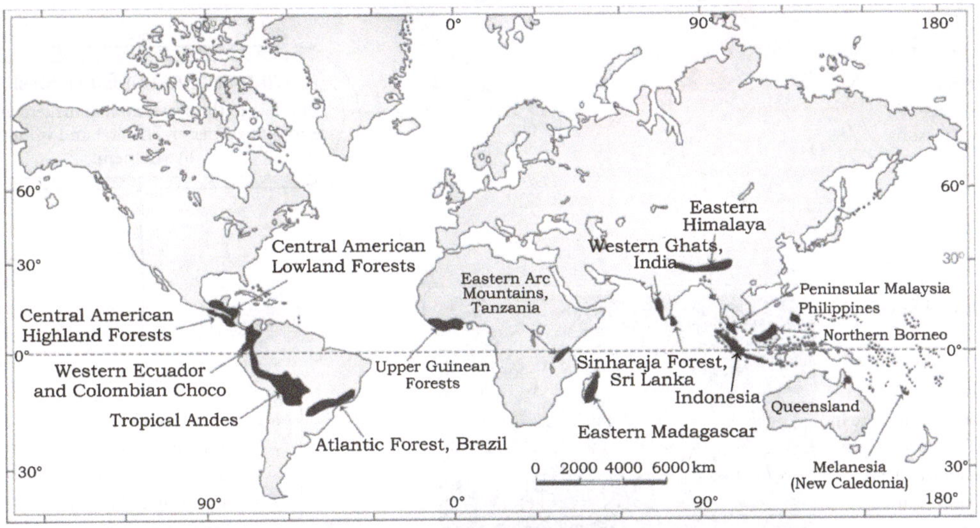

▲ *Some Ecological Hotspots in the World*

Check Point 2

1. Mention any two reasons due to which biodiversity loss take place.
2. In how many categories IUCN classified the threatened species of plants and animals?
3. What is the importance of the Earth Summit?
4. What do you mean by Mega Diversity Centres?

9 Forage Plants Those plants which are used as food for animals.

Mind Map

BIODIVERSITY AND CONSERVATION

1 Biodiversity

It refers to number and variety of organisms found in a given region.

Levels of Biodiversity

- **Genetic Biodiversity** It refers to variation of genes within species.
- **Species Biodiversity** It refers to varieties as well as number of species in a given area.
- **Ecosystem Biodiversity** It refers to variety of ecosystem in a given area.

2 Importance of Biodiversity

Biodiversity plays three important role within its define boundaries.

- **Ecological Role** This involves significant role of species for ecosystem function and human survival, e.g., biodiversity help in regulation of climate.
- **Economic Role** This involve significant role in the promotion of economic benefits, e.g., biodiversity as a reservoir used for manufacturing of food.
- **Scientific Role** This involve significant role of ecosystem in scientific fields, e.g., biodiversity helps in understanding how life functions.

3 Loss of Biodiversity

The decline or disappearance of biodiversity due to various reasons.

Classification of Threatened Species

- This classification is done by International Union of Conservation of Nature and Natural Resource
- **Endangered Species** Species which are in danger of extinction are listed in Red list.
- **Vulnerable Species** Species which are likely to be in danger in near future.
- **Rare Species** Species that are found in very small population.

4 Conservation of Biodiversity

It refers to the protection, management or restoration of natural habitat and wildlife that live in them.

Measures for Conservation

- Earth Summit (1992)
- Wildlife Protection Act (1972)
- Sustainable use of resources
- Awareness among people regarding Environment

NCERT Folder

Choose the right answer from the four alternatives given below

(i) **Conservation of biodiversity is important for**

(a) Animals (b) Animals and Plants
(c) Plants (d) All organisms

Ans (d) all organisms

(ii) **Threatened species are those which**

(a) threaten others
(b) lion and tiger
(c) are abundant in numbers
(d) are suffering from the danger of extinction.

Ans (d) are suffering from the danger of extinction.

(iii) **National parks and sanctuaries are established for the purpose of**

(a) Recreation (b) Hunting (c) Pets (d) Conservation

Ans (d) Conservation

(iv) **Biodiversity is richer in**

(a) Tropical regions (b) Polar regions
(c) Temperate regions (d) Oceans

Ans (a) Tropical regions

(v) **In which one of the following countries, the 'Earth Summit' was held?**

(a) UK (b) Mexico (c) Brazil (d) China

Ans (c) Brazil

Answer the following questions in about 30 words

(i) **What is biodiversity?**

Ans Biodiversity refers to the variety of plants, animals and micro-organisms, the genes they contain and the ecosystem they form.

In other words, it is the variety of organisms found within a specified geographical region.

(ii) **What are the different level of biodiversity?**

Ans There are three levels of biodiversity. These are

- **Genetic diversity** It refers to variation of genes within species.
- **Species diversity** It refers to the variety of species.
- **Ecosystem diversity** It refers to the diversity of habitats and ecological processes occurring within each ecosystem type.

(iii) **What do you understand by 'hotspots'?**

Ans The areas rich in species biodiversity are known as hotspots. IUCN has identified biodiversity hotspots in order to concentrate resources on most vulnerable areas. Hotspots are identified on the basis of dominant vegetation.

(iv) **Discuss briefly the importance of animals to human kind.**

Ans The importance of animals to human kind are as follows

- The animals are an integral part of ecosystem as human being. Animal helps in maintaining ecosystem.
- Animals are the part of food chain and they capture and store energy, produce organic material to the ecosystem.
- As both are the part of ecosystem, therefore, their existence is dependent upon each other.

(v) **What do you understand by 'exotic species'?**

Ans The species which are introduced from outside into a native area are called exotic species. There are many examples when the natural biotic community of the ecosystem suffered intensive damage, due to the introduction of exotic species.

Answer the following questions in about 150 words

(i) **What are the roles played by biodiversity in the shaping of nature?**

Ans The biodiversity plays its role in following forms in shaping the nature

Ecological Role

- Various species perform various functions which are ecologically important.
- All the species are inter-related and dependent upon each other for their survival.
- Every organism contributes for the sustenance of ecosystem. Thus, the more diverse an ecosystem is the more stable it will be.
- Diversity increases the resilience of ecosystem to withstand adversities.

Economic Role

- It supports pollination, water purification and climate control.
- It helps ecosystems recover, reducing economic losses.
- It boosts the economy through ecotourism.
- It manifests itself in the form of crop diversity.
- It provides commodities like food crops, livestock, forests, fish, medicinal resources, etc.

Scientific Role

- Biodiversity gives insights about evolution and future of life.

- It helps us in understanding about how the life functions.
- It also talks about role of every species in sustaining the ecosystem.

(ii) What are major factors that are responsible for the loss of biodiversity? What steps are needed to prevent them?

Ans Some of the major factors responsible for loss of biodiversity are given as under

- The accelerated rate of growth of human population in last few decades has caused overexploitation of natural resources, clearing of forests, etc.
- About 3/4 of the world population lives in tropical areas. Since these areas are critical for biodiversity, a massive damage has been done to the biodiversity.
- Natural calamities like earthquakes, floods, volcanic eruptions, forest fires, droughts, etc cause damage to biodiversity.
- Pollutants like toxic heavy metals, pesticides, hydrocarbons etc cause damage to biodiversity.
- Introduction of new species or exotic species degrades native species.
- Poaching of animals for commercial use of their body parts has dwindled the biodiversity to a great extent.

Steps needed to prevent them are

- There should not be any construction or infrastructural activities in the ecologically sensitive areas.
- Population explosion must be controlled.
- Ban on poaching should be implemented strictly.
- Chemically hazardous wastes should be treated for discharging in the ecosystem.
- No new exotic species should be introduced in the native areas.
- Community efforts should be made to protect and conserve biodiversity.

Exam Pattern Questions

Objective Type Questions

Multiple Choice Questions (MCQs)

1. Biodiversity is described as the variability among living organisms on Earth based on which of the following aspects?

(a) Genetic differences within a species.
(b) Diversity of habitats and ecosystems.
(c) Number and variety of species in a region.
(d) All of the above

2. Biodiversity plays which of the following roles within its defined boundaries?

(a) Ecological role of biodiversity
(b) Economic role of biodiversity
(c) Scientific role of biodiversity
(d) All of the above

3. Which of the following has been classified by IUCN as the threatened species?

(a) Endangered species (b) Vulnerable species
(c) Rare species (d) All of these

4. What is the primary goal of the Convention on Biological Diversity signed at the Earth Summit in Rio de Janeiro, Brazil?

(a) Preservation of endangered species worldwide.
(b) Prevention of natural disasters impacting biodiversity.
(c) Sustainable development with conservation of biodiversity.
(d) Increase in human population to support biodiversity.

5. The objective of biodiversity conservation is to ....

(a) Increase the genetic diversity among human populations.
(b) Ensure the sustainable use of resources while preserving species.
(c) Maximise the economic profit from natural resources.
(d) Reduce the number of species in an ecosystem.

6. The primary purpose of the Wild Life (Protection) Act of 1972 in India is to ....

(a) promote hunting as a recreational activity.
(b) establish national parks and sanctuaries to protect wildlife.
(c) convert forest land into agricultural fields.
(d) increase population in biodiversity hotspots.

7. To protect, preserve and propagate the variety of species within natural boundaries, the Government of India passed which of the following Act? CBSE Diksha

(a) The Wildlife(Protection) Act, 1972
(b) The Wildlife Protection and Conservation Act, 1927
(c) The Conservation of Biodiversity Act, 1972
(d) All of the above

8. Which of the following statements is incorrect?
(a) Biodiversity can be discussed at three levels.
(b) Genes are the basic building blocks of various life forms.
(c) The diversity of species can be measured through its richness, abundance and types.
(d) Areas which are not rich in species diversity are called hotspots of diversity.

9. What do we call the areas rich in species diversity? Choose the correct option from the following ones. CBSE Diksha
(a) Mega diversity centres
(b) Hotspots of diversity
(c) National parks
(d) None of the above

10. Which of the following statements regarding the ecological role of biodiversity is correct?
I. Every species performs a function contributing to the ecosystem's balance.
II. Biodiversity helps in the cycle of water and nutrients in the ecosystem.
III. Ecosystems with high biodiversity are less stable and productive.
IV. A diverse ecosystem improves the chances of species survival through environmental changes.

Choose the correct option.
(a) I, II, IV (b) I, III, IV
(c) II, III, IV (d) I, II, III

11. Biodiversity can be discussed at three levels, each playing a crucial role in maintaining ecological balance. Identify the correct levels of biodiversity discussed in the context of conservation.
I. Genetic Diversity II. Population Diversity
III. Species Diversity IV. Ecosystem Diversity

Codes
(a) Both I and III (b) Only II
(c) I, III and IV (d) Both II and III

12. Identify the type of region from the information given below.
The International Union for the Conservation of Nature and Natural Resources (IUCN) has identified certain areas.These are defined according to their vegetation. For example, in Madagascar about 85 per cent of the plants and animals are found nowhere else in the world. Most of these regions rely on species-rich ecosystems for food, firewood, cropland and income from timber.

Options
(a) Hotspots regions
(b) Temperate regions
(c) Polar regions
(d) Sub-tropical regions

13. Identify the role of biodiversity from the information given below.
This type of biodiversity is important because each species can give us some clue as to how life evolved and will continue to evolve. Biodiversity also helps in understanding how life functions and the role of each species in sustaining ecosystems of which we are also a parts. This fact must be drawn upon every one of us so that we live and let other species also live their lives.

Options
(a) Ecological Role of Biodiversity
(b) Scientific Role of Biodiversity
(c) Economic Role of Biodiversity
(d) Political role of Biodiversity

14. Which of the following is a characteristic of species diversity?
I. It relates to the number of species in a defined area.
II. Areas with fewer species are considered hotspots.
III. It is measured through richness, abundance and types of species.
IV. Species diversity is not influenced by the local climate.

Choose the correct option.
(a) I, II, III (b) I, III, IV
(c) II and III (d) I and III

15. Identify the statement that is not true with regard to biodiversity conservation.
I. Biodiversity is crucial for human survival as all life forms are interconnected and imbalance in one affects the others.
II. Conservation of biodiversity only requires the protection of endangered species and not their natural habitats.
III. Mega diversity centers are countries with a large variety of species, mostly found in tropical regions.
IV. Conservation strategies should include involvement of local communities and sustainable practices.

Options
(a) Statements I and III (b) Only II
(c) Only IV (d) Statements II and IV

16. Identify the statement that is not true with regard to ecosystem diversity.
I. Ecosystem diversity refers to the variety of habitats within an ecosystem.
II. Ecosystem boundaries are very rigid and clearly defined.
III. Ecosystems with greater biodiversity are more stable and resilient.

IV. Ecosystem diversity contributes to the health and productivity of an environment.

Options

(a) Only I
(b) Only II
(c) Statements II and III
(d) Statements III and IV

Arrange the Following

17. Arrange the following events related to biodiversity conservation in sequence.

(i) The Convention on Biological Diversity was signed at the Earth Summit in Rio de Janeiro in 1992.

(ii) The IUCN Red List of Threatened Species was developed to categorise species based on their conservation status.

(iii) The Wildlife Protection Act of 1972 was passed in India to protect national parks and sanctuaries.

(iv) The concept of biodiversity hotspots was introduced to focus conservation efforts on areas with high species diversity and vulnerability.

Codes

(a) (iii), (ii), (iv), (i)
(b) (iv), (i), (iii), (ii)
(c) (ii), (iii), (i), (iv)
(d) (iii), (iv), (ii), (i)

Match the Following

18.

List I (Classification of Threatened Species)	List II (Meaning)
A. Endangered species	1. Species which are in danger of extinction.
B. Vulnerable species	2. Species which are likely to be in danger of extinction in near future.
C. Rare species	3. Species which are found in very small population in the world.

Codes

	A	B	C		A	B	C
(a)	1	2	3	(b)	2	3	1
(c)	3	1	2	(d)	1	3	2

19.

List I	List II
A. Genetic Diversity	1. Refers to the variety of species in a given area
B. Species Diversity	2. Species that are in danger of becoming extinct
C. Ecosystem Diversity	3. Refers to the variation of genes within a species
D. Endangered Species	4. Refers to the differences in ecosystems and habitats

Codes

	A	B	C	D		A	B	C	D
(a)	3	1	4	2	(b)	2	3	1	4
(c)	4	3	1	2	(d)	1	3	4	2

Assertion-Reason

Directions (Q. Nos. 20-23) In the questions given below are two statements labelled as Assertion (A) and other is labelled as Reason (R). In the context of two statements, which one of the following is correct?

Codes

(a) Both A and R are true and R is the correct explanation of A
(b) Both A and R are true, but R is not the correct explanation of A
(c) Both A and R are incorrect
(d) A is correct, but R is incorrect

20 **Assertion** (A) Biodiversity decreases from the equator towards the poles.

Reason (R) The Biodiversity is evenly distributed on the Earth.

21 **Assertion** (A) The demarcation of ecosystem boundaries is difficult and complex.

Reason (R) The boundaries of communities and ecosystems are not clearly defined.

22. **Assertion** (A) Biodiversity plays a significant role in maintaining ecosystem stability.

Reason (R) The more the variety of species in an ecosystem, the more stable the ecosystem is likely to be.

23. **Assertion** (A) Biodiversity hotspots are areas with a high concentration of endemic species.

Reason (R) Hotspots are located in tropical regions and are vital for maintaining global biodiversity.

Answers

1. (d) All of the above
2. (d) All of the above
3. (d) All of these
4. (c) Sustainable development with conservation of biodiversity.
5. (b) Ensure the sustainable use of resources while preserving species.
6. (b) Establish national parks and sanctuaries to protect wildlife.
7. (a) The Wildlife(Protection) Act, 1972
8. (d) Areas which is not rich in species diversity are called hotspots of diversity.
9. (b) Hotspots of diversity
10. (a) I, II, IV
11. (c) I, III and IV
12. (a) Hotspots regions
13. (b) Scientific Role of Biodiversity
14. (d) I and III
15. (b) Only II
16. (b) Only II
17. (a) (iii), (ii), (iv), (i)
18. (a)
19. (a)
20. (d) A is correct, but R is incorrect
21. (a) Both A and R are true and R is the correct explanation of A
22. (a) Both A and R are true and R is the correct explanation of A
23. (a) Both A and R are true and R is the correct explanation of A

Subjective Questions

Short Answer Type Questions

1. What do you mean by diversity? What are its types? Why diversity is important?

Ans. The physical or biological complexity of a system is known as diversity.

There are three main types of diversity. These are

(i) **Genetic Diversity** Diversity of genes within a species.

(ii) **Species Diversity** Diversity of species within an ecosystem.

(iii) **Ecosystem Diversity** Diversity of ecosystem within the biosphere.

Importance of Diversity

The importance of diversity are given as under

- The diversity of life forms is essential to maintain balance in the ecosystem.
- The diversity of species is essential for survival of life forms.
- Diversity of associations smoothens flow of energy, water and nutrients.

2. What is the economic role of biodiversity? Explain. CBSE Diksha

Ans. Biodiversity is an important resource for all humans in their day-to-day life. Some of the key economic roles of biodiversity are as follows

- One important part of biodiversity is crop diversity which is also called agro-biodiversity.
- Biodiversity is seen as reservoir of resources to be drawn upon for the manufacture of food, pharmaceutical and cosmetic products.
- Some of the important economic commodities that biodiversity supplies to humankind are food crops, livestock, forests, fish, medicinal resources, etc.

3. Explain why biodiversity is important for an ecosystem? CBSE Diksha

Ans. Biodiversity is very important for an ecosystem. Following features establish importance of an ecosystem

- Various functions performed by various species are essential for functioning of ecosystem. These functions include capture of energy, cycling of nutrients, fixing up gases, etc.
- Greater the amount of diversity in an ecosystem, more the productive species will be.
- Biodiversity maintains the balance of ecosystems by ensuring all species play a role in food chains.
- With greater diversity, ecosystem has greater chances of adaptation with environment.
- Biodiversity provides stability to the ecosystem.

4 Explain ecological role of biodiversity. Competency Based Que

Ans Biodiversity plays a very significant role in the ecosystem. In an ecosystem, every organism depends on other organism for survival.

Some of the important ecological roles played by the biodiversity are given as under

- Species capture and store energy which is a part of flow of energy in the ecosystem.
- In an ecosystem, the organic materials are produced and decomposed by various species.
- Various species help in cycling of nutrients and water in the ecosystem.
- Species fix up atmospheric gases which are used in the food chain.
- Species also help in regulation of climate.

5. "Biodiversity is an important resource for all human beings in their day to day life". Analyse the statement. Competency Based Que

Ans Biodiversity is an important resource for all human beings in their day to day life because

- Crop diversity also known as agro biodiversity is an important part of biodiversity.
- Biodiversity as a reservoir of resources is used for manufacturing of food, medicines and cosmetic products.
- Some of the important economic commodities that biodiversity supplies to human kind are food crops, livestock, forests, fish, medicinal resources, etc.

6. What is the scientific role of biodiversity? Explain. Competency Based Que

Ans The scientific role of biodiversity is given as under

- Each species provides insight about how life has evolved in the history and how life will evolve in the future.
- Biodiversity also gives us an understanding about how life functions.
- Biodiversity explains about the role of each species in sustaining ecosystem.
- Biodiversity gives us an idea about what is the place and the role of human beings in the ecosystem.
- It gives us a responsibility to ensure existence of other species also and to live in harmony with other species.

7. Why are tropical forests so important with the point of view of biodiversity? Explain. Competency Based Que

Ans Out of all the types of biomes, tropical rainforests are very important with the point of view of biodiversity.

Following factors make tropical rainforests so important:

- Tropical rainforests are found in tropical regions of the globe. These areas are 1/4 area of Earth and 3/4 of the world population lives there.
- These tropical rain forests contain 50% species of the Earth.
- The biodiversity is highest in these forests. They are called lungs of the Earth.
- All the 12 hotspots and mega diversity centres are located in the tropical rainforests areas.
- New species are being discovered in the tropical areas regularly.

8. Concept of biodiversity is an integral part of many human cultures". Give arguments to support this statement highlighting the scientific role of biodiversity. CBSE Diksha

Ans This is true that biodiversity is an integral part of human cultures because

- Each species can give us some clue as to how life evolved and will continue to evolve.
- It helps us in understanding how life functions and the role of each species in sustaining ecosystems of which we are also a part.
- The level of biodiversity is a good indicator of the state of our relationships with other living species. It is our ethical responsibility to consider that each and every species along with us have intrinsic right to exist.

9. "Economic importance of biodiversity is responsible for its deterioration". Analyse the statement. Competency Based Que

Ans. Economic importance of biodivesity is responsible for its own deterioration because biodiversity is seen as a reservoir of resources. It can be used for the manufacturing of food, pharmaceutical and cosmetic products.

Biodiversity supplies various commodities for the day to day life use for all humans such as food crops, livestock, forest, fish, medicinal resources, etc.

To obtain these resources as much as it is available, human beings are exploiting nature more than its ecological footprint.

Mass level of deforestation, mining, illegal trafficking of plants and animals results into the deterioration of biodiversity.

10. What is the role of the International Union for Conservation of Nature (IUCN) in the conservation of biodiversity? Explain. Competency Based Que

Ans The International Union for Conservation of Nature (IUCN) plays a crucial role in the conservation of biodiversity by classifying species into categories based on their risk of extinction. The IUCN publishes the Red List of Threatened Species, which provides valuable information about endangered, vulnerable and rare species worldwide.

The organisation also identifies biodiversity hotspots, which are regions rich in species but under threat and advocates for the protection of these areas. Furthermore, IUCN promotes international efforts to conserve biodiversity, such as ensuring the sustainable use of natural resources and the regulation of wildlife trade. Through its global network, the IUCN fosters cooperation and awareness to protect biodiversity and prevent species loss.

11. **"The more diverse an ecosystem, better are the chances for the species to survive through adversity and attacks. Explain** **Competency Based Que**

Ans The more diverse an ecosystem, better are the chances for the species to survive and consequently is more productive. If there is diversity of species it will assist in the other survival of species. Hence, the loss of species would decrease the ability of the system to maintain itself. An ecosystem with high biodiversity may have a greater chance of adapting to environmental change. Therefore, extinction of species have wider impact on decreasing of the biodiversity.

The species which survive will transfer their genes to their next generation due to which ecosystem will continue to evolve. Also diverse ecosystem has more chances to withstand natural disasters.

12. **"Discuss the human activities which are responsible for deteriorating the biodiversity." Also suggest some measures to come out from this problem.**

Ans The growth in human populations has increased the rate of consumption of natural resources which has accelerated the loss of species and habitation in different parts of the world.

Some major human activities responsible for loss of biodiversity are

- Changes in land usage i.e. conversion of forest land to agriculture or residential land.
- Increasing pollution which includes air pollution, water pollution and soil pollution.
- Emission of carbon and change in CO_2 concentration in the atmosphere. These have increased the global temperature and give rise to global warming which is responsible for loss of biodiversity.
- Change in nitrogen cycle and acid rain. This change is also responsible for biodiversity destruction because change in nitrogen cycle will decrease the amount of nitrogen content into soils which is much needed for plant growth. Acid rain is equally harmful for biodiversity.

Some measures to reduce deterioration of biodiversity are

- To come out from this challenge, we need to adopt sustainable mode of development.
- We should use resources judiciously.
- We should also consume our nature and ecology.

13. **"Biodiversity is important for human existence". Explain the measures which are necessary to develop for the conservation of biodiversity.** **Competency Based Que**

Ans For conservation of biodiversity following measures should be adopted

- To educate people about environment friendly activities is the need of the hour.
- There is a need to reorient our activities in such a way that development process is sustainable and is harmonious with other life forms.
- Involvement and cooperation of local communities should be promoted for conservation and sustainable use of resources.
- Development of institutional structures at local level is necessary for the effectiveness of these efforts.

14. **Tropical regions are the most diverse regions of the world. Justify the statement.**

Ans. Tropical regions are the most diverse regions of the world because

- These regions which occupy only about one-fourth of the total area of the world, contain about three-fourth of the world human population.
- Abundant rainfall in these areas creates ideal conditions for diverse ecosystems.
- Rainforests, wetlands and coral reefs in tropical regions provide diverse habitats for many organisms.

15. **Explain the threatened species of plants and animals classified into three categories by IUCN for the purpose of their conservation.**

Ans. The International Union of Conservation of Nature and Natural Resources (IUCN) has classified the following threatened species of plants and animals into three categories for the purpose of their conservation

(i) **Endangered Species** It includes those species which are in danger of extinction. The IUCN publishes information about endangered species world-wide as the Red List of threatened species.

(ii) **Vulnerable Species** This includes the species which are likely to be in danger of extinction in near future if the factors threatening to their extinction continue.

(iii) **Rare Species** Population of these species is very small in the world. They are confined to limited areas or thinly scattered over a wider area.

Long Answer Type Questions

1. Explain the relationship between weathering processes, climatic zones and biodiversity. How do variations in the weathering mantle affect the types of vegetation and species found in different regions? Competency Based Que

Ans Weathering processes, climatic zones and biodiversity are closely interconnected. Weathering, the breakdown of rocks into smaller particles, varies across different climatic zones. In regions with high solar energy and abundant water, such as tropical climates, weathering is more intense, creating a fertile weathering mantle that supports diverse vegetation. This fertile soil allows a wide range of plant species to thrive, which, in turn, supports a variety of animals and microorganisms, leading to high biodiversity.

In contrast, areas with extreme climates, such as deserts or polar regions, experience slower weathering processes due to limited water and temperature extremes. The weathering mantle in these regions is often less fertile, supporting fewer plant species, and consequently, biodiversity is lower.

Thus, variations in the weathering mantle, influenced by climate, directly affect the types of vegetation and species that can survive in different regions, shaping the overall biodiversity.

2. Discuss some important steps taken on national and international level for conservation of biodiversity.

Ans Various significant steps have been taken on national and international level for the conservation of biodiversity are

On International Level

Earth Summit United Nations Conference on Environment and Development (UNCED) also called Earth Summit held in 1992 at Rio de Janeiro. It was the first instrument to address all the aspects of biodiversity. Every year, Summit held in the form of Conference of Parties (COP) meeting to discuss the issues for conservation of biodiversity.

International Union of Conservation of Nature and Natural Resources It is an international organisation which has classified the threatened species of plants and animals into three categories for the purpose of their conservation.

Hotspots In order to concentrate resources on those areas that are most vulnerable, the IUCN has identified certain areas as biodiversity hotspots. These hotspots are defined according to their vegetation.

On National Level

- Government of India alongwith 155 other nations have signed the Convention of Biodiversity at the Earth Summit.
- Government of India passed the Wildlife Protection Act 1972 to protect, preserve and propagate the variety of species within the national boundaries.

Apart from that, various NGOs, voluntary groups are active in the field of conservation of biodiversity on national and global level.

3. What do you understand by mega diversity centres? Why are they so important and provide a list of these centres?

Ans **Mega Diversity Centres** Ecological centres, situated in the tropical areas of the earth, which have very high amount of biodiversity, are known as Mega diversity centres.

List of Mega Diversity Centres

The Mega diversity centres are located in following countries:

- Mexico
- Columbia
- Ecuador
- Peru
- Brazil
- Madagascar
- China
- India
- Malaysia
- Indonesia
- Democratic Republic of Congo
- Australia

Importance of Mega Diversity Centres

- They are located in tropical areas where around 3/4 of world population lives.
- These areas have around 50% of the world species.
- They have world's highest biodiversity.
- Many researches are being done in these areas to classify newly discovered species.
- Revival of endangered species is being tried in these areas.

4. "The critical problem is not merely the conservation of species nor the habitat but the continuation of process of conservation." Give your argument in support of this statement. Competency Based Que

Ans Many national and international level initiatives have been taken for the conservation of biodiversity in last two decades.

The Earth Summit which was held in 1992 at Rio de Janeiro set up some major objectives to achieve at world level such as

- Conservation of Biodiversity.
- Sustainable use of the component of biodiversity.
- Fair and equitable use of biodiversity and equal sharing of benefit.

After this, various summits held timely and many protocols have been signed to attain the objectives such as Cartagena Protocol (1999), Nagoya Protocol (2010).

But the effectiveness of these efforts is not upto the desirable limit.

Limitations Although there is proper mechanism on world level to discuss the issue, but not effective mechanism for implementation of provision as

- Developed countries have accessability to all resources due to their economic prosperity, which are misused by these countries.
- Underdeveloped countries have less resources for the conservation of their biodiversity.
- Least developed nations are highly vulnerable as their resources are utilised by other rich countries.
- Due to lack of funding, process is unable to continue, which causes ineffectiveness in the efforts and initiatves.

5. "Conservation of biodiversity is crucial for the well-being of humanity". Justify this statement. Competency Based Que

Ans. Conservation of biodiversity is essential for the well-being of humanity as it provides numerous ecological, economic, and scientific benefits.

Ecologically, biodiversity helps maintain ecosystem stability by ensuring the proper functioning of processes such as nutrient cycling, water purification, and climate regulation. A diverse range of species helps in the resilience of ecosystems, making them more adaptable to environmental changes.

Economically, biodiversity is a valuable resource, contributing to sectors like agriculture, forestry, and pharmaceuticals. Crop diversity, for instance, ensures food security, while medicinal plants offer potential cures for various diseases. Additionally, biodiversity supports industries like tourism and fisheries, which are crucial for the global economy.

Scientifically, studying biodiversity helps us understand the processes of evolution, disease resistance, and ecosystem services. It also offers insights into the development of new technologies and medicines. Thus, protecting biodiversity is fundamental for human survival, health and progress.

6. What are the main factors that are responsible for the loss of biodiversity? CBSE Diksha

Ans. Factors responsible for the loss of biodiversity are as follows

- **Growth of human population** Since the last few decades, growth in human population has increased the rate of consumption of natural resources. It has accelerated the loss of species and habitation in different parts of the world.
- **Over-exploitation of resources and deforestation** Ever increasing population has caused overexploitation of resources and deforestation to fulfill the needs of large population.
- **Natural calamities** Natural calamities such as earthquakes, floods, volcanic eruptions, forest fires, droughts etc. cause damage to the flora and fauna of the earth, bringing change the biodiversity of respective affected regions.
- **Pesticides and other pollutants** Hydrocarbons and toxic heavy metals destroy the weak and sensitive species.
- **Exotic species** There are many species of a natural biotic community of an ecosystem which have suffered extensive damage because of the introduction of exotic species.
- **Hunting and poaching** During the last few decades, some animals like tigers, elephants, rhinoceros, crocodiles, minks and birds were hunted mercilessly by poachers for their horn, tusks etc. This has resulted in the rendering of certain types of organisms as endangered category.

7. Mention the steps for conservation of biodiversity that has been suggested by the world conservation Strategy. CBSE Diksha

Ans. The world conservation strategy has suggest the following steps for biodiversity conservation

- Efforts should be made to preserve the species that are endangered.
- Prevention of extinction requires proper planning and management.
- Varieties of food crops, forage plants, timber trees, livestock, animals and their wild relatives should be preserved.
- Each country should identify habitats of wild relative and ensure their protection.
- Habitats where species feed, breed, rest and nurse their young should be safeguarded and protected.
- International trade in wild plants and animals be regulated.

Source Based Questions

1. Read the passage carefully and answer the questions that follow.

Since the last few decades, growth in human population has increased the rate of consumption of natural resources. It has accelerated the loss of species and habitation in different parts of the world. Tropical regions which occupy only about one-fourth of the total area of the world, contain about three-fourth of the world human population. Overexploitation of resources and deforestation have become rampant to fulfil the needs of large population. As these tropical rain forests contain 50 per cent of the species on the earth, destruction of natural habitats have proved disastrous for the entire biosphere. Natural calamities such as earthquakes, floods, volcanic eruptions, forest fires, droughts, etc. cause damage to the flora and fauna of the earth, bringing change in the biodiversity of respective affected regions. Pesticides and other pollutants such as hydrocarbons and toxic heavy metals destroy the weak and sensitive species. Species which are not the natural inhabitants of the local habitat but are introduced into the system, are called exotic species. There are many examples when a natural biotic community of the ecosystem suffered extensive damage because of the introduction of exotic species. During the last few decades, some animals like tigers, elephants, rhinoceros, crocodiles, minks and birds were hunted mercilessly by poachers for their horn, tusks, hides, etc. It has resulted in the rendering of certain types of organisms as endangered category.

(i) Which of the following is the most important factor that has led to decline in biodiversity?

(a) Earthquakes (b) Rising population
(c) Agriculture (d) Mining and quarrying

Ans (b) Rising population

(ii) Which of the following species is originally not a part of an ecosystem and are introduced from the outside?

(a) Vulnerable species (b) Endangered species
(c) Exotic species (d) Near threatened species

Ans (c) Exotic species

(iii) Which of the following biome has the highest biodiversity?

(a) Deserts (b) Coastal region
(c) Rainforests (d) Oceans

Ans (c) Rainforests

2 Read the passage carefully and answer the questions that follow.

Biodiversity is important for human existence. All forms of life are so closely interlinked that disturbance in one gives rise to imbalance in the others. If species of plants and animals become endangered, they cause degradation in the environment, which may threaten human being's own existence. There is an urgent need to educate people to adopt environment-friendly practices and reorient their activities in such a way that our development is harmonious with other life forms and is sustainable. There is an increasing consciousness of the fact that such conservation with sustainable use is possible only with the involvement and cooperation of local communities and individuals. For this, the development of institutional structures at local levels is necessary. The critical problem is not merely the conservation of species nor the habitat but the continuation of process of conservation.

To protect, preserve and propagate the variety of species within natural boundaries, the Government of India passed the Wild Life (Protection) Act, 1972, under which national parks and sanctuaries were established and biosphere reserves declared. There are some countries which are situated in the tropical region; they possess a large number of the world's species diversity. They are called mega diversity centres. There are 12 such countries, namely Mexico, Columbia, Ecuador, Peru, Brazil, Democratic Republic of Congo, Madagascar, China, India, Malaysia, Indonesia and Australia in which these centres are located.

In order to concentrate resources on those areas that are most vulnerable, the International Union for the Conservation of Nature and Natural Resources (IUCN) has identified certain areas as biodiversity hotspots. Hotspots are defined according to their vegetation. Plants are important because these determine the primary productivity of an ecosystem. Most, but not all, of the hotspots rely on species-rich ecosystems for food, firewood, cropland, and income from timber.

(i) Why the development of institutional structures at local level is necessary?

Ans. The development of institutional structure is necessary at the local level because there is an increasing consciousness of the fact that conservation with sustainable use is possible only with the involvement and cooperation of local communities and individuals.

(ii) Why there is a need to reorient the human activities?

Ans. There is a need to reorient human activities because of the growing degradation of biodiversity, which can have severe consequences for human health and future generations.

(iii) How does the IUCN help in focusing conversation efforts globally?

Ans. The IUCN helps focus conservation efforts globally by identifying biodiversity hotspots, concentrating resources on vulnerable areas, and promoting sustainable practices through international cooperation and awareness.

Map Based Question

1. Mark the following ecological hotspots on the map of the world.

(i) Eastern Himalayas
(ii) Upper Guinean Forests
(iii) Atlantic Forest, Brazil
(iv) Western Ghats
(v) Eastern Madagascar
(vi) Indonesia
(vii) Tropical Andes

Ans

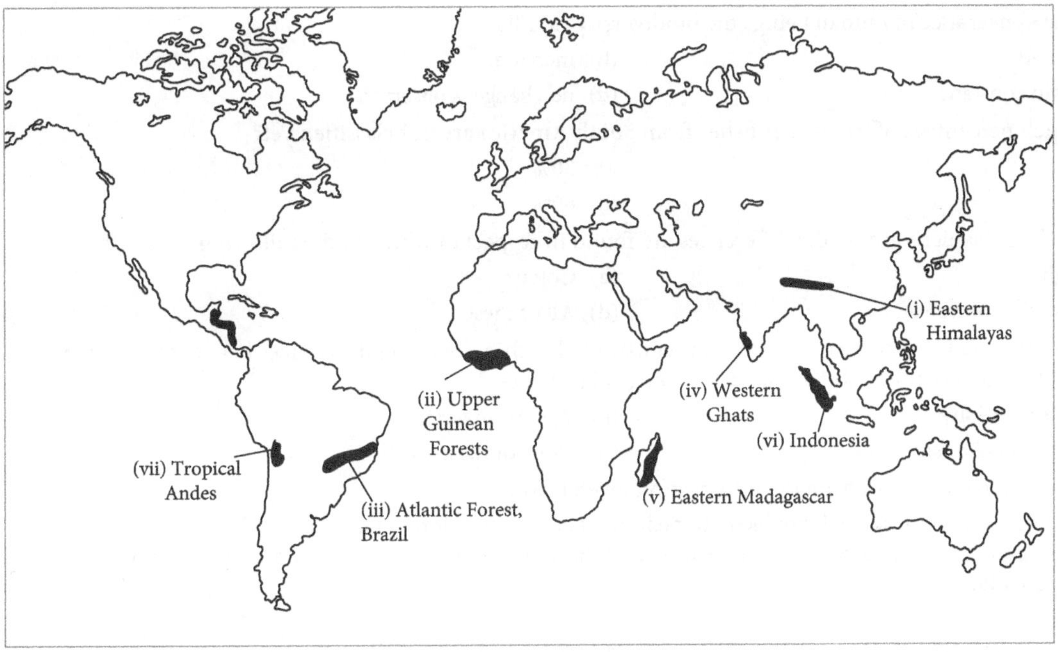

SELF ASSESSMENT TEST

Objective Type Questions

1. After the appearance of human beings the biodiversity rapidly
   (a) declined (b) increased
   (c) remain constant (d) no change is observed
2. How much percentage of freshwater fishes from South America are not classified yet?
   (a) 10% (b) 30%
   (c) 40% (d) 60%
3. Within Homo sapiens group, the differences are found in respect of which of the following?
   (a) Height (b) Colour
   (c) Physical appearance (d) All of these
4. Which of the following types of diversities is constituted within the broad differences between ecosystem types and the diversity of habitats and also ecological processes?
   (a) Species diversity (b) Genetic diversity
   (c) Ecosystem diversity (d) None of these
5. Identify the type of species from the information given below.
   This includes the species which are likely to be in danger of extinction in near future if the factors threatening to their extinction continue. Survival of these species is not assured as their population has reduced greatly.
   Options
   (a) Endangered species (b) Vulnerable species
   (c) Critically endangered species (d) Rare species

Short Answer Type Questions

6. Establish the relationship among genes, species and ecosystems.
7. Growth in the human population has increased the rate of consumption of natural resources. Explain the impacts of humans on biodiversity in context of this statement.
8. How all life forms are interlinked with each other? Explain.
9. What is the main aim of the Earth Summit and list down the suggested steps for biodiversity conservation by the summit?
10. Explain in detail the role played by IUCN for conservation of species.

Long Answer Type Questions

11. What do you understand by hotspots? What are their main characteristics?
12. Explain the main provisions of Wildlife Protection Act, 1972 of Government of India.
13. What is the responsibility of human beings towards other species? Write in detail.
14. Biodiversity also helps in understanding how life functions and the role of each species. Explain the scientific role of biodiversity.
15. 'Countries which are situated in the tropical region, possess a large number of the world's species diversity'. Justify the statement with valid reasons.

CHAPTER 1

India - Location

This chapter deals with location and size of India. It also highlights the neighbouring countries, international and state boundaries of India that determine its territorial reach and significance.

The mainland of India, extends from **Kashmir** in the North to **Kanniyakumari** in the South and **Arunachal Pradesh** in the East to **Gujarat** in the West.

YOUR STUDY GOALS

1.1 Location and Extent
1.2 Size
1.3 India and its Neighbours

YOUR PRACTICE GOALS

- Objective Type Questions (21 Qs ; MCQs, Matching, A-R)
- Subjective Questions (13 SAs, 4 LAs)
- Source Based Questions (2 Qs)
- Map Based Question (1 Qs)

1.1 Location and Extent

- India's territorial limit extends towards the sea upto **12 nautical miles**[1] (about 21.9 km) from the coast.
- The Southern boundary of India extends upto **6°45′ N latitude** in the Bay of Bengal.
- The latitude and longitudinal extent of India is roughly about **30 degrees.**
- Actual distance measured from **North to South** is **3214 km** and that from **East to West** is **2933 km**. This difference is based on the fact that the distance between two longitudes decreases towards the poles whereas the distance between two latitudes remains the same everywhere.
- Southern part of the country lies within the tropics[2] and the Northern part lies in the sub-tropical zone[3] or the warm temperate zone.
- This location of India is responsible for large variations in land forms, climate, soil types and natural vegetation in the country.
- There is longitudinal variation of nearly 30 degrees, which causes a time difference of nearly two hours from the Easternmost and the Westernmost parts of India.

1 Nautical miles It is a unit for measuring distance at sea.
2 Tropics Zone that lies between Tropic of Cancer and Tropic of Capricorn.
3 Sub-tropical zone Zone beyond the Tropic of Cancer and Tropic of Capricorn in the Northern and Southern hemisphere.

▲ *India : Administrative Divisions*

Standard Meridian

- 82°30′ E is the Standard Meridian of India. Indian Standard Time is ahead of Greenwich Mean Time by 5 hours and 30 minutes.
- There are some countries where there are more than one standard meridian due to their vast East-to-West extent. For example, the USA has seven time zones.

1.2 Size

- India with its area of **3.28 million sq. km** accounts for 2.4 per cent of the world's land surface area. It is the seventh largest country in the world.
- India's large size has led to great physical diversity. In the North huge mountains like **Himalayas** are present.

- Rivers like **Ganga, Brahmaputra, Mahanadi, Krishna, Godavari** flows through India.
- The North-East and South regions are home to dense, green forested hills. There's a vast sandy area in West called **Marusthali.**
- The country is geographically surrounded by
  - **Himalayas** in the North
  - **Hindukush and Sulaiman** ranges in the North-West
  - **Purvachal hills** in the North-East
  - The **Indian Ocean** in the South.
- This unique geographic setup is known as the **Indian subcontinent.**
- Indian subcontinent includes countries like Pakistan, Nepal, Bhutan, Bangladesh and India.
- The Himalayas have acted as a barrier to the Indian subcontinent which has resulted in developing the unique regional identity of the Indian subcontinent.
- Peninsular part of India extends towards the Indian ocean.
- India has a coastline of 7,517 km including coastlines of Andaman & Nicobar in Bay of Bengal and Lakshadweep in the Arabian Sea. The mainland coastline of India is 6,100 km.

1.3 India and its Neighbours

- India is located in the **South-Central part** of the continent of Asia, bordering the Indian ocean (Bay of Bengal and Arabian Sea).
- **Sri Lanka and Maldives** are the two island countries located in the Indian Ocean, which are India's neighbours.
- Sri Lanka is separated from India by the **Gulf**[4] of Mannar and **Palk Strait**[5].

Quick Test

1 What is the total land area of India?
2 What is the rank of India in terms of area in the world?
3 Which latitude divides the country into two equal parts?
4 Name a country which has more than one time zone.
5 Palk Strait separates which country from India?

4 **Gulf** A narrow stretch of water enclosed by land on three sides with a narrow opening
5 **Strait** A narrow stretch of water that divides two landmasses and joins two water bodies.

Mind Map

INDIA-LOCATION

1 Location and Extent

Latitudinal Extent
- 8° 4′ N to 37° 6′ N latitudes.
- The Tropic of Cancer divides India into two climatic zones.

Longitudinal Extent
- 68°7′ E to 97°25′ E longitudes
- Longitudes causes time differences in the country.

Time Zone
The local time of 82°30′ E longitude is followed all over the country as Indian Standard Time.

2 Size

Area
India covers an area of 3.28 million square km which leads to great physical diversity.

North-South Extent
The actual distance measured from North to South is 3214 km.

East-West Extent
The actual distance measured from East to West is 2,933 km.

Coastline
India has a coastline of 6,100 km in the mainland and 7517 km in the entire geographical coast of the mainland plus the two island groups.

3 Physical Diversity

- Himalayas in the North
- Deccan plateau in the South
- Sandy deserts in the West
- Fertile plains and forested hills in the East

4 Geographical Importance

- Himalayas and other ranges acted as a physical barrier.
- Strategic maritime location provides links to global trade routes.

5 India and its Neighbours

- India is located in the South-Central part of the continent of Asia.
- India has land borders with Pakistan, Bangladesh, Myanmar.
- Its island neighbours are Sri Lanka, Maldives.
- Sri Lanka is separated from India by the Gulf of Mannar and Palk Strait.

NCERT Folder

Intext Question

Q. Differentiate between a Gulf and a Strait. (Pg 5)

Ans. Differences between Gulf and a Strait are as follows

Gulf	Strait
It is a large body of water partially enclosed by land.	It is a narrow waterway connecting two larger bodies of water
Connected to an ocean.	Separates two landmasses.

Choose the right answer from the four alternatives given below

(i) Which one of the following latitudinal extent is relevant for the extent of India's area?

(a) 8°41′ N - 35°7′ N
(b) 8°4′ N - 37°6′ N
(c) 8°4′ N - 35°6′ N
(d) 6°45′ N - 37°6′ N

Ans (b) 8°4′ N - 37°6′ N

(ii) Which one of the following countries shares the longest land frontier with India?

(a) Bangladesh (b) China
(c) Pakistan (d) Myanmar

Ans (a) Bangladesh

(iii) Which one of the following countries is larger in area than India?

(a) China (b) Egypt
(c) France (d) Iran

Ans (a) China

(iv) Which one of the following longitudes is the Standard Meridian for India?

(a) 69°30′ E (b) 82°30′ E
(c) 75°30′ E (d) 90°30′ E

Ans (b) 82°30′ E

Answer the following questions in about 30 words

(i) Does India need to have more than one standard time? If yes, why do you think so?

Ans Yes, India needs to have more than one standard time. This is because its East-West extension is very large and there is a difference of about 2 hours in the time of its Eastern and Western ends, whereas the time zones of the world have been made at the difference of 30 minutes or 7°30′ longitudes.

(ii) What are the implications of India having a long coastline?

Ans India's long coastline gives several advantages to the country which are as follows

- It helps to connect the countries of the Western world to the countries of the Eastern world through trans-oceanic routes.
- It is a source of various marine resources.
- It helps in domestic and international trade.

(iii) How is the latitudinal spread of India advantageous to it?

Ans The latitudinal spread of India is advantageous because it provides a large variety of

- Landforms such as mountains, hills, plains, deserts, valleys, plateaus, etc.
- Climate types such as tropical, temperate, extreme and maritime climate.
- Soil types such as alluvial, black, laterite, arid, etc.
- Natural vegetation like forests, grassland, etc.

(iv) While the Sun rises earlier in the East, say Nagaland and also sets earlier, how do the watches at Kohima and New Delhi show the same time?

Ans Watches at Kohima and New Delhi show the same time because watches all over India are set according to the local time of the Standard Meridian of India i.e. 82°30′ E longitude known as the Indian Standard Time (IST).

Exam Pattern Questions

Objective Type Questions

Multiple Choice Questions (MCQs)

1. What is the actual distance of India from North to South?

(a) 2,933 km (b) 3,214 km
(c) 3,124 km (d) 5,325 km

2. Which of the following latitudes divides India into two climatic zones?

(a) Tropic of Capricorn (b) Tropic of Cancer
(c) Equator (d) Arctic Circle

3. How many time zones are there in USA?

(a) 3 (b) 5 (c) 7 (d) 9

4. Which of the following mountain ranges lies on the North-Western part of India?

(a) Hindukush and Sulaiman ranges
(b) Purvachal hills
(c) Himalayas
(d) None of the above

5. Which of the following reasons explains the difference in distance between latitudes and longitudes?

(a) The distance between longitudes decreases towards the poles, whereas the distance between latitudes remains constant.
(b) The distance between latitudes decreases towards the poles, while longitudes remain constant.
(c) Latitudes and longitudes have equal distances at all points.
(d) The difference is based on the Earth's rotation, not its shape.

6. India's coastal length is about 6,100 km in the mainland. How much is the total coastline including island groups?

(a) 5,500 km (b) 7,517 km
(c) 6,500 km (d) 8,000 km

7. Which of the following is a true statement regarding the physical geography of India?

(a) India's physical diversity results from its vast latitudinal and longitudinal extent.
(b) India has a flat terrain with minimal variations in landforms.
(c) The Himalayas have no impact on India's regional identity.
(d) India's geographical size does not influence its climate or vegetation.

8. Which of the following Indian States shares its border with as many as three countries? CBSE Diksha

(a) Himachal Pradesh (b) Sikkim
(c) Arunachal Pradesh (d) Punjab

9. How many Union Territories India does have? CBSE Diksha

(a) 7 (b) 6
(c) 8 (d) 9

10. India's territorial limit further extends towards the sea upto CBSE Diksha

(a) 22 nautical miles (b) 12 nautical miles
(c) 12.9 nautical miles (d) 22.9 nautical miles

11. Which of the following statements are correct related to the geographical features of India?

I. India has a vast latitudinal and longitudinal extent, with variations in time and climate.
II. The Southernmost part of India lies in the Tropic of Cancer, while the Northernmost part lies in the sub-tropical zone.
III. The Standard Meridian of India passes through multiple states and the country has a single time zone, Indian Standard Time (IST).
IV. India's coastline spans about 7,100 km and the country shares borders with nine neighbouring countries.

Choose the correct option.

(a) I, II, III
(b) II, III, IV
(c) I, III, IV
(d) I, II, IV

12. Choose the correct pair of geographical boundaries of India.

I. Northern boundary: Himalayas; Western boundary: Arabian Sea
II. Southern boundary: Kanniyakumari; Eastern boundary: Bay of Bengal
III. Western boundary: Assam; Eastern boundary: Gujarat
IV. Eastern boundary: Himalayas; Southern boundary: Nagaland

Options

(a) I and II (b) II and III
(c) I and IV (d) III and IV

13. Which of the following statements are correct about India's physical diversity?

I. India is home to a variety of landforms including mountains, plains, deserts and coastal areas.

II. The Himalayas and other mountain ranges form physical barriers to interaction with neighbouring countries.

III. The large rivers in India such as the Ganga, Brahmaputra and Godavari are important for irrigation and transportation.

IV. India has no deserts and is known for its tropical forests.

Choose the correct option.

(a) I, II, III (b) II, III, IV
(c) I, II, IV (d) I, III, IV

14. Identify the statement that is not true with regard to India's location and physical features.

(i) India's mainland extends from Kashmir in the North to Kanniyakumari in the South and from Arunachal Pradesh in the East to Gujarat in the West.

(ii) India's territorial limit extends only up to 12 nautical miles from the coast.

(iii) The country's Southern boundary extends up to 6°45′ N latitude in the Bay of Bengal.

(iv) India's total area is about 5 million sq. km.

Options

(a) Statements (i) and (iv) (b) Only (ii)
(c) Only (iii) (d) Statement (iv)

15. Which of the following statements are correct about India's neighbouring countries?

I. India shares a land border with Nepal, Bhutan, Pakistan, China and Bangladesh.

II. Sri Lanka and the Maldives are island nations to the South of India.

III. India's Northern boundary is formed by the Bay of Bengal.

IV. India is separated from Sri Lanka by the Gulf of Mannar and the Palk Strait.

Choose the correct option.

(a) I, II, IV (b) I, III, IV
(c) II, III, IV (d) I, II, III

16. Which of the following nations is/are larger than India in terms of area?

I. USA II. Canada
III. China

Codes

(a) Only I (b) I and II
(c) II and III (d) All of these

17. Identify the statement that is not true about the concept of Indian Standard Time (IST).

(i) Indian Standard Time is ahead of Greenwich Mean Time by 5 hours and 30 minutes.

(ii) The Standard Meridian of India is 82°30′ E.

(iii) Indian Standard Time is based on the meridian passing through New Delhi.

(iv) There are multiple standard meridians in India due to its vast East-to-West extent.

Options

(a) Statements (i) and (iv) (b) Only (iii)
(c) Only (ii) (d) Only (iv)

Arrange the Following

18. Arrange the following countries correctly in terms of their rank in area in the world. **Competency Based Que**

(i) Russia (ii) Canada
(iii) China (iv) Brazil

Options

(a) (i), (ii), (iii), (iv) (b) (ii), (i), (iv), (iii)
(c) (iv), (iii), (ii), (i) (d) (i), (iv), (iii), (ii)

Assertion-Reason

Directions (Q. Nos. 19-21) In the questions given below are two statements labelled as Assertion (A) and other is labelled as Reason (R). In the context of two statements which one of the following is correct?

Codes

(a) Both A and R are true, but R is not the correct explanation of A
(b) Both A and R are true and R is the correct explanation of A
(c) Both A and R are incorrect
(d) A is correct, but R is incorrect

19. Assertion (A) The distance between two latitudes remains the same everywhere.

Reason (R) Latitudes are parallel and equidistant to the equator.

20. Assertion (A) India has 2 hours time difference between the Easternmost and Westernmost parts of the country.

Reason (R) India has variation of nearly 30 degrees in its longitudinal extent.

21. Assertion (A) The tropic of cancer affects the distribution of heat across the country.

Reason (R) The tropic of cancer divides India into Northern and Southern halves, leading to different temperate zones, which influence the climate.

Answers

1. (b) 3,214 km
2. (b) Tropic of Cancer
3. (c) 7
4. (a) Hindukush and Sulaiman ranges
5. (a) The distance between longitudes decreases towards the poles, whereas the distance between latitudes remains constant.
6. (b) 7,517 km
7. (a) India's physical diversity results from its vast latitudinal and longitudinal extent.
8. (b) Sikkim
9. (c) 8
10. (b) 12 nautical miles
11. (a) I, II, III
12. (a) I and II
13. (a) I, II, III
14. (d) Statement (iv)
15. (d) I, II, IV
16. (d) All of these
17. (d) Only (iv)
18. (a) (i), (ii), (iii), (iv)
19. (b) Both A and R are true and R is the correct explanation of A
20. (b) Both A and R are true and R is the correct explanation of A
21. (b) Both A and R are true and R is the correct explanation of A

Subjective Questions

Short Answer Type Questions

1. Give the extent of India in terms of latitude and longitude and also in kilometres.

Ans The latitudinal extent of India is 8°4′ N to 37°6′ N and the longitudinal extent of India is 68°7′ E to 97°25′ N.

The latitudinal and longitudinal extent of India is roughly about 30 degrees, whereas the actual distance measured from North to South extremity is 3,214 km and from East to West is 2,933 km. Total area of India is 3.287 million sq km. It is 7th largest country in the world.

2. Which physical feature has contributed to the evolution of a unique identity of the Indian sub-continent?

Ans The Himalayas have contributed to the evolution of a unique identify of the Indian sub-continent. These mountains are unique in nature. It is because the Himalayas together with other mountains ranges have acted as a physical barrier between the countries of the Indian sub-continent in the past. It is very difficult to cross these mountain ranges which lie in the Northern part of India.

A few mountain passes such as the Khyber, the Bolan, the Shipki la, the Nathula, the Bomdila, have enabled people to cross these mountain ranges easily.

These are the reasons due to which the Himalayas are considered very important physical feature which have contributed to the evolution of a unique identity of the Indian sub-continent.

3. Explain about the neighbouring countries of India.

Ans. India shares its 15,200 km long land border with Bangladesh and Myanmar in the East, China, Nepal and Bhutan in the North, Pakistan and Afghanistan in the North-West.

India is located in South central part of the continent of Asia connecting Africa and Europe in West and China, Japan and Australia in the East through trans-oceanic routes bordering the Indian Ocean, the Bay of Bengal and the Arabian Sea.

Sri Lanka and Maldives are the two island countries located in the Indian ocean. Sri Lanka is separated from India by the Gulf of Mannar and the Palk Strait.

4. Distinguish between the tropical and the temperate zones.

Ans. Differences between the tropical and the temperate zones are as follows

The Tropical Zone	The Temperate Zone
The zone or area that lies below the tropics is known as the tropical zone.	The zone or area that lies in the North or above the tropics is known as the temperate zone.
It experiences the position of the overhead Sun twice a year.	It never experiences overhead Sun as the angle of the sun rays is above 90° or slanting.
It experiences high temperature throughout the year.	In temperate zone, the temperature is high in summer and low in winters.

5. Why does India have a time difference of 2 hours between the Eastern and the Western margins of it? Explain. CBSE Diksha

Ans India has a time difference of 2 hours between the Eastern and Western margins because India has a vast extent of 30° longitudes between its West and East. As difference between two longitudes is 4 minutes.

Therefore, the time difference between India's East-West is calculated as 4×30=120 minutes or 2 hours.

6. 'Although the latitudinal and longitudinal extent of India is almost the same i.e. 30°, the North-South extent of the country in terms of kilometres is more than its East-West extent.' Explain.

Ans North-South extent of India in terms of kilometres is more than East-West extent because the distance between two longitudes decreases towards the poles due to spherical shape of the earth and convergence of meridians at the poles. Whereas the distance between two latitudes remains the same everywhere as the latitudes are parallel to the equator.

Hence, even if latitudinal and longitudinal extent of India are almost same, the distance of North-South extent in kilometres is more than East-West extent in kilometres.

7. Differentiate between a gulf and a strait.

Ans Differences between a gulf and a strait are as follows

Gulf	Strait
A gulf is a deep inlet of the sea which is surrounded by land on three sides.	A strait is a naturally formed narrow waterway that connects two large bodies of water.
Gulfs are formed due to the movements of the tectonic plates.	A strait can be formed by tectonic shifts or land that has been subsided or been eroded.
Gulfs are generally broader and have a more rounded or curved shape	Strait are typically narrow and long.
Gulf is sometimes also known as a large bay.	If a strait is formed by human activities, it is called as canal, e.g. the Suez Canal.

8. India is known for its unity in diversity. Explain. Competency Based Que

Ans. Though, India has large geographical, regional, social, cultural and economic diversity but it exhibits a high degree of unity in diversity because of the following factors

- Monsoonal rythm of seasons has provided a strong element of uniformity.
- Inter-regional contacts and exchange have generated strong bonds and cultural fusion.
- Along with the political system, the above factors have played the role of unification and integration of the country.

9. India's territorial limits extend up to 12 nautical miles from its coastline. Explain the significance of this maritime boundary.

Ans. India's territorial limits extend up to 12 nautical miles from its coastline, signifying its sovereignty over the surrounding waters. This boundary grants India exclusive rights to explore and manage resources like fisheries and mineral deposits within this zone.

It also plays a crucial role in ensuring national security, allowing control over maritime activities and preventing foreign interference in its territorial waters.

10. India's vast latitudinal extent places it in both the tropics and the sub-tropical zone. Explain how this geographical positioning affects India's agricultural practices, climate zones and biodiversity. Competency Based Que

Ans. India's positioning between the tropics and sub-tropical zone results in diverse climatic conditions, from tropical monsoon in the south to temperate climates in the north. This variation supports a wide range of agricultural practices, with rice, cotton spices in the south and wheat and barley in the north.

The diversity of climates also promotes rich biodiversity, with distinct ecosystems ranging from tropical forests to alpine meadows, supporting a variety of flora and fauna.

11. Why is the standard meridian of India set at 82°30′ E? Explain its significance in relation to India's timekeeping and its impact on daily life.

Ans. India's standard meridian is set at 82°30′ E to create a uniform time system across the country, despite its vast east-west extent. This meridian ensures that Indian Standard Time (IST) is 5 hours and 30 minutes ahead of GMT, allowing consistent timekeeping.

It helps keep daily activities like work, travel, and communication on the same schedule across the country, so everyone follows the same time, no matter where they are.

12. The size of India has endowed her great physical diversity. Explain. Competency Based Que

Ans. The size of India has endowed her great physical diversity due to

- The presence of lofty mountains in the North.
- Green forested hills in the North-East and South India.
- Vast sandy expanse of Marusthali.

- Large expanse of Indian Ocean in the South.
- The group of islands in the Arabian Sea and Bay of Bengal.

13. The Himalayas together with other ranges have acted as a formidable physical barrier in the past. Justify.
Competency Based Que

Ans. The Himalayas together with other ranges have acted as a formidable physical barrier in the past because it was difficult to cross it. This isolation helped in shaping a unique regional identity in the Indian subcontinent. The Himalayas acted as a barrier which protects us from foreign invaders.

These ranges can be accessed through certain mountain passes such as the Khyber, the Bolan, the Shipkila and the Bomdila, etc.

Long Answer Type Questions

1. Explain the importance of the central location of India.

Ans The importance of central location of India can be seen through the following points

- India occupies a unique position on the globe and enjoys a unique closeness with Europe, Africa and Australia.
- Geographically, India has central location between East and West Asia.
- Indian ocean provides favourable route for international trade.
- The long coastline provides many deep and natural harbours.
- The water bodies on three sides of the Indian Peninsula help in the origin of monsoon.
- The Himalayan mountains act as a climatic barrier. It protects North India from polar cold winds and forces the monsoon winds to give rainfall.
- The Tropic of Cancer passes through the center of India. Therefore, North India enjoys the temperate climate, whereas South India experiences the tropical climate.

2. India has been endowed with unique physical diversity. Justify the statement.

Ans. India has been endowed with unique physical diversity such as

- The presence of high mountains in the North bounded by the Himalayas, the Hindukush, the Sulaiman, the Karakoram and the Purvachal hills.
- The large perennial rivers like the Ganga, the Yamuna, the Indus and the Brahmaputra of North India which are connected with most of the countries of the sub-continent.
- The plateau in South is bounded by hills such as the Vindhayas, the Satpura, the Eastern and the Western Ghats.
- Large rivers of the peninsular India form deltas, estuaries in the coastal plains. The vast sandy expanse of desert or *Marusthalies* in the West.
- The long coastline with island groups of Lakshadweep and Andaman and Nicobar.

3. Do you think that physical barrier is a hindrance in interaction with our neighbouring countries in modern times? Give some examples how we have overcome these difficulties in the present day.
Competency Based Que

Ans. No, physical barrier is not a hindrance in interaction with our neighbouring countries in modern times because of the development of transportation and communication systems. For example

- With the help of latest technologies it is possible to cross mountains like Himalayas by making tunnels and through passes e.g. Pir Panjal tunnel, Rohtang tunnel, Chennai-Nashri tunnel, the Bolan pass, the Shipkila pass, the Nathula pass, the Bomdila pass, etc. These are helpful to move to neighbouring countries.
- Through ships and ocean going vessels, it is possible to send and receive large cargoes of trade to and from India all over the world.
- Airways made it possible to cross difficult terrains like, deserts, forests and oceans. It is a fast going mode of transport which reduced time distance from many days or weeks to few hours.
- Besides these, communication system plays an important role to shorten long distance problems, as one can easily contact with another and also can do online trade and business through internet, satellite communication system, telephone, fax, etc.

4. Explain the significance of India's latitudinal and longitudinal extent. How does this affect the country's climate, soil, vegetation and landforms?

Ans. India's latitudinal and longitudinal extent plays a crucial role in shaping its climate, soil, vegetation and landforms. The country spans approximately 30 degrees of latitude, from 6°45′ N in the south to about 37° N in the north, and around 30 degrees of longitude, from 68°7′ E to 97°25′ E.

This vast span results in a diversity of climatic zones, ranging from the tropical climate in the south to the temperate and cold climate in the north, influencing the types of vegetation and landforms. The varied climate leads to diverse soils, from the alluvial soils of the Indo-Gangetic plains to the desert soils of Rajasthan.

The climatic differences also support a wide range of vegetation, including tropical forests, grasslands and temperate forests. The landforms are equally diverse, with the snow-capped Himalayas in the north, the fertile Ganga-Brahmaputra plains and the rugged Peninsular Plateau, contributing to the country's rich geographical diversity.

Source Based Questions

1 Read the passage carefully and answer the questions that follow.

The mainland of India, extends from Kashmir in the North to Kanniyakumari in the South and Arunachal Pradesh in the East to Gujarat in the West. India's territorial limit further extends towards the sea upto 12 nautical miles (about 21.9 km) from the coast. Our Southern boundary extends upto 6°45′ N latitude in the Bay of Bengal. The latitudinal and longitudinal extent of India are roughly about 30 degrees, whereas the actual distance measured from North to South extremity is 3,214 km, and that from East to West is only 2,933 km. This difference is based on the fact that the distance between two longitudes decreases towards the poles whereas the distance between two latitudes remains the same everywhere.

From the values of latitude, it is understood that the Southern part of the country lies within the tropics and the Northern part lies in the sub-tropical zone or the warm temperate zone. This location is responsible for large variations in land forms, climate, soil types and natural vegetation in the country. From the values of longitude, it is quite discernible that there is a variation of nearly 30 degrees, which causes a time difference of nearly two hours between the Easternmost and the Westernmost parts of our country. While the Sun rises in the North-Eastern states about two hours earlier as compared to Jaisalmer, the watches in Dibrugarh, Imphal in the East and Jaisalmer, Bhopal or Chennai in the other parts of India show the same time.

There is a general understanding among the countries of the world to select the standard meridian in multiples of 7°30′ of longitude. That is why 82°30' E has been selected as the 'standard meridian' of India. Indian Standard Time is ahead of Greenwich Mean Time by 5 hours and 30 minutes.

(i) **India's Southern boundary extends upto 6°45′N latitudes in the Bay of Bengal. India's territorial limit further extends upto .... from the coast.**

(a) 24 nautical miles (b) 12 nautical miles
(c) 36 nautical miles (d) 22 nautical miles

Ans (b) 12 nautical miles

(ii) **The landmass of India to the North of Tropic of Cancer lies in which of the following zones?**

(a) Tropical zone
(b) Equatorial zone
(c) Warm temperate zone
(d) Tundra zone

Ans (c) Warm temperate zone

(iii) **Why India chose 82°30′ E as the 'Standard Meridian'?**

(a) It is near the Greenwich longitude.
(b) Standard meridian is chosen as multiple of 7°30° ′ longitude.
(c) It is exact central meridian that passes through India.
(d) It crosses maximum states of India

Ans (b) Standard meridian is chosen as multiple of 7°30° longitude.

2. Read the passage carefully and answer the questions that follow.

The size of India has endowed her with great physical diversity. Thus, you may appreciate the presence of lofty mountains in the North; large rivers such as Ganga, Brahmaputra, Mahanadi, Krishna, Godavari and Kaveri; green forested hills in North-East and South India; and the vast sandy expanse of Marusthali. Bounded by the Himalayas in the North, Hindukush and Sulaiman ranges in the North-West, Purvachal hills in the North-East and by the large expanse of the Indian ocean in the South, it forms a great geographic entity known as the Indian sub-continent. It includes the countries — Pakistan, Nepal, Bhutan, Bangladesh and India. The Himalayas, together with other ranges, have acted as a formidable physical barrier in the past. Except for a few mountain passes such as the Khyber, the Bolan, the Shipkila, the Nathula, the Bomdila, etc. it was difficult to cross it. It has contributed towards the evolving of a unique regional identity of the Indian sub-continent. By referring to the physical map of India you can now describe the physical variations which you would come across while travelling from Kashmir to Kanniyakumari and from Jaisalmer in Rajasthan to Imphal in Manipur. Peninsular part of India extends towards the Indian Ocean. This has provided the country with a coastline of 6,100 km in the mainland and 7,517 km in the entire geographical coast of the mainland plus the island groups Andaman and Nicobar located in the Bay of Bengal and the Lakshadweep in the Arabian Sea. Thus India, as a country, is a physically diverse land providing occurrence of varied resources.

(i) **What geographical feature in the North of India acts as a physical barrier?**

Ans. The Himalayas in the North of India act as a physical barrier, isolating the Indian subcontinent from Central Asia and influencing its climate, culture and regional identity throughout history.

(ii) **How does India's geographical location affect its physical variations?**

Ans. India's diverse geographical location, from the Himalayas in the North to the Indian Ocean in the South, results in varied climates, landforms, vegetation and resources, contributing to its physical diversity.

(iii) **How did the Himalayas contribute to the regional identity of the Indian subcontinent?**

Ans. The Himalayas acted as a natural barrier, limiting external invasions and fostering unique regional cultures, languages, and traditions, thus shaping the distinct regional identity of the Indian subcontinent.

Map Based Question

1 Mark the following on the map of India.

(i) Latitudinal extent
(ii) Longitudinal extent
(iii) Standard Meridian
(iv) States through which Tropic of Cancer passes
(v) Southern most point of mainland of India

Ans.

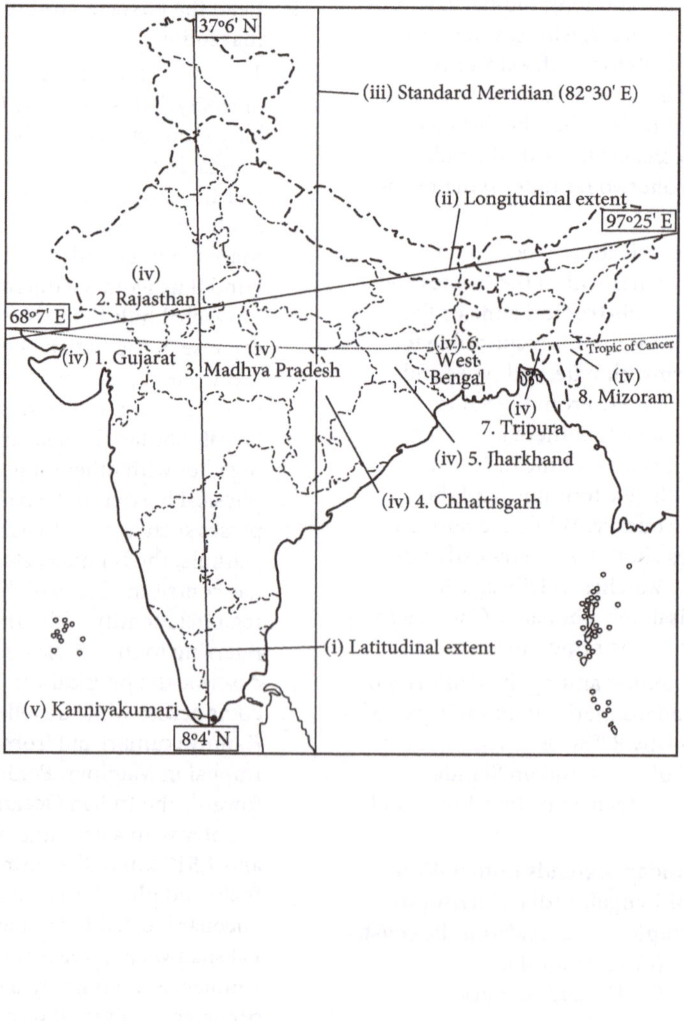

SELF ASSESSMENT TEST

Objective Type Questions

1. India lies entirely in which of the following hemisphere?
   (a) Northern (b) Southern
   (c) Eastern (d) Western
2. The actual distance of India from East to West extremity is
   (a) 2933 km (b) 3214 km
   (c) 4322 km (d) 3933 km
3. The IST stands for
   (a) Indian Space Terminal (b) Indian Standard Time
   (c) International Standard Time (d) None of these
4. Which of the following is/are the large rivers of India?
   I. Ganga II. Brahmaputra III. Mahanadi

   Codes
   (a) Only I (b) I and II
   (c) II and III (d) All of these
5. Match the following.

	List I		List II
A.	Southern boundary of India	1.	8°4′ N
B.	Standard Meridian of India	2.	82°30′ E
C.	Latitudinal value of the Tropic of Cancer	3.	23°30′ N
D.	World's land surface area of India	4.	2.4%

Codes

	A	B	C	D		A	B	C	D
(a)	1	2	3	4	(b)	4	3	2	1
(c)	3	2	4	1	(d)	1	3	4	2

Short Answer Type Questions

6. 'The North-South of India in kms is longer than the East-West extent.' Give reasons.
7. 'Two longitudes have a time difference of 4 minutes and India has a time difference of 120 minutes between its Eastern and Western ends.' Explain.
8. 'Indian farmers can grow a variety of crops.' Give reasons.

Long Answer Type Questions

9. Explain the importance of the central location of India.
10. Why do you think that physical barrier is not a hindrance in interaction with our neighbouring countries in modern times? Give some examples, how we can overcome these difficulties in the present day?

2

CHAPTER

Structure and Physiography

The Earth is approximately 4600 million years old. Over these years, it has undergone many changes due to endogenic and exogenic forces.
Due to these endogenic and exogenic forces and lateral movements of the plates, the present geological structure and geomorphologic processes in the Indian subcontinent came into existence.

YOUR STUDY GOALS

2.1 Geological Division of India
2.2 Physiography of India

YOUR PRACTICE GOALS

- Objective Type Questions (22 Qs ; MCQs, Matching, A-R)
- Subjective Questions (15 SAs, 4 LAs)
- Source Based Questions (4 Qs)
- Map Based Questions (6 Qs)

Over millions of years, the location of Indian plate was South of the equator. It was much larger in size and connected to Australia through Indian-Australian plate.

Later this broke into many parts and started to drift. The Australian plate moved towards the South-Eastern direction and the Indian plate to the North.

This Northward movement of the Indian plate is still active and it has significant consequences on the physical environment of the Indian subcontinent.

2.1 Geological Divisions of India

Based on the variations in India's geological structure and formations, India can be divided into three geological divisions

The Peninsular Block

- The Indian Peninsula is made up of metamorphic rocks and igneous rocks such as gneisses and granite.
- Since the **Cambrian period**[1], the Peninsula has been standing like a rigid block but some of its part like Western coast is submerged below the sea and some other parts changed due to tectonic activity.

1 **Cambrian period** It is a period (541-485 million years ago) when most of the major animal groups emerged, leading to a rapid diversification of life on Earth.

- As a part of the Indo-Australian Plate, it has been affected by various vertical movements and **block faulting**[2]. This faulting resulted in the formation of Narmada, the Tapi, the Mahanadi and the Satpura block mountains.
- This block is also called as a **Relict and Residual mountains** like the Aravali hills, the Nallamala hills, the Javadi hills, the Veliconda hills, the Palkonda range and the Mahendragiri hills.
- The Northern boundary of the Peninsular Block extends as an irregular line running from Kachchh along the Western side of the Aravali Range near Delhi and then run parallel to the Yamuna and the Ganga to the Rajmahal Hills and the Ganga delta.
- Apart from these, the Karbi Anglong and the Meghalaya Plateau in the North-East and Rajasthan in the West are also extensions of this block.
- The North-Eastern parts of the block are separated by the Malda fault in West Bengal from the Chotanagpur plateau.
- In Rajasthan, the desert and other desert-like features overlay this block.
- Most of the East flowing rivers form deltas before entering the Bay of Bengal. The deltas formed by the Mahanadi, the Krishna, the Kaveri and the Godavari are important examples.

The Himalayas and Other Peninsular Mountains

- The Himalayas along with other Peninsular mountains are young, weak and flexible in their geological structure unlike the rigid and stable Peninsular Block.
- These mountains are tectonic in origin, divided by fast-flowing rivers which are in their youthful stage.
- The geomorphic processes results in the development of faults, folds and thrust plains.

Indo-Ganga-Brahmaputra Plain

- This is the third geological division of Indian subcontinent. This was formed by the river Indus, Ganga and Brahmaputra.
- Originally, it was a geo-synclinal depression which was developed during the third phase of the Himalayan mountain formation approximately about **64 million years ago**.
- It has been gradually filled by the sediments brought by the Himalayan and Peninsular rivers. Average depth of alluvial deposits in these plains ranges from **1,000-2,000** m.

2.2 Physiography of India

- 'Physiography' of an area is the result of structure, process and the stage of development. India has great diversity in terms of physical features.
- There are significant variations among the different regions of India in terms of their geological structure. Variations in the physiography and relief are important among these.
- The relief and physiography of India has been greatly affected by the geological and geomorphological processes active in the Indian subcontinent.
- The North has a vast expanse of rugged topography, consisting of a series of mountain ranges with varied peaks, beautiful valleys and deep gorges.
- The South consists of stable table land with highly divided plateaus, eroded rocks and developed series of steep cliff. The vast North Indian plain lies between the Himalayas and Southern Plateau.

2 **Block Faulting** Block faulting is often associated with tectonic activity. When the crust breaks, some blocks of rock rise up while others drop down, creating a series of peaks and valleys.

- Based on these macro variations, India can be divided into the following physiographic divisions:
  1. The Northern and North-Eastern Mountains
  2. The Northern Plain
  3. The Peninsular Plateau
  4. The Indian Desert
  5. The Coastal Plains
  6. The Islands

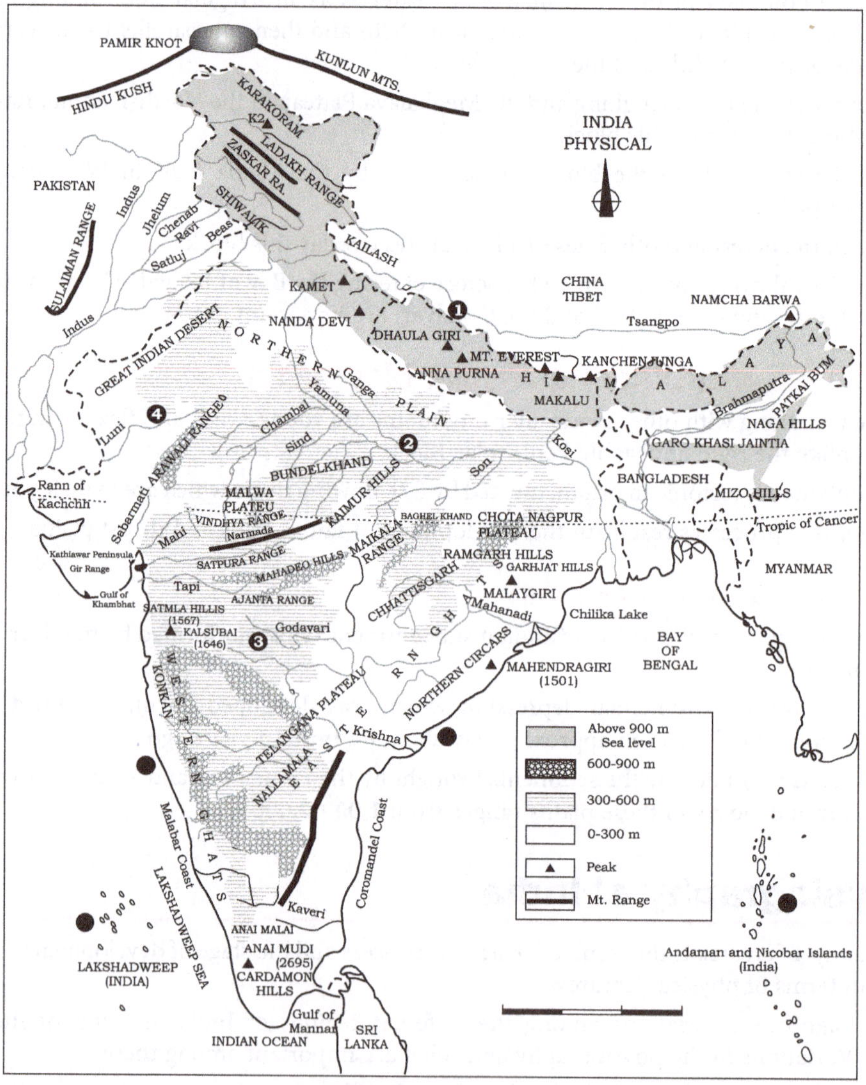

▲ *India : Physical*

The North and North-Eastern Mountains

- The North and North-Eastern mountains consist of the Himalayas and the North-Eastern hills. The Himalayas consist of a series of parallel mountain ranges.
- Some of the important ranges are the Greater Himalayan range, which includes the Great Himalayas and the Shiwalik.
- The general arrangement of these ranges is from **North-West** to the **South-East** direction in the North-Western part of India.

▲ *The Himalayas*

- Himalayas lies in the Darjiling and Sikkim regions in an East-West direction, while in Arunachal Pradesh they are from South-West to the North-West direction.
- In Nagaland, Manipur and Mizoram, they are in the North-South direction.
- The approximate length of the Great Himalayan range, also known as the **central axial range**, is 2,500 km from East to West and their width varies between 160-400 km from North to South.
- The Himalayas stand almost like a strong and long wall between the Indian subcontinent and the Central and East Asian countries.
- Himalayas are not only the physical barrier, they also act as climatic, drainage and cultural divide between India and its neighbouring countries.

Quick Test 1

1. What are the geological divisions of India?
2. In how many macro physiographic variations India can be divided?
3. What is the length of great Himalayan Mountain range?
4. Give examples of few landforms formed in the Himalayan region.

The Northern Plains

- The Northern Plains are formed by the alluvial deposits brought by the rivers the Indus, the Ganga and the Brahmaputra.

▲ *The Northern Plain*

- These plains extend approximately 3,200 km from East to West. The average width of these plains varies between 150-300 km.
- The maximum depth of alluvium deposits varies between 1,000-2,000 m.
- From North to South, these can be divided into three major zones: **the Bhabar, the Tarai** and **the alluvial plains**. The alluvial plains can be further divided into the **Khadar** and the **Bhangar**.

Bhabar

- It is a narrow belt ranging between 8-10 km parallel to the Shiwalik foothills at the break-up of the slope.
- As a result of this, the streams and rivers coming from the mountains deposit heavy materials of rocks and boulders and rivers disappear in this zone.

Tarai

- It lies in the South of Bhabar. It has width of 10-20 km.
- Here most of the streams and rivers re-emerge without having any properly defined channel and these creates marshy and swampy conditions.
- This region has dense growth of natural vegetation and variety of wildlife.

Bhangar and Khadar

- The South of Tarai is a belt consisting of old and new alluvial deposits known as the Bhangar and Khadar.

- These plains consist of erosional landforms like alluvial plains and depositional landforms such as sand bars, meanders, ox bow lakes and braided channels.
- Brahmaputra plains have large riverine islands and sand bars[3]. Most of these areas are subjected to periodic floods and shifting river courses forming braided streams[4].
- The mouths of these mighty rivers also form some of the largest deltas of the world, for example, the famous **Sundarbans delta**.
- Brahmaputra plains are featureless with a general elevation of 50-150 m above the mean sea level.
- The states of Haryana and Delhi form a water divide between the Indus and the Ganga river systems.
- The Brahmaputra river flows from the North-East to the South-West direction. It takes an almost 90° turn towards South at Dhubri before it enters Bangladesh.
- These river valley plains have a fertile alluvial soil cover which supports a variety of crops like wheat, rice, sugarcane and jute and hence, supports a large population.

The Peninsular Plateau

- The Peninsular plateau is the **irregular triangle** that rises from the height of 150 m above the river plains up to an elevation of 600-900 m.
- The Peninsular plateau extended to Jaisalmer in the West, where it has been covered by the longitudinal sand ridges and crescent-shaped sand dunes called **barchans**. This region has the presence of metamorphic rocks such as marble, slate, gneiss, etc.
- Delhi ridge in the North-West, (extension of Aravalis), the Rajmahal hills in the East, Gir range in the West and the Cardamom hills in the South are the outer extent of the Peninsular plateau.
- An extension of this is also seen in the North-East, in the form of Shillong and Karbi-Anglong plateau.
- The Peninsular India is made up of a series of patland plateaus such as the Hazaribagh plateau, the Palamu plateau, the Ranchi plateau, the Malwa plateau, the Coimbatore plateau and the Karnataka plateau, etc. This is one of the oldest and the most stable landmass of India.
- The general elevation of the plateau is from the West to East, which is also proved by the pattern of the flow of rivers.
- Some of the important physiographic features of this region are tors, block mountains, rift valleys, spurs, bare rocky structures, series of hills and wall-like quartzite dykes.
- The Western and North-Western part of the plateau have black soil.
- This Peninsular plateau has undergone through many phases of upliftment and submergence, accompanied by crustal faulting and fractures. The **Bhima fault** is special example because of its regenerated seismic activities.
- The North-Western part of the plateau has a complex relief of ravines[5] and gorges[6]. The ravines of Chambal, Bhind and Morena are some of the well-known examples.
- Based on the prominent relief features, the Peninsular plateau can be divided into three broad groups: The Deccan Plateau, the Central Highlands and the Northern Plateau.

i. The Deccan Plateau

- This is bordered by the Western Ghats in the West, Eastern Ghats in the East and the Satpura, Maikal range and Mahadeo hills in the North.
- Western Ghats are locally known by different names such as **Sahyadri** in Maharashtra, **Nilgiri hills** in Karnataka and Tamil Nadu, and **Anaimalai hills** and **Cardamom hills** in Kerala.

---

3 Sand bars It is a ridge of sand or sediments that forms in a body of water such as a river, lake, lagoon, etc.
4 Braided streams It is the structure made by multiple channels of rivers that joins together in the form of braids.
5 Ravines It is a landform that is narrower than a canyon but larger than gullies.
6 Gorges It is a narrow, steep-sided valley that is usually formed by a river cutting through mountains or hills.

- Western Ghats are higher in elevation and more continuous than the Eastern Ghats. Their average elevation is about 1,500 m with the height increasing from North to South.
- **Anaimudi** (2,695 m) is the highest peak of Peninsular plateau which is located on the Anaimalai hills of the Western Ghats followed by **Dodabetta** (2,637 m) on the Nilgiri hills.
- Most of the Peninsular rivers have their origin in the Western Ghats. Eastern Ghats are highly eroded by the rivers such as the Mahanadi, the Godavari, the Krishna, the Kaveri, etc.
- Some of the important ranges include the Javadi hills, the Palconda range, the Nallamala hills, the Mahendragiri hills, etc.
- The Eastern and the Western Ghats meet each other at the Nilgiri hills.

ii. The Central Highlands

- They are bounded to the West by the Aravali range.
- The Satpura range is formed by a series of eroded plateaus on the South, generally at an elevation varying between 600-900 m above the mean sea level. This forms the Northernmost boundary of the Deccan plateau. It is an example of the relict mountains which are highly denuded and form discontinuous ranges.
- The general elevation of the Central Highlands ranges between 700-1,000 m above the mean sea level and it slopes towards the North and North-Eastern directions.
- Most of the tributaries of the river Yamuna have their origin in the Vindhyan and Kaimur ranges.
- **Banas** is the only significant tributary of the river Chambal that originates from the Aravali in the Western ranges.
- An Eastern extension of the Central Highland is formed by the Rajmahal hills. Towards South of Rajmahal hills lies a large reserve of minerals in the Chotanagpur plateau.

iii. The North-Eastern Plateau

- It is an extension of the main Peninsular plateau.
- It is believed that due to the force exerted by the North-Eastward movement of the Indian plate at the time of the Himalayan origin, a huge fault was created between the Rajmahal hills and the Meghalaya plateau.
- Later, this depression got filled up by the deposition activity of the numerous rivers.
- Today, the Meghalaya and Karbi Anglong plateau are seperated from the main Peninsular Block.
- The Meghalaya plateau is further sub-divided into three:

  (i) The Garo Hills; (ii) The Khasi Hills; (iii) The Jaintia Hills
- These are named after the tribal groups inhabiting this region. An extension of this is also seen in the Karbi Anglong hills of Assam.
- Like the Chotanagpur plateau, the Meghalaya plateau is also rich in mineral resources like coal, iron ore, sillimanite, limestone and uranium.
- This area receives maximum rainfall from the South-West monsoon. As a result, the Meghalaya plateau has a highly eroded surface.
- Cherrapunji is covered with a bare rocky surface with the absence of any permanent vegetation cover.

Quick Test 2

1. Name the hill that form the Western and Eastern edge of the Deccan Plateau.
2. Where is Eastern extention of central highlands marked?
3. What is the highest peak of Western Ghats?
4. Which two plateaus are detached from the mainland of Peninsular Plateaus?

The Indian Desert

▲ *The Indian Desert*

- It lies to the North-West of the Aravali hills. It is a land of undulating topography dotted with longitudinal dunes and *barchans*.
- This region receives low rainfall below 150 mm per year and hence, it has arid climate with low vegetation cover. It is because of these characteristic features that this is also known as ***Marusthali***.
- The evidence available at wood fossils park at Aakal and marine deposits around Brahmsar, near Jaisalmer shows that during the Mesozoic era, this region was under the sea.
- The rock structure of the desert is an extension of the Peninsular plateau but due to extreme arid conditions, its surface features have been carved by physical weathering and wind actions.
- Some of the desert land features present here are mushroom rocks, shifting dunes and oasis[7] (mostly in its Southern part).
- Based on the arrangement, the desert can be divided into two parts:
  (i) The Northern part is sloping towards Sindh. (ii) The Southern towards the Rann of Kachchh.
- Most of the rivers in this region are ephemeral[8]. For example, the Luni river flowing in the Southern part of the desert.
- Low precipitation and high evaporation make Indian Desert a water deficit region.
- There are some streams which disappear after flowing for some distance and present a typical case of inland drainage by joining a lake or playa[9].
- The lakes and the playas have brackish water which is the main source of obtaining salt.

The Coastal Plains

- Based on the location and active geomorphological processes, coastal plains can be broadly divided into two

(i) The Western Coastal Plains

- The Western coastal plains are an example of submerged coastal plain.
- It is believed that the city of Dwaraka which was once a part of the Indian mainland, situated along the West coast is submerged under water. Because of this submergence, it is a narrow belt and provides natural conditions for the development of ports and harbours.

▲ *Coastal Plains*

- Kandla, Mazagaon, JLN Port Nhava Sheva, Marmagao, Mangalore, Cochin, etc are some of the important natural ports located along the West coast.
- The Western coast, extending from the Gujarat coast in the North to the Kerala coast in the South, may be divided into following divisions
  - The Kachchh and Kathiawar coast in Gujarat
  - Konkan coast in Maharashtra
  - Goan coast and Malabar coast in Karnataka and Kerala.
- The Western coastal plains are narrow in the middle and get broader towards North and South. The rivers flowing through this coastal plain do not form any delta.
- The Malabar coast has distinguishing features in the form of Kayals[10] (backwaters), which are used for fishing, inland navigation and due to its special attraction for tourists.
- Every year the famous **Nehru Trophy Vallamkali** (boat race) is held in Punnamada Kayal in Kerala.

---

7 **Oasis** It is an area made fertile by the source of fresh water in an otherwise desert area.
8 **Ephemeral** The rivers that doesn't flow all year long, but only for short time after rainstorm.
9 **Playa** It is flat, dry area in a desert which was once covered by a temporary lake but has dried up.
10 **Kayals** Backwaters or lakes on the coast of Malabar.

(ii) The Eastern Coastal Plains

- The Eastern coastal plain is broader and is an example of an emergent coast. There are well developed deltas here which are formed by the rivers flowing Eastward into the Bay of Bengal.
- These include the deltas of the Mahanadi, the Godavari, the Krishna and the Kaveri. Because of its emergent nature, it has less number of ports and harbours.
- The continental shelf extends up to 500 km into the sea, which makes it difficult for the development of good ports and harbours.

The Islands

There are two major island groups in India, one in the Bay of Bengal and the other in the Arabian Sea.

The Bay of Bengal Island groups

- The Bay of Bengal Island groups consist of about **572 islands/islets**. These are situated roughly between 6°N-14°N and 92°E -94°E.

▲ *An Island*

- The entire group of islands is divided into two broad categories - the **Andaman** in the North and the **Nicobar** in the South.
- Some important mountain peaks in Andaman and Nicobar Islands are Saddle peak (North Andaman - 738 m), Mount Diavolo (Middle Andaman - 515 m), Mount Koyob (South Andaman - 460 m) and Mount Thuiller (Great Nicobar - 642 m).
- The two principal groups of islets[11] include the **Ritchie's archipelago** and the **Labrynth island**. They are separated by a waterbody which is called the **Ten-degree channel**. It is believed that these islands are an elevated portion of submarine mountains.
- Some smaller islands are volcanic in origin. Barren island, the only active volcano in India is also situated in the Nicobar Islands.
- The coastal line has some coral deposits and beautiful beaches. These islands receive convectional rainfall and have an equatorial type of vegetation.

The Islands of the Arabian Sea

- The islands of the Arabian sea include Lakshadweep and Minicoy.
- These are spread between 8°N-12°N and 71°E -74°E longitude. These islands are located at a distance of 220 km-440 km off the Kerala coast.
- The entire island group is built of coral deposits. There are approximately **36 islands** of which 11 are inhabited.
- Minicoy is the largest island with an area of 453 sq. km.
- The entire group of islands is broadly divided by the **Nine-degree channel**, North of which is the Amini Island and to the South of the Cannanore Island.
- The Islands of this archipelago have storm beaches[12] consisting of unconsolidated pebbles, shingles, cobbles and boulders on the Eastern seaboard.

Quick Test 2

1. Name three major ports of Western Coastal Plains.
2. What is the total extent of the Coastal plains?
3. What is the main source of salt in the desert regions?
4. Name two islands of the Arabian Sea.

---

11 **Islets** Very small islands that are generally uninhabited.

12 **Storm Beaches** Storm beaches are often steep, with a slope of up to 45°. They're made of rounded cobbles, shingle and sometimes sand.

Mind Map

The Peninsular Block
- It is made up of metamorphic and igneous rocks, e.g., geneisses, granite.
- Northern boundary of the Peninsular Block extends as an irregular line running from Kachchh along the Western side of the Aravali Range near Delhi and then run parallel to the Yamuna and the Ganga to the Rajmahal Hills and the Ganga delta.
- North-Eastern parts of the block are separated by the Malda fault.

Indo-Ganga Brahmaputra Plains
- These are formed by the deposits of river Indus, Ganga and Brahmaputra.
- Gradually filled by the sediments brought by the Himalayan and Peninsular rivers.
- The average depth of alluvial deposits in these plains ranges from 1,000-2,000 m.

1 Geological Division of India
This division is based on the geological structure and formation of India.

The Himalayas and Other Mountains
- These are of tectonic origin, divided by fast flowing rivers.
- These are young, weak and flexible in their geological structure.

STRUCTURE AND PHYSIOGRAPHY

The Northern Plains
Formed by the alluvial deposits from Indus, Ganga and Brahmaputra.
- **Bhabar** It is a narrow belt ranging between 8-10 km parallel to the Shiwalik foothills.
- **Tarai** It lies in the South of Bhabar and has width of 10-20 km. This region has dense growth of natural vegetation and variety of wildlife.
- **Bhangar and Khadar** (Old and new alluvial deposits respectively)These plains consist of erosional landforms like alluvial plains and depositional landforms,(e.g. sand, bars, meanders, ox bow lakes).

The Peninsular Plateau
- Oldest and most stable landmass of India. It extended to Jaisalmer in the West, where it has been covered by the longitudinal sand ridges and crescent-shaped sand dunes(barchans).
- **The Deccan Plateau** This is bordered by the Western Ghats in the West, Eastern Ghats in the East and the Satpura, Maikal range and Mahadeo hills in the North.
- **The Central Highlands** They are bounded to the West by the Aravali range.
- **The North-Eastern Plateau** It is an extension of the main Peninsular plateau.

2 Physiography of India

The North and North-Eastern Mountains
- Consists of Himalayas and North-Eastern hills.
- Important Himalayan ranges are Great Himalayas, Middle Himalayas, Shiwaliks.

The Islands
- The Arabian Sea Island Group
- The Bay of Bengal Island Group

The Coastal Plains
Long coastline that runs along Bay of Bengal and Arabian Sea.
- **The Western Coastal plains** These are an example of submerged coastal plain. They are narrow in the middle and get broader towards North and South. The rivers flowing through this coastal plain do not form any delta.
- **The Eastern Coastal plains** It is an example of an emergent coast. The continental shelf extends up to 500 km into the sea. It is broader and contains well developed deltas.

The Indian Desert
- Lies to the North-West of Aravali hills.
- Receives rainfall below 150 mm per year.
- Irregular topography consisting of sand dunes and barchans, e.g., Rann of Kutch, Jaisalmer.

NCERT Folder

Choose the right answer from the four alternatives given below

(i) Which one of the water bodies separates the Andaman from the Nicobar?

(a) 11° Channel (b) Gulf of Mannar
(c) 10° Channel (d) Andaman Sea

Ans. (c) 10° Channel

(ii) On which of the following hill range is the 'Dododabetta' peak situated?

(a) Nilgiri hills (b) Anaimalai hills
(c) Cardamom hills (d) Nallamala hills

Ans. (a) Nilgiri hills

Answer the following questions in about 30 words

(i) If a person is to travel to Lakshadweep, from which coastal plain does he prefer and why?

Ans. If a person is to travel to Lakshadweep, he will prefer the Southern part of Western Coastal Plain. This is because Lakshadweep is very close to the Kerala coast, about 280-480 km off the coast.

(ii) Where in India will you find a cold desert? Name some important ranges of this region.

Ans. A cold desert in India is Leh-Ladakh which is found in Kashmir Himalayas. It lies between the Greater Himalayas and the Karakoram ranges. The important ranges in this region are Zaskar, Ladakh, Karakoram and Pir Panjal.

(iii) Why is the Western Coastal Plain devoid of any delta?

Ans. The Western Coastal Plain is devoid of any delta because several fast flowing rivers originating from the Western Ghats do not have much sediments to deposit as they flow on hard rocky surface.

Answer the following questions in not more than 125 words

(i) Make a comparison of island groups of the Arabian Sea and the Bay of Bengal.

Ans. Differences between the island groups of the Arabian Sea and the Bay of Bengal are as follows

Basis	Islands of the Arabian Sea (Lakshadweep)	Islands of the Bay of Bengal (Andaman and Nicobar)
Number of Islands	There are approximately 36 islands.	They consist of about 572 islands.
Location	They are located between 8° N to 12° N latitudes and 71° E to 74° E longitudes.	They are situated between 6° N to14° N latitudes and 92° E to 94° E longitudes.
Origin	These islands are built of coral deposits.	These are mainly formed by volcanic activities.
Beaches	Beaches on the coast consist of shingles pebbles, cobbles, boulders, etc.	Some coastline beaches are very beautiful made up of coral deposits.
Parts	Minicoy is the largest island which is known for its tourist attraction.	They have a volcanic island i.e. Barren Island (active volcano).
Separation	The group of island is divided by 11° channel, North of which is Amini island and South is Cannanore island.	The water body separating Andaman and Nicobar islands is 10° channel.
Distance	These islands lie opposite to the coast of Kerala in Arabian Sea approximately at a distance of 280-240 km.	It lies 1200 km far away from mainland in the Bay of Bengal.

(ii) What are the important geomorphological features found in the river valley plains?

Ans. The geomorphological (land) features found in the river valley plains are stated according to the size of sediments and their areas of deposition. These features are discussed below

Bhabar

A narrow belt of 8-16 km wide along the foot hills of the Shiwalik from the Indus to the Tista, comprising of pebbles and boulders, where almost all streams disappear is known as Bhabar.

The Tarai

It lies parallel to Bhabar in its South, made up of smaller sediments where streams and rivers re-appear, turning a large area into marshy and swampy land known as Tarai region.

The Alluvial Plain

It is divided into following types

(i) **Bhangar** It is an area of old alluvium deposited above the level of the flood plains. It is not so fertile due to presence of kankar deposits.

(ii) **Khadar** The flood plain which has new alluvium is called Khadar. It is the most fertile layer suitable for intensive agriculture, as it is replenished every year after the floods.

Some other geomorphological features found in the plains formed by the running water are alluvial fans, flood plains, sand bars, meanders, ox-bow lakes, braided streams, etc.

(iii) If you move from Badrinath to Sunderbans delta along the course of the river Ganga, what major geomorphological features will you come across?

Ans If we move from Badrinath to Sunderbans delta along the course of the river Ganga, we will come across the following major geomorphological features:

- **Gorge** It is a narrow valley between hills or mountains, typically with steep rocky walls and a stream running through it.
- **Canyon** A canyon is characterised by steep step-like side slopes and may be as deep as a gorge. A canyon is wider at its top than at its bottom. In fact, a canyon is a variant of gorge.
- **Waterfall** When the rivers start falling in pits in mountainous regions, they make waterfall.
- **V Shaped Valleys** Valleys start as small and narrow rills; the rills will gradually develop into long and wide gullies; the gullies will fur̀ther deepen, widen and lengthen to give rise to valleys.
- **Plunge Pools** At the foot of waterfalls large potholes, quite deep and wide, form because of the sheer impact of water and rotation of boulders. Such large and deep holes at the base of waterfalls are called plunge pools.

Exam Pattern Questions

Objective Type Questions

Multiple Choice Questions (MCQs)

1. Over million of years ago, Indian plate was in which direction with respect to the Equator?

(a) South
(b) North
(c) Exactly on the Equator
(d) None of the above

2. Which of the following is the example of relict and residual mountains of India?

(a) Aravalli hills (b) Javadi hills
(c) Nallamala hills (d) All of these

3. Choose from the following, the East flowing rivers of the Peninsular block.

(a) Mahanadi (b) Krishna
(c) Kaveri (d) All of these

4. Which one of the following does not indicate that Peninsular Block is an ancient landmass? CBSE Diksha

(a) The rift valleys of the river Narmada
(b) Residuals mountains
(c) Deep narrow valleys of the rivers
(d) The gneisses and granites rock masses

5. Which of the following ports is located on the Western coastal plains?

(a) Nhava Sheva (b) Tuticorin
(c) Chennai (d) All of these

6. The Eastern and Western Ghats converge at which of the following range?

(a) Patkai hills (b) Garo hills
(c) Nilgiri hills (d) Rajmahal hills

7. What is the latitudinal extent of the Andaman and Nicobar Island?

(a) 6°N-20°N (b) 6°N-14°N
(c) 20°N-23°N (d) 14°N-18°N

8. The North-Eastern part plateau regions are separated from the main Chotanagpur plateau by CBSE Diksha

(a) The Ganga river (b) Garo Hills
(c) Malda Fault (d) Dun Valley

9. The Himalayas are different from Peninsular Block due to which one of the following reasons? CBSE Diksha

(a) Young geological structure and volcanic peaks
(b) Rounded hills and pointed summit
(c) Weak and flexible structure
(d) Stable and rigid landmass

10. **Choose the correct statement from the following.**

I. The Indian Peninsula is made up of metamorphic rocks.
II. The Indian Peninsula is made up of igneous rocks.
III. The Indian Peninsula is made up of rocks like granite.
IV. The Indian Peninsula is made up of sedimentary rocks.

Options

(a) I, II, III (b) I and II
(c) II and IV (d) All of these

11. **Consider the following statement about Indo-Ganga Brahmaputra and choose the incorrect one.**

I. This is one of the geological divisions of Indian subcontinent.
II. This is formed by the river Indus, Ganga and Yamuna.
III. Average depth of Alluvial deposits in these plains ranges from 1,000-2,000 m.

Options

(a) Only I (b) I and II (c) Only III (d) Only II

12. **Consider the following about the Great Indian Desert and choose the option which is correct?**

I. It lies to the West of Aravali hills.
II. It is covered with Barchans.
III. It has tropical semi-evergreen climate.

Codes

(a) I and II (b) I and III
(c) II and III (d) I, II and III

13. **Due to which of the following processes/forces, the geological structure and geomorphological processes came into existence in the Indian subcontinent?**

I. Endogenic Force
II. Exogenic Force
III. Lateral movements of the plates

Codes

(a) I and II (b) Only III
(c) I and III (d) All of these

14. **Consider the following statements regarding the Great Indian Desert and choose the correct one.**

I. It lies to the South-West of the Aravali hills.
II. This region receives low rainfall below 90 mm per year.
III. The Luni river flowing in the Southern part of the desert.
IV. The rock structure of the desert is an extension of the Peninsular plateau.

Options

(a) Only I (b) I and II
(c) III and IV (d) All of these

15. **Consider the following statements regarding the island groups of Arabian Sea and choose the incorrect one.**

I. The islands of the Arabian Sea include Lakshadweep and Minicoy.
II. Minicoy is the largest island with an area of 453 sq. km.
III. The entire group of islands is broadly divided by the ten-degree channel.

Options

(a) I and II (b) II and III (c) Only III (d) Only I

16. **Identify the type of Alluvial plain from the given description.**

These plains consist of features of mature stage of fluvial erosional and depositional landforms such as sand bars, meanders, ox bow lakes and braided channels. These lies to the South of Tarai and consisting of old and new Alluvial deposits.

Options

(a) Bhangar and Khadar (b) Bhabar
(c) Tarai (d) Brahmaputra Plain

Arrange the Following

17. **Arrange the following division of Indian Physiography from North to South.**

(i) North Plains (ii) Himalayas
(iii) Peninsular plateau (iv) Islands of India

Codes

(a) (ii), (i), (iii), (iv) (b) (iv), (iii), (ii), (i)
(c) (i), (ii), (iii), (iv) (d) (ii), (i), (iv), (iii)

Match the Following

18.

	List I (Peaks)		List II (Hill Region)
A.	Mahendragiri	1.	Eastern Ghats
B.	Anaimudi	2.	North Andaman
C.	Everest	3.	Himalayas
D.	Saddle	4.	Western Ghats

Codes

	A	B	C	D		A	B	C	D
(a)	2	1	4	3	(b)	1	4	3	2
(c)	1	4	2	3	(d)	2	1	3	4

19.

	List I		List II
A.	The North and North-Eastern Mountains	1.	Formed by the Alluvial deposits
B.	The Northern Plain	2.	Shiwalik
C.	The Peninsular Plateau	3.	Irregular triangle
D.	The Indian Desert	4.	Mushroom rocks

Codes

	A	B	C	D		A	B	C	D
(a)	2	1	3	4	(b)	1	4	3	2
(c)	4	3	2	1	(d)	3	2	1	4

20.

List I		List II	
A.	Bhabar	1.	It lies in the South of Bhabar
B.	Tarai	2.	Runs 8-10 km parallel to the Shiwalik foothills
C.	Bhangar	3.	Bordered by the Western Ghats in the West
D.	Deccan plateau	4.	Consisting of old and new alluvial deposits

Codes

	A	B	C	D		A	B	C	D
(a)	2	1	4	3	(b)	1	2	3	4
(c)	3	4	2	1	(d)	2	3	1	4

Assertion-Reason

Directions (Q. Nos. 21-22) In the questions given below are two statements labelled as Assertion (A) and other is labelled as Reason (R). In the context of two statements which one of the following is correct?

Codes

(a) Both A and R are true, but R is not the correct explanation of A

(b) Both A and R are true and R is the correct explanation of A

(c) Both A and R are incorrect

(d) A is correct, but R is incorrect

21. **Assertion** (A) The Indian desert is ephemeral.

Reason (R) The Indian desert receives low rainfall and has high temperature along with arid climate.

22. **Assertion** (A) The Northern plains of India are made of alluvial soil.

Reason (R) This soil is brought by the rivers making the plains highly fertile for agriculture.

Answers

1. (a) South
2. (d) All of these
3. (d) All of these
4. (c) Deep narrow valleys of the rivers
5. (a) Nhava Sheva
6. (c) Nilgiri hills
7. (b) 6°N–14°N
8. (c) Malda Fault
9. (c) Weak and flexible structure
10. (a) I, II, III
11. (d) Only II
12. (a) I and II
13. (d) All of these
14. (b) I and II
15. (c) Only III
16. (a) Bhangar and Khadar
17. (a) (ii), (i), (iii), (iv)
18. (b)
19. (a)
20. (a)
21. (b) Both A and R are true and R is the correct explanation of A
22. (b) Both A and R are true and R is the correct explanation of A

Subjective Questions

Short Answer Type Questions

1. Briefly describe the Indo-Ganga- Brahmaputra Plain.

Ans The Indo-Ganga-Brahmaputra Plain was formed by the river Indus, the Ganga and the Brahmaputra. It was a geo-synclinal depression or a shallow low lying area.

The depression was gradually filled by the sediments brought by the Himalayan and Peninsular rivers to form the plain area. It has an average thickness of 1000-2000 m. The relief and physiography of India has been greatly influenced by geological and geomorphological processes resulting in diverse physical features such as the Indo-Ganga-Brahmaputra Plain.

2. How were the Northern Plains formed? Briefly describe the extent of the Northern Plains.

Ans **Formation of the Northern Plains**

The Northern Plains have been formed by the alluvial deposits or the sediments brought by the rivers, such as the Indus, the Ganga and the Brahmaputra along with their tributaries.

Extent of the Northern Plains

The approximate length of the plain from the East to the West is 3200 km, width of its alluvial deposits varies between 150-300 km, maximum depth of its alluvial deposits varies between 1000-2000 m.

According to the size of sediments deposited from North to South, the Northern Plain can be divided into the following three zones

(i) Bhabar Zone (ii) Tarai Zone

(iii) Alluvial Plains

3. The Peninsular plateau has undergone various phases of upliftment and submergence, which has contributed to the formation of its present features. Discuss the important features of the Peninsular Plateau. Competency Based Que

Ans. The Peninsular plateau of India has undergone various phases of upliftment and submergence, which has contributed to the formation of its present features.

The important features of the Peninsular plateau are as follows

- It is the oldest and the most stable landmass of India with the outer extent of Delhi ridge in the North-West, Rajmahal hills in the East, Gir range in the West and Cardamom hills in the South.
- The Peninsular plateau is made up of a series of patland plateaus (made up of lava deposits) such as the Hazaribagh, the Palamu, the Ranchi, the Malwa, the Coimbatore and the Karnataka plateaus.
- The elevation of the plateau is between 600-900 m from the West to the East, which is proven by the flow of rivers towards the Bay of Bengal.

4. The Central Highlands is an example of the old and relict mountains. Briefly describe the features of the central highlands. Competency Based Que

Ans. The central highlands are a part of the Peninsular plateau of India. The features of this region are

- They are relict (old) mountains and are highly denuded (eroded). They form discontinuous ranges.
- They are bounded to the West by Aravalis, and to the South by Satpura range.
- They are extended in the West till Jaisalmer where it is covered by sand dunes and barchans.
- The general elevation of central highlands is 700-1000m.
- An Eastern extension of central highlands is formed by Rajmahal hills.
- Important rivers flowing in this region are Banas and Chambal.

5. Explain the islands of India located in the Bay of Bengal.

Ans The Andaman and Nicobar islands are located in the Bay of Bengal. The features of the islands of India located in the Bay of Bengal are

- They are about 572 islands/islets. They are situated between 6°N-14°N and 6°E-14°E.
- This group of island is divided into Andaman islands in the North and Nicobar islands in the South Nicobar. These two groups are separated from each other by the ten degree channel.
- The Bay of Bengal islands are believed to be volcanic in origin.
- They are also considered as elevated portions of the submarine mountain.
- Barren island, the only active volcano is located in the Nicobar islands.

6. Distinguish between Bhabar and Tarai.

Ans Differences between Bhabar and Tarai are as follows

Basis	Bhabar	Tarai
Location	It lies parallel to foothills of Shiwalik.	It lies in the South of the Bhabar belt.
Width	It is 8-10 km wide.	It is 10-20 km wide.
Rivers	Streams and rivers disappear in this zone due to covering of this region by heavy materials of rocks and boulders.	Rivers in this zone re-emerge without having demarcated channels making it swampy and marshy.
Vegetation	It is not suitable for growth of vegetation and agriculture.	It is suitable for thick growth of natural vegetation and varied wildlife.

7. Distinguish between the Northern Plains and Coastal Plains.

Ans. Differences between the Northern Plains and Coastal Plains are as follows

Basis	Northern Plains	Coastal Plains
Location	They are located on the foot hills of Himalayas.	They are located along the Arabian Sea and the Bay of Bengal.
Divisions	They are divided as the Bhabhar, Tarai and Alluvial plains.	They are divided as the Konkan plains, Goan plains, Malabar plains, North Circar and Coromandel plains.
Characteristics	Important characteristics of these plains are riverine islands and sandbars.	Important characteristics of these plains are ports, harbours and kayals (backwaters).

8. Distinguish between Bhangar and Khadar.

Ans. Differences between Bhangar and Khadar are as follows

Basis	Bhangar	Khadar
Composition	It is composed of old alluvium deposits.	It is composed of new alluvium deposits.
Agriculture	It is not much suited for agriculture.	It is suitable for agriculture.
Fertility of Soil	It is less fertile due to concretion (kankar) in it.	It is the most fertile soil due to new layer of alluvium deposits every year.

9. Why we see a smaller number of ports on the Eastern coastal plain in comparison to Western coastal plain? **CBSE Diksha**

Ans Western coastal plain is a kind of submerged coastal plain and the Eastern part of this coastal plain is an emergent coast. Due to this reason, the Eastern coast has a shallow, wide continental shelf, which makes it difficult to develop ports and harbours on the Eastern Coastal plain.

On the other hand rivers on Western coast forms estuaries and provide natural harbours. Hence, there are more ports found Western coastal plains the than Eastern coastal plains.

10. Why are the Himalayan mountains considered as weak and unstable in its youthful stage?

Ans According to the Geological history, the youthfull Himalayan mountains have been formed recently. These have been formed by the collusion of Eurasian and Indian tectonic plates. They are still subjected to an interplay of exogenic and endogenic forces acting upon them. Due to these forces, a number of faults, folds and thrust plains are formed in the Himalayas. These features result in instability and weak structure of the Himalayas.

Thus, in its youthful stage, the Himalayas are considered as weak and unstable which also leads to a number of hazards like landslides in the Himalayan regions.

11. Write a brief description of the physiography of India.

Ans India is characterised by great diversity in its physical features which are

- In the North, it has vast expanse of rugged (uneven) topography consisting of a series of mountain ranges with high peaks, beautiful valleys and deep gorges.
- In the South, it has stable table land with highly dissected plateaus, denuded rocks and developed series of scarps.
- In between these two, lies the vast North-Indian plain formed by the sediments of many large rivers.
- The islands of India in the Bay of Bengal and the Arabian sea have been formed by millions of years of geological processes.

12. What activities do the people living in different physical divisions need to do for the development or growth of the country?

Ans India is bestowed with a variety of physical divisions such as high mountains, low hills, desert, fertile plains, long coastline and plateaus. They are rich in different resources but no region has all the resources available there or is self-sufficient. The people of Himalayas depend for food and minerals on plains and plateaus whereas source of water is in mountains and hills. For fishing and international trade, people need to depend on the coasts.

Thus, for overall growth and development of the country, people of different regions need to help and cooperate, respect others and their resources, exchange resources, goods, knowledge, technology support, at the time of crisis to maintain peace and harmony.

13. Northern plains are important for Indian economy. Explain Why? **Competency Based Que**

Ans The importance of Northern plains for Indian economy are as follows

- The plain is made up of the alluvial soil brought down by the rivers. This soil is very soft and fertile. Major crops such as wheat, rice, sugarcane, pulses, oilseeds and jute are grown here. This plain is also called the food bowl of India.
- The plain is soft, level and flat. Therefore, wells, tubewells and canals can be dug for irrigation. Due to proper irrigation, this regions is the largest producer of foodgrains in india.
- The plain is very important for the economic development in India. This plain has a network of roads and railway as well for the development of various industries.
- This is one of the most thickly populated plains of the world., providing a significant labour force for various industries and services.

14 What is the significance of the Peninsular plateau in India's structure?

Ans. The Peninsular plateau is a fundamental part of India's structure, it is one of the oldest and most stable landmasses. Peninsular plateau is significant in India's structure due to

- Its geological stability, rich mineral resources and variety of landforms like the Deccan Plateau, Vindhyan Range and Western and Eastern Ghats make it economically and geographically significant.
- The plateau has a hard rock foundation that is less susceptible to seismic activity, ensuring geological stability.

- They provide water for irrigation to the vast region of the plateau. Major rivers such as the Godavari, Krishna and Kaveri flow across it.

15 **'The Himalayas play an important role for the entire Indian subcontinent'. Discuss.** Competency Based Que

Ans The role of the Himalayas for the entire Indian subcontinent can be seen through the following points

- The Himalayan mountains separate India from the rest of the Asian continent and give it a unique identity known as the subcontinent.
- Most of the neighbouring countries can be travelled due presence of passes in the Himalayan mountains.
- The mountains check the cold Siberian winds and the wet South-Western monsoon winds and save India from being a cold and dry desert.
- The Perennial and large rivers of the Himalayas are the source of water, affecting all economic activities such as agriculture, irrigation, industrial growth, generation of hydel power, inland water transportation, etc.

Long Answer Type Questions

1. **Write the main differences between the two edges of the Deccan plateau.**

Ans Two edges that form the East-West extent of the Deccan plateau are the Western Ghats and the Eastern Ghats

Basis	The Western Ghats	The Eastern Ghats
Location	The Western Ghats form continuous chain from Maharashtra to Kanniyakumari.	The Eastern Ghats form a discontinuous chain of low hills from Odisha to the Nilgiri hills.
Altitude	They have an average altitude of 1500 m.	They have an average altitude between 600-900 m.
Hills	Sahyadri, Nilgiri, Anaimalai and Cardamom hills form the Western Ghats.	Some important ranges are Javadi, Palconda, Nallamala and Mahendragiri.
Highest Peak	The highest peaks are Anaimudi (2,695 m) and Dodabeta (2,637 m) in these ghats.	Mahendragiri (1,501 m) is the highest peak in these ghats.
Rivers	The Western Ghats are the important source of many large rivers like Mahanadi, Godawari, etc.	No rivers originate from these Ghats.

2. **Indian desert is an important physiographic division of India in terms of location and features. Discuss.** Competency Based Que

Ans. **Location**

The Great Indian desert or Thar desert lies to the North-West of the Aravali hills. It is a land of undulating (not a levelled surface) topography with various types of sandunes located in the North-Western part of India. The marine deposits and wood fossils are estimated to be 180 million years old, indicating that the area was submerged or underwater during mesozoic era. At present, it is also known as *Marusthali* because it has arid climate, with low vegetation cover due to low rainfall below 150 mm per year.

The characteristics of the Indian desert are as follows

- Due to extreme arid conditions like physical weathering and action of wind, the land features such as mushroom rocks, shifting sand dunes, oasis are seen in this area.
- The desert tract has two regional parts, the Northern part slopes to the West or Sindh and the Southern part slopes towards South or the Rann of Kachchh.
- Most of the rivers in this region are ephemeral or seasonal like Luni river in the Southern part.
- Low rainfall and high evaporation make it a water deficit region.
- The seasonal streams form inland drainage (streams disappear after flowing for some distance) by joining a lake or playa (shallow saline lake).
- These lakes have brackish water (saline water unfit for drinking) which is the main source of obtaining salt.

3. **Central highlands form one of the important parts of Peninsular plateau. Discuss some features of central highland.** Competency Based Que

Ans Following are the features of central highland.

- They are bounded to the West by the Aravali range.
- The Satpura range is formed by a series of scarped plateaus on the South, generally at an elevation varying between 600-900 m above the mean sea level.
- This forms the Northernmost boundary of the Deccan plateau.
- The extension of the Peninsular plateau can be seen as far as Jaisalmer in the West, where it has been covered by the longitudinal sand ridges and crescent-shaped sand dunes called barchans.
- This region has the presence of metamorphic rocks such as marble, slate, gneiss, etc.
- The general elevation of the Central Highlands ranges between 700-1,000 m above the mean sea level and it slopes towards the North and North-East directions.
- The Chotanagpur region in Eastern part of the plateau has a large reserve of minerals.
- Banas is the only significant tributary of the river Chambal that originates from the Aravali in the Western ranges.

4. Differentiate between Western coastal plains and Eastern coastal plains. **Competency Based Que**

Ans. Differences between the Western coastal plains and the Eastern coastal plains are as follows

Basis	The Western Coastal Plains	The Eastern Coastal Plains
Type of coast	The Western coastal plains are an example of a submerged coastal.	The Eastern Coastal plains are an example of emergent coastal.
Location	These plains are located between the Western Ghats and the Arabian Sea.	These coastal plains extend between the Eastern Ghats and the Bay of Bengal.
Width	These are narrow plains and slope steeply towards the Arabian Sea.	These are wider plains and slope gently Eastwards.
Rivers	These plains are drained by many short and swift streams which are unable to form delta.	These plains are drained by big rivers like Mahanadi, Godavari, Krishna, Kaveri, etc. These rivers form large deltas.
Known For	These coastal plains are known for Kayals that are used for fishing and Inland transportation.	These coastal plains are known for deltas formed by rivers that are used for agriculture.

Source Based Questions

1 Read the passage carefully and answer the questions that follow.

The rift valleys of the Narmada, the Tapi and the Mahanadi and the Satpura block mountains are some examples of it. The Peninsula mostly consists of relict and residual mountains like the Aravali hills, the Nallamala hills, the Javadi hills, the Veliconda hills, the Palkonda range and the Mahendragiri hills, etc. The river valleys here are shallow with low gradients. Most of the East flowing rivers form deltas before entering into the Bay of Bengal. The deltas formed by the Mahanadi, the Krishna, the Kaveri and the Godavari are important examples.

(i) Which geological landform is formed by river Narmada in the peninsular block of India?

(a) V-shaped valley (b) U-shaped valley
(c) Canyons (d) Rift valley

Ans (d) Rift valley

(ii) The Peninsular Block of India consists of which of the following type of mountains?

(a) Young fold mountains (b) Block mountains
(c) Relict mountains (d) Both (b) and (c)

Ans (d) Both (b) and (c)

(iii) Which of the following river forms delta before entering into the Bay of Bengal?

(a) Tapi (b) Narmada
(c) Godavari (d) Luni

Ans (c) Godavari

2. Read the passage carefully and answer the following questions that follow.

The North and North-Eastern Mountains consist of the Himalayas and the North-Eastern hills. The Himalayas consist of a series of parallel mountain ranges. Some of the important ranges are the Greater Himalayan range, which includes the Great Himalayas and the Shiwalik. The general orientation of these ranges is from North-West to the South-East direction in the North-Western part of India. Himalayas in the Darjiling and Sikkim regions lie in an East-West direction, while in Arunachal Pradesh they are from South-West to the North-West direction. In Nagaland, Manipur and Mizoram, they are in the North-South direction. The approximate length of the Great Himalayan range, also known as the central axial range, is 2,500 km from East to West, and their width varies between 160-400 km from North to South. It is also evident that the Himalayas stand almost like a strong and long wall between the Indian sub-continent and the Central and East Asian countries.

(i) The Himalayas separate India from which of the following region?

(a) Central Asia (b) Europe
(c) South-East Asia (d) North America

Ans (a) Central Asia

(ii) In which direction are the Himalayas in Nagaland, Manipur and Mizoram?

(a) East-West (b) North-South
(c) North-West (d) East

Ans (b) North-South

(iii) In which direction Himalayas in Darjeeling and Sikkim region lies?

(a) East (b) East-West
(c) North-South (d) West

Ans. (b) East-West

3 Read the passage carefully and answer the questions that follow.

The Northern plains are formed by the alluvial deposits brought by the rivers – the Indus, the Ganga and the Brahmaputra. These plains extend approximately 3,200 km from the East to the West. The average width of these plains varies between 150-300 km. The maximum depth of alluvium deposits varies between 1,000-2,000 m. From the North to the South, these can be divided into three major zones: the Bhabar, the Tarai and the alluvial plains. The alluvial plains can be further divided into the Khadar and the Bhangar. Bhabar is a narrow belt ranging between 8-10 km parallel to the Shiwalik foothills at the break-up of the slope.

As a result of this, the streams and rivers coming from the mountains deposit heavy materials of rocks and boulders, and at times, disappear in this zone. South of the Bhabar is the Tarai belt, with an approximate width of 10-20 km where most of the streams and rivers re-emerge without having any properly demarcated channel, thereby, creating marshy and swampy conditions known as the Tarai.

This has a luxurious growth of natural vegetation and houses a varied wildlife. The South of Tarai is a belt consisting of old and new alluvial deposits known as the Bhangar and Khadar respectively. These plains have characteristic features of mature stage of fluvial erosional and depositional landforms such as sand bars, meanders, oxbow lakes and braided channels. The Brahmaputra plains are known for their riverine islands and sand bars. Most of these areas are subjected to periodic floods and shifting river courses forming braided streams. The mouths of these mighty rivers also form some of the largest deltas of the world, for example, the famous Sunderbans delta.

Otherwise, this is a featureless plain with a general elevation of 50-150 m above the mean sea level. The states of Haryana and Delhi form a water divide between the Indus and the Ganga river systems. As opposed to this, the Brahmaputra river flows from the North-East to the South-West direction before it takes an almost 90° Southward turn at Dhubri before it enters into Bangladesh. These river valley plains have a fertile alluvial soil cover which supports a variety of crops like wheat, rice, sugarcane and jute, and hence, supports a large population.

(i) **How the Northern plains are formed?**

Ans. The Northern plains are formed by the alluvial deposits brought by the rivers namely, the Indus, the Ganga and the Brahmaputra.

(ii) **Why river disappear in Bhabar region?**

Ans. Bhabar is the region South of the Lower Himalayas and the Shivalik Hills. After descending from the mountains, the rivers deposit pebbles in a slim belt. It accommodates pebble- studded rocks within the porous beds. Due to the porosity of the rocks, the streams disappear and flow underground.

(iii) **What makes the Bhangar and Khadar plains unique?**

Ans. The Bhangar and Khadar plains are unique because these plains have characteristic features of mature stage of fluvial erosional and depositional landforms. For example, sand bars, meanders, oxbow lakes and braided channels.

4. Read the following passage and answer the questions that follow.

On the basis of the location and active geomorphological processes, it can be broadly divided into two: (i) the Western coastal plains; (ii) the Eastern coastal plains.

The Western coastal plains are an example of submerged coastal plain. It is believed that the city of Dwaraka which was once a part of the Indian mainland situated along the West coast is submerged under water. Because of this submergence it is a narrow belt and provides natural conditions for the development of ports and harbours. Kandla, Mazagaon, JLN port Nhava Sheva, Marmagao, Mangalore, Cochin, etc. are some of the important natural ports located along the West coast. Extending from the Gujarat coast in the North to the Kerala coast in the South, the Western coast may be divided into following divisions - the Kachchh and Kathiawar coast in Gujarat, Konkan coast in Maharashtra, Goan coast and Malabar coast in Karnataka and Kerala respectively. The Western coastal plains are narrow in the middle and get broader towards North and South. The rivers flowing through this coastal plain do not form any delta. The Malabar coast has got certain distinguishing features in the form of 'Kayals' (backwaters), which are used for fishing, inland navigation and also due to its special attraction for tourists. Every year the famous *Nehru Trophy Vallamkali* (boat race) is held in *Punnamada Kayal* in Kerala.

(i) **What makes the Malabar coast a unique tourist attraction and how does it contribute to local activities?**

Ans. The Malabar coast consists of 'Kayals' (backwaters) that serves multiple purposes in nature such as fishing, inland navigation and tourism, including the famous Nehru Trophy boat race.

(ii) **How do the Western coastal plains' natural features influence India's maritime trade development?**

Ans. The submerged nature creates natural harbours that enables the development of major ports like Kandla, Mangalore, and Cochin, facilitating maritime trade development in India.

(iii) **How does the significance of Dwaraka contribute to our understanding of the Western coastal plains' geological history?**

Ans. Dwarka's submergence shows the submerged nature of Western coastal plains, which suggests the geological changes over time in India's Western coastline.

Map Based Questions

1. Mark the following mountains on the map of India.

(i) Karakoram Range
(ii) Garo-Khasi Hills
(iii) Jaintia Hills
(iv) Aravali Range
(v) Vindhyan Range
(vi) Satpura Range
(vii) Western Ghats
(viii) Eastern Ghats

Ans

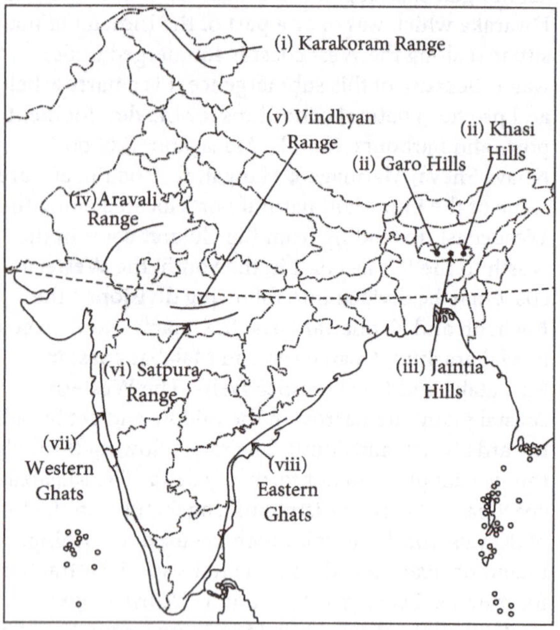

2. **On the map of India, mark the following.**

(i) K2 (ii) Kanchenjunga
(iii) Nandadevi (iv) Nanga Parbat
(v) Namcha Barwa (vi) Anaimudi

Ans

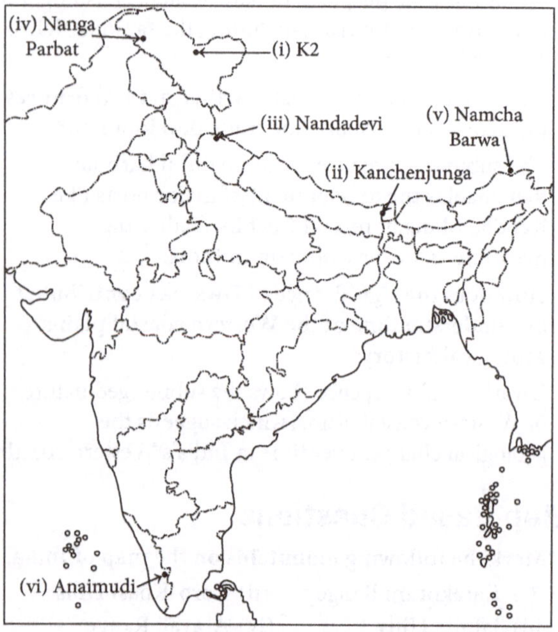

3. **On the map of India, mark the following passes.**

(i) Shipkila (ii) Nathula
(iii) Palghat (iv) Bhorghat (v) Thalghat

Ans

4 **On the map of India, mark the following plateaus.**

(i) Malwa (ii) Chotanagpur
(iii) Meghalaya (iv) Deccan Plateau

Ans

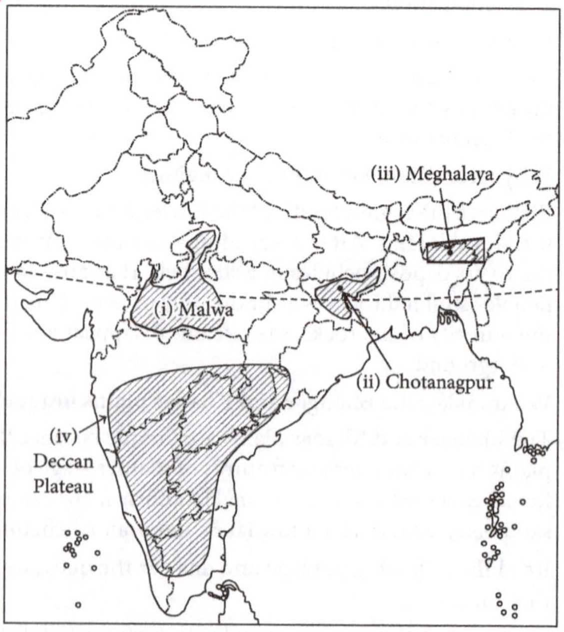

5. **On the map of India, mark the following coastal plains.**

(i) Saurashtra (ii) Konkan
(iii) Malabar (iv) Coromandel
(v) Northern Circars

Ans

6. **On the map of India, mark the following islands.**

(i) Andaman & Nicobar Islands
(ii) Lakshadweep Islands

Ans

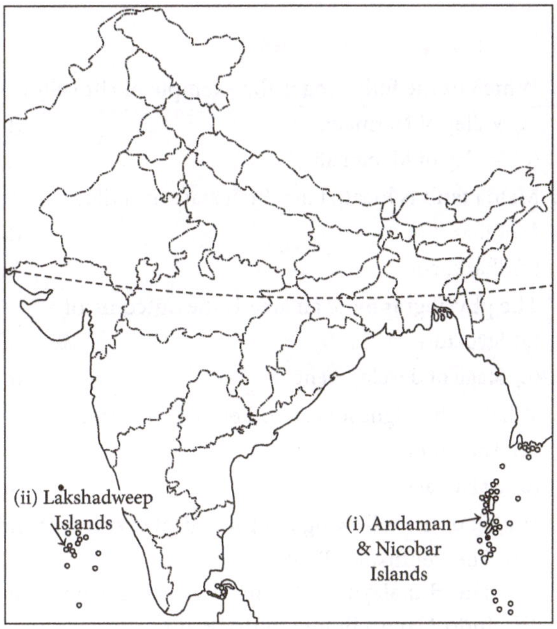

SELF ASSESSMENT TEST

Objecive Type Questions

1. Which of the following is the example of rift valley of India?
   (a) Valley of Narmada
   (b) Valley of Tapi
   (c) Valley of Mahanadi
   (d) All of these
2. Malda fault is located in which state of India?
   (a) Bihar
   (b) West Bengal
   (c) Jharkhand
   (d) Odisha
3. The physiography of an area is the outcome of
   (a) Structure
   (b) Process
   (c) Stage of development
   (d) All of these
4. What is the highest peak of Peninsular plateau
   (a) Anaimudi
   (b) Palkonda Range
   (c) Nallamala
   (d) Javadi
5. Which of the following is a geological division of India?
   I. The Peninsular Block
   II. The Himalayas and other Peninsular Mountains
   III. Indo-Ganga-Brahmaputra Plain

   Codes
   (a) I and II
   (b) II and III
   (c) I and III
   (d) All of these

Short Answer Type Questions

6. What do you know about the features of the Indian desert? Why do streams form inland drainage pattern there?
7. Which coast has more natural ports and why? Why is it difficult to develop ports on the other coast?
8. Why are the Island groups great attraction for tourists?

Long Answer Type Questions

9. Describe the major parts of the Northern plains on the basis of the size of the sediments.
10. Briefly write about the three geological divisions of the Peninsular India.
11. 'North-Eastern plateau is an important physical feature of Indian subcontinent.' Elucidate the statement.
12. 'There are two major islands groups in India.' Discuss about them briefly.

3
CHAPTER

The flow of water through well-defined channels is known as 'drainage' and the network of such channels is called a 'drainage system'.

▼ **YOUR STUDY GOALS**

3.1 Drainage Pattern
3.2 Indian Drainage System
3.3 Extent of Usability of River Water

▼ **YOUR PRACTICE GOALS**

- Objective Type Questions (22 Qs ; MCQs, Matching, A-R)
- Subjective Questions (13 SAs, 6 LAs)
- Source Based Questions (3 Qs)
- Map Based Questions (5 Qs)

Drainage System

- There are two major types of drainage systems in India: **Perennial** and **Seasonal**. Perennial rivers originate from the Himalayan glaciers and flow throughout the year. Seasonal rivers are found in Peninsular India and the amount of water they carry depends on rainfall.
- A **catchment area** is a region where all the rain or melted snow drains into a single place, like a river, lake, or pond. The edges of this area are usually marked by high ground, like hills or ridges, which guide the flow of water.
- A **drainage basin** is an area drained by a river and its tributaries. **Watershed** is the boundary line separating one drainage basin from the other.

3.1 Drainage Pattern

The drainage pattern of an area is the outcome of the geological time period, nature and structure of rocks, topography, slope, amount of water flowing and the periodicity of the flow.

Important Drainage Patterns

(i) A **dendritic drainage pattern** resembles the branches of a tree, where streams branch out and form a network. This pattern is commonly seen in the rivers of the Northern plains.

(ii) A **radial drainage pattern** occurs when rivers flow outward in all directions from a central hill or elevated region. Rivers originating from the Amarkantak range is a prime example of this pattern.

(iii) A **trellis drainage pattern** is formed when primary tributaries flow parallel to each other, with secondary tributaries joining them at right angles.

(iv) A **centripetal drainage pattern** appears when rivers converge and drain into a central lake or depression, with water flowing inward from all directions.

3.2 Indian Drainage System

- The Indian drainage system consists of many small and big rivers. It is the result of the evolutionary process of the three major physiographic units and the nature and characteristics of precipitation.
- Based on the **discharge of water** (orientations to the sea) Indian drainage system may be grouped into the **Arabian Sea drainage** and the **Bay of Bengal drainage**.

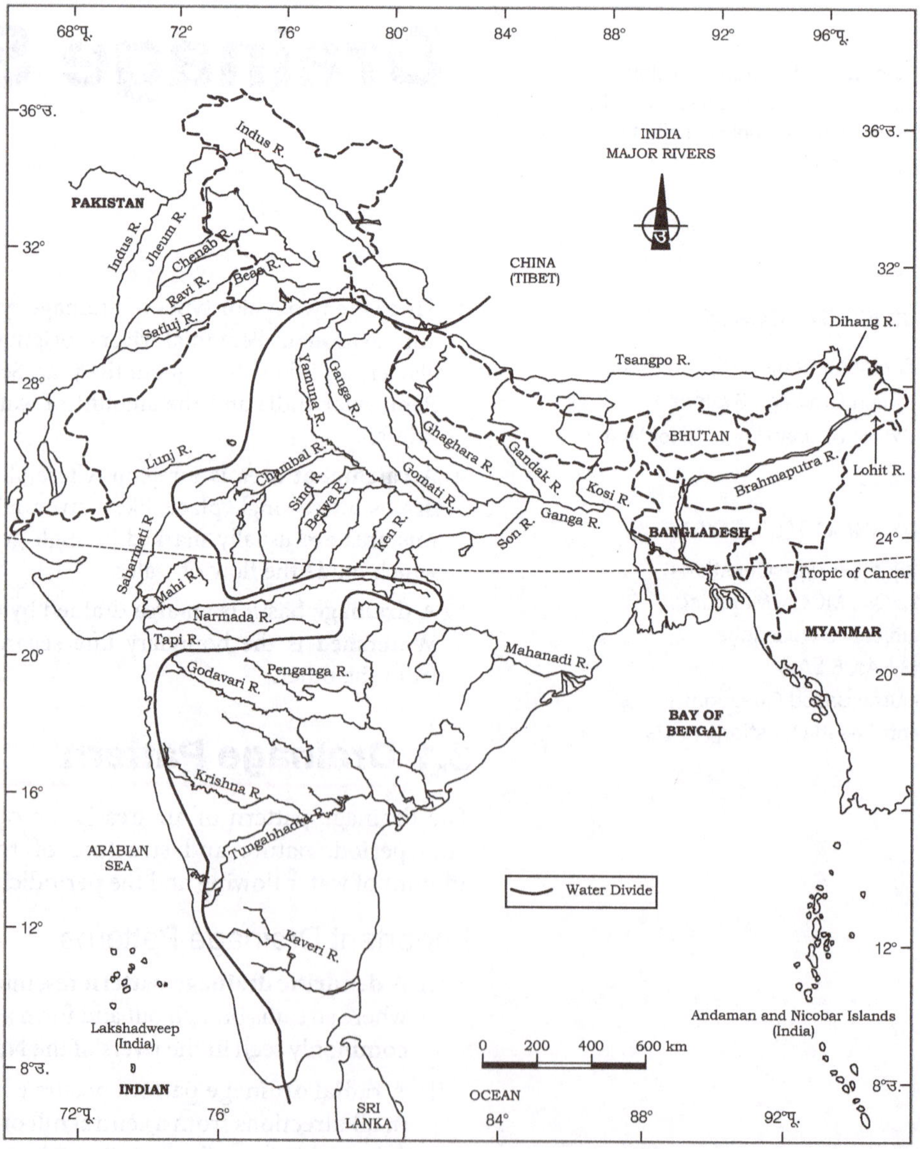

- They are separated from each other through the Delhi ridge, the Aravalis and the Sahyadris.
- Nearly 77 per cent of the drainage area consisting of the Ganga, the Brahmaputra, the Mahanadi, the Krishna, etc flows into the Bay of Bengal while 23 per cent comprising the Indus, the Narmada, the Tapi, the Mahi and the Periyar systems discharge their waters in the Arabian Sea.
- Based on the **size of the watershed**, the drainage basins of India are grouped into the following three categories
  (i) **Major river basins** These are river basins with more than 20,000 sq. km of catchment area. They include 14 drainage basins such as the Ganga, the Brahmaputra, the Krishna, the Tapi, the Narmada, the Mahi, the Pennar, the Sabarmati, the Barak, etc.
  (ii) **Medium river basins** These are river basins with a catchment area between 2,000-20,000 sq. km. They include 44 river basins such as the Kalindi, the Periyar, the Meghna, etc.
  (iii) **Minor river basins** These are river basins with a catchment area of less than 2,000 sq. km. They include a fairly good number of rivers flowing in the area of low rainfall.
    - Based on the mode of origin, nature and characteristics, the Indian drainage may also be classified into the **Himalayan drainage** and the **Peninsular drainage**.

The Himalayan Drainage

- It mainly includes the Ganga, the Indus and the Brahmaputra river basins.
- These rivers receive their water from the melting of snow and precipitation hence, they are perennial.
- These rivers form deep gorges, V-shaped valleys, **rapids**[1] and waterfalls in their mountainous course. In plains, they form depositional features like flat valleys, oxbow lakes, flood plains, braided channels and **deltas**[2] near the **river mouth**[3].
- In the plains, they display a strong **meandering**[4] tendency and shift their courses frequently. River Kosi, also known as the **sorrow of Bihar**, frequently changes its course.

▲ *Rapids*

- The Kosi brings a huge quantity of sediments from its upper parts and deposits it in the plains, therefore the course of the river gets blocked and it changes its path frequently.

Evolution of the Himalayan Drainage

- The Himalayan drainage system has evolved through a long geological history.
- There are different opinions about the evolution of the Himalayan rivers.
- Geologists believe that a mighty river called Shiwalik or Indo-Brahma crossed the entire longitudinal extent of the Himalayas from Assam to Punjab and onwards to Sind. It finally discharged into the **Gulf of Sind** near lower Punjab during the **Miocene period** some 5-24 million years ago.
- The remarkable continuity of the Shiwalik and its origin and alluvial deposits consisting of sands, silt, clay, boulders and conglomerates support this viewpoint.
- It is opined that in due course of time Indo- Brahma river was divided into three main drainage systems
  (i) The Indus and its five **tributaries**[5] in the Western part
  (ii) The Ganga and its Himalayan tributaries in the central part
  (iii) The stretch of the Brahmaputra in Assam and its Himalayan tributaries in the Eastern part.

---

1 **Rapids** These are sections of a river where the river bed has a relatively steep gradient, causing an increase in water velocity and turbulence.
2 **Delta** It is a triangular alluvial deposit at the mouth of a river.
3 **River Mouth** The place where a river empties itself into the sea or lake is known as its mouth.
4 **Meander** It is a winding curve or bend of a river.
5 **Tributaries** A tributary is a stream or river that flows into a larger river or lake, but does not flow directly into the ocean.

- The division was due to the Pleistocene upliftment in the Western Himalayas, including the uplift of the **Potwar Plateau** (Delhi Ridge), which acted as the water divide[6] between the Indus and Ganga drainage systems.
- Likewise, the down pushing of the Malda gap area between the Rajmahal hills and the Meghalaya plateau during the mid-pleistocene period, diverted the Ganga and the Brahmaputra systems to flow towards the Bay of Bengal.

Major River Systems of the Himalayan Drainage

The Indus System

- It is one of the largest river basins of the world, covering an area of 11,65,000 sq. km. It covers an area of 321, 289 sq. km. Its total length is 2,880 km and in India its length is 1,114 km.
- The Indus, also known as the Sindhu, is the Westernmost of the Himalayan rivers in India. It originates from a glacier near **Bokhar Chu** (31°15′ N latitude and 81°40′ E longitude) in the Tibetan region at an altitude of 4,164 m in the Kailash Mountain range.
- In Tibet, it is known as ***Singi Khamban*** or **Lion's mouth.** After flowing in the North-West direction between the Ladakh and Zanskar ranges, it passes through Ladakh and Baltistan.
- It cuts across the Ladakh range, forming a spectacular gorge near Gilgit in Jammu and Kashmir. It enters Pakistan near Chilas in the Dardistan region.
- The Indus is joined by several Himalayan tributaries such as the Shyok, the Gilgit, the Zaskar, the Hunza, the Nubra, the Shigar, the Gasting and the Dras. It finally emerges from the hills near Attock where it joins the Kabul river on its right bank.
- The Indus river flows Southward. The five rivers of Punjab, namely the Satluj, the Beas, the Ravi, the Chenab and the Jhelum together form 'Panjnad', and merges with Indus. It finally discharges into the Arabian Sea, East of Karachi.
- The Indus flows in India only through Jammu and Kashmir.
- The important tributaries joining the right bank of the Indus are the Khurram, the Tochi, the Gomal, the Viboa and the Sangar. They all originate in the Sulaiman ranges.

Tributaries of the Indus River

- **Jhelum** The Jhelum, rises from a spring at Verinag, situated at the foot of the Pir Panjal in the South-Eastern part of the Valley of Kashmir. It flows through Srinagar and the Wular lake before entering Pakistan through a deep narrow gorge. It joins the Chenab near Jhang in Pakistan.
- **Chenab** The Chenab is the **largest tributary** of the Indus. It is formed by two streams, the Chandra and the Bhaga, which join at Tandi near Keylong in Himachal Pradesh. Hence, it is also known as **Chandrabhaga**. The river flows for 1,180 km before entering into Pakistan.
- **Ravi** The Ravi rises West of the Rohtang Pass in the Kullu hills of Himachal Pradesh and flows through the Chamba valley of the state. Before entering Pakistan and joining the Chenab near Sarai Sidhu, it drains the area lying between the South-Eastern part of the Pir Panjal and the Dhauladhar ranges.
- **Beas** The Beas originates from the Beas Kund near the Rohtang Pass at an elevation of 4,000 m above the mean sea level. The river flows through the Kullu Valley forming a gorge[7] at Kati and Largi in the Dhauladhar range. It enters the Punjab plains where it meets the Satluj near Harike.
- **Satluj** The Satluj originates in the 'Raksas tal' near Mansarovar at an altitude of 4,555 m in Tibet where it is known as **Langchen Khambab**. It flows almost parallel to the Indus for about 400 km before entering India and comes out of a gorge at Rupar. It passes through the Shipki La on the Himalayan ranges and

6 Water divide The upland that separates two drainage systems is known as the water divide.
7 Gorge A gorge is a narrow valley with steep, rocky walls that is usually located between hills or mountains.

- **Satluj** The Satluj originates in the 'Raksas tal' near Mansarovar at an altitude of 4,555 m in Tibet where it is known as **Langchen Khambab.** It flows almost parallel to the Indus for about 400 km before entering India and comes out of a gorge at Rupar. It passes through the Shipki La on the Himalayan ranges and enters the Punjab plains. It is an antecedent river[8]. It provides water to the canal system of the Bhakra Nangal project.

The Ganga System

- The Ganga rises in the Gangotri glacier near **Gaumukh** (3,900 m) in the Uttarkashi district of Uttarakhand. Here, it is known as the **Bhagirathi**.
- It flows through the Central and the Lesser Himalayas in narrow gorges. **At Devprayag**, the Bhagirathi meets the Alaknanda and from here it is known as the Ganga.
- The Ganga enters the plains at Haridwar. The Ganga flows from the South to the South-East and East. It splits into two distributaries, the **Bhagirathi** and the **Padma**.
- Ganga has a length of 2,525 km. It flows through Uttarakhand (110 km) and Uttar Pradesh (1,450 km), Bihar (445 km) and West Bengal (520 km).
- The Ganga basin covers about 8.6 lakh sq. km area in India. The Ganga river system is the largest in India having several perennial and non-perennial rivers originating in the Himalayas in the North and the Peninsula in the South, respectively.

Alaknanda River

- The Alaknanda has its source in the Satopanth glacier above Badrinath. The Alaknanda consists of the Dhauli and the Vishnu Ganga which meet at Joshimath or Vishnu Prayag.
- The other tributaries of Alaknanda such as the Pindar join it at Karna Prayag while Mandakini or Kali Ganga meet it at Rudra Prayag.

Tributaries of the River Ganga

- **Yamuna** The Yamuna is the Westernmost and **longest tributary** of the Ganga. It originated from the Yamunotri glacier on the Western slopes of the Banderpunch range (6,316 m). It joins the Ganga at Prayag (Allahabad). It is joined by the Chambal, the Sind, the Betwa and the Ken on its right bank which originates from the Peninsular plateau while the Hindan, the Rind, the Sengar, the Varuna, etc. join it on its left bank. Much of its water feeds the Western and Eastern Yamuna and the Agra canals for irrigation purposes.
- **Chambal** The Chambal rises near Mhow in the Malwa plateau of Madhya Pradesh and flows Northwards through a gorge upwards of Kota in Rajasthan, where the Gandhisagar dam has been constructed. From Kota, it moves down to Bundi, Sawai Madhopur and Dholpur and finally joins the Yamuna. The Chambal is famous for its badland topography called the **Chambal** ravines[9].
- **Gandak** The Gandak rises in the Nepal Himalayas between the Dhaulagiri and Mount Everest and drains the central part of Nepal. It enters the Ganga plain in Champaran district of Bihar and joins the Ganga at Sonpur near Patna. The Gandak comprises two streams, namely Kaligandak and Trishulganga.
- **Ghaghara** The Ghaghara originates in the glaciers of Mapchachungo. The major tributaries of Ghaghara are Tila, Seti and Beri.
- **Kali** The river Kali (Sarda) joins the Ganga at Chhapra.
- **Kosi** The Kosi is an antecedent river. It originates from the North of Mount Everest in Tibet. Its mainstream is Arun. After crossing the Central Himalayas in Nepal, it is joined by the **Son Kosi** from the West and the **Tamur Kosi** from the East. It forms **Sapt Kosi** after merging with the river Arun.

---

8 Antecedent river An antecedent river is a river that maintains its original course and pattern despite changes in the underlying rock topography.

9 Ravine It is a landform narrower than a canyon and is often the product of stream cuttting erosion. It is typically classified as larger in scale than gullies, although smaller than valleys.

- **Ramganga** The Ramganga is a small river originating from the Garhwal hills near Gairsain. It changes its course to the South-West direction after crossing the Shiwalik and enters into the plains of Uttar Pradesh near Najibabad. It joins the Ganga near Kannauj.
- **Damodar** The Damodar occupies the Eastern margins of the Chotanagpur Plateau where it flows through a rift valley[10] and finally joins the Hugli. The Barakar is its main tributary. The Damodar is known as the **sorrow of Bengal**. The Damodar Valley Corporation is a multipurpose project on the river.
- **Saryu** The Saryu rises in the Milam glacier in the Nepal Himalayas. It is known as the Goriganga there. It is called Kali or Chauk around the Indo-Nepal border, where it joins the Ghaghara.
- **Mahananda** The Mahananda rises in the Darjeeling hills. It joins the Ganga as its last left bank tributary in West Bengal.
- **Son** The Son is a large South-bank tributary of the Ganga, originating in the Amarkantak plateau. It forms a series of waterfalls at the edge of the Deccan plateau and reaches Arrah, West of Patna, to join the Ganga.

Namami Gange Programme

- It is an Integrated Conservation Mission, approved as "Flagship Programme" by the Union Government in June 2014. It has twin objectives of effective reduction of pollution, conservation and rejuvenation of the National River Ganga.
- Main pillars of the Namami Gange Programme are
  - Sewerage Treatment Infrastructure
  - River-Surface Cleaning
  - Afforestation
  - Industrial Effluent Monitoring
  - River-Front Development
  - Bio-Diversity
  - Public Awareness
  - Ganga Gram

The Brahmaputra System

- The Brahmaputra is one of the largest rivers in the world. It originates from the **Chemayungdung glacier** of the Kailash range near the Mansarovar lake. From here, it bends Eastward horizontally for nearly 1,200 km in a dry and flat region of Southern Tibet, where it is known as the **Tsangpo**, which means **the purifier**.
- The Rango Tsangpo is the major right-bank tributary of the Brahmaputra in Tibet. It emerges as a stormy and dynamic river after carving out a deep gorge in the Central Himalayas near Namcha Barwa (7,755 m).
- The river emerges from the foothills under the name of Siang or Dihang. It enters India from West of Sadiya town in Arunachal Pradesh. Flowing South-West, it forms its left bank tributaries, viz., Dibang or Sikang and Lohit from here it is known as the Brahmaputra.
- The Brahmaputra is joined by numerous tributaries in its 750 km long journey through the Assam valley. Its major **left bank tributaries** are the Burhi Dihing and Dhansari (South) whereas the important **right bank tributaries** are the Subansiri, Kameng, Manas and Sankosh.
- The Subansiri which has its origin in Tibet, is an antecedent river.
- The Brahmaputra enters Bangladesh near Dhubri and flows Southward.
- In Bangladesh, the Tista joins it on its right bank from where the river is known as the Jamuna. It finally merges with the river Padma, which falls in the Bay of Bengal.
- The Brahmaputra is well-known for floods, shifting in flow and bank erosion. This is because most of its tributaries which are large and bring large quantities of sediments because of heavy rainfall in its catchment area.

10 Rift valley It is a linear-shaped lowland between several highlands or mountain ranges created by the action of a geologic rift or fault.

Quick Test 1

1 Which physical feature separates the Arabian sea drainage system and the Bay of Bengal drainage system?
2 Name a river in Northern India that has a major river basin.
3 Which river forms gorges at Kati and Largi in the Dhauladhar range?
4 Name the major right bank tributary of Brahmaputra.

The Peninsular Drainage System

- The Peninsular drainage system is older than the Himalayan river system. This is evident from the broad, largely-graded shallow valleys and the maturity of the rivers.
- The Western Ghats running close to the Western coast act as the water divide between the major Peninsular rivers, discharging their water in the Bay of Bengal and as small **rivulets**[11] joining the Arabian Sea.
- Most of the major Peninsular rivers except Narmada and Tapi flow from West to East.
- The Chambal, the Sind, the Betwa, the Ken and the Son are major Peninsular rivers that originates in the Northern part of Peninsula and belong to the Ganga river system.
- The other major river systems of the Peninsular drainage are - the Mahanadi, the Godavari, the Krishna and the Kaveri.
- Peninsular rivers have fixed courses, there is absence of meanders and non, perennial water flow.
- The Narmada and the Tapi which flow through the rift valley are, however, exceptions.

The Evolution of the Peninsular Drainage System

- The following major geological events in the past have shaped the present drainage systems of Peninsular India
  - Sinking of the Western side of the Peninsula led to its submergence below the sea during the early tertiary period. Generally, it has disturbed the symmetrical plan of the river on either side of the original watershed.
  - The process of upliftment of Himalayas leads to the submergence of Northern side of the Peninsular block and this resulted in the formation of **trough faulting**[12]. The Narmada and the Tapi flow in trough faults and fill the original cracks with their sediments. Hence, there is a lack of alluvial and deltaic deposits in these rivers.
  - Slight tilting of the Peninsular block from the North-West to the South-Eastern direction led to the development of the entire drainage system which flows towards the Bay of Bengal during the same period.

Major River Systems of the Peninsular Drainage

Mahanadi

- The Mahanadi rises near Sihawa in the Raipur district of Chhattisgarh and runs through Odisha to discharge its water into the Bay of Bengal.
- It is 851 km long and its catchment area spreads over 1.42 lakh sq. km. Some navigation is carried on in the lower course of this river.
- 53 per cent of the drainage basin of this river lies in Madhya Pradesh and Chhattisgarh, while 47 per cent lies in Odisha.

---

11 **Rivulets** It is a small stream of water or another liquid.
12 **Trough faulting** It is a geological process due to which a long and narrow depression formed on Earth's surface, which is bounded by faults on either side.

Godavari

- The Godavari is the **largest Peninsular river system**. It is also called the **Dakshin Ganga**. It rises in the Nasik district of Maharashtra and discharges its water into the Bay of Bengal.
- Its tributaries run through the States of Maharashtra, Madhya Pradesh, Chhattisgarh, Odisha and Andhra Pradesh. The Penganga, the Indravati, the Pranhita and the Manjra are its principal tributaries.
- It is **1,465 km long** with a catchment area spreading over 3.13 lakh sq. km, 49 per cent of this, lies in Maharashtra, 20 per cent in Madhya Pradesh and Chhattisgarh and the rest in Andhra Pradesh.
- The Penganga, the Indravati, the Pranhita and the Manjrira are principal tributaries of the Godavari.
- The Godavari have heavy floods in its lower parts in the South of Polavaram, where it forms a picturesque gorge. It is navigable only in the deltaic stretch.
- Godavari splits into many branches after Rajamundri (a city in Andhra Pradesh) and forms large deltas.

Krishna

- The Krishna is the **second largest East-flowing Peninsular river** which rises near Mahabaleshwar in Sahyadri.
- Its total length is **1,401 km**. The Koyna, the Tungbhadra and the Bhima are its major tributaries.
- Of the total catchment area of the Krishna, 27 per cent lies in Maharashtra, 44 per cent in Karnataka and 29 per cent in Andhra Pradesh and Telangana.

Kaveri

- The Kaveri rises in Brahmagiri hills (1,341m) of Kogadu district in Karnataka. Its length is **800 km** and it drains an area of 81,155 sq. km.
- Since the upper catchment area receives rainfall during the South-West monsoon season (summer) and the lower part during the North-East monsoon season (winter), the river carries water throughout the year with comparatively less fluctuation than the other Peninsular rivers.
- About 3 per cent of the Kaveri basin lies in Kerala, 41 per cent in Karnataka and 56 per cent in Tamil Nadu. Its important tributaries are the Kabini, the Bhavani and the Amravati.

Narmada

- The Narmada originates on the Western side of the Amarkantak plateau at a height of about 1,057 m.
- Flowing in a rift valley between the Satpura in the South and the Vindhyan range in the North, it forms a picturesque gorge in marble rocks and Dhuandhar waterfall near Jabalpur.
- After flowing a distance of about 1,312 km, it meets the Arabian Sea South of Bharuch, forming a broad 27 km long estuary[13]. Its catchment area is about 98,796 sq. km.
- The **Sardar Sarovar Project** has been constructed on this river.

Tapi

- The Tapi originates from Multai in the Betul district of Madhya Pradesh.
- It is 724 km long and drains an area of 65,145 sq. km. Nearly 79 per cent of its basin lies in Maharashtra, 15 per cent in Madhya Pradesh and the remaining 6 per cent in Gujarat.

---

13 Estuary It is an arm or inlet of the Sea at the lower end of a river.

Luni

- Luni is the largest river system in Rajasthan and flows West of Aravali. It originates near Pushkar in two branches, the Saraswati and the Sabarmati.
- They join each other at Govindgarh. From here, the river comes out of Aravali and is known as Luni.
- It flows towards the West till Telwara and then takes a South-West direction to join the Rann of Kuchchh. The entire river system is ephemeral[14].

3.3 Extent of Usability of River Water

- The rivers of India carry huge volumes of water per year but it is unevenly distributed both in time and space.
- The rivers of North India are perennial (have water throughout the year), whereas the rivers of South India are non-perennial (have very little water during the dry season).
- The volume of water increases in the rainy season and decreases in the dry season. If rainfall is above average, some areas suffer from floods and if it is below average, the dry regions face drought conditions.
- Problems in using river water are as follows
  - No availability in sufficient quantity.
  - The uneven flow of water
  - Load of silt in river water
  - River water disputes between states
  - Shrinking of channels due to the extension of settlements towards the Thalweg[15]
  - River water is polluted due to
    - Natural factors such as landslides, mudflow, etc.
    - Economic factors such as industrial development, untreated wastes in river water and urban growth discharge
    - Socio-cultural factors such as large-scale bathing and washing, cremation grounds on the banks, throwing of dead bodies, immersing flowers and statues on many festivals.

Quick Test 2

1. Which Peninsular river is navigable only in the deltaic stretch?
2. From where does the river Kaveri emerge?
3. Where does river Luni drain?
4. Mention two economic and natural factors that cause water pollution.

---

14 Ephemeral A stream that has flowing water only during or for a short duration after precipitation events in a typical year.

15 Thalweg It is a line that connects the lower most point of a river channel or a valley.

Mind Map

DRAINAGE SYSTEM

1 Drainage Pattern

- It is the outcome of geological time, topography, slope, structure of rock. This pattern is commonly seen in the river of the Northern Plains.
- **Dendritic Pattern** It resembles the branches of a tree.
- **Radial Pattern** In this, rivers originates and flow in all directions, e.g., Amarkantak range.
- **Trellis Pattern** In this, primary tributaries flow parallel to each other and secondary tributaries join them at right angles.
- **Centripetal Pattern** In this, water from all directions gets discharged into a lake.

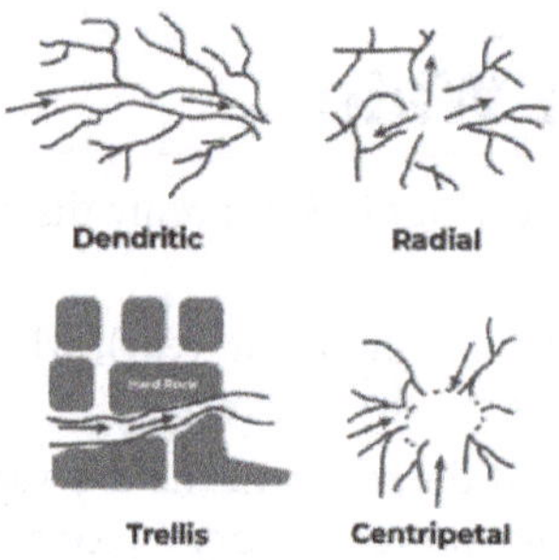

2 Indian Drainage System

Based on Mode of Origin, Nature and Characteristics

Himalayan Drainage System

- It originates from the Himalayas. These rivers receive their water from the melting of snow and precipitation.
- **Key Features** Deep gorges, meandering in plains and frequent change of river course.
- **Examples** Indus, Ganga, Brahmaputra river system

Peninsular Drainage System

- These are older system with mature and shallow valleys. They have fixed courses.
- **Key Features** East flowing rivers are there, except Narmada and Tapi.
- **Examples** Godavari, Krishna, Kaveri, Mahanadi, Luni, Narmada, Tapi river system.

Based on Discharge of Water

- **Arabian Sea Drainage** It covers 23% of total drainage area. It comprises Indus, Narmada, Tapi, Mahi and Periyar systems.
- **Bay of Bengal Drainage** It covers 77% of the total drainage area. It comprises Ganga, Brahmaputra, Mahanadi, Krishna, etc.

Based on Size of Watershed

- **Major River Basins** Catchment area of this river basin is more than 20,000 km^2.
- **Medium River Basins** Catchment area of this river basin is between 2,000-20,000 km^2.
- **Minor River Basin** Catchment area of this river basin is less than 2,000 km^2.

NCERT Folder

Choose the right answer from the four alternatives given below

(i) **Which one of the following rivers is known as the 'Sorrow of Bengal'?**

(a) The Gandak (b) The Son
(c) The Kosi (d) The Damodar

Ans. (d) The Damodar

(ii) **Which one of the following rivers has the largest river basin in India?**

(a) The Indus
(b) The Brahmaputra
(c) The Ganga
(d) The Krishna

Ans. (c) The Ganga

(iii) **Which one of the following rivers is not included in Panjnad?**

(a) The Ravi (b) The Chenab
(c) The Indus (d) The Jhelum

Ans. (c) The Indus

(iv) **Which one of the following rivers flows in a rift valley?**

(a) The Son
(b) The Narmada
(c) The Yamuna
(d) The Luni

Ans. (b) The Narmada

(v) **Which one of the following is the place of confluence of the Alaknanda and the Bhagirathi?**

(a) Vishnu Prayag (b) Rudra Prayag
(c) Karan Prayag (d) Deva Prayag

Ans. (d) Deva Prayag

State the differences between the following

(i) **River Basin and Watershed**

Ans. Differences between river basin and watershed are as follows

Basis	River Basin	Watershed
Meaning	The catchment area of large rivers is called river basin.	The catchment area of small rivulets and rills (streams) is known as watershed.
Area	River basin covers a very large area.	Watershed is smaller in area.

(ii) **Dendritic and Trellis drainage pattern**

Ans. Differences between dendritic and trellis drainage pattern are as follows

Basis	Dendritic Drainage Pattern	Trellis Drainage Pattern
Meaning	It is the pattern that resembles the branches of a tree. The rivers flow at slope terrain from one direction to another one direction to another.	It is formed in the area of levelled surface where the primary tributaries of the river flow parallel to each other and secondary tributaries join them at right angle.
Example	Such patterns are formed by the rivers of the Northern plains.	Such patterns are seen in the upper parts of the Himalayas.

(iii) **Radial and Centripetal drainage pattern**

Ans. Differences between radial and centripetal drainage pattern are as follows

Basis	Radial Drainage Pattern	Centripetal Drainage Pattern
Formation	It is formed on hill slopes where the rivers originate and flow in all directions.	It is formed in the dry areas where short and seasonal rivers discharge their waters from all directions in a lake or depression. It is also known as inland drainage.
Example	It is found on Amarkantak range.	It is found on Loktak lake rivers.

(iv) **Delta and Estuary**

Ans. Differences between delta and estuary are as follows

Basis	Delta	Estuary
Shape	It is more or less triangular flat area of alluvium deposit at the mouth of a river.	The sharp edged mouth of rivers like V-shaped valley, devoid of any deposits is known as an Estuary.
Suitability	They are formed in the regions of low tides and coastal plains and are fertile for agricultural purpose.	They are rich fishing grounds and are suitable for inland transportation.

Answer the following questions in about 30 words

(i) **What are the socio-economic advantages of interlinking of rivers in India?**

Ans. The socio-economic advantages of interlinking of rivers in India are

- It provides employment to lakhs of people for constructing canals, links, storage, etc.
- It engages marginal farmers in agricultural activities through irrigation and increase in the food production will increase the average income of farmers.
- It helps in generation of electricity that will promote industrial growth and many other economic activities.
- It helps to control the problems of floods and drought that will prevent the loss of millions of rupees.

(ii) **Write three characteristics of the Peninsular rivers.**

Ans. Characteristics of the Peninsular rivers are

- The Peninsular river are ephemeral or seasonal in nature as they do not get water from melting glaciers.
- They are old rivers with graded profile and have shallow valleys and flat mountain peaks.
- They are characterised by fixed course and absence of meanders.

Answer the following questions in not more than 125 words

(i) **What are the important characteristic features of North Indian rivers?**

Ans. Some important characteristics features of the North-Indian rivers are as follows

- They are fed by melting of snow and precipitation.
- These are perennial in nature or have water throughout the year.
- In their mountainous course, they form deep gorges, V-shaped valleys, rapids, waterfalls, etc due to the erosional activity. These rivers flow with high velocity on steep slopes. In Himalayan reaches, course of these rivers is highly tortous (having many turns).
- When they enter the plains, the rivers form depositional features like flat valleys, alluvial fans, meanders, ox-bow lakes, flood plains, braided channels and deltas. Over the plains, these rivers shift their courses frequently.

(ii) **Suppose you are travelling from Haridwar to Siliguri along the foothills of the Himalayas. Name the important rivers you will come across. Describe the characteristics of any one of them.**

Ans. While travelling from Haridwar to Siliguri along the foothills of the Himalayas, we shall come across the Ganga, the Ram Ganga, the Saryu, the Gomti, the Ghaghra, the Gandak and the Kosi.

Characteristics of the Ganga river are

- The Ganga is the most important river in this region. It covers the largest river basin in India having a number of perennial and non-perennial rivers and also has cultural significance.
- It rises in the Gangotri glacier near Gaumukh in Uttarkashi district of Uttarakhand.
- At Deva Prayag it is known as the Ganga where the Bhagirathi and the Alaknanda meet.
- It flows through the states of Uttarakhand (110 km), Uttar Pradesh (1,450 km), Bihar (445 km) and West Bengal (520 km) for a distance of 2,525 km.
- The Ganga basin covers about 8.6 lakh sq km area in India.
- The Son is its major right bank tributary and the left bank tributaries of Ganga are the Ramganga, the Gomti, the Ghagara, the Gandak, the Kosi and the Mahananda.
- Before forming the Sundarban delta, it splits into distributaries namely the Bhagirathi and the Hugli.

Exam Pattern Questions

Objective Type Questions

Multiple Choice Questions (MCQs)

1. Which one of the following is true to indicate an area where all the precipitation flows to a single stream or a set of streams?

(a) Water divide
(b) Submerged area
(c) Catchment area
(d) Levees

2. The flow of water through well-defined channels is ....

(a) catchment area (b) watershed
(c) drainage (d) river basin

3. Which of the following drainage patterns is also known as inland drainage?

(a) Dendritic (b) Centripetal
(c) Trellis (d) Radial

4. Which of the following rivers is part of the Bay of Bengal drainage system?

(a) Ganga (b) Brahmaputra
(c) Mahanadi (d) All of these

5. Which of the following pairs of rivers have a medium drainage basin?

(a) The Ganga and the Yamuna
(b) The Kalindi and the Periyar
(c) The Narmada and the Tapi
(d) The Brahmaputra and the Yamuna

6. Which of the following rivers is known as 'Sorrow of Bihar'?

(a) Damodar (b) Kosi
(c) Son (d) Chambal

7. Which of the following rivers is known as Singi Khamban in Tibetan range?

(a) Indus (b) Brahmaputra
(c) Satluj (d) Kosi

8. Which is largest tributary of the Indus river?

(a) Beas (b) Chenab
(c) Ravi (d) Jhelum

9. Which is the major right bank tributary of the Ganga river?

(a) Gandak (b) Mahananda
(c) Son (d) Gomti

10. Which of the following is incorrect about Subansiri river?

(a) It is antecedent river.
(b) It originates in Tibet.
(c) It is left bank tributary of Brahmaputra.
(d) All of the above

11. .... river is also known as Dakshin Ganga.

(a) Krishna (b) Godavari
(c) Mahanadi (d) Kaveri

12. Which river forms Dhuandhar waterfall?

(a) Tapi (b) Kaveri
(c) Shravati (d) Narmada

13. Which of the following pairs is incorrect?

(a) Mahanadi – Raipur
(b) Godavari – Nasik
(c) Krishna – Mahabaleshwar
(d) Kaveri – Raichuru

14. Consider the following about peninsular rivers.

I. They are seasonal in nature.
II. They have fixed course.
III. They are younger than Himalayan rivers.
IV. They have less or no meanders.

Which of the given statement(s) is/are correct?

(a) I, II, III (b) I, II, IV
(c) II, III, IV (d) I, III, IV

15. Consider the following statements about tributaries of the Ganga.

I. Barakar river is main tributary of Mahananda.
II. River Ghaghara makes deep gorge at Shishapani.

Which of the statement is correct?

(a) Only I (b) Only II
(c) Both I and II (d) None of these

16. Which of the following are the right bank tributaries of Indus?

I. Kabul river II. Beas
III. Khurram IV. Sangar
V. Chenab

Codes

(a) I, II, III (b) III, IV, V
(c) I, III, IV (d) II, III, IV

17. Identify the river based on the characteristics given below.

It is an important tributary of the Indus and rises from a spring at Verinag situated at the foot of the Pir Panjal in the South-Eastern part of the Valley of Kashmir. It flows through Srinagar and the Wular Lake before entering Pakistan through a deep narrow gorge. It joins the Chenab near Jhang in Pakistan.

Options

(a) Satluj (b) Chenab (c) Ravi (d) Jhelum

Arrange the Following

18. Arrange the following rivers from North to South.

(i) Chenab (ii) Jhelum
(iii) Ravi (iv) Satluj

Codes

(a) (i), (ii), (iii), (iv) (b) (iv), (iii), (ii), (i)
(c) (ii), (i), (iii), (iv) (d) (ii), (iv), (iii), (i)

19. Arrange the following rivers in ascending order according to their length

(i) Mahanadi (ii) Kaveri
(iii) Tapi (iv) Krishna

Codes

(a) (iv), (iii), (ii), (i) (b) (iii), (ii), (i), (iv)
(c) (i), (ii), (iii), (iv) (d) (iii), (iv), (ii), (i)

Match the Following

20.

	List-I (River)		List-II (Tributary)
A.	Indus	1.	Kameng
B.	Brahmaputra	2.	Bhavani
C.	Godavari	3.	Shigar
D.	Kaveri	4.	Pranhita

Codes

	A	B	C	D
(a)	1	3	4	2
(b)	3	1	4	2
(c)	3	1	2	4
(d)	1	4	3	2

21.

	List I (River)		List II (Glacier)
A.	Brahmaputra	1.	Mapchachungo
B.	Ghaghra	2.	Bokhar chu
C.	Alaknanda	3.	Chemayungdung
D.	Indus	4.	Satopanth

Codes

	A	B	C	D		A	B	C	D
(a)	1	2	3	4	(b)	2	1	4	3
(c)	3	2	4	1	(d)	3	1	4	2

Assertion-Reason

In the questions given below are two statements labelled as Assertion (A) and other is labelled as Reason (R). In the context of two statements which one of the following is correct?

Codes

(a) Both A and R are true, but R is not the correct explanation of A
(b) Both A and R are true and R is the correct explanation of A
(c) Both A and R are incorrect
(d) A is correct, but R is incorrect

22. Assertion (A) Narmada and Tapi flow in rift valley.

Reason (R) Narmada and Tapi drain in the Bay of Bengal.

Answers

1. (c) Catchment area
2. (c) drainage
3. (b) Centripetal
4. (d) All of these
5. (b) The Kalindi and the Periyar
6. (b) Kosi
7. (a) Indus
8. (b) Chenab
9. (c) Son
10. (c) It is left bank tributary of Brahmaputra.
11. (b) Godavari
12. (d) Narmada
13. (d) Kaveri – Raichuru
14. (b) I, II, IV
15. (b) Only II
16. (c) I, III, IV
17. (d) Jhelum
18. (c) (ii), (i), (iii), (iv)
19. (b) (iii), (ii), (i), (iv)
20. (b)
21. (d)
22. (d) A is correct, but R is incorrect

Subjective Questions

Short Answer Type Questions

1. In what categories can the drainage basins be classified on the basis of their watershed?

Or **Explain three main categories of drainage basin of India that are classified on the basis of the size of the watershed.** **CBSE Diksha**

Ans. On the basis of the size of watershed, drainage basin is classified into the following

- **Major river basin** with more than 20,000 sq km of catchment area, e.g. the Ganga.
- **Medium river basin** with catchment area of 2,000-20,000 sq km, e.g. the Periyar.
- **Minor river basin** with catchment area of less than 2000 sq km, e.g. Bhadra river in Karnataka has catchment area of 1968 sq km.

2. Where does the Brahmaputra originate? Briefly state three important features of Brahmaputra.

Ans. Brahmaputra is one of the largest rivers in the world. It has its origin in the Chemayungdung glacier of Kailash Mountain Range, near Mansarovar lake. It is known as Tsangpo in Tibet.

Three important features of Brahmaputra are as follow

(i) It carves out a deep gorge in the central Himalayas, near Namcha Barwa due to its turbulent and dynamic nature.

(ii) It is known for causing flood, channel shifting and bank erosion as most of its tributaries are large.

(iii) It receives various tributaries throughout its journey in Assam. Its major left bank tributaries are Burhi Dihing and Dhansiri whereas right bank tributaries include Subansiri, Kameng, Manas.

3. The Indo-Brahma river dismembered into how many drainage systems? Why did it happen?

Ans. According to the geologist, during the miocene period (5-24 million years ago) there was a mighty river known as the Indo-Brahma. It was dismembered into three main drainage systems

(i) Indus and its five tributaries in Western part.

(ii) Ganga and its tributaries in Central part.

(iii) Brahmaputra in Assam and its Himalayan tributaries in Eastern part.

The dismemberment was due to the following reasons

- Pleistocene upheaval in the Western Himalayas, including the uplift of the Potwar plateau which acted as a water divided between Indus and Ganga.
- Mid-Pleistocene down thrusting of Malda Gap between Rajmahal hills and Meghalayas plateau which diverted Ganga and Brahmaputra's flow.

4. Study the table carefully and answer the questions that follow

River	Length	Catchment Area
The Ganga	2525 km	8.61 lakh km^2
The Indus	1114 km	3.21 lakh km^2
The Brahmaputra	1100 km	1.94 lakh km^2

(i) Which is the longest and the largest river in India?

(ii) In India, the Indus covers a length of only 1114 km and area of 3.21 lakh km^2. What is its total length and total catchment area?

(iii) Where does the river Brahmaputra make a very deep gorge in the Himalayas?

Ans. (i) The longest and the largest river in India is Ganga. It originates in the Gangotri glacier near Gaumuk. Its length is 2525 km and it has a catchment area of 8.61 lakh km^2.

(ii) The total length of river Indus is 2880 km and its total area is 11.65 lakh km^2.

(iii) The river Brahmaputra makes very deep gorge near Namcha Barwa in Central Himalayas.

5. What do you mean by drainage? What are the different drainage patterns formed by the rivers?

Ans. The flow of water through well defined channels is known as 'drainage'. The drainage pattern of an area is the outcome of geological time period, nature and structure of rocks, topography, slope, amount of water and periodicity of flow.

For major types of drainage pattern refer to text on page no. 311-312 under the heading 'Important Drainage Patterns'.

6. What is the place of origin of river Kaveri? Why it has water in its catchment throughout the year?

Ans. River Kaveri originates in Brahmagiri hills of Kodagu district in Karnataka. Its length is 800 km and drains an area of 81,155 sq km in Kerala, Karnataka and Tamil Nadu. Its important tributaries are the Kabini, the Bhavani and the Amravati.

It has water in its catchment throughout the year as this is the only river of the Peninsular India which receives rainfall from South-West monsoon as well as North-East monsoon winds.

7. Mention three geological events that have shaped the present drainage system of the Peninsular India.

Ans. The three geological events that have shaped the present drainage system of the Peninsular India are

(i) Sinking of the Western flank of the Peninsula leading to its submergence below the sea during the early tertiary period (5 million years ago).

(ii) Upheaval of the Himalayas when the Northern flank of the Peninsular block was subjected to sinking and the consequent trough faulting.

(iii) Slight tilting of the Peninsular block from North-West to the South-Eastern direction gave orientation to the entire drainage system towards the Bay of Bengal.

8. In modern times, direct use of river water is restricted. Why?

Ans. In modern times direct use of river water is restricted due to the following reasons

- No availability of water in sufficient quantity.
- River water pollution.
- Problem of sedimentation or load of silt in water.
- Uneven seasonal flow of water.
- River water disputes between states.
- Shrinking of channels due to the extension of settlements towards the banks and lower valleys.
- Damage to natural ecology of rivers.

9. Write a short note on Gorges and Rift Valleys.

Ans. **Gorges** Gorges are the narrow, steep sided valleys having almost vertical edges. These are associated with compressional forces in which folding occurs. There is much tearing and wearing down of rocks. These valleys came into existence during the deep cutting into the rocks by fast flowing rivers.

Rift Valleys A depression formed by faulting processes through which river begins to flow is termed as a rift valley. There is negligent wearing and tearing of rocks as the rock strata (layer) is very hard and resistant. Rift valleys occur due to the sliding down of the rock strata.

10. What is the difference between tributary and distributary?

Ans. Differences between tributary and distributary are as follows

Tributary	Distributary
It is a river or stream which contributes its water to a main river by discharging it into the latter.	It is a branch or outlet which leaves a main river and does not rejoin it, carrying its water to the sea or a lake.
It is generally found in the upper or the middle course of a river.	It is found in the lower course of the river.
It increases the activity of the main river.	It is formed near the river's mouth before it falls into the sea. There it flows very sluggishly (slowly).

11. 'Rainwater is losing its economic and asthetic values due to pollution'. Explain the causes of river pollution and its impact on our health. Competency Based Que

Ans. Most of the Indian rivers and their tributaries are highly polluted due to the following reasons

- Discharge of untreated sewage disposal and industrial effluents directly into the rivers. These wastes usually contain a wide variety of organic and inorganic pollutants including solvents, grease, plastics, heavy metals and pesticides.
- A large amount of waste generated by big colonies, slums, hotels, hospital with no proper disposal system and dumping grounds near settlements pollute river water.

The polluted water has negative impact on human health such as

- High quantity of calcium in water is one of the causes for gastrointestinal diseases and increased kidney stone problems in people.
- Excess presence of chlorine in water leads to diarrhoea and skin allergies.

12. Write a short note on Namami Devi Narmada.

Ans. Namami Devi Narmada is a campaign conceived and coordinated by Government of Madhya Pradesh as a people's movement to protect the environment.

The objectives of Namami Devi Narmada are

- To increase awareness about need for conservation of river Narmada and sustainable use of its resources.
- Plantation at banks of river Narmada for protection of riparian zone and reduction in soil erosion.
- To suggest remedial action in the field of river conservation and promotion of eco-friendly agricultural practices.
- To identify various sources on river pollution and to resolve same through public awareness and participation.
- It also includes planting 60 million trees along the river's bank and promotion of fruit cultivation among farmers.

13. **Would there be life without freshwater? Can rainwater harvesting preserve the water resources?** Competency Based Que

Ans. No, life is not possible without freshwater. Water is no longer an abundant resource as we have been over exploiting surface and groundwater to meet the increasing demands. This has resulted in an alarming fall in the quantity and quality of water.

Yes, rainwater harvesting can be practised to save our water resources. Rainwater harvesting is a simple, economical and eco-friendly method of water conservation. It is an ideal solution to recharge the groundwater by controlling the flow of surface water.

Benefits of rainwater harvesting are

- Quality of groundwater improves.
- Raises the water levels in wells and borewells.
- Mitigates the effects of drought conditions.
- Reduces soil erosion as the surface runoff is reduced.
- Choking of drains and flooding of roads decreases.

Long Answer Type Questions

1. **On the basis of mode of origin, nature and characteristics, the Indian drainage system is classified into how many groups? Discuss in brief.**

Ans. On the basis of the mode of origin, nature and characteristics, the Indian drainage system is classified into two groups

(i) **The Himalayan Drainage**

Many geologists believe that mighty river called Shivalik or Indo-Brahma came into being due to Earth's movement in the Miocene (tertiary) period (5-24 million years ago). It flowed in the entire longitudinal extent of the Himalayas from Assam to Punjab and finally discharged into the Gulf of Sindh.

It has also been proved by the remarkable continuity of Shivalik and its lacustrine origin (sediments in the beds of lakes) consisting of sand, silt, clay, boulders and conglomerates. Then, the Indo-Brahma river was dismembered (separated or divided) into three main drainage systems i.e.

(a) The Indus and its five tributaries in the Western part.

(b) The Ganga and its Himalayan tributatries in Central part.

(c) The Brahmaputra and its Himalayan tributaries in the Eastern part.

This dismemberment was due to upheaval in the Western Himalayas and the Potwar plateau (Delhi Ridge) which acted as water divide between the Indus and the Ganga.

In the East, the Ganga and the Brahmaputra dismembered from Shiwalik due to the submergence of Malda gap area between the Rajmahal hills and the Meghalaya plateau.

(ii) **The Peninsular Drainage System** Three major geological events in the distant past have shaped the present drainage systems of Peninsular India.

Sinking of the Western flank of the Peninsula leading to its submergence below the sea during the early tertiary period (5 milion years ago).

Upheaval of the Himalayas when the Northern flank of the Peninsular block was subjected to sinking and the consequent trough faulting. For example, the Narmada and the Tapi flow in trough/faults.

Slight tilting of the Peninsular block from North-West to the South-Eastern direction gave orientation to the entire drainage system towards the Bay of Bengal.

Important rivers of this drainage system includes Mahanadi, Godavari, Krishna, Kaveri, Narmada, Tapi and Luni river.

2. **Give five points of difference between the Himalayan rivers and Peninsular river.** CBSE Diksha

Ans. The difference between the Himalayan rivers and Peninsular rivers is discussed below

Himalayan River System	Peninsular Rivers System
This system is younger than the Peninsular river system.	This sytem is older than the Himalayan river system.
These rivers receive water from melting of glaciers, snow and rainfall.	These rivers generally depends on rainfall for water.
They are perennial which means flow throughout the year.	They are seasonal.
They do not have fixed courses and there is presence of meanders.	They have fixed courses and there is absence of meanders.
Examples The Ganga, the Indus, etc.	**Examples** The Mahanadi, the Godavari, etc.

3. **Why are rivers considered as the 'Lifeline of Indian Economy'?**

Ans. Rivers are considered as the lifeline of Indian economy because of the following reasons

Source of Freshwater Rivers are the major source of freshwater which has made the survival possible as most of our requirements are met by these rivers. The total flow of surface water in India is estimated about 1,350 cubic kms.

Agriculture and Irrigation The fertile river banks and perennial rivers made India an agricultural country. Rainfall in India is seasonal and unevenly distributed, therefore rivers become the main source of irrigation. By constructing canal 33% of annual flow of the Indian rivers is used for irrigation.

Navigation In the past, rivers were the only mode of transportation, that's why people settled in the river valleys and they still use them for navigation. The country has a navigable waterways of about 10,600 km and the major navigable rivers are the Ganga, the Brahmaputra, the Mahanadi, the Godavari and the Krishna.

Hydro-Electric Production Large rivers have great water power potential and they are also used for generating hydro-power. India's hydro-electric power potential is estimated at 84,000 MW and in March 2016, its installed utility scale was 42,783 MW.

Rivers Provide Shelter Rivers provide shelter or a home to wide variety of rare plants and marine animals. Diversity of these living beings still have not been explored to its fullest but a large number of fish, birds and other living organisms survive in river water.

4. Which is the Westernmost Himalayan river in India? Describe its features in detail.

Ans. Indus river, also known as Sindhu is the Westernmost Himalayan river in India. In Tibet region, it is known as Singi Khambab or Lion's Mouth.

The main features of the Indus river system are as follows

- The Indus is one of the largest river basins in the world. It covers area of 11,65,000 sq km (321,289 sq km in India).
- The total length of it is 2,880 km out of which 1,114 km is in India.
- It rises from a glacier near Bokhar Chu in the Kailash mountain range and falls into the Arabian sea forming a large delta.
- It flows between the Ladakh and Zaskar ranges and forms a gorge near Gilgit cutting across the Ladakh range.
- It enters into Pakistan near Chilas in the Dardistan region and meets with five tributaries of Punjab above Mithankot.
- These fives rivers are called Panjnad and they include Sutlaj, Beas, Ravi, Chenab and Jhelum.
- It flows only through Jammu and Kashmir in India and drains into Arabian sea, after crossing Pakistan. It is joined by many Himalayan rivers on its left bank such as the Shyok, the Zaskar, the Nubra, the Hunza, etc and many of them join it from the right bank such as the Kabul, the Khurram and the Gomal, etc.

5. Give the main features of the two long rivers of the Peninsular India, one flowing towards the East and one towards the West.

Ans. In the Peninsular region, the longest river flowing towards the East is the Godavari and towards the West is the Narmada.

Characteristics of Godavari are

- It is 1,465 km long with the catchment area of 3.13 lakh sq km.
- It rises in the Nasik district of Maharashtra and forms a large delta before it discharges its water into the Bay of Bengal.
- It covers the maximum distance in Maharashtra, then flows through the states of Madhya Pradesh, Chhattisgarh, Odisha and Andhra Pradesh.
- Its main tributaries are the Penganga, the Indravati, the Pranhita and the Manjira. It is navigable only in the deltaic stretch and splits into distributaries after Rajamundri. It is also known as Dakshin Ganga.

Characteristics of Narmada are:

- It has total length of about 1,312 km with the catchment area of 98,796 sq km.
- It rises at a height of 1,057 m from the Western flank of the Amarkantak plateau in Madhya Pradesh.
- Flowing in a rift valley between the Satpura and the Vindhyan ranges, it forms a picturesque gorge and Dhuadhar waterfall near Jabalpur in Madhya Pradesh.
- Sardar Sarovar Project is one of the largest dams constructed on this river.

6. Explain the factors responsible for river pollution in India. Suggest a few measures to solve the problem. **CBSE Diksha**

Ans. In India, river pollution is mainly due to human activities. Untreated sewage from cities and industrial waste are major contributors, dumping harmful chemicals and pathogens directly into rivers. Cultural practices, such as the immersion of idols and other religious offerings, also introduce pollutants. Additionally, excessive agricultural runoff containing pesticides and fertilisers contaminates river water.

To address river pollution, several measures can be implemented

- Improve sewage treatment facilities to prevent untreated waste from entering rivers.
- Strictly regulate and monitor industrial discharges, ensuring effluents are treated before disposal.
- Promote eco-friendly practices for religious and cultural events to reduce waste in rivers.

- Encourage sustainable farming to minimise pesticide and fertiliser runoff.
- Increase public awareness about the impact of pollution on river ecosystems.

Source Based Questions

1. Read the passage carefully and answer the questions that follow.

There are a large number of river systems in the Peninsular drainage. The Mahanadi rises near Sihawa in Raipur district of Chhattisgarh and runs through Odisha to discharge its water into the Bay of Bengal. Some navigation is carried on in the lower course of this river. Fifty three per cent of the drainage basin of this river lies in Madhya Pradesh and Chhattisgarh, while 47 per cent lies in Odisha. The Godavari is the largest Peninsular river system. It is also called the Dakshin Ganga. It rises in the Nasik district of Maharashtra and discharges its water into the Bay of Bengal. Its tributaries run through the states of Maharashtra, Madhya Pradesh, Chhattisgarh, Odisha and Andhra Pradesh. It is 1,465 km long with a catchment area spreading over 3.13 lakh sq. km 49 per cent of this, lies in Maharashtra, 20 per cent in Madhya Pradesh and Chhattisgarh, and the rest in Andhra Pradesh.

(i) Which of the following statements is correct for the Mahanadi River?

(a) It rises near Surat in Gujarat.
(b) 49% of this river lies in Maharashtra.
(c) It runs through Odisha to discharge into the Bay of Bengal.
(d) It is 750 km long.

Ans. (c) It runs through Odisha to discharge into the Bay of Bengal.

(ii) Why Godavari river is known as 'Dakshin Ganga'?

(a) It is the largest Peninsular river
(b) Due to its cultural significance
(c) It rises in Raipur
(d) All of the above

Ans. (a) It is the largest Peninsular river

(iii) Identify the following states of tributaries of the Godawari river from the following.

(a) Maharashtra, Odisha, Rajasthan
(b) Odisha, Madhya Pradesh, Haryana
(c) Chhattisgarh, Andhra Pradesh, Odisha
(d) Maharashtra, Madhya Pradesh, Odisha

Ans. (d) Maharashtra, Madhya Pradesh, Odisha

2. Read the passage carefully and answer the questions that follow.

The Himalayan drainage system has evolved through a long geological history. It mainly includes the Ganga, the Indus and the Brahmaputra river basins. Since these are fed both by melting of snow and precipitation, rivers of this system are perennial. In the Himalayan reaches, the course of these rivers is highly tortous, but over the plains they display a strong meandering tendency and shift their courses frequently. River Kosi, also know as the 'sorrow of Bihar', has been notorious for frequently changing its course. The Kosi brings huge quantity of sediments from its upper reaches and deposits it in the plains. The course gets blocked, and consequently, the river changes its course.

However, geologists believe that a mighty river called Shiwalik or Indo-Brahma traversed the entire longitudinal extent of the Himalaya from Assam to Punjab and onwards to Sind, and finally discharged into the Gulf of Sind near lower Punjab during the Miocene period some 5-24 million years ago. The remarkable continuity of the Shiwalik and its lacustrine origin and alluvial deposits consisting of sands, silt, clay, boulders and conglomerates support this viewpoint. It is opined that in due course of time Indo– Brahma river was dismembered into three main drainage systems

(i) The Indus and its five tributaries in the western part.
(ii) The Ganga and its Himalayan tributaries in the Central part.
(iii) The stretch of the Brahmaputra in Assam and its Himalayan tributaries in the Eastern part.

The dismemberment was probably due to the Pleistocene upheaval in the Western Himalayas, including the uplift of the Potwar Plateau (Delhi Ridge), which acted as the water divide between the Indus and Ganga drainage systems.

(i) What is the most important reason behind river Kosi being called as 'sorrow of Bihar'?

Ans. The river Kosi is known as 'sorrow of Bihar' because of frequent floods in the river.

(ii) Why did Shivalik river divided into various river systems?

Ans. Due to upliftment of Western Himalayas, Shivalik river got divided into various river systems.

(iii) Which physical features acts as a water divide between Indus and Ganga river systems?

Ans. Potwar plateau acts as a water divide between Indus and Ganga river systems.

3. Read the passage carefully and answer the questions that follow.

The Ganga is the most important river of India both from the point of view of its basin and cultural significance. It rises in the Gangotri glacier near Gaumukh (3,900 m) in the Uttarkashi district of Uttarakhand. Here, it is known as the Bhagirathi. It cuts through the Central and the Lesser Himalayas in narrow gorges. At Devprayag, the Bhagirathi meets the Alaknanda; hereafter, it is known as the Ganga. The Alaknanda has its source in the Satopanth glacier above Badrinath. The Alaknanda consists of the Dhauli and the Vishnu Ganga which meet at Joshimath or Vishnu Prayag.

The other tributaries of Alaknanda such as the Pindar joins it at Karna Prayag while Mandakini or Kali Ganga meets it at Rudra Prayag. The Ganga enters the plains at Haridwar. From here, it flows first to the South, then to the South-East and East before splitting into two distributaries, namely the Bhagirathi and the Padma. The river has a length of 2,525 km. It is shared by Uttarakhand (110 km) and Uttar Pradesh (1,450 km), Bihar (445 km) and West Bengal (520 km). The Ganga basin covers about 8.6 lakh sq. km area in India alone.

The Ganga river system is the largest in India having a number of perennial and non-perennial rivers originating in the Himalayas in the North and the Peninsula in the South, respectively. The Son is its major right bank tributary. The important left bank tributaries are the Ramganga, the Gomati, the Ghaghara, the Gandak, the Kosi and the Mahananda. The river finally discharges itself into the Bay of Bengal near the Sagar Island.

(i) How the Ganga river is formed?

Ans. The Ganga river rises in the Gangotri glacier near Gaumukh (3,900 m) in the Uttarkashi district of Uttarakhand. Here, it is known as the Bhagirathi. It cuts through the Central and the Lesser Himalayas in narrow gorges. At Devprayag, the Bhagirathi meets the Alaknanda; hereafter, it is known as the Ganga.

(ii) How many Prayags are formed by the Alaknanda river on its course?

Ans. The Alaknanda in its upper course is joined by its tributaries and forms important pilgrimage sites known as five Prayags. These are Vishnu Prayag, Nanda Prayag, Karna Prayag, Rudra Prayag and Dev Prayag.

(iii) Which states are benefitted by the Ganga river?

Ans. Following states are benefitted by the Ganga river

- Uttarakhand (110 km)
- Uttar Pradesh (1,450 km)
- Bihar (445 km)
- West Bengal (520 km)

Map Based Questions

1 On a political map of India, mark the following rivers.

(i) Indus (ii) Narmada (iii) Tapi
(iv) Godavari (v) Krishna

Ans.

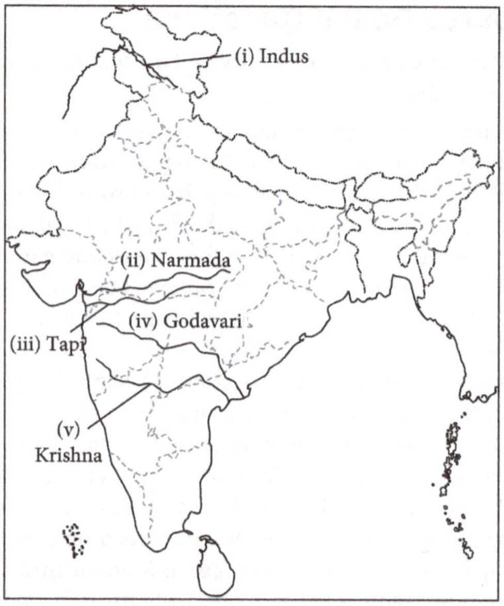

2 Locate the following rivers on the political map of India.

(i) Kaveri
(ii) Mahanadi
(iii) Tsangpo (Brahmaputra)
(iv) Satluj
(v) Ganga

Ans.

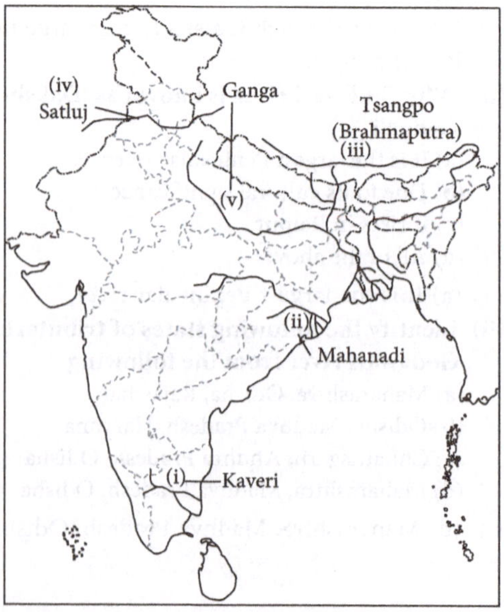

3. **On the map of India, mark the following rivers.**

(i) Yamuna (ii) Chambal

(iii) Damodar (iv) Luni

Ans.

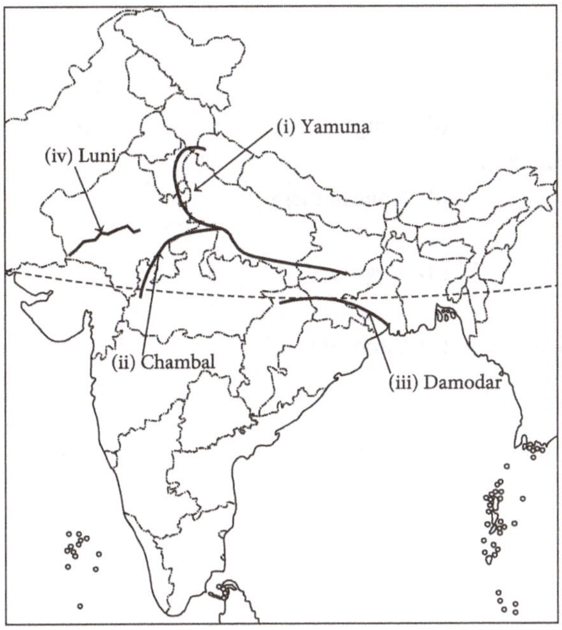

4. **Identify the lakes marked on the map given below.**

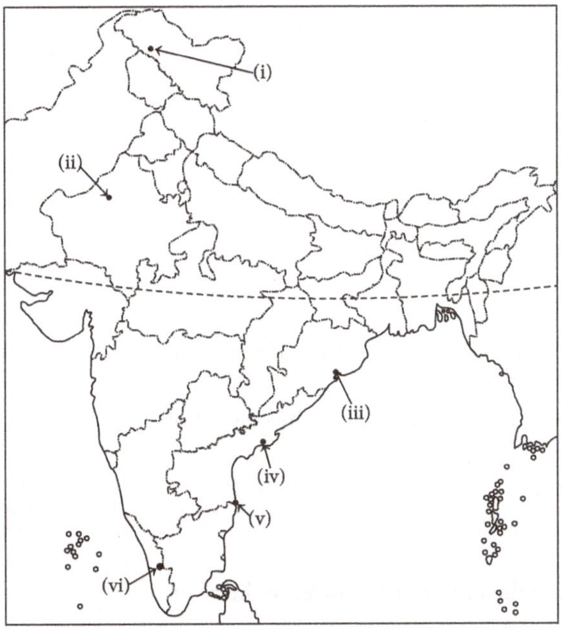

Ans.

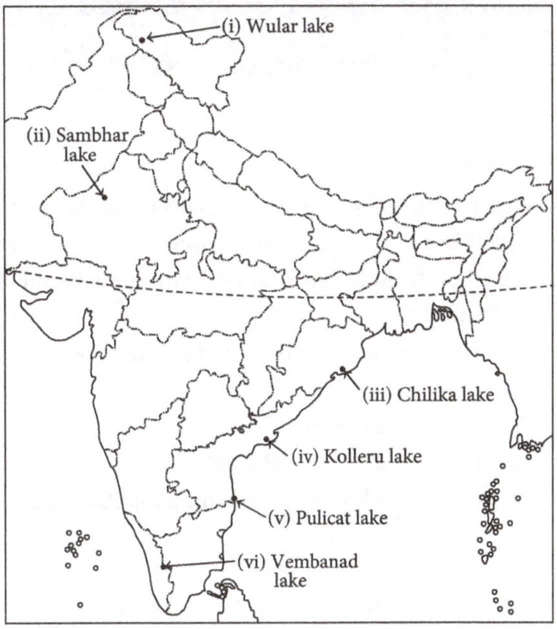

5. **On the map of India, mark the following**

(i) Palk Strait (ii) Rann of Kutch

(iii) Gulf of Kutch (iv) Gulf of Mannar

(v) Gulf of Khambat

Ans.

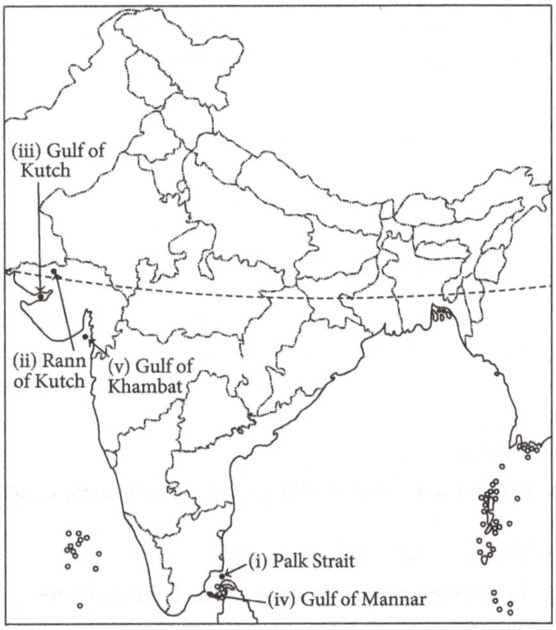

SELF ASSESSMENT TEST

Objective Type Questions

1. Which of the following rivers drains in the Arabian sea?
   (a) Krishna (b) Periyar (c) Mahanadi (d) Ganga
2. Which of the following drainage patterns is found on the Amarkantak range?
   (a) Dendritic (b) Trellis (c) Radial (d) None of these
3. Which of the following river basins is not medium river basin?
   (a) Kalindi (b) Pennar (c) Periyar (d) Meghna
4. The river Saryu rises in .... glacier.
   (a) Bandarpunch (b) Milam (c) Mapchachungo (d) Satopanth
5. Consider the following statements about the Himalayan rivers.
   I. They are perennial.
   II. They have no meanders.
   III. They shift their course frequently.
   IV. They are younger than peninsular rivers.

   Which of the given statement are correct?
   (a) II, III, IV (b) I, II, III (c) I, III, IV (d) I, II, IV
6. Match the following

	List I (River)		List II (Tributary)
A.	Ganga	1.	Gasting
B.	Indus	2.	Manjra
C.	Brahmaputra	3.	Mahananda
D.	Godavari	4.	Sankosh

Codes

	A	B	C	D
(a)	3	4	1	2
(b)	4	1	2	3
(c)	2	1	4	3
(d)	3	1	4	2

Short Answer Type Questions

7. Distinguish between Dendritic and Trellis drainage pattern.
8. The Himalayan drainage system has evolved through a long geological history. Explain the Himalayan river system.
9. The Ganga is the most important river of India. Describe Namami Gange Programme in the context of the statement.
10. Differentiate between the features of the Ganga and the Jhelum river.

Long Answer Type Questions

11. 'In the Himalayan drainage system, Ganga is the major river'. Write the important features of the river Ganga.
12. 'The Brahmaputra is one of the largest rivers of the world'. Explain the Brahmaputra drainage system along with its tributaries.
13. Explain the evolution of the Peninsular Drainage System and also include some major rivers of this system.

4 CHAPTER

Climate

This chapter deals with the climate of India and its variations. It describes the climate of India using different factors like weather, rainfall and winds. It discusses the working of monsoon. It also shows how India's climate affects farming.

YOUR STUDY GOALS

YOUR PRACTICE GOALS

- Objective Type Questions (18 Qs ; MCQs, Matching, A-R,)
- Subjective Questions (13 SAs, 7 LAs)
- Source Based Questions (2 Qs)
- Map Based Questions (2 Qs)

- Weather conditions vary during different seasons. These changes occur due to the changes in the elements of weather (temperature, pressure, wind direction and velocity, humidity and precipitation, etc).
- **Weather** is the momentary state of the atmosphere while **climate** refers to the average of the weather conditions over a longer period.
- Weather changes quickly, maybe within a day or week but climate changes are not felt and may be noted after 50 years or even more.

4.1 Unity and Diversity in the Monsoon Climate

- Monsoon refers to the climate associated with a seasonal reversal in the direction of winds. India has a hot monsoonal climate which is the prevalent climate in South and South-East Asia.
- The monsoon emphasises the unity of India with the rest of the South-East Asian region. However, there are regional variations in Indian weather and climate. For example, the climate of Kerala and Tamil Nadu in the South are different from that of Uttar Pradesh and Bihar in the North.
- The climate of India has many regional variations in terms of the pattern of winds, temperature and rainfall, rhythm of seasons and the degree of wetness or dryness. These regional diversities may be described as sub-types of monsoon climate.

For example,

- **Difference based on the pattern of winds** In the summer, the mercury occasionally touches 55°C in Western Rajasthan and it drops down to as low as minus 45°C in winter around Leh.
- **Difference based on precipitation** While snowfall occurs in the Himalayas, it only rains over the rest of the country. The amount of precipitation too varies from region to region. While **Cherrapunji** and **Mawsynram** in the Khasi Hills of Meghalaya receive rainfall over 1,080 cm in a year, Jaisalmer in Rajasthan rarely gets more than 9 cm of rainfall during the same period.
- **Difference based on the pattern of winds** The Ganga delta and the coastal plains of Odisha are hit by strong rain-bearing storms almost every third or fifth day in July and August while the Coromandel coast, a thousand km to the South, is generally during these months.

4.2 Factors Determining the Climate of India

- **Latitude** As the Tropic of Cancer passes through the central part of India in an East-West direction, the Northern part of India lies in the sub-tropical and temperate zone. The part lying South of the Tropic of Cancer falls in the tropical zone. The tropical zone being nearer to the equator, experiences high temperatures throughout the year with small daily and annual ranges. Area North of the Tropic of Cancer being away from the equator, experiences extreme climate with high daily and annual range of temperature.
- **The Himalayan Mountains** The lofty Himalayas in the North and its extensions act as an effective climatic divide. The tall mountain chain provides a shield to protect the subcontinent from the cold Northern winds. These cold and chilly winds originate near the Arctic Circle and blow across central and Eastern Asia. The Himalayas also trap the monsoon winds, forcing them to shed their moisture within the subcontinent.
- **Distribution of Land and Water** India is surrounded by the Indian Ocean on three sides in the South and covered by high and continuous mountains in the North. As compared to the landmass, water heats up or cools down slowly. This differential heating of land and sea creates different air pressure zones in different seasons in and around the Indian subcontinent. Difference in air pressure causes a reversal in the direction of monsoon winds.
- **Distance from the Sea** Along the coastal area there is less or no climate variation. Areas in the interior of India are far away from the moderating influence of the sea. Such areas have extremes of climate. That is why, the people of Mumbai and the Konkan coast have hardly any idea of extremes of temperature and the seasonal rhythm of weather. On the other hand, the seasonal contrasts in weather at places in the interior of the country such as Delhi, Kanpur and Amritsar affect the entire sphere of life.
- **Altitude** Temperature decreases with height. Due to thin air, places in the mountains are cooler than places on the plains. For example, Agra and Darjeeling are located on the same latitude, but the temperature of January in Agra is 16°C whereas it is only 4°C in Darjeeling.
- **Relief** The physiography or relief of India also affects the temperature, air pressure, direction and speed of wind and the amount and distribution of rainfall. The windward sides of Western Ghats and Assam receive high rainfall during June-September whereas the Southern plateau remains dry due to its leeward situation along the Western Ghats.

4.3 The Nature of Indian Monsoon

- Systematic studies of the causes of rainfall in the South Asian region help to understand the causes and salient features of the monsoon, such as the onset of the monsoon and break in the monsoon.

The Onset of the Monsoon

- The differential heating of land and sea during the summer months is the mechanism that sets the monsoon winds to drift towards the Indian subcontinent.
- During April and May when the Sun shines vertically over the Tropic of Cancer, the large landmass in the North of the Indian Ocean gets intensely heated. This causes the formation of low pressure in the North-Western part of the subcontinent.
- As the pressure towards South of Indian Ocean is high, the wind starts to move towards the low pressure areas towards equator.
- These conditions help in the Northward shift in the position of the ITCZ[1]. The South-West monsoon may thus, be seen as a continuation of the South-East trade winds deflected towards the Indian subcontinent after crossing the Equator. These winds cross the Equator between 40°E and 60°E longitudes.
- The shift in the position of the ITCZ is also related to the phenomenon of withdrawal of the Westerly jet stream[2] from its position over the North Indian plain, South of the Himalayas.
- The Easterly jet stream sets along 15°N latitude when the Western jet stream withdraws itself from the region. This Easterly jet stream is held responsible for the burst of the monsoon in India.

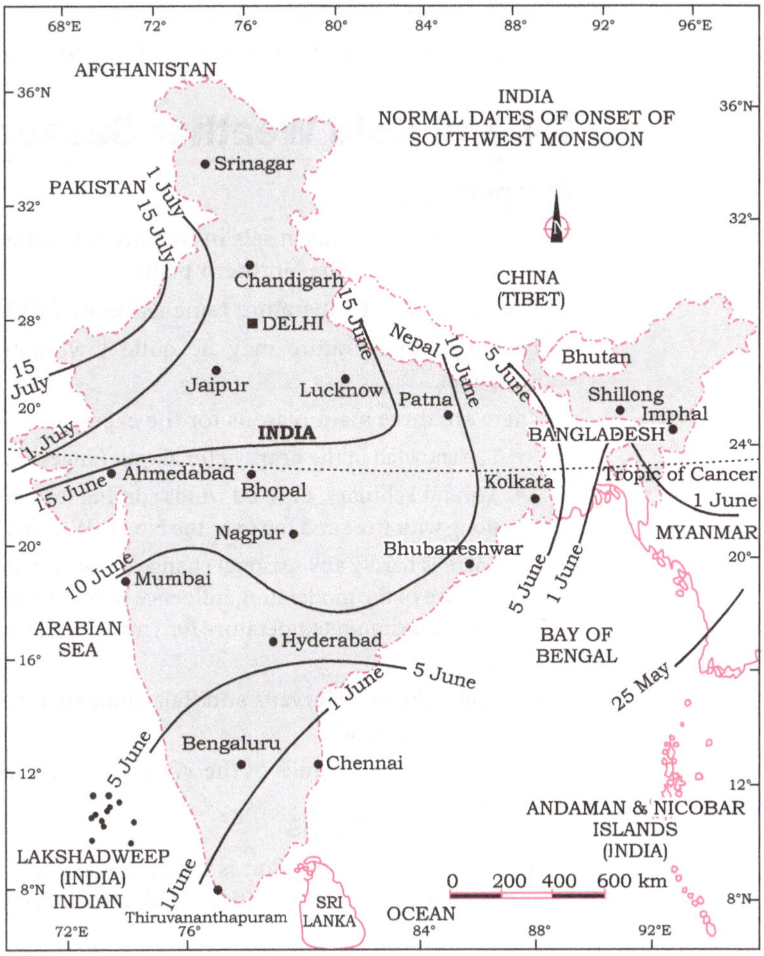

▲ *The onset of the Monsoon*

- The South-West monsoon sets in over the Kerala coast by the 1st of June and moves towards Mumbai and Kolkata between the 10th and 13th of June. By mid-July, South-West monsoon enters the entire subcontinent.

Break in the Monsoon

- During the South-West monsoon period after having rains for a few days, if rain fails to occur for one or more weeks, it is known as a break in the monsoon.
- These dry periods are quite common during the rainy season. These breaks in the different regions are due to different reasons
  - In Northern India rains are likely to fail if the rain-bearing storms are not very frequent along the monsoon trough or the ITCZ over this region.
  - Towards West coast, there is dry period (less rainfall) when wind blow parallel to the coast.

1 **ITCZ** It is a region around the equator where trade winds from Northern hemisphere and Southern hemisphere intersect.
2 **Jet streams** These are fast flowing air currents in the upper atmosphere of the Earth.

Quick Test 1

1. How can regional variations in Indian climate be identified?
2. What is the impact of Himalayas in maintaining India's climate?
3. Which phenomenon is related with withdrawl of the Westerly jet streams?
4. Which period is considered as dry towards the West coast of India?

4.4 The Cold Weather Season

Temperature

- The cold weather season sets in by **mid-November** in Northern India. **December** and **January** are the coldest months in the Northern plain.
- The mean daily temperature remains below 21°C and cover most parts of Northern India.
- The night temperature may be quite low, sometimes going below freezing point in Punjab and Rajasthan.
- There are three main reasons for the excessive cold in North India during this season
    - The snowfall in the nearby Himalayan ranges creates a cold wave situation.
    - Around February, the cold winds coming from the Caspian Sea and Turkmenistan bring cold waves along with frost and fog over the North-Western parts of India.
    - There is hardly any seasonal change in the distribution pattern of the temperature in coastal areas because of the moderating influence of the sea and the proximity to the equator. For example, the mean maximum temperature for January at Thiruvananthapuram is as high as 21°C and for June, it is 29.5°C.
- States like Punjab, Haryana and Rajasthan are far away from the moderating influence of sea experience continental climate.
- Temperatures at the hills of the Western Ghats remain comparatively low.

Pressure and Winds

- By December 22nd, the Sun is directly over the Tropic of Capricorn in the Southern hemisphere. This leads to high-pressure conditions in the Northern plains of India, while Southern India has slightly lower air pressure.
    - **Isobars** of 1019 mb and 1013 mb pass through North-West India and far South India.
    - Winds start blowing from the high-pressure area in the North-West towards the lower-pressure area over the Indian Ocean to the South. As the pressure difference is low, these winds are light, blowing at about 3-5 km per hour.
    - The shape of the land affects the direction of these winds
        - In the Ganga Valley, winds blow West or North-West.
        - In the Ganga-Brahmaputra delta, they blow North.
        - Over the Bay of Bengal, the winds are North-Easterly.
- During winter, India generally has pleasant weather. Sometimes, this calm weather is interrupted by shallow cyclonic depressions that form over the Eastern Mediterranean Sea.
- These depressions travel East across West Asia, Iran, Afghanistan and Pakistan before reaching North-Western India. They pick up moisture from the Caspian Sea and the Persian Gulf, bringing occasional changes in the weather in Northern India.

Rainfall

- Winter monsoons do not cause rainfall as they move from land to the sea. As they have little humidity and anti-cyclonic circulation on land, the possibility of rainfall from them is reduced. So, most parts of India do not have rainfall in the winter season. There are some exceptions to it.
- In North Western India, some weak temperate cyclones from the Mediterranean Sea cause rainfall in Punjab, Haryana, Delhi and Western Uttar Pradesh. It is highly beneficial for **rabi crops.**
- The precipitation is in the form of snowfall in the lower Himalayas. This snow sustains the flow of water in the Himalayan rivers during the summer months.
- The precipitation decreases from West to East in the plains and from North to South in the mountains. The average winter rainfall in Delhi is around 53 mm. In Punjab and Bihar, rainfall remains between 25 mm and 18 mm respectively.
    - Central parts of India and Northern parts of the Southern Peninsula also get winter rainfall occasionally.
    - Arunachal Pradesh and Assam in the North-Eastern parts of India also have rains between 25 mm and 50 mm during these winter months.
    - During October and November, North-East monsoon while crossing over the Bay of Bengal, picks up moisture and causes torrential rainfall over the Tamil Nadu coast, Southern Andhra Pradesh, South-East Karnataka and South-East Kerala.

4.5 The Hot Weather Season

Temperature

- In March, as the Sun moves **towards the Tropic of Cancer**, temperatures in North India start rising.
- **April, May** and **June** are the summer months in North India, with most areas recording temperatures between 30°C and 32°C. In March, the Deccan Plateau records the **highest daytime temperature**, around 38°C.
- By April, temperatures between 38°C and 43°C are common in Gujarat and Madhya Pradesh.
- In May, the heat spreads Northward and in North-West India, temperatures can reach up to 48°C.
- Summer in South India is milder because of the surrounding oceans, with temperatures generally staying between 26°C and 32°C.
- In the Western Ghats hills, the altitude keeps temperatures below 25°C.
- Coastal areas show that temperatures don't decrease from North to South but instead increase from the coast toward the interior.
- The daily minimum temperature during summer in most regions stays above 26°C.

Pressure and Winds

- The summer months bring extreme heat and lower air pressure in the Northern part of India. As the land heats up, the Inter-Tropical Convergence Zone (ITCZ) moves North and is positioned around 25°N by July.
- This low-pressure monsoon trough stretches from the Thar Desert to Patna and the Chotanagpur plateau.
- The location of the ITCZ causes a surface circulation of winds.
    - On the West coast and along West Bengal and Bangladesh, the winds are South-Westerly.
    - These South-Westerly monsoon winds actually originate from the displaced equatorial Easterlies. By mid-June, these winds bring the start of the rainy season.

- In North Bengal and Bihar, winds are Easterly or South-Easterly.
- In the North-West, dry, hot winds known as **Loo** blow in the afternoon and can continue until midnight.

- In May, dust storms are common in Punjab, Haryana, Eastern Rajasthan and Uttar Pradesh. They provide relief from heat through light rain and cool breezes.
- Sometimes, moist winds are pulled towards the edge of the low-pressure trough, causing intense local storms. These local storms can bring strong winds, heavy rains, and even hailstorms.

Some Famous Local Storms of Hot Weather Season

(i) ***Mango Shower*** Towards the end of summer, there are pre-monsoon showers which are a common phenomenon in Kerala and coastal areas of Karnataka. Locally, they are known as mango showers since they help in the early ripening of mangoes.

(ii) **Blossom Shower** With this shower, coffee flowers blossom in Kerala and nearby areas.

(iii) **Nor Westers** They are also known as **Kalbaishakhi**. These winds blow in region of Bengal and Assam along with heavy rainfall and thunderstorm. These showers are useful for tea, jute and rice cultivation. In Assam, these storms are known as **Bardoisila**.

(iv) **Loo** These are hot, dry and oppressing winds blowing in the Northern plains from Punjab to Bihar with higher intensity between Delhi and Patna.

4.6 The South-West Monsoon Season

- In May, temperatures in the North-Western plains of India increase rapidly, creating stronger low-pressure areas.
- By early June, this low-pressure zone attracts South-East trade winds from the Southern Hemisphere over the Indian Ocean.
- These South-East trade winds cross the equator, and turn toward the Bay of Bengal and Arabian Sea. The South-East trade winds absorb lots of moisture present over the warm equatorial currents.
- After crossing the equator, they shift to a South-West direction, becoming the South-West monsoons.
- The South-West monsoon rains begin suddenly, often bringing a drop-in temperature, lightning and thunder, called the **break** or **burst** of the monsoons.
- Monsoon rains start in early June along the coast of Kerala, Karnataka, Goa and Maharashtra and reach interior regions by early July. Temperatures drop by 5°C to 8°C from mid-June to mid-July as these winds cover the land.
- The South-West monsoon approaches India in two branches : the **Arabian Sea** branch and the **Bay of Bengal** branch.

Monsoon Winds of the Arabian Sea

- **Western Ghats Branch** Winds hit the Western Ghats, rising to altitudes between 900-1200 meters. They cool and release heavy rainfall (250-400 cm) on the windward side of the Ghats and coastal plains. After crossing, the winds warm up, lose moisture, and bring little rainfall to the region East of the Ghats, known as the **'rain-shadow'** area.
- **Central India Branch** This branch moves North along the Narmada and Tapi river valleys, spreading rainfall over central India. It reaches the Chotanagpur Plateau, causing about 15 cm of rainfall, then moves into the Ganga plains, where it merges with the Bay of Bengal branch.

- **Saurashtra and Kachchh Branch** Winds hit Saurashtra Peninsula and Kachchh, bringing minimal rainfall as they move over West Rajasthan along the Aravalli mountains. These winds eventually meet the Bay of Bengal branch over Punjab and Haryana, intensifying rains in the Western Himalayas.
- The Tamil Nadu coast remains dry during Arabian Sea branch of South-West monsoon. Tamil Nadu coast is rainshadow zone/area of this branch.
- As the coast's position is parallel to the Bay of Bengal branch of the South-West monsoon, it doesn't receive direct rainfall.

Bay of Bengal Branch

- This branch first hits the coast of Myanmar and parts of South-East Bangladesh. The Arakan Hills deflect it towards India, where it enters West Bengal and Bangladesh from the South and South-East.
- This branch splits into two sub-branches under the influence of the Himalayas as follows

(i) **Ganga Plains Branch** It moves Westward along the Ganga plains, reaching the Punjab plains and causing rain across Northern India.

(ii) **Brahmaputra Valley Branch** It moves up the Brahmaputra valley in the North, bringing widespread rainfall to the North-Eastern states. A sub-branch reaches the Garo and Khasi hills in Meghalaya, where **Mawsynram** receives the **world's highest average annual rainfall**.

4.7 Season of Retreating Monsoon

- The months of **October** and **November** are known for **retreating monsoons**. By the end of September, the South-West monsoon becomes weak as the low-pressure belt of the Ganga plain starts moving Southward in response to the Sun's movement towards the South.
- The monsoon retreats from the Western Rajasthan by the first week of September. It withdraws from Rajasthan, Gujarat, Western Ganga Plain and the Central Highlands by the end of September.
- By the beginning of October, the low pressure covers Northern parts of the Bay of Bengal and by early November, it moves over Karnataka and Tamil Nadu. By the middle of December, the centre of low pressure is completely removed from the Peninsula.
- The retreating South-West monsoon season is characterised by clear skies and a temperature rise.
- Due to moist land with high temperature and humidity, the weather becomes heated. This is commonly known as the **October heat**.
- In the second half of October, the temperature begins to fall rapidly, in Northern India.
- The weather in the retreating monsoon is dry in North India but it is rainy in the Eastern part of the Peninsula. Here, October and November are the rainiest months of the year.
- The widespread rain in this season is associated with the cyclonic depressions that originated over the Andaman Sea and crossed over the Eastern coast of the Southern Peninsula. These tropical cyclones are very destructive.
- The thickly populated deltas of the Godavari, Krishna and Kaveri are affected by these cyclones. A few cyclonic storms also strike the coast of West Bengal, Bangladesh and Myanmar.
- A bulk of the rainfall of the Coromandel coast is derived from these depressions and cyclones. Such cyclonic storms are less frequent in the Arabian Sea.

EI-Nino and the Indian Monsoon

- EI-Nino is a complex weather system that appears once every three to seven years. This brings drought, floods and other weather extremes to different parts of the world.
- The system involves oceanic and atmospheric phenomena with the appearance of warm currents off the coast of Peru in the Eastern Pacific and affects weather in many places including India.
- EI-Nino is an extension of the warm equatorial current which gets replaced temporarily by cold Peruvian current or Humboldt current (locate these currents in your atlas). This current increases the temperature of water on the Peruvian coast by 10°C. This results in
  - The distortion of equatorial atmospheric circulation;
  - Irregularities in the evaporation of sea water;
  - Reduction in the amount of planktons which further reduces the number of fishes in the sea.
- The word EI-Nino means 'Child Christ' because this current appears around Christmas in December. December is a summer month in Peru (Southern Hemisphere).
- EI-Nino is used in India for forecasting long range monsoon rainfall.
- In 1990-91, there was a wild EI-Nino event and the onset of South-West monsoon was delayed over most parts of the country ranging from five to twelve days.

Quick Test 2

1. Mention any one reason due to which North India face excessive cold.
2. Why winter monsoon do not cause rainfall in Northern part of India?
3. In which region 'mango shower' phenomenon is observed?
4. Which region is rainshadow area of Arabian Sea branch of monsoon?
5. What is October heat?

4.8 Traditional Indian Seasons

- In the Indian tradition, a year is divided into **six seasons**. These seasons are set for two months as per Indian tradition.
- This cycle of seasons is based on the practical experience and age-old perception of weather phenomena of people from Northern and Central India. However, this system does not match with the seasons of South India where there is little variation in the seasons.

Seasons	**Months** (According to the Indian Calendar)	**Months** (According to the Gregorian Calendar)
Vasanta	Chaitra-Vaisakha	March-April
Grishma	Jyaistha-Asadha	May-June
Varsha	Sravana-Bhadra	July-August
Sharada	Asvina-Kartika	September-October
Hemanta	Margashirsa-Pausa	November-December
Shishira	Magha-Phalguna	January-February

Distribution of Rainfall

The average annual rainfall in India is about 125 cm, but it has great spatial variations.

- **Areas of High Rainfall** The highest rainfall occurs along the West coast, on the Western Ghats and in the sub-Himalayan areas in the North-East and the hills of Meghalaya. Here the rainfall exceeds 200 cm. In some parts of Khasi and Jaintia hills, the rainfall exceeds 1,000 cm. In the Brahmaputra valley and the adjoining hills, the rainfall is less than 200 cm.

- **Areas of Medium Rainfall** Rainfall between 100-200 cm is received in the Southern parts of Gujarat, East Tamil Nadu, North-Eastern Peninsula covering Odisha, Jharkhand, Bihar, Eastern Madhya Pradesh, Northern Ganga plain along the sub-Himalayas and the Cachar Valley and Manipur.
- **Areas of Low Rainfall** Western Uttar Pradesh, Delhi, Haryana, Punjab, Jammu and Kashmir, Eastern Rajasthan, Gujarat and Deccan Plateau receive rainfall between 50-100 cm.
- **Areas of Inadequate Rainfall** Parts of the Peninsula, especially in Andhra Pradesh, Karnataka, Maharashtra, Ladakh and most of Western Rajasthan receive rainfall below 50 cm.

Monsoon and Economic Life of India

- The entire agricultural cycle of India revolves around the monsoon. This is because about 64 per cent people of India depend on agriculture for their livelihood and agriculture itself is based on the South-West monsoon.
- Except Himalayas, all the parts of the country have suitable temperature to grow crops or plants throughout the year.
- Regional variations in monsoon climate help in growing various types of crops.
- The variability of rainfall brings droughts or floods every year in some parts of the country.
- The agricultural prosperity of India depends very much on timely and adequately distributed rainfall. If it fails, agriculture is adversely affected particularly in those regions where means of irrigation are not developed.
- Sudden monsoon burst creates the problem of soil erosion over large areas in India.
- Winter rainfall by temperate cyclones in North India is highly beneficial for rabi crops.
- Regional climatic variation in India is reflected in the vast variety of food, clothes and house types.

Global Warming

- The climate has changed in the past, both globally and locally.
- Large-scale industrialisation and polluting gases in the atmosphere contribute significantly to global warming.
- The **greenhouse effect** is a major factor in global warming and human-made carbon dioxide emissions are a major concern.
- Carbon dioxide levels in the atmosphere are rising due to fossil fuel burning. Other greenhouse gases, like methane, chlorofluorocarbons and nitrous oxide are present in smaller amounts. These gases are better in trapping terrestrial heat.
- These gases are increasing global temperatures, causing glaciers and polar ice caps to melt and adding more water to the oceans.
- Over the past 150 years, Earth's average surface temperature has risen. By 2100, it's expected that global temperatures will rise by about 2°C, leading to higher sea levels.
- The sea level is predicted to rise by 48 cm by the end of the 21st century, causing more frequent flooding.
- Climate change will increase the spread of insect-borne diseases, like malaria.
- Some areas will become wetter, while others will get drier, affecting farming and ecosystems.
- These changes will impact human populations and natural environments worldwide.

Quick Test 3

1. In how many season Indian climate is divided as per Indian tradition?
2. Which regions are identified as areas of low rainfall in India?
3. Mention any one impact of monsoon on economic life of India.
4. Which gases are included as green house gas?

Mind Map

CLIMATE

1 Unity and Diversity in Monsoon Climate

Regional Variation in Temperature
Example, on the same day, Rajasthan records 55°C, while Leh records minus 45°C.

Regional Variation in Rainfall
Example, on the same day, Cherrapunji records more than 1080 cm of rainfall while Jaisalmer records 9 cm of rainfall.

2 Factors Determining the Climate of India

- Latitude
- Himalayan mountains
- Distribution of land and water
- Distance from the sea
- Altitude
- Relief

3 The Nature of Indian Monsoon

Onset of the Monsoon
The arrival of the South-West monsoon over Indian sub-continent.

Break in Monsoon
The period when there is no rainfall for one week or more.

4 Seasons in India

Hot season
- April, May and June are the months of summer in North India .
- The weather is mild in South India.
- Heat waves like loo are common.

Cold Season
- Mild temperature in Southern region.
- Extreme temperature in North region.
- December and January are the coldest months in Northern plains.

Retreating Monsoon
Dry spells with cyclonic rainfall in October-November.

South-West Monsoon Season
Heavy rainfall occurs from June to September.

5 Traditional Indian Seasons

Distribution of Rainfall
The average annual rainfall in India is about 125 cm.
- **Areas of High Rainfall** Highest rainfall occurs along the West coast and in the sub-Himalayan areas in the North-East and the hills of Meghalaya(200cm).
- **Areas of Medium Rainfall** Rainfall between 100-200 cm is received in the Southern parts of Gujarat, East Tamil Nadu, North-Eastern Peninsula, etc.
- **Areas of Low Rainfall** Western Uttar Pradesh, Delhi, Haryana, Punjab, Jammu and Kashmir, Eastern Rajasthan, Gujarat and Deccan Plateau (50-100 cm).
- **Areas of Inadequate Rainfall** Parts of the Peninsula, especially in Andhra Pradesh, Karnataka, Maharashtra, Ladakh and most of Western Rajasthan (below 50 cm).

Monsoon and Economic Life of India
- Agricultural cycle of India revolves around the monsoon.
- About 64 per cent people of India depend on agriculture for their livelihood.
- Variations in monsoon climate help in growing various types of crops.

Global Warming
- Causes due to large-scale industrialisation and polluting gases in the atmosphere.
- Greenhouse effect is a major factor.
- Greenhouse gases, like methane, chlorofluorocarbons and nitrous oxide are increasing global temperatures, causing glaciers and polar ice caps to melt.

NCERT Folder

Choose the right answer from the four alternatives given below

(i) **What causes rainfall on the coastal areas of Tamil Nadu in the beginning of winters?**

(a) South-West monsoon
(b) Temperate cyclones
(c) North-Eastern monsoon
(d) Local air circulation

Ans. (c) North-Eastern monsoon

(ii) **What is the proportion of area of India which receives annual rainfall less than 75 cm?**

(a) Half
(b) One-third
(c) Two-third
(d) Three-fourth

Ans. (b) One-third

(iii) **Which one of the following is not a fact regarding South India?**

(a) Diurnal range of temperature is less here.
(b) Annual range of temperature is less here.
(c) Temperatures here are high throughout the year.
(d) Extreme climatic conditions are found here.

Ans. (d) Extreme climatic conditions are found here.

(iv) **Which one of the following phenomenon happens when the Sun shines vertically over the Tropic of Capricorn in the Southern hemisphere?**

(a) High pressure develops over North- Western India due to low temperature.
(b) Low pressure develops over North-Western India due to high temperature.
(c) No changes in temperature and pressure occur in North-Western India.
(d) 'Loo' blow in the North-Western India.

Ans. (a) High pressure develops over North-Western India due to low temperature.

Answer the following questions in about 30 words

(i) **What is the Inter-Tropical Convergence Zone?**

Ans. The Inter Tropical Convergence Zone (ITCZ) is a low pressure zone located at the equator where trade winds meet, which results in high humidity, frequent rainstorms and heavy rainfall.

(ii) **What is meant by 'bursting of monsoon'? Name the place of India which gets the highest rainfall.**

Ans. The sudden onset of South-West monsoon causing sudden and continuous heavy rains is known as the 'burst of monsoon'.

Mawsynram in Meghalaya gets the highest rainfall in India.

(iii) **Which types of cyclone cause rainfall in North-Western India during winter? Where do they originate?**

Ans. Temperate cyclones or Western disturbance causes rainfall in North-Western India during winter. Temperate cyclones originates in India from the Mediterranean Sea. They also cause snowfall in Northern India.

Answer the following questions in not more than 125 words

(i) **Not withstanding the broad climatic unity, the climate of India has many regional variations. Elaborate this statement giving suitable examples.**

Ans. Though, India has the tropical monsoon climate but it has many regional variations in temperature and rainfall that can be explained by the following examples

- On a summer day, Churu in Rajasthan may record a temperature of 50° C or more but Tawang in Arunachal Pradesh hardly touches 19° C on the same day.
- On a winter night, temperature at Drass (Ladakh) may drop down to -45° C while the places on the coasts in South India, records 20° C to 22° C temperature.
- Annual range of temperatures may be hardly 7° C to 8° C in Kerala and Andaman islands whereas, Thar desert experiences more than 20° C annual range of temperature.
- High mountains of Himalayas receive snowfall while rest of the country gets rainfall.
- Meghalaya gets more than 400 cm of rainfall while Western Rajasthan receives 20 cm of rainfall.
- Most parts of the country get rainfall during June to September, while coastal plains of Tamil Nadu receives rainfall in beginning of winter season.
- North India experiences continental or extreme climate, while South India has maritime climate.

(ii) How many distinct seasons are found in India as per the Indian Meteorological Department? Discuss the weather conditions associated with any one season in detail.

Ans. Indian Meteorological Department has recognised four distinct seasons such as cold weather season, hot weather season, South-West monsoon season and retreating monsoon season.

Season of Retreating Monsoon

The months of October and November are known for retreating monsoon. The pressure conditions start changing in the Northern India due to the apparent movement of Sun towards South. The South-West monsoon winds becomes weak as the low pressure trough of the Ganga plain moves towards South India.

The monsoon retreats from the Western Rajasthan by the first week of September and the low pressure is completely removed by the Peninsula by mid of December. The retreating season is marked by clear skies, rise in temperature and high humidity. This makes the weather oppressive commonly known as the 'October heat'.

This season is dry in North India but the South-Eastern part of the Peninsula gets most of its rain in these months. It is also marked by cyclonic depressions or tropical cyclones which originate over the Andaman Sea. These depressions are affected by the Easterly jet streams towards the coasts of Bangladesh, West Bengal, and cause destruction on these coasts.

Exam Pattern Questions

Objective Type Questions

Multiple Choice Questions (MCQs)

1. The momentary state of atmosphere is known as

(a) Climate (b) Temperature
(c) Weather (d) None of these

2. The climate of India exhibit regional variations in which of the following element?

(a) Pattern of winds (b) Rainfall
(c) Temperature (d) All of these

3. Choose the correct option regarding the consequence of El-Nino.

(a) Presence of cold Humbolt current along Peru coast
(b) Distortion of equatorial atmospheric circulation
(c) Increase in amount of plankton
(d) Early onset of monsoon in India

4. The pleasant weather conditions during winter in India are disturbed by cyclonic depressions originating in

(a) Mediterranean sea (b) South China sea
(c) Aral sea (d) Black sea

5. Which of the following region receive rainfall in winter season from North-East monsoon?

(a) Punjab
(b) Western Uttar Pradesh
(c) Southern Andhra Pradesh
(d) All of the above

6. Which of the following examples justify that there are seasonal variations in temperature from place to place and from region to region in India? CBSE Diksha

(a) In summer 55°C in the Western Rajasthan, -45°C in winter around Leh.
(b) On a June day temperature in Churu 50°C or more whereas in Tawang it is 19°C.
(c) On a December night, temperature in Drass - 45°C while in Thiruvananthapuram records 20°C on the same night.
(d) All of the above

7. There is widespread distribution of annual rainfall throughout India. Identify the region based on the given description.

Here the rainfall exceeds 200 cm. In some parts of Khasi and Jaintia hills, the rainfall exceeds 1,000 cm. In the Brahmaputra valley and the adjoining hills, the rainfall is less than 200 cm. This region includes the West coast, on the Western Ghats and the sub-Himalayan areas in the North-East and the hills of Meghalaya.

(a) Areas of high rainfall
(b) Areas of moderate rainfall
(c) Areas of low rainfall
(d) Areas of inadequate rainfall

8. **Winter rainfall is beneficial for cultivation of which type of crop?**

(a) Rabi crops (b) Kharif crops
(c) Zaid crops (d) All of these

9. **Consider the following statements and choose the correct statement.**

I. Areas North of Tropic of Cancer experience small daily and annual range of temperature.
II. The leeward side of mountain receives heavy rainfall.

Codes

(a) Only I (b) Only II
(c) Both I and II (d) None of these

10. **Consider the following statement regarding retreating monsoon and choose the incorrect ones.**

I. The months of October and November are known for retreating monsoons.
II. The monsoon retreats from the Eastern Rajasthan by the first week of September.
III. It withdraws from Rajasthan, Gujarat by the end of September.
IV. A few cyclonic storms also strike the coast of Maharashtra, Bangladesh and Myanmar.

Options

(a) I and II (b) II and IV
(c) I and IV (d) I and III

11. **Consider the following statements about Nor Westers and choose the correct statement**

I. They blow in Bengal and Assam.
II. Locally, they are known as Kalbaisakhi.
III. In Bengal, they are known as Bardoisila.
IV. They are useful for tea, jute and rice cultivation.

Codes

(a) I, II and III (b) II, III and IV
(c) I, II and IV (d) I, III and IV

Arrange the Following

12. **Which of the following are correctly arranged in ascending order according to the annual rainfall received by them?**

(i) Andhra Pradesh
(ii) Bihar
(iii) Khasi Hills
(iv) Western Uttar Pradesh

Codes

(a) (i), (ii), (iii), (iv) (b) (iii), (ii), (i), (iv)
(c) (i), (iv), (ii), (iii) (d) (ii), (iv), (i), (ii)

Match the Following

13.

List I (Traditional Season)		List II (Months)	
A.	Vasanta	1.	September-October
B.	Grishma	2.	March-April
C.	Sharada	3.	November-December
D.	Hemanta	4.	May-June

Codes

	A	B	C	D		A	B	C	D
(a)	4	2	3	1	(b)	2	4	1	3
(c)	4	3	2	1	(d)	3	2	4	1

14.

List I		List II	
A.	Tropic of Cancer	1.	Temperature decreases with height
B.	The Himalayan Mountains	2.	Traps the monsoon winds
C.	Distribution of Land and Water	3.	High temperatures throughout the year
D.	Altitude	4.	Creates different air pressure zones

Codes

	A	B	C	D		A	B	C	D
(a)	3	2	4	1	(b)	1	2	3	4
(c)	4	3	2	1	(d)	1	4	3	2

Assertion-Reason

Directions (Q. Nos. 15-18) In the questions given below are two statements labelled as Assertion (A) and other is labelled as Reason (R). In the context of two statements, which one of the following is correct?

Codes

(a) Both A and R are true, but R is not the correct explanation of A
(b) Both A and R are true and R is the correct explanation of A
(c) Both A and R are incorrect
(d) A is correct, but R is incorrect

15. **Assertion** (A) Mountains are cooler than plains.
Reason (R) Air is thick near sea level and density of air decreases with height.

16. **Assertion** (A) Peninsular region do not have well defined cold season.
Reason (R) Peninsular region has sea on two sides and close proximity to equator.

17. **Assertion** (A) East of Western Ghats receive high rainfall.
Reason (R) The winds after crossing Western Ghats descend and get cooled which reduces humidity in the winds.

18. **Assertion** (A) South-East trade winds are attracted towards the Indian subcontinent from the South of the equator.
Reason (R) An intense low pressure is formed in the North-Western part of the subcontinent due to vertical sun rays over the Tropic of Cancer.

Answers

1. (c) Weather
2. (d) All of these
3. (b) Distortion of equatorial atmospheric circulation
4. (a) Mediterranean sea
5. (c) Southern Andhra Pradesh
6. (d) All of the above
7. (a) Areas of high rainfall
8. (a) Rabi crops
9. (d) None of these
10. (b) II and IV
11. (c) I, II and IV
12. (c) (i), (iv), (ii), (iii)
13. (b)
14. (a)
15. (b) Both A and R are true and R is the correct explanation of A
16. (d) A is correc, but R is incorrect
17. (c) Both A and R are incorrect
18. (b) Both A and R are true and R is the correct explanation of A

Subjective Questions

Short Answer Type Questions

1. Explain the spatial temperature variations in India.

Ans. India is a vast country with different physiology and temperature. Some examples of spatial variation in temperature are as follows

- In Western Rajasthan, the temperature rises to 55° C in summer and drops down to -45° C in winters in Leh region in Jammu and Kashmir.
- Churu in Rajasthan may record a temperature of 50° C or more on a day in June, while the mercury hardly touches 19° C in Tawang in Arunachal Pradesh on the same day.
- On a December night, the temperature in Drass in Jammu and Kashmir may drop to -45° C, while Chennai or Thiruvananthapuram records 20° C or 22° C.
- The difference between day and night temperature in Kerala and Andaman islands is low, may be 7° C or 8° C, whereas the difference in day and night in the Thar desert may be 30° C to 35° C.

2. Briefly describe the South-West monsoon season in India.

Ans. South-West monsoon season begins in June and ends in September. The low pressure conditions over the North-Western plains get further intensified and are powerful enough to attract the trade winds of the Southern hemisphere. The South-East trade winds cross the equator and are deflected towards the right due to the coriolis force and blow into the Indian landmass as South-West monsoon winds.

Due to the tapering shape of Peninsular India, the South-West monsoon winds get divided into two branches

(i) The Arabian Sea branch.
(ii) The Bay of Bengal branch.

3. Why is there excessive cold in North India during winter?

Ans. The following are the reasons for excessive cold in North India during winters

- Punjab, Haryana and Rajasthan being far away from the moderating influence of sea experience continental climate.
- The snowfall in the nearby Himalayan ranges creates cold wave situation.
- The cold waves come from the Caspian Sea and Turkmenistan cause frost and fog over North-Western parts of India.
- On the other hand, in Peninsular region there is no well defined cold season due to moderating effect of the sea and proximity to equator.

4. "The climate of India is best described in terms of an annual cycle of seasons". Describe the characteristics of the hot weather season of India. Competency Based Que

Ans. The climate of India is characterised by a rhythm of seasons. The hot weather season starts from the months of March-April.

The characteristics of hot weather season are

Temperature April, May and June are the months of summer in North India where temperature ranges between 35° C to 45° C due to the apparent movement of the Sun towards the Tropic of Cancer. In South India, it is not so intense, as the surrounding water bodies keep the temperature low between 26° C to 32° C.

Pressure and Winds High temperature in North India leads to low pressure condition and the ITCZ moves Northwards at 25° N in July. This elongated low pressure trough, extends from Thar desert decent to Patna and Chotanagpur plateau.

Local Storms The dry conditions prevail in the larger part of North but temporary storms or the local winds bring a welcome respite from the oppressing heat. For example, Loo which are hot, dry and oppressing winds blow in the Northern plains from Punjab to Bihar and with higher intensity between Delhi and Patna.

5. The monsoon winds flowing in the South-Westerly direction approach the landmass of India in two branches. Describe how the Arabian sea branch of the monsoon causes rainfall in various regions. Competency Based Que

Ans.. The monsoon winds of the Arabian Sea branch split into three branches and cause rainfall in following regions

(i) One branch is obstructed by Western Ghats. As the winds climb the slopes of Western Ghats from 900-1200m, the winds become cool. This results in heavy rainfall on the windward side of Sahyadris and Western coastal plain.

After crossing the Western Ghats, these winds descend and get heated up which reduces humidity in the winds. This results in little rainfall East of Western Ghats.

(ii) The second branch strikes the coast North of Mumbai and cause rainfall in Central Highlands. The Chotanagpur plateau gets 15 cm of rainfall from this branch. The amount goes on decreasing towards East and then enters the Ganga plain to mingle with the Bay of Bengal branch.

(iii) The third branch of these winds strike the Saurashtra Peninsula and the Kachchh and move further towards Rajasthan, Punjab and Haryana. It causes little rain in Rajasthan, as the Aravalis are parallel to these winds. In Punjab and Haryana, it too joins Bay of Bengal branch. These two branches reinforce each other and cause rain in Western Himalayas.

6. Monsoon connotes the seasonal reversal in the direction of winds. Discuss about the causes of this reversal of winds. Competency Based Que

Ans. Monsoon type of climate is prevalent in South and South-East Asia. The monsoon winds shift their directions seasonally.

This seasonal shift is accompanied by changes in the patterns of rainfall.

The main causes of seasonal reversal of winds are

(i) Formation of low pressure Inter Tropical Convergence Zone (ITCZ) during the summer season over the Northern Ganga plains.

(ii) Formation of high pressure zone at 20°S latitude over the Indian Ocean in the Arabian Sea.

(iii) There is replacement of sub-tropical Westerly jet stream by the Easterly jet stream.

Thus, there is reversal of winds from North East to South and South-West direction and vice-versa.

7. What do you understand by global warming? What are causes of global warming?

Ans. The increase in the overall temperature of the Earth due to the presence of greenhouse gases in the atmosphere is known as global warming.

Following are the major causes of global warming

Man Made Causes

- **Deforestation** The forests have been cut down for various developmental activities. This leads to increase in levels of carbon dioxide.
- **Industrial Development** Industries lead to increase in Greenhouse gases in the environment. The harmful emissions from industries raise the temperature of atmosphere.
- **Use of ACs and Refrigerators** With the excessive use of ACs and Refrigerators, human beings are adding chloroflourocarbons in the atmosphere which causes warming of Earth.
- **Use of Vehicles** Increase in use of vehicles lead to increasing fossil fuel emissions that increase Earth's temperature.

Natural Causes

- **Volcanoes** The ash and smoke which is emitted out of the volcanoes goes into the atmosphere and increases the temperature of atmosphere.
- **Forest Fires** Forest fires, caused due to natural reasons emit a large amount of carbon containing smoke. This also leads to rising temperature.

8. Through which methods temperature and pressure are represented on a map? Where do you notice the high and low temperature in India during winter months?

Ans. On maps, temperatures are represented through method of isotherms. These are lines that join the places of same temperature.

Pressure can be represented through method of isobars which join the places of same pressure.

During winters, the isotherm of 10° C passes through the lower Himalayan region, while isotherm of 25° C passes South-Western coast and South India.

The highest isobar of 1019 mb is seen in the North-Western part of India, whereas isobar of 1013 mb is seen through extreme South and over the Bay of Bengal.

Thus, the Isobar and Isotherm maps clearly indicate the temperature and pressure condition over the Indian sub-continent during winters.

9. What is the cause of dry spells during rainy season in different parts?

Ans. During the South-West monsoon, after the rain occurs for a few days, the rain fails to occur for one or more weeks. These dry spells or breaks are common in rainy season in the different regions due to different reasons

- In Northern India, rains are likely to fail if rain bearing storms are not very frequent along the monsoon trough or ITCZ over this region.
- On the West coast, the dry spells are associated with days when winds blow parallel to the coast.
- According to a research, the dry spells may also occur due to large scale deforestation for various purposes, this ultimately results in longer breaks in monsoon.

10. What is El Nino ? Describe the effects of El Nino.

Ans. El Nino means child christ. It is a complex weather system that appears every three to seven years and brings drought, floods and other weather extremes to different parts of the world.

El Nino is an extension of the warm equatorial Pacific current which gets replaced temporarily by the cold Peruvian current or Humboldt current. The system of El Nino involves the atmospheric and weather phenomenon with the appearance of warm currents on the Peru coast and Eastern Pacific.

The effects of El Nino include

(i) It affects weather in many parts of India and the world.

(ii) It raises the temperature of water on the Peruvian coast by 10°C.

(iii) It results in distortion of equatorial atmospheric circulation.

(iv) Results in irregularities in sea water evaporation and reduction in Planktons, which reduces the amount of fish in the sea.

11. Explain how monsoon play an important role in our economy.

Ans. Importance of monsoon for economic condition in India are

- Monsoon is the axis around which the entire agricultural cycle of India revolves.
- Regional variations in monsoon climate help in growing various types of crops.
- Variability of rainfall brings drought or floods every year in one or the other parts of the country affecting the economic condition of the farmers.
- Sudden and heavy monsoon creates problem of soil erosion over large areas affecting the productivity of crops.
- Winter rainfall in the Northern part of India is highly beneficial for rabi crops.

12. What are Western disturbances? Which part of India is influenced by these disturbances and how? CBSE Diksha

Ans. Western disturbances are shallow cyclonic depression (low pressure system) formed over Mediterranean Sea and these low-pressure systems move towards its West during winter months. This phenomenon affects different parts of India. These are mentioned below

- North-West part of India is influenced by these disturbances. Little rainfall in Punjab, Haryana, Delhi and Western Uttar Pradesh occurs which is beneficial for rabi crop.
- Due to this disturbance there is snowfall in the lower Himalayas which is the source of our perennial rivers.

13. Why do Chennai receive more rainfall during winters than in summers?

Ans. Chennai, the capital of Tamil Nadu lies on the Eastern coastal plain on the coromandel coast. This region mostly receives its rainfall during the cold winter season as compared to the summers. This region is located on the rainshadow zone of the Western Ghats and that is why the rainfall received in the summers is very less.

During October, November, the Sun shifts. The Tropic of Capricorn in the Southern Hemisphere. There is high pressure above the Northern plains and in the South, the air pressure is very low. The 1019mb and 1013mb isobars pass through North and South India respectively. Due to this pressure gradient the North-East monsoon winds blow and pick up moisture from the Bay of Bengal and cause torrential rainfall near the Coromandal coast. Thus, Chennai receives most of its rainfall during the winter season.

Long Answer Type Questions

1. Describe in details the process of onset of monsoon season during the summer months in India.

Ans. The phenomenon of monsoon has been studied at the global level which has helped in understanding the causes and salient features of monsoon in the South-Eastern region. The onset of the monsoon season begins during the summer months.

It can be described by the following process

- The Sun shines vertically over the Tropic of Cancer during summer months and the large landmass in the North of the Indian Ocean gets intensely heated. This causes an intense low pressure in the North-Western part of the subcontinent. The pressure in the Indian Ocean is high due to slow heating of water.
- The ITCZ shifts Northwards and the South-East trade winds cross the equator due to the intense low pressure cell formed over the Northern part.
- The shift of ITCZ is also related to the phenomenon of the withdrawal of the Westerly jet streams from the Northern plain and South of the Himalayas. Then, the Easterly jet streams sets in along 15° N latitude from the eastern coast and held responsible for the 'burst of monsoon' which means continuous heavy rainfall for few days.
- The South-East trade winds are deflected towards the subcontinent between 40° E to 60° E longitudes. The direction of the winds change due to coriolis force and start blowing from South-West and are known as South- West monsoons.
- The monsoon sets in over the Kerala coast by 1st June, Mumbai by 10th, Kolkata by 13th June and by mid-July it enters the entire sub-continent.

2. Monsoon winds of the Bay of Bengal branch blow and affect the rainfall pattern in different parts. Explain how? Competency Based Que

Ans. The monsoon winds approaching the land of the Indian subcontinent from the South-Westerly directions are bifurcated into two branches. The Arabian Sea and the Bay of Bengal branch.

The Bay of Bengal branch strikes the coast of Myanmar and part of South-East Bangladesh. Instead of the South-West direction. It is deflected by the Arakan mountains along the coast of Myanmar and then blow into West Bengal and Bangladesh as South Easterly monsoon winds.

From here, this branch splits into two under the influence of the Himalayas and thermal low pressure in the North-West. One branch moves Westward along the Ganga plain upto the Punjab plains. The other branch moves up the Brahmaputra valley in the North-East causing widespread rain.

They cause heavy rainfall (more than 1000 cm) in Cherrapunji and Mawsynram lying on the windward sides of the Garo and the Khasi hills.

The Tamil Nadu or Coromandal coast remains dry because it is parallel to the Bay of Bengal branch of South-West monsoon and it also lies in the rain shadow area of the Arabian Sea branch of South-West monsoon.

3. Explain the nature of Indian monsoon. CBSE Diksha

Ans. Monsoon is familiar though a complex climate phenomenon as no single theory has been able to explain monsoon fully. At the global level, systematic studies have helped to understand the causes and salient features of the monsoon such as

- **Onset of the Monsoon** When the Sun shines vertically over the Tropic of Cancer during summer months, the large landmass in the North of the Indian Ocean gets intensely heated. This causes an intense low pressure in the North-Western part of the sub-continent. The pressure in the Indian Ocean is high due to slow heating of water. The ITCZ shifts Northwards and the South-East trade winds cross the equator due to the intense low pressure cell formed over the Northern part of India.
- **Break in Monsoon** After having rains for a few days during the monsoon period, the rain fails to occur for one week or more, this dry spell is known as 'Break in the Monsoon' which are quite common during rainy reason. This break can be seen on the West coast when winds blow parallel to the coast.

In the Northern part of India, the break in the monsoon occur when rain bearing storms are not very frequent along the monsoon trough or low pressure zone or ITCZ.

4. The climate of India is divided into four seasons. Discuss about the characteristics of cold weather season in India.

Ans. The characteristics of cold weather season are as follows

Temperature In the Northern hemisphere, the cold weather season begins in mid-November upto the month of February. In the North parts of India, mean daily temperature remains below 21° C. This region is excessively cold because it is away from the moderating influence of sea, the snowfall occurs on the high mountain ranges of the Himalayas and the cold waves caused by the winds coming from the Caspian Sea and Turkmenistan.

Pressure and Winds

Due to the Sun's position over the Tropic of Capricorn and low temperature conditions in Northern plains and the Central Asia, a weak high pressure is formed over North and slightly low pressure in South. As a result, wind start blowing from North-Western high pressure zone to low pressure zone over the Indian Ocean. Wind direction is influenced by the topography.

They are North-Westerly down the Ganga valley, become Northerly in the Ganga- Brahmaputra delta and North-Easterly over the Bay of Bengal.

Rainfall

Winter monsoons do not cause rainfall because they have little humidity and also due to anti-cyclonic circulation on land. So, most parts of India do not have rainfall in winter season except central parts of India and Northern parts of Southern Peninsula which gets rainfall occasionally. Arunachal Pradesh and Assam in the North-Eastern parts of India also gets rainfall between 25 mm and 50 mm during winter season.

The temperate cyclones from the Mediterranean sea cause rainfall in Punjab, Harayana, Delhi and Western Uttar Pradesh. Though the amount is not enough but highly beneficial for rabi crops. The precipitation is in the form of snowfall in the lower Himalayas and it goes on decreasing from West to East in the plains and from North to South in the mountains.

5. Describe the conditions associated with retreating monsoon season and distribution of rain.

Ans. The monsoon winds start retreating in the months of October and November from the Indian subcontinent. The low air pressure over the Northern India is replaced by the high pressure and the monsoon retreats from Western Rajasthan, Gujarat, Western Ganga plains and Cultural highlands first.

The conditions associated with this season are

(i) Clear skies and rise in temperature.
(ii) Extreme weather due to high humidity.
(iii) In second half of October, temperature falls rapidly in North India.
(iv) Dry weather in North India region.
(v) Rainfall in Eastern part of Peninsula.

Distribution of rain is as follows

(i) The rain in this season is associated with cyclonic depressions originating over Andaman Sea.
(ii) These depressions manage to cross the Eastern coast and the Indian Peninsula, causing rain.
(iii) Majority of the rainfall on the East coast is due to these cyclonic depressions.
(iv) These cyclones cause very heavy rainfall which is very destructive in the highly populated regions of Godavari, Krishna, Kaveri deltas.
(v) Every year, the cyclonic depressions bring disasters here due to their high rainfall and thunderstorms.

6. Explain any five factors related to location and relief which influence the climate of India. **CBSE Diksha**

Ans.. Following are the factors related to the location and relief which influences the climate of India.

(i) The latitude creates climatic variation as the Northern region experiencing an extreme range of temperatures due to its sub-tropical and temperate zones, while the Southern tropical region remains warm with a smaller temperature range.
(ii) The Himalayas protects India from cold Arctic winds and trap monsoon winds, leading to significant rainfall within the subcontinent.
(iii) Coastal areas enjoy a moderate climate due to closeness to the sea, whereas interior regions have a more extreme climate.
(iv) Land-water distribution influences seasonal air pressure and causes the monsoon wind reversal, with the Indian Ocean surrounding the South and the Himalayas to the North.
(v) Altitude affects temperature by making higher regions cooler than plains at the same latitude. For instance, in January, Agra (at a lower altitude) averages 16°C, while Darjeeling (higher altitude) experiences a much cooler 4°C. Together, these factors produce diverse climatic conditions across India.

7. A number of geological evidences suggest that once, a large part of the earth was under ice cover. Why does this ice cover melt?

Ans. The melting of the ancient ice cover on earth can be due to a combination of natural and human-induced factors. Geological evidence suggests that the earth has undergone several cycles of glaciation and deglaciation due to natural climatic changes over millions of years. These changes were primarily due to variations in earth's orbit, axial tilt, and solar radiation, known as Milankovitch cycles, which altered the distribution of sunlight across the planet.

Volcanic activity and tectonic shifts also contributed by releasing greenhouse gases like carbon dioxide and methane, which trapped heat in the atmosphere, leading to gradual warming.

In recent times, human activities have accelerated the melting of ice through industrialisation, deforestation, and the burning of fossil fuels. These activities release significant amounts of greenhouse gases, enhancing the greenhouse effect. Consequently, global temperatures have risen, causing polar ice caps and glaciers to melt at an alarming rate, further exacerbated by feedback mechanisms like reduced reflectivity from diminishing ice cover.

Source Based Questions

1. Read the passage carefully and answer the questions that follow.

In North-Western India, some weak temperate cyclones from the Mediterranean sea cause rainfall in Punjab, Haryana, Delhi and Western Uttar Pradesh. Although the amount is meagre, it is highly beneficial for rabi crops. The precipitation is in the form of snowfall in the lower Himalayas. It is this snow that sustains the flow of water in the Himalayan rivers during the summer months. The precipitation goes on decreasing from West to East in the plains and from North to South in the mountains. The average winter rainfall in Delhi is around 53 mm. In Punjab and Bihar, rainfall remains between 25 mm and 18 mm Respectively. Central parts of India and Northern parts of Southern Peninsula also get winter rainfall occasionally. Arunachal Pradesh and Assam in the North-Eastern parts of India also have rains between 25 mm and 50 mm during these winter months. During October and November, the northeast monsoon while crossing over the Bay of Bengal, picks up moisture and causes torrential rainfall over the Tamil Nadu coast, Southern Andhra Pradesh, South-East Karnataka and South-East Kerala.

(i) What is the form of precipitation in the lower Himalayas during winter?

(a) Rainfall
(b) Snowfall
(c) Hailstorm
(d) Dew

Ans. (b) Snowfall

(ii) What is the average winter rainfall in Delhi?

(a) 18 mm
(b) 25 mm
(c) 53 mm
(d) 100 mm

Ans. (c) 53 mm

(iii) During the cold winter season (October-November), most of the rainfall in South India occurs in which of the following states?

(a) Tamil Nadu (b) Karnataka
(c) Kerala (d) All of these

Ans. (d) All of these

2. Read the passage carefully and answer the questions that follow.

Towards the end of the nineteenth century, it was believed that the differential heating of land and sea during the summer months is the mechanism which sets the stage for the monsoon winds to drift towards the subcontinent. Since the pressure in the Indian Ocean in the South of the landmass is high as water gets heated slowly, the low pressure cell attracts the South-East trades across the Equator. These conditions help in the Northward shift in the position of the ITCZ. The South-West monsoon may thus, be seen as a continuation of the South-East trades deflected towards the Indian sub-continent after crossing the Equator. These winds cross the Equator between 40°E and 60°E longitudes. The shift in the position of the ITCZ is also related to the phenomenon of the withdrawal of the westerly jet stream from its position over the North Indian plain, South of the Himalayas. The easterly jet stream sets in along 15°N latitude only after the Western jet stream has withdrawn itself from the region. This easterly jet stream is held responsible for the burst of the monsoon in India.

(i) What was the earlier concept about the mechanism of monsoon winds in India?

Ans. The earlier concept about the mechanism of monsoon winds in India was that the differential heating of land and sea during the summer months is responsible for the arrival of the monsoon winds in the sub-continent.

(ii) How is intense low pressure formed in the North-Western part of the Indian sub-continent?

Ans. During April and May, when the Sun shines vertically over the Tropic of Cancer, the large landmass in the North of Indian Ocean gets intensely heated. This causes the formation of an intense low pressure in the North-Western part of the Indian sub-continent.

(iii) Which phenomenon is related to the withdrawal of the westerly jet stream from its position over the north Indian plain, South of the Himalayas?

Ans. The shift in the position of the ITCZ is related to the phenomenon of the withdrawal of the westerly jet stream from its position over the North Indian plain, South of the Himalayas.

Map Based Question

1 On the map of India, mark the following.

(i) Area with highest rainfall in India.

(ii) Area with lowest rainfall in India.

Ans.

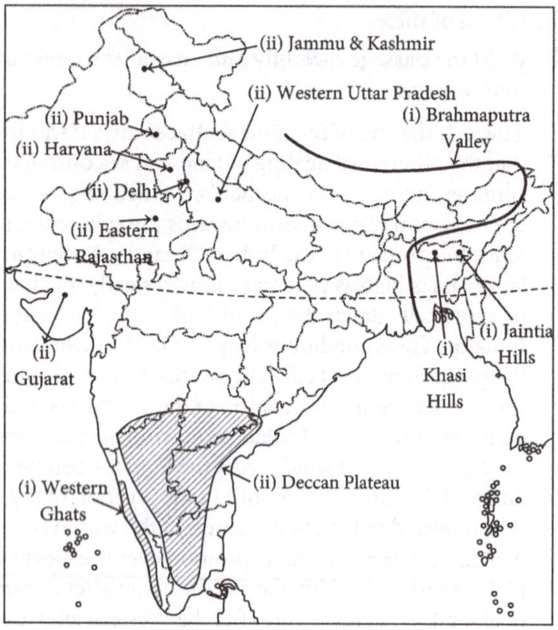

2 Mark the following on the map of India.

(i) Areas with highest temperature in India.

(ii) Areas with lowest temperature in India.

Ans.

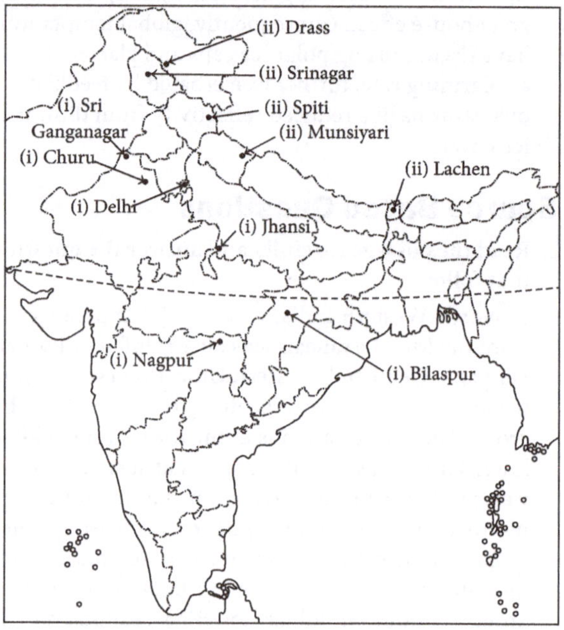

SELF ASSESSMENT TEST

Objective Type Questions

1 The monsoon sets the earliest in which of the following states?

(a) Delhi
(b) Kerala
(c) Haryana
(d) Tamil Nadu

2 Break in monsoon in Northern India occurs due to

(a) Low frequency of rain bearing storms
(b) Presence of ITCZ over the region
(c) Both (a) and (b)
(d) None

3 El-Nino occurs in which month?

(a) September
(b) March
(c) December
(d) June

4 The local storm helpful in rice cultivation are

(a) Loo
(b) Nor Wester
(c) Mango shower
(d) Blossom shower

5. In spite of variation in the climate of Kerala and Tamil Nadu in the South and Uttar Pradesh and Bihar in the North there is unity in climate of India due to

(a) Vast Latitudinal extent
(b) Varied Relief features
(c) Monsoon
(d) Proximity to Indian ocean

6. Which of the following factors governing climate of India is concerned with upper air circulation?

(a) Trade winds
(b) Jet stream
(c) Cyclone
(d) Land breeze and sea breeze

7. Which of the following is not a characteristic of monsoon rain?

(a) It occur in wet and dry spell.
(b) Spatial distribution is also uneven.
(c) Rainfall is largely governed by relief.
(d) Occurs throughout the year.

Short Answer Type Questions

8. Distinguish between weather and climate.
9. What do you understand by range of temperature? In which part of India do you find higher range of temperature and why?
10. Temporary storms bring a welcome respite from the oppressing heat since they bring with them light rains and a pleasant cool breeze. Give significance of any three temporary storms of wind.
11. The rain in the South-West monsoon season begins rather abruptly. How?

Long Answer Type Questions

12. Write the important features of the winter monsoon season.
13. Analyse the rainfall pattern of India.
14. Describe the pattern of rainfall distribution in India.

5

CHAPTER

Natural vegetation refers to a plant community that has not been disturbed over a long time and this allows the species to adjust themselves to climate and soil conditions.

YOUR STUDY GOALS

5.1 Types of Forests
5.2 Forest Conservation
5.3 Wildlife

YOUR PRACTICE GOALS

- Objective Type Questions (25 Qs ; MCQs, Matching, A-R)
- Descriptive Type Questions (11 SAs, 5 LAs)
- Source Based Questions (2 Qs)
- Map Based Questions (3 Qs)

Natural Vegetation

- India is a land of great variety of natural vegetation. Himalayas are marked with temperate vegetation; the Western Ghats and the Andaman and Nicobar Islands have tropical rain forests; the deltaic regions have tropical forests and mangroves; the desert and semi desert areas of Rajasthan are known for cacti and a wide variety of bushes and thorny vegetation.
- Depending upon the variations in the climate and the soil, the vegetation of India changes from one region to another.

5.1 Types of Forests

- Based on certain common features such as predominant vegetation type and climatic regions, Indian forests can be divided into the following groups
  - (i) Tropical Evergreen and Semi-Evergreen Forests
  - (ii) Tropical Deciduous Forests
  - (iii) Tropical Thorn Forests
  - (iv) Montane Forests
  - (v) Littoral and Swamp Forests

Tropical Evergreen and Semi Evergreen Forests

- Tropical evergreen forests are found in warm and humid areas with an annual precipitation of **over 200 cm** and mean annual temperature above 22°C.
- These forests are found in the Western slope of the Western Ghats, hills of the North-Eastern region and the Andaman and Nicobar islands.
- Species found in these forests include rosewood, mahogany, aini, ebony, etc.
- Tropical evergreen forests have layers closer to the ground and are covered with shrubs and creepers, with short trees followed by tall variety of trees.
- There is no definite time for trees to shed their leaves, flowering and bearing fruit.
- In these forests, trees reach great heights up to 60 m or above.
- Semi evergreen forests are found in the less rainy parts of these regions. Such forests have a mixture of evergreen and moist deciduous trees.
- Main species of these forests are white cedar, hollock and kail.
- The **undergrowing climbers**[1] are the reason that this forest looks so evergreen.

Value of Forests

- The British were aware of the economic value of the forests in India. Therefore, large scale exploitation of these forests was started by Britishers.
- This exploitation changed the structure of forests. The oak forests in Garhwal and Kumaon were replaced by pine (chirs) which was used to lay railway lines.
- Forests were also cleared for activities like plantations of tea, rubber and coffee.
- The British also used timber for construction activities as it acts as an insulator of heat. The use of forests was more towards the commercial use.

▲ *Evergreen Forests*

Tropical Deciduous Forests

- These are the most widespread forests in India. They are also called as the **monsoon forests**.
- They spread over regions which receive rainfall between **70-200 cm**.
- Based on the availability of water, these forests are further divided into moist and dry deciduous forest.

Moist Deciduous Forests

- These are found in the regions which record rainfall between **100-200 cm**.
- These forests are found in the North-Eastern states along the foothills of Himalayas, Eastern slopes of the Western Ghats and Odisha.
- Teak, sal, shisham, hurra, mahua, amla, semul, kusum, sandalwood, etc. are the main species of these forests.

Dry Deciduous Forests

- These covers vast areas of the country, where rainfall ranges between **70 -100 cm**.
- On the wet regions, they act like moist deciduous, while on the drier margins they act like thorn forests.
- These forests are found in rainy areas of the Peninsula and the plains of Uttar Pradesh and Bihar.

---

1 **Undergrowing climbers** These are plants with weak stem that cannot stand straight alone.

- In the higher rainfall regions of the Peninsular plateau and the Northern Indian plain, these forests have a **parkland landscape**[2] with open stretches in which teak and other trees with patches of grass are common.
- As the dry season begins, the trees shed their leaves completely and the forest appears like a vast grassland with naked trees all around.
- Tendu, palas, amaltas, bel, khair, axlewood, etc. are the common trees of these forests.
- In the Western and Southern part of Rajasthan, vegetation cover is very scanty due to low rainfall and overgrazing.

▲ *Tropical Thorn Forests*

▲ *Montane Forests*

Tropical Thorn Forests

- Tropical thorn forests occur in the areas which receive rainfall **less than 50 cm.**
- These consist of a variety of grasses and shrubs. It includes semi-arid areas of South-West Punjab, Haryana, Rajasthan, Gujarat, Madhya Pradesh and Uttar Pradesh.
- In these forests, plants remain leafless for most part of the year and give rise to scrub vegetation.
- Important species found are *babool, ber* and wild date palm, *khair, neem, khejri, palas,* etc. Tussocky grass grows up to a height of 2 m as the under growth.

Montane Forests

- These forests are found in the high-altitude region.
- In mountainous areas, natural vegetation changes because of decrease in temperature with increasing height.
- The Himalayan ranges show a succession of vegetation from the tropical to the tundra, which change with the altitude.
- Mountain forests can be classified into two types, the **Northern mountain forests** and the **Southern mountain forests**.

The Northern Mountain

- The Northern mountain forests can be divided into three types, these are discussed below

1. Wet Temperate Forest

- These forests are found between an **altitude of 1,000-2,000 m.**
- In the higher hill ranges of North-Eastern India, hilly areas of West Bengal and Uttarakhand, evergreen broad leaf trees such as oak and chestnut are predominant.
- Between 1,500-1,750 m, pine forests are also well-developed in this zone, with **Chir Pine** as a very useful commercial tree.
- Deodar, a highly valued economic species grows mainly in he Western part tof the Himalayan range. It is durable wood mainly used in construction activities.

2. Alpine Forests and Pastures

- Alpine forests and pastures are found at the height of **3,000-4,000 m.** Temperate grasslands are also found at many places.
- Silver firs, junipers, pines, birch and rhododendrons, etc are the common trees that are found here.
- Blue pine and spruce are found at altitudes of 2,225-3,048 m.

2 **Parkland Landscape** It is an open area of grass with trees usually in a temperate region.

- These pastures are used extensively for **transhumance**[3] by tribes like the Gujjars, the Bakarwals, the Bhotiyas and the Gaddis.

3. Tundra Vegetation

- **Mosses** and **lichens** are found in tundra vegetation at higher altitudes.
- Trees are not found here as it is permanently frozen.
- The Southern slopes of the Himalayas carry a thicker vegetation cover because of relatively higher precipitation than the North-facing slopes.

The Southern Mountain Forest

- These forests include the forests found in three distinct areas of Peninsular India which are the Western Ghats, the Vindhyas and the Nilgiris.
- As they are closer to the tropics and only 1,500 m above the sea level, vegetation is temperate in the higher regions and subtropical on the lower regions of the Western Ghats, especially in Kerala, Tamil Nadu and Karnataka.
- The temperate forests are called ***Sholas*** in the Nilgiris, Anaimalai and Palani hills.
- Some of the other trees of these forests that are economically significant include, magnolia, laurel, cinchona and wattle. Such forests are also found in the Satpura and the Maikal ranges.

Littoral and Swamp Forests

- India has a rich variety of wetland habitats. About 70 per cent of this comprises areas under paddy cultivation.
- In India, **3.9 million hectares** of total wetland has been grouped into eight categories, these are mentioned below
  - (i) The reservoirs of the Deccan Plateau in the South together with the lagoons and other wetlands of the Southern West coast.
  - (ii) The vast saline expanses of Rajasthan, Gujarat and the Gulf of Kachchh.
  - (iii) Freshwater lakes and reservoirs from Gujarat Eastwards through Rajasthan (Keoladeo National Park) and Madhya Pradesh.
  - (iv) The delta wetlands and lagoons of India's East coast (Chilika lake).
  - (v) The freshwater marshes of the Gangetic Plain.
  - (vi) The floodplains of the Brahmaputra; the marshes and swamps in the hills of North-East India and the Himalayan foothills.
  - (vii) The lakes and rivers of the montane region of Kashmir and Ladakh.
  - (viii) The mangrove forest and other wetlands of the island arcs of the Andaman and Nicobar islands.
- **Chilika Lake** (Odisha) and **Keoladeo National Park** (Bharatpur) are protected as water-fowl habitats under the **Convention of Wetlands of International Importance** (Ramsar Convention).

Mangroves

- Mangroves grow along the coasts in the salt marshes, tidal creeks, mud flats and estuaries.
- They consist of several salt-tolerant species of plants.
- These forests are bounded by **creeks**[4] of stagnant water and tidal flows. These forests also provide shelter to a wide variety of birds.

▲ *Mangroves*

3 **Transhumance** It is the seasonal movement of livestock (such as sheep) between mountain and lowland pastures.
4 **Creeks** It is a watercourse which carries water from river or stream.

- In India, the mangrove forests spread over 6,740 sq. km which is 7 per cent of the world's mangrove forests.
- They are highly developed in the Andaman and Nicobar islands and the Sundarbans of West Bengal. Other areas of significance are the Mahanadi, the Godavari and the Krishna deltas.
- However, these important ecosystem are threatened due to encroachment and require the conservation[5] efforts.

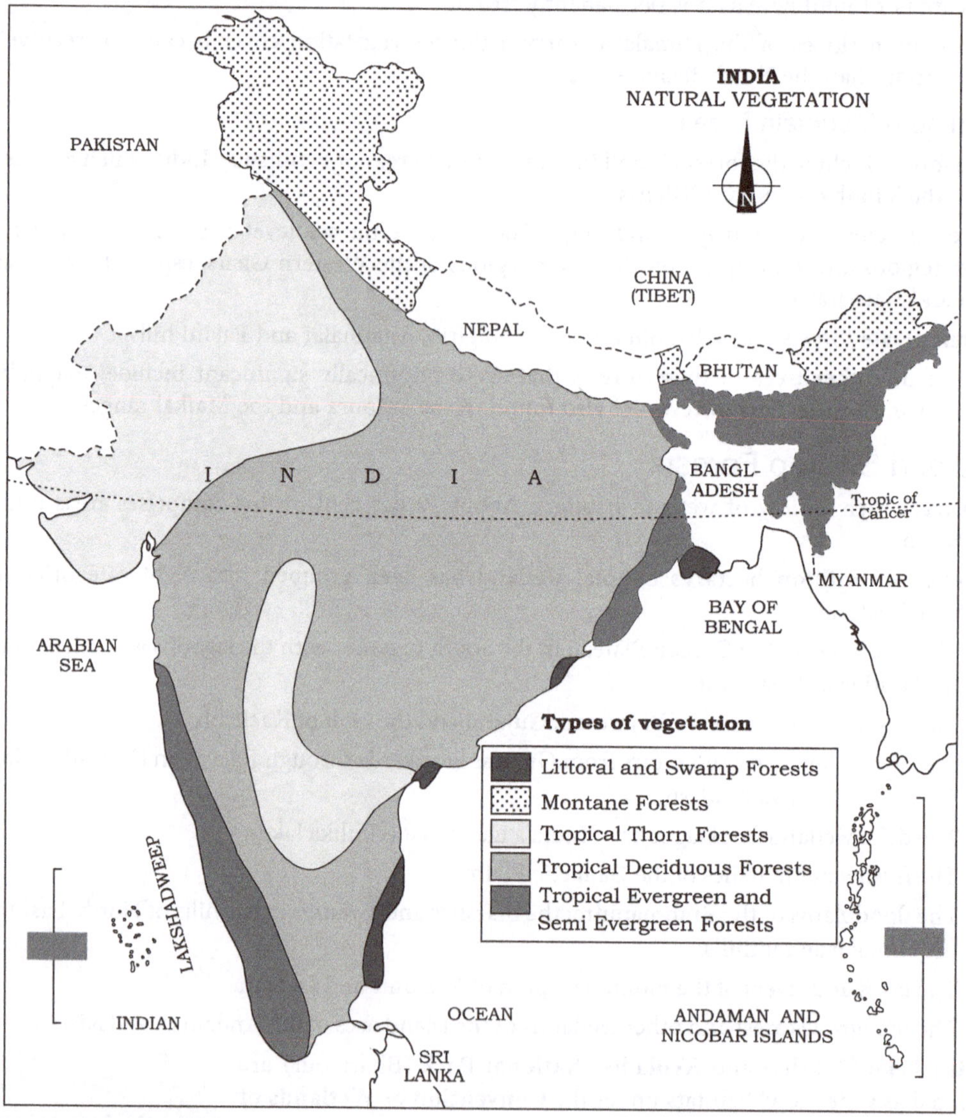

▲ *Natural Vegetation*

Quick Test 1

1. Give an example of tree found in evergreen forest.
2. Mosses are a part of which type of vegetation?
3. In which state Keoladeo National Park is situated?
4. Mention the climatic conditions required for the growth of Mangrove forests.

5 **Conservation** It is the act of protection of natural environment and natural resources for future.

5.2 Forest Conservation

- The Government of India adopted a forest policy in **1952**, which was further modified in 1988.
- According to the new forest policy, the Government will emphasise sustainable forest management to conserve and expand forest reserve and to meet the needs of local people.
  The forest policy aimed at
  (i) Bringing 33 per cent of the geographical areas under forest cover.
  (ii) Maintaining environmental stability and to restore forests where ecological balance was disturbed.
  (iii) Conserving the natural heritage of the country, its biological diversity and genetic pool.
  (iv) Checking soil erosion, extension of the desert lands and reduction of floods and droughts.
  (v) Increasing the forest cover through social forestry and afforestation on degraded land.
  (vi) Increasing the productivity of forests to make timber, fuel, fodder and food available to rural population who are dependent on forests and encourage the replacement of wood.
  (vii) Creation of a massive people's movement involving women to encourage planting of trees and stop cutting of trees.

Forests and Life

- Forests are source of sustenance and livelihood for tribal communities. It provides them food, fruits of all kinds, edible leaves, honey, nourishing roots and hunting.
- It provides them with material to build their houses and items for practising their arts.
- It is commonly believed that the tribal communities live in harmony with nature and protect forests.

Social Forestry

- Social forestry means the management and protection of forests and afforestation on barren lands with the purpose of helping in the environmental, social and rural development.
- The National Commission on Agriculture (1976) has classified social forestry into three categories
  (i) **Urban forestry** It means growing and managing trees on public and privately-owned lands in and around urban centres such as green belts, parks, roadside avenues, industrial and commercial green belts, etc.
  (ii) **Rural forestry** It gives emphasis on promotion of agro-forestry and community-forestry.

  Agro-forestry
  - It combines forestry with agriculture.
  - It is the raising of trees and agriculture crops on the same land inclusive of the waste patches.
  - It is done so that production of food, fodder, fuel, timber and fruit can be done at the same time.

  Community Forestry
  - It involves growing trees on public or community land such as the village pasture and temple land, roadside, canal bank, strips along railway lines and schools, etc.
  - Community forestry programme aims at providing benefits to the community.
  - Community forestry provides a means under which the people of landless classes can associate themselves in growing trees and thus, get those benefits which are restricted for landowners.

  (iii) **Farm Forestry**
  - Farm forestry refers to the practice where farmers grow trees for commercial and non-commercial purposes on their farm lands.

- Forest departments of various states distribute seedlings of trees free of cost to small and medium farmers.
- Several lands such as the margins of agricultural fields, grasslands and pastures, land around homes and cow sheds may be used for growing trees under non-commercial farm forestry.

Quick Test 2

1. In which year forest policy modified?
2. Who classified social forestry into three types?
3. What is community forestry?
4. What is the areal extent of Mangrove forest in India?

5.3 Wildlife

- About 4-5 per cent of all known plant and animal species on the Earth are found in India.
- The main reason for this diversity of life forms is the great diversity of the ecosystem found in India.
- Over the years, this habitat has been disturbed by human activities and as a result, their numbers have reduced. There are certain species that are at the rate of extinction.
- The reasons for the decline in wildlife are as follows
  - Forests have been exploited on large scale due to industrial and technological advancement that has affected the habitat of animals.
  - To fulfil the needs of growing population, forests were cleared for agriculture, human settlement, roads, mining, reservoirs, etc.
  - Pressure on forests increased due to cutting trees for fodder and fuelwood and removal of small timber by the local people.
  - Hunting and overgrazing has affected the wildlife adversely. Now commercial poaching is uncontrolled.
  - Risk of forest fire also affects the wildlife in a negative way.
- Conservation of wildlife is of great significance to the national as well as the world heritage along with the promotion of ecotourism[6].

Wildlife Conservation in India

- In 1972, a comprehensive Wildlife Act was enacted, which provides the main legal framework for conservation and protection of wildlife in India.
- The two main objectives of the Act are
  - (i) To provide protection to the endangered species listed in the schedule of the Act.
  - (ii) To provide legal support to the conservation areas classified as National parks[7], sanctuaries and closed areas.
- This Act has been comprehensively amended in 1991. It strengthened rules to better protect wildlife and endangered plants by setting penalties for those who harm them. As on February 2025, there are 106 National parks and 573 Wildlife Sanctuaries in the country.
- There are 103 National parks and 563 wildlife sanctuaries in the country.
- For effective conservation of flora and fauna, special steps have been initiated by the Government of India in Collaboration with UNESCO's **'Man and Biosphere Programme'**.

6 Ecotourism It is a form of nature-oriented tourism intended to contribute to the conservation of the natural environment

7 National Parks It is an area which is strictly reserved for the protection of the wildlife and where activities of forestry, grazing or cultivation is not allowed.

- Special schemes like **Project Tiger** (1973) and **Project Elephant** (1992) have been launched to conserve these species and their habitat in a sustainable manner.
- Project Tiger has been implemented since 1973. The main objective of the scheme is to ensure maintenance of population of tigers in India for scientific, aesthetic, cultural and ecological values.
- The objective of the Project Tiger includes preservation of areas of biological importance as natural heritage for the benefit, education and enjoyment of the people.
- Initially, the Project Tiger was launched in nine tiger reserves by covering an area of 16,339 sq. km, now it has increased to 50 tiger reserves, encompassing 71,027.10 sq. km of core tiger habitats distributed in 18 states.
- The tiger population in the country has registered an increase from 1,411 in 2006 to 2,967 in 2020 which is 70 per cent of the global tiger population.
- Project Elephant, started in 1992, is a program to help states that have wild elephant populations roaming freely.
- The main goal is to make sure that these elephants can survive for a long time in their natural habitats.
- The project provides support for protecting elephants and their environments in 16 states across India, helping to keep these elephant populations safe and healthy in the wild.
- Apart from these, some other projects such as **Crocodile Breeding Project**, **Project Hangul** and **Conservation of Himalayan Musk Deer** have also been launched by the Government of India.

List of Biosphere Reserves

Name of the Biosphere Reserve and Total Geographical Area (km^2)	Date of Designation	Location in the States/UT
Nilgiri (5520)	01.08.1986	Part of Wynad, Nagarhole, Bandipur and Mudumalai, Nilambur, Silent Valley and Siruvani Hills (Tamil Nadu, Kerala and Karnataka).
Nanda Devi (5860.69)	18.01.1988	Part of Chamoli, Pithoragarh and Almora Districts in Uttarakhand.
Nokrek (820)	01.09.1988	Part of East, West and South Garo Hill Districts in Meghalaya.
Manas (2837)	14.03.1989	Part of Kokrajhar, Bongaigaon, Barpeta, Nalbari, Kamrup and Darrang Districts in Assam.
Sunderban (9630)	29.03.1989	Part of delta of Ganga and Brahamaputra river system in West Bengal.
Gulf of Mannar (10500)	18.02.1989	Indian part of Gulf of Mannar extending from Rameswaram island in the North to Kaniyakumari in the South of Tamil Nadu.
Great Nicobar (885)	06.01.1989	Southern most island of Andaman and Nicobar Islands.
Similipal (4374)	21.06.1994	Part of Mayurbhanj District in Odisha.
Dibru-Saikhowa (765)	28.07.1997	Part of Dibrugarh and Tinsukia Districts in Assam.
Dehang Debang (5111.5)	02.09.1998	Part of Upper Siang, West Siang and Dibang Valley Districts in Arunachal Pradesh.
Pachmarhi (4981.72)	03.03.1999	Part of Betul, Hoshangabad and Chhindwara Districts in Madhya Pradesh.
Kangchenzonga (2619.92)	07.02.2000	Part of North and West Districts in Sikkim.
Agasthyamalai (3500.36)	12.11.2001	Part of Thirunelveli and Kaniyakumari Districts in Tamil Nadu and Thiruvananthapuram, Kollam and Pathanmthitta districts in Kerala.
Achanakmar-Amarkantak (3835.51)	30.03.2005	Part of Anuppur and Dindori Districts of Madhya Pradesh and Bilaspur district of Chhattisgarh.

Name of the Biosphere Reserve and Total Geographical Area (km^2)	Date of Designation	Location in the States/UT
Kachchh (12, 454)	29.01.2008	Part of Kachchh, Rajkot, Surendranagar and Patan Districts in Gujarat.
Cold Desert (7770)	28.08.2009	Pin Valley National Park and surroundings; Chandratal and Sarchu and Kibber Wildlife sanctuary in Himachal Pradesh.
Seshachalam (4755.997)	20.09.2010	Sechachalam hill ranges in Eastern Ghats encompassing part of Chittoor and Kadapa Districts in Andhra Pradesh.
Panna (2998.98)	25.08.2011	Part of Panna and Chhattarpur Districts in Madhya Pradesh.

*** Sites with bold letters have** *been included in the World Network of Biosphere Reserves of UNESCO.*

Source : Annual Report 2018-19, Ministry of Environment and Forests, Government of India.

Biosphere Reserves

- A Biosphere Reserve is a special area of land or coast that represents a unique ecosystem and is recognised globally.
- These reserves are part of **'UNESCO's Man and Biosphere (MAB) Program'**, which focuses on conserving nature while supporting the people who live there.
- The objectives of Biosphere Reserves are
  - **Conservation** Provide conservation of biodiversity and ecosystem.
  - **Development** Provide space for development along with environment conservation.
  - **Logistics** Provide international network for research and monitoring.
- There are 18 Biosphere Reserve in India out of which 11 have been recognised by the UNESCO on World Network. As on February 2025, there are 12 Biosphere Reserve in India that are recognized by the UNESCO World Network.

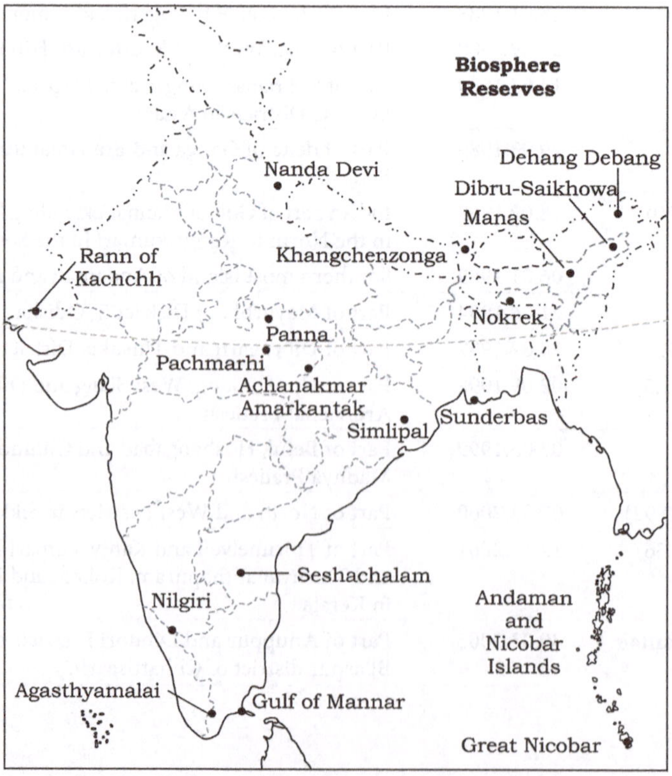

Mind Map

NATURAL VEGETATION

1 Types of Forests

Tropical Evergreen and Semi-Evergreen Forests
- Rainfall ranges between 150-200 cm, e.g., Hills of North-East Region.
- Species include rosewood, mahogany, aini, ebony, white cedar, hillock, etc.
- No definite time for trees to shed their leaves.

Tropical Deciduous Forests
- Rainfall ranges between 70-200 cm.
- **Moist Deciduous Forest** Found in regions which record rainfall between 100-200 cm. Species include teak, sal, sheesham, amla, etc.
- **Dry Deciduous Forest** Found in regions which receive rainfall between 70-100 cm. Species include tendu, palas, bel, khair, etc.

Littoral and Swamp Forests
Example, Sundarban, Chilika lake

Tropical Thorn Forest
- Rainfall is less than 50 cm, e.g., Rajasthan, Haryana.
- Species include babool, ber, neem, etc.

Mangroves
- Grow along the coasts in the salt marshes, tidal creeks, mud flats and estuaries.
- Spread over 6,740 sq km in India.
- Highly developed in the Andaman and Nicobar islands and the Sundarbans of West Bengal.

Montane Forests
- The Northern mountain forests
  - (i) **Wet Temperate Forests** Found between altitude of 1000-2000m.
  - (ii) **Alpine Forests and Pastures** Found at the height of 3000-4000m.
  - (iii) **Tundra Vegetation** Permanently frozen area. Only mosses and lichens are found.
- The Southern Mountain Forests

2 Forest Conservation

It is a practice of maintaining, protecting and restoring forests through various ways.

Based on Conservation Policy of Forests
- **Social Forestry** It is the management and protection of forests and afforestation on barren land.
- **Farm Forestry** It is the process by which farmers grow trees for commercial and non-commercial purposes.

3 Wildlife

There is remarkable diversity of life-forms in India

4 Wildlife Conservation in India

- Wildlife Act (1972)
- Man and Biosphere Programme (MAB)
- Project Tiger (1973)
- Project Elephant (1992)

5 Biosphere Reserves

It is a unique ecosystem of terrestrial and coastal areas under MAB programme.

Objectives
- **Conservation** It involves conservation of biodiversity and ecosystem.
- **Development** It involves development of the area in any environment.
- **Logistics** It involves linking of area internationally for research and monitoring.

NCERT Folder

Choose the right answer from the four alternatives given below

(i) Sandalwood is an example of

(a) Evergreen forest (b) Deciduous forest
(c) Deltaic forest (d) Thorny forest

Ans. (b) Deciduous forest

(ii) Which one of the following was the purpose of Project Tiger?

(a) To kill tigers
(b) To put tigers in the zoo
(c) To protect tigers from illegal hunting
(d) To make films on tigers

Ans. (c) To protect tigers from illegal hunting

(iii) In which one of the following states is the Nandadevi Biosphere Reserve situated?

(a) Bihar (b) Uttar Pradesh
(c) Uttarakhand (d) Odisha

Ans. (c) Uttarakhand

(iv) How many of the Biosphere Reserves from India are recognised by the UNESCO? As on February 2025, there are 12 UNESCO Biosphere Reserve in India.

(a) One (b) Two (c) Three (d) Eleven

Ans. (d) Eleven

(v) Which one of the following proportion of area of the country was targeted to be under forest in Forest Policy of India?

(a) 33% (b) 44% (c) 55% (d) 22%

Ans. (a) 33%

Answer the following questions in about 30 words

(i) What is natural vegetation? Under what climatic conditions do Tropical Evergreen Forests develop?

Ans. Natural vegetation refers to a plant community that has been left undisturbed over a long time. Tropical Evergreen forests develop in the areas where rainfall is above 200 cm and annual mean temperature is above 22°C.

(ii) What do you undertand by social forestry?

Ans. Social forestry means the management and protection of forests and afforestation on barren lands for environmental, social and rural development.

(iii) Define Biosphere Reserves.

Ans. Biosphere reserves are large areas of unique ecosystem of land and water which have been reserved for conservation, research and development.

These areas are recognised by UNESCO under Man and Biosphere (MAB) programme. There are 18 Biosphere Reserves in India out of which 11 have been recognised by UNESCO on World Network. As on February 2025, there are 12 UNESCO Biosphere Reserve in India.

(iv) What is the difference between forest area and forest cover?

Ans. The area which has been notified and recorded as forest land irrespective of existence of trees in the records of State Revenue Department is known as forest area.

The area which is actually covered by trees with canopy as shown by aerial photographs and satellite images is known as forest cover.

Answer the following question in not more than 150 words

(i) What steps have been taken up to conserve forests?

Ans. In order to conserve forests, Forest Policy was adopted by government in 1952 which was modified in 1988. Based on the Forest Conservation Policy, social forestry was initiated.

Social forestry is the management and protection of forests and afforestation on barren land with objective of helping in environmental, social and rural development. Social forestry involves the following steps

(i) **Urban Forestry** It involves raising and management of trees on public and privately owned lands in and around urban centres such as green belts, parks, roadside avenues, etc.

(ii) **Rural Forestry** It involves emphasis on promotion of Agro-forestry and Community forestry.

- **Agro-Forestry** It is raising of trees and agriculture crops on same land inclusive of waste patches.
- **Community Forestry** It involves raising of trees on public or community land such as village pasture and temple land, canal bank, etc.

(iii) **Farm Forestry** It is the process under which farmers grow trees for commercial and non-commercial purposes on their farm lands.

(ii) How can people's participation be effective in conserving forests and wildlife?

Ans. For the conservation of forest and wildlife people participation is prerequisite. Without their participation this task cannot be completed.

The role of people in conserving forest and wildlife is discussed below

- People play both direct as well as indirect role in the conservation of the forests and wildlife.
- Population explosion, enhancing rate of industrialisation and urbanisation are responsible for deforestation. Therefore, people should follow measures to control their population.
- All the people should adopt principle of sustainable development. They should promote development which is in harmony with the nature.
- Civil societies should promote sensitisation among the people about the importance of forest and wildlife.
- When people visit forest for tourism, they should not litter over there.
- People should not buy clothes and other accessories which are made up of animals skins. Also, they should not consume meats of wild animals.
- People should not pollute the environment, as pollution is quite injurious to plants and animals.
- Tribal people who are living in the forest area should be aware about the disadvantages of the shifting cultivation on forest.

Exam Pattern Questions

Objective Type Questions

Multiple Choice Questions (MCQs)

1. Which region of India has less than 10 per cent of the forest area? CBSE Diksha

(a) North-East (b) South-West
(c) North-West (d) South-East

2. Which of the following tree do not belong to Tropical Evergreen Forests?

(a) Rosewood (b) Kusum
(c) Aini (d) None of these

3. Which of the following were the reasons for the exploitation of forest resources by Britishers?

(a) To lay railway lines
(b) To introduce plantations
(c) For construction activities
(d) All of the above

4. Which of the following species grows upto height of 2 m as undergrowth in Tropical Thorn Forest?

(a) Khair (b) Khejri
(c) Tussocky grass (d) All of these

5. Pine forests are well developed between an altitude of

(a) 1500 - 1750 m (b) 2000 - 2100 m
(c) 1900 - 2100 m (d) 1000 - 1500 m

6. Identify the type of forest from the given description.
In mountainous areas, natural vegetation changes because of decrease in temperature with increasing height. These forests are found in the high-altitude region between 1500-1750 m, pine forests are also well developed in this zone.

(a) Montane Forest (b) Dry Deciduous Forest
(c) Tropical Thorn Forest (d) Wet Temperate Forest

7. Combining forestry with agriculture is known as

(a) Urban Forestry (b) Farm Forestry
(c) Agro-Forestry (d) Community Forestry

8. The main reason behind declining wildlife is CBSE Diksha

(a) Industrial advancement lead to exploitation of forest.
(b) Being prey and predator they are important for ecological development.
(c) Vital role in economic development.
(d) Helps in diversity conservation.

9. When was Project Elephant launched?

(a) 1986 (b) 1972
(c) 1992 (d) 1973

10. Which of the following project is not the part of India's UNESCO Man and Biosphere programme?

(a) Project Tiger (b) Crocodile Breeding project
(c) Project Elephant (d) Project Leopard

11. How many Biosphere Reserves are there in India?

(a) 10 (b) 11
(c) 14 (d) 18

12. Consider the following statement regarding Tropical Deciduous Forest and choose the correct one.

I. These are the most widespread forests in India.
II. They are also called the monsoon forests.
III. They receive rainfall between 70-200 cm.

Options
(a) Only I (b) II and III
(c) I and III (d) All of these

13. Consider the following statements regarding Mangroves and choose the incorrect option.
I. These forests grow along the coasts in the salt marshes.
II. They consist of several plants that can not survive in salt water.
III. In India, the Mangrove forests spread over 8,000 sq. km
IV. The Sundarbans of West Bengal is one of the examples of Mangrove.

Options
(a) Only I (b) Both II and III
(c) Only IV (d) All of these

14. Consider the following statements about semi-evergreen forests and choose the correct one.
I. These forests have mixture of evergreen and moist deciduous trees.
II. White Cedar is main species of this forest.

Codes
(a) Only I (b) Only II
(c) Both I and II (d) None of these

15. Which of the following is characteristic of dry deciduous forests?
I. Rainfall between 100-200 cm
II. Parkland landscape
III. Open stretches of teak interspersed with grasses
IV. Tendu is a common tree found here

Codes
(a) I, II and III (b) II, III and IV
(c) I, II, III and IV
(d) I, III and IV

16. Which of the following is characteristic of mangroves?
I. Grows along coast in tidal creeks.
II. Consist of salt-tolerant plant species.
III. Give shelter to birds.
IV. Highly developed in Sunderbans of West Bengal.

Codes
(a) I, II and III (b) II, III and IV
(c) I, II, III and IV (d) I, III and IV

17. Consider the following statements about Forest Policy of India and choose the correct one.
I. It was adopted in 1986.
II. It aimed at bringing 50 per cent of geographical area under forest cover.

Codes
(a) Only I (b) Only II
(c) Both I and II (d) None of these

18. Which of the following is the reason for decline in wildlife?
I. Hunting II. Over grazing
III. Poaching IV. Forest fire
V. Deforestation

Codes
(a) I, III and V (b) II, IV and V
(c) I, II, III and IV (d) All of these

Arrange the Following

19. Arrange the following Biosphere Reserves from North to South regions where they found.
(i) Seshachalam (ii) Panchmari
(iii) Cold desert (iv) Nilgiri

Codes
(a) (iii), (ii), (i), (iv) (b) (i), (ii), (iii), (iv)
(c) (iv), (ii), (iii), (i) (d) (iii), (iv), (i), (ii)

Match the Following

20.

List I (Biosphere Reserve)		List II (Location)	
A.	Nanda Devi	1.	Andhra Pradesh
B.	Simlipal	2.	Uttarakhand
C.	Cold Desert	3.	Himachal Pradesh
D.	Seshachalam	4.	Odisha

Codes

	A	B	C	D		A	B	C	D
(a)	1	3	2	4	(b)	2	4	3	1
(c)	3	2	1	4	(d)	1	4	2	3

21.

List I (Project/Policy)		List II (Year)	
A.	Forest Policy	1.	1973
B.	Wildlife Act	2.	1952
C.	Project Tiger	3.	1992
D.	Project Elephant	4.	1972

Codes

	A	B	C	D		A	B	C	D
(a)	1	2	3	4	(b)	3	1	2	4
(c)	2	4	1	3	(d)	2	1	4	3

22.

List I (Forest type)		List II (Characteristics)	
A.	Tropical Evergreen	1.	Receive rainfall less than 50 cm
B.	Tropical Deciduous	2.	Receive rainfall between 70-200 cm.
C.	Alpine Forest	3.	Receive rainfall more than 200 cm
D.	Tropical Thorn Forest	4.	They are situated at the height of 3,000-4,000 m

Codes

	A	B	C	D		A	B	C	D
(a)	3	2	4	1	(b)	3	4	2	1
(c)	1	2	3	4	(d)	2	3	4	1

Assertion-Reason

Directions (Q. Nos. 23-25) In the questions given below are two statements labelled as Assertion (A) and other labelled as Reason (R). In the context of two statements which one of the following is correct?

Codes

(a) Both A and R are true, but R is not the correct explanation of A
(b) Both A and R are true and R is the correct explanation of A
(c) Both A and R are incorrect
(d) A is correct, but R is incorrect

23. **Assertion** (A) Southern slopes of Himalayas have thick cover of vegetation.

Reason (R) Southern slopes of Himalayas receive high precipitation.

24. **Assertion** (A) Deodar is used for construction activity.

Reason (R) Sandalwood is main species of evergreen forest

25. **Assertion** (A) The Himalayan ranges show a succession of vegetation from the tropical to the tundra.

Reason (R) In mountainous region, change in temperature affects the type of vegetation.

Answers

1. (c) North-West
2. (b) Kusum
3. (d) All of the above
4. (c) Tussocky grass
5. (a) 1500 - 1750 m
6. (a) Montane Forest
7. (c) Agro-Forestry
8. (a) Industrial advancement lead to exploitation of forest.
9. (c) 1992
10. (d) Project Leopard
11. (d) 18
12. (d) All of these
13. (b) Both II and III
14. (c) Both I and II
15. (b) II, III and IV
16. (c) I, II, III and IV
17. (d) None of these
18. (d) All of these
19. (a)
20. (b)
21. (c)
22. (a)
23. (b) Both A and R are true and R is the correct explanation of A
24. (d) A is correct, but R is incorrect
25. (b) Both A and R are true and R is the correct explanation of A

Subjective Questions

Short Answer Type Questions

1. The desert region of Rajasthan is known for a number of bushes and thorny vegetation. What are the characteristics of this type of vegetation?

Ans. Thorny vegetation is mainly found in the desert region of Rajasthan. Due to less availability of moisture and rainfall, the plant leaves turn themselves into thorns to conserve water.

The important characteristics of this type of vegetation are

- These forests occur in the areas which receive rainfall less than 50 cm.
- These consist of a variety of grasses and shrubs. Plants remain leafless for most part of the year and gives an expression of scrub vegetation.
- Important species found in this region are babool, ber, khair, neem, khejri, palas, wild date palm, etc.

- Tussocky grass grows upto a height of 2 m in these areas.
- These forests are also found in semi-arid areas of Punjab, Haryana, Rajasthan, Gujarat, Madhya Pradesh and Uttar Pradesh.

2. What are Montane forests? Describe any one type of montane vegetation.

Ans. Montane forests are found in mountain regions. In these regions, vegetation changes due to decrease in temperature with increase in height, from Tropical to Tundra.

Montane forests are classified into Northern and Southern Montane forrests.

Northern Montane Forests

The characteristics of Northern Montane forests are as follows

- In the Northern Montane forests, deciduous forests are found in the foothills of Himalayas.
- They are succeeded by wet temperate forests at an altitude of 1000-1200 m.
- Pine forests are well developed between 1500-1750 m.
- Temperate grasslands are also found in many places in this zone.
- Blue pine and spruce appear at an altitude of 2225- 3048 m.
- There is transformation to Alpine forests and pastures at 3000-4000 m.
- At much higher altitudes, Tundra vegetation is found which includes mosses and lichens.

3. Exploitation of forest in India is associated with the British policies. Discuss.

CBSE DIksha, Competency Based Que

Ans. The Britishers exploited the forests in India in the following ways

- The British were aware of the economic value of the forests in India, hence, large scale exploitation of these forests was started.
- The structure of forests was also changed. The oak forests in Garhwal and Kumaon were replaced by pine (chirs) which was needed to lay railway lines.
- Forests were also cleared for introducing plantations of tea, rubber and coffee.
- The British also used timber for construction activities as it acts as an insulator of heat.
- The protectional use of forests was replaced by commercial use.

4. Wetland groups of India has been divided into 8 categories. Discuss them.

Ans. The eight wetland groups in India are

(i) The reservoirs of the Deccan plateau with lagoons and other wetlands of West coast.

(ii) The vast saline area of Rajasthan, Gujarat and the Gulf of Kachchh.

(iii) The fresh water marshes of the Gangetic Plains.

(iv) The flood plains of Brahmaputra; marshes and swamps in hills of North-East India and Himalayan foothills.

(v) The reservoirs, lakes and rivers of the montane region in Kashmir and Ladakh.

(vi) The mangrove forest and other wetlands of the island arcs of the Andaman and Nicobar islands.

(vii) Delta wetlands and lagoons of Chilika lake (India's East coast).

(viii) Fresh water lakes and reservoirs from Gujarat Eastwards through Rajasthan (Keoladeo National Park in Bharatpur and Madhya Pradesh).

5 What are Mangrove forests? Explain how they form a unique type of vegetation? Where are they found in India?

Ans. Mangrove forests are forests of small tree or shrubs, that grow in coastal or saline areas. Mangroves occur in the tropical region having roots submerged under the water. They form a unique type of vegetation because

- They grow along the coast in salty marshes, tidal creeks, mud flats or estuaries.
- They consist of plant species, which are salt tolerant and survive in saline water.
- These forests provide shelter to a wide variety of birds.
- They are adapted to low oxygen conditions as their roots are submerged.

In India, Mangroves cover 6740 km^2 of area. It is almost 7% of the world's mangroves. These are well developed in Andaman and Nicobar islands and Sunderbans of West Bengal. They are also found between Mahanadi, Godavari and Krishna deltas.

6. Various measures have been taken by the government to protect and conserve wildlife in India. Explain the objectives of any two of these. **Competency Based Que**

Ans. Government of India has taken various measures to conserve and protect wildlife.

These includes Wildlife Protection Act, establishment of National Parks, Biosphere Reserves, special Projects like Project Tiger, Project Elephant, etc.

Wildlife Protection Act, 1972

The main objectives of Wildlife Protection Act include

- To provide protection to endangered species listed in the Schedule of the Act.
- To provide legal support to the conservation areas of the country classified as National Parks and Wildlife Sanctuaries.

Biosphere Reserves

The main objectives of establishing the Biosphere Reserves include

(i) **Conservation** To conserve Biodiversity and Ecosystem.

(ii) **Development** Development of area in an integrated manner.

(iii) **Logistics** Area should be linked internationally for research and monitoring.

7. What were the main objectives of Project Tiger launched by the Government? Explain, how it has contributed to the protection of tiger.

Ans. Project Tiger was launched in 1973 by the Government of India with the aim of protecting the tiger species and preserving and conserving the population of tigers.

It has the following objectives

- To ensure that there is a viable population of tigers in India for scientific, aesthetic, cultural and ecological values.
- To preserve areas of biological importance as natural heritage for the benefit, education and enjoyment of the people.
- Eliminating all forms of human exploitation and disturbance from habitat of tigers.

It has contributed to protection of tiger in the following ways

(i) The area under Tiger Reserves have increased from earlier 16,339 km^2 to 36,988 km^2.

(ii) The total number of tiger reserves have increased from earlier 9 to 44 (Now 57).

(iii) The tiger population has significantly increased from 1, 411 to 3,642.

8. What do you understand by social forestry? What are various ways in which rural areas practise rural forestry?

Ans. Social forestry refers to the management and protection of forest and planting forests on barren land for the purpose of environmental, social and rural development.

In rural areas, rural forestry is practised as agro-forestry and community forestry.

Agro-Forestry It combines forestry with agriculture. It means growing trees and agriculture crops on the same land, including the waste patches.

It helps in the production of food, fodder, fuel, timber, fruits, etc. at the same time.

Community Forestry It involves the raising of trees on public or community land such as the village pasture, temple land, roadside, canal bank, river bank, strips along railway lines and schools.

It provides a means under which the people of landless class can associate themselves in cultivating trees for their own benefits.

9. There is decline in certain species of plant and animals. Explain why? **Competency Based Que**

Ans. Reasons for declining wildlife are as follows

- Forests have been exploited on a large scale due to industrial and technological advancement that has affected the habitat of animals.
- To fulfil the needs of the growing population, forests have been cleared for agriculture, human settlement, roads, mining industries, reservoirs, etc.
- Pressure on forests increases when trees and their branches are cut for fuel, fodder and timber by local people.
- Hunting and overgrazing has caused adverse effect on wildlife and its habitat.
- Forest fire often in tropical forests disturbs wildlife as well.

10. How should we contribute in conservation of forests and wildlife? Suggest some ways to control the exploitation of the wildlife and forests.

Ans. Flora and Fauna are integral part of our lives directly or indirectly so the conservation of them is our responsibility. For effective conservation, we should plant as many trees as we can by participating in programs like Van Mahotsav. We should take pledge never to kill any animal, neither for fun or food and convince others to do so.

Every species has a key role to play in the ecosystem. Hence, the exploitation of the plant and animal resources by human beings is essential to be controlled through the following ways

- Hunting by greedy hunters for commercial purposes should be stopped at all cost.
- Reckless cutting of forests to bring land under cultivation and inhabitation should be minimised.
- Pollution due to chemical and industrial wastes should be checked.

11. Wildlife in India suffers from many threats especially by humans. Discuss them.

Ans. Wildlife in India suffers from many threats sepecially by humans which results in extinction of species. Some of the important reasons are discussed below

- The primary threat is habitat loss due to large-scale deforestation for industrial expansion, agriculture, human settlements and infrastructure development.
- Growing population demands have led to increased logging for fuel, fodder and construction, further disturbing natural habitats.
- Additionally, commercial poaching has increased the hunting of animals for their fur, bones and other body parts, this has reduced populations of endangered species.
- Overgrazing by livestock and the risk of forest fires further degrade ecosystems, while pollution from industrial waste and chemicals contaminates water and soil, affecting both flora and fauna.

Long Answer Type Questions

1. Briefly describe the Tropical Evergreen and Semi-Evergreen Forests.

Ans. Tropical Evergreen Forests

Conditions These are found in warm and humid areas having an average annual rainfall of over 200 cm and mean annual temperature of 22 degree celcius.

Regions They are found on the Western slopes of Western Ghats, hill of North-East region and the Andaman and Nicobar islands.

Features There is no definite time for the trees to shed their leaves, flowering and fruition. They appear green all the year round. In these forests, the trees reach great height upto 60m or above. Forests are well stratified and creepers, short structured trees followed by tall variety of trees.

Species Species in this region are rosewood, mahagony, aini, ebony, etc.

Semi-Evergreen Forests

Conditions The semi evergreen forests are found in the less rainy parts of these regions having rainfall between 150-200 cm and temperature of 26 degree celcius.

Regions They are located on the Western coast, lower slopes of Eastern Himalayas, Assam, Odisha, etc.

Features Such forests have a mixture of evergreen and moist deciduous trees and they are less dense than the evergreen forests. The undergrowing climbers provide an evergreen character to these forests.

Species Main species are white cedar, hollock and kail.

2. Distinguish between Moist Deciduous and Dry Deciduous Forests.

Ans. Differences between Moist Deciduous Forests and Dry Deciduous Forests are as follows

Basis	Moist Deciduous Forests	Dry Deciduous Forests
Rainfall	They are found in the regions where rainfall is between 100-200 cm.	They are found in the areas where rainfall ranges between 70-100 cm.
Species	Teak, sal, shisham, mahua, amla, semul, kusum, sandalwood, etc. are the main species of this forest.	Tendu, palas, bel, khair, axlewood, amaltas, etc. are found in this region.
Location	These forests are found in the North-Eastern states along the foothills of Himalayas, Eastern slopes of the Western Ghats.	These forests are found in rainier areas of the Peninsula and the plains of Uttar Pradesh and Bihar. As the dry season begins, the trees shed their leaves and forests appears like a vast grassland with naked trees all around.

3 The Himalayan ranges show a succession of vegetation from the tropical to the tundra. Justify.

Competency Based Que

Ans. As we know, temperature decreases with height and, so, the type of vegetation also changes. The Himalayan ranges show a succession of vegetation from the tropical tundra. It can be justified by the following points

- Deciduous forests are found in the foothills of the Himalayas which are succeeded by the wet temperate forest. These forests are found between on altitude of 1000-2000m.
- Evergreen broad leaf trees such as oak and chestnut are predominant in these areas.
- Pine forest are well developed between 1,500-1750m.
- At the height of 3000-4000m, there is a transition to alpine forests and pastures.
- Temperate grasslands are also found at many places in this zone.
- Blue pine and spruce appear at altitudes of 2,225-3,048m. Common trees in Alpine forests are silver firs, junipers, pines, birch and rhododendrons.
- At the higher altitudes, mosses and lichens forms a part of tundra vegetation. In this region, trees and scrubs are mainly absent, they cannot survive in the permafrost region.

Hence, we can show that Himlayan region show cases unique nature in the terms changes nature of vegetation from low to high altitude.

4. Discuss the usefulness of wildlife for human beings and explain the institutional efforts made by the government for protection and conservation of biodiversity.

Ans. The wildlife includes all undomesticated living plant and species.

Usefulness of Wildlife

- Large number of medicinal plants grow in forests.
- They are used as a mode for recreational activities.
- They provide lot of ecological services such as foods, prevent soil erosion, etc.

Wildlife of India is a great natural heritage. Almost 4-5% of all known plant and animal species are found in India. Wildlife also plays an important role in maintaining the ecological balance in nature.

Over the years, wildlife has been hunted indiscriminately and their habitats have been disturbed. So, various efforts to protect and conserve biodiversity have been made. These efforts include

- In 1972, a comprehensive Wildlife Act was enacted, which provides a legal framework for conservation and protection of wildlife in India. It provides protection to the endangered species.
- 106 National parks and 573 Wildlife sanctuaries have been constructed to protect the wildlife.
- For the purpose of conservation of biodiversity, special steps have been initiated by the Government in collaboration with the UNESCO's man and Biosphere Reserve program.
- Special schemes such as Project Tiger (1973) and Project Elephant (1992) have been launched to conserve these species and habitats in a sustainable manner.
- Apart from these, other projects like Crocodile Breeding Project, Project Hangul and Conservation of Himalayan Musk Dear have been launched by the Government.

5. Tropical thorn forests have some important characteristics and they are found in certain favourable location. Justify the statement. **Competency Based Que**

Ans. Following are the characteristics of Tropical Thorn Forests

- Tropical thorn forest occurs in those areas that receive rainfall less than 50 cm in a year.
- These types of forests consist of a variety of grasses and shrubs.
- In India, these forests are found in the semi-arid areas of south west Punjab, Haryana, Rajasthan, Gujarat, Madhya Pradesh and Uttar Pradesh.
- One of the main characteristics of Tropical thorn forest is that the plants remain leafless for most part of the year and this results in the rise of scrub type of vegetation.
- Important species that are found in Tropical Thorn Forest are babool, ber, and wild date palm, khair, neem, khejri, palas, etc.
- Tussocky grass are found in these areas that grows up to a height of 2 m as the under growth.

Source Based Questions

1. Read the passage carefully and answer the questions that follow.

Social forestry means the management and protection of forests and afforestation on barren lands with the purpose of helping in the environmental, social and rural development. The National Commission on Agriculture (1976) has classified social forestry into three categories. These are urban forestry, rural forestry and farm forestry. Urban forestry pertains to the raising and management of trees on public and privately owned lands in and around urban centres such as green belts, parks, roadside avenues, industrial and commercial green belts, etc.

Rural forestry lays emphasis on promotion of agro-forestry and community-forestry. Agro-forestry is the raising of trees and agriculture crops on the same land inclusive of the waste patches. It combines forestry with agriculture, thus, altering the simultaneous production of food, fodder, fuel, timber and fruit. Community forestry involves the raising of trees on public or community land such as the village pasture and temple land, roadside, canal bank, strips along railway lines, and schools etc. Community forestry programme aims at providing benefits to the community as a whole. Community forestry provides a means under which the people of landless classes can associate themselves in tree raising and thus, get those benefits which otherwise are restricted for landowners.

Farm forestry is a term applied to the process under which farmers grow trees for commercial and non-commercial purposes on their farm lands.

(i) **What is the most important component of rural forestry?**

(a) Community
(b) Agriculture
(c) Industrialisation
(d) Both (a) and (b)

Ans. (d) Both (a) and (b)

(ii) **Farm forestry includes which of the following?**
(a) Planting of trees
(b) Planting horticulture crops
(c) Animal husbandry
(d) Planting low water crops

Ans. (a) Planting of trees

(iii) **Which of the following is an essential component of social forestry?**
(a) Pesticides
(b) Afforestation
(c) Sustainable development
(d) Organic manure

Ans. (b) Afforestation

2. Read the passage carefully and answer the questions that follow.

Tropical Evergreen Forests are found in the Western slope of the Western Ghats, hills of the North-Eastern region and the Andaman and Nicobar islands. They are found in warm and humid areas with an annual precipitation of over 200 cm and mean annual temperature above 22°C. Tropical Evergreen Forests are well stratified, with layers closer to the ground and are covered with shrubs and creepers, with short structured trees followed by tall variety of trees.

In these forests, trees reach great heights up to 60 m or above. There is no definite time for trees to shed their leaves, flowering and fruition. As such these forests appear green all the year round. Species found in these forests include rosewood, mahagony, aini, ebony, etc. The semi evergreen forests are found in the less rainy parts of these regions. Such forests have a mixture of evergreen and moist deciduous trees. The undergrowing climbers provide an evergreen character to these forests. Main species are white cedar, hollock and kail.

The British were aware of the economic value of the forests in India, hence, large scale exploitation of these forests was started. The structure of forests was also changed. The oak forests in Garhwal and Kumaon were replaced by pine (chirs) which was needed to lay railway lines. Forests were also cleared for introducing plantations of tea, rubber and coffee. The British also used timber for construction activities as it acts as an insulator of heat. The protectional use of forests was, thus, replaced by commercial use.

(i) **Why Tropical Evergreen Forests are found in the Western slope of the Western Ghats, hills of the North-Eastern region and the Andaman and Nicobar islands?**

Ans. Tropical Evergreen Forests are found in the Western slope of the Western Ghats, hills of the North-Eastern region and the Andaman and Nicobar islands. It is due to the fact that these regions have warm and humid areas with an annual precipitation of over 200 cm and mean annual temperature above 22° C.

(ii) **Why evergreen forests are named so?**

Ans. The evergreen forests have no definite time for trees to shed their leaves, flowering and fruition. So, these forests appear green all the year round thus, are known by this name.

(iii) **The British changed the composition of forests of India for which purpose?**

Ans. The British changed the composition of forests of India for the following purposes
- Pine for rail lines
- Timber for construction activities

Map Based Questions

1. On the map of India, mark the wildlife reserves in India.

Ans.

2. On the map of India, mark the following.

(i) Corbett National Park
(ii) Kaziranga National Park
(iii) Ranthambore National Park
(iv) Shivpuri National Park
(v) Simplipal National Park

Ans.

3. Mark the following on the map of India.

(i) Keoladeo Ghana Bird Sanctuary
(ii) Ranganathittu Bird Sanctuary
(iii) Periyar Wildlife Sanctuary
(iv) Rajaji Wildlife Sanctuary
(v) Mudumalai Wildlife Sanctuary
(vi) Dachigam Wildlife Sanctuary

Ans.

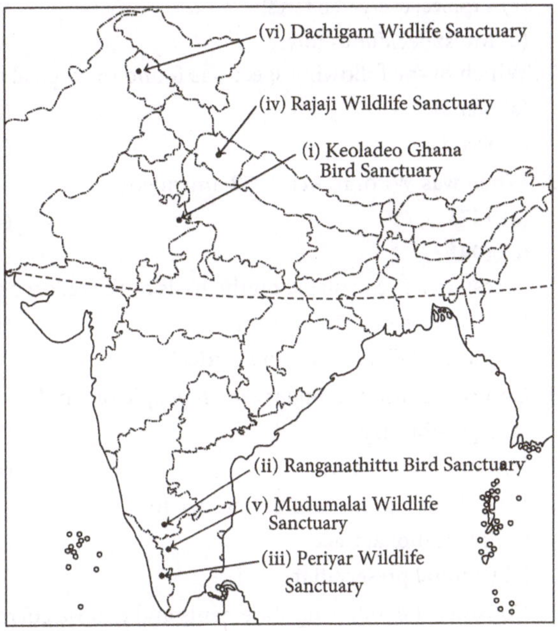

SELF ASSESSMENT TEST

Objective Type Questions

1. Kail is a species found in
   (a) Tropical evergreen forest
   (b) Semi-evergreen forest
   (c) Moist deciduous forest
   (d) Tropical thorn forest
2. Which of the following species is found in tropical thorn forest?
   (a) Semul
   (b) Neem
   (c) Deodar
   (d) Cinchona
3. When was Wildlife Act, 1972 amended?
   (a) 1973
   (b) 1992
   (c) 1991
   (d) 2019
4. Forest area is calculated on the basis of the records procured by?
   (a) State Revenue Department
   (b) Forest Survey of India
   (c) National Commission on Agriculture
   (d) National Remote Sensing Institute
5. Choose the process under which people of landless classes can associate themselves in tree raising.
   (a) Agro-forestry
   (b) Urban forestry
   (c) Community forestry
   (d) Farm forestry
6. Wild life is a great natural heritage for
   (a) International trade
   (b) Ecological diversity
   (c) Cultural preservation
   (d) Biological development
7. Consider the following statements and choose correct ones.
   I. Chilika lake is protected under Ramsar convention.
   II. The temperate forests are called Sholas in the Nilgiris, Anaimalai and Palani hills.

   Codes
   (a) Only I
   (b) Only II
   (c) Both I and II
   (d) None of these

Short Answer Type Questions

8. 'The protection of wildlife has a long tradition in India'. Write down the steps taken by the government of India for wildlife protection.
9. 'To a vast number of tribal people, the forest is a home, a livelihood and their very existence'. Explain.
10. 'India is a land of great variety of natural vegetation'. Justify.

Long Answer Type Questions

11. 'Indian forests are divided into many types'. Describe the Evergreen , Deciduous and Thorn Forests of India.
12. 'In mountainous areas, the decrease in temperature with increasing altitude leads to a corresponding change in natural vegetation'. Justify the statement.
13. 'India has a rich variety of wetland habitats'. Explain the littoral and swamp forests in the context of the given statement.
14. There is a great diversity of flora and fauna in India. Justify.

6 CHAPTER

Natural Hazards and Disasters

This chapter deals with the study of natural hazards and disasters, focusing on their types such as earthquakes, Tsunami, cyclones, floods and landslides. It also examines their causes, impacts and measures for disaster management and mitigation.

YOUR STUDY GOALS

YOUR PRACTICE GOALS

- Objective Type Questions (24 Qs ; MCQs, Matching, A-R)
- Descriptive Type Questions (11 SAs, 7 LAs)
- Source Based Questions (2 Qs)

- Change is a continuous process which involve phenomena that are big and small, material and non-material that make our physical and socio-cultural environment.
- Disasters in general and natural disasters in particular, are some such changes that are negative for humankind.

6.1 Disaster

- Disaster is an undesirable occurrence resulting from forces that are largely not in human control.
- It causes or threatens serious disturbances to life and property including death and injury to a large number of people.
- Apart from natural forces there are some human activities that also causes disaster.
- Bhopal Gas tragedy, Chernobyl nuclear disaster, wars, release of CFCs (Chlorofluorocarbons) and increase of greenhouse gases, environmental pollutions like noise, air, water and soil are some of the disasters which are caused directly by human actions.
- There are some other activities of human beings that intensify disasters indirectly. Landslides and floods due to deforestation, unscientific **land use**[1] and construction activities in weak areas are some of the disasters that are the results of indirect human actions.

1 **Land Use** It is defined as the use of land for different purposes like residential, industries, etc.

Natural Hazard and Disaster

- According to scholars, the terms Natural Hazard and Disaster are interchangeable. They are related to phenomena but they are quite different from each other.
- Natural Hazards are elements of circumstances in the Natural environment that have the power to cause harm to people and property.
- These may be fast or permanent change in environmental settings like currents in the oceans, steep slope and unstable structural features in the Himalayas or extreme climatic conditions in deserts or glaciated areas.
- Natural disasters are relatively sudden and can cause large scale, widespread death, loss of property and disturbance to social systems and life.
- Any event with very high magnitude of destruction and damage can be classified as disaster.

Changing Perspective on Natural Disaster and Hazards

- Previously, hazards and disasters were seen as two closely related phenomena, i.e. areas prone to natural hazards, were more vulnerable to disasters. Hence, people avoided increase of their activities in such areas and that is how disasters were less damaging.
- Technological power has encouraged humans to interrupt the natural condition of the environment. Now, human beings tend to intensify their activities into disaster prone areas which increases the chances of more damage.
- Floodplains and coastal areas in India, like those near major cities and ports such as Mumbai and Chennai, are heavily populated because they offer valuable land for living, business and trade. However, construction of buildings near rivers and coast makes these areas highly vulnerable to natural disasters like cyclones, hurricanes and tsunamis.
- Floodplains can overflow and coastal locations are directly exposed to powerful storms and high waves.

6.2 Natural Disasters and Hazards in India

- India is vast and diverse in terms of its physical and socio-cultural dimension. It is largely due to its vast geographical area, environmental and cultural diversity. Scholars described it as the 'Indian-subcontinent' and the **'land of unity in diversity'**.
- India is vulnerable to natural disasters because of its vastness in natural settings, social discrimination and large population structure.

Some of the major natural disasters are discussed below

Earthquake

- Earthquakes are the sudden shaking of the Earth's surface. Earthquakes that are of tectonic origin are the most devastating and they affect large area.
- On the other hand, the earthquakes associated with volcanic eruption, rock fall, landslides, **subsidence**[2], particularly in the mining areas, failure of dams and reservoirs, etc. affects a limited area and the scale of damage is also small.
- The Indian plate is moving at a speed of one centimetre per year towards the North and North-Eastern direction. This movement of plates is being constantly opposed by the Eurasian plate from the North.
- As result of this, both the plates are said to be locked with each other resulting in accumulation of energy at different points of time.
- Excessive accumulation of energy results in building up of stress, which ultimately results in the breaking up of the lock and the sudden release of energy causes earthquakes along the Himalayan arch.

2 **Subsidence** It is the gradual sinking or downward setting of the Earth's surface. It can lead to surface cracks, sinking of land.

- Some of the most vulnerable Union Territories/States are Jammu and Kashmir, Ladakh, Himachal Pradesh, Uttarakhand, Sikkim and the Darjeeling subdivision of West Bengal and all the seven states of the North-East.
- Apart from these regions, the Central-Western parts of India, particularly Gujarat (in 1819, 1956 and 2001) and Maharashtra (in 1967 and 1993) have also experienced some severe earthquakes.
- The occurrence of earthquakes in Peninsular block (oldest and most stable) was difficult to explain for a long time.
- Recently, a fault line is discovered along river Bhima (Krishna), near Latur and Osmanabad (Maharashtra). It can lead to breaking down of the Indian plate.

▲ *A damaged building due to an earthquake*

Earthquake Prone Areas

- Organisations like National Geophysical Laboratory, Geological Survey of India, Department of Meteorology, Government of India, along with the recently formed National Institute of Disaster Management, have studied previous occurrences of earthquake in India.
- An intensive analysis of more than 1,200 earthquakes that occurred in India over years have been done. On the basis of this India is divided into **five** earthquake zones
  (i) **Very High Damage Risk Zone** It includes North-East states, areas to the North of Darbhanga and Araria along Indo-Nepal border in Bihar, Uttarakhand, Western Himachal Pradesh (around Dharamshala), Kashmir Valley in Himalayan region and Kachchh region in Gujarat.
  (ii) **High Damage Risk Zone** It includes the remaining parts of Jammu and Kashmir, Ladakh, Himachal Pradesh, Northern parts of Punjab, Eastern parts of Haryana, Delhi, Western Uttar Pradesh and Northern Bihar.
  (iii) **Moderate Damage Risk Zone** It includes areas between the plateaus of Deccan and Central Highland and Southern part of Indo-Gangetic Plains.
  (iv) **Low Damage Risk Zone** It includes areas surrounding Malwa plateau, Karnataka plateau, Chhotanagpur Plateau, Telangana plateau and Southern parts of Eastern Ghats.
  (v) **Very Low Damage Risk Zone** It includes old and stable landmasses of the Peninsular plateau and inner parts of Central Highlands.

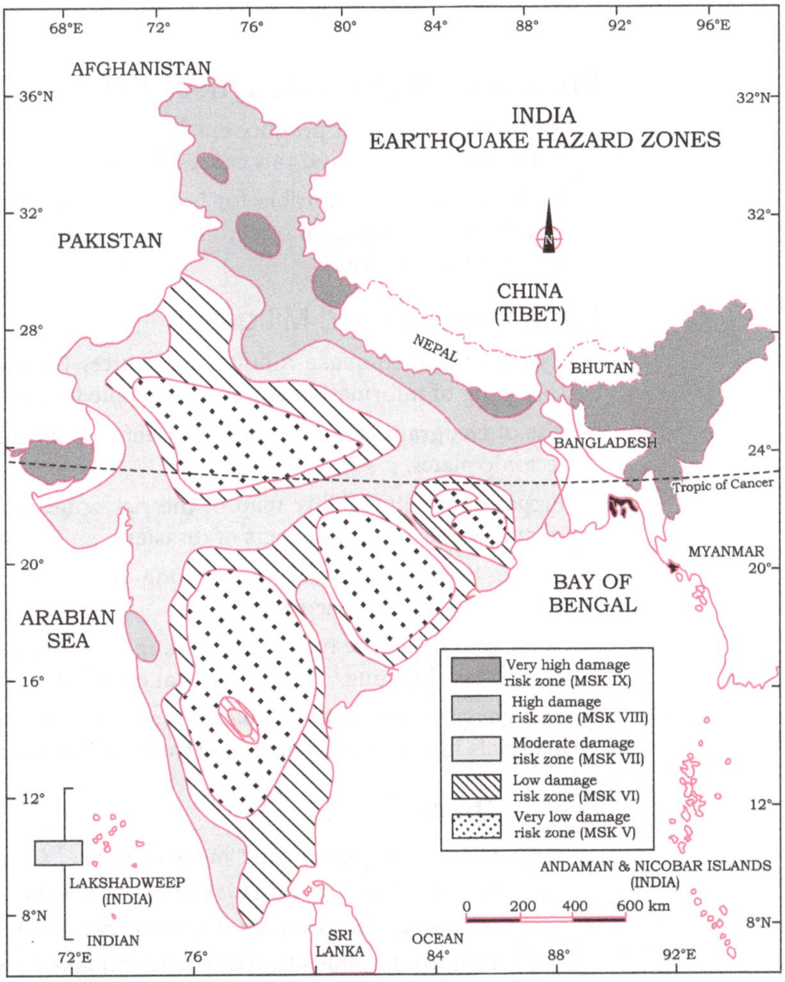

▲ *India : Earthquake Hazard Zones*

Socio-Economic Consequences of Earthquake

- Earthquake causes huge loss of life and property in the areas of high-density population.
- It damages and destroys settlements, infrastructure, transport and communication network, industries and other developmental activities.
- It makes people homeless and puts extra pressure and stress on the weak economy of the developing countries.
- It reduces the material and social-cultural gains of people that they have preserved for years.

Effects of Earthquakes

Earthquakes have disastrous effects on the area of their occurrence.

Effects of Earthquakes

On Ground Structures	On Manmade Structures	On Water
• Fissures Settlements	• Cracking Slidings	• Waves Hydro-Dynamic Pressure
• Landslides	• Overturning	• Tsunami
• Liquefaction	• Buckling	• Possible-Chain-Effects
• Earth Pressure	• Collapse	
• Possible Chain-Effects	• Possible Chain Effects	

Environmental Consequences of Earthquake

- Surface seismic waves produce cracks on upper layer of Earth's crust through which water and volatile[3] materials is released and this causes floods in neighbouring areas.
- Earthquakes are responsible for landslides and these causes obstructions in river flow and channels resulting in formation of reservoirs. Sometimes rivers also change their course causing flood and other calamities in the area.

Earthquake Hazard Mitigation

- Establishing earthquake monitoring centres (seismological centres) for regular monitoring and fast spreading of information among the people in the vulnerable areas.
- Use of **Geographical Positioning System** (GPS) can be of great help in monitoring the movement of tectonic plates.
- Preparing a vulnerability map of the risk zones and educating people about the ways and means to minimise the adverse impacts of disasters.
- Proper link to be established among the various groups for fast spreading of vulnerability risk information among the people.
- Modifying the house types and building-designs in the vulnerable areas and discouraging construction of high-rise buildings, large industrial establishments and big urban centres in the vulnerable areas.
- The government should make it mandatory to adopt Earthquake resistant designs and use light materials in major construction activities in the vulnerable areas.

Quick Test 1

1. Give an example of fault line earthquake.
2. Name a plateau region that lies in the low damage earthquake risk zone.
3. Name a plateau that lies in the high damage risk zone of earthquake.
4. Eastern Haryana falls in which earthquake zone?

3 **Volatile** Those material which are likely to damage due to sudden and unexpected changes.

Tsunami

- Tsunamis or harbour waves or seismic sea waves are high vertical waves in ocean water. These are caused by the sudden displacement of ocean water due to earthquake and volcanic eruptions that causes the sea floor to move abruptly.
- Normally, the seismic waves cause only one sudden vertical wave, but after the initial disturbance, a series of afterwaves are created in water that oscillate between high crest and low trough to restore the water level.
- The speed of wave in the ocean depends upon the depth of water. It is more in the shallow water than in ocean deep. As a result of this, the impact of tsunami is less over the ocean and more near the coast.
- During tsunami, a ship is not much affected over deep water as it has long wavelength and limited wave height so, it raises the ship only by few metres and rise and fall takes several minutes.
- The wavelength of Tsunami reduces near the coast, where water is shallow and the wave height increases.
- Sometimes, the wave height can be up to 15 m or more, which causes large scale destructions along the shores. Thus, these are also called **shallow water waves**.

▲ *Earthquake*

Tsunami Prone Area

Tsunamis are frequently observed over the Pacific Ring of Fire, particularly along the coast of Alaska, Japan, Philippines and other islands of South-East Asia, Indonesia, Malaysia, Sri Lanka and India.

Effects of Tsunami

- Destruction of ports, cities, towns, structures, building and other settlements.
- Loss of life and property in coastal areas. As coastal areas are densely populated and are centres of intense activity, this loss is higher in case of tsunami than by any other natural hazard. Due to tsunami that occurred on 26th December, 2004 about 3,00,000 people lost their lives.

Mitigation of Hazards Created by Tsunami

- The mitigation of hazards created by tsunami is difficult because losses are on a much larger scale. Thus, it is beyond the capacity of individual state or government to mitigate the damage. Hence, combined efforts at the international levels are the possible ways of dealing with these disasters.
- The only mitigation is to observe **Tsunami Warning System**, so that loss can be reduced by a timely evacuation (removal) programme from the coastal areas. India has volunteered to join the International Tsunami Warning System.

Tropical Cyclones

- These are intense low-pressure areas confined to the area lying **between 30° N to 30° S latitudes** in the atmosphere around which high velocity winds blow.
- They extend up to 500 to 1,000 km horizontally and 12-14 km vertically from the surface.
- A tropical cyclone or hurricane is like a heat engine that is energised by the release of latent heat.
- The wind gathers after moving over the oceans and seas due to the condensation of moisture.
- Some conditions for the emergence of tropical cyclones are
    - Large and continuous supply of warm and moist air that can release enormous latent heat.
    - Strong coriolis force that can prevent filling of low pressure at the centre. Absence of coriolis force near the equator prohibits the formation of tropical cyclone between 0°-5° latitude.

- Unstable condition through the troposphere that creates local disturbances around which a cyclone develops.
- Absence of strong vertical wind wedge (block), which disturbs the vertical transport of latent heat.

Spatio-Temporal Distribution of Tropical Cyclones in India

- Tropical cyclones originate in India in the Bay of Bengal and the Arabian Sea. Most of the cyclones originate between 10°-15° North latitudes during the monsoon season.
- In case of the Bay of Bengal, cyclones mostly develop during the months of October and November. Here, they originate between 16°-20° N latitudes and to the West of 92° E longitude.
- In July, the place of these storms shifts to around 18° N latitude and West of 90° E longitude near the Sunderban Delta.

Consequences of Tropical Cyclones

- Generally, with the increase in distance from the sea, the force of the cyclone decreases as energy of the tropical cyclone comes from latent heat released by warm moist air.
- In the same way, in India, the force of the cyclone decreases with increase in distance from the Bay of Bengal and the Arabian Sea.
- So, the coastal areas are often struck by severe cyclonic storms with an average velocity of 180 km/h. This results in abnormal rise in the sea level which is known as **Storm Surge**[4].
- A surge is generated due to interaction of air, sea and land. The cyclone provides the driving force in the form of very high horizontal pressure-gradient and very strong surface winds. The sea water flows across the coast along with strong winds and heavy downpour.
- This results in dense human settlements, agricultural fields, damaging crops and destruction of structures created by human beings.

Risk Reduction Measures for Tropical Cyclones

- By creating awareness, knowledge and preparedness on the part of the members of communities.
- Avoid constructing heavy and expensive infrastructure and other activities in the vulnerable areas.
- Proper timely warning and evacuation of people.
- Latest monitoring system should be installed to keep an eye on the speed and frequency of the storm.
- Construction of cyclone shelters, embankments, **dykes**[5], reservoirs and afforestation to reduce speed of winds.

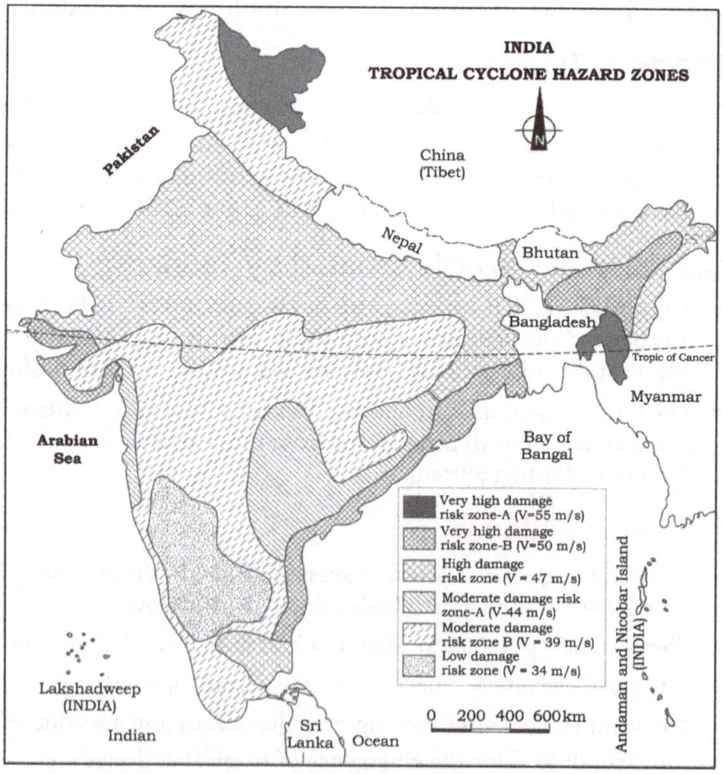

▲ *Tropical Cyclones*

4 **Storm Surge** It is defined as the abnormal rise in the sea level.
5 **Dykes** It is a long thick wall that is built to prevent the sea or a river from flooding low land.

Floods

- Flood is the condition of excessive water that flows over land and human properties. It happens due to the rise of water in the channels.
- Floods are relatively slow in occurrences and they occur in well identified regions and within expected time in a year.

Causes of Floods

- Floods occur commonly when water in the form of surface runoff exceeds the carrying capacity of the river channels, streams, lakes and other inland water bodies and flows into the neighbouring low-lying flood plains.
- It can also be caused due to cyclone or storm surge in the coastal areas.
- It can be caused due to high intensity of rainfall for a longer time.
- It can also take place when temperature rises leading to fast melting of ice and snow.
- Large cemented urban areas reduce the **infiltration**[6] rate and leads to overflowing.
- Huge amount of eroded material in the water due to higher rate of soil erosion causes blockage in the drains leading to flooding of the area.
- Human activities also play an important role in the origin as well as spread of floods such as indiscriminate deforestation, unscientific agricultural practices, disturbances along the natural flow of channels and colonisation of flood-plains and river-beds which increase the intensity, magnitude and gravity of floods.

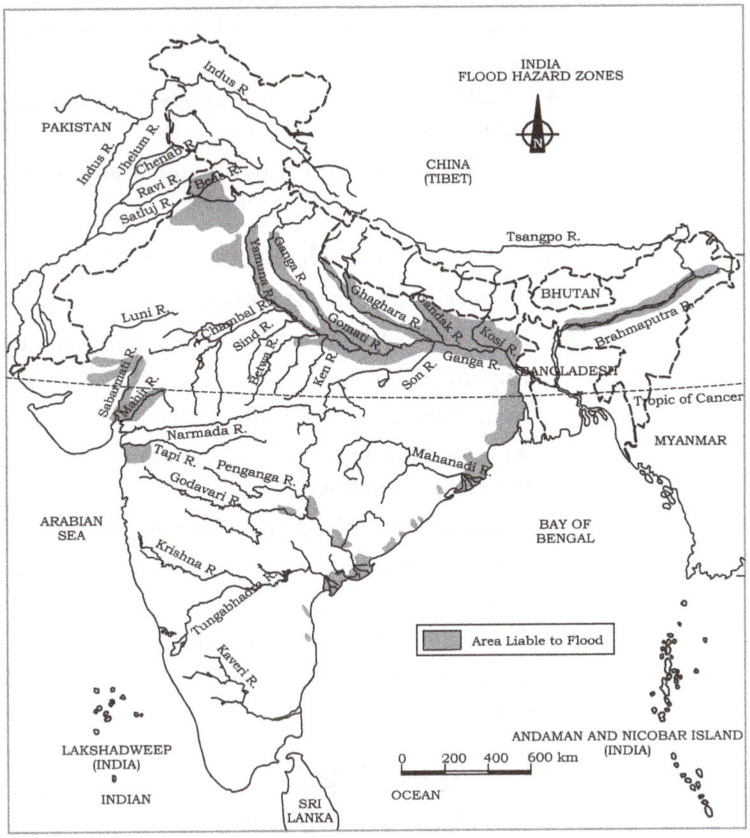

▲ *Effects of Floods*

Flood Prone Areas

- Flood occur frequently over wide geographical area, having disastrous results in many parts of the world.
- Floods in South, South-East and East Asian countries, particularly in China, India and Bangladesh are frequent and equally disastrous.
- Floods occur in almost all the river basins of the country. **Rastriya Barh Ayog** (National Flood Commission) identified 12 per cent or 40 million hectares of land in India as flood prone regions.
- Most of the flood affected areas are the Ganga basin, Brahmaputra basin, Indus basin and river basins of Peninsular India and their tributaries.
- Assam, West Bengal and Bihar are among high flood prone states of India. Apart from these, most of the rivers in Northern States like Punjab and Uttar Pradesh are vulnerable to occasional floods.
- States like Rajasthan, Gujarat, Haryana and Punjab are also getting flooded due to flash floods. This is because of the pattern of monsoon and blocking of streams and river channels by human activities.
- The retreating monsoon is responsible for flooding in Tamil Nadu during November-January.

6 **Infiltration** it is the process by which water enters the ground through rocks.

Effects of Floods

- Floods particularly in Assam, West Bengal, Bihar and Eastern Uttar Pradesh (flooding rivers), coastal areas of Odisha, Andhra Pradesh, Tamil Nadu and Gujarat (cyclone) and Punjab, Rajasthan, Northern Gujarat and Haryana (flash floods) have serious impact on national economy and society.
- Floods not only damage valuable crops every year but also damage physical infrastructure like houses, bridges, roads, railways, etc get damaged by the gushing water.
- Millions of people become homeless with their cattle due to floods.
- Lack of clean drinking water facilities and contamination of water leads to outbreak of diseases like cholera, hepatitis, gastro-enteritis and other water-borne diseases also spread in flood affected area.
- Flooding of large agricultural lands leads to huge crop loss and results in shortage of food and fodder.
- The land may become infertile due to erosion of the top layer or may turn to saline if sea water floods the area.
- Apart from negative effects, floods also make a few positive contributions. Every year, agricultural fields get deposition of silt due to floods.
- Floods increase fertility of the soil. **Majuli** in Assam is the best example of good paddy crops after the annual floods in Brahmaputra.

Risk Reduction Measures for Floods

- Removal of human engagement from the river channels and removing people from the flood plain area.
- No major development should be permitted in the areas which are subjected to high flooding.
- Important facilities like hospitals, schools, offices should be built in safe areas.
- In urban areas, ponds and lakes can be created in low lying areas.
- Afforestation, protection of vegetation, clearing of debris from streams can be done to reduce the amount of runoff water.
- Construction of flood protection **embankments**[7] and dams, channel improvement, etc.
- Flood proofing can reduce the damage by use of sand bag, blocking or sealing of doors and windows of houses, etc.
- The building should be constructed on elevated areas or platforms.
- Flood hazard mapping will give the proper indication of water flow and warning can be issued in an organised manner to shift and evacuate people on time to reduce the risk.

Quick Test 2

1. On which factors speed of Tsunami waves depends?
2. What is abnormal rise in sea level during tropical cyclone called?
3. Mention one risk reduction measures for floods.
4. Name a state which is flooded due to flash flood.

Droughts

- It is an extended period when there is a shortage of water availability due to inadequate rainfall; excessive rate of evaporation and overutilisation of water from reservoirs and other storages including groundwater.

7 **Embankments** It is a raised banks or wall made of stones. These are used to protect against flooding from tides, sea waves or streams.

Types of Droughts

(i) **Meteorological Drought** It occurs when there is inadequate rainfall for a prolonged period with irregular distribution of rainfall over space and time.

(ii) **Hydrological Drought** It occurs when the availability of water in different storages, natural streams and reservoirs like aquifers, lakes, etc. fall below that the precipitation can replenish.

(iii) **Agricultural Drought** It occurs when the moisture level in the soil is insufficient to maintain average crop yields resulting in crop failure. Thus, it is also known as soil **moisture drought**. If an area has more than 30 per cent of its gross cropped area under irrigation, the area is excluded from drought prone category.

(iv) **Ecological Drought** It occurs when the productivity of a natural ecosystem fails due to shortage of water and because of ecological distress, damages are induced in the ecosystem.

▲ *Drought*

Drought Prone Areas in India

- According to some estimates, 30 per cent of total country's area is drought prone, affecting 50 million people. 19 per cent of total area and 12 per cent of its total population suffer due to drought every year.
- Based on intensity of droughts, India can be divided into the following regions
  - **Extreme Drought Affected Areas** These regions receive less than 90 mm average rainfall. Most parts of Rajasthan, particularly areas to the West of the Aravali hills. i.e. Marusthali and Kachchh regions of Gujarat and mainly the districts like Jaisalmer and Barmer fall in this category.
  - **Severe Drought Affected Areas** These regions receive 50-80 per cent less rainfall than the normal. It includes parts of Eastern Rajasthan and Eastern Maharashtra most parts of Madhya Pradesh, interior parts of Andhra Pradesh, Karnataka plateaus, Odisha, Northern parts of interior Tamil Nadu and Southern parts of Jharkhand.
  - **Moderate Drought Affected Areas** These regions receive 26-50 per cent less rainfall than the normal. Northern parts of Rajasthan, Haryana, Southern Uttar Pradesh, the remaining parts of Gujarat, Maharashtra except Konkan, Jharkhand and Coimbatore plateau of Tamil Nadu and interior parts of Karnataka, etc fall in this category.

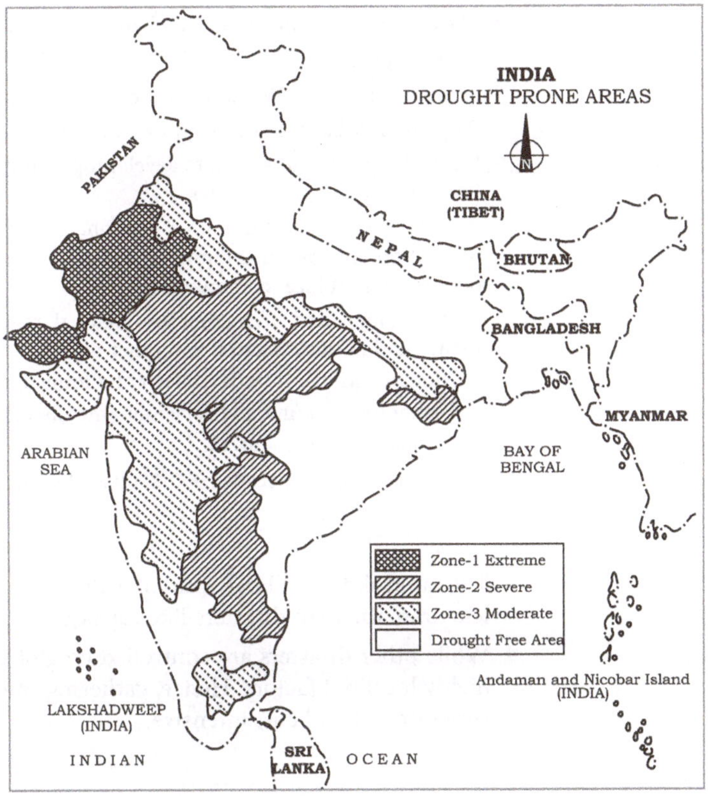

▲ *Drought Prone Areas in India*

Consequences of Drought

- Crop failure leading to scarcity of food grains (*akal*) and fodder (*trinkal*).
- Inadequate rainfall resulting in shortage of water (*jalkal*).

- Shortage of food grains, fodder and water together has most devastating effect.
- Large scale death of cattle and other animals.
- Migration of humans and livestock.
- Scarcity of water compels people to consume contaminated water resulting in spread of many waterborne diseases like gastro-enteritis, cholera, hepatitis, etc.

Risk Reduction Measures for Droughts

- Provision for distribution of safe drinking water and medicines for victims.
- Availability of fodder and water for cattle.
- Shifting of people and their livestock to safer places.
- Identification of groundwater potential in form of aquifers with the help of remote sensing and satellite imageries.
- Transfer of river water from surplus to deficit areas and particularly planning for inter-linking of rivers and construction of reservoirs and dams.
- Spreading of knowledge about drought resistant crops and proper training to practice the same.
- Rainwater harvesting can also be an effective method in minimising effects of drought.

Yokohama Strategy and International Decade for Natural Disaster Reduction (IDNDR)

- In 1994, from May 23rd to 27th, all the members of the UN and other states met at World Conference on Natural Disaster Reduction in Yokohama (Japan) to finalise a plan, known as Yokohama Strategy and Action Plan for a Safer World.
- The conference adopted the Yokohama Strategy as a guide to mitigate the losses due to the disaster particularly in developing countries, which are ill-equipped to cope with them.

The resolution of the World Conference on Natural Disasters Reduction is mentioned below

- Each country has the sovereign responsibility to protect its citizens from natural disasters.
- It will give priority attention to developing countries particularly the least developed, landlocked countries and small-island developing states.
- It will develop and strengthen national capabilities through legislation for natural and other disaster prevention, mitigation and preparedness, including the mobilisation of non-governmental organisations and participation of local communities.
- It will promote and strengthen sub-regional, regional and international co-operation in activities to prevent, reduce and mitigate natural and other disasters, with particular emphasis on
  - Human and institutional capacity building and strengthening.
  - Technology sharing; the collection, the dissemination and utilisation of information.
  - Mobilisation of resources.
- It also declared the decade 1990-2000 as the International Decade for Natural Disaster Reduction (IDNDR).

Landslides

- The rapid sliding of large mass of bedrocks is known as landslide. Disasters due to landslides are usually less dramatic than disasters like earthquakes, volcanic eruptions, tsunamis and cyclones.
- While other disasters are controlled by global or regional factors, landslides are mainly controlled by highly localised factors. Hence, gathering information and monitoring the possibilities of landslides is very difficult and cost intensive.

Landslide Vulnerability Zones

- Based on frequency, geology, geomorphic agents, slope, vegetation covers and land use, India has been divided into several zones, which are as follows

Very High Vulnerability Zone

- It includes highly unstable areas like young mountainous areas in the Himalayas and Andaman and Nicobar, high rainfall regions with steep slopes in the Western Ghats and Nilgiris, the North-Eastern regions areas that experience frequent grounds shaking due to earthquakes, etc.
- The areas of intense human activities in mountains like construction of roads, dams are also included in this zone.

High Vulnerability Zone

- These are the areas that have almost similar conditions to those included in the very high vulnerability zone. The only difference between these two is combination, intensity and frequency of controlling factors.
- All the Himalayan states, and the states from the North-Eastern regions except plains of Assam are included in this zone.

Moderate to Low Vulnerability Zone

- It includes areas that receive less precipitation such as Trans-Himalayan areas of Ladakh and Spiti (Himachal Pradesh), areas in Aravalli with undulated and stable relief and low precipitation, rain shadow areas in the Western and Eastern Ghats and Deccan plateau.
- It also includes the States of Jharkhand, Odisha, Madhya Pradesh, Maharashtra, Karnataka, Tamil Nadu, Chhattisgarh and Andhra Pradesh, Goa and Kerala where landslide occurs due to mining and subsidence.

Other Areas

- The States like Rajasthan, Haryana, Uttar Pradesh, Bihar, West Bengal (except Darjeeling district), Assam (except Karbi Anglong district) and coastal regions of Southern states are safe from landslides.

Effects of Landslides

- It causes roadblock, destruction of railway lines, channel blocking due to rock falls.
- It causes diversion of river courses which lead to flood and loss of life and property.
- It makes spatial interaction difficult, risky and costly and adversely affects the developmental activities.

Risk Reduction Measures for Landslides

- Adopt area-specific measures to deal with landslides.
- Restriction on the construction and other developmental activities such as roads, dams, irrigation canal, etc. in high vulnerability areas.
- Limiting agricultural activities to valleys and areas with moderate slope.
- Control on development of large settlements in high vulnerability zones.
- Promoting large-scale afforestation programmes. Construction of bunds to reduce the flow of water.
- Terrace farming should be encouraged in the North-Eastern states where **Jhumming**[8] (Slash and Burn/ Shifting cultivation) is practiced.
- Surface drainage control works, underground pipes and cables, etc. should be installed to withstand forces caused by landslides.
- Awareness, education and insurance will assist individuals to cope up with the damage.

---

8 **Jhumming** It is the process of growing crops by first clearing the land of trees and vegetation and burning them thereafter.

6.3 Disaster Management

- Disasters can be natural or result of human activities. It is possible to prevent human-made disasters. However, it is not possible to prevent occurrence of natural disasters. Thus, there is emphasis on natural disaster's mitigation and management.
- The fundamental steps taken for disaster management at different level includes establishment of **National Institute of Disaster Management**, (India); **Earth summit at Rio de Janeiro**, (Brazil) in 1993 and **World Conference on Disaster Management** in May 1994 at Yokohama, (Japan), etc.
- Mitigation includes measures taken to reduce both the effect of the hazard and the vulnerability and also conditions in order to reduce the intensity of future disasters.
- There are three stages involved in disaster mitigation and management

  (i) **Pre-Disaster Management**
  - Generating data and information about the disasters.
  - Preparing vulnerability zoning maps.
  - Spreading awareness among the people.
  - Adopting disaster planning, preparedness, and preventive measures in the vulnerable areas.

  (ii) **During Disaster**
  - Evacuation through rescue and relief programmes.
  - Construction of shelter and relief camps.
  - Supply of water, food, clothing and medical aids should be ensured on an emergency basis.

  (iii) **Post-Disaster Operations**
  - Rehabilitation and recovery of victims.
  - Capacity building to deal with future disasters, such as contingency funds, insurance, etc.

Disaster Management Bill, 2005

- The Government of India has established National Institute of Disaster Management and introduced the **Disaster Management Bill**, 2005 to handle or manage any disasters.
- The Disaster Management Bill, 2005, defines disaster as a catastrophe, mishap, calamity, or grave occurrence affecting any area, arising from natural or man-made causes, or by accident or negligence.

Quick Test 3

1. Name an area moderately affected by drought.
2. Name a region in India that is safe from landslide.
3. What measures should be adopted in North-Eastern states to mitigate landslide?
4. Where was World Conference on Natural Disaster Reduction in 1994 held?

Mind Map

NATURAL HAZARDS AND DISASTERS

1 Disasters

Disaster is an undesirable occurence that occurs very quickly with no warning.

2 Classification of Natural Disasters

Floods

- **Causes** Heavy rainfall, river overflow, deforestation
- **Effects** Crop damage, property loss, disease
- **Mitigation** Afforestation, proper drainage

Droughts

- **Causes** Low rainfall, over-irrigation
- **Effects** Crop failure, water scarcity
- **Mitigation** Rainwater harvesting

Tropical Cyclones

- **Causes** Low pressure system
- **Effects** Strong winds, flooding
- **Mitigation** Early warning systems

Earthquake

- **Causes** Tectonic movement, volcanic activity
- **Effects** Building collapse, landslides
- **Mitigation** Earthquake resistant designs

Landslides

- **Causes** Heavy rainfall, deforestation
- **Effects** Road-blockage, loss of life
- **Mitigation** Proper land-use planning

Tsunami

- **Causes** Earthquake under the sea
- **Effects** Coastal destruction, high death tolls
- **Mitigation** Tsunami warning system

3 Human-caused Disasters

- **Example** Industrial accidents, mining
- **Effects** Air pollution, water contamination
- **Mitigation** Sustainable practices and strict rules and regulations

4 Disaster Management

It is the process of protecting lives and property from the effect of disasters.

- **Pre Disaster Management** Involves data collection, awareness and planning.
- **During-Disaster Management** Involves rescue, relief camps and medical aid.
- **Post Disaster Management** Involves rehabilitation, recovery and rebuilding.

NCERT Folder

Choose the right answer from the four alternatives given below

(i) **Which one of the following states of India experiences floods frequently?**

(a) Bihar (b) West Bengal
(c) Assam (d) Uttar Pradesh

Ans (c) Assam

(ii) **In which one of the following districts of Uttarakhand did Malpa landslide take place?**

(a) Bageshwar (b) Almora
(c) Champawat (d) Pithoragarh

Ans (d) Pithoragarh

(iii) **Which one of the following states receives floods in winter months?**

(a) Assam (b) West Bengal
(c) Kerala (d) Tamil Nadu

Ans (d) Tamil Nadu

(iv) **In which of the following rivers is the Majuli river island situated?**

(a) Ganga (b) Brahmaputra (c) Godavari (d) Indus

Ans (b) Brahmaputra

(v) **Under which type of natural hazards do blizzards come?**

(a) Atmospheric (b) Aquatic
(c) Terrestrial (d) Biological

Ans (a) Atmospheric

Answer the following questions in about 30 words

(i) **When can a hazard become a disaster?**

Ans When a natural hazard causes widespread destruction, damage, death etc., and fail to reduce its effects on the human life, then it becomes a disaster. Natural hazards are the elements of circumstances in the natural environment that can cause harm to people and property whereas natural disasters are sudden and cause widespread destruction, deaths and disturbances.

(ii) **Why are there more earthquakes in the Himalayas and in the North-Eastern region of India?**

Ans There is movement of Indian plate towards the North and North-Eastern direction and constants obstruction by the Eurasian plate from the North. As a result of this, both the plates are said to be locked with each other resulting in accumulation of energy at different point of time, that builds up stress, which ultimately leads to the breaking up of the locks and sudden release of energy and causes earthquake along the Himalayan arch.

Thus, there are more earthquakes in the Himalayas and in the North-Eastern regions of India.

(iii) **What are the basic requirements for the formation of a cyclone?**

Ans The basic requirements for the formation of a cyclone are

(i) Large and continuous supply of warm and moist air that can release enormous latent heat.

(ii) Strong Coriolis force that can prevent filling of low pressure at the centre.

(iii) Unstable condition through troposphere that creates local disturbances around which a cyclone develops.

(iv) **How are floods in Eastern India different from the ones in Western India?**

Ans The difference between floods in Eastern and Western India is as follows

Floods in Eastern India	Floods in Western India
It is due to rivers and cyclones.	It is due to flash floods.
Volume and area of discharge of East flowing rivers is more. Thus, floods in Eastern India are more severe.	Volume and area of disharge of West flowing rivers is less. Thus, floods in Western India are less severe.
Change in river courses, e.g. Kosi river in Bihar, leads to more severe floods.	Rivers do not change their course.

(v) **Why are there more droughts in Central and Western India?**

Ans There are more droughts in Central and Western India because of the following reason

- These areas receive very less rainfall in comparison to other areas.
- Scarcity in groundwater and water bodies as Western India consists of deserts and Central India consists of plateaus.

Answer the following questions in about 150 words

(i) **Identify the landslide-prone regions of India and suggest some measures to mitigate the disasters caused by these.**

Ans Landslide-prone areas of India has been divided into a number of zones

(i) **Very High Vulnerability Zone** It includes young mountainous areas in the Himalayas and Andaman and Nicobar, high rainfall regions with steep slopes in the Western Ghats and Nilgiris, the North-Eastern regions, the areas that experience ground shaking due to earthquakes and areas of intense human activities.

(ii) **High Vulnerability Zone** Areas that have almost similar conditions to those included in the very high vulnerability zone are included in this category. All the Himalayan states and the states from the North-Eastern regions except the plains of Assam fall under this zone.

(iii) **Moderate to Low Vulnerability Zone** Areas that receive less precipitation such as Trans- Himalayan areas of Ladakh and Spiti, areas in Aravalis, rainshadow areas in the Western and Eastern Ghats and Deccan plateau.

Also the states of Jharkhand, Odisha, Madhya Pradesh, Maharashtra, Karnataka, Tamil Nadu, Goa and Kerala are prone to landslide due to mining and subsidence.

Some measures to mitigate the disasters caused by landslides are as follows

- Restriction on the construction and other developmental activities such as roads, dams, irrigation canal, etc in high vulnerability areas.
- Limiting agriculture to valleys and areas with moderate slopes.
- Control on development of large settlements in high vulnerability zones.
- Promoting large-scale afforestation programmes and construction of bunds to reduce the flow of water.
- Terrace farming should be encouraged in the North-Eastern states.

(ii) What is vulnerability? Divide India into natural disaster vulnerability zones based on droughts and suggest some mitigation measures.

Ans Vulnerability refers to the risk of becoming a victim to a disaster. For instance, people who live in coastal areas are more vulnerable to cyclone than people who live in interior parts.

On the basis of severity of droughts, India can be divided into the following regions

Extreme Drought Affected Areas These regions receive less than 90 mm average rainfall. Most parts of Rajasthan, particularly areas to the West of the Aravali hills i.e. Marusthali and Kachchh regions of Gujarat and mainly the districts like Jaisalmer and Barmer fall in this category.

Severe Drought Affected Areas Areas which have 50-80 percent less rainfall than normal. It includes parts of Eastern Rajasthan and Maharashtra, most parts of Madhya Pradesh, interior parts of Andhra Pradesh, Karnataka, Odisha, Northern parts of interior Tamil Nadu and Southern parts of Jharkhand, fall in this category.

Moderate Drought Affected Areas Areas which have 26-50 per cent less rainfall than normal. It includes Northern parts of Rajasthan, Haryana, Southern Uttar Pradesh and the remaining parts of Gujarat, Maharashtra except Konkan, Jharkhand and Coimbatore plateau of Tamil Nadu and interior Karnataka, etc.

The measures to reduce the risk of drought are as follows

- Distribution of safe drinking water and medicines for the victims.
- Availability of fodder and water for cattle.
- Shifting of people and their livestock to safer places.
- Identification of groundwater potential in form of aquifers.
- Transfer of river water from surplus to deficit areas and planning for inter-linking of rivers and construction of reservoirs and dams.
- Dissemination of knowledge about drought resistant crops and proper training to practice the same.

(iii) When can developmental activities become the cause of disasters?

Ans Intensive developmental activities carried out in disaster prone areas which are unable to keep pace with ecology and environment have severe consequences and cause large scale disasters.

The causes of disasters are

- Constructional activities and deforestation in the mountainous and coastal areas causes floods and landslides. Structures on the sea coast are prone to storm surges and cyclones.
- Human activities such as mining, blast, etc. causes landslide.
- Human activities in fragile areas can be very harmful in earthquake prone areas.
- Excessive industrial development can also be disastrous if there is any leakage of poisonous gases or incidence of fire. For example, Bhopal Gas Tragedy and Chernobyl Nuclear Disaster.

Exam Pattern Questions

Objective Type Questions

Multiple Choice Questions (MCQs)

1. Which of the following disaster has been caused by direct human action?

(a) Bhopal Gas Tragedy (b) Chernobyl nuclear disaster
(c) Wars (d) All of these

2. Which of the following region belongs to very high damage risk zone of earthquake?

(a) Sikkim (b) Kashmir valley
(c) Delhi (d) Eastern Haryana

3. Which of the following is a measure to mitigate earthquake?

(a) Establishing earthquake monitoring centres.
(b) Use light materials in construction in vulnerable areas.
(c) Discouraging industrial establishment in vulnerable areas.
(d) All of the above

4. Which of the following is true regarding Tsunami?

(a) Impact of tsunami is less near the coast and more over ocean.
(b) It is easy to mitigate damage of tsunami.
(c) It is high vertical wave in ocean water caused by its sudden displacement due to earthquake or volcanic eruptions.
(d) India has not joined International Tsunami Warning System.

5. Which of the following statements is not true regarding the Tsunamis? **CBSE Diksha**

(a) Tsunamis occur due to the earthquakes and volcanic eruptions at the sea-floor.
(b) After reaching the coast, the tsunami waves release enormous energy stored in them.
(c) The Tsunamis are frequently observed along with the coastal areas of the Atlantic Ocean.
(d) The height of these waves rarely exceeds 1 metre in the deep sea. Whereas, on reaching the shallow coastal water their height can reach up to 15m or more.

6. Which steps can be taken in mitigation of tropical cyclone?

(a) Construction of dykes
(b) Afforestation
(c) Installation of monitoring system
(d) All of the above

7. What percentage of area was identified as a drought area?

(a) 10 per cent (b) 12 per cent
(c) 18 per cent (d) 30 per cent

8. Which of the following can help in mitigation of drought?

(a) Inter-linking of rivers
(b) Identification of groundwater potential in form of aquifer
(c) Rainwater harvesting
(d) All of the above

9. Identify the type of natural disaster from the given statement.

It is the rapid sliding of large mass of bedrocks. Disasters due to this are usually less dramatic than disasters like earthquakes, volcanic eruptions, tsunamis and cyclones.

(a) Landslide (b) Earthquake
(c) Temperate cyclone (d) Volcanic eruption

10. Landslide can be mitigated by

(a) Limiting agriculture to valleys and areas with moderate slope.
(b) Large scale afforestation programs.
(c) Construction of bunds to reduce flow of water.
(d) All of the above

11. Choose from the following the correct statement regarding steps in Post Disaster Management.

I. Preparing vulnerability zoning maps
II. Evacuation
III. Capacity building
IV. Spreading awareness.

Options

(a) Both I and II (b) Both II and IV
(c) Only III (d) All these

12. Consider the following statements and choose the correct one.

I. Natural hazards are relatively sudden events and cause large scale, widespread death, loss of property and disturbance to social systems and life over which people have little or no control.
II. Natural disasters are elements of circumstances in natural environment that have potential to harm people or property, or both.

Codes

(a) Only I (b) Only II
(c) Both I and II (d) None of these

13. **Consider the following statements and choose the correct statements.**

I. Earthquakes of tectonic origin are more devastating and have large area of influence.
II. Earthquakes associated with volcanic eruption have limited area of influence and scale of damage.

Codes

(a) Only I (b) Only II
(c) Both I and II (d) None of these

14. **Which of the following is socio-economic consequence of earthquake?**

I. Destroys infrastructure
II. Makes people homeless
III. Cause landslides
IV. Robs population of material and socio-cultural gains.

Codes

(a) I, II and III (b) I, II and IV
(c) II, III and IV (d) I, III and IV

15. **Consider the following statements about Tropical cyclone and choose the correct one**

I. Strong Coriolis force is required for its formation.
II. It has a high pressure centre.
III. It extends 500 to 1000 km horizontally.

Codes

(a) I and II (b) II and III
(c) I and III (d) I, II and III

16. **Which of the following is responsible for causing landslide?**

I. Intense rainfall
II. Geological weak material
II. Earthquake

Codes

(a) I and II (b) II and III
(c) I and III (d) I, II and III

17. **Consider the following statements. Which of them is responsible for causing floods?**

I. Surface run off beyond carrying capacity of river
II. Storm surge
III. High rainfall
IV. Blockage in drains due to huge amount of eroded material in water

Codes

(a) I and II (b) I, II, III and IV
(c) II, II and IV (d) I, III and IV

18. **Which of the following is consequence of flood?**

I. Loss of infrastructure
II. Outbreak of diseases
III. Shortage of food
IV. Infertile land

Codes

(a) I, II, III and IV (b) I, II and III
(c) II, III and IV (d) I, III and IV

Arrange the Following

19. **Arrange the following stages required in disaster mitigation and management in correct order.** **CBSE Diksha**

(i) Preparing vulnerability map and spreading awareness among the people about the risk.
(ii) Construction of shelters and rehabilitation centers for the victims.
(iii) Rescue and relief operation such as evacuation
(iv) Supply of water, food, clothing and medical aids.

Options

(a) (i), (iii), (iv), (ii) (b) (i), (ii), ((iii), (iv)
(c) (i), (iv), (iii), (ii) (d) (i), (ii), (iv), (iii)

Match the Following

20.

List I (Type of Drought)	List II (Definition)
A. Meteorological	1. Insufficient moisture level in soil
B. Hydrological	2. Fall in productivity of natural ecosystem
C. Agricultural	3. Fall in availability of water in different storages, lakes, etc.
D. Ecological	4. Inadequate rainfall for prolonged period

Codes

	A	B	C	D		A	B	C	D
(a)	4	3	1	2	(b)	3	4	2	1
(c)	3	4	1	2	(d)	4	3	2	1

21.

List I (Earthquake prone area)	List II (Places include)
A. Very digh damage risk zone	1. Central Highlands.
B. High damage risk zone	2. Eastern parts of Haryana
C. Low damage risk zone	3. Southern parts of Eastern Ghats.
D. Very low damage risk zone	4. Uttarakhand

Codes

	A	B	C	D		A	B	C	D
(a)	4	2	3	1	(b)	1	2	3	4
(c)	4	3	2	1	(d)	2	3	4	1

Assertion-Reason

Directions (Q. Nos. 22-24) In the questions given below are two statements labelled as Assertion (A) and other is labelled as Reason (R). In the context of two statements, which one of the following is correct?

Codes

(a) Both A and R are true, but R is not the correct explanation of A
(b) Both A and R are true and R is the correct explanation of A
(c) Both A and R are incorrect.
(d) A is correct, but R is incorrect

22. **Assertion** (A) Kachchh region in Gujarat is an extremely drought affected area.

Reason (R) Kachchh region in Gujarat is low damage risk zone of earthquake.

23. **Assertion** (A) Strong vertical wind wedge should be absent for emergence of tropical cyclone.

Reason (R) Strong vertical wind wedge disturbs vertical transport of latent heat.

24. **Assertion** (A) Due to storm, there is an increase in the loss of life and property in India, Bangladesh, Myanmar, etc.

Reason (R) It is largely due to high vulnerability of huge population residing in the coastal area.

Answers

1. (d) All of these
2. (b) Kashmir valley
3. (d) All of the above
4. (c) It is high vertical wave in ocean water caused by its sudden displacement due to earthquake or volcanic eruptions.
5. (c) The Tsunamis are frequently observed along with the coastal areas of the Atlantic Ocean.
6. (d) All of the above
7. (d) 30 per cent
8. (d) All of the above
9. (a) Landslide
10. (d) All of the above
11. (c) Only III
12. (d) None of these
13. (c) Both I and II
14. (b) I, II and IV
15. (c) I and III
16. (d) I, II and III
17. (b) I, II, III and IV
18. (a) I, II, III and IV
19. (a) (i), (iii), (iv), (ii)
20. (a)
21. (a)
22. (d) A is correct, but R is incorrect
23. (b) Both A and R are true and R is the correct explanation of A
24. (b) Both A and R are true and R is the correct explanation of A

Subjective Questions

Short Answer Type Questions

1. Distinguish between Natural hazards and Natural disasters.

Ans Differences between Natural hazards and Natural disasters are as follows

Basis	Natural Hazards	Natural Disasters
Meaning	Natural hazards are elements of circumstances in the natural environment that have the potential to cause harm to people or property or both.	Natural disaster is an undesirable occurrence resulting from forces that are largely outside human control, strikes quickly with little or no warning, causing serious disruption of life and property.
Scope	Every natural hazard is not a disaster.	Every natural disaster is a result of a natural hazard.
Example	Earthquakes in Japan is a natural hazard.	Earthquake in Nepal in 2015 proved to be a great disaster.

2. Differentiate between Man-made disaster and Natural disaster.

Ans Differences between Man-made disaster and Natural disaster are as follows

	Man-made Disaster	Natural Disaster
Meaning	Man-made disasters are undesirable occurrence resulting from human actions.	Natural disaster is an undesirable occurrence resulting from forces that are largely outside human control, strikes quickly with little or no warning, causing serious disruption of life and property.
Prevention	Man-made disasters can be prevented upto a large extent.	However; it is not easy to prevent the occurrence natural disaster.
Example	Bomb blast, fire, industrial explosions, wars, accidents, etc.	Earthquakes, tsunami, landslides, floods, droughts, cyclones, etc.

3. Earthquakes are the most unpredictable and highly destructive of all the natural disasters. But their classification into certain zones on the basis of vulnerability have reduced their impacts on humans. Explain. **Competency Based Que**

Ans Earthquakes are the most unpredictable and destructive natural disasters. They cause huge damage to life and property. Their impact on human life has been reduced by classifying zones on the basis of vulnerability to an earthquake.

India has been classified into following zones

(i) **Very High Damage Risk Zone** It includes North-Eastern states, , Kashmir valley, Uttarakhand, Western Himachal Pradesh, etc.

(ii) **High Damage Risk Zone** It includes Northern Punjab, Eastern Haryana, Delhi, Western Uttar Pradesh, Northern Bihar, Sikkim and the remaining parts of Jammu and Kashmir, Himachal Pradesh and Uttarakhand.

(iii) **Moderate Damage Risk Zone** It includes areas between the plateaus of the Deccan and Central Highland and Southern part of Indo-Gangetic plains.

(iv) **Low Damage Risk Zone** It includes areas surrounding Malwa plateau, Karnataka plateau, Chhotanagpur plateau, Telangana plateau.

(v) **Very Low Damage Risk Zone** It includes old stable landmasses of the Peninsular plateau.

4. Suggest the measures that can be adopted to mitigate the effects of earthquake on human lives and property.

Ans To prevent the losses, it is important to put emphasis on disaster preparedness and mitigation by taking following measures

- Establishing earthquake monitoring system for regular monitoring and fast dissemination of information among the people in the vulnerable areas.
- Use of Global Positioning System (GPS) to monitor the movement of tectonic plates.
- Preparing a vulnerability map of the risk zones and educating the people about the ways and means to minimise the adverse impacts of disasters.
- It should be mandatory to adopt earthquake resistant designs and use light materials in major construction activities in vulnerable areas.
- Proper link to be established among institutions for fast dissemination of vulnerability risk information among people.

5. Earthquakes are devastating for human lives and property. Explain socio-environmental effects of earthquakes. **Competency Based Que**

Ans The socio-environmental effects of earthquakes are

- It causes huge loss of life and property in areas of high density of population.
- Earthquakes damages and destroys the settlement, infrastructure, transport, communication network, industries and other development activities.
- It robs the population of their material and socio-cultural gains that they have preserved over generations.
- It also causes landslides and floods that obstructs channels and disturbs the entire ecosystem and environment.

6. What is a Tropical cyclone? Explain its spatio-temporal distribution in India.

Ans Tropical cyclones are intense low pressure areas confined to the areas lying between 30°N and 30°S latitudes. It is a heat engine which gets its energy from the release of latent heat due to the condensation of moisture that wind has gathered after moving over oceans and seas.

Spatio-temporal distribution of tropical cyclone in India is explained below

- The tropical cyclones originating in the Arabian sea and Bay of Bengal affect the East and West coasts of India.
- In the Bay of Bengal, they originate in the months of October and November between 16°–20°N latitudes and West of 92°E.

- By the month of July, they shift to around 18°N latitude and to the West of 90°E. As they come near the landmass of India, they struck the coastal areas with wind speeds of 180km/hr. It causes huge damage to these areas.

7. Floods are relatively slow in occurrence and occur in well defined regions. Do you agree that the effects of floods can be mitigated easily. What measures can be taken to reduce their effects? Competency Based Que

Ans Yes, floods are slow in occurrence and occur in well defined regions and with in expected time in a year. Thus, their effects can be reduced easily with the help of some well planned measures.

The measures to reduce the effects of floods are as follows

- No major development should be permitted in the areas which are subjected to high flooding.
- Removal of human encroachment from river channels and depopulating flood plains.
- Important facilities like hospitals, schools, offices should be built in safe areas.
- In urban areas, ponds and lakes can be created in low lying areas.
- Construction of flood protection embankments, dams, channel improvement, etc.

8. Flood affected areas have increased in India. Enumerate the causes for the increase in food affected areas. Competency Based Que

Ans. There has been an increase in flood affected areas due to following reasons

- Changing climatic conditions leading to high intensity rainfall for longer time period and melting of ice and snow.
- Reduction in infiltration rate and presence of eroded material in water due to soil erosion.
- Unregulated deforestation and grazing.
- Disturbance along natural drainage channels.
- Colonisation of flood plains and river beds.
- Increase in flash floods in states of Rajasthan, Gujarat, Haryana and Punjab due to pattern of monsoon and blocking of streams and channels.
- Due to retreating monsoon, increase in flooding on Southern coast during November-January.

In India, every year, various regions are affected by droughts that cause damage to the social, cultural and economic aspects of life.

9. Droughts have cascading effects on various aspects of environment and society. Justify. Competency Based Que

Ans Drought is the shortage of water availability due to inadequate precipitation, excessive evaporation and over utilisation of water. It affects various aspects of environment and society.

The effects of droughts are as follows

- Scarcity of food and fodder due to failure of crops.
- Shortage of water.
- Large scale death of cattle.
- Migration of humans and livestock.
- Spread of water borne diseases due to contaminated water.
- Low moisture and precipitation creates hazardous conditions in forests, creating wildfires.
- Agrarian distress and loss of agro-based industries.

Hence, drought effects the overall economic, environmental and social life of people.

10. Why it is difficult to detect a tsunami in the deeper parts of the sea? CBSE Diksha

Ans It is difficult to detect tsunami in deeper parts of the oceans because in the deep ocean, a tsunami has a small amplitude (less than 1 metre) but very long wavelength (hundreds of kilometres). This means that the slope, or steepness of the wave is very small, which is why they are not noticed by sailors.

Once a tsunami reaches shallow water near the coast, its wavelength gets reduced and the period remains unchanged, which increases the wave- height up to 15m or more, which causes large-scale destructions along the shores.

11. Why was the Yokohama strategy adopted? What were the resolutions of natural disaster reduction?

Ans The Yokohama strategy was adopted by the United Nations as it was believed that the impact of natural disasters in terms of human and economic losses has risen in the recent years and the society was become vulnerable to natural disasters. These disasters affected the poor and the vulnerable the most in developing countries. The Yokohama strategy was adopted as a guide for the decade of 1990-2000.

The resolutions at the World Conference on Natural Disaster Reduction were

- Each country has the responsibility to protect its citizens from natural disasters.
- Priority attention to be given to developing and least developed countries.
- To prevent, reduce and mitigate the disasters by regional and international co-operation.

Long Answer Type Questions

1. Why do Tsunamis occur? State the effects of Tsunamis.

Ans Tsunamis or harbour waves or seismic sea waves are high vertical waves in ocean water that occur due to the sudden displacement of ocean water due to earthquake and volcanic eruptions that cause the sea floor to move abruptly.

The speed of wave in the ocean depends upon the depth of water. It is more in the shallow water than in deep ocean. As a result of this, the impact of tsunami is less over the ocean and more near the coast.

It can be proved with an example that a ship is not much affected over deep water as it has long wave length and limited wave height, whereas near the coast where it enters shallow water, its wavelength gets reduced and wave height increases and causes large scale devastation. Tsunami waves after reaching the coast release enormous energy stored in them and water flows turbulently onto land leading to following effects

- Destruction of ports, cities, towns, structures, building and other settlements.
- Loss of life and property in coastal areas. As coastal areas are densely populated and are centres of intense activity, this loss is higher in case of tsunami than by any other natural hazard.
- e.g. Due to tsunami that occurred On 26th December, 2004 more than 300,000 people lost their lives.

2. What are the effects of tropical cyclones? What measures can be taken to reduce its impact?

Ans The effects of tropical cyclones are as follows

- The coastal areas are often struck by severe cyclone storms with an average velocity of 180 km/h.
- This results in abnormal rise in the sea level which is known as storm surge.
- This results in flooding of human settlements, agricultural fields, damaging crops and destruction of structures created by human being.
- It causes huge life and economic loss of the state and the nation as well, if timely action is not taken.

The risk of tropical cyclones can be reduced by the following measures

- By creating awareness, knowledge and preparedness among the members of communities.
- Not to have heavy and expensive infrastructure and activities in the areas affected every year.
- Proper timely warning and evacuation plan should be displayed and taught to the people.
- Latest monitoring system should be installed to keep an eye on the speed and frequency of the storm.
- Construction of cyclone shelters, embankments, dykes, reservoirs and afforestation to reduce speed of wind.
- Swift mobilisation of disaster forces in the case of emergency.
- Promoting mangrove plantation, as it reduces the impact of the cyclone.
- Avoiding residential complexes in the vulnerable areas.

3. There are certain areas in India, that are prone to floods. State risk reduction measuress to reduce the effects of floods.

Ans Most of the flood affected areas are the Ganga basin, Brahmaputra basin, Indus basin, and river basins of Peninsular India and their tributaries.

Assam, West Bengal and Bihar are among high flood prone states of India. Apart from these, most of the rivers in Northern states like Punjab and Uttar Pradesh are vulnerable to occasional floods. States like Rajasthan, Gujarat, Haryana and Punjab are getting inundated due to flash floods.

The pattern of monsoon and blocking of streams and river channel by human activities is responsible for it. The retreating monsoon is responsible for flooding in Tamil Nadu during November-January.

The measures to reduce the risk of floods are as follows

- No major development should be permitted in the areas which are subjected to high flooding.
- Removal of human encroachment from the river channels and depopulating flood plains.
- Important facilities like hospitals, schools, offices should be built in safe areas.
- In urban areas, ponds and lakes can be created in low lying areas.
- Reforestation, protection of vegetation, clearing of debris from streams can be done to reduce the amount of run-off water.
- Construction of flood protection embankments, dams, channel improvement, etc.
- Flood proofing can reduce the damage by use of sand bag, blocking or sealing of doors and windows of houses, etc.
- The building should be constructed on an elevated areas platforms.
- Flood hazard mapping will give the proper indication of water flow and warning can be issued in an organised manner to shift and evacuate people on time to reduce the risk.

4. Droughts have immense disastrous consequences thus it is necessary to reduce the risks related to droughts. Elucidate measures to minimise the effects of droughts. **Competency Based Que**

Ans Droughts have both immediate and long term disastrous consequences. Thus mitigation of droughts require both these effects into consideration.

Immediate Measures

- Provision for distribution of safe drinking water and medicines for victims.
- Availability of fodder and water for cattle.
- Shifting of people and their livestock to safer places.

Long term Measures

- Identification of groundwater potential in form of aquifers.
- Transfer of river water from surplus to deficit areas.
- Inter-linking of rivers
- Construction of reservoirs and dams.
- Spread of knowledge about drought resistant crops.
- Rainwater harvesting.
- Restoring pastures and balancing land and water resources.
- Diversifying rural livelihoods through social protection, cash transfer programs or improving access to markets and rural services.

5. There are various type of droughts that occurs in India. Elucidate. **Competency Based Que**

Ans. Drought is an unusual dry period which results in shortage of water due to absence or deficiency of rainfall from its normal pattern in a region or excessive rate of evaporation or overutilisation of water from reservoirs and other storages including groundwater.

In India, every year, various regions are affected by droughts that cause damage to the social, cultural and economic aspects of life.

The different types of droughts are as follows

- **Meteorological Drought** It is inadequate rainfall for a prolonged period of time marked with its irregular distribution over space and time.
- **Hydrological Drought** It results when the availability of water in different storages, natural streams and reservoirs like aquifers, lakes, etc. fall below that the precipitation can replenish.
- **Agricultural Drought** It is the drought when the moisture level in the soil is insufficient to maintain average crop yields resulting in crop failure. An area having more than 30 per cent of its gross cropped area under irrigation is excluded from drought prone category.
- **Ecological Drought** It is the drought when the productivity of a natural ecosystem fails due to shortage of water and as a consequence of ecological distress, damages are induced in the ecosystem.

6. How can we cope up any disaster effectively through mitigation and management?

Ans Mitigation includes measures taken to reduce both the effect of the hazard and the vulnerability and it also reduces the scale of future disaster.

There are three stages involved in disaster mitigation and management

(i) **Pre-Disaster Management** It involves
- Generating data and information about the disasters.
- Preparing vulnerability zoning maps.
- Spreading awareness among the people.
- Adopting disaster planning, preparedness and preventive measures in the vulnerable areas.
- Creating awareness among the people about the various aspects of disaster.
- Organising mock practices to show people how to response at the time of disaster.

(ii) **During Disaster** It involves rescue and relief operations such as
- Evacuation of people and livestock
- Construction of shelter and relief camps.
- Supply of water, food, clothing and medical aids should be done on an emergency basis.
- Restoring the communication, so that disaster can be carried out effectively.

(iii) **Post-Disaster Operations** It involves
- Rehabilitation and recovery of victims.
- Capacity building in order to cope up with future disasters, such as contingency funds, insurance, etc.

7. Why earthquake hazard mitigation is more important than any other hazard? Discuss some mitigation measures and preparedness of such a disaster. **CBSE Diksha**

Ans. Unlike other disasters, the damages caused by earthquakes are more devastating. It destroys most of the transport and communication links, due to which it becomes difficult to provide timely relief to the victims. Moreover, it is not possible to prevent the occurrence of an earthquake.

Therefore, the best option is to put emphasis on mitigation measures and preparedness such as

- Establishing earthquake monitoring centres (seismological centres) for regular monitoring and fast spreading of information among the people in the vulnerable(weak) areas.
- Use of Geographical Positioning System (GPS) can be of great help in monitoring the movement of tectonic plates.
- Preparing a vulnerability map of the country and spreading of vulnerability risk information among the people and educating them about the ways and means minimising the adverse impacts of disasters.
- Modifying the house types and building- designs in the vulnerable areas and discouraging construction of high-rise buildings, large industrial establishments and big urban centres in such areas.
- Finally, making it mandatory to adopt earthquake-resistant designs and use light materials in major construction activities in vulnerable areas.

Source Based Questions

1. Read the passage carefully and answer the questions that follow.

Earthquakes and volcanic eruptions that cause the sea-floor to move abruptly resulting in sudden displacement of ocean water in the form of high vertical waves are called tsunamis (harbour waves) or seismic sea waves. Normally, the seismic waves cause only one instantaneous vertical wave; but, after the initial disturbance, a series of afterwaves are created in the water that oscillate between high crest and low trough in order to restore the water level. The speed of wave in the ocean depends upon the depth of water. It is more in the shallow water than in the ocean deep. As a result of this, the impact of tsunami is less over the ocean and more near the coast where they cause large-scale devastations. Therefore, a ship at sea is not much affected by tsunami and it is difficult to detect a tsunami in the deeper parts of sea. It is so because over deep water the tsunami has very long wave-length and limited wave-height. Thus, a tsunami wave raises the ship only a metre or two and each rise and fall takes several minutes. As opposed to this, when a tsunami enters shallow water, its wave-length gets reduced and the period remains unchanged, which increases the waveheight. Sometimes, this height can be up to 15m or more, which causes large-scale destructions along the shores. Thus, these are also called Shallow Water Waves.

Tsunamis are frequently observed along the Pacific ring of fire, particularly along the coast of Alaska, Japan, Philippines and other islands of South-East Asia, Indonesia, Malaysia, Myanmar, Sri Lanka, and India etc. After reaching the coast, the tsunami waves release enormous energy stored in them and water flows turbulently onto the land destroying port-cities and towns, structures, buildings and other settlements. Since the coastal areas are densely populated the world over and these are also centres of intense human activity, the loss of life and property is likely to be much higher by a tsunami as compared to other natural hazards in the coastal areas.

(i) Tsunamis are caused by which of the following?

(a) Seismic waves
(b) Moon's gravitational attraction
(c) Sun's gravitational repulsion
(d) Tropical cyclone

Ans (a) Seismic waves

(ii) The most intense tsunamis occurs in which of the following regions?

(a) Indian Ocean (b) Atlantic Ocean
(c) Pacific Ocean (d) None of these

Ans (c) Pacific Ocean

(iii) The tsunamis mainly affect which of the following regions?

(a) Plains (b) Mountain valleys
(c) Coastal plains (d) All of these

Ans (c) Coastal plains

2. Read the passage carefully and answer the questions that follow.

Inundation of land and human settlements by the rise of water in the channels and its spill-over presents the condition of flooding. Unlike other natural disasters, the causes of floods are well established. Floods are relatively slow in occurrences and often, occur in well-identified regions and within expected time in a year. Floods occur commonly when water in the form of surface run-off exceeds the carrying capacity of the river channels and streams and flows into the neighbouring low-lying flood plains. At times, this even goes beyond the capacity of lakes and other inland water bodies in which they flow. Floods can also be caused due to a storm surge (in the coastal areas), high intensity rainfall for a considerably longer time period, melting of ice and snow. reduction in the infiltration rate and presence of eroded material in the water due to higher rate of soil erosion. Though floods occur frequently over wide geographical area having disastrous ramifications in many parts of the world, floods in the South, South-East and East Asian countries, particularly in China, India and Bangladesh, are frequent and equally disastrous. Once again, unlike other natural disasters, human beings play an important role in the genesis as well as spread of floods. Indiscriminate deforestation, unscientific agricultural practices, disturbances along the natural drainage channels and colonisation of flood-plains and river-beds are some of the human activities that play an important role in increasing the intensity, magnitude and gravity of floods. Frequent inundation of agricultural land and human settlement, particularly in Assam, West Bengal, Bihar and Eastern Uttar Pradesh (flooding rivers), coastal areas of Odisha, Andhra Pradesh, Tamil Nadu and Gujarat (cyclone) and Punjab, Rajasthan, Northern Gujarat and Haryana (flash floods) have serious consequences on the national economy and society.

(i) **How might human activities contribute more to flooding than natural causes in Asian countries?**

Ans. Through deforestation, poor farming practices, and settlement in flood-prone areas, humans significantly increase the flood impacts.

(ii) **How could deforestation potentially worsen flooding situations?**

Ans. Deforestation reduces the natural water absorption and increases surface runoff which leads to higher flood intensity and frequency.

(iii) **Why might floods be considered more predictable than other natural disasters?**

Ans. Floods is considered more predictable than other natural disasters due to their slow occurrence in identifiable regions during expected times of year which makes them more foreseeable.

SELF ASSESSMENT TEST

Objective Type Questions

1. India is highly vulnerable to natural calamities because of
   (a) Vastness in terms of natural attributes
   (b) Colonial past
   (c) Large population
   (d) All of these
2. India has been divided into how many earthquake zones?
   (a) Three
   (b) Five
   (c) Four
   (d) None of these
3. Which of the following is characteristic of centre of cyclone?
   (a) Cold
   (b) Cloudless
   (c) High pressure
   (d) None of these
4. Meteorological drought is
   (a) Lack of availability of water in different storages.
   (b) Condition of insufficient moisture level in soil.
   (c) Condition of ecological distress.
   (d) Inadequate rainfall for prolonged period.
5. Which of the following factor responsible for floods in India?
   I. Excessive rainfall
   II. Climate change
   III. Construction of dams

   Codes
   (a) I and II
   (b) I and III
   (c) II and III
   (d) All of these

Short Answer Type Questions

6. What has IDNDR emphasised on to prevent, reduce and mitigate disasters?
7. Give brief note on socio-environmental consequences of earthquakes.
8. Classify drought affected areas of India according to its severity.
9. 'Droughts have both immediate as well as long-term disastrous consequences on social and physical environments'. Suggest any two ideas that should be kept in mind while mitigating the drought.
10. Divide landslide prone areas into different vulnerability zone.

Long Answer Type Questions

11. Recall the consequences of recent landslide occurred in North India. Suggest some measures to cope up with it.
12. 'Floods are very frequent in India'. Explain its causes and effects of it.
13. Enumerate the mitigation action plan for cyclones.
14. 'Flood as a disaster has so many adverse effects in the region where it occurs'. Justify the statement.

PRACTICAL WORK

1. Introduction to Map

Maps

Maps are essential tools in geography, representing the Earth's surface in a simplified manner. Since, it is impossible to represent all features of the Earth's surface in their actual size and form, maps are drawn at a reduced scale, allowing for a detailed representation.

The choice of scale, symbols, colours and generalisation techniques help make maps effective and informative.

> **Globe**
>
> Globe is a 3D structure. It is known as a true representation of the Earth.

Essentials of Map Making

Cartography is the art and science of map-making. It involves several key processes that ensure the accuracy and usability of the map. These processes that may also be referred to as essential to maps are

- **Scale** Scales are used to find the actual distance between two points on the map. Maps are reductions of actual areas, and the scale determines the level of detail included. A carefully chosen scale ensures that the map serves its intended purpose effectively.

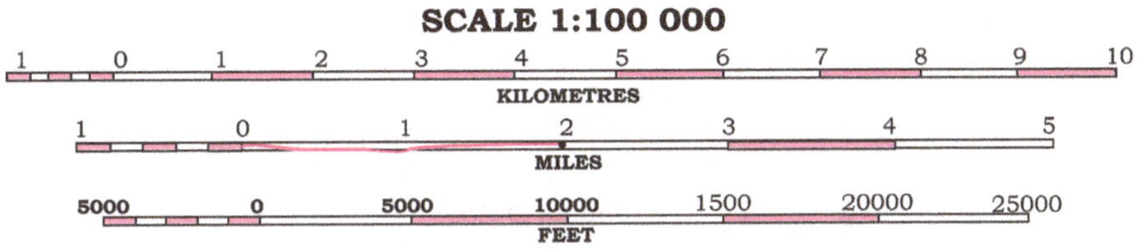

Scale

- **Map Projection** Since the Earth is a geoid, its curved surface must be transformed into a flat representation. This transformation is called projection. It reduces unavoidable distortions in shape, area, distance, or direction.
- **Generalisation** Maps must focus on relevant information, omitting unnecessary details. Generalisation involves selecting, simplifying, and refining the data to match the map's purpose.
- **Map Design** Effective map design includes the choice of symbols, colours, lettering styles, and arrangement of elements. A well-designed map enhances readability and communication.

- **Map Construction and Production** The creation of maps has evolved from manual drawing to computer-assisted mapping and digital printing techniques, making modern maps more accurate and accessible.

History of Map Making

Map-making dates back to ancient civilisations. The earliest known maps were found in Mesopotamia. It was drawn on clay tablets from 2500 B.C. Greek and Arab geographers contributed significantly to modern cartography by introducing geographical coordinates and calculating the Earth's circumference.

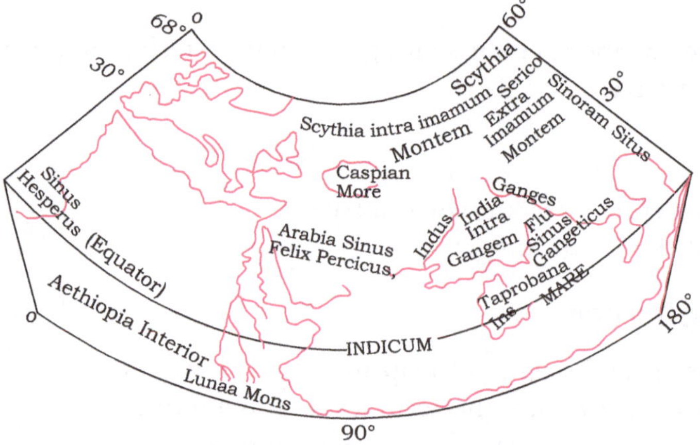

Ptolemy's World Map

During the Vedic period in India, astronomical and cosmological concepts influenced map-making, as seen in ancient Indian texts. Ancient Indian scholars divided the known world into seven 'dwipas'.

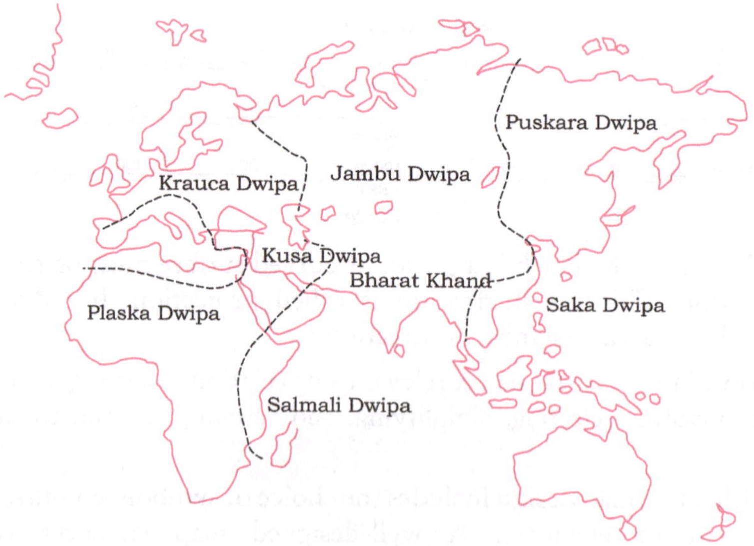

Seven Dwipas of the World as conceived in Ancient India

The Survey of India, established in 1767, was crucial in developing accurate maps for administrative and planning purposes.

Types of Maps

Maps can be classified based on scale and function.

Classification Based on Scale

1. **Large-Scale Maps** These maps depict smaller areas in greater detail.

- **Cadastral Maps** The term 'cadastral' is derived from the French word 'cadastre' meaning 'register of territorial property'. These are generally used for property boundaries and land ownership records. These maps are drawn at scales of 1:500 to 1:4000.
- **Topographical Maps** These maps provide detailed representations of terrain, settlements, and infrastructure, often at scales of 1:250,000, 1:50,000, or 1:25,000. The topographical maps are based on precise surveys and are prepared as a series of maps made by the national mapping agencies of almost all countries.

Topographical Map

2. **Small-Scale Maps** These maps cover larger areas but with less detail.
    - **Wall Maps** Such maps are typically smaller than topographical maps but larger than atlas maps. These are used in lectures or classrooms.
    - **Atlas Maps** These are very small-scale maps. These are highly generalised to provide a broad overview of continents countries and regions.

Classification Based on Function

1. **Physical Maps** These maps represent the natural features of the Earth. For example, geology, soils, drainage, elements of weather, climate, vegetation, etc.
    - **Relief Maps** Such maps show mountains, valleys, plains and drainage patterns.
    - **Geological Maps** These maps indicate rock formations, fault lines and mineral deposits.
    - **Climatic Maps** Such maps are used to depict temperature, precipitation, wind patterns and other climatic conditions.
    - **Soil Maps** These maps represent different soil types and their distribution.
2. **Cultural Maps** These maps display human-made features and demographic information.
    - **Political Maps** These maps show administrative boundaries like countries, states, and districts.
    - **Population Maps** These maps illustrate population density, growth and demographic composition.
    - **Economic Maps** These maps depict agricultural zones, industrial centres and trade routes.
    - **Transportation Maps** These maps highlight roads, railway networks and airports.

Uses of Maps

Maps are used by geographers, planners and policymakers. They facilitate various types of spatial analysis, including

- **Measurement of Distance** Distances can be measured between two points using dividers, scales, or rotameters.
- **Measurement of Direction** Cardinal and intermediate directions help users navigate accurately. Cardinal points on a map are North [N], South [S], East [E] and West [W].
- **Measurement of Area** The area of features can be calculated using graph paper methods. The area is then determined by a simple equation

Area = Sum of whole squares+ Sum of partial squares/2 * map scale

The area can also be calculated by using a fixed-area polar planimeter.

2. Map Scale

A map scale is an essential element of any map. Without a scale, a map cannot accurately show distances and proportions. A drawing without a scale is called a sketch. The scale helps in measuring distances and areas on a map.

Definition of Scale

A scale shows the relationship between a map and the real world. It helps in finding the actual ground distance by measuring the map distance. It is usually represented as a ratio or in graphical form. For example, if a map has a scale of 1:50,000, it means that one unit on the map equals 50,000 units on the ground.

Systems of Measurement

There are two systems of measurement of distances used in different countries of the world. These are

- **Metric system** The distances calculated as kilometers, meters, centimetres, etc., are part of this method. India uses a metric system of measurement.
- **English system** The distances calculated as miles, furlongs, yards, feet, etc., are part of this method. This is generally used in the USA and UK.

Importance of Scale

Scales are important for understanding and using maps correctly. They help in

- Measuring distances accurately between locations.
- Comparing different maps of the same area with different levels of detail.
- Calculating areas for planning and land use.
- Navigating and understanding geographical features.

Methods of Representing Scale

There are three main ways to show scale on a map. Each method has its advantages and limitations.

1. Statement of Scale

This method expresses scale in words. It states how much distance on the ground is represented by a certain distance on the map. For example, '1 cm represents 10 km' means that 1 cm on the map equals 10 km in reality.

This method is simple and easy to understand. However, if the map is resized, the statement of scale becomes incorrect.

2. Graphical or Bar Scale

This method uses a line with divisions marked to represent distances. It is also called a bar scale. The map user can directly measure distances using this scale.

This method remains accurate even if the map is resized. However, users need to know how to read the bar scale properly.

R.F. 1: 50, 000

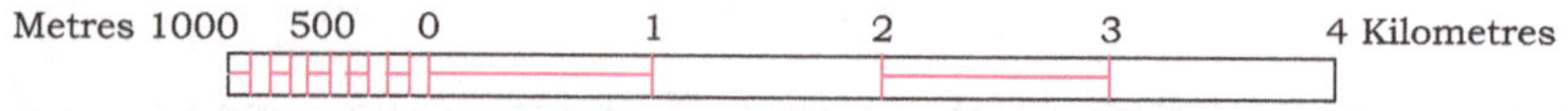

3. Representative Fraction (RF)

This method of the scale is expressed as a fraction showing the ratio between a unit distance on the map or plan.

The distance is measured in the same units as on the ground. For example, a scale of 1:50,000 means that 1 unit on the map equals 50,000 units on the ground.

This method is universal and can be used with any unit of measurement. However, it does not provide direct distance readings like the graphical scale.

Conversion of Scale

A scale can be converted from one form to another. The most common conversions include

- **Statement of Scale to RF** A statement scale can be converted to RF by changing the ground distance to the same unit as the map distance.

  For example, if a scale of 1 inch represents 4 miles then the RF scale will represent it as 1:253,440. Because 1 mile is equal to 63,360 inches, and in scale, 1 inch represents 1 inch as four miles, hence it will be 4* 63360 inches (253,440).
- **RF to Statement of Scale** Similarly, the RF scale can be converted into the statement scale.

  For example, if an RF of 1:253,440 is given, it can be converted into a statement like '1 cm represents 2.53 km' by using simple mathematical calculations. As 253,440 represents the units on the ground then, 1 cm will represent 253440/100000 (1 km= 10000 cm). In other words, 1 cm will represent 2.5344 km.

Construction of the Graphical/ Bar Scale

The bar scale is the graphical representation of the statement and scale. Example, construct a graphical scale when the given statement of scale is 1 inch representing 1 mile and read the distance in miles and furlongs. As 1 inch represents 1 mile, 6 inches represent 6 miles. Through the following steps, we an construct the graphical scale.

- Draw a straight line of 6 inches and divide it into 6 equal parts and assign a value of 1 mile each for 5 right side divisions.
- Divide the extreme left side division into 4 equal parts and mark each division by a value of 2 miles each, beginning from 0.

RF 1: 63360

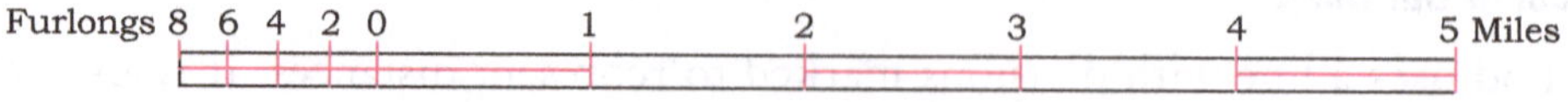

3. Latitude, Longitude and Time

The Earth is nearly spherical, but it is not a perfect sphere. Due to its rotation, it bulges at the Equator and flattens at the poles. This shape is called an oblate spheroid.

To locate places on the Earth's surface, an imaginary grid system is used. This system consists of lines called latitudes and longitudes. These lines help in identifying locations, measuring distances, and calculating time differences across the world.

Parallels of Latitude

Parallels of latitude refers to the angular distance, in degrees, minutes and seconds of a point North or South of the Equator. Lines of latitude are referred to as parallels.

Latitudes measure the distance North or South of the Equator in degrees. The equator is at 0° latitude, and the poles are at 90°N and 90°S.

Lines joining places with the same latitudes are called parallels. The total number of latitudes is 180, with 90 in the Northern Hemisphere and 90 in the Southern Hemisphere.

The length of one degree of latitude varies slightly, measuring about 111 km on average.

Important latitudes include the Tropic of Cancer (23.5°N), the Tropic of Capricorn (23.5°S), the Arctic Circle (66.5°N), and the Antarctic Circle (66.5°S).

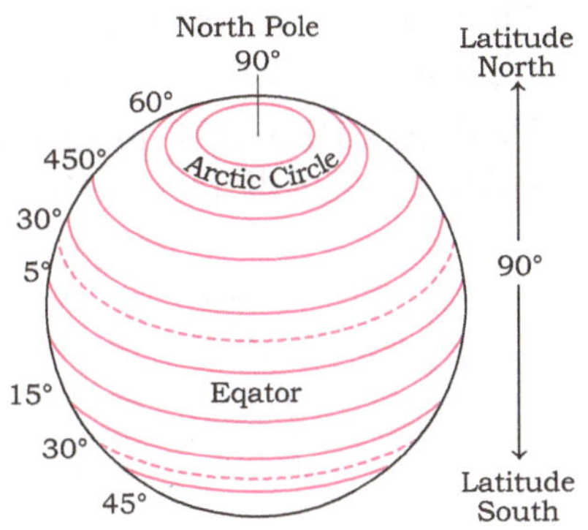

Parallels of Latitudes

Drawing the Parallels of Latitudes

Steps to draw the parallels of latitudes are as follows

- Draw a circle and divide it into two halves, by drawing a horizontal line in the centre. This will act as the Equator.
- Place a protractor on this circle in a way that 0° and 180° lines on the protractor coincide with the Equator on the paper.
- To draw 20°S, mark two points at an angle of 20° from the Equator, on the East and West of the lower portion of the circle.
- The arms of the angle cut the circle at two points. Joining these two points with a parallel line to the Equator will be 20°S.

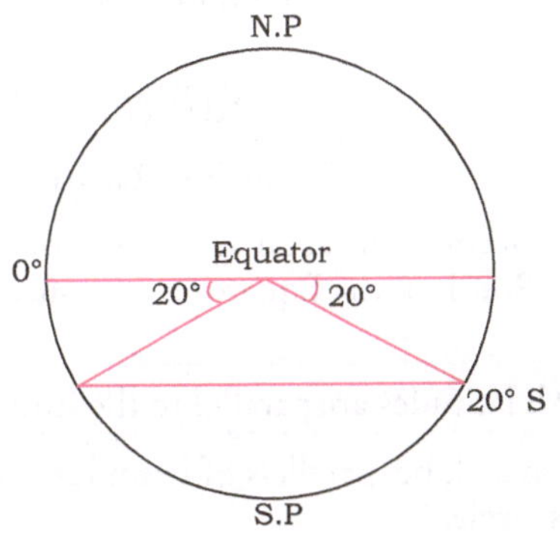

Drawing of Parallels of Latitudes

Meridians of Longitude

The meridians of longitude refer to the angular distance, in degrees, minutes and seconds of a point East or West of the Prime (Greenwich) Meridian. Lines of longitude are often referred to as meridians.

Longitudes measure the distance East or West of the Prime Meridian, which is set at 0° and passes through Greenwich, England. There are 360 longitudes, with 180 in the Eastern Hemisphere and 180 in the Western Hemisphere.

The distance between longitudes is widest at the Equator (111 km) and narrows as they approach the poles. The 180° longitude is called the International Date Line, which plays a role in changing calendar dates.

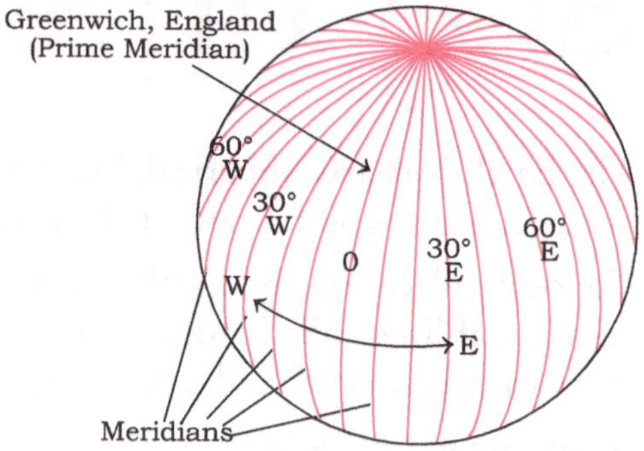

Meridians of Longitude

Drawing the Meridians of Longitude

- Draw a circle with a centre representing the North pole.
- Draw a vertical line through the centre of the circle, i.e. crossing the North pole. This represents 0° and 180° meridians, which meet at the North pole.
- To draw 45°E and W, place a protractor along the vertical line drawn and mark 45° on both sides. These will denote 450°E on the left and 45°W on the right.

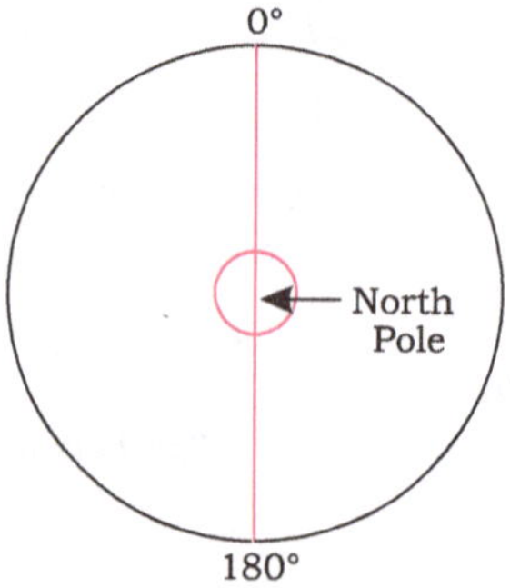

Meridians of 0° and 180° join at the North Pole

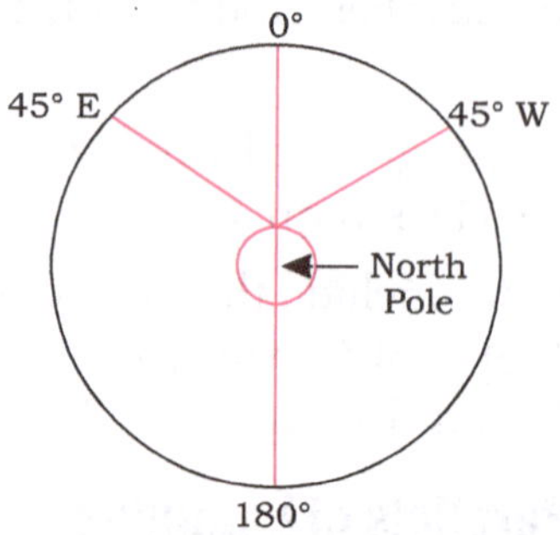

Drawing of Meridians of Longitude

Difference between Latitudes and Longitudes

Parallels of Latitude	Meridians of Longitude
Latitude is the angular distance of a point North or South of the Equator as measured in degrees.	Longitude is the angular distance along the Equator measured in degrees. It is measured East or West of Greenwich (0°) from 0° to 180°
All latitudes are parallel to the Equator.	All meridians of longitude converge at the poles.
On a globe, parallels of latitudes appear as circles.	All meridians of longitude appear as circles running through the poles.

Parallels of Latitude	Meridians of Longitude
The distance between two latitudes is approximately 111km.	The distance between two longitudes is maximum at the equator (111.3km) and minimum at the poles (0km). Midway at 45° of latitude it is 79 km.
The 0° latitude is referred to as the equator and the 90° as the poles.	There are 360° longitudes, 180 each in the East and West of the Prime Meridian.
The latitudes from the Equator to the poles are used to demarcate temperature zones, i.e. 0° to 23½ North and South as the torrid zone, 23 ½° to 66 ½° as the temperate zone and 66 ½° to 90° as the frigid zone.	The longitudes are used to determine the local time with reference to the time at Prime Meridian.

Longitude and Time

The Earth rotates 360° in 24 hours, which means it moves 15° every hour. This movement creates different time zones across the world. Each degree of longitude represents a time difference of 4 minutes. Moving Eastward, the time increases, while moving Westward, the time decreases.

The Indian Standard Time (IST) is based on 82.5°E longitude and is 5 hours 30 minutes ahead of Greenwich Mean Time (GMT). The rate of the time at which the sun traverses over certain degrees of longitudes is used to determine the local time of an area concerning the time at Prime Meridian.

Example If we want to determine the local time of New Orleans, which is located at 900° W longitude and when the time at Greenwich is 12:00 noon, we will reduce the time because cities left for Greenwich lags in time from 0° longitude. At every longitude, the time decreases by 4 minutes towards the West of prime meridian. So, if time at Greenwich is 12 noon then at New Orleans it will be 6:00 AM.

International Date Line

The International Date Line (IDL) is located at approximately 180° longitude. It helps to maintain the same data across the globe.

When crossing the IDL from East to West, the calendar moves a day backwards. When crossing from West to East, the calendar moves a day forward. This line prevents confusion in keeping track of time and dates globally.

4. Map Projections

Map projection is the technique of representing the Earth's curved surface on a flat plane. This involves transforming the spherical network of latitude and longitude into a two-dimensional format. The Earth, being a geoid, poses challenges in accurately depicting its features on flat surfaces.

Need for Map Projections

The primary reasons for creating map projections include

- It facilitates detailed studies of regions that are impractical to analyse using a globe.
- It enables comparisons between different geographical areas.
- It allows for accurate representation of distances, shapes and directions.

Elements of Map Projection

- **Reduced Earth** A model representing the Earth at a smaller scale for easier mapping is called the 'reduced Earth'. This model should be more or less spheroid having the length of polar diameter lesser than equatorial and on this model, the network of graticule can be transferred.
- **Parallels of Latitude** These are the circles that run parallel to the Equator, varying in length and ranging from 0° at the Equator to 90° at the poles.
- **Meridians of Longitude** These are the semi-circles that extend from pole to pole, intersecting at right angles with parallels.
- **Global Properties to Preserve** When creating map projections, certain properties must be maintained like
  - **Distance** Accurate measurement between points.
  - **Shape** Correct representation of regional outlines.
  - **Size/Area** Accurate depiction of area proportions.
  - **Direction** Correct orientation between points.

Classification of Map Projections

Map projections can be classified based on various criteria

Drawing Techniques

- **Perspective Projections** These are drawn using light sources to project images of latitudes and longitudes.
- **Non-Perspective Projections** These are developed without light sources.
- **Mathematical Projections** These are derived from mathematical calculations and formulae. They have little relation with the projected image.

Developable Surface

- **Cylindrical Projections** These are created using a cylindrical surface.
- **Conical Projections** These projections are made by wrapping a cone around the globe.
- **Zenithal Projections** These are directly obtained when a plane touches the globe at a point.

Global Properties

- **Equal Area Projections** These maintain area accuracy (e.g., Homolographic).
- **Orthomorphic Projections** These preserve shape (e.g., Mercator).
- **Azimuthal Projections** These correctly represent direction from a central point.
- **Equi-Distant Projections** These maintain accurate distances along specific lines.

Source of Light

- **Gnomonic projection** These are obtained by putting a light source at the centre of the globe.
- **Stereographic projections** These are drawn when the source of light is placed at the periphery.
- **Orthographic projection** These are drawn when the light source is placed at infinity from the globe, and opposite to the point at which the plane surface touches the globe.

Construction of Some Selected Projections

Conical Projection with One Standard Parallel

A conical projection is one, which is drawn by projecting the image of the graticule of a globe on a developable cone, which touches the globe along a parallel of latitude called the standard parallel. As the cone touches the globe located along AB, the position of this parallel on the globe coinciding with that on the cone is taken as the standard parallel. The length of other parallels on either side of this parallel is distorted.

Example Construct a conical projection with one standard parallel for an area bounded by 10° N to 70° N latitude and 10° E to 130° E longitudes when the scale is 1:250,000,000 and latitudinal and longitudinal interval is 10°.

Calculation

$$\text{Radius of reduced Earth R} = \frac{640,000,000}{250,000,000} = 2.56 \text{ cm}$$

Standard parallel is 40° N (10, 20, 30, 40, 50, 60, 70)

Central meridian is 70° E (10, 20, 30, 40, 50, 60, 70, 80, 90, 100, 110, 120, 130)

Construction

- Draw a circle or a quadrant of 2.56 cm radius marked with angles COE as 10° interval and BOE and AOD as 40° standard parallel.
- A tangent is extended from B to P and similarly from A to P, so that AP and BP are the two sides of the cone touching the globe and forming standard parallel at 40° N.

- The arc distance CE represents the interval between parallels. A semi-circle is drawn by taking this arc distance.
- X-Y is the perpendicular drawn from OP to OB.
- A separate line N-S is taken on which BP distance is drawn representing standard parallel. The line NS becomes the central meridian.
- Other parallels are drawn by taking arc distance CE on the central meridian.
- The distance XY is marked on the standard parallel at 40° for drawing other meridians.
- Straight lines are drawn by joining them with the pole.

Properties

- All the parallels are arcs of concentric circle and are equally spaced.
- All meridians are straight lines merging at the pole. The meridians intersect the parallels at right angles.
- The scale along all meridians is true, i.e. distances along the meridians are accurate.
- An arc of a circle represents the pole.
- The scale is true along the standard parallel but exaggerated away from the standard parallel.
- Meridians become closer to each other towards the pole.
- This projection is neither equal-area nor orthomorphic.

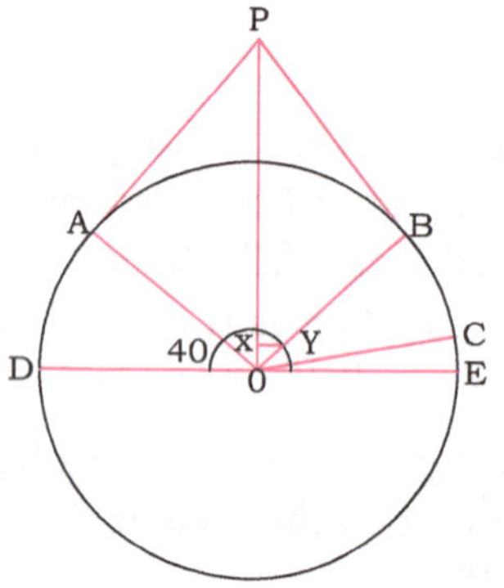

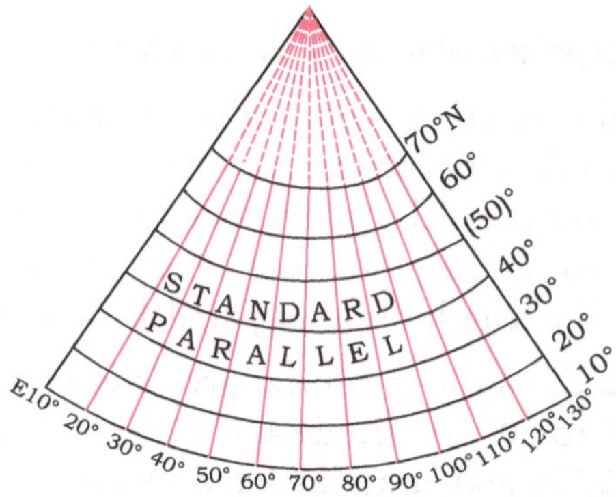

Simple Conical Projection with one standard parallel.

Limitations

- It is not suitable for a world map due to extreme distortions in the hemisphere opposite the one in the standard parallel selected.
- Even within the hemisphere, it is not suitable for representing larger areas as the distortion along the pole and near the Equator is larger.

Uses

- This projection is commonly used to showcase areas of mid-latitudes with limited latitudinal and larger longitudinal extent.
- A long narrow strip of land running parallel to the standard parallel and having an East-West stretch is correctly shown on this projection.

- The direction along the standard parallel is used to showcase railways, roads, narrow river valleys and international boundaries.
- This projection is suitable for showing the Canadian Pacific Railways, Trans-Siberian Railways, international boundaries between the USA and Canada and the Narmada Valley.

Cylindrical Equal Area Projection (Lambert of Projection)

The cylindrical equal area projection, also known as the Lambert's projection, has been derived by projecting the surface of the globe with parallel rays on a cylinder touching it at the Equator. Both the parallels and meridians are projected as straight lines intersecting one another at right angles. The pole is shown with a parallel equal to the Equator; hence, the shape of the area gets highly distorted at the higher latitude.

Example Construct a cylindrical equal area projection for the world when the RF of the map is 1:300,000,000 taking latitudinal and longitudinal interval as 15°.

Calculation Radius of the reduced Earth $R = \frac{640,000,000}{300,000,000} = 2.1$ cm

$$\text{Length of the Equator } 2\pi R \text{ or } = \frac{2 \times 22 \times 2.1}{7} = 13.2 \text{ cm}$$

$$\text{Interval along the Equator} = \frac{13.2 \times 15°}{360°} = 0.55 \text{ cm}$$

Construction

- Draw a circle of 2.1 cm radius.
- Mark the angles of 15°, 30°, 45°, 60°, 75° and 90° for both, Northern and Southern hemispheres.
- Draw a line of 13.2 cm and divide it into 24 equal parts at a distance of 0.55cm apart. This line represents the Equator.
- Draw a line perpendicular to the Equator at the point where 0° is meeting the circumference of the circle.
- Extend all the parallels equal to the length of the Equator from the perpendicular line and complete the projection.

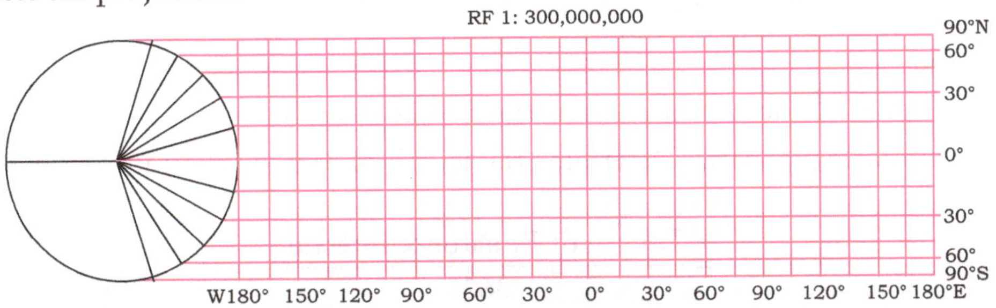

Cylindrical Equal Area Projection

Properties

- All parallels and meridians are straight lines intersecting each other at the right angle.
- The polar parallel is also equal to the Equator.
- Scale is true only along the Equator.

Limitations

- Distortion increases as we move towards the pole.
- The projection is non-orthomorphic.
- Equality of area is maintained at the cost of distortion in shape.

Uses

- The projection is most suitable for the area lying between 45° N and S latitudes.
- It is suitable to show the distribution of tropical crops like rice, tea, coffee, rubber and sugarcane.

Mercator's Projection

A Dutch cartographer Mercator Gerardus Karmer developed this projection in 1569. The projection is based on mathematical formulae. So, it is an orthomorphic projection in which the correct shape is maintained. The distance between parallels increases towards the pole. Like cylindrical projection, the parallels and meridians intersect each other at a right angle. It has the characteristics of showing correct directions. A straight line joining any two points on this projection gives a constant bearing, which is called a Laxodrome or Rhumb line.

Example Draw a Mercator's projection for the world map on the scale of 1:250,000,000 at 15° interval.

Calculation

$$\text{Radius of the reduced Earth is } R = \frac{250{,}000{,}000}{250{,}000{,}000} = 1'' \text{ inch}$$

$$\text{Length of the Equator } 2\pi R \text{ or } \frac{1 \times 22 \times 2}{7} = 6.28'' \text{ inches}$$

$$\text{Interval along the Equator} = \frac{6.28 \times 15^\circ}{360^\circ} = 0.26'' \text{ inches}$$

Construction

- Draw a line of 6.28″ inches representing the Equator as EQ.
- Divide it into 24 equal parts. Determine the length of each division using the following formula

$$= \frac{\text{Length of Equator} \times \text{Interval}}{360}$$

Practical Work

- Calculate the distance for latitude with the help of the table given below

Latitude	Distance
15°	0.265 × 1 = 0.265″ inch
30°	0.549 × 1 = 0.549″ inch
45°	0.881 × 1 = 0.881″ inch
60°	1.317 × 1 = 1.317″ inches
75°	2.027 × 1 = 2.027″ inches

- Complete the projection as shown in fig. below

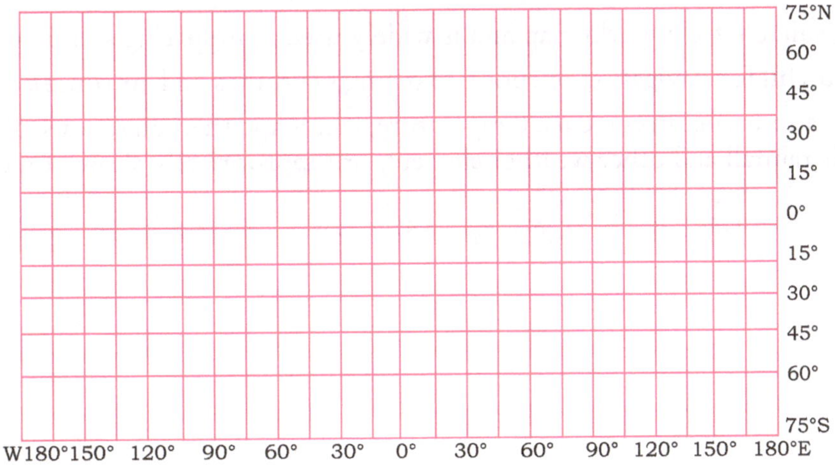

RF 1:250,000,000

Mercator's Projection

Properties

- All parallels and meridians are straight lines and intersect each other at right angles.
- All parallels have the same length,i.e. of the Equator.
- All meridians have the same length and equal spacing. But they are longer than the corresponding meridian on the globe.
- Spacing between parallels increases towards the pole.
- The scale along the Equator is correct as it is equal to the length of the Equator on the globe, but other parallels are longer than the corresponding parallel on the globe; hence the scale is not correct along them. For example, the 30° parallel is 1.154 times longer than the corresponding parallel on the globe.
- The shape of the area is maintained, but at higher latitudes distortion takes place.
- The shape of small countries near the Equator is truly preserved while it increases towards the poles.

- It is an angle-based projection.
- This is an orthomorphic projection as the scale along the meridian is equal to the scale along the parallel.

Limitations

- There is a greater exaggeration of scale along the parallels and meridians in high latitudes. As a result, the size of the countries near the pole is highly exaggerated. For example, the size of Greenland equals the size of the USA, whereas it is 1/10th of the USA.
- Poles in this projection cannot be shown as 90° parallel and the meridian touching them is infinite.

Uses

- It is more suitable for a world map and is widely used in preparing atlas maps.
- It is very useful for navigation purposes showing sea routes and air routes.
- Drainage patterns, ocean currents, temperature, winds and their directions, distribution of worldwide rainfall and other weather elements are appropriately shown on this map.

5. Topographical Maps

It is a map of a small area drawn on a large scale depicting detailed surface and both natural and man- made features. Topographical maps are also known as general-purpose maps. They serve as the base maps and are used to draw other maps.

Importance of Topographical Maps

- Topographical maps are useful in understanding the physical and cultural landscape of an area.
- These maps are drawn at relatively large scales, which allows them to depict important features such as mountains, valleys, rivers and human settlements in great detail.
- The information provided by these maps is invaluable for researchers, planners and outdoor enthusiasts alike.
- In India, the Survey of India is responsible for preparing these maps. Their work ensures that topographical maps are accurate and up-to-date, which is essential for urban planning, environmental studies and disaster management.

Topographical Maps in India

In India, topographical maps are published in two main series

(i) **India and Adjacent Countries Series** These were developed by the Survey of India before 1937 and focused on Indian geography. The topographical maps of India are prepared on 1: 10,00,000, 1: 250,000, 1: 125,000, 1:50,000 and 1: 25,000.

(ii) **International Map Series of the World** These aim to create standardised maps for the entire world. These are made using the scales like 1:10,000,000 and 1:250,000.

Methods of Relief Representation

Relief representation is a key feature of topographical maps. The Earth's surface is not uniform; it consists of various landforms such as mountains, hills, plateaus, and plains. To accurately depict these variations in elevation and depression, several methods are employed.

Contours

Contours are imaginary lines that connect points of equal elevation above sea level.

The spacing between contour lines indicates the steepness or gentleness of slopes; closely spaced lines represent steep areas while widely spaced lines indicate gentle slopes.

Other methods include hachures (short lines indicating slope direction), hill shading (to give a three-dimensional appearance), layer tints (colour gradients representing elevation), benchmarks (specific points with known elevations), and spot heights (exact elevation points).

Drawing of Contours and Their Cross Sections

The topographical features show varying degrees of slopes. For example, a flat plain exhibits gentler slopes and the cliffs and gorges are associated with the steep slopes. Similarly, valleys and mountain ranges are also characterised by the varying degree of slopes, i.e. steep to gentle. Hence, the spacing of contours is significant since it indicates the slope.

Type of Slopes

- **Gentle Slope** When the degree or angle of the slope of a feature is very low, the slope will be gentle. The contours representing this type of slope are far apart.
- **Steep Slope** When the degree or angle of the slope of a feature is high and the contours are closely spaced, they indicate a steep slope.

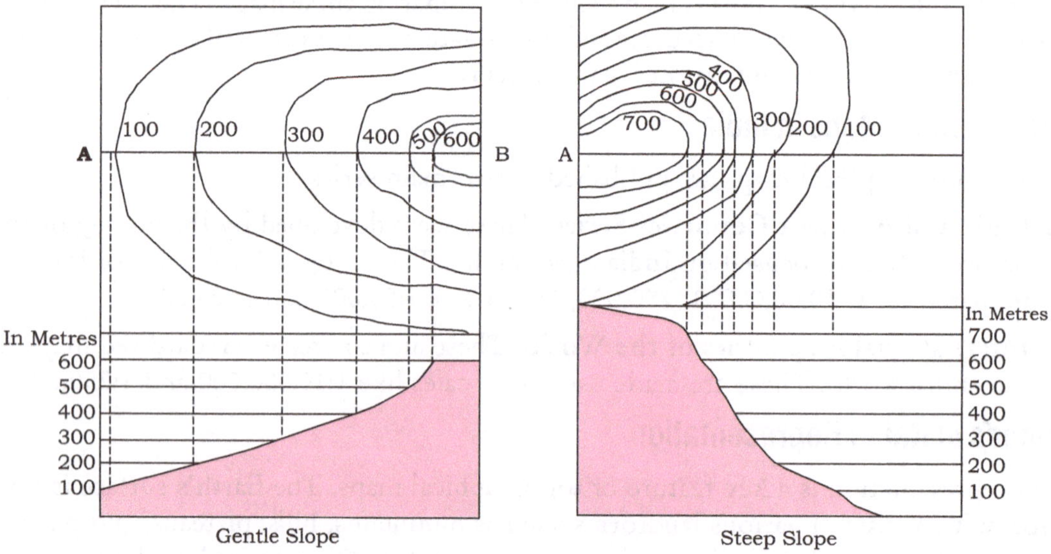

Gentle and Steep Slope

- **Concave Slope** A slope with a gentle gradient in the lower parts of a relief feature and steep in its upper parts is called a concave slope. Contours in this type of slope are widely spaced in the lower parts and are closely spaced in the upper parts.
- **Convex Slope** Unlike the concave slope, the convex slope is fairly gentle in the upper part and steep in the lower part. As a result, the contours are widely spaced in the upper parts and are closely spaced in the lower parts.

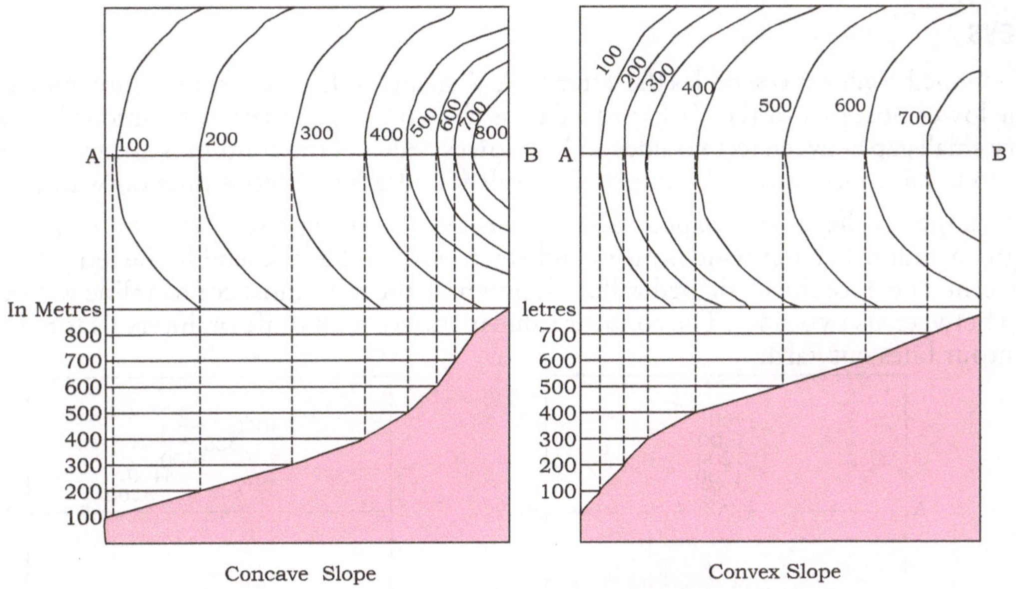

Concave and Convex Slope

Types of Landforms Represented by Contours

Topographical maps illustrate various landforms through contour lines. Some major landforms include

- **Conical Hills** These hills rise uniformly from the surrounding land and are represented by concentric contours spaced at regular intervals.
- **Plateaus** Flat-topped areas with steep sides show closely spaced contours at their edges.

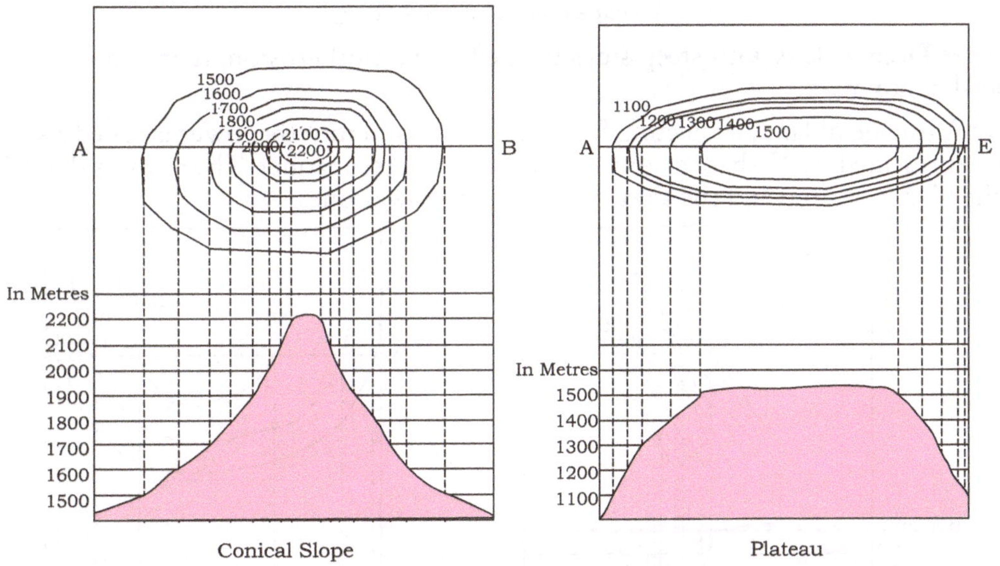

Conical Hills and Plateau

Practical Work

Valleys

- **'V'-shaped Valley** It resembles the letter V. A V-shaped valley occurs in mountainous areas. The lowermost part of the V-shaped valley is shown by the innermost contour line with a very small gap between its two sides and the lowest value of the contour is assigned to it. The contour value increases with uniform intervals for all other contour lines outward.
- **'U'-shaped Valley** A U-shaped valley is formed by strong lateral erosion of glaciers at high altitudes. The flat wide bottom and steep sides make it resemble the letter 'U'. The lowermost part of the U-shaped valley is shown by the innermost contour line with a wide gap between its two sides. The contour value increases with uniform intervals for all other contour lines outward.

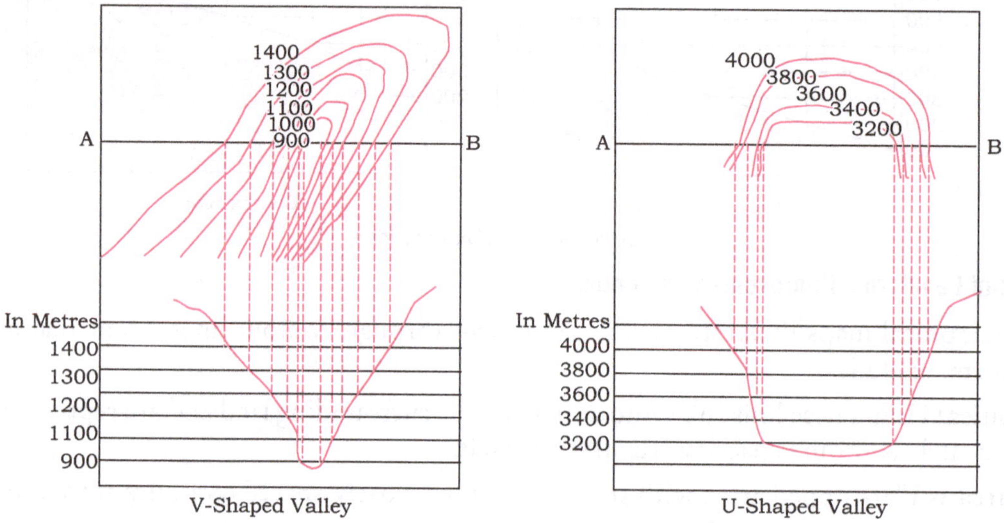

V-shaped and U-shaped Valley

- **Gorges** Deep valleys with steep sides formed by vertical erosion; represented by closely spaced contours.
- **Spur** A tongue of land, projecting from higher ground into the lower is called a spur. It is also represented by V-shaped contours but in a reverse manner. The arms of the 'V' point to the higher ground and the apex of 'V' to the lower ones.

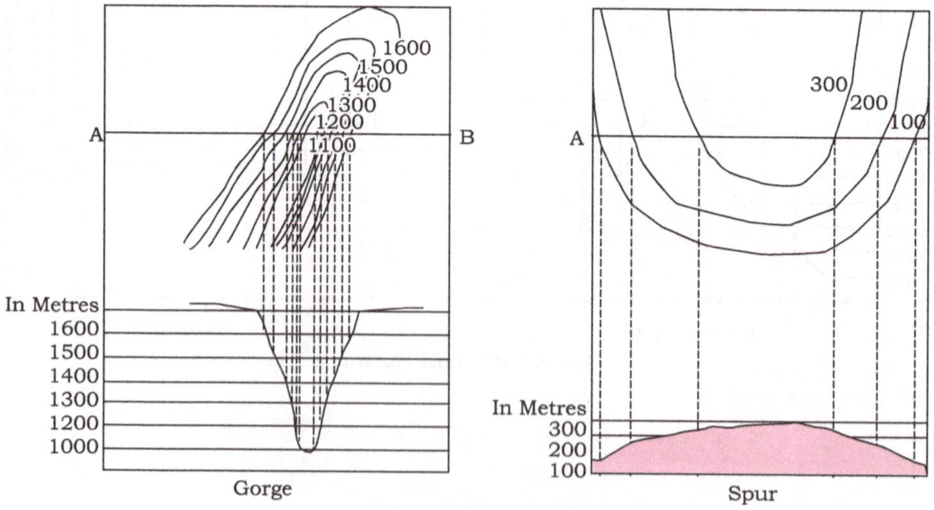

Gorge and Spur

Practical Work

- **Cliff** It is a very steep or almost perpendicular face of landform. On a map, a cliff may be identified by the way the contours run very close to one another, ultimately merging into one.
- **Waterfall and Rapids** A sudden and more or less perpendicular descent of water from a considerable height in the bed of a river is called a waterfall. Sometimes, a waterfall succeeds or precedes with a cascading stream forming rapids upstream or downstream of a waterfall. The contours representing a waterfall merge into one another while crossing a river stream and the rapids are shown by relatively distant contour lines on a map.

Steps for Drawing a Cross-section

To draw a cross-section of relief features from contour maps, follow these steps

- Draw a straight line across the contours on the map and label it as AB.
- Take a strip of white paper or graph paper and place its edge along line AB.
- Mark the position and value of each contour that crosses AB.
- Select a vertical scale, such as $\frac{1}{2}$ cm = 100 metres.
- Draw horizontal lines parallel to each other, equal in length to AB. Ensure there are enough lines to match the total contour lines.
- Label the contour values along the vertical axis, starting with the lowest value.
- Place the marked paper along the bottom line of the cross-section so that AB on the paper matches AB on the map. Mark the contour points.
- Draw perpendicular lines from the AB line to intersect contour lines.
- Connect all points smoothly to complete the cross-section.

Identifying Cultural Features in Topographical Maps

Cultural features such as settlements, buildings, roads and railways are represented using conventional signs, symbols and colours. These features help in understanding the landscape of the area.

Distribution of Settlements

Settlements are identified based on site, pattern, alignment and density. By comparing the settlement map with the contour map, different settlement types can be understood.

Types of rural settlements are

- Compact
- Scattered
- Linear
- Circular

Types of urban settlements are

- Cross-road town
- Market centre
- Coastal resort centre
- Manufacturing centre with suburban villages
- Religious centre
- Nodal point
- Hill station
- Port
- Capital town

Factors Affecting Settlement Location

1. Availability of water
2. Food supply
3. Type of land (relief)
4. Nature of occupation
5. Need for defence

Settlement locations should be examined using contour and drainage maps. The density of settlements is often related to food supply. Linear settlements occur along rivers, roads, embankments and coastlines.

Urban settlements may have specific patterns. For example, cross-road towns have a fan shape with houses along roadsides and the market at the centre. Nodal towns have roads radiating in all directions.

Transport and Communication Patterns

Transport and communication networks depend on relief, population, size and resource development. Conventional signs and symbols on maps represent these networks.

Roads, railways and communication lines provide useful information about accessibility and connectivity in the area shown on the map.

Interpretation of Topographical Maps

Reading topographical maps requires familiarity with their symbols and conventions. Each map includes a legend that explains the conventional signs used to represent different features.

Key elements to consider when interpreting these maps include marginal information (such as sheet number and scale), relief details (identifying hills or plains), drainage patterns (rivers and tributaries), land use (agricultural or urban areas), and human settlements (cities or towns).

Conventional Symbols Used in Map

Roads, metalled : According to importance; distance stone
Roads, unmetalled : According to importance, bridge Cart-track pack-track and pass. Foot-path with bridge.
Streams : with track in bed; undefined, canals
Dams: masonary or rock-filled; Earthwork, Weir.
River dry with water channel: with islands and rocks. Tidal river, Swamp, Reeds
Wells, lined, unlined. Spring Tanks, pernnial:dry
Embankments: road or rail
Railway, broad gauge: double, single with station, under construction.
Railway other gauges; double; single with distance stone, under construction. Light Railway or tramway telegraph line cutting with tunnel

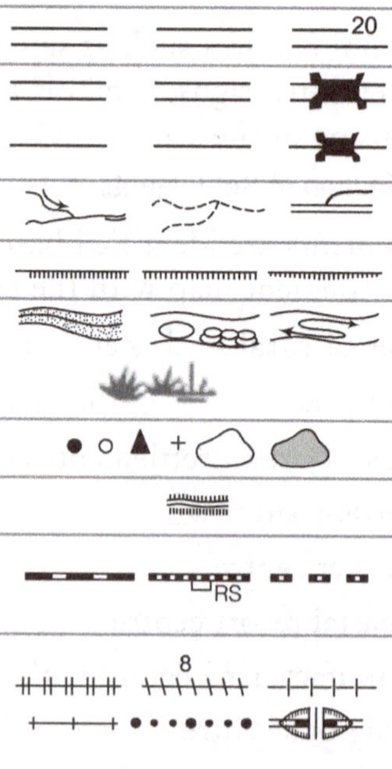

Contours Cliffs	
Sand features (1) Flat, (2) Sand-hills (permanent), (3) Dunes (shifting).	
Towns or villages: inhabited; deserted, Fort.	
Huts: Permanent, temporary, Tower, Antiquities	
Temple, Chhatri, Church, Mosque, Idgah, Tomb, Graves	
Lighthouse, Lightship, Buoys, lighted, unlighted Anchorage.	
Mine, Vine on trellis, Grass, Scrub.	
Palms : palmyra : other, plantain conifer Bamboo Other trees	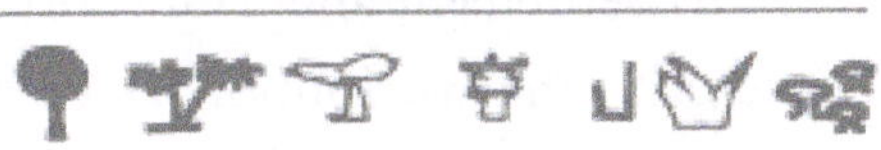
Boundary, international.	
Boundary, state: demarcated; undemarcated.	
Boundary, district; sub-division, tahsil or taluk, forest.	
Boundary, pillars: surveyed; unlocated; village trijunction.	
Heights, triangulated, station, point, approximate	△200 •200 •200
Bench-mark, geodetic; tertiary; canal	BM 63.3 DM63.3 .63
Post Office. Police Station	PO PS
Bungalows; Dak or travellers; inspection, Rest-house.	DB IB (Canal), RH (Forest)
Circuit house. Camping ground	CH, CG
Forest; reserved; protected	RF, PF

To interpret a topographical map effectively

- **Start with Marginal Information** This includes details about the map's location and scale.
- **Examine Relief Features** Identify hills, plateaus, plains, or mountains based on contour patterns.
- **Analyse Drainage Patterns** Look for rivers and their tributaries to understand water flow in the area.
- **Assess Land Use** Determine how land is utilised-whether for agriculture, industry, or natural reserves.
- **Identify Human Settlements** Recognise urban centres and rural settlements based on their distribution patterns.
- **Occupation** May be identified with the help of land use and the type of settlement. For example, in rural areas the main occupation of the majority of the people is agriculture; in tribal regions, lumbering and primitive agriculture dominate and in coastal areas, fishing is practised.

Map Interpretation Procedure

The following steps will help in map interpretation

- Find out from the index number of the topographical sheet, the location of the area in India. This would give an idea of the general characteristics of the major and minor physiographic divisions of the area. Note the scale of the map and the contour interval, which will give the extent and general landform of the area.
- Trace out the following features on tracing sheets.
  (a) **Major landforms** As shown by contours and other graphical features.
  (b) **Drainage and water features** The main river and its important tributaries.
  (c) **Land use** i.e. forest, agricultural land, wastes, sanctuary, park, school, etc.
  (d) Settlement and Transport pattern.
- Describe the distributional pattern of each of the features separately by drawing attention to the most important aspect.
- Superimpose pairs of these maps and note down the relationship, if any, between the two patterns. For example, if a contour map is superimposed over a land use map, it provides the relationship between the degree of slope and the type of land used.
- Aerial photographs and satellite imageries of the same area and scale can also be compared with the topographical map to update the information.

6. Introduction to Remote Sensing

The term remote sensing was introduced during the 1960s. It was defined as the total processes used to acquire and measure the information of some property of objects and phenomena by a recording device (sensor) that is not physically touching the objects or phenomena being studied. Remote sensing devices react to a wider range of radiations reflected/ emitted, absorbed and transmitted by all object surfaces at a temperature above 0 kelvin (-273 C).

Stages in remote sensing

The basic processes that help in the collection of information about the properties of the objects and phenomena of the Earth's surface are as follows

- **Source of Energy** The Sun is the main energy source for remote sensing. Artificial energy sources like flashguns and radar beams are also used.
- **Transmission of Energy** Energy travels from the source to the Earth's surface in waves at the speed of light. This is called Electromagnetic Radiation (EMR). Waves differ in size and frequency, forming the Electromagnetic Spectrum. Remote sensing mainly uses visible, infrared and microwave energy.
- **Interaction with Earth's Surface** When energy reaches the Earth, it is absorbed, transmitted, reflected, or emitted by objects. Different objects respond differently to energy. For example, freshwater absorbs more energy and appears dark in satellite images, while turbid water reflects more and appears lighter.
- **Energy Propagation through Atmosphere** Reflected energy travels back through the atmosphere, where gases, water molecules, and dust particles modify it. Some energy is absorbed or scattered and does not reach the sensor.
- **Detection by Sensors** Sensors on satellites record the energy they receive. Remote sensing satellites orbit 700.900 km above Earth (e.g., Indian Remote Sensing Series). Weather satellites, like INSAT, orbit much higher at 36,000 km in a geostationary position.
- **Conversion of Energy into Data** Sensors convert energy into digital images made of numbers arranged in rows and columns. These are sent to Earth stations, like the one in Shadnagar, Hyderabad.
- **Extracting Information from Data** Once the image data is received, it is processed to remove errors. Information is extracted using digital processing techniques or visual interpretation.

Creating Maps and Tables The extracted information is used to create thematic maps and tabular data for analysis and decision-making.

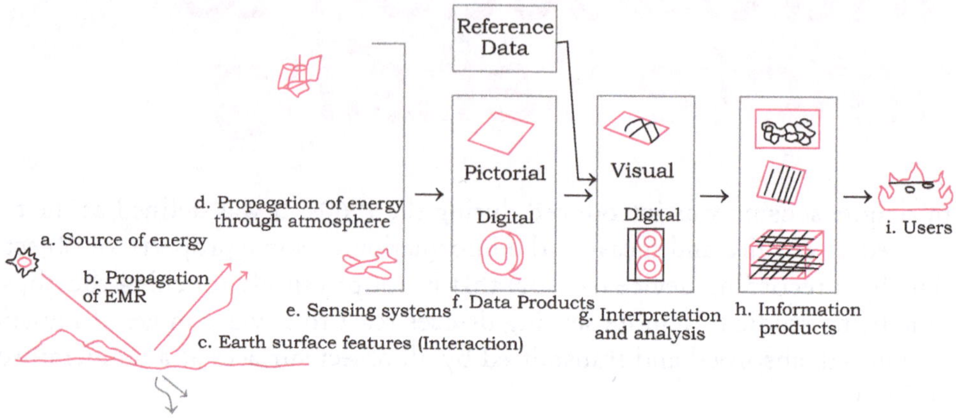

Stages in Remote Sensing Data Acquisition

Sensors

A sensor collects electromagnetic radiation, converts it into a signal, and helps gather information about objects. Sensors are of two types

- **Photographic sensors** (cameras) take images at once.
- **Non-photographic sensors** (scanners) collect images bit by bit.

Scanners

Multi-Spectral Scanners (MSS)

In satellite remote sensing, Multi-Spectral Scanners (MSS) are used to capture images. They scan the Earth by sweeping across a field of view using mirrors and detectors. The collected energy is converted into digital numbers (DN Values) for storage and analysis.

Types of Multi-Spectral Scanners

(i) **Whiskbroom Scanners** It has a rotating mirror and a single detector. The mirror moves between 90° and 120° to collect images. It covers visible to middle infrared spectral bands. It uses Total Field of View (TFOV) and Instantaneous Field of View (IFOV) to collect data.

(ii) **Pushbroom Scanners** These have multiple detectors arranged in a line. Each detector captures energy from a small ground area (pixel).

Example The **SPOT HRV-1 sensor** has 3000 detectors, covering a swath of 60 km with a spatial resolution of 20 metres.

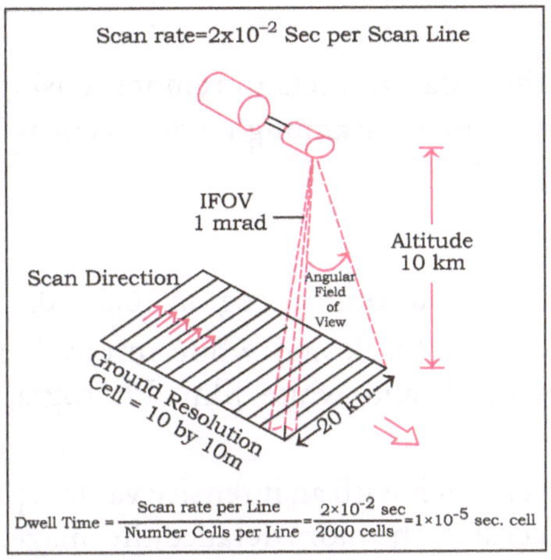

Whiskhroom Scanners

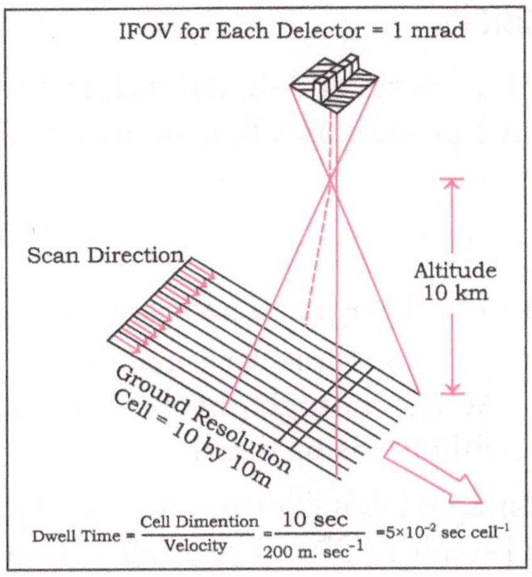

Pushbroom Scanners

Temporal Resolution in Satellite Remote Sensing

In satellite remote sensing, a **sun-synchronous polar orbit** allows satellites to capture images of the same location at regular intervals. This interval is known as **temporal resolution** or **revisit time.**

By comparing images taken at different times, we can study changes on the Earth's surface. For example, satellite images of the Himalayas help track vegetation changes over time. Similarly, images taken before and after the **2004 Indian Ocean tsunami** reveal its impact. The **pre-tsunami image** (June 2004) shows the undisturbed landscape of Banda Aceh, Indonesia, while the **post-tsunami image** highlights the widespread damage caused by the disaster.

Sensor Resolutions

- **Spatial Resolution** In remote sensing, **spatial resolution** refers to a sensor's ability to distinguish two closely spaced objects as separate. Higher resolution allows the detection of even smaller objects on the Earth's surface.
- **Spectral Resolution** It refers to the sensor's ability to detect and record information in different bands of the electromagnetic spectrum. Just like a prism splits light into colours, sensors capture different wavelengths to highlight various features.

  Example Infrared bands show water bodies as dark, while green bands highlight dry surfaces.
- **Radiometric Resolution** It determines how well a sensor can detect small differences in energy levels between objects. Higher radiometric resolution means better detection of slight variations in brightness and surface properties. The spatial, spectral, and radiometric resolutions of some of the remote sensing satellites of the world are shown below

Data Products

Photographic images and digital images are the data products in remote sensing. The photographic process uses light-sensitive film, while a scanning device records images digitally.

Types of Data Products

- **Photographic Images** These are captured in the optical region (0.3 . 0.9 μm) using different types of film-black and white, colour, black and white infrared, and colour infrared. Aerial photography mostly uses black and white film. Photographs can be enlarged without losing detail.
- **Digital Images** Digital images consist of pixels, each with an intensity value represented as a Digital Number (DN). The smaller the pixel size, the more detailed the image. However, excessive zooming can lead to loss of detail. Digital images can be enhanced using image processing algorithms to improve visibility and analysis.

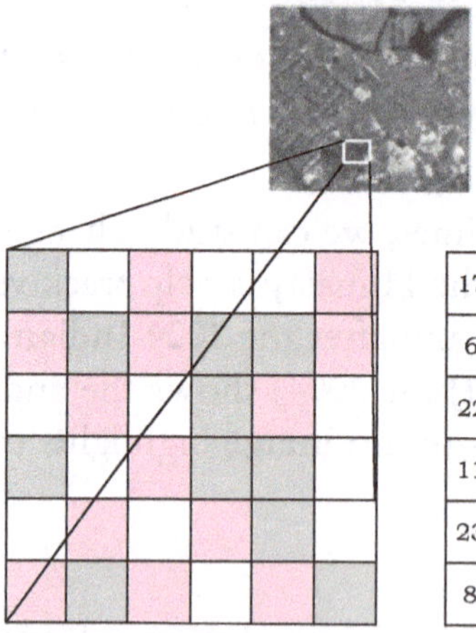

170	230	85	255	221	0
68	136	17	170	119	68
221	0	238	138	0	255
119	255	85	170	136	238
238	17	221	68	19	255
85	170	119	221	17	136

Digital image (top) and Part of it zoomed showing Pixel's brightness (left) and the associated Digital Numbers (right)

Interpretation of Satellite Imageries

Satellites capture images of the Earth's surface using special sensors. These images help us understand the shapes, patterns and features of different objects and natural phenomena. The data collected can be in the form of photographs or digital images. To study this data, we can use two main methods **visual interpretation** and **digital image processing.**

(i) **Visual Interpretation** This is a manual process where experts carefully examine satellite images to identify objects and patterns.

(ii) **Digital Image Processing** This method uses computers and specialised software to analyse images and extract useful information.

Elements of Visual Interpretation

In everyday life, we identify objects based on their shape, size, location, and surroundings. These features are called elements of visual interpretation. They can be grouped into two categories

(i) **Image Characteristics** These include tone or colour, texture, shape, size, pattern and shadow.

(ii) **Terrain Characteristics** It refers to the location of objects and their relationship with surrounding features.

The following elements help in interpreting images and understanding different land features

1. Tone or Colour

- Objects absorb, transmit and reflect energy. The reflected energy is recorded by sensors in shades of grey (black and white images) or different colours.
- Smooth and dry surfaces reflect more energy, appearing brighter, while rough and moist surfaces appear darker.
- Healthy vegetation reflects infrared light and appears bright red in false-colour images.
- Clearwater absorbs most radiation and looks dark or black, while turbid water appears lighter due to suspended particles.

S. No.	Earth Surface Feature	Colour(In Standard FCC)
1.	**Healthy Vegetation and Cultivated Areas**	
	• Evergreen	Red to magenta
	• Deciduous	Brown to red
	• Scrubs	Light brown with red patches
	• Cropped land	Bright red
	• Fallow land	Light blue to white
2.	**Waterbody**	
	• Clear water	Dark blue to black
	• Turbid waterbody	Light blue
3.	**Built – up area**	
	• High density	Dark blue to bluish green
	• Low density	Light blue
4.	**Waste lands/Rock outcrops**	
	• Rock outcrops	Light brown
	• Sandy deserts/River sand/	Light blue to white
	• Salt affected	
	• Deep ravines	Dark green
	• Shallow ravines	Light green
	• Water logged/Wet lands	Metalled black

2. Texture

- Texture refers to small variations in colour or tone caused by groups of small objects. It can be smooth or coarse.
- Dense residential areas appear as fine textures, while low-density areas appear coarse.
- Crops like sugarcane and millet create coarse textures, whereas rice and wheat fields have fine textures.

3. Size

- The size of an object in an image helps in identification.
- Large industrial areas are distinguishable from residential areas. Stadiums, settlements, and other structures can be identified based on their relative size.

4. Shape

- The outline or form of an object helps in recognition. Some objects have distinct shapes, making them easy to identify.
- The circular shape of the Sansad Bhawan is unique.
- Railway tracks are long and straight, distinguishing them from roads.
- Religious places like mosques and temples have distinct architectural shapes.

5. Shadow

- Shadows depend on the sun's angle and the height of objects. They help in identifying tall structures like minarets, towers and water tanks.
- However, in cities, shadows can obscure objects.
- Shadows are less useful in satellite images but important in aerial photography.

6. Pattern

- Many natural and man-made structures form repetitive patterns. Recognising these patterns helps in interpretation.
- Planned residential areas have similar house layouts.
- Orchards and plantations have trees in a uniform arrangement.
- Drainage networks and settlement types can be identified by their patterns.

7. Association

- Association refers to how objects are related to their surroundings.
- Schools are usually near residential areas and have playgrounds.
- Stadiums, racecourses and golf courses are common in big cities.
- Industries are often near highways, while slums develop along railway tracks or drains.

Viva Voce Questions

1. ***What is a map?***

Ans. A map is a representation of the Earth's surface or a part of it, drawn to scale on a flat surface.

2. ***What are the essential elements of map-making?***

Ans. The essential elements include scale, projection, generalisation, map design, and map construction.

3. ***What is cartography?***

Ans. Cartography is the science and art of making maps.

4. ***What are the different types of maps based on scale?***

Ans. There are two different types of maps based on scale i.e., large scale and small-scale maps. Large-scale maps (e.g., cadastral maps, topographical maps) and small-scale maps (e.g., wall maps, atlas maps).

5. ***What is the difference between physical and cultural maps?***

Ans. Physical maps show natural features like mountains and rivers, while cultural maps depict human-made features like roads and cities.

6. ***What is a map scale?***

Ans. A map scale represents the ratio between the distance on the map and the actual ground distance.

7. ***What are the three ways to represent scale?***

Ans. The three ways to represent scale are statement of scale, graphical or bar scale, and representative fraction (RF).

8. ***How can a statement scale be converted to RF?***

Ans. By converting ground distance to the same unit as the map distance and expressing it as a ratio.

9. ***What is the difference between latitude and longitude?***

Ans. Latitude measures the distance North or South of the Equator, while longitude measures the distance East or West of the Prime Meridian.

10. ***Why is the International Date Line important?***

Ans. It helps in maintaining uniform dates globally by adjusting calendar days when crossing it.

11. ***How does longitude affect time zones?***

Ans. The Earth rotates 360° in 24 hours, meaning every 15° longitude corresponds to a time difference of 1 hour.

12. ***What is a map projection?***

Ans. It is a method used to represent the curved surface of the Earth on a flat surface.

13. ***Name different types of map projections.***

Ans. The different types of map projections are cylindrical, conical, and mercator projections.

14. ***Why do distortions occur in map projections?***

Ans. Distortions on the maps occur due to the curved surface of Earth being represented on a flat plane. Distortions lead to changes in shape, area, distance, or direction.

15. ***What are topographical maps?***

Ans. Topographical maps are detailed maps that show both natural and human-made features of an area.

16. *What is a contour line?*

Ans. A line that joins points of equal elevation on a map is a contour line.

17. *How can we identify a steep slope and a gentle slope on a topographical map?*

Ans. We can identify slopes based on the distance between the contours. Steep slopes have closely spaced contour lines, while gentle slopes have widely spaced contour lines.

18. *What is a V-shaped valley and a U-shaped valley?*

Ans. A V-shaped valley is formed by river erosion, while a U-shaped valley is formed by glacial erosion.

19. *What is remote sensing?*

Ans. It is the technique of gathering information about the Earth's surface without direct contact, using sensors and satellites.

20. *What is the difference between spatial and spectral resolution?*

Ans. Spatial resolution refers to the ability of a sensor to distinguish small objects, while spectral resolution refers to its ability to capture data in different wavelengths of the electromagnetic spectrum.

21. *What is temporal resolution?*

Ans. It is the frequency at which a satellite revisits the same area to capture images.

22. *What are the two types of remote sensing data products?*

Ans. The two types of remote-sensing data products are photographic images and digital images.

23. *What is the difference between visual interpretation and digital image processing?*

Ans. Visual interpretation is the manual identification of objects in images, while digital image processing uses computer algorithms for analysis.

SAMPLE
QUESTION PAPERS (1-3)

SAMPLE QUESTION PAPER 1

A Highly Simulated Sample Question Paper for CBSE Class XI

(SOLVED)

GEOGRAPHY

General Instructions

- This question paper contains 30 questions. All questions are compulsory.
- This question paper is divided into five sections – Sections A, B, C, D and E.
- Section A – Questions no. 1 to 17 are Multiple Choice (MCQ) Type Questions carrying 1 mark each.
- Section B – Questions no. 18 and 19 are Source Based Questions carrying 3 marks each.
- Section C – Questions no. 20 to 23 are Short Answer (SA) Type Questions carrying 3 marks each. Answer to these questions shall be written in 80 to 100 words.
- Section D – Questions no. 24 to 28 are Long Answer (LA) Type Questions carrying 5 marks each. Answer to these questions shall be written in 120 to 150 words.
- Section E – Questions no. 29 and 30 are Map Based Questions. Carrying 5 marks each.

Time : 3 hours **Max. Marks : 70**

SECTION A

1. **A branch of physical geography called as climatology deals with which of the following.** **(1)**

(a) Geology (b) Hydrology (c) Meteorology (d) Pedology

2. **The term given to the study of map making ....** **(1)**

(a) Researcher (b) Analyst (c) Cartography (d) Demography

3. **Which of the following are correctly arranged in ascending order according to the rainfall received by them?** **(1)**

(a) Khasi Hills, Bihar, Western Uttar Pradesh, Andhra Pradesh
(b) Bihar, Andhra Pradesh, Western Uttar Pradesh, Khasi Hills
(c) Andhra Pradesh, Western Uttar Pradesh, Bihar, Khasi Hills
(d) Western Uttar Pradesh, Andhra Pradesh, Bihar, Khasi Hills

4. **Consider the following statements and choose the correct option from the given options.** **(1)**

I. The temperature and precipitation determine density, type and distribution of vegetation.
II. Rocks with differences in their structure under similar climatic condition offer similar resistance to various geomorphic processes.

Codes
(a) Only statement I is correct
(b) Both the statements are true and statement II correctly present the reason for statement I
(c) Only statement II is correct
(d) Both the statements I and II are incorrect

5. **Arrange the following biosphere reserves of India in chronological order from their date of establishment.** **(1)**

I. Nilgiri **II. Nanda Devi**
III. Nokrek **IV. Manas**

Codes
(a) I, II, III, IV (b) III, IV, I, II (c) IV, III, II, I (d) II, I, IV, III

6. Assertion (A) Asthenosphere is the main source of magma.
Reason (R) Outer core is in solid state while inner core is in liquid state. (1)

Codes
(a) Both (A) and (R) are true but (R) is not the correct explanation of (A)
(b) Both (A) and (R) are true and (R) is the correct explanation of (A)
(c) Both (A) and (R) are incorrect
(d) (A) is correct, but (R) is incorrect

7. Which of the following is incorrectly matched? (1)
(a) Maritime tropical - mT
(b) Continental tropical - cT
(c) Maritime polar - mC
(d) Continental polar - cP

8. The movement of ocean water are primarily studied through (1)
(a) Waves
(b) Tides
(c) Ocean currents
(d) All of the above

9. Assertion (A) Physical weathering process cause great damage to rocks. (1)

Reason (R) The rocks suffer from continued fatigue due to repetition of contraction and expansion.

Codes
(a) Both (A) and (R) are true but (R) is not the correct explanation of (A)
(b) Both (A) and (R) are true and (R) is the correct explanation of (A)
(c) Both (A) and (R) are incorrect
(d) (A) is correct, but (R) is incorrect

10. In Tibetan range 'Indus' river is known as .... ? (1)
(a) Singi Khamban (b) Gangotri (c) Tsangpo (d) Gandak

11. Which of the following pairs is correctly matched? (1)
(a) Mahendragiri – Eastern Ghats
(b) Anaimudi – North Andaman
(c) Everest – Western Ghats
(d) Saddle – Himalayas

12. Which of the following is not a reason for landslide in Western Ghat and Nilgiri region? (1)
(a) Steeper slopes
(b) Mechanical weathering due to temperature changes
(c) Heavy rainfall
(d) Tectonic instability

13. Identify the type of topography based on the given description. (1)

Groundwater plays an important role in eroding and shaping this landform. these landforms are found in the areas of rocks like limestone, dolomites which are rich in calcium carbonate.
(a) Fluvial topography
(b) Karst topography
(c) Aeolian topography
(d) Glacial topography

14. Which of the following were the reasons for the exploitation of forest resources by Britishers? (1)
(a) To lay railway lines
(b) To introduce plantations
(c) For construction activities
(d) All of the above

FULLY SOLVED

Study the following map and answer the following questions no. 15-17.

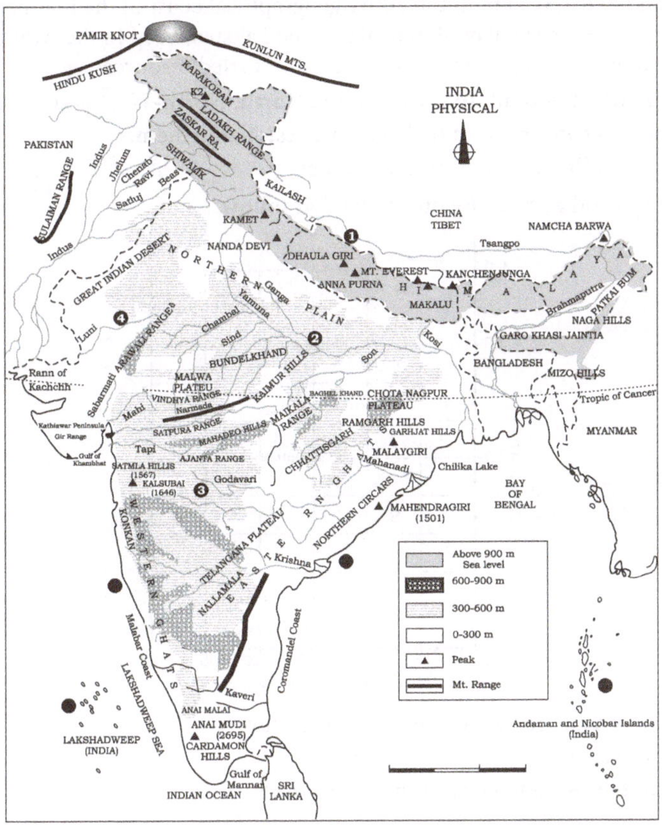

15. **In which part of India, the Great Indian desert is situated?** **(1)**

(a) Northern part (b) North-Western part (c) Southern part (d) Central part

16. **Choose from the following the peaks situated in the Greater Himalaya Range.** **(1)**

(a) Karakoram (b) Kamet (c) Naga Hills (d) Nanda Devi

17. **Which part of India consists of the Ramgarh Hills?** **(1)**

(a) Chhotanagpur Plateau (b) North-Eastern Plateau
(c) Meghalaya Plateau (d) The Central Highlands

SECTION B

18. **Read the given passage and answer the questions that follow.**

The size of India has endowed her with great physical diversity. Thus, you may appreciate the presence of lofty mountains in the North; large rivers such as Ganga, Brahmaputra, Mahanadi, Krishna, Godavari and Kaveri; green forested hills in North-East and South India; and the vast sandy expanse of Marusthali. You may further appreciate that bounded by the Himalayas in the North, Hindukush and Sulaiman ranges in the North-West, Purvanchal Hills in the North-East and by the large expanse of the Indian Ocean in the south, it forms a great geographic entity is known as the Indian sub-continent. It includes the countries — Pakistan, Nepal, Bhutan, Bangladesh and India.

The Himalayas, together with other ranges, have acted as a formidable physical barrier in the past. Except for a few mountain passes such as the Khyber, the Bolan, the Shipkila, the Nathula, the Bomdila, etc it was difficult to cross it. It has contributed towards the evolving of a unique regional identity of the Indian sub-continent. By referring to the physical map of India you can now describe the physical variations which you would come across while travelling from Kashmir to Kanniyakumari and from Jaisalmer in Rajasthan to Imphal in Manipur.

Peninsular part of India extends towards the Indian Ocean. This has provided the country with a coastline of 6,100 km in the mainland and 7,517 km in the entire geographical coast of the mainland plus the island groups Andaman and Nicobar located in the Bay of Bengal and the Lakshadweep in the Arabian Sea. Thus India, as a country, is a physically diverse land providing occurrence of varied resources.

(i) **India is bounded by which mountain ranges in the North, North-West and North-East?** **(1)**

(ii) **Indian sub-continent is comprised of which countries? Name them.** **(1)**

(iii) **How one can cross the Himalayan mountain range?** **(1)**

19. **Study the following graph and answer the questions that follow.**

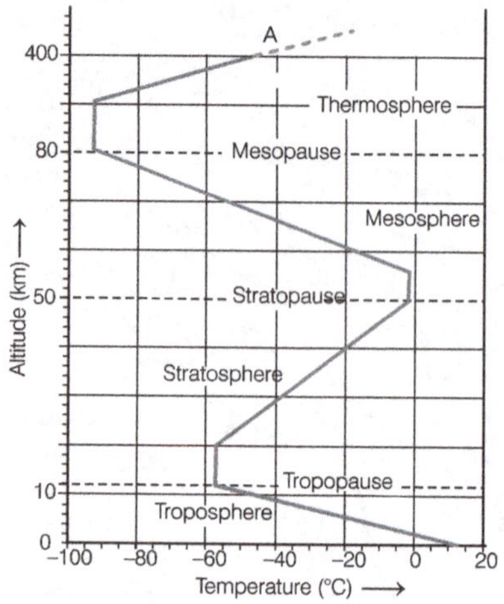

(i) Which layer of the atmosphere has the lowest temperature? **(1)**

(ii) Name the region marked as 'A'. **(1)**

(iii) State two features of mesosphere layer of the atmosphere. **(1)**

SECTION C

20. Explain briefly the nature of South-West monsoon season in India. **(3)**

Or Monsoon connotes the seasonal reversal in the direction of winds. What causes the reversal of winds?

21. Study the diagram of 'fronts' and answer the following questions. **(3)**

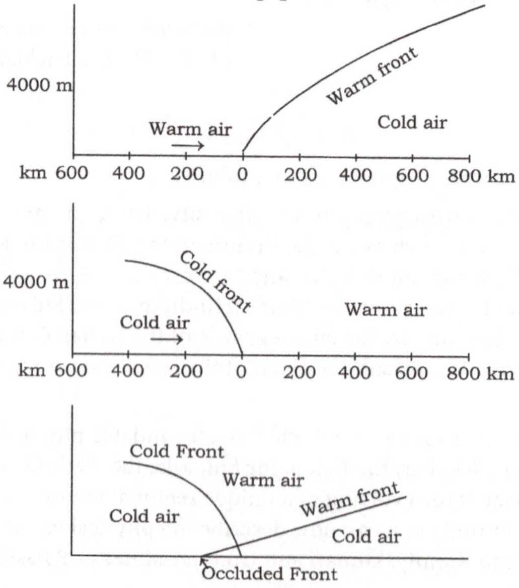

(i) Name the type of air mass that is dominant during the formation of occluded front.
(ii) Write one characteristics of warm front.
(iii) What type of weather condition is associated with the formation of a warm front dominant?

22. Differentiate between continental shelf and continental slope. **(3)**

23. 'The climate of India is best described in terms of an annual cycle of seasons'. Describe the characteristics of the hot weather season of India. **(3)**

SECTION D

24. Do you think that physical barrier is a hindrance in interaction with our neighbouring countries in modern times? Give some examples how we have overcome these difficulties in the present day. **(5)**

25. 'Rivers are considered as the 'lifeline of Indian Economy'. Elucidate the statement. **(5)**

Or 'The Himalayan river system has distinct characteristics in terms of drainage pattern and water availability.' Elucidate the statement.

26. Distinguish between the Moist Deciduous and Dry Deciduous Forests. **(5)**

Or Wildlife is immensely useful for humans in several ways. Discuss and explain the institutional efforts made by the government for protection and conservation of biodiversity.

27. 'Along with multiple merits, tides are also supportive to economy of the nation'. Give your argument in support of this statement. **(5)**

Or 'Coriolis force influences the direction of wind in both the hemispheres and impacts the global air circulation pattern.' Explain.

28. Discuss the effect of general circulation of atmosphere. **(5)**

Or "The temperature cyclone has greater significance in the region it occurs." Give your argument in support of this statement.

SECTION E

29. **On the given outline map of India, seven features are marked as i, ii, iii, iv, v, vi and vii. Identify any five features with the help of the information given below.** **(5)**

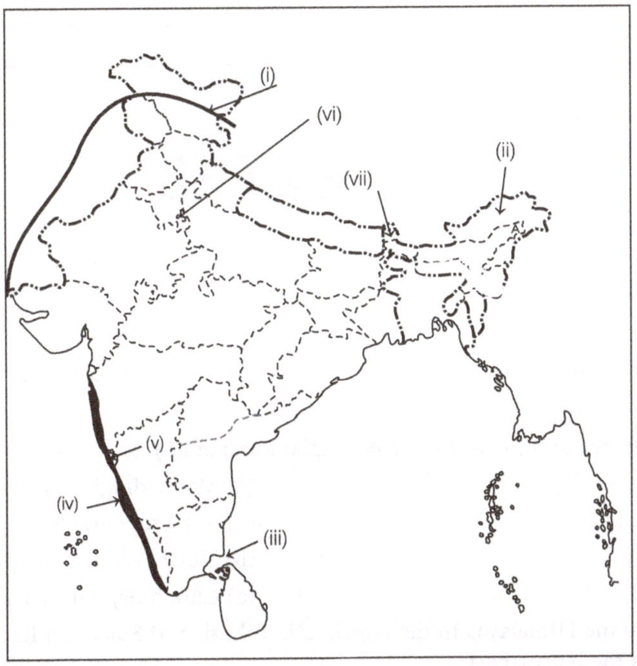

FULLY SOLVED

(i) The Northern flowing river
(ii) Easternmost state of India
(iii) Strait that divides India and Sri Lanka
(iv) The Western Mountain range parallel to the Western coast of the Indian peninsula
(v) Smallest state of India
(vi) An area of low rainfall
(vii) A country of Indian sub-continent

30. **On the given map of world, mark any five of the following features.** **(5)**

(i) Central American Low Land Forest (ii) Upper Guinean Forest
(iii) Atlantic Forest, Brazil(iv) Sinharaja Forest, Sri Lanka
(v) Eastern Madagascar (vi) Queensland
(vii) Eastern Arc Mountains, Tanzania

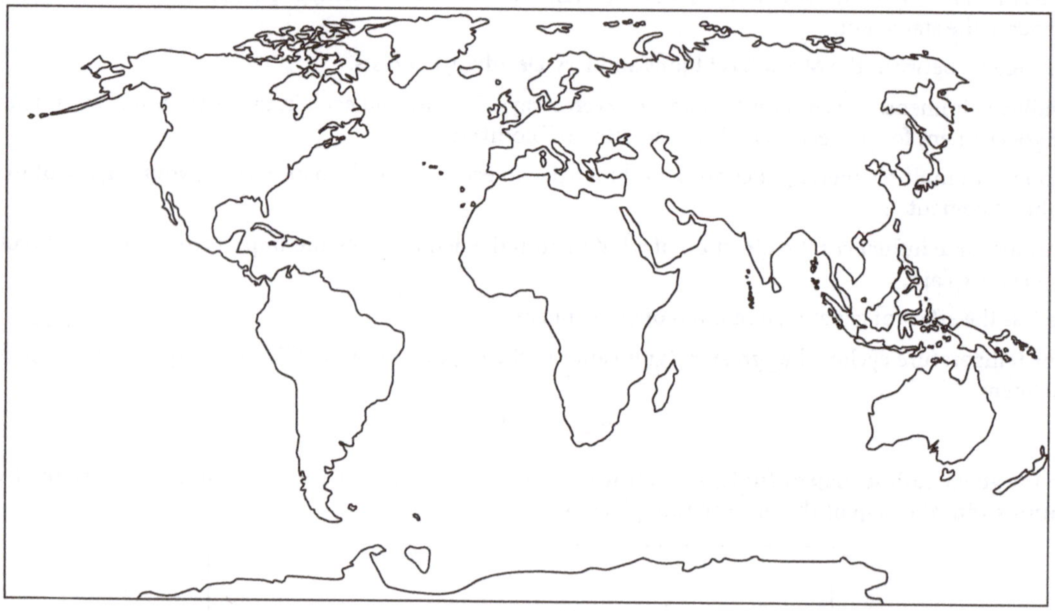

ANSWERS

1. (c) Meteorology
2. (b) Cartography
3. (c) Andhra Pradesh, Western Uttar Pradesh, Bihar, Khasi Hills
4. (a) Only statement I is correct
5. (d) II, I, IV, III
6. (d) (A) is correct, but (R) is incorrect.
7. (c) Maritime polar - mC
8. (d) All of the above
9. (b) Both (A) and (R) are true and (R) is the correct explanation of (A)
10. (a) Singi Khamban
11. (a) Mahendragiri – Eastern Ghats
12. (d) Tectonic instability
13. (b) Karst topography
14. (d) All of the above
15. (b) North-Western part
16. (a) Karakoram
17. (a) Chhotanagpur Plateau
18. (i) India is bounded by the Himalayas in the North, Hindukush and Sulaiman Ranges in the North-West, Purvanchal Hills in the North-East.

(ii) Indian sub-continent is comprised of seven countries such as India, Nepal, Bangladesh, Pakistan, Bhutan, Sri Lanka and the Maldives.

(iii) One can cross the Himalayan mountains through many mountain passes such as the Khyber pass, the Bolan pass, the Shipkila pass, the Nathula pass, the Bomdila pass, etc. These passes make it possible to cross the vast range of the Himalayas.

19. (i) Mesopause is the layer of the atmosphere which has the lowest temperature.

(ii) Exosphere is the region marked as 'A'. It is the outermost layer of the atmosphere.

(iii) Two features of mesosphere layer of the atmosphere are as follows

(a) The mesosphere is directly above the stratosphere and below the thermosphere. It extends from about 50 to 85 km above the Earth's surface.

(b) Temperature decreases with height throughout the mesosphere.

20. South-West monsoon season begins in June and ends in September. The low pressure condition over the North-Western plains get further intensified and are powerful enough to attract the trade winds of the Southern Hemisphere. The South-East trade winds cross the equator and are deflected towards the right due to the coriolis force and blow into the Indian landmass as South-West monsoon winds.

Due to the tapering shape of Peninsular India, the South-West monsoon winds get divided into two branches

(i) The Arabian Sea branch

(ii) The Bay of Bengal branch

Or Monsoon type of climate is prevalent in South and South-East Asia. The monsoon winds shift their directions seasonally. This seasonal shift is accompanied by changes in the patterns of rainfall.

The main causes of seasonal reversal of winds are

(*i*) Formation of low pressure Inter Tropical Convergence Zone (ITCZ) during the summer season over the Northern Ganga plains.

(*ii*) Formation of high pressure zone at 20°S latitude over the Indian Ocean in the Arabian Sea.

(*iii*) There is replacement of sub-tropical Westerly jet stream by the Easterly jet stream. Thus, there is reversal of winds from North-East to South and South-West direction and vice-versa.

21. (*i*) During the formation of Occluded, the air mass that is more dominant is the Cold air mass.

(*ii*) Warm front has a characteristic that it moves slowly as compared to the cold front because the air is less dense and lighter.

(*iii*) Warm front is associated with stormy weather as the less dense air rises above the cold air mass. This results in the process of condensation and the air starts cooling down. This ultimately results in the formation of clouds and storms.

22. Differences between continental shelf and continental slope are as follows

Continental Shelf	Continental Slope
It is the extended margin of each continent.	It is the connecting link between continental shelf and ocean basin.
The average depth is 200 m.	The depth varies between 200 m to 3000 m.
The mean width is about 70 km.	It begins where the bottom of continental shelf drop off.
The average gradient is 1° or even less.	The average gradient is 2-5° C.
Continental shelf covers approximately 5 per cent of Earth's surface.	It cover 6.4 per cent of Earth's surface.

23. The climate of India is characterised by a rhythm of seasons. The hot weather season starts from the months of March-April. The characteristics of hot weather season are

Temperature April, May and June are the months of summer in North India where temperature ranges between 35° C to 45° C due to the apparent movement of the Sun towards the Tropic of Cancer. In South India, it is not so intense, as the surrounding water bodies keep the temperature low between 26° C to 32° C.

FULLY SOLVED

Pressure and Winds High temperature in North India leads to low pressure condition and the ITCZ moves Northwards at 25° N in July. This elongate's low pressure trough, extends from Thar desert decent to Patna and Chotanagpur plateau.

Local Storms The dry conditions prevail in the larger part of North but temporary storms or the local winds bring a welcome respite from the oppressing heat. Loo which are hot, dry and oppressing winds blow in the Northern plains from Punjab to Bihar and with higher intensity between Delhi and Patna.

Mango showers or pre-monsoon showers occur in Kerala and coastal karnataka Nor Westers are storms of notorious nature in Bengal and Assam. In Assam, these are known as Bardoli Chheerha.

24. No, physical barrier is not a hindrance in interaction with our neighbouring countries in modern times because of the development of transportation and communication systems. For example

(*i*) With the help of latest technologies it is possible to cross mountains like Himalayas by making tunnels and through passes e.g. Pir Panjal tunnel, Rohtang tunnel, Chennai-Nashri tunnel, the Bolan pass, the Shipkila pass, the Nathula pass, the Bomdila pass, etc. These are helpful to move to neighbouring countries.

(*ii*) Through ships and ocean going vessels, it is possible to send and receive large cargoes of trade to and from India all over the world.

(*iii*) Airways made it possible to cross difficult terrains like, deserts, forests and oceans. It is a fast going mode of transport which reduced time distance from many days or weeks to few hours.

25. Rivers are vital to the Indian economy in the following ways

- Rivers play a critical role in supporting agriculture, industry, transportation, and energy production.
- Agriculture is the primary livelihood for millions of people in India, it depends heavily on river-fed irrigation, especially in the fertile plains of the Ganges, Brahmaputra, and Indus.
- These river systems provide essential water resources for cultivating crops like rice, wheat, and sugarcane, which sustain rural communities and contribute to food security.
- Rivers are crucial for hydroelectric power generation, contributing significantly to India's renewable energy capacity. Rivers also serve as natural waterways, facilitating transport and trade in regions.
- Additionally, they support fisheries, tourism, and cultural activities, providing employment for millions of people.
- Major cities and industrial hubs located along riverbanks also rely on these water sources for the economic benefit.

Or Distinct characteristics of Himalayan rivers are mentioned as below

- The Himalayan River System is distinct for its unique drainage pattern and abundant water availability.
- They get the water from melting glaciers and monsoon rains; the rivers are perennial which has a continuous flow throughout the year.
- The system's drainage pattern features both dendritic and antecedent drainage, where rivers like the Ganga, Brahmaputra, and Indus, cut through mountain ranges, forming deep gorges and steep valleys in their upper courses.
- This results from the rivers' ancient origin, predating the rise of the Himalayas, and their erosive power as they flow downward with high velocity.
- As the rivers goes down the slope, they spread across vast plains and deposit nutrient-rich alluvial soil which is essential for agriculture.
- These perennial rivers support extensive irrigation, drinking water needs, and hydroelectricity, which makes the Himalayan rivers crucial for India's ecology and economy.

26. Difference between Moist Deciduous Forests and Dry Deciduous Forests are as follows

Basis	Moist Deciduous Forests	Dry Deciduous Forests
Rainfall	They are found in the regions where rainfall is between 100-200 cm.	They are found in the areas where rainfall ranges between 70-100 cm.
Species	Teak, sal, shisham, mahua, amla, semul, kusum, sandalwood, etc are the main species of this forests.	Tendu, palas, bel, khair, axlewood, amaltas, etc are found in this region.
Location	These forests are found in the North-Eastern states along the foothills of Himalayas, Eastern slopes of the Western Ghats.	These forests are found in rainier areas of the Peninsula and the plains of Uttar Pradesh and Bihar. As the dry season begins, the trees shed their leaves and forests appears like a vast grassland with naked trees all around.

Or The wildlife includes all undomesticated living plant and species.

Over the years, wildlife has been hunted indiscriminately and their habitats have been disturbed. So, various efforts to protect and conserve biodiversity have been made. These efforts include

- In 1972, a comprehensive Wildlife Act was enacted, which provides a legal framework for conservation and protection of wildlife in India. It provides protection to the endangered species.
- 106 National parks and 573 Wildlife sanctuaries have been constructed to protect the wildlife.
- For the purpose of conservation of Biodiversity, special steps have been initiated by the Government in collaboration with the UNESCO's man and Biosphere Reserve program.
- Special schemes such as Project Tiger (1973) and Project Elephant (1992) have been launched to conserve these species and habitats in a sustainable manner.
- Apart from these, other projects like Crocodile Breeding Project, Project Hangul and Conservation of Himalayan Musk Dear have been launched by the Government.

27. Tides generally help in navigation, desilting of sediments and wash out pollutants from estuaries. Apart from all these significances, there are various economic importance of tides, some of them are:

- **Shipping** Harbours located near the mouth of rivers and estuaries having shallow bars at entrance prevent the ship and boats from entering into the harbours. Tides help ships to move in and come out smoothly.
- **Electricity** Tidal force is also used as a source for generating electricity. The generation of tidal energy was started by France. India also produces tidal energy in the Gulf of Khambhat and Kuchchh.
- **Minerals** Tides bring gems and minerals near the coast which are used by the industries to produce the products.
- **Fishery** Due to tides, fish comes nearer to coast and help the fishermen to catch them easily. Tides can be predicted in advance and hence fishermen can plan their activities.
- **Salt Industries** Tides also provides support to salt industries as sea water accumulates in the depressions near the coasts which is further converted into salt.

Or The Coriolis effect is caused by the Earth's rotation. It deflects the path of moving air to the right in the Northern Hemisphere and to the left in the Southern Hemisphere. This deflection is stronger at higher latitudes and weaker near the equator. In the Northern Hemisphere, winds are deflected to the right which causes the trade winds to blow from the North-East and the westerlies from the South-West.

In the Southern Hemisphere, winds are deflected to the left, with trade winds blowing from the South-East and westerlies from the North-West. This effect shapes global air circulation patterns and contributes to the formation of the Hadley, Ferrel, and Polar cells, which help in distributing the heat and moisture across the Earth and influences the weather and climate systems.

28. The movement of air is known as atmospheric circulation and when the average of the entire globe is considered, the motion is referred to as the general circulation of the atmosphere.

Earth's atmospheric circulation is an important transfer mechanism for both energy and mass. In this process, the imbalances between equatorial energy surplus and polar energy deficit is partly resolved, Earth's weather patterns are generated, and ocean currents are produced.

The general circulation of the atmosphere also affects the oceans. The large scale winds of the atmosphere initiate large and slow moving currents on the ocean.

Ocean in turn provides input of energy and water vapours into the air. For example, warming and cooling of the Pacific Ocean is the most important in terms of general atmospheric circulation. The warm water of the central Pacific ocean slowly drift towards South American coast and replaces the cold Peruvian current which is known as El-Nino. The El-Nino event is closely associated with the pressure changes in the central Pacific and Australia which is called Southern Oscillation.

The combination of both El-Nino and Southern Oscillation is known as ENSO. In the years where the ENSO is strong, the large scale variations in weather occur over the world.

Or The temperate cyclone occurs in mid-latitude of Southern hemisphere which are born along the polar front. The temperate cyclone covers may be 1000 km wide area. These cyclones move at a gentle pace of 5 to 25 km per hour. The weather condition in different parts of the cyclone varies significantly. Temperature increases suddenly when the cyclone comes very close to the observation point.

Significance for the region are:

- Temperate cyclone gives light shower which are highly beneficial for the agriculture.
- It causes snowfall in the region which causes attraction for tourism.
- The snowfall becomes the fresh source of water for rivers.
- Since the movement of wind is low, it does not cause any harm to life and property.
- These temperate cyclones do not require, so much disaster management machinery due to their less violent nature.

Thus, this way temperate cyclones has greater significance to the region it occurs.

29.

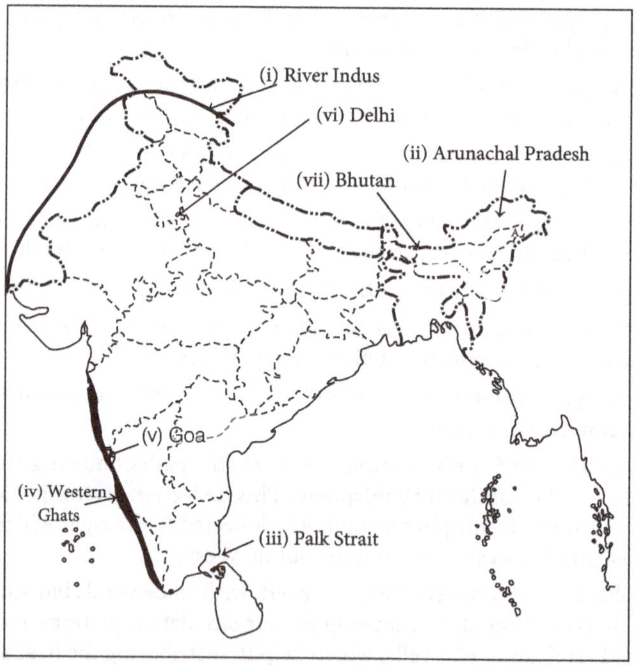

FULLY SOLVED

30.

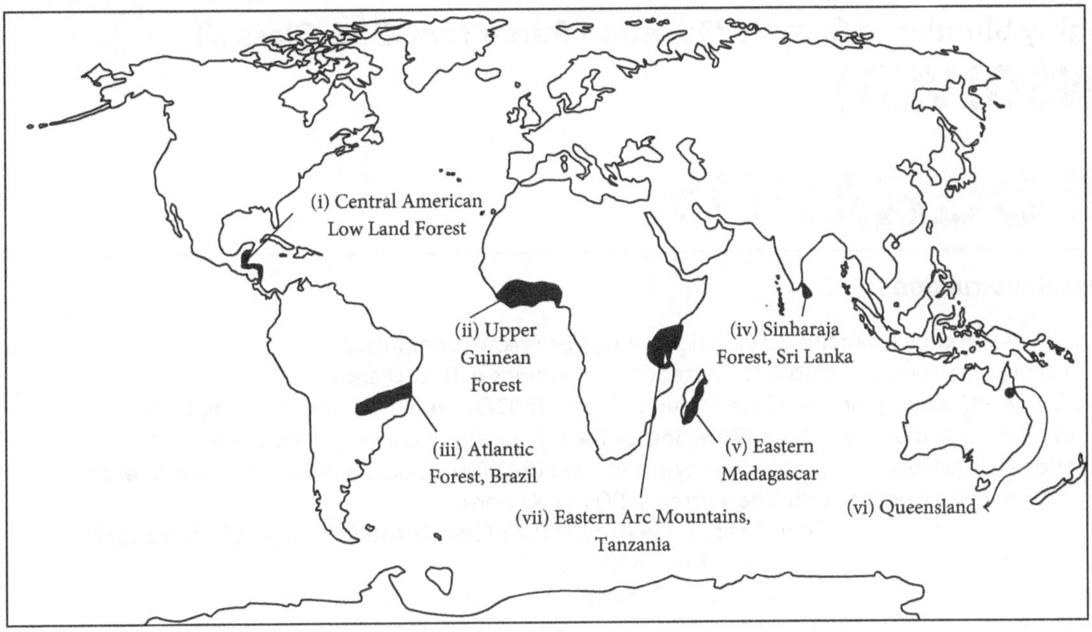
(i) Central American
Low Land Forest
(ii) Upper
Guinean
Forest
(iii) Atlantic
Forest, Brazil
(iv) Sinharaja
Forest, Sri Lanka
(v) Eastern
Madagascar
(vi) Queensland
(vii) Eastern Arc Mountains,
Tanzania

SAMPLE QUESTION PAPER 2

A Highly Simulated Sample Question Paper for CBSE Class XI

(UNSOLVED)

GEOGRAPHY

General Instructions

- This question paper contains 30 questions. All questions are compulsory.
- This question paper is divided into five sections – Sections A, B, C, D and E.
- Section A – Questions no. 1 to 17 are Multiple Choice (MCQ) Type Questions carrying 1 mark each.
- Section B – Questions no. 18 and 19 are Source Based Questions carrying 3 marks each.
- Section C – Questions no. 20 to 23 are Short Answer (SA) Type Questions carrying 3 marks each. Answer to these questions shall be written in 80 to 100 words.
- Section D – Questions no. 24 to 28 are Long Answer (LA) Type Questions carrying 5 marks each. Answer to these questions shall be written in 120 to 150 words.
- Section E – Questions no. 29 and 30 are Map Based Questions. Carrying 5 marks each.

Time : 3 hours **Max. Marks : 70**

SECTION A

1. **Which of the following countries is/are included in the Indian sub-continent?** **(1)**

(a) Pakistan (b) Nepal (c) Bhutan (d) All of these

2. **Arrange the following personalities in sequence according to the period of their theories.** **(1)**

I. Wegener **II. Arthur Holmes**
III. McKenzie **IV. Hess**

Codes

(a) II, I, III, IV (b) IV, III, II, I (c) I, II, IV, III (d) III, I, II, IV

3. **There is a term given to the activity which is the combination of forestry and agriculture. Choose from the following.** **(1)**

(a) Urban forestry (b) Farm forestry (c) Agro-forestry (d) Community forestry

4. **Many factors acts upon the ocean water that causes waves, choose from the following the correct factor.**

(a) Temperature (b) Precipitation (c) Winds (d) None of these

5. **Choose the correct statement regarding the feature of Himalayan drainage system.** **(1)**

(a) The rivers of this drainage system are fed by melting of snow and precipitation.
(b) These are perennial in nature or have water throughout the year.
(c) These rivers pass through the giant gorges carved out by the erosional activity carried on simultaneously with the uplift of the Himalayas.
(d) All of the above

6. Which of the following pairs is incorrectly matched? **(1)**

(a) Great Himalayas – Shiwaliks
(b) Great Indian Desert – Rajasthan
(c) Kaimur Hills – Madhya Pradesh and Bihar
(d) Cold Desert – Uttarakhand

7. Identify the type of source about interior of the Earth from the following given description. **(1)**

These source of information uses the technique that extract core samples from the Earth's interior. These samples offer information about the Earth's sub-surface layers, temperature, and mineral content.

(a) Core drilling (b) Volcanic eruption (c) Satellite imagery (d) Earthquakes

8. Assertion (A) Carbon dioxide is meteorologically a very important gas. **(1)**

Reason (R) CO_2 is transparent to the incoming solar radiation but opaque to the outgoing terrestrial radiation.

Codes

(a) Both (A) and (R) are true but (R) is not the correct explanation of (A)
(b) Both (A) and (R) are true and (R) is the correct explanation of (A)
(c) Both (A) and (R) are incorrect
(d) (A) is correct, but (R) is incorrect

9. Choose from the following the incorrect statement regarding Isobars. **(1)**

I. Isobars are lines drawn on a weather map that connect points of equal atmospheric pressure.
II. The closer the isobars are to each other, the stronger the pressure gradient.
III. Isobars does not help predict changes in weather conditions.
IV. Wider spacing between isobars indicates lighter winds.

(a) I, II, III (b) II and III (c) Only III (d) Only II

10. Consider the following statements and choose the correct option from the given options. **(1)**

I. Southern slopes of Himalayas have thick cover of vegetation.
II. Southern slopes of Himalayas receive high precipitation.

Codes

(a) Only statement I is correct
(b) Both the statements are true and statement II correctly present the reason of statement I
(c) Only statement II is correct
(d) Both the statements I and II are incorrect

11. The Eastern and Western Ghats converge at which of the following ranges? **(1)**

(a) Patkai Hills (b) Garo Hills (c) Nilgiri Hills (d) Rajmahal Hills

12. Assertion (A) The work of groundwater cannot be seen in all types of rocks. **(1)**

Reason (R) Physical or mechanical removal of materials by moving groundwater is insignificant in developing landforms.

Codes

(a) Both (A) and (R) are true but (R) is not the correct explanation of (A)
(b) Both (A) and (R) are true and (R) is the correct explanation of (A)
(c) Both (A) and (R) are incorrect
(d) (A) is correct, but (R) is incorrect

13. The highest point of a wave is called as **(1)**

(a) Crest (b) Trough (c) Gyre (d) Surge

14. Which of the following is a feature of Tropical Evergreen Forests? **(1)**

(a) These are found in warm and humid areas with average annual precipitation of over 200 cm and mean temperature above 22°C.

(b) They are found on the Western slope of the Western Ghats, hill of the North-Eastern region and the Andaman and Nicobar Islands.

(c) Species found in the forests include rosewood, mahogony, ebony, etc.

(d) All of the above

Study the given diagram and answer the following questions no. 15-17.

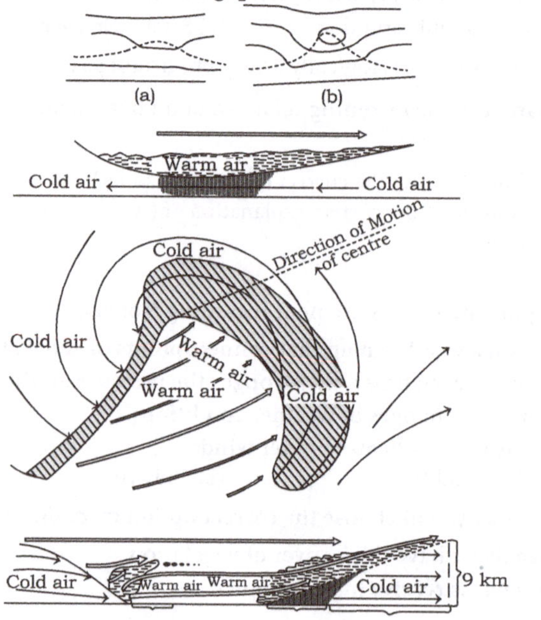

15. Which type of front is formed when the cold and warm air mass stays still? **(1)**

(a) Cold front (b) Occluded front (c) Stationary front (d) Warm front

16. Which air mass is active during the second stage of formation of temperate cyclone? **(1)**

(a) Cold air mass (b) Warm air mass (c) Both (a) and (b) (d) None

17. Identify from, the following the weather condition in the last stage of temperate cyclone. **(1)**

(a) Stormy weather (b) Calm weather (c) Heavy rainfall (d) Snowfall in the area

SECTION B

18. Read the following paragraph and answer the questions that follow.

The Himalayas along with other Peninsular mountains are young, weak and flexible in their geological structure unlike the rigid and stable Peninsular Block. Consequently, they are still subjected to the interplay of exogenic and endogenic forces, resulting in the development of faults, folds and thrust plains. These mountains are tectonic in origin, dissected by fast-flowing rivers which are in their youthful stage. Various landforms like gorges, V-shaped valleys, rapids, waterfalls, etc are indicative of this stage.

The third geological division of India comprises the plains formed by the river Indus, the Ganga and the Brahmaputra. Originally, it was a geo-synclinal depression which attained its maximum development during the third phase of the Himalayan mountain formation approximately about 64 million years ago. Since then, it has been gradually filled by the sediments brought by the Himalayan and Peninsular rivers.

UNSOLVED

Average depth of alluvial deposits in these plains ranges from 1,000-2,000 m. It is evident from the above discussion that there are significant variations among the different regions of India in terms of their geological structure, which has far-reaching impact upon other related aspects. Variations in the physiography and relief are important among these. The relief and physiography of India has been greatly influenced by the geological and geomorphological processes active in the Indian sub-continent.

(i) **How is the Himalayan mountain range different from the Peninsular Block?** **(1)**

(ii) **Which features highlight the youthful stage of the Himalayas?** **(1)**

(iii) **Which rivers play an important role in the formation of the Northern plains of India?** **(1)**

19. **Study the given diagram and answer the questions that follow.**

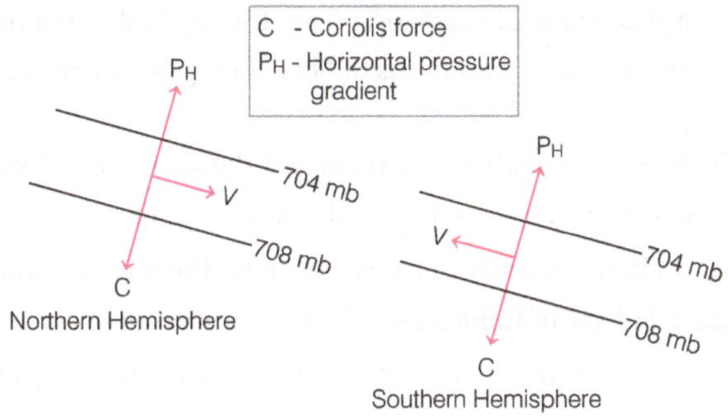

(i) Name the phenomenon is shown in the given diagram. **(1)**

(ii) Which force determines the velocity of a wind? **(1)**

(iii) State two features of coriolis force. **(1)**

SECTION C

20. Which physical feature has contributed to the evolution of a unique identity of the Indian sub-continent? **(3)**

21. **Study the map and Answer the following questions** **(3)**

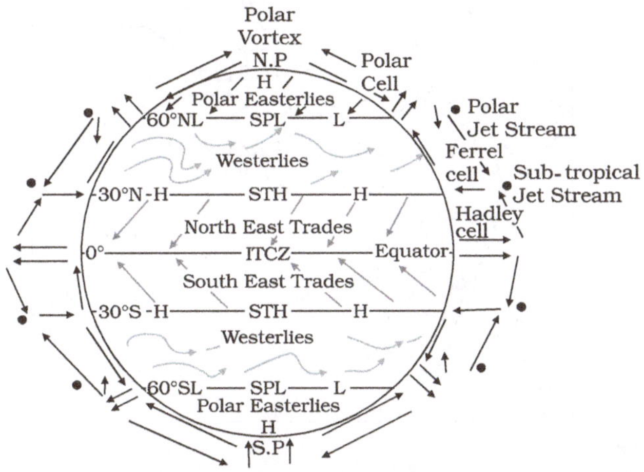

Simplified General Circulation of the Atmosphere

(i) Name the type of cell that is generated between 0° to 30° latitude.

(ii) Write one characteristic of Subtropical high-pressure belt.

(iii) Why there is subsidence of air in the polar cell?

22. There are two sources of energy for the Earth. Insolation and terrestrial radiations, they differs from each other, Explain how? **(3)**

23. Dew is not formed on the cloudy nights". Give reason for the specification of statement. **(3)**

Or "Excess evaporation and less precipitation is the main reason behind the dry climate". Discuss the economic activities which are important for human being in such climate.

SECTION D

24. The two peninsular rivers, Godavari and Narmada display interesting differences in their regimes compared to Himalayan rivers like Ganga plain. Explain. **(5)**

25. Several Biodiversity Reserves have been established to protect its unique flora and fauna. Explain. **(5)**

Or The Himalayan ranges show a succession of vegetation from the tropical to the tundra. Justify.

26. 'Different parts of the Earth receive varying amounts of Solar Energy throughout the year'. Elucidate the statement. **(5)**

Or 'Evaluate the relationship between temperature inversion and the occurence of specific weather phenomena'.

27. The ocean floor is divided into major divisions. Briefly discuss about these divisions. **(5)**

Or Give reasons for the differences in the Salinity of the oceans near the Equator and poles.

28. The Western and Eastern coastal plains of India differs from each other in many terms. Justify the statement. **(5)**

Or 'Tropical Rainforests in India have ecological importance and they contribute to biodiversity conservation and climate regulation. Explain how?

SECTION E

29. On the given outline map of India, seven features are marked as (i), (ii), (iii), (iv), (v), (vi) and (vii). Identify any five features with the help of the information given below. **(5)**

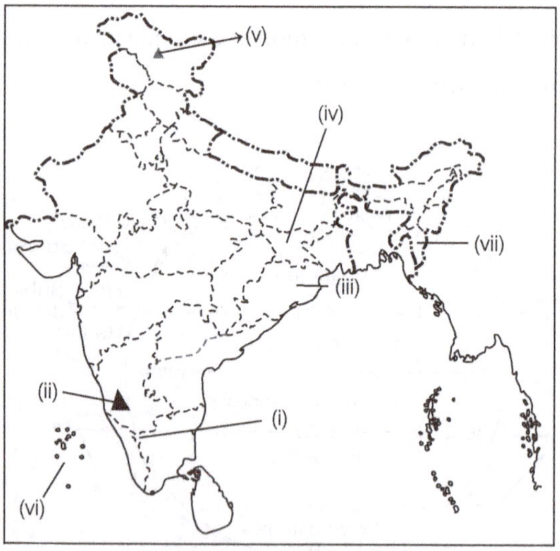

(i) A biosphere reserve
(ii) One mountain peak
(iii) An area that receive 100-200 cm of rainfall
(iv) A plateau that covers most of the Jharkhand state
(v) A mountain peak in the Northernmost India
(vi) An island group in the South-West of India
(vii) A North-Eastern state of India

UNSOLVED

30. **On the given map of world, mark the following features.** **(5)**

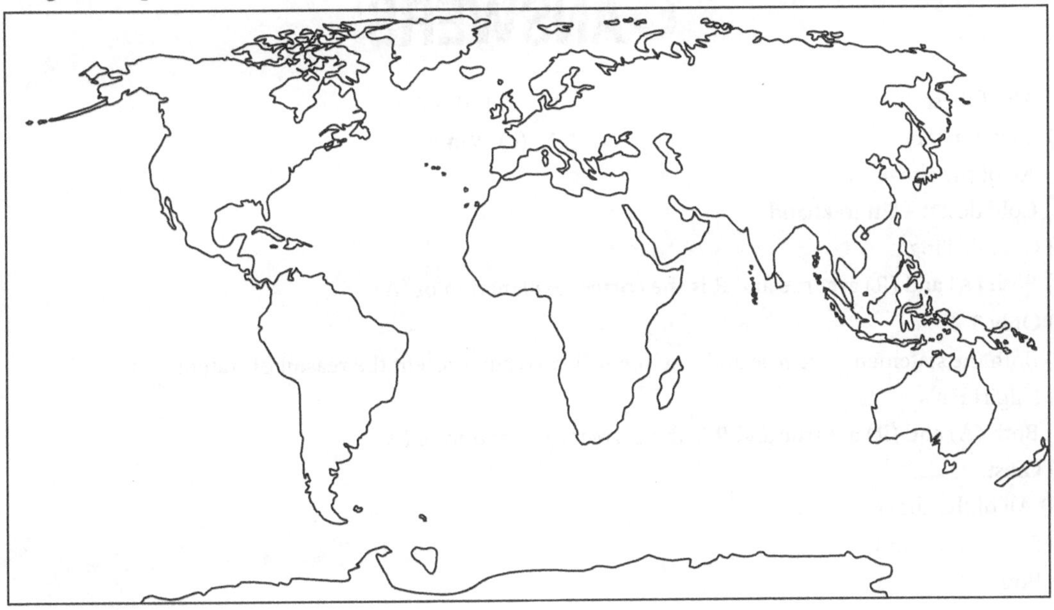

(i) Arabian Plate
(ii) South Equatorial Current
(iii) A biodiversity hotspot in Asia
(iv) Cocos Plate
(v) Upper Guinean Forest
(vi) Western Ghats, India
(vii) Northern Borneo

ANSWERS

1. (d) All of these
2. (c) I, II, IV, III
3. (c) Agro forestry
4. (c) Winds
5. (d) All of the above
6. (d) Cold desert - Uttarakhand
7. (a) Core drilling
8. (b) Both (A) and (R) are true and R is the correct explanation of (A)
9. (c) Only 3
10. (b) Both the statements are true and statement II correctly present the reason of statement I
11. (c) Nilgiri Hills
12. (b) Both (A) and (R) are true and R is the correct explanation of (A)
13. (a) Crest
14. (d) All of the above
15. (a) Stationary Front
16. (c) Both (a) and (b)
17. (b) Calm weather

29.

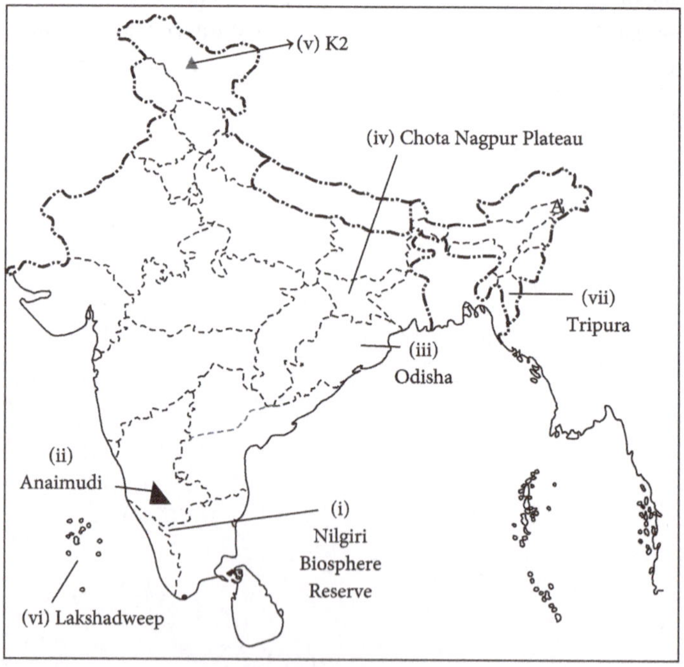

30.

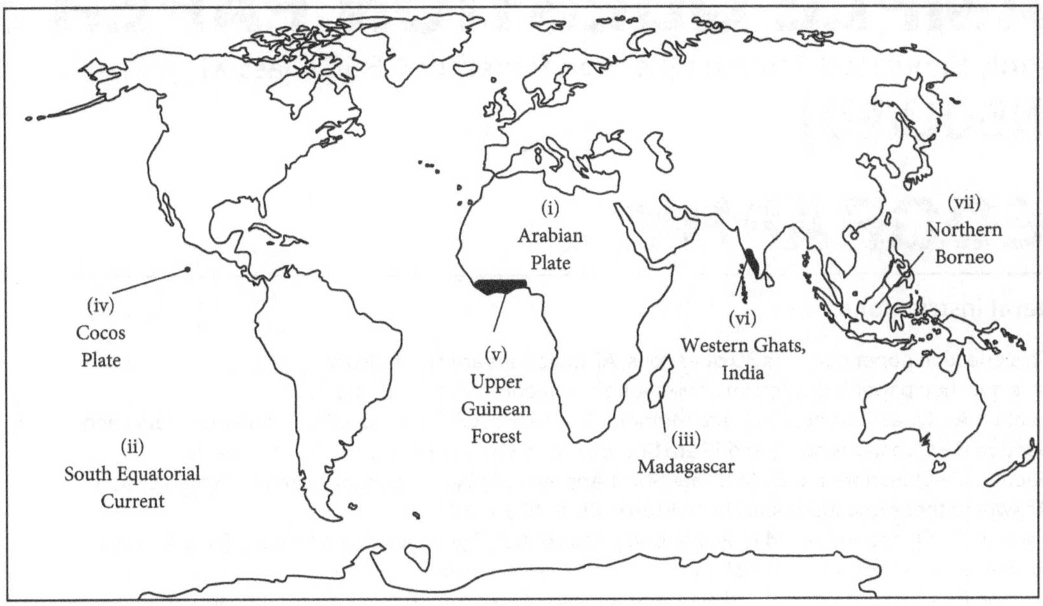
(i)
Arabian
Plate
(ii)
South Equatorial
Current
(iii)
Madagascar
(iv)
Cocos
Plate
(v)
Upper
Guinean
Forest
(vi)
Western Ghats,
India
(vii)
Northern
Borneo

UNSOLVED

SAMPLE QUESTION PAPER 3

A Highly Simulated Sample Question Paper for CBSE Class XI

(UNSOLVED)

GEOGRAPHY

General Instructions

- This question paper contains 30 questions. All questions are compulsory.
- This question paper is divided into five sections - Sections A, B, C, D and E.
- Section A - Questions no. 1 to 17 are Multiple Choice (MCQ) Type Questions carrying 1 mark each.
- Section B - Questions no. 18 and 19 are Source Based Questions carrying 3 marks each.
- Section C - Questions no. 20 to 23 are Short Answer (SA) Type Questions carrying 3 marks each. Answer to these questions shall be written in 80 to 100 words.
- Section D - Questions no. 24 to 28 are Long Answer (LA) Type Questions carrying 5 marks each. Answer to these questions shall be written in 120 to 150 words.
- Section E - Questions no. 29 and 30 are Map Based Questions. Carrying 5 marks each.

Time : 3 hours **Max. Marks : 70**

SECTION A

1. Which of the following rivers is known as sorrow of Bihar? **(1)**

(a) Damodar (b) Kosi (c) Son (d) Chambal

2. Consider the following statements and choose the correct option from the given options. **(1)**

I. The amount of heat causes pressure differences in the atmosphere.

II. The amount of heat received by different parts of the Earth is not same.

Codes

(a) Only statement I is correct

(b) Both the statements are true and statement II correctly present the reason for statement I

(c) Only Statement II is correct

(d) Both the statements I and II are incorrect

3. 'El-Nino is known to have which of the following consequences?

(a) Presence of cold Humbolt current along Peru coast **(1)**

(b) Distortion of equatorial atmospheric circulation

(c) Increase in amount of plankton

(d) Early onset of monsoon in India

4. Arrange the types of clouds as per their height (from highest to lowest elevation). **(1)**

I. Cumulus clouds **II. Cirrus clouds**

III. Nimbus clouds **IV. Stratus clouds**

Codes

(a) II, I, IV, III (b) I, II, III, IV

(c) II, IV, III, I (d) III, II, I, IV

5. Identify from the following the feature of Indo-Ganga-Brahmaputra plain. **(1)**

(a) This was formed by the river Indus, the Ganga and the Brahmaputra.
(b) Earlier, it was a geo-synclinal depression.
(c) It attained its maximum development during the third phase of the Himalayan mountain formation, approximately about 64 million years ago.
(d) All of the above

6. Which of the following features is related to Montane Forests? **(1)**

(a) In mountainous areas, the decrease in temperature with increasing altitude leads to a corresponding change in natural vegetation.
(b) Mountain forests can be classified into two types, the Northern mountain forests and the Southern mountain forests.
(c) The Himalayan ranges show a succession of vegetation from the tropical to the Tundra, which change in with the altitude.
(d) All of the above

7. Which of the following pairs is incorrectly matched? **(1)**

(a) Latitude	–	Distance from North and South of the equator measured in degrees up to 90 degree.
(b) Radiation	–	The emission of energy in the form of rays or waves.
(c) Scattering	–	The process in which radiation or particles are deflected or diffused.
(d) Isotherm	–	The line which joins the places having equal height.

8. Assertion (A) Deodar is used for construction activity.
Reason (R) Sandalwood is main species of evergreen forest. **(1)**

Codes

(a) Both (A) and (R) are true but (R) is not the correct explanation of (A)
(b) Both (A) and (R) are true and (R) is the correct explanation of (A)
(c) Both (A) and (R) are incorrect
(d) (A) is correct, but (R) is incorrect

9. Arrange the following according to the increasing salinity. **(1)**

(i) Lake Van **(ii) Black Sea**
(iii) Great Salt Lake **(iv) Dead Sea**

Options

(a) (i), (ii), (iii), (iv)
(b) (ii), (iii), (iv), (i)
(c) (ii), (iii), (i), (iv)
(d) (iii), (i), (ii), (iv)

10. Identify the correct order of Indian rivers which is arranged from West to East direction. **(1)**

(a) The Ganga, Yamuna, Gomati, Ghaghra
(b) The Gomati, Yamuna, Ganga, Ghaghra
(c) The Yamuna, Ganga, Gomati, Ghaghra
(d) The Yamuna, Ghaghra, Ganga, Gomati

11. The movement of ocean water is influenced by which of the following features? **(1)**

I. Temperature **II. Salinity** **III. Density**

Codes

(a) I and II
(b) II and III
(c) I and III
(d) All of these

UNSOLVED

12. **Assertion (A)** Tamil Nadu lies in rain shadow area of Arabian Sea branch of South West Monsoon.
Reason (R) Tamil Nadu coast receives high rainfall during South-West monsoon season. **(1)**

Codes

(a) Both (A) and (R) are true but (R) is not the correct explanation of (A)
(b) Both (A) and (R) are true and (R) is the correct explanation of (A)
(c) Both (A) and (R) are incorrect
(d) (A) is correct, but (R) is incorrect

13. **Which of the following pairs is matched correctly?** **(1)**

(a) Perigee – When Moon's orbit is farthest from the Earth
(b) Apogee – When moon is closest to the Earth
(c) Perihelion – When the Earth is closest to the Sun
(d) Aphelion – When the Earth is closest to the Moon

14. **Identify the type of river system based on the given description.** **(1)**

It is the most important river of India both in terms of its basin and cultural significance. It rises in the Gangotri glacier near Gaumukh in the Uttarkashi district of Uttarakhand. It flows from the South to the South-East and East. It splits into the Bhagirathi and the Padma.

(a) Indus (b) Ganga (c) Brahmaputra (d) Mahanadi

Study the following diagram and answer the following questions from 15 to 17.

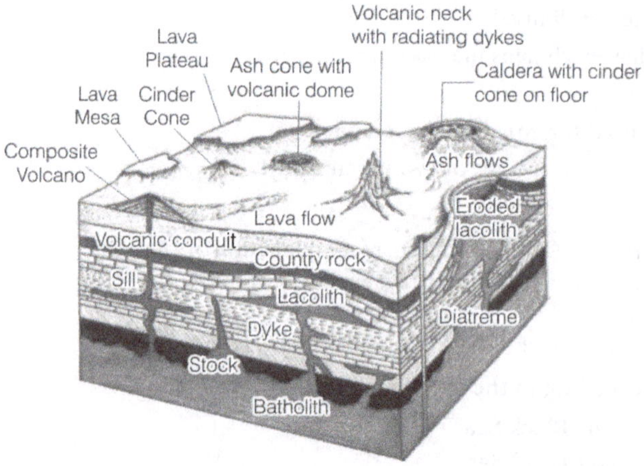

15. **Identify the intrusive landforms from the following.** **(1)**

(a) Laccolith (b) Lava flow (c) Cinder (d) Lava Mesa

16. **Which landform from the following are large mass of igneous rocks in dome shaped at the base.** **(1)**

(a) Laccolith (b) Dyke (c) Batholith (d) Lopolith

17. **Identify which feature is formed by the deposition of layers of lava outside the surface of the Earth.** **(1)**

(a) Lava Plateau (b) Composite Volcano (c) Lava Mesa (d) Sills

SECTION B

18. **Read the following paragraph and answer the questions that follow.**

Rising from the height of 150 m above the river plains up to an elevation of 600-900 m is the irregular triangle known as the Peninsular plateau. Delhi ridge in the North-West, (extension of Aravalis), the Rajmahal Hills in the East, Gir range in the West and the Cardamom Hills in the South constitute the outer extent of the Peninsular Plateau. However, an extension of this is also seen in the North-East, in the form of Shillong and Karbi-Anglong Plateau.

UNSOLVED

The Peninsular India is made up of a series of Patland plateaus such as the Hazaribagh Plateau, the Palamu Plateau, the Ranchi Plateau, the Malwa Plateau, the Coimbatore plateau and the Karnataka plateau, etc. This is one of the oldest and the most stable landmass of India. The general elevation of the plateau is from the West to the East, which is also proved by the pattern of the flow of rivers.

Some of the important physiographic features of this region are tors, block mountains, rift valleys, spurs, bare rocky structures, series of hummocky hills and wall-like quartzite dykes offering natural sites for water storage. The Western and North-Western part of the plateau has an emphatic presence of black soil. This Peninsular Plateau has undergone recurrent phases of upliftment and submergence accompanied by crustal faulting and fractures. (The Bhima fault needs special mention, because of its recurrent seismic activities). These spatial variations have brought in elements of diversity in the relief of the Peninsular Plateau. The North-Western part of the plateau has a complex relief of ravines and gorges. The ravines of Chambal, Bhind and Morena are some of the well-known examples.

On the basis of the prominent relief features, the Peninsular plateau can be divided into three broad groups: (i) The Deccan Plateau (ii) The Central Highlands (iii) The North-Eastern Plateau.

(i) The Peninsular plateau is surrounded by which geographical features of India? **(1)**

(ii) The Peninsular India is made up of a series of Patland plateau. Name these. **(1)**

(iii) Which special feature of the Peninsular India proves the general elevation of the plateau? **(1)**

19. **Observe the map of India and answer the following questions.**

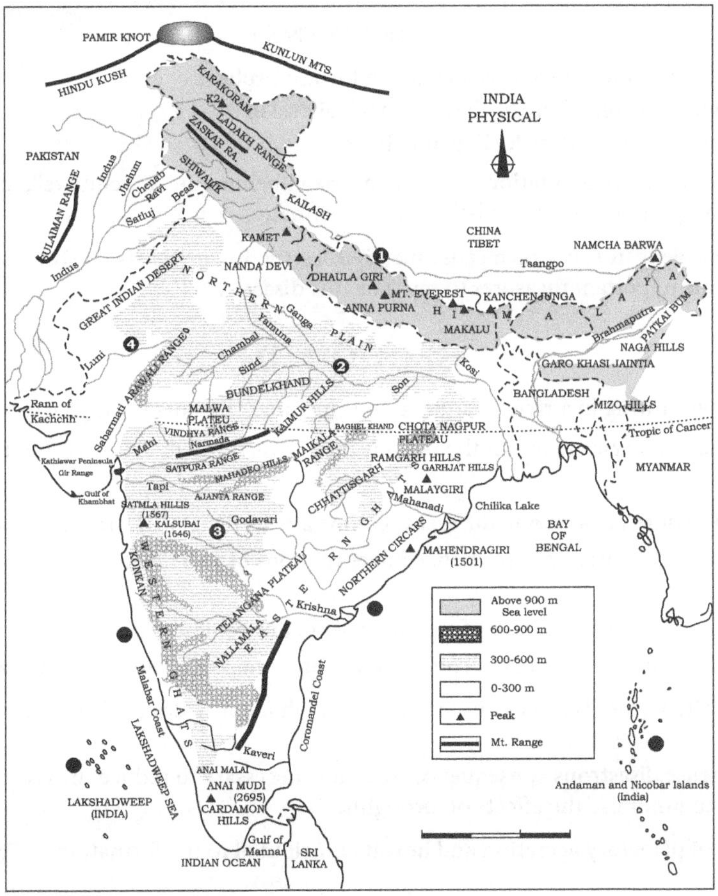

(i) Name the ranges which are part of the Greater Himalayas. **(1)**

(ii) Which mountain range lies between the Narmada and Tapi rivers? **(1)**

(iii) The Northern Circars consist of the deltas of which Indian rivers? **(1)**

SECTION C

20. How should we contribute in conservation of forests and wildlife? Suggest some ways to control the exploitation of the wildlife and forests. **(3)**

Or What were the main objectives of Project Tiger launched by the Government. Explain, how it has contributed to the protection of tiger.

21. **Study the following diagram and Answer the following Questions.** **(3)**

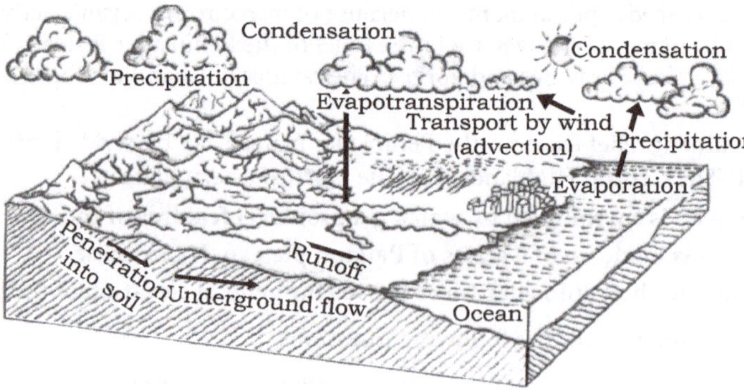

Hydrological Cycle

(i) Name the process by which clouds are formed in the atmosphere.
(ii) How does evaporation contribute to the hydrological cycle?
(iii) Runoff affect the hydrological cycle. Explain How?

22. 'Excess evaporation and less precipitation is the main reason behind the dry climate". Discuss the economic activities which are important for human being in such climate. **(3)**

23. "Tornadoes are the violent storms which cause massive destruction on its way". Discuss its impact on human life. Also suggest some important measures to mitigate this disaster. **(3)**

SECTION D

24. 'The quantity of water flowing in a river channel is not the same.' Discuss through examples. **(5)**

25. Tropical Cyclones have adverse effects on the regions they cross through. Discuss about the measures taken to reduce the impact. **(5)**

Or 'The movement of Pressure belts during different seasons affects the global wind patterns'. Justify the statement.

26. 'The Composition of Earth's atmosphere changed over millions of years due to natural and human factors'. Explain. **(5)**

Or The Himalayan ranges show a succession of vegetation from the tropical to the tundra. Justify.

27. Give reasons why Plate Tectonic Theory is considered as an important theory in Physical Geography? **(5)**

Or "The Continental Drift Theory is a very important theory which provides evidences from the past." Discuss the theory in brief.

28. Droughts have immense disastrous consequences thus it is necessary to reduce the risks related to droughts. Elucidate measures to minimise the effects of droughts. **(5)**

Or Discuss the process of planetory accretion and how it contributed to the formation of Earth.

SECTION E

29. **On the given outline map of India, seven features are marked as (i), (ii), (iii), (iv), (v), (vi) and (vii). Identify any five features with the help of information given below.** **(5)**

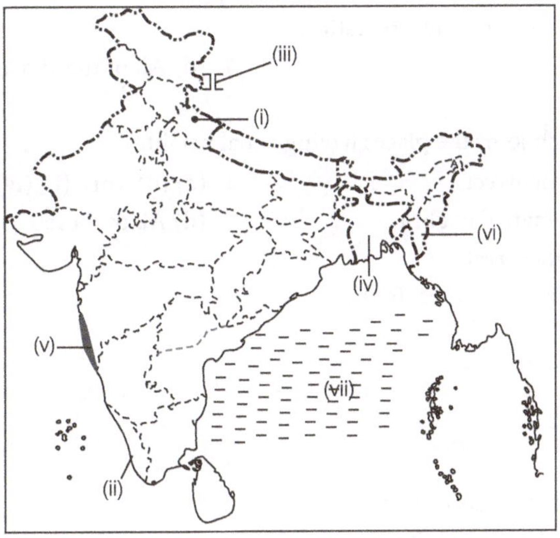

(i) A biosphere reserve
(ii) The Union Territory located close to Kerala coast
(iii) A mountain pass
(iv) Country having largest border with India
(v) A coast of India
(vi) A North-Eastern state of India
(vii) The North-Eastern part of the Indian Ocean

30. **On the given map of world, mark the following features.**

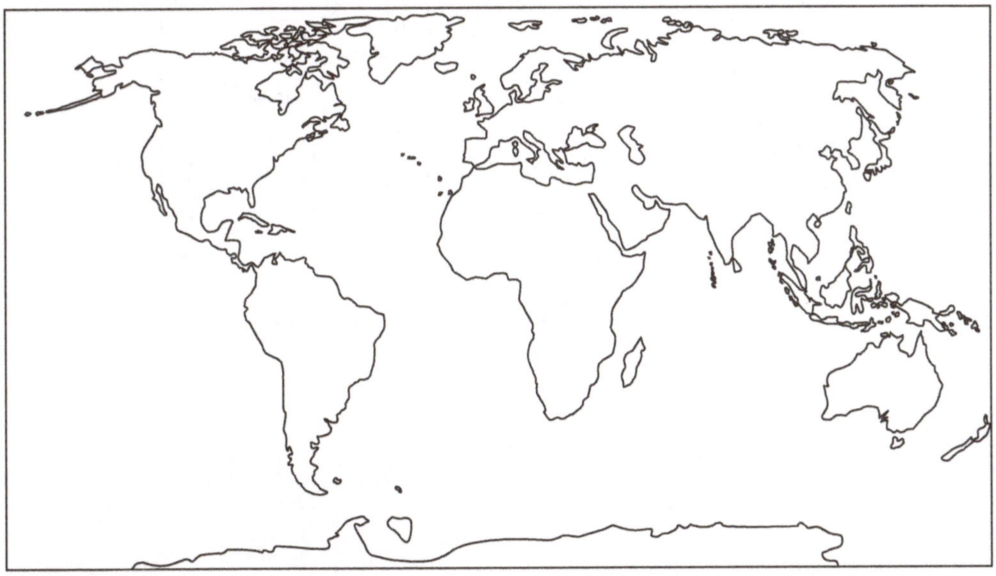

(i) Benguela Current
(ii) A biodiversity hotspot in South America
(iii) Caroline Plate
(iv) Atlantic Forest
(v) Eastern Madagascar
(vi) Philippines
(vii) Eurasian Plate

ANSWERS

1. (b) Kosi
2. (b) Both the statements are true and statement II correctly present the reason for statement I
3. (b) Distortion of equatorial atmospheric circulation
4. (a) II, I, IV, III
5. (d) All of the above
6. (d) All of the above
7. (d) Isotherm – The line which joins the places having equal height.
8. (d) (A) is correct but (R) is incorrect
9. (c) (ii), (iii), (i), (iv)
10. (c) The Yamuna, Ganga, Gomati, Ghaghra
11. (d) All of these
12. (d) (A) is correct but (R) is incorrect
13. (c) Perihelion – When the Earth is closest to the Sun
14. (b) Ganga
15. (a) Laccolith
16. (c) Batholiths
17. (b) Composite Volcano
29.

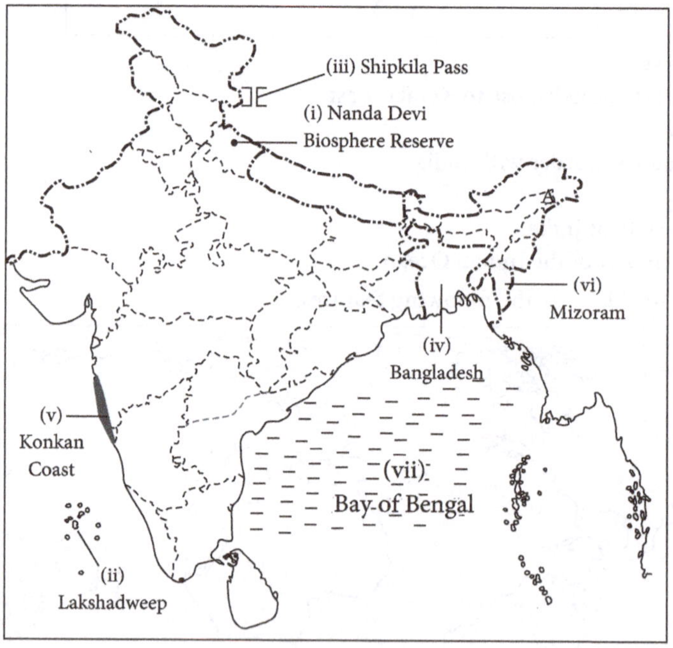

30.

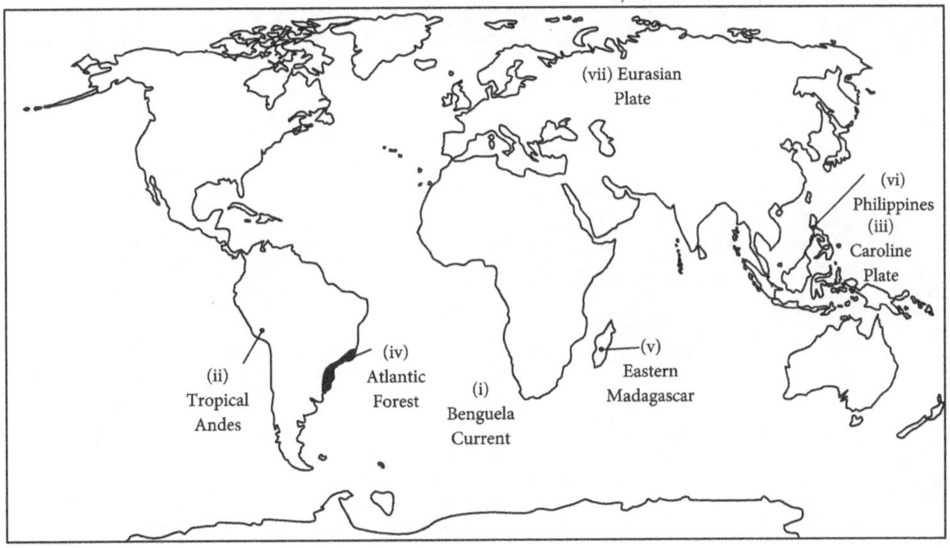
(vii) Eurasian
Plate
(vi)
Philippines
(iii)
Caroline
Plate
(ii)
Tropical
Andes
(iv)
Atlantic
Forest
(i)
Benguela
Current
(v)
Eastern
Madagascar